MW00852034

2

The Korean War

The Korean War

An Exhaustive Chronology

BUD HANNINGS

Foreword by General P.X. Kelley,
USMC (Ret.), 28th Commandant

Volume 2
(September 23, 1950–November 12, 1951)

McFarland & Company, Inc., Publishers
Jefferson, North Carolina, and London

Volume 2

LIBRARY OF CONGRESS CATALOGUING-IN-PUBLICATION DATA

Hannings, Bud.
The Korean war : an exhaustive chronology / Bud Hannings ;
foreword by General P.X. Kelley, USMC (Ret.).
p.   cm.
Includes index.

3 volume set—
ISBN-13: 978-0-7864-2814-4
illustrated case binding : 50# alkaline paper

1. Korean War, 1950–1953 — Chronology.   2. Korean War, 1950–1953.
3. Korean War, 1950–1953 — United States — Chronology.
4. United Nations — Armed Forces — Korea — Chronology.   I. Title.
DS918.H336   2007   951.904'20202 — dc22   2007010570

British Library cataloguing data are available

©2007 Bud Hannings. All rights reserved

*No part of this book may be reproduced or transmitted in any form
or by any means, electronic or mechanical, including photocopying
or recording, or by any information storage and retrieval system,
without permission in writing from the publisher.*

On the cover: Situation Map of Korea November 25, 1950;
Elements of Eighth Army retire from Sunch'on
and move south towards P'yongyang, December 2, 1950

Manufactured in the United States of America

*McFarland & Company, Inc., Publishers
Box 611, Jefferson, North Carolina 28640
www.mcfarlandpub.com*

Contents

September 23 The Swedish Red Cross Field Hospital contingent arrives at Pusan.

Inchon–Seoul vicinity: X Corps Headquarters relocates from Inchon to Ascom City. General Almond impatiently complains of what he considers a slow Marine advance. He suggests to General O.P. Smith that the 1st Marines should execute an envelopment attack by utilizing the terrain south of the Han River.

In turn, General O.P. Smith rejects the idea, choosing not to divide the 1st and 5th Marines by a river. General Almond, determined to give MacArthur the city of Seoul, issues an ultimatum to Smith, giving him twenty-four hours to break through the stiff resistance or he would commit the 7th Infantry Division by ordering the 32nd Regiment to envelop the enemy positions in Seoul.

Seoul, a strategic military objective, is becoming an equally important political prize, fraying the nerves on both sides of the argument. Meanwhile, three days of resolute enemy resistance at the city continues to forestall its capture.

In the 1st Marine Division zone, the 1st Marines Regiment advances nearly without incident to the Han River. The 3rd Battalion captures Hill 108, the strategic high ground that controls the damaged bridges that span the river. Later, at 2200, headquarters issues an order instructing the 1st Marines to ford the Han River on the following morning, essentially confirming an earlier verbal directive.

In the 5th Marines sector, the 2nd Battalion, S.K. Marines, resumes its attack toward Hill 105 Center, but the resistance on the two knolls (Hills 66 and 88), designated Hill 56 by the U.S. Marines, remains tenacious, and the South Koreans continue to take additional casualties without making any significant progress.

At about 1300, Colonel Roise (2nd Battalion, 5th Marines) pushes his command post forward to the base of Hill 104. By the middle of the afternoon, upon authorization from Colonel Murray, Roise's 2nd Battalion, 5th Marines, replaces the South Korean Marines and carries the fight. At this time, it is still not known to the Marines that they are encountering the enemy's main line of resistance.

After a moderate artillery barrage, the 2nd Battalion advances, bolstered by one platoon of tanks. Companies D and F attack while Company E offers support fire from the eastern slopes of Hill 104. Company F, on the right, jumps off from its positions south of the railroad to capture the heights below the railroad tunnel.

Meanwhile, Company D, led by 1st Lieutenant H.J. Smith, advances along a sunken road, moving toward Hill 56 north of the tunnel. Complications quickly develop when the assault troops begin crossing about 1,000 yards of rice paddies. The point tank, unable to pass through a huge ditch, becomes immobilized. Consequently, the four trailing tanks stall. Three of the tanks divert and shadow the railroad tracks, while a fourth remains in the paddy to shepherd the ground Marines.

Meanwhile, Company F, led by Captain Peters, is incurring heavy casualties. A mortar section is ordered to move up to support Company F, but the instructions, according to Lt. Sansing, are not received on his radio. This snafu costs the company heavily when its three platoons, lacking 60-mm support fire, ascend Hill 56 against sheets of heavy enemy fire.

In the meantime, Company D, commanded by Lieutenant H.J. Smith, successfully navigates the sunken road. It easily reaches its initial objective. However, the 1st Platoon, led by Lieutenant Heck, launches its attack on the primary objective, Smith's Ridge (so named in honor of Lt. H.J. Smith).

The 1st Platoon swings to the left to lead the assault, while the 2nd and 3rd Platoons move against the slopes of Hill 56. The 1st Platoon advances effortlessly until it reaches open ground about halfway from the objective. Suddenly, menacing layers of fire, originating from a huge knob on the southern slope of Smith's Ridge, crash violently upon the exposed Marines, slimming their numbers.

The 1st Platoon contains less than half its strength following the several-minute ordeal. The platoon leader, Lieutenant Heck, receives a mortal wound, and his top NCO, Sergeant T. Crowson, receives a severe wound.

Meanwhile, Lieutenant H.J. Smith enters the field of fire to personally extricate the beleaguered 1st Platoon. The 2nd and 3rd Platoons (Company D) maintain their efforts to seize the northeastern slopes of Hill 56. Nevertheless, the enemy remains entrenched, giving little ground.

Simultaneously, counterattacks are mounted. The 2nd Battalion repulses the enemy attacks, but it is unable to secure the enemy held ridges by dark. Lt. Smith directs his embattled command to establish night positions on the high ground; however, the unit is out of contact with friendly forces.

On the eastern slopes, Company F has also spent the day in a wild slugfest. It doggedly advances against heavy resistance to seize the railroad tunnel (northeastern slopes, Hill 56). The 1st Platoon, led by Lieutenant Anderson, attacks an enemy strong point near the tunnel, but ferocious enemy fire cuts the platoon down to 27 men. Undaunted, the weary contingent forges ahead and engages the enemy at close-quarters, exchanging grenades while they also fire from point-blank range.

The enemy force, estimated to be company strength, is annihilated. Seven Marines of the 1st Platoon remain unscathed, while the remainder have been either killed or wounded. The survivors of the 1st Platoon receive orders to return to the company positions.

All the wounded and most of the Marine dead are brought back. The troops of Anderson's 1st Platoon and Lieutenant Nolan's 2nd Platoon are consolidated as Company F and establish night positions about fifty yards from the isolated 3rd Platoon of Lieutenant Albert Belbusti.

Both Company D and Company F hold precarious

positions and each is isolated, but anticipated enemy counterattacks never develop during the night (23rd-24th). The incessant firing of the 11th Marines' howitzers upon the enemy positions throughout the night might have been the neutralizer.

In the 3rd Battalion, 5th Marines sector, enemy troop positions near Nokpon-ni come under effective bombardment as weapons company troops, poised on Hill 296, experiment and blast the troop formations with fire from a captured enemy howitzer. Also, Company H, augmented by tanks, engages the enemy throughout the day. The 1st Battalion, 5th Marines, similar to the 3rd Battalion, had been assigned defensive duties, but its positions on Hill 105 South remain under fire throughout the day. The opposition's fire is especially effective.

Companies B and C are unable to move about and the troops lack a resupply of ammo, food and water until after dusk. Nevertheless, the Marine air support, although hindered by enemy smoke pots, successfully carries out six missions, including a stunning blow that occurs when planes (attached to VMF-214) led by Lt. Colonel Lischeid pummel an enemy troop concentration, thereby aborting a counterattack against Hill 105 South.

In other activity, the recently arrived 7th Marines, commanded by Colonel Homer Litzenberg, receives orders to advance from Inchon to the Han River. The orders stipulate that the regiment is to cross the river and deploy behind the 5th Marines. Headquarters (Regimental) and the 3rd Battalion ford the river during the latter part of the morning. Later, slightly after 1700, Colonel Litzenberg establishes his command post on the north bank of the river. The 2nd Battalion, 7th Marines, remains in position northwest of Kimpo until it is relieved on the following day by a U.S. Army unit. Meanwhile, the 1st Battalion, 7th Marines, continues to debark at Inchon.

In the 7th Infantry Division area, the 1st Battalion, 32nd Regiment, secures Hill 290, located about three miles below the Han River and about seven miles southeast of Yongdungp'o. Seizure of the hill gives the 7th Division strategic high ground that commands the southeastern approaches to the Han River and to Seoul.

Meanwhile, the 31st Regiment, operating about thirty miles south of Seoul, assumes responsibility for Suwon and its airfield, and has the responsibility to secure the town and capture the heights south of the airfield. The reconnaissance company, which captures prisoners in Suwon, is informed by the POWs that the N.K. 105th Armored Division had been in Choch'i-won on the 18th, en route to bolster the Seoul defenders. The 31st Regiment maintains a steady eye on the southern approach routes to Suwon in search of the enemy armor.

In the Eighth Army area, Army Headquarters moves from Pusan to Taegu and reopens there at 1400. The IX Corps (U.S. 2nd and 25th Divisions and their supporting units), commanded by Major General John B. Coulter, becomes operational at 1400. In conjunction, since 21 September, the 2nd and 25th Divisions have shoved the N.K. 4th, 6th, 7th and 9th Divisions back about fifteen miles from the area around Mason to Chinju.

A shortage of equipment and communications personnel has played a big part in the IX Corps' delay in becoming operational. These same crucial needs continue to hinder the IX Corps operations. Many of its intended personnel and equipment had been transferred to X Corps. IX Corps has been saddled with running supplies for the I Corps, due to the inability of the rails to maintain pace with the ground troops.

The 2nd and 25th Divisions, during the northward advance of Eighth Army beyond the 38th Parallel, will forfeit a portion of the spine of its motor pool. In one instance, the 2nd Division loses 320 trucks to establish a Red Ball Express to provide support for I Corps once it crosses the Han River. Nonetheless, between this day and September 30th, IX Corps fares well. Participating units capture twenty-two antitank guns, forty-one artillery pieces, four self-propelled guns, forty-two mortars and four enemy tanks. It also seizes nearly 500 tons of ammunition.

General Coulter confers with General Walker at the 25th Division command post. Coulter receives permission to modify the axis of his attack, switching it from a southwest direction to a westward and a southwestward course. But Coulter is ordered to maintain the corps' boundaries as they stand.

In other activity, it is now apparent that the colossal enemy ring around the Pusan Perimeter has vanished, and it is now equally obvious that the successful invasion of Inchon by the Marines has caused the turnabout. Eighth Army and the South Korean Army are finally on the threshold of the long-awaited offensive needed to regain their honor after the long period of defeat and at times humiliation.

The South Koreans had been matched against the N.K. 5th, 8th, 12th and 15th Divisions on the northern front of the Pusan Perimeter. Beginning this day, the South Koreans will advance about 70 miles within a week. At present, about 160,000 U.N. troops are deployed within the Pusan Perimeter, about 76,000 in Eighth Army area and 75,000 in the South Korean Army sector.

In the I Corps area, 1st Cavalry Division sector, 7th Cavalry zone, TF-777 continues the advance, spearheaded by TF Lynch. At 0430, the ground troops cross the Naktong River to resume the chase. Companies I and K walk through the chilled river water, and in near cadence with the soggy march, an enemy ammo depot on the opposite bank detonates and creates a rousing boom. Nonetheless, the two companies seize the far bank at 0530, about twenty-two hours after the task force had departed Tabu-dong. The 36-mile drive has scooped up 5 enemy tanks, about 50 trucks, 20 pieces of artillery and 10 motorcycles. In addition, the task force has killed or captured about 500 enemy troops.

The 1st Battalion, commanded by Major William

O. Witherspoon, bolts the river and drives northwest to Sangju, which is discovered to be free of the enemy. In the meantime, engineers modify the crossing site by establishing a ferry and using rafts, each strong enough to transport the tanks and trucks across the river. The task is complete by the following day.

In the 8th Cavalry sector, Lt. Colonel Hallett Edson replaces Colonel Raymond Palmer as regimental commanding officer. Palmer embarks for Japan. Later, during early November, Palmer regains his command. Other ranking officers in the regiment are unhappy with the decision by the corps commander, General Milburn, to bring in Edson.

In the 24th Division sector, General Church orders the division to initiate its attack. Three regiments advance northwest in a drive that plows along the Taejon–Seoul Highway moving toward Kumch'on. The 21st Regiment spearheads the assault, but General Church has modified his plans to permit the regiments to leap-frog to maintain pressure against the enemy. The advance encounters stiff resistance, which is raised by units of the N.K. 105th Armored Division. The route is blocked at various points by an array of concealed and entrenched weapons, including antitank guns and tanks. The roads are saturated with minefields to further hinder the advance, but the Americans push forward.

During the afternoon, a ferocious exchange erupts between the tanks of Company C, 6th Medium Tank Battalion, and those of the enemy. Four Patton M-46 tanks succumb to the combined enemy fire of tanks and antitank guns. But three enemy tanks are knocked out by air strikes and U.S. tank fire. Toward midnight,

the 5th RCT is poised to jump ahead of the 21st Regiment and take the lead to Kumch'on. Meanwhile, the 1st Battalion, 19th Regiment, continues its advance. The regiment drives south along the Waegwan–Kumch'on Highway moving toward Songju, which it seizes during the early morning hours of the 24th.

In the IX Corps area, 2nd Division sector, the N.K. 2nd, 4th and 9th Divisions, which have been deployed on the opposing side of the Naktong Bulge, retreat west under the pressure of the Eighth Army attacks. The N.K. 9th Division, in the lead, heads through Hyopch'on, but its dust barely dissipates as contingents of the 2nd Division arrive. The N.K. 4th Division departs Sinban-ni and swings toward Hyopch'on, while the 2nd Division moves through Ch'ogye, heading toward Hyopch'on. At Ch'ogye, the 38th Regiment battles fiercely and overwhelms the enemy rear-guards. The U.S. 38th Regiment closes against Hyopch'on on the 24th, in synchronization with the 23rd Regiment.

In the 25th Division sector, in accordance with the change in the direction of attack by division, the 27th Regiment moves from the south flank to redeploy on the division's north flank.

In other activity, General Kean establishes Task Force Torman, commanded by Captain Charles Torman (CO, 25th Reconnaissance Co.). During the evening, the task force passes through the 27th Regiment at Paedun-ni. The 27th Regiment then redeploys on the north flank at Chungam-ni, from where it will attack and establish a bridgehead on the opposite side of the Nam River. From there, it is to attack through Uiryong and then drive to Chinju.

ROK troops are aboard trains at Inchon, en route to participate in the attack to regain Seoul.

In other activity, the enemy resistance against the 35th Regiment at the Chinju Pass dissipates as the North Korean 6th Division contingents withdraw during the night of the 23rd-24th.

In Air Force activity, Fifth Air Force relocates its Korea headquarters to Taegu from Pusan. Also, Far East Air Force initiates the first known special operations mission of the Korean War when on this day, SB-17 aircraft, attached to the 3d Air Rescue Squadron based in Japan, execute a classified flight over Korea.

The SB-17 is a long-range four-engine search and rescue aircraft that is manned by a crew of nine or ten men. Initially, the aircraft was a prototype of the B-17 and received its first flight in July 1935. The plane is heavily armed with thirteen 50-inch machine guns and has the capacity to carry a bomb-load of 17,600 pounds. These Flying Fortresses also played a huge part in the air campaign in Europe during World War II.

Afterward, about fifty of the Flying Fortresses (B-17Gs) were converted specifically for search and sea rescue missions and re-designated as SB-17s. Two of these, attached to 3rd Air Rescue Squadron, serve during the Korean Conflict from their base in Japan. Two other RB-17s (reconnaissance attached to photo mapping flight), based in the Philippines at Clark Air Base, also serve the U.S. in Korea by executing special missions to gather intelligence. The planes contain radar and they carry boats that can be dropped into the sea to rescue downed pilots.

— *In the United States:* Congress overrides a presidential veto, enabling the McCarran Internal Security Act to become law. The legislation mandates that all Communist organizations must open their membership records and disclose their finances. In addition, the act requires all members of the Communist Party in the U.S. to register with the Justice Department.

— *In Japan:* General MacArthur, upon his return to Tokyo, sends a message to the Joint Chiefs of Staff in Washington explaining that at the earliest opportunity, he is going to restore President Syngman Rhee, his cabinet and other government officials to power.

September 24   *Inchon–Seoul vicinity:* The 17th Regiment, 7th Division, arrives at Inchon from Pusan, where it had been floating reserve, Eighth Army. The regiment debarks on the 25th, and within four additional days, the unit will be engaged in combat. In enemy-held Seoul, the N.K. 18th Division, which had fought in the vicinity of Yongdungp'o, regroups and prepares to evacuate Seoul and evade the Marines by heading north on Uijongbu Road toward Ch'orwon.

In the 1st Marine Division zone, as usual, the Marine aviators are overtaxed. On this day, the 2nd Battalion receives abundant air support. Marine squadron VMF-214, commanded by Lt. Colonel Lischeid, strikes enemy positions every two hours, with each strike executed by 5 planes. In addition, VMF-212 establishes a record by executing 12 flights that include 46 sorties.

In the 5th Marines sector, the North Koreans retain control of Hills 66 (Marines' Hill 56) and 88 to the front of Hill 105 Center, having repulsed the S.K. Marines and the 2nd Battalion, 5th Marines, since the 22nd. According to OpnO 26–50, Hill 105 North is the final objective of the 2nd Battalion. However, Smith's Ridge and Hill 88 must also be taken by the beleaguered 2nd Battalion.

Company D, 2nd Battalion, drives against Hill 66 (56) in synchronization with contingents of the 3rd Battalion that attack from their positions on Hill 296 to strike the enemy's flank. Company D had watched the previous night pass under relative calm. Company F, 2nd Battalion, has been hit especially hard, and its three platoon leaders (Nolan, Anderson and Belbusti) have all been wounded.

About 2,500 Communist troops stand in front of the two scheduled attacking Marine companies. At 0610, the heavy guns of the 11th Marines signal the imminent attack, and planes (VMF-323) arrive to bolster the twenty-minute bombardment. At 0630, Company F drives from the eastern slope of Hill 56 (Lt. Harry Nolan has been evacuated). Lieutenant Belbusti leads about 20 troops toward the heights east of the railroad tunnel, while Lieutenant Anderson jumps off with the able-bodied men of the 2nd and 3rd platoons, which combined, number about 20 men.

The attack receives some added muscle when planes (VMF-323) zoom overhead at low levels and drop their bombs in close proximity, but ahead of the charging Marines. The attack on the east slope succeeds and F Company seizes high ground, from which it gains the advantage. Later, planes attached to VMF-214 arrive to assure control of the area.

Following the fierce firefights, both platoons are ordered to push forward toward a stone wall on the enemy's flank, giving the Marines targets at 300 yards distant. The Communists, caught naked in an open field, are quickly shredded, and the objective is taken.

Meanwhile, Company D attacks under the cover of a thick mist and permeating smoke that hover over the burning dwellings. The Marines advance toward the base of Hill 56. Suddenly, as the contingent encroaches the objective, enemy fire, originating on Smith's Ridge, creates a wall of fire that temporarily prevents further progress. The incessant barrage includes artillery and mortar fire as well as automatic weapons.

Marine armor roars forward to assist, but one vehicle strikes a mine and another sustains a direct hit by a mortar shell, which disables it. Casualties continue to mount as Company D attempts to break from its untenable positions. The company commander, Lieutenant H.J. Smith, commits every man in the outfit. Still, no advance occurs and the ammunition is rapidly being expended. Relentlessly, the enemy fire continues, answered with equal fervor by the stalled Marines.

A donnybrook ensues during the stalemate. In some instances, the opposing sides are within grenade-throwing distances. The Marines, however, score much more accurately with their tosses. A squad led by Sergeant Robert Smith moves around the southern flank of the hill to strike from the flank, but it encounters rock solid resistance. Nine men, including a corpsman, are slain. Sergeant Smith and two other wounded Marines survive.

At about 1000, Colonel Roise receives word by radio that Lieutenant H.J. Smith's Company D is in dire need of reinforcements, but the battalion commander is compelled to deny the request, stating that the reserve troops (Company E) must be retained for the assault against the ultimate objectives. Meanwhile, Colonel Roise, the battalion commander, becomes wounded, but it is not serious. After receiving medical attention for his injured arm, Roise returns to his headquarters to complete the mission.

By about 1030, the fog and smoke vanish and the skies clear, providing the Marines with an opportunity. The artillery of the 11th Marines, the mortars of Lieutenant George Grimes' 81-mm section (2nd Battalion) and Marine planes arrive to bolster the ground troops. Initially, four Corsairs of VMF-323 execute repeated low-level sweeps. Subsequently, additional planes arrive.

During two of the air attacks, enemy antiaircraft fire damages 5 of 10 attacking planes. There is no lapse of enemy fire. Mortars and automatic weapons turn up the heat. Undaunted, despite being held up for about two hours, the remnants of Company D, commanded by Lieutenant Smith, remain determined to seize the hill.

During the first part of the afternoon, the 30 remaining riflemen of Company D and 14 other Marines (Weapons Platoon) form to attack. Marine aircraft again soar overhead and deposit bombs and napalm while strafing the objective. Soon after, a Corsair executes two dry runs over the target, the latter signaling the commencement of the attack. The Marines find themselves advancing over and through large numbers of enemy bodies that have been slain, in great part, by the thunderous fire of the artillery and aircraft.

Marines spring toward the crest in awe of the numbers of Communist dead, which explains the lack of fierce resistance. Short of the summit, Smith halts the attack to regroup for the final push. Shortly thereafter, 32 Marines, with Smith at the front, dart from their positions and sprint toward the crest. The charge surprises the enemy, but not sufficiently to halt their return fire, which pours down the slope.

Lieutenant H.J. Smith is killed during the ascent. The remaining able-bodied Marines maintain the thrust, and twenty-six Marines place their clamps on the summit. The defenders react in various ways. Some feign death, while others gallop down the reverse slopes. Some others resist ferociously. Undaunted, despite the weary 100-yard dash up the treacherous slope, the Marines crush the resistance and secure the hill. The foxholes are corroded with layers of corpses and the rest of the summit is carpeted with other enemy dead. Even the bunkers have been transformed into crypts.

Meanwhile, 11 trailing Marines bring up the machine guns and ammunition to ensure retention of the bloody crest. The enemy survivors come under vicious fire as they dash down the slope. In the meantime, more Company D troops arrive at the peak to bring the defending force to 56 men. Of these, 26 are wounded. Nevertheless, the wounded refuse to be evacuated.

At 1300, Lieutenant Karle Seydel, the lone unwounded officer of Company D, radios word to battalion headquarters that its objectives, including Hill 66 (56), are secure. The North Koreans mount a futile counterattack to retake Hill 66. At day's end, battle-weary Company D has sustained 176 casualties, including 36 killed and 116 wounded (and evacuated). The company's complement of 206 Marines now stands at twenty-six able-bodied men and the additional four wounded men who had remained on the crest.

On the following day, the 2nd Battalion reinitiates the attack against Hill 105 Center. In other 2nd Battalion activity, Company E is restrained from attacking until the other two companies secure their objectives. Following the victories of Companies D and F, Company E strikes against Hill 105 North.

At 1500, while en route to its objective, enemy fire rains upon Company E shortly after it passes Hill 56. The menacing mortar and automatic weapons fire hinders the advance, and other obstacles remain in the path. The Communists had laid mines along the approaches. Five tanks (1st Platoon, Company B, 1st Tank Battalion) push forward to augment the assault, but they get snagged in a minefield. One tank is lost to mortar fire and another is destroyed after striking a mine. The remaining three tanks are stymied, unable to navigate through the minefield.

Quick action by one daring engineer, Sergeant Stanley McPherson (Company A, 1st Engineer Battalion), forestalls disaster when he ventures onto the blocked road, and while under strong fire, he singlehandedly clears a path for the armor. The tanks then speed forward and unleash their firepower, which decimates a few machine gun strongholds and knocks out two antitank guns. However, the delay is costly; twilight begins to overtake the area and forces a postponement against what appears to be the prominent obstacle facing Company E — Hill 72, which is straddled between Hills 105 North and 105 Center.

In the 3rd Battalion sector, the enemy launches two unsuccessful predawn assaults against Marine positions on Hill 296. The 3rd Battalion is scheduled to drive down the eastern spur of Hill 296 to execute a flanking attack and to supply cover fire for the 2nd Battalion. The 1st Battalion is to relieve the 3rd Battalion on Hills 216 and 296. Following the shattering of the predawn attacks, Company H remains engaged with the Communists on the eastern slopes of Hill 296, but at 1550, Company G swings out and smashes into the enemy's right flank in a coordinated attack with Company H to terminate the resistance there.

The 3rd Battalion incurs five killed and thirty-three wounded on this day. By about 2000, the 1st Battalion completes the relief of Company I and various other 3rd Battalion troops on Hill 216.

In other activity, the 1st Battalion, 5th Marines, atop

Hill 105 South, guards the site on the Han where the 1st Marines will cross.

In the 1st Marines sector, dawn sparks the initiation of the attack. Company C, 1st Engineer Battalion, moves out and secures a crossing site on the Han at a point about 2,000 yards south of Hill 105 South, but it is an exhausting ordeal, as enemy mines permeate the area. Nevertheless, elements of the 2nd Battalion, 1st Marines, begin the move from their positions near Yongdungp'o at about 0800. LVTs (Company A, 1st Tractor Bn.) speed the battalion across the river, completing the trek by about 0945. The 2nd Battalion sustains 2 men killed and 9 wounded, due to unexpected fire from Hill 105 South, thought to have been reduced previously by the 1st Battalion, 5th Marines. Later, Colonel Sutter's troops establish contact with units of the 5th Marines on the north bank.

Meanwhile, the 1st Battalion, commanded by Lt. Colonel Jack Hawkins, and Regimental Headquarters follow the 2nd Battalion across the Han. The 1st Battalion receives orders to drive east and jump through the 2nd Battalion, which is easier said than done. The 2nd Battalion is sprinting toward Hill 79, the regimental objective. At about 1300, unexpected enemy fire again erupts from concealed positions on Hill 105 South. The hostile fire inflicts 4 casualties on the 1st Battalion.

At 1500, Colonel Hawkins' Marines seize Hill 79. They decorate it with Old Glory so enemy troops in nearby railroad marshaling yards could clearly see that the Stars and Stripes had entered the southwest section of Seoul.

In other activity, at 1515, the 3rd Battalion, 1st Marines, commanded by Lt. Colonel Thomas Ridge, receives orders from Division to relinquish its defense of Hill 108 south of the Han bridges. The battalion is to revert to regimental control and begin to cross the Han. Ridge's unit completes the crossing by 2000. Again, enemy fire zips into the newest occupants of the north bank of the Han. Ridge's Marines engage in a heated but brief exchange of fire with the enemy on Hill 105 South. Company I is committed to permanently extinguish the nagging opposition. Ten Communist troops are taken prisoner, but the Marines lose one man killed and two wounded.

The 1st and 2nd Battalions, 1st Marines, relieve the 1st Battalion, 5th Marines, and assume responsibility for the southern flank of the Marines' line along the western fringe of Seoul. The 3rd Battalion, 1st Marines, settles down in an assembly area slightly to the rear.

Meanwhile, the 2nd Battalion, 187th Airborne RCT, relieves the 2nd Battalion, 7th Marines, permitting the Marine battalion to cross the Han and join the regiment. Also, the 1st Battalion, 7th Marines, having concluded debarkation at Inchon, rejoins the regiment. The 7th Marines, on the left flank of the 5th Marines, is ordered to sweep across the northern tip of Seoul to guard the north flank and the rear of the 5th Marines. Simultaneously, it is to block the escape routes to the north.

In the 7th Infantry Division sector, General Almond arrives at Division headquarters at 0930. He confers with Generals Barr and Henry Hodes, the commanding officer and assistant CO, respectively, and with Colonel Louis Heath, the divisional chief of staff. The discussions include the possibility of a 7th Division attack into Seoul on the following day. Later, when Almond arrives back at his headquarters, he informs S.K. Colonel Paik to prepare for battle, in case his S.K. 17th Regiment is attached to the 32nd Regiment for the attack into Seoul.

In the meantime, General Almond decides that he will order the 7th Division to attack into Seoul. At 1400, Army Generals Barr and Hodes, Marine General O.P. Smith and other officers, including Colonel Forney, USMC, X Corps deputy chief of staff, and Colonel Beauchamp, CO, 32nd Regiment, are informed by Almond during a meeting at Yongdungp'o Circle that the attack will commence at 0600 on the 25th.

X Corps supplements the 7th Division, attaching the Marine 1st Amphibious Tractor Battalion (minus one company) and two platoons of Company A, 56th Amphibious Tank and Tractor Battalion, to it. In addition, the S.K. 17th Regiment is attached to the 7th Division. The three main objectives of the 32nd Regiment's attack are to capture South Mountain, drive two miles east and secure Hill 120, then capture Hill 348, the dominating feature five miles east of Seoul.

In other activity, the 2nd Battalion, 32nd Regiment, launches a successful predawn attack against enemy positions on the south side of the Han River across from Seoul. The surprise attack becomes a deadly wake-up call for some sleeping North Koreans. The battalion easily reduces the opposition, while it also seizes supplies and captures a regimental headquarters. The 2nd Battalion then continues the attack and secures the south bank of the Han at a bend in the river southeast of Seoul.

In the meantime, the 31st Regiment is in the Suwon vicinity. The 2nd Battalion, 31st Regiment, deployed on Hill 142 about two miles south of the airfield, comes under severe attack at about 2300. Enemy tanks storm the left flank along the Suwon–Osan road. The battalion holds tough and receives some strong assistance from both the 57th FABn and Battery B, 15th FABn. The attack is repelled and four T-34 tanks are destroyed.

In the Eighth Army area, the Army modifies its previous breakout operation order. It directs IX Corps to launch unlimited attacks to seize Chonju and Kanggyong.

In Air Force activity, planes continue to seek enemy troop concentrations, but some of the pilots complete their sorties and arrive back at their bases without having discovered any targets.

In the I Corps area, 1st Cavalry Division sector, Division focuses on the area around Sangju–Naktong-ni until the 25th, but the 7th Cavalry continues to advance.

In the 7th Cavalry zone, the tanks of TF-777 cross the Naktong by noon, and they advance 10 miles to Sanju to join the task force there. Colonel William Harris dispatches one platoon of tanks and Company K, 7th Cavalry, to Poun, a thirty-mile jaunt. Meanwhile, General Gay orders a contingent of tanks and infantry to advance toward Kumch'on to bolster the 24th Division elements that are slugging it out with the enemy on the Waegwan–Taejon–Seoul Highway. The 7th Cavalry contingent reaches the 24th Division, but in so doing, it exits the cavalry zone of action and soon after receives orders to return to its operating area.

In the 24th Division sector, during the first moments of the 24th, the 5th RCT takes the point and drives toward Kumch'on. A concentration of enemy troops on Hill 140, about three miles outside of Kumch'on, raises tenacious resistance. The advance stalls and the enemy on the hill buys some time to permit other units to withdraw. The N.K. 9th Division retreats toward Taejon, but it is diverted to the area around Hill 140. Other enemy units are committed at Kumch'on to hold back the surging Eighth Army. The rear guard forces include the surviving tanks of the N.K. 105th Armored Division and the 849th Independent Anti-Tank Regiment. The slugfest accelerates as the Americans encroach the objective. Air strikes destroy five enemy tanks and U.S. ground fire finishes off another three.

Meanwhile, the ground troops pound the enemy. The 849th Independent Anti Tank Regiment is nearly annihilated. Six Patton tanks are lost to enemy fire. Later in the day, the 21st Regiment drives forward north of the highway, establishes contact with the 5th RCT and bolsters its attack. In conjunction, some enemy contingents lay back along the Waegwan Highway and engage the Division's trailing unit, the 19th Regiment. By day's end, the 5th RCT and its supporting contingents sustain about 100 casualties, due mostly to tank and mortar fire.

In related activity, the 1st Battalion, 19th Regiment, seizes Songju at 0200. Later, the unit moves out to hook up with the 27th British Brigade to conduct mop-up operations in the area. In the meantime, the N.K. 10th Division begins to bury its artillery before initiating its withdrawal.

In the IX Corps area, 2nd Division sector, the 23rd Regiment rapidly drives from the south in coordination with the 38th Regiment, which closes against Hyopch'on from the northeast to unleash a double envelopment assault. A contingent of 38th Regiment establishes a roadblock that severs the Chinju–Kumch'on Road and blocks the northeastern escape route from Hyopch'on. About two battalions of enemy troops are trapped in the town.

During the afternoon, the 23rd Regiment drives into the town and pushes the enemy out. Unwittingly, they flee northeast directly into the roadblock. About 300 enemy troops are killed. But the plight of the enemy is only beginning; soaring Air Force F-51 fighters join the fight. The planes fly fifty-three sorties and further pulverize the survivors while they flee for the hills. Later, after dusk, the 1st Battalion, 38th Regiment, moves into Hyopch'on, and joins the 23rd Regiment there.

In the 25th Division sector, Task Force Torman drives along the coastal road heading toward Chinju, but it encounters resistance from elements of the N.K. 3rd Battalion, 104th Security Regiment. By dusk, the task force secures the heights at the road junction about three miles outside Chinju. The enemy force is composed of about 200 troops, according to information later gained from the battalion commanding officer, Lt. Colonel Pak Chong Song, during an interrogation.

In other activity, the 35th Regiment regroups at the Chinju pass, subsequent to the withdrawal of the enemy. During the night, a patrol probes to the Nam River and discovers that the enemy has knocked out the bridge span. Also, General Kean, to better handle his area of responsibility with regard to IX Corps objectives, establishes two key task forces, TF Matthews and TF Dolvin. TF Dolvin had formerly been TF Torman.

Task Force Matthews is composed of the 25th Reconnaissance Company, Company A, 79th Tank Battalion; one platoon of Company B, 67th Engineer Combat Battalion; an Air TAC party; and the medical section of the 27th Regiment. Two additional task forces also are involved with the attack. TF Matthews spearheads the assault, but is closely trailed by TF Blair, commanded by Major Melvin Blair (CO, 3rd Bn., 24th Regiment), and TF Corley, commanded by Colonel John Corley (CO, 24th Regiment).

The two primary task forces are to attack simultaneously, but TF Matthews (on the left) is unable to execute the mission until the 27th, due to the three demolished bridges west of Chinju. TF Dolvin, commanded by Lt. Colonel Welborn G. Dolvin, CO, 89th Tank Battalion, commences its attack from the division right on the 26th. The primary components of the task force are Companies A and B, 89th Tank Battalion, and Companies B and C, 35th Regiment.

Task Force Dolvin will split into two units, each composed of tanks and infantry contingents. Other units attached to TF Dolvin are the 1st Platoon, Company A, 65th Engineer Combat Battalion; 2nd Platoon, Heavy Mortar Company, 35th Regiment; the medical detachment, 89th Tank Bn., and some task force trains.

In the ROK II Corps area, the S.K. 6th and 8th Divisions push rapidly through the mountains and gain about sixteen miles on this day. The 6th Division reaches Andong before midnight. Meanwhile, the N.K. 8th and 12th Divisions abandon their positions in the vicinity of Andong, but they raise resistance during the withdrawal. Forward units of the S.K. force enter the city. Other S.K. troops arrive to block some of the escape routes, which forces elements of the N.K. 8th Division to divert and move into the mountains. Most of the survivors (about 1,500) make it to the Yalu River.

In the meantime, most of the N.K. 12th Division has exited the town. The S.K. 6th Division, operating on the left, drives toward Hamch'ang.

September 25 On or about this date, the N.K. I Corps orders all units still south of Waegwan to retire

A Sherman medium tank (M4) pauses along a road in the vicinity of Kumch'on while infantry troops pass by.

northward. This is the final day of action for the USS *Sicily* and VMF-214 during the Seoul-Inchon campaign. During the latter part of the day it embarks to receive required maintenance. The USS *Badoeng Strait* and its VMF-323 assume responsibility for further action in support of the ground troops.

The commanding officer of the *Badoeng Strait* bans the number 17 from the carrier. The first plane lost by the Carrier on D-Day plus 2 was numbered 17. Two days later, a sergeant examining the new aircraft, also designated number 17, was mortally wounded when the guns accidentally fired. And then on September 23, the ill-fated Corsair 17 is again plagued when its pilot, Major Robert Floeck, is killed. Today, Plane Number 17 leaves the carrier and yet another life is lost, prompting Captain John Thach to permanently banish the number 17.

Also on this day, Captain Leslie E. Brown, who on September 9 became the first Marine pilot to fly a jet against an enemy force, is killed on another mission. His plane is downed by antiaircraft fire.

Inchon–Seoul vicinity: In the X Corps area, slightly before dark, aerial observance detects enemy columns moving out of Seoul. General Almond places an urgent request for Far East Air Forces to illuminate the escape route with flares to aid Marine Night Fighters. A B-29 arrives and its crew obliges and soon after spends about three hours' flying time over the area to deposit the flares above the enemy. Two gigan-

tic enemy columns receive some punishing blows from the Marine planes. In conjunction, X Corps artillery units unleash their guns and deliver an enfilade of blazing fire upon the closer portions of the retiring enemy.

General Almond makes what some construe as a premature proclamation slightly before midnight. He proclaims the liberation of Seoul. The announcement is made precisely three months to the day since the city had been captured by the Communists, and coincidentally, it is on the same day that Almond had promised General MacArthur that it would fall.

In other activity, the 3rd Battalion, 187th Airborne Regiment, arrives at Kimpo Airfield by air from Ashiya, Japan. The airborne troops take responsibility for the airfield.

In the 1st Marine Division zone, today, all the Division's regiments will be north of the Han River and linked together. At 0700 the Division commences the final phase of its attack to seize Seoul. According to OpnO 11–50, RCT 1 and the attached 2nd Korean Marine Battalion is to capture that portion of Seoul within its zone (South Mountain and Ducksoo Palace area). Following these seizures, it is to advance about 6 additional miles and seize Objective Able, the heights beyond the northeastern suburbs. RCT-5 its attached division reconnaissance company and the 1st Korean Marine Battalion are to secure the northwest sector of Seoul.

Following this gain, they are to capture Objective Baker, the heights above the Seoul–Uijongbu Road, which lie about 6 miles outside the city. RCT-7 is to seize Objective Charlie, the heights above the Seoul–Kaesong Road near Chonsong-ni, about 6 miles northwest of the city's center-point. The combat team is to simultaneously cover the division's left flank. In conjunction, the 3rd Battalion, 187th Airborne RCT, is to remain under the control of the 1st Marine Division with orders to guard the left flank, both south and west of the Han River.

Also, the attached South Korean Marine units are utilized for mop-up operations. The Korean Marine Regiment (minus the 1st and 2nd Battalions) is to remain as division reserve. Subsequent to the recapture of the city, it is to resume control of its detached battalions and occupy the capital.

At 2040, the 1st Marine Division receives a somewhat confusing order, directing it to launch an immediate attack: "X Corps TACair commander, reports enemy fleeing city of Seoul on road north.... He is conducting heavy air attack and will continue same. You will attack now to the limit of your objective to insure maximum destruction of enemy forces." But Colonel Alpha Bowser, 1st Marine Division G-3, remains unconvinced that the Communists are abandoning the city. He inquires at X Corps headquarters and he is informed that the order, issued by General Almond, stands. General O.P. Smith is adamantly opposed to the order, and he, too, calls headquarters, only to receive a similar rebuff from the chief of staff, General Ruffner, who explains that General Almond insists on an immediate attack.

At 2200, Smith reluctantly and against his instincts directs the 1st and 5th Marines, commanded by Colonels Puller and Murray respectively, to attack, but he stipulates that they move only along routes that can be easily identified in the dark. The 1st Marines receives the orders at 2205, and the 5th Marines is informed at 2215, the latter having just turned back an enemy attack about two hours earlier. Both regiments take measures to prepare their exhausted troops to again attack, and the word is passed to the 7th and 11th Marines. Within minutes after the orders to attack are received, the 5th Marines is hit by an enemy counterattack.

In the 5th Marines sector, the 1st Battalion, commanded by Colonel Newton, having completed its relief of the 3rd Battalion units on Hills 216 and 296, is poised to advance on the left of the 3rd Battalion upon orders. The leftward shift by the 1st Battalion postures it to protect the steep entrances to both hills. Meanwhile, artillery and air strikes pummel the enemy line throughout the morning. The Marine air support (VMF-214), sustains another loss, its second in two days, when Lt. Colonel Lischeid is shot from the sky over the western portion of Seoul. Within about two additional hours, Lt. Colonels Wyczawski and Volcansek, the commanders of VMF-212 and VMF(N)-542 respectively, also are downed by enemy fire, but these two pilots survive.

Subsequent to the preparatory barrages, the 3rd Battalion, under Taplett, drives down Hill 296, in concert with the 2nd Battalion, under Roise, which grinds toward Hill 105 North. The 3rd Battalion is to secure the two southeastern knobs of Hill 296. The 2nd Battalion assault is bolstered by fire from the 3rd Battalion on Hill 296 and one platoon of tanks. Company E spearheads the attack. Company D (less than full strength), on its left, drives northward from Hill 66 (Smith's Ridge) and follows the ridge line that leans southwest from Hill 296. From there, Company D, led by Lieutenant Seydel, pivots southeast and continues its hard fought advance. At 1320, following a grueling contest, Hill 88 falls to Company D. Meanwhile, Company E, led by Captain Jaskilka, encounters fierce fire originating on enemy-held Hill 72. Despite the horrific fire and mounting casualties, the 1st Platoon, led by Lieutenant Deptula, silences the mortars and the automatic weapons fire. Hill 72 is secured at 1335. Company F, held in reserve, then advances to occupy Hill 72.

During the ongoing melee, at 1310, air strikes are requested to thump the enemy positions on Hill 105 North to lessen the resistance against the final attack by the remaining two platoons of Company E. At 1325, the artillery roars and signals the imminent assault by the platoons of Lieutenants James Epley and Samuel Eddy. The attacking Marines relentlessly grind forward, and by 1545, Hill 105 North falls to the 2nd Battalion.

Meanwhile, the 3rd Battalion gnaws forward. Like the 2nd Battalion, it, too, receives powerful blows from enemy artillery, as long-range interdiction fire arrives from Hill 105 North and from Hill 338, on its right and left respectively. After being temporarily held up by Colonel Murray, while Hill 105 North is being secured by the 2nd Battalion, Companies G and H resume the attack at 1435 against extremely dense fire originating from their left. The Marines plow forward, taking heavy casualties as they advance. Company H is hit especially hard as it grinds forward along the giant knob on the open left flank. Nevertheless, it reaches the objective, an intermediate peak, by 1635.

In the meantime, Company G secures an unnamed peak north of the 2nd Battalion's positions, but on the same ridge. Contact is quickly made between the two battalions. Following the seizures, Company I jumps off to continue the assault at about 1700; however, the enemy launches a counterattack and draws blood. The Communist attack is augmented by effective support fire that presses both Companies H and I. The Marines maintain their positions and pound the attacking Reds. Finally, by about dusk, the enemy losses climb to about 100 killed and they abort the assault.

The beleaguered Marines then prepare for the next task. Company H reverts to battalion reserve. Company I assumes responsibility for the front lines, and it prepares to drive into Seoul on the following day.

In related activity, other elements of the 2nd Battalion successfully attack Hill 105 Center to reduce the resistance there by mid-afternoon. According to information ascertained from enemy prisoners, about 500 North Koreans are killed on Hill 105 Center. Consequently, the Marine advances have destroyed the western defenses of Seoul and inflicted severe casualties upon the enemy. About 1,200 Communist dead are strewn about the hills and in the foxholes. The Marines estimate total enemy dead along the western defenses by all weaponry at 1,750.

The 5th Marines enter the northwest sector of the city and advance toward Sodaemun Prison and Government House. A synchronized attack by the 1st and 5th Marines on the following day is planned by the two regiments during the evening of the 25th. But, while the 5th Marine Regiment is preparing the attack, new orders arrive at slightly after 2200 for an immediate attack into the city by the 1st and 5th Marines. However, the enemy strikes first and the 3rd Battalion, 5th Marines, is attacked by about 200 North Koreans. A savage night-long battle ensues, but the Marines repel the Communists and terminate the action at 0445.

While the fighting is raging between the Marines and the enemy, the 5th Marines also has patrols out in an attempt to establish contact with the 1st and 7th Marines. Contingents extending south and southeast fail to make contact with the 1st Marines, and the patrols to the north are unable to locate the 7th Marines. General O.P. Smith had directed the regiments to make contact before assaulting Seoul in the darkness. The divisional attack will be postponed and the 5th Marines does not advance from its positions during the night, except for the patrols.

In the 1st Marines sector, the 1st Battalion maintains a blocking position at Hill 79 along the southern portion of Seoul during the morning, while it waits for the 3rd Battalion to alter its course of attack against Seoul. The 3rd Battalion, led by Lt. Colonel Thomas Ridge, advances prior to dawn and moves east through the positions of the 2nd Battalion in a column of companies. At that point, it pivots sharply, then drives north toward the center of Seoul.

At about the same time, the 1st Battalion shifts slightly backward from its positions, and then it too drives north, operating on the right flank of the 3rd Battalion. The maneuver puts great strength against Seoul, but it creates a hole between the 1st and 5th Marines. Due to an unexpected crisis at Hill 105 South, the 1st Marines lack tank support. The tank column expects to encounter mines along the route, which parallels the rail lines that lead into Seoul. Therefore, the two tank platoons of Company B (commanded by Captain Bruce Williams), 1st Tank Battalion, are bolstered by engineers and by one infantry platoon of Company F to safeguard its passage through the lines of the 2nd Battalion, 5th Marines.

Infantry take the point and the engineers are couched between the tanks. The advance through the gap in the lines occurs without incident. But when the column reaches the midway point, an ambush is sprung. Enemy fire rings out from Hill 105 South, thought to have previously been secured by the 1st Battalion, 5th Marines, and swept clean by mop-up teams of the 3rd Battalion, 1st Marines. The ambush, perpetrated by about 300 troops, catches the column off guard and its ripping fire inflicts casualties.

Lieutenant Babe, commanding officer 2nd Platoon, Company C, Engineers, is struck immediately. The debilitating wound prevents him from ordering the infantry under Sergeant Farrington to strike the left flank of the enemy to eliminate the blockage. Soon after, Sergeant Paolino assumes command of Babe's engineers, but the enemy force appears much too powerful.

Meanwhile, the commanding officer of the tanks, Captain Bruce Williams, ponders a withdrawal to avoid being overrun, but he decides to commit his equalizers. He sends out a flamethrower tank and an M-26 escort. By circuitous route, the armor maneuvers into position on the left flank of the infested slope. The tanks immediately roar into action. Bellowing bursts of napalm bounce along the entire string of enemy entrenchments, compelling the inhabitants to seek cooler ground. They flee directly into the menacing machine gun fire of Lieutenant Cummings' platoon and then, his tanks shred the fleeing enemy troops. All the while, the engineers and infantry reorganize along the rails and lower slopes by Sergeants Paolino and Farrington respectively. A sharp line of cover fire begins to emerge, but yet another hazard threatens the Marines.

Nearby, enemy grenades begin to explode, and they activate the Marines' instinctive alarms. They spot the problem: three primitive huts that sit on the slope just under the enemy trenches on the left flank. They also discover that an enemy cave is concealed by the third hut. Sergeant Paolino receives permission from Captain Williams to apply tank fire. Lieutenant Cummings responds to a string of hefty bangs on his tank by Paolino. He swivels his turret and pummels the trio of huts with several devastating 90-mm shells.

While adjusting his fire to ring the newest target, Cummings and the others observe about ten enemy troops as they file out of the cave with their hands extended high above their heads. After this initial surrender, a steady stream of Communist troops pours out of the endangered cave. Soon after, 131 North Koreans are captured, including two weapon-carrying women in uniform. About 150 enemy troops are killed. Hill 105 South, thought benign, is finally dormant.

The column, outnumbered by its prisoners, reinitiates the march and pushes forward after searching the women prisoners. They claim to be nurses, not soldiers, and they complain that they had not been treated fairly. The media fans the incident and the people in the States read some sensational stories. Nevertheless, the

Marines maintain they had treated them properly under the circumstances, and had given them clothes that make them look more like women.

At about 1200, the small armored task force reaches the positions of the 1st Marines and pulls up to the intersection where the rail tracks converge with the boulevard that leads into Seoul. Lieutenant Cummings reports to Colonel Puller, and then, the push into the city begins. The Marines, spearheaded by tanks, grind forward against roadblocks and fierce resistance. Antitank weapons, mortars and automatic weapons attempt to stall the advance. Nonetheless, the Marines gnaw forward and move down both sides of the boulevard. Two of the lead tanks, including that of Cummings, strike mines, but both are saved. The 1st Marines drives toward the main Seoul railroad and several other key points, including the American and Russian consulates, City Hall and the ancient Ducksoo Palace. By evening, the 1st and 3rd Battalions each penetrate about two thousand yards. The former halts in the heights to the right of the 3rd Battalion. The 3rd Battalion drills directly into the city and halts at positions next to the rail lines and on the western slope of Hill 97. Both units then converge and take up defensive positions on Hill 82 to prepare for the following day's attack.

Engineers begin removing mines, previously set by them, to clear the path for the attack. The 2nd Battalion (Reserve) deploys to the rear of the 1st Battalion to provide cover on the right flank and for the rear. Like the other Marine regiments, the 1st Marines receives orders at about 2200 instructing it to immediately launch an attack into Seoul. At about 0145, subsequent to a fifteen-minute artillery barrage, the 1st Marines are poised to advance. But, Colonel Puller, at about seven minutes before jump off, concludes that the bombardment is insufficient. He requests a repeat performance to bolster the assault.

The attack is rescheduled for 0200, but the enemy nixes the attack by striking first. At 0153, an emergency message arrives that proclaims that a fierce enemy assault, including armor, is pushing from the city, driving toward the 1st Marines positions to the southwest. The urgent news suggests that self-propelled guns are also with the attack units.

Meanwhile, a 3rd Battalion patrol, led by Corporal Charles Collins and composed of eight Marines and three South Koreans, probes to establish contact with the 5th Marines. Instead, at about 0130, the patrol encounters the surging enemy. A fire fight ensues about four hundred yards to the front of the 1st Marines' lines. Several men of the patrol make it back to their zone and give the alert. Corporal Collins is not among them; he is presumed killed.

In the meantime, Major Edwin Simmons detects the absolute sounds of tracked vehicles, and they are not sporting Marine insignia. Simmons receives word that two enemy tanks are encroaching George Company's roadblock, which is bolstered with 3.5 rocket launchers, heavy machine guns and some hefty 75-mm re-coilless rifles. Without hesitation, the enemy tanks are plastered with seething fire; one is knocked out and the other retreats.

The uninvited visitors derail the Marine assault scheduled for 0200; however, both sides still gather in the darkness. The enemy attack force numbers about battalion strength and it is fortified by tanks. The enemy advance is intercepted by the 11th Marines' artillery and by mortar fire. The attack reaches its pinnacle at about 0230, but it falls prey to an iron hailstorm, which literally blows the attackers back and stalls the attack. Subsequent enemy infantry advances are ineffective. The surviving armor launches sporadic advances, but they also fail to cross through the Marines' line.

By dawn, the counterattack sizzles and the survivors disengage, then retire hurriedly. Marine fire slays the last two enemy T-34 tanks at 0630. Daylight emphasizes the horror of the killing grounds, which are permeated with the stench of death, the peculiar odor of scorched armor and the scores of mangled corpses. Corporal Collins, thought to have been lost, is not among the deceased. After his patrol encountered the attack force, he had concealed himself in Korean civilian garb. He walks back into friendly lines at about 0630.

The N.K. 25th Brigade sustains 475 to 500 killed and a great deal more wounded. In addition, 83 prisoners are collected by the 1st Marines. Interrogation of the POWs, coupled with the combing of the battlefield, determines that seven enemy tanks and two self-propelled guns were destroyed. If this 700-man enemy force was in the process of abandoning Seoul, as described by General Almond, it had apparently been retiring in the wrong direction.

In the 7th Marines sector, the 1st Battalion sends out continuous reconnaissance patrols to maintain contact with RCT-5 and RCT-7 and to sweep the terrain lying between both units. The 2nd Battalion moves out at 0630 to secure Objective Charlie, then takes it without incident at 1215. In the meantime, the 3rd Battalion remains in a defensive arc-like posture to protect the highways and trails near the ferry-crossing site at Haengju.

In the 7th Infantry Division zone, the 17th Regiment comes ashore to join the 7th Division as its 3rd Regiment. In other activity, the scheduled attack by the 32nd Regiment, reinforced, is being prepared. The spearheading 2nd Battalion and the 96th FABn are deployed east of the town. The 1st and 3rd Battalions, deployed northwest of it, are commanded by Colonels Faith and Schumann respectively. Both units will trail Colonel Mount's 2nd Battalion when it crosses the Han.

Company A, 56th Amphibian Tractor Battalion, and the Marine 1st Amphibian Tractor Battalion (minus Company B) had spent an exhausting night to assure success. They were compelled to execute a 25-mile round-trip to transport the troops to a jump-off site about 5,000 yards east of a rail bridge at Yongdungp'o.

At 0600, a thirty-minute artillery barrage is initiated by the 48th FABn, and its thunderous roar is enjoined by heavy mortars that sizzle the bluffs beyond the river bank. At 0630, the 2nd Battalion, 32nd Regiment, spearheaded by Company F, begins crossing the river during an usually foggy morning, and it completes the trek without incident. The LVTs transport the troops inland about 200 yards. From that point, they dart across the tiny beach area and ascend the 30 to 60 foot bluffs bringing the vanguard to the slopes of South Mountain. The sun emerges through the fog at about 0730. At about the same time, air strikes pound Hill 120, and South Mountain, the latter standing ominously on the north bank, leans northwest and extends backward directly into Seoul.

By about noon, the 3rd Battalion brings up the rear, and soon after, it fords the river and traces the steps of the 1st Battalion. It moves east, jumps through the 1st Battalion and occupies Hill 120. The 1st Battalion then deploys in positions between the 2nd and 3rd Battalions. In the meantime, the vanguard is swiftly ascending South Mountain. It overcomes moderate resistance as it surges to the summit and claims it by 1500.

The 2nd Battalion immediately establishes a night defensive perimeter on the summit. The regiment is unable to proceed from the heights into the city because the movement might impede the ongoing operations of the 1st and 5th Marines. In conjunction, the ROKs cross behind the 3rd Battalion against heavy fire, but the LVTs safely deliver the S.K. 17th Regiment. The 32nd Regiment and the ROKs deploy within a zone of action from which they can expeditiously advance on the right flank of the Marines at the prescribed time.

Meanwhile, Colonel Mount deploys Company F on South Mountain's low eastern knob, and he places Company G on the more elevated western knob. During the night of the 25th-26th, while one enemy battalion is being vanquished by a night-long battle with the 1st Marines on the outskirts of Seoul, another enemy battalion assaults the 2nd Battalion, 32nd Regiment. At 0500 (26th), the Communists pound the 2nd Battalion and make some progress. The troops holding the forward positions are temporarily shoved back, but then a counterattack ignites a fierce battle that regains the lost ground.

By about 0700, the lines are fully restored and the Reds are shoved off the ridge. The victors count 394 dead Communist troops on the battlefield and another 174 taken prisoner. At 2150, the S.K. 17th Regiment, on the far right flank of the 32nd Regiment, jumps off at 2150 to seize Hill 348. The battle continues throughout the night (25th-26th). By mid-afternoon on September 26, the South Koreans secure Hills 292 and 348.

In the 31st Regiment's sector at Suwon, aerial intelligence determines that the series of hills that lie about ten miles south of Suwon and about two or three miles south of the U.S. positions are heavily fortified by the enemy. These hills command both sides of the road and the railroad lines slightly north of Osan. The 92nd FABn arrives at Suwon to augment the forces there.

In the Eighth Army area, during the day, General Walker pays homage to the South Korean forces in tribute to the tremendous progress they have made against the enemy. Walker states: "Too little has been said in praise of the South Korean Army which has performed so magnificently in helping turn this war from the defensive to the offensive."

In other activity, the British 27th Brigade is detached from the U.S. 24th Division and attached to I Corps control.

In the I Corps area, 1st Cavalry Division sector, General Gay becomes perturbed during the evening of the 25th when orders arrive from I Corps that direct him to retain the 1st Cavalry Division at its present positions. Gay attempts unsuccessfully to contact Eighth Army headquarters to clarify what appears to have been erroneous orders. He wants authorization to resume the attack and hook up with X Corps. General Gay dispatches an urgent message by liaison plane to Eighth Army.

Toward midnight and subsequent to the installation of phone lines, Gay receives a call from Colonel Edgar J. Conley, Jr. (Eighth Army G-1). Conley informs him that Walker has authorized 1st Cavalry to attack toward Suwon to establish contact with X Corps if he believes the mission can be accomplished. The cavalry assault force moves out the morning of the 26th.

In the 7th Cavalry zone, the unit is to remain in Poun until notified otherwise.

In the 24th Division sector, Kumch'on falls to the 5th RCT. The 3rd Battalion, commanded by Colonel Benjamin Heckemeyer, enters the ruins during the morning to eliminate the remaining resistance, and secures it by 1445.

In other activity, mop-up operations continue in the vicinity of Songju. The enemy defenders become further exasperated. The N.K. 10th Division, reduced to about twenty-five percent of its strength, has expended nearly all of its ammunition and depleted its fuel supply. Its withdrawal, which had begun on the previous day, moves into high gear. By dusk, the U.S. 21st Regiment jumps off and continues the attack. The regiment drives west along the highway against dissipating enemy resistance.

In the IX Corps area, 2nd Division sector, the 23rd Regiment is ordered to move against Koch'ang via a road that supposedly lies south of the route of the 38th Regiment; however, reconnaissance (air and ground) concludes that the road is either nonexistent or impenetrable. General Keiser then orders the 23rd Regiment to alter its route and advance along a road to the north. At 1600, the regiment (less the 1st Battalion) departs for Koch'ang. The march is tedious and opposition is encountered. Three separate heavy firefights occur, and in addition, the regiment must reconstruct four bridges.

Nonetheless, the 23rd Regiment arrives at Koch'ang on the following morning.

In the meantime, the 38th Regiment departs Hyopch'on at dawn and it, too, drives toward Koch'ang. Meanwhile, the N.K. 2nd Division abandons its vehicles and equipment as it retreats haphazardly. The debris hinders and then stalls the 38th Regimental vehicles, which cannot navigate around the obstacles. The infantry begins to pursue on foot. The day-long thirty-mile chase nets 450 prisoners, and about 260 Communists are slain. At 2030, the 38th Regiment halts several miles from Koch'ang.

Air Force planes hammer Koch'ang during the late afternoon and the target is inundated with rockets, napalm and bombs. The swift pace of the 38th Regiment and the heavy steel claws of the Air Force have combined to thwart the plans of the enemy. The N.K. 2nd, 4th, 9th and 10th Divisions had planned to converge on Koch'ang and regroup, but those plans are now impossible. The N.K. 2nd Division is down to about 2,500 troops (maximum), and most are under duress from the U.S. onslaught. The sweep to Koch'ang captures fourteen antitank guns, four artillery pieces, nine mortars and seventeen vehicles. In addition, the 38th Regiment seizes ten motorcycles and about 300 tons of ammunition.

The regiment enters Koch'ang on the following morning. By the end of September, most of the North Korean 2nd Division has dispersed into the hills, leaving the commanding officer, Major General Choe Hyon, with only about 200 troops.

In the 25th Division sector, Task Force Torman approaches the Nam River bridge, which leads into Chinju. One of the supporting tanks runs over a mine and fragments fly in every direction. Captain Torman is struck and wounded, then evacuated. Captain Charles M. Matthews, CO, Company A, 79th Tank Battalion, assumes command.

In the meantime, the 2nd Battalion, 35th Regiment, begins to cross the Nam about two and one-half miles southeast of Chinju at 0200 and then drives against Chinju, which is defended by about 300 enemy troops. The 2nd Battalion, bolstered by TF Torman's tank fire from the opposite bank of the Nam, overcomes the opposition and secures Chinju. During the afternoon, the 1st and 3rd Battalions ford the Nam and join the 2nd Battalion. During the evening, and thanks to an underwater bridge constructed by the 65th Engineers, TF Torman also moves into Chinju. The engineers work throughout the night, and by noon on the following day, vehicles ford the river several miles south of the damaged bridge.

Farther south near Uiryong, about 1,000 Korean refugees and U.S. engineers, while under sporadic mortar fire, construct another sandbag crossing of the Nam. The 8th FABn commits its guns and the mortars are put out of commission. During the night (25th–26th), the 1st Battalion, 27th Regiment, crosses to the north bank, completing the trek by dawn on the 26th.

In the ROK II Corps area, the S.K. 6th Division pushes into Hamch'ang after dark. Within two additional days, it presses through the most rugged part of the Sobaek Mountain Range to draw closer to Chungju.

In other activity, the S.K. 8th Division overcomes minefields. It begins eliminating the remaining resistance in Andong and secures it on the following day.

In ROK Army Headquarters area, the S.K. 3rd Division, bolstered by the guns of U.S. naval surface vessels, attacks Yongdok, defended by the N.K. 5th Division. The defenders, unable to retreat east by the sea, attempt to evacuate and head inland toward the mountains. The Navy's guns redesigned the landscape of the town; it is scarred and charred and the rising smoke blankets the skyline. The Communists apparently evacuate swiftly. The South Koreans enter the town to discover horse-drawn carts complete with hitched ponies. The assault troops also capture other equipment, including Russian-made trucks that are abandoned with the motors running. The South Koreans initiate immediate pursuit.

One U.S. officer, Major Curtis Ivey (KMAG), has procured 25 trucks through the ingenuity of Colonel McPhail, an advisor to the ROK I Corps. The South Koreans roar up the coastal road to finish off the division, which by now is reduced to about one regiment. In conjunction, most of the time the South Korean forces advance by foot. The trucks are a luxury.

In Air Force activity, during encounters with MiGs on this day, Lieutenant Booth T. Holker (334th Fighter-Interceptor Squadron, 4th Fighter-Interceptor Group) receives two victories in the vicinity of Taechon. Lieutenant Charles F. Loyd, also of the 334th Fighter-Interceptor Squadron, downs a MiG in the vicinity of Sinanju. In another air duel, Lieutenant Paul E. Roach, 334th Fighter-Interceptor Squadron, and his wingman combine to knock out another MiG near Anju.

September 26–October 21 1950

Subsequent to the Eighth Army breakout from the Pusan Perimeter and up to October 1, 1950, seven damage survey teams scour the area to attempt to arrive at accurate numbers concerning destroyed or captured enemy equipment. The information is required to offset what apparently have been inflated figures calculated from the units' daily records. The troops comb every primary route of transportation used by armor between the 38th Parallel and the Perimeter. The Kaesong–Sariwon–Pyongyang Road above the 38th Parallel is also scoured.

The detachments discover sixty demolished U.S. tanks. Enemy equipment discovered: 239 enemy T-34s, either destroyed or abandoned, and 76 self-propelled 76-mm guns. Evidence indicates the Air Force should receive credit for sixty of the enemy tanks. U.S. tanks gain credit for killing thirty-nine enemy tanks and the rocket launcher teams receive

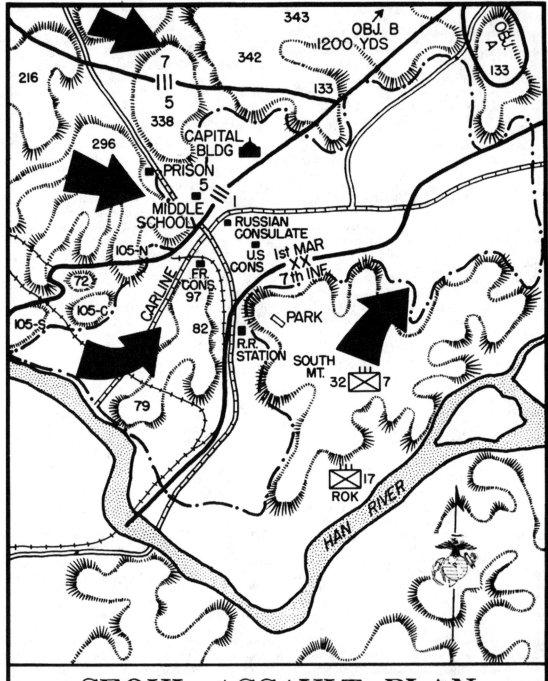

SEOUL ASSAULT PLAN

26 SEP 50

SHOWING DIVISION & REGTL BOUNDARIES

0   4000

YARDS

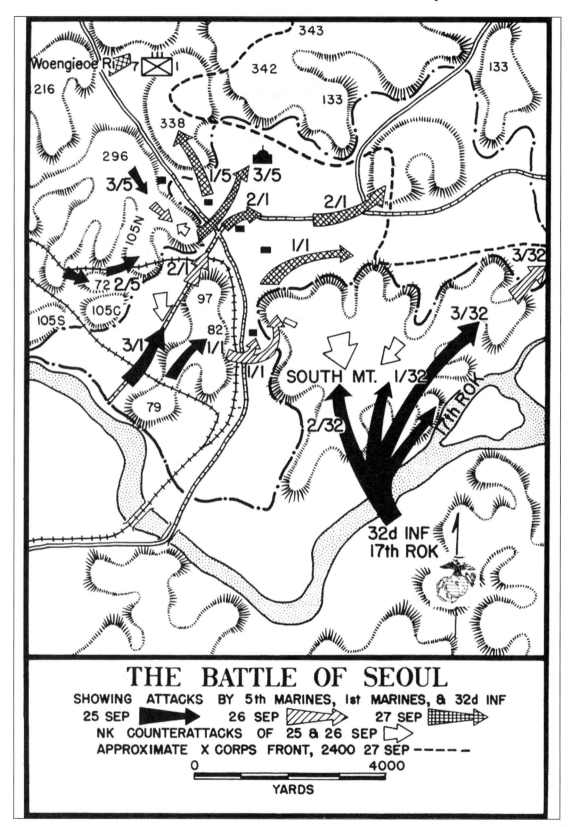

THE BATTLE OF SEOUL
SHOWING ATTACKS BY 5th MARINES, 1st MARINES, & 32d INF

25 SEP   26 SEP   27 SEP

NK COUNTERATTACKS OF 25 & 26 SEP

APPROXIMATE X CORPS FRONT, 2400 27 SEP ----

0   4000

YARDS

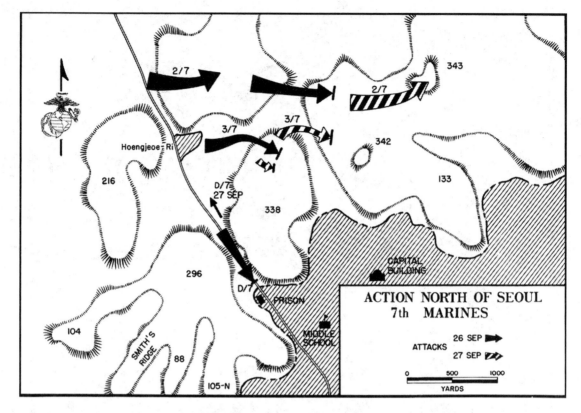

ACTION NORTH OF SEOUL
7th MARINES

ATTACKS   26 SEP ▶
           27 SEP ⚡

0   500   1000
YARDS

credit for thirteen kills, but it is certain that the bazookas accounted for many more enemy tanks than the figures state. The Air Force may have gotten credit for some tanks that had been taken out earlier by the bazookas.

U.S. tank losses, since their introduction to the conflict in July and continuing through September, from all causes is 136. The most startling statistic is that nearly 100 (70 percent) of the tanks had been lost to enemy mines. The figure is in sharp contrast to the tank losses attributable to mines during World War II, which totaled 20 percent.

September 26 *In Naval activity,* the destroyer USS *Brush* sustains damage by an enemy mine off the east coast of Korea.

Inchon–Seoul vicnity: In the X Corps area, the 1st Marine Division zone, after daylight the Marines execute the orders of the previous night. Division issues OpnO 12–50 at 1230. The directive mandates the resumption of the attack against Seoul, and it is slightly altered by committing the 7th Marines to the quest. Prior to the attack, the 1st Marine Division is deployed in a half-moon formation that stretches from the northwest to the south and encompasses the ground between the Kaesong Highway and Hill 82.

In the 1st Marines sector, the 2nd Battalion, 1st Marines, commanded by Colonel Sutter, starts early and passes through the positions of the 3rd Battalion. Coming out of reserve, it drives down Ma-Po Boule-

vard to seize Seoul. Companies F and G, led by Baker Company tanks, sprint forward. But Lieutenant Cummings' tank strikes a mine (U.S. M-6) that the engineers had missed during a clearing operation the previous night. The detonation knocks out the tank and inflicts casualties to some ground Marines on both sides of the tank.

The advance continues, but the situation gets no better. The Communists have made roadblocks out of rice bags piled eight feet high and about five feet thick, placed about 300 to 400 yards apart. The obstacles are augmented by defenders and anti-tank guns. Nevertheless, the Marine infantry and armor plow forward. Engineers, covered by sharpshooters, move methodically to open a path. Once the mines are eliminated the tanks burst through the barriers, followed by the infantry.

As the Marines terminate the individual blockages, other North Koreans continue to fire from nearby buildings. Seemingly, every rooftop, window and alley is launching shells at the charging Marines, who must defend against fire coming from all points. The progress is measured by yards, and the attack is hindered by even more unexpected obstacles, such as groups of civilians, including women and children, scattered along the line of advance. The tanks continue to crash through the bunkers and the ground troops drill deeper, disregarding the intense heat, smoke and flames emerging from the burning buildings.

The battle rages furiously, and it includes suicidal

missions by individuals carrying demolition charges who attack the armor. The first attempt succeeds when one North Korean dashes fearlessly toward a flamethrower tank and damages it while the vehicle is shadowing two M-26s. However, the crew escapes the burning vehicle and nearby infantrymen cut down subsequent demolition-men well before they reach the armor.

The dogged pace of the advance expends the ammunition and consumes the fuel at an alarming rate, which forces the vehicles to move to the rear to procure the necessary fuel and supplies. In the meantime, the infantry wisely pauses to await the return of the tanks before it jumps to the next blockade. Following the return of the armor, the Marines reinitiate the tedious drive into Seoul. Company F, led by Captain Groff, and Company E pound against the enemy resistance until dark and gain about 1,200 yards. At one key intersection, Company F encounters such stiff resistance that Company E, scheduled to peel off to the right, is compelled to throw its weight into the fight to ensure advancement.

Meanwhile, the 1st Battalion, 1st Marines, operating on the right flank of the regimental sector, begins its descent from its positions on Hill 82. Companies A and B are to advance on the right and secure the promontory on the northwestern edge of South Mountain and the finger extending out below it. In conjunction, Company C's objective is the primary railroad station and the nearby slopes of South Mountain, where the enemy remains active, slightly east of the sector of the 32nd Infantry Regiment. Marine planes plaster enemy positions, and a heavy artillery and mortar barrage commences prior to jump off.

Upon cessation of the preparatory bombardments, Captain Wray's Company C spearheads the attack. It descends down the slope and regroups near a stream that runs alongside the railroad yard. From there, the company drives north after fording the river. The Marines encounter moderate resistance that is amplified due to the pesky positions. The Communists are intertwined in buildings and railcars. Nonetheless, the Marines grind forward, yard by yard. The rail station is seized and its yard is secured. Once inside the station, the Marines discover some executed Korean women and children and a few dead Communist troops. By dusk, the area is secure.

In the 5th Marines sector, during the early morning hours and following a heavy artillery and mortar barrage, the 3rd Battalion jumps off to finish clearing the remaining opposition from the Hill 296 group. The descent is rugged for both companies; G Company departs its positions on a ridge above Hill 105 North to secure the low terrain to the right of Company I. Meanwhile, Company I descends the huge spur on Hill 296 that leads to the center of Seoul.

Both missions are eventful. Company G encounters tenacious opposition throughout the day. In one instance, while Company G is pinned down, PFC Eugene Obregon spots a wounded Marine. Disregarding the tenacious fire, he dashes out to rescue him. After he drags the wounded man to the side of the road, an enemy contingent closes on them. Obregon covers the wounded Marine with his body and he returns effective fire, but eventually he is fatally struck by a burst of enemy machine gun fire. PFC Obregon receives the Medal of Honor posthumously for his selfless heroism under fire.

Company I, lacking support weapons, attacks. Its commanding officer, Captain McMullen, convinced that his organic weapons can suffice, cancels the preparatory artillery. Almost immediately, the rugged advance by Company I is met by ferocious resistance. The Marines attack down the slopes, but the resistance on the lower section of the slope is much stronger than anticipated. The lack of support weapons takes its toll. The Communists deliver sheets of fire against the two platoons of descending Marines and inflict casualties. The North Korean fire continues without pause, but the Marines push to a knob and seize it, despite both attacking platoon leaders being wounded.

To bolster the assault, Captain McMullen throws in his reserve platoon to offset the losses sustained on the right by the 3rd Platoon, and then he takes personal command of the attack. As Company I drills downward, it plows into an enemy labyrinth that contains about 200 troops. Close-quartered bloody fighting ensues, but when it concludes, the Marines evict the North Koreans and send them fleeing to lower positions on the slope. However, Company I is thoroughly drained of strength, unable to advance farther.

Company I takes a slight pause to rejuvenate itself, but the tranquility on the knob is short-lived. The Communists mount an unexpected counterattack to retake the positions. The exhausted company reaches inward for a second breath to thwart the assault, but ammunition is becoming scarce. The enemy pushes hard and the donnybrook intensifies as the situation becomes grave. The Marines are pushed to the brink as the casualty list, which includes Captain McMullen, soars. McMullen has just sustained his seventh wound, including World War II and Korea; he is evacuated.

To forestall disaster, a small but impetuous supply party led by Lieutenant Wallace Williamson arrives. It barrels into the inferno, and without missing a step, the ammunition is passed out. The infusion of supplies gives the Marines a B-12 shot, and the exhausted company then pours out the iron. It breaks up the assault and destroys the enemy defense system there. Fighting continues the rest of the day. The threat of being dislodged is terminated, but Company I is too weak to seize the peak of the knob before dark.

In other activity, the 2nd Battalion, 5th Marines, operating south of the 3rd Battalion, spends the day mopping up. Also, the 1st KMC Battalion deploys between the Reconnaissance Company and the 3rd Battalion, the former holding the summit of Hill 296 in the northwest. Meanwhile, the 1st Battalion remains in regimental reserve. Due to the heavy resistance encountered on this day, the 5th Marines are unable to move into Seoul and establish contact with the 1st Marines.

In the 7th Marines sector, the regiment receives orders to drive north of Seoul and secure the mountain pass. From there they are to sever the road running from Seoul to Uijongbu and Ch'orwon, at a point about one mile beyond Government House. The 7th Marines is bolstered by the divisional recon company and the 5th S.K. Marine Battalion. The orders also specify that the regiment is to pinch out the 5th Marines there, and begin an attack alongside the 1st Marines, which is driving northeast.

The 5th Marines is ordered to support the 7th Marines until it is pinched out. At that point, the 5th Marines is to revert to division reserve and relieve units of the 7th Marines. The objectives of the 7th Marines: Baker (Hill 171); Dog (northern half of 338); Easy (Hill 342); Fox (Hill 133) and George (Hill 343). The ground is nasty, which ensures a difficult task for the fresh regiment. The 1st Battalion, 7th Marines, commanded by Lt. Colonel Raymond G. Davis, relieves the 2nd Battalion (minus Company D) and the 3rd Battalion at their northeastern positions along the Kaesong Highway during the morning. The relief operation frees both battalions for the attack on Seoul.

Meanwhile, at 0630, Colonel Homer Litzenberg orders Company D, 7th Marines, to head southwest along the Kaesong Highway and establish contact with the 5th Marines at Seoul. Initially, the trip is uneventful and at times surprising. Throngs of seemingly happy Korean civilians bellow loud cheers of welcome; however, the unexpected string of greeters prevents the Marines from employing flank guards. The column effortlessly travels through Hoengjeoe, and by about 0900, the convoy nears Hills 338 and 296, two huge slopes on the left and right respectively. The ominous slim valley pass that splits the two overwhelming slopes also is in view. When the column reaches a point slightly in front of Sodaemun Prison in the northwest sector of Seoul, the enemy strikes. Menacing machine guns pour their shells into the approaching convoy and inflict casualties. Among the wounded is the machine gun officer, Lieutenant Goggin. The Marines bolt from the vehicles and take cover to return fire.

The target remains about 400 yards down the highway, where the enemy is utilizing a huge tower to deliver their storm of fire. The Marines, lacking flank protection, are caught off guard on flat terrain. Instinctively, they begin to return fire, but the enemy answers with more fire, some originating within 100 yards of the convoy. Both flanks are at risk, making the positions nearly untenable. The commanding officer, Captain Richard Breen, directs the 2nd Platoon, led by Lieutenant Seeburger, to assault the heights near the prison.

In the meantime, two mortars are set up and although in naked positions, their 60-mm shells destroy one enemy machine gun position. However, return fire remains relentless. Undaunted, the mortar crews, led by Lieutenant Paul Sartwell, continue to exchange blows. Sartwell becomes wounded twice, but he continues fighting until he is struck by a third and debilitating wound.

All the while, the 2nd Platoon closes on the prison, and the 1st Platoon, led by Lieutenant Paul Mullaney, attacks on the left to ascend Hill 338 and break the pressure, but to no avail. Enemy fire forbids success. The struggling company is dangerously stretched out, and lacking armor and artillery, the convoy is guarded only by the 1st Platoon, led by Lieutenant James D. Hammond.

Captain Breen, himself wounded, receives a call on his radio from Major Raymond Fridrich (Regimental S-3). Fridich asks how bad the situation has become, and Breen assures him that his beleaguered Company D will hold its ground. While the Marines seek solutions to extricate the isolated company, the Communists attempt to encircle the command. Enemy contingents rush to the rear of the trapped Marines to prevent rescue. A support column is rushed to the area, but the enemy roadblock forces it to return. The crisis becomes more grave as ammunition and supplies are being rapidly expended. Captain Breen reels in his troops to gain more tenable positions and to prevent annihilation.

In the meantime, Marine planes pound the enemy positions to alleviate some of the pressure. Company D (carrying all of its wounded and dead) relocates about 1,000 yards from where it was ambushed, at a split in the road between the two towering enemy-infested slopes. The regrouping is complete by 1600. After taking the new positions, Captain Breen takes defensive measures to ensure that the unit makes it through the night. Additional planes arrive and successfully drop supplies within the tiny perimeter. Two planes are damaged during the mission, and one of them is forced to make an emergency landing at Kimpo.

At about dawn on the following day (27th), a rescue unit composed of the tanks and infantry rolls down the highway and extricates besieged Company D. The weary command is transported back to Hoengjeoe-ri. In the meantime, the remainder of the 2nd Battalion had followed the steps of Company D, but as scheduled and unaware of the dilemma, the battalion swings to the left and moves into the hills at Hoengjeoe about one mile from where Company D is trapped. From its positions in the heights, the 2nd Battalion dispatches reconnaissance units to check the area above Hoengjeoe, but they too remain unaware of Company D's predicament.

Then, at 1400, Companies E and F, 2nd Battalion, drive east to capture Hill 343. The assault gains about 1,000 yards, but then enemy fire originating on Hill 338 plugs the hole and stalls the advance. Lt. Colonel Hinkle, to avoid the risk of losing his right flank, orders his men to halt and dig in for the night.

In the meantime, the 3rd Battalion, 7th Marines, led by Major Roach, concludes an eight-mile march and arrives in an assembly area to prepare to assault Hill 338 (north). Companies G and H advance to seize it. At 1700, Company G, led by Captain Thomas Cooney, moves around the northern half of the objective, and then he dispatches two platoons to seize the summit. Without opposition, Company G takes the northern summit of Hill 338. Meanwhile, Company H, led by Captain Nicholas Shields, advances to the right of Company G, but as it reaches a draw, heavy fire prevents further advance. Shields, rather than risk his right flank to heavy fire, orders his company to establish defensive positions on the slopes for the night.

In the 7th Infantry Division zone, during the mid-afternoon, Generals Walker and Partridge arrive at Suwon Airfield from Taegu to conduct an impromptu meeting with the 31st Regimental staff. During the meeting, Walker informs those in attendance that the 1st Cavalry Division is advancing quickly and that it will apparently reach X Corps lines within about thirty-six hours. It is possible that, because of the arrival of Walker in Suwon and the warning messages that arrive in X Corps Headquarters, an advance unit of the 1st Cavalry is spared annihilation during the later part of today; unannounced, it plunges into the 31st Regimental lines.

In the 31st Regimental sector, the commanding officer, Colonel Ovenshine, orders the 2nd Battalion to secure the heights near Osan. The task force assigned to seize the high ground is composed of Companies E and F, reinforced by a contingent of Company G and two tank platoons. In conjunction, the 3rd Battalion is poised to bolster the attack, if required. Colonel Ovenshine also establishes another task force, composed of contingents of Companies G and H, and Company A, 73rd Tank Battalion. The task force is to drive south along the highway. The two task forces are to attack simultaneously on the following day.

In other activity, an advance contingent of TF Lynch (1st Cavalry Div.) establishes contact with the 31st Regiment during the latter part of the night, but the encounter is not expected by the 31st Regiment. (*See also,* **September 26**, 1950, *In the 1st Cavalry Division, 7th Cavalry sector.*)

In the 32nd Regimental zone, having crossed the Han on the previous day, the regiment awaits a counterattack, but the night passes quietly. Then, at 0430, the silence is shattered. In the 2nd Battalion zone, automatic weapons fire is heard and the distinct noise of rumbling T-34s is also picked up. Within about one-half hour, the view to the front displays about 1,000 North Koreans moving toward the Americans on South Mountain. A bloody contest begins as the enemy hordes speed up the pace and charge forward. The 2nd Battalion pours its firepower into the enemy ranks, but the advance continues.

On the lower eastern knob of South Mountain, Company F is unable to withstand the onslaught and it is overcome, but to the west, Company G defiantly holds the knob and repulses the enemy while it inflicts heavy losses. Colonel Mount commits his entire reserve, and the attack is halted. Lost terrain is retaken by 0700. The 32nd further clobbers the attackers with everything available as they retreat down the slopes.

Company E, 2nd Battalion, mops up the reverse slopes of South Mountain and the ground near its base by the river. The regiment counts 394 dead Communists, including 110 who had been slain within the perimeter. Another 134 enemy troops are captured.

In the 1st Battalion sector, north of South Mountain, heavy firefights develop in the streets of Seoul. Following the 2nd Battalion's victory, the 1st Battalion encounters what apparently is a straggler contingent of the original attacking force against South Mountain. Eighty North Koreans are captured during the skirmish. In the meantime, at 0800, the 3rd Battalion drives four miles east from its positions on Hill 120 to seize Hill 106 (aka 348).

En route, an enemy column is detected as it attempts to evacuate Seoul. Company L, commanded by Lieutenant Harry McCaffrey, attacks and devastates a strongly defended fortification, while Company I moves to the base of the objective. Company L's attack captures a headquarters, seemingly that of a corps and possibly the primary enemy headquarters posted in Seoul. Planes arrive to hammer the retreating column, just as the U.S. soldiers bolt into action. The enemy troops are bludgeoned and rocked into a state of shock.

Meanwhile, Company I storms the crest of the hill. The combined effort of the planes and the 32nd Regiment demolishes five enemy tanks and destroys or captures about forty other vehicles. Additional prizes include seven machine guns, several artillery pieces and two ammunition depots. The enemy force loses about 500 killed.

In other activity, the S.K. 17th Regiment controls Hills 292 and 348, following its night-long assault. The seized terrain commands the highway four miles east of Seoul. By day's end, all enemy resistance is cleared from the 32nd Regiment's sector, giving it an impressive record covering its actions over the past eight days. The 32nd has secured all of its assigned objectives, about 15 percent of the fortified portion of Seoul and South Mountain.

Also, patrols of the 1st Marines probe the right flank and establish contact with Company E, 32nd Regiment, at the western foundation of South Mountain. During today's fighting, the 32nd Regiment sustains 6 killed, 92 wounded and three MIAs.

In the Eighth Army area, there is some apprehension at headquarters. General Walker and his staff prefer that X Corps be incorporated under the control of Eighth Army. Walker is convinced that there should be a unified command over all U.N. troops in Korea. However, no written record shows Walker ever bringing his concerns directly to MacArthur. Today, Walker does request of MacArthur that he be kept informed of X Corps' progress, to afford Walker a clearer focus to prepare for the imminent convergence of the two forces. On the following day, Walker receives a response from MacArthur.

In the I Corps area, 1st Cavalry Division sector, General Gay meets with his commanders and he issues the order to attack at 1200. The 7th Cavalry will spearhead the advance.

In the 7th Cavalry zone, TF Lynch departs Poun at 1130 and speeds northwest to link with the 7th Division (X Corps). Task Force Lynch remains unchanged, except that the artillery unit is composed of only Battery C, 77th FABn. The vanguard is composed of the Regimental I&R Platoon and the 3rd Platoon of tanks (70th Tank Bn.), commanded by Lieutenant Robert W. Baker.

Colonel Lynch orders Baker to withhold his fire unless the enemy initiates the action. The armor and infantry speed along the highway without incident and encounter only South Korean civilians. During the middle of the afternoon, the column passes through deserted Ch'ongju, and later, it halts at Ipchang-ni. The column halts after traveling about sixty-four miles due to lack of gasoline, and no refueling truck accompanies the convoy. Extra gas cans are collected from the other vehicles and the troops refuel three of the six tanks.

At about the same time, several men of the I&R Platoon spot what they believe to be an approaching enemy tank. The U.S. tanks prepare for action, but the approaching danger turns out to be three enemy trucks. When they notice they are within the clutches of the Americans, all three drivers bolt from their moving vehicles. One of the careening trucks comes to a stop after crashing into an I&R Platoon jeep. The Americans commandeer the enemy's gasoline to refuel the remaining armor, and the convoy resumes the advance at about 2000.

Colonel Lynch, having received permission to use his discretion, orders the convoy to turn on its vehicles' lights. Lynch also grants Lieutenant Baker permission to fire at the enemy if necessary. The convoy increases its speed and about 2030, it reaches the main Seoul Highway, slightly south of Ch'onan.

The task force soon discovers that the town is full of enemy troops. Undaunted, Baker advances in the lead vehicle and the convoy reaches a guarded intersection. Undecided about which way to lead the convoy, he points his finger and inquires of an enemy sentry: "Osan?" The sentry nods, but looks as if he has seen a ghost. He vanishes in the darkness.

The convoy roars through the town while congregations of enemy troops merely meander about and watch the task force pass. The convoy holds its fire until it is through the town and on the heels of an enemy contingent of about company strength. The enemy contingent is raked with machine gun fire. The three point tanks advance too far and lose communications with the main force.

Meanwhile, Colonel Lynch forms a new point and the task force resumes the advance, spearheaded by one platoon of infantry and bolstered by a bazooka team and a .50-caliber ring mounted machine gun. At a point about ten miles south of Osan, the distinct sounds of tank and artillery fire are heard. Immediately, Colonel Lynch orders the convoy's lights turned off. In the meantime, the three lead tanks continue their rapid advance and pass through Osan at full throttle, then they pause to check out the situation. Baker believes he hears the vehicles of the TF to his rear, but his detachment spots enemy tank tracks. A large number of T-34s are nearby, but due to the darkness and probably poor communications, the enemy assumes Baker's tanks are part of their force, and they pass without incident.

When the tanks reach a point about three miles north of Osan, they come under enemy fire. The three tanks blaze through the barrage and soon after, discover American M-26 tank tracks, which signal that Baker's tanks are approaching X Corps lines. However, X Corps expects no friendly tanks. As Baker's column approaches the perimeter, elements of the 31st Regiment, 7th Division, commence fire, including that of recoilless rifles. Eighth Army has now established contact with X Corps, but it isn't exactly as planned.

One of the incoming shells hits the third tank in line, severing its .50-caliber machine gun and decapitating one crewman. Baker's tanks continue to race through the friendly fire and burst into the U.S. lines. Baker's small force receives a bonus. Engineers have just removed the mines along his approach route to accommodate an imminent attack by the 31st Regiment. Additionally, the X Corps tanks purposely hold their fire. The crews think they might be American, once they see the tanks are coming in with lights on and traveling at high speed. Nonetheless, the triggers are ready and only the first tank is to be permitted an unmolested entrance. The second tank is destroyed. Suddenly, and fortuitously, a white phosphorous grenade illuminates the American white star on one of TF Lynch's tanks, and it is seen by the X Corps tanks.

Subsequent to the jubilant link-up, Lieutenant Baker and the tankers with the 31st Regiment try unsuccessfully to contact Colonel Lynch. The main body of the task force lags behind Baker by about one hour, and the route is becoming much more precarious. The convoy proceeds with its lights out and reaches a point shy of Habong-ni at about 2400.

The midnight hour rings of potential danger. Colonel Lynch glances at a T-34 that is about twenty yards from the road; it appears to be out of action, like most of the enemy armor encountered along the route. Lynch motions to Captain James B. Webel (Regimental S-3), and he mentions that the Air Force had probably taken the tank out. At about this time, the tank commences firing, and in an instant, an undiscovered tank begins to pound the column. The infantry scatters for cover and a bazooka team speeds back from the point to exterminate the ambush contingent. The first T-34 is blown away, but the second tank rams the column. It maintains its fire and crashes into several vehicles. A recoilless rifle batters the charging tank, and afterward, it becomes entangled with a damaged U.S. vehicle and finally stalls, but its guns remain operable. A bazooka team attempts to destroy it, but the bazooka doesn't fire. Captain Webel creeps up to the immobilized tank and attempts to board it to deposit a grenade down the hatch.

Meanwhile, the T-34 breaks loose and nearly crushes Webel in the process. Webel commandeers a five-gallon can of gasoline and reinitiates his attack. He douses the rear of the T-34 with the combustible fuel and then funnels some directly onto the engine. It explodes immediately and Webel is catapulted from the inferno. He lands about twenty feet behind the burning tank. Webel emerges with only some superficial wounds on his face and hands and two broken ribs. In the meantime, the exchange of fire and the flames from the burning tank attract the attention of other nearby tanks.

Colonel Lynch hears the approaching armor, but he cannot verify that they are the tanks with Lieutenant Baker. Taking precautions, Lynch orders the road blocked with a truck. Soon after, two tanks encroach and they are definitely T-34s. One of the North Koreans in his native tongue yells: "What the Hell goes on here?" At the first sound of the inquiry, the Americans open fire. The T-34s snap their hatches closed and begin firing. The truck that blocks their passage explodes in flames. Meanwhile, the three remaining U.S. tanks move up to neutralize the enemy advantage. And then, the enemy ups the ante. Eight additional T-34s arrive on the scene.

The armor exchanges bloody blows in the darkness, and the Americas are being struck hard. One T-34 is destroyed, but the North Koreans knock out two of the three task force tanks. Captain Webel disregards his wounds and rushes forward to end the threat. He dashes past several Americans who are holding a bazooka with ammunition, but no one in the detachment knows how to operate the weapon. Webel grabs the bazooka and goes into action. He knocks out two tanks. The enemy troops bolt from their disabled tank only to be met by Webel, who greets them with a submachine gun. Hurriedly, they flee.

Meanwhile, Sergeant Willard H. Hopkins boards an enemy tank and slides a grenade down the open hatch to destroy the crew and the tank. Hopkins then forms an improvised bazooka team to continue the hunt. The enemy tanks are being eliminated, one by one, as the battle rages outside of Habong-ni. The remaining enemy tanks continue to fire against the Americans. Some manage to advance well into the depth of the convoy. One tank crashes forward, ringing fire and smashing into vehicles as it moves, until it reaches the southern end of the convoy — point-blank range for a waiting 105 howitzer. The raging T-34 is transformed into debris.

Hopkins had attempted to take out this tank, but he became caught in a cross-fire and was killed. The ferocious contest lasts for about one hour and is costly, but the U.S. infantry takes the day. Seven of the ten T-34s are destroyed and the remaining three scoot in the opposite direction. TF Lynch sustains 2 men killed and 28 wounded. In addition to the loss of two tanks, the TF loses 15 vehicles. Subsequent to the action, Task Force Lynch remains in place until daylight.

In the 24th Division sector, the 19th Regiment leapfrogs over the 21st Regiment and drives to Yongdong,

seizing it without incident. Three Americans discovered in the local jail are freed. The 19th Regiment then drives toward Okch'on, about 10 miles east of Taejon. The column reaches the objective at 0200 on the 27th.

In the IX Corps area, 2nd Division sector, at 0830, the 38th Regiment pushes contingents into Koch'ang. An enemy hospital is seized and 45 enemy wounded are captured. The 23rd Regiment arrives shortly thereafter. Later, during the evening, the regiment advances fourteen miles without incident and reaches Anui at 1930. The regiment discovers the area to be a labyrinth of soggy, flooded rice paddies. The town's roads are capable of handling the vehicles, but they cannot stray from the highway. The area still contains enemy contingents. They will strike during the night (26th-27th).

In the 25th Division sector, the 1st Battalion, 27th Regiment, crosses the Nam and then as vanguard, it drives northwest to Uiryong and seizes it before noon. The remainder of the regiment follows. TF Matthews is to attack west toward Hadong and from there it is to swing northwest and drive against Iri, Kumje, Kunsan, Kurye, Namwon and Sunch'ang, but the drive does not begin until the following day. The 228-mile drive from Chinju to the Kum River culminates on September 30.

In the meantime, Task Force Dolvin, operating on the right, jumps off at 0600. The column departs Chinju, its infantry transported atop the rear of the tanks. The column drives northwest toward Hamyang, tracing the steps of the retreating N.K. 6th Division. The 35th Regiment follows TF Dolvin through this dense, nasty terrain, which has been a sanctuary for guerrillas and other Communist forces. The task force must maneuver through the eastern and northern sides of the rugged, mountainous Chiri-san area. TF Dolvin travels 138 miles during its advance from Chinju to the Kum River, and it encounters mines early on.

Several miles out, the lead tank hits a mine and the entire column stalls. Engineers dislodge 11 additional mines from the road and the column resumes its advance, but it enters a new minefield and another tank is damaged. At a third minefield, an enemy contingent unsuccessfully attempts to block the column. The North Koreans are quickly dispersed. The task force discovers 9 vehicles about seven truckloads of ammunition, plus six antitank guns. Later, at about dark, the enemy blows a bridge just north of Hajon-ni. Task Force Dolvin fabricates another crossing and fords the stream during the night (26th-27th). On the following day, the task force again encounters resistance.

In the ROK II Corps area, the S.K. 8th Division seizes Andong. Some forward contingents advance farther northwest and drive into Yech'on.

In Air Force activity, The 22nd Bomber Group strikes targets in the vicinity of Haeju. The mission is executed by 22 B-29s and they hit an ammunition manufacturing complex. Also, B29s attached to the 92nd Bomber Group attack targets in the vicinity of Hungnam, including the Pujon hydroelectric plant. The air strikes executed this day terminate the first strategic bombing phase against North Korean targets.

In other activity, at Taegu, Fifth Air Force establishes the provisional 543rd Tactical Support Group for the purpose of overseeing the Air Force's tactical reconnaissance squadrons in Korea.

— *In the United States:* The Marine Corps announces that on this day, its 138 organized reserve ground units have within the last 43 days reported for duty.

— *In Japan:* At 1410, General MacArthur signs and publicizes United Nations Command Communique 9, which states that Seoul is liberated. Similarly to the announcement of General Almond, the proclamation is premature. Bloody fighting still ensues throughout the city and by dusk, X Corps controls only about half of it. The proclamation states: "Seoul, the capital of the Republic of Korea, is again in friendly hands. United Nations forces including the 17th Regiment of the ROK Army and elements of the U.S. 7th and 1st Marine Divisions, have completed the envelopment and seizure of the city." Nonetheless, more of the enemy will have to be eliminated before the entire city is secure.

In other activity, MacArthur's headquarters in Tokyo dispatches a radio message to X Corps in Korea explaining that Eighth Army is closing on X Corps positions and contact should occur at any time. Identical messages are forwarded to NAVFE and to Far East Air Forces. All parties are instructed to take every precaution to ensure that these advancing units are not brought under fire.

In other activity, General Edwin Wright receives a memorandum from General Hickey (deputy of chief of staff, FEC), informing him that MacArthur wants a plan developed that would incorporate X Corps as the amphibious invasion force to be committed at Wonsan. General Wright (G-3), head of JSPOG, has the plans forwarded to MacArthur within several hours. The plan, detailing the advance into North Korea, calls for X Corps to land at Wonsan on the east coast or "elsewhere" while Eighth Army concentrates to the west. The plan sparks controversy, as it creates two separate field commands that will split the forces.

Wonsan is a likely candidate for the invasion site. It has been the bloodline of Russian supplies being shipped by sea from Vladivostok, and its rail line leads directly north to Vladivostok. The east coast seaport of Wonsan also fills the bill of a geographic swivel, capable of catapulting troops to various strategic locations. These include the prime real estate at Hamhung–Hungnam, fifty miles north. A force also could easily be shot west across the peninsula to P'yongyang.

September 27 *Inchon–Seoul vicinity:* Seoul
still contains an abundance of snipers in buildings and the remaining fortified blockades. One by one, the roadblocks are crumbling. The 1st Battalion, 1st Marines, advances north through the city against fierce opposition. Enemy guns hold up Company C near the rail station. Tanks roll forward to take the brunt of the resistance and blow holes in the defenses. Flamethrow-

ers and M-26s fire incessantly, but enemy fire knocks out one armored vehicle and a mine takes out another before the blockage is clear. Soon after, the attack grinds eastward to reduce the remaining opposition. Company E moves on the left while Company A drives on the right, each eliminating the barricades that stand in its path.

Meanwhile, the 2nd Battalion, 1st Marines, grinds down Ma-Po Boulevard against rigid opposition during the first phase of its assault. The battalion drives to the French Consulate and captures it just prior to 1100. The Marines briskly propel Old Glory up the staff. The flag-raising event is the prelude to the recapture of the U.S. Embassy. During the struggle for the streets of Seoul, a pitched battle erupts at the city's primary intersection, and the arrival of Lieutenant Cummings' tanks is a welcome sight. Company D, under the umbrella of the armor, penetrates directly into the hornet's nest, defended by self-propelled guns.

Cummings' tank knocks two guns out of commission, but then his tank strikes a mine and becomes damaged. Meanwhile, one enemy truck, with a howitzer in tow, is destroyed by Sergeant Mcdonald's tank as it attempts escape. The advance maintains a steady pace, despite the inability of the 7th Marines to connect with the 1st Marines. By 1530, the Marines whip through the rugged urban streets and secure the Russian Consulate Embassy.

Elements of Company E, 2nd Battalion, commanded by Captain Charles D. Frederick, remove the Russian colors and replace them with the Stars and Stripes. Within ten minutes, the Marines dash another 350 yards to the U.S. Consulate, and at 1537, Old Glory is unfurled atop the nearby U.S. Embassy, which still contains a contingent of North Koreans that control a machine gun. The North Koreans capitulate without firing a shot.

Company D, operating south of the government compound, drives east, but severe incoming fire from three separate directions halts progress. The Marines take cover in buildings while Corsairs zoom overhead and lace the street with deadly iron streamers that crash within one block of the stalled company. In conjunction with the air strikes, the 1st Platoon, again covered by tank fire, jumps farther ahead in the wake of each pass of the aircraft. The 1st Platoon then lunges forward, taking a wide leap to terminate the resistance. The riflemen and BARmen fire incessantly as they advance and crush the resistance by 1630.

The city of Seoul belongs to the U.S. Marines. Although the battle is won, some remnant snipers and several small pockets of Communist troops remain. The Marines, the S.K. Marines and the S.K. police execute mop-up operations. Subsequent to the termination of the organized opposition, the 1st and 2nd Battalions of Chesty Puller's 1st Marines ignore the lingering sniper fire and march to the eastern sector of the city to establish night positions there.

In the 5th Marines sector, at the northern part of Seoul, the enemy resistance finally dissipates, permitting a more rapid advance. Sodaemun is seized without incident by Company E, but too late. A Korean civilian reports that the Communists, anticipating the loss of Seoul, had recently removed about 400 American POWs and shipped them north.

Meanwhile, the primary attack of the 5th Marines occurs farther south. At 0645, the 3rd Battalion advances to seize the eastern knob of Hill 296, and then its principal objective, Government House. All the while, huge spirals of smoke still ring upward from the charred and shattered city, half-choking the men of Companies G and I as they clear the heights. To their surprise, they encounter no heavy fire; rather, the remnant defenders on the ridge offer only sporadic sniper fire. Once the high ground is secured, the Marines drive to seize their sector of Seoul.

By about 0730, Companies G and I descend the heights and begin plowing through the streets in the western sector of the city. The ground Marines, with supporting engineers and tanks, encounter resistance. Individually, the obstacles along the streets are destroyed and within two hours, elements of Company G establish contact with the 1st Marines. Without pause, the 3rd Battalion presses forward, driving north. Prior to 1030, it secures Seoul Middle School and the heights (Hill 79) north of the school. From here, the Marines lurch against Kwang Who Moon Circle, which boasts the final enemy barricade that raises organized resistance.

The Marine tanks advance to crush the barrier. One tank, a flamethrower, nudges close to the blockade at the intersection and unleashes steady bursts of flame that terminate the opposition. From the reduced plaza, Company G, 3rd Battalion, moves without incident to Government House. At 1508, simultaneously, the Marines run down North Korean flags that are flying on two poles at opposite ends of the building. In quick motion, twin U.S. flags are immediately catapulted to the top of the flagpoles, signaling the retaking of the capital. The occupants of the Government House apparently had not expected to be evicted. When Marines enter the unoccupied building, they discover warm food. After vanquishing the organized resistance, the 3rd Battalion reverts to eliminating the remaining snipers and stragglers.

In the evening the 3rd Battalion establishes its command post in Government House. In the meantime, the 1st Battalion, 5th Marines, which is trailing the 3rd Battalion, reaches the Seoul Middle School during the morning. From there, it swings left and drives north toward another strategic target, Hill 338, situated about one mile northwest of Government House. The attack commences at 1300, following air strikes and an artillery and mortar barrage. Initially, the 1st Platoon, Company A, surges forward and gains some high ground. Then the 2nd Platoon, led by Lieutenant Edward Collins, shoots around the left of a wall and climbs to seize the summit. But heavy enemy fire causes a temporary suspension of the advance to allow planes to arrive and quell the resistance.

The Marine pilots roar over the area and plunder the enemy positions on the crest. This devastating fire is followed by a heavy concentration of mortars, which provides ample cover fire. The Marines advance behind the whizzing shells and hammer the enemy. The 1st Platoon, led by Lieutenant Nicholas Trapnell, springs to a knoll just below the towering peak. In conjunction, the 2nd Platoon reinitiates its assault against the summit and it advances to the left of the wall.

At about the same time, the 3rd Platoon, led by Sergeant George Bolkow, operating on the right, bolts to the front and becomes the vanguard. The 3rd Platoon bursts through the final resistance and secures the summit of Hill 338 at 1508, to complete the mission of the 3rd Battalion. It now controls the Seoul–Pyongyang Highway at the northwest edge of Seoul. After dark, the bulk of the remaining enemy troops in Seoul abscond.

In the 7th Marines sector, in the 1st Battalion zone, near the area dubbed "Haengju Front," the enemy pops out of the northern hills at about 1200 and drives toward the old ferry crossing at Hill 125. En route, the Communists encounter Company A, commanded by Captain David Banks, the designated guardians of a roadblock at Ryokokyu. Soon after, Company C, commanded by Captain Richard Delamar III, is thrown into the fight to ensure the safety of the bridgehead. The heated exchange ensues without pause and causes the Marines to add more punch. One platoon of Company B bolsters the bridgehead and the slugfest ends. The enemy disengages and bolts for Kaesong.

In the 2nd Battalion zone, a contingent that includes tanks, infantry and engineers rolls down the Kaesong Highway and easily establishes contact with Company D. The battle-weary troops, isolated between Hills 238 and 296 since the 25th, are easily rescued. The column then returns to Hoengjeoe, again against no significant resistance.

At about the same time, the 3rd Battalion, supported by fire from the 2nd Battalion, jumps off to reduce the northern portion of Hill 338. The assault meets rigid resistance. Companies H and G advance on the left and right respectively. Company H then maneuvers through a precarious draw on the right of Company G, while Company I advances on the left flank of G Company.

And then, unexpected heavy fire pours down from the heights. One platoon (Company H), the 3rd, led by Lieutenant Paul Denny, shoots forward, but the 1st and 2nd platoons remain stalled, forcing Captain Shields, the company commander, to reel it back rather than risk isolation.

In the meantime, Company I temporarily shifts its positions to bolster Company H, but still the stiff enemy fire prevents advance. Company I then reinitiates its original mission and begins to drive north to reduce the remaining obstinate resistance on the far-strung knobs of Hill 338. Later, Company G is ordered to depart from its ridge line position and strike against Hill 342 to the east. To bolster the assault, Colonel

Litzenberg, during mid-morning, orders his 2nd Battalion to strike Hill 343, located about 2,500 yards north of its lines. Like the other ongoing assaults, this, too, is a methodical advance against ferocious enemy fire and over nasty ground. Companies E and F, commanded by Captains Walter Phillips and Elmer Zorn, respectively, launch the attack.

Company F advances on the left while Company E, to the right, plows straight ahead. Following a tedious contest, the Marines take the objective by dusk. Company E commands the summit. Meanwhile, Company G, commanded by Captain Cooney, is heavily engaged at Hill 342. Initially, the advance progresses well. It

safely passes through a complicated enemy minefield without incident, compliments of South Koreans who had marked the mines. However, upon reaching the objective, the Marines are greeted by sniper fire. The 1st Platoon advances to provide cover fire while the 2nd and 3rd Platoons assault the objective. Enemy fire bars the 1st Platoon from reaching its designated positions in the heights. Meanwhile, the other two platoons advance, but lacking cover fire, they, too, are unable to ascend from the low ground on the slope.

For the rest of the day, the enemy on Hill 342 continues to hold the high ground. The 7th Marines have reduced Hill 343 but it still shares occupancy with the

A Marine rifleman, from inside a damaged building, fires at the enemy while two others hold under some cover.

enemy on Hills 338 and 342. In conjunction, the 7th Marines, covering the period September 23–27, report 375 enemy dead and 34 prisoners. The regiment captures six rifles, four machine guns and about 600 bayonets.

In the 7th Infantry Division zone, at Suwon, the 31st Regiment prepares to initiate its assault to seize the heights at Osan. At about dawn, when the flanking force arrives at Osan, it is fired upon by an N.K. tank, but a bazooka team takes action and knocks the tank out. The contingent then passes through Osan and drives north toward the high ground. Simultaneously, the other task force begins to drive south, but it encounters resistance that, as suspected, is part of the 105th N.K. Armored Division. Enemy tanks and antitank guns bolster the ground troops.

The combat that emerges along the highway continues to intensify as the day passes, but progress is slow. Toward the end of the grueling day, the 31st Regiment's two task forces converge near Hill 113, which contains the bulk of the enemy force. The task forces establish a night perimeter there. During the two attacks, the enemy sustains the loss of 300 troops. In addition, 14 enemy tanks, 6 antitank guns and a few mortars are destroyed. Lt. Colonel Robert Summers, 2nd Battalion, commanding officer, and Major Lester Olson, Regimental S-3, become seriously wounded.

In the 32nd Regimental zone, at South Mountain, the day remains relatively tranquil, while the regiment awaits the arrival of the 1st Marines at the conclusion of its attack. Later in the day, the Marines come abreast of the 32nd, facing east.

In other activity, the 32nd Regiment reports its casualties for this day as 32 killed, 33 wounded and nine MIAs; however, many of these had been sustained during the previous day's heavy fighting at South Mountain. (*See also, In the I Corps area, 1st Cavalry Division sector, 7th Cavalry zone,* this date.)

In other activity, General Gay, commanding officer, 1st Cavalry Division, arrives at Osan prior to noon. The 1st Cavalry's TF-777 does not participate in the ongoing attack of the 31st Regiment, but Gay, upon conferring with a 31st regimental battalion commander, offers to commit the 8th Cavalry to bolster the assault. Gay also agrees to commit the 77th and 99th FABns and one tank company. The battalion commander (31st Regiment), according to Gay, informs him that he will need authorization from higher authority. There is no confirmation of any conversations concerning 1st Cavalry participation, but the cavalry is not called upon to assist.

In the Eighth Army area, General Walker receives a response from General MacArthur regarding his inquiry of the previous day. If Walker had retained any hope that X Corps would be coming under the authority of Eighth Army, he now knows it will not occur. MacArthur informs Walker that X Corps will be retained as GHQ Reserve and that it will be confined to occupation of the Inchon-Seoul vicinity, while awaiting new GHQ orders. MacArthur tells Walker that he will be "appraised" of the X Corps situation at an "early date."

In the I Corps area, 1st Cavalry Division sector, 7th Cavalry zone, the enemy lies in wait for the approach of TF Lynch, which resumes its advance at 0700, but the marching column expects trouble. The point detachment comes under fire by a tank, but the threat is quickly eradicated by a bazooka team. Shortly thereafter, the column is fired upon by an enemy machine gun crew. Lieutenant William Woodside mounts an immediate charge that crushes the resistance. Then, the task force encounters two abandoned enemy tanks, but this time, Colonel Lynch takes no chances. Both tanks are destroyed.

Task Force Lynch enters Osan at 0800. In less than one half-hour, at 0826, contingents of Companies K and L, 7th Cavalry, encounter contingents of Company H, 31st Regiment, 7th Division, at a bridge slightly north of Osan. Task Force 777 informs General Gay that contact has been established between Eighth Army and X Corps this day, at 0826 near Osan.

In the 24th Division sector, the 19th Regiment pulls into Okch'on at 0200 and takes a slight pause. Once the tanks are refueled, the attack resumes. At 0530, the regiment rolls out of town and the enemy is there to meet it. One tank stumbles upon a mine, and immediately following the detonation, an antitank gun demolishes the tank. This is enjoined by heavy fire originating in the heights west of Okch'on. The 1st Battalion mounts an attack, but it gains little ground against the granite resistance.

Meanwhile, thousands of enemy troops continue to abandon the Taejon vicinity. The Air Force maintains heat on the besieged city and the nearby strong points, while the ground troops continue to gnaw forward. About 300 enemy prisoners, representing seven separate divisions, are captured during the day. This makes it clear that Taejon is a major point of convergence for the units, which are retreating from positions both south and west of Waegwan.

The reports of tanks destroyed conflict; the figures are inflated: the Air Force claims twenty kills, including thirteen near Taejon and eight additional tanks damaged. The ground forces also report thirteen kills outside Taejon; Company A, 19th Regiment bazooka teams claim three of these.

At day's end, the 19th Regiment prepares to launch another attack in the morning.

In the IX Corps area, 2nd Division sector, the 23rd Regiment remains in Anui, its troops confined to the town due to flooded paddies. At 0400, the enemy commences a deadly mortar and artillery attack. The commanding officer of the 3rd Battalion, Lt. Colonel R.G. Sherrard, is severely wounded when the command post is struck and his staff is decimated. The battalion executive officer, the S-2, assistant S-3, the artillery liaison officer and one antiaircraft officer are killed by the blast. The pre-dawn bombardment also wounds twenty-five enlisted men (Regimental and Headquarters Companies).

A Marine fires a sub machine gun (.45-caliber M3) during fighting in Seoul, while another uses a radio.

teen aircraft arrive to extinguish the threat. The firepower of the F-51s is strongly felt by the enemy, and following the delivery of the bombs, napalm and rockets, the task force reinitiates the assault. The charge succeeds and the infantry pushes through, bypassing about 600 North Koreans, but again the column stalls when it arrives at a blown bridge.

In other activity, TF Matthews, trailed by the 2nd Battalion, 24th Regiment, attacks at 1000. It drives toward Hadong. Along the route, the column continues to hear news of retreating North Koreans and their American captives.

The pace accelerates to close the gap, but the enemy remains about four hours ahead. When the column reaches Hadong at 1730, refugees report that one contingent of enemy troops and its captives are only about one-half hour ahead. The column swings northwest in hot pursuit.

TF Matthews reaches Komdu, about ten miles distant, and rescues eleven American soldiers (3rd Battalion, 29th Regiment). Most are unable to walk, and it is evident that the North Koreans have administered no medical treatment to their wounds.

In the ROK II Corps area, S.K. 8th Division sector, elements advance to Tanyang, near the upper Han River.

In the Capital Division sector, the Division advances north through the mountains and moves into Ch'unyang, about thirty-one miles east of the advancing S.K. 8th Division.

— *In Japan:* General MacArthur is informed by the Joint Chiefs of Staff that he is now authorized to cross the 38th Parallel to complete the destruction of the North Korean forces. The orders stipulate that no U.N. troops are to cross the Yalu River into Chinese or Soviet territory and they mandate that only South Korean units should proceed to the border. The instructions also direct MacArthur, if feasible, to unite all of Korea under the leadership of Syngman Rhee. However, MacArthur is informed that this directive is subject to change, depending on the unfolding circumstances. The JCS mandate in their directive that MacArthur is to focus on the intentions of the Soviets and Chinese and inform the JCS immediately if he

In other activity, Hill 409 near Hyongp'ung is abandoned prior to dawn by elements of the N.K. 10th Division. The remaining contingents cross to the west bank of the Naktong, terminating organized enemy resistance east of the river. Contingents of the U.S. 9th Regiment enter Hyongp'ung during the afternoon. In the meantime, two companies of the 2nd Battalion, 9th Regiment, secure Hill 409 without incident. On the following day, the 2nd Battalion crosses the Naktong.

In other activity, on or about this date, the commanding officer of the N.K. I Corps disbands his headquarters at Choch'iwon. He and some other N.K. officers head for the Taebaek Mountains.

In the 25th Division sector, Task Force Dolvin resumes its attack toward Hamyang, but the enemy mounts heavy opposition. The lead tank in the column becomes damaged after it hits a mine. In the meantime, enemy troops scattered about the nearby ridges initiate mortar and small arms fire. The U.S. infantry fails to dislodge the enemy on the right side of the highway, but the tanks eliminate the resistance on the left side of it. Planes are called upon to subdue the resistance and bolster another infantry assault.

Meanwhile, General Kean arrives on the scene. Six-

concludes that they might be preparing to enter the conflict.

General MacArthur is also ordered to dispatch his plan of operations concerning the crossing of the 38th Parallel to the JCS for their approval. MacArthur balks at the suggestion that he should seek approval. He requests authorization to cross the 38th Parallel if the North Koreans refuse to surrender. MacArthur receives an answer on the 29th.

September 28   *Inchon-Seoul vicinity:* Seoul

falls to X Corps. The North Koreans are retreating north toward Uijongbu. However, prior to evacuating the city, the Communists wreak havoc on the suspected families of the S.K. troops, guerrillas and policemen. Despicable atrocities occur. During the latter part of the day, Generals O.P. Smith and Edward Craig transfer the 1st Marine Division's CP from Oeoso-ri to Seoul.

In the 1st Marines sector, the 1st and 2nd Battalions resume the attack at 0645, while the 3rd Battalion remains in reserve. It and the 2nd S.K. Marine Battalion execute mop-up missions in the rear. The 2nd Battalion, 1st Marines, sweep the northeast section of Seoul. The battalion overcomes mines and advances against light opposition. In contrast, the 1st Battalion encounters many mines and some solid opposition even though organized resistance has been shattered. Combined, the 1st and 2nd Battalions clear the remainder of Seoul.

By dark, the 1st Marines advances to Hill 133 to afford the regiment domination of the Seoul–Uijongbu–Ch'orwon Highway at the northeast fringe of Seoul. The 7th Marines' attack against Hill 224, about one mile farther north, and becomes stalled by fierce resistance.

In the 5th Marines sector, patrols are dispatched throughout the day, but all are without incident. The 5th Marines, subsequent to gaining its objectives, is pinched out by the 1st and 7th Marines. The regiment

assembles near the Women's University in Seoul. Colonel Murray establishes his headquarters with the perimeter of the university.

In the 7th Marines sector, elements of the 7th Marines drive down the main road and secure the heights between Seoul and Uijongbu. The enemy raises stiff resistance to protect their escape routes to Uijongbu. During the day's fighting, Lt. Colonel Thornton Hinkle, commanding officer of the 2nd Battalion, becomes wounded, and he is evacuated. Major Sawyer replaces him.

The day's prizes include about 75 tons of dynamite, all of it manufactured in the U.S. and thought to have been captured by the North Koreans from the ROKs during the initial stages of the invasion into the south. Colonel Litzenberg establishes his headquarters slightly west of Ducksoo Palace, where Colonel Puller establishes the 1st Marines headquarters.

In the 7th Infantry Division zone, in the 31st Regimental sector, naval air strikes are scheduled to hit enemy-held Hills 92 and 113 at about noon to crack the remaining resistance there. The infantry, as ordered, at 0830 begins pulling back from its positions of the previous night as a precaution against being bombed by mistake. The planes arrive on schedule and attack the targets, including a rail tunnel near Hill 92, for about fifty minutes.

After the air strikes, artillery (57th and 92nd FABn) and mortar fire begin pounding the slopes until just before 1330. When the guns cease firing, Companies K and L drive against Hill 113. They overcome nominal resistance and seize it by 1515. Company K deploys on Hill 113 and it provides cover fire for Company L, which drives to Hill 92. The objective is quickly seized, giving the regiment domination of both hills within one hour. Enemy survivors retire eastward. The 31st Regiment sustains no casualties during the mission, which clears the highway between Suwon and Osan. The regiment buries more than 100 Communists troops.

U.S. Marines and tanks move through Seoul during the battle for control of the city.

Supplies on a pier in Pusan.

On the previous day, General Gay had offered to commit elements of the 1st Cavalry to bolster the 31st Regimental attack, but the 8th Cavalry remained out of the fight. General Barr, commanding officer, 7th Infantry Division, states that he was never informed of General Gay's offer.

In the Eighth Army area, since Eighth Army's crossing of the Naktong, the Communists continue to increase the massacre of South Koreans. At Sach'on, the jail is torched, and about 280 police, government officials and civilians are burned to death. Other enemy occupied towns, such as Chonju, Hamyang, Kongju, Mokp'o and Anui, are found to contain mass burial sites. The victims include women and children.

In other activity, the 3rd Battalion, Royal Australian Regiment, arrives at Pusan. Soon after, it will join the British 27th Brigade at Kumch'on.

In the I Corps area, 1st Cavalry Division sector, the swift advance of the Division has caught many enemy units in a clamp. Contingents of the N.K. 105th Armored Division are isolated in the vicinity of Ansong and P'yongt'aek. Very few of these enemy troops reach North Korea. Other remnant forces of various units are trapped in the vicinity of Taejon.

In the 7th Cavalry zone, ten enemy tanks pound a contingent of the 16th Reconnaissance Company near P'yongt'aek. The detachment sustains casualties, but reinforcements arrive to extricate the besieged unit. Contingents of both Company K, 7th Cavalry, and Company C, 70th Tank Battalion, arrive and encounter the enemy tanks. Fighter bombers also arrive overhead. The combined thrust of the 7th Cavalry and the aircraft destroys 7 of the 10 tanks. The planes destroy five of the T-34s.

In the 24th Division sector, at 0700, the Air Force again lambastes the enemy positions in the heights west of Okch'on, preceding an attack by the 2nd Battalion, 19th Regiment. After the air strike, the battalion drives up the slopes. Surprisingly, it encounters no resistance. During the previous night, the enemy had abandoned the slopes. However, about 800 enemy troops are detected by aircraft as they flee from Taejon while the air strikes are in progress. One other retreating contingent is discovered west of Taejon, moving toward Choch'i-won.

Just west of Taejon, the Air Force targets a group of about 1,000 enemy troops. The planes strafe the columns and scorch the area with napalm. In the meantime, the 19th Regiment and engineers prepare to retake the city, which had been seized from them during July. At 1630, a forward detachment of scouts (2nd Bn., 19th Reg.) and engineers (Company C, 3rd Eng. Bn.) move into Taejon, followed within an hour by the main column of the 19th Regiment.

Meanwhile, a 24th Division liaison plane lands at the airstrip at 1800, and by 1830, the regiment secures Taejon. The recapture of the city brings exhilaration to the 19th Regiment and the engineers of Company C. The two units were among the final elements to abandon the city on July 20.

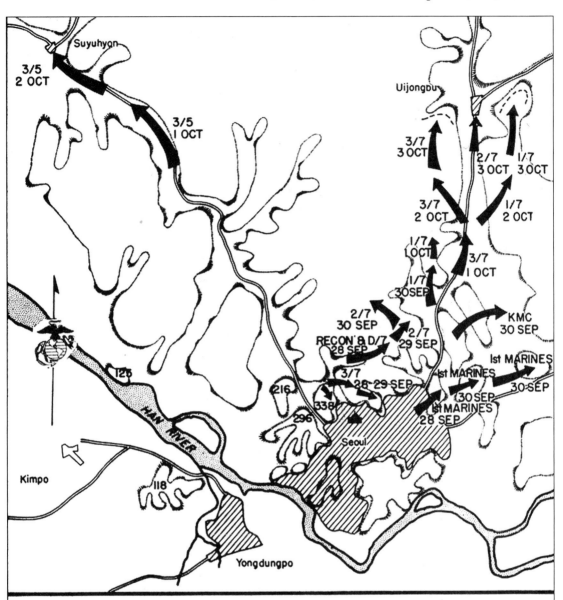

PURSUIT OF THE NKPA

&

CAPTURE OF UIJONGBU

28 SEP -- 3 OCT 1950

0   5   10

MILES

However, the good spirits are short-lasting, as the Americans discover more atrocities. In and around Taejon, about 5,000 to 7,000 South Koreans have been massacred. The scenes are grisly. The dead had been tied together in groups, ranging between 100 and 200 people, and each had his hands bound behind his back prior to execution. Forty American soldiers captured during the earlier fighting and 17 South Korean soldiers are among the murdered masses.

Only 6 people cheat death. Two Americans, one S.K. soldier and three civilians remain alive when the city is taken. The six survivors, thought to be dead, had only been wounded and were feigning death when buried alive.

A group of 500 massacred South Korean troops, each with their hands tied behind their backs, is discovered near the Taejon airstrip. The appalling sights are witnessed by hundreds of American troops, including Generals Milburn and Church, and the innumerable official reports are not exaggerated.

In the IX Corps area, 2nd Division sector, elements of the 23rd Regiment, driving from the east, approach Hamyang. Contact is made with TF Dolvin at an intersection east of the town.

In the 9th Regiment sector, the 2nd Battalion, subsequent to being relieved by the 65th Regimental Combat Team at Hill 409, crosses the Naktong River and rejoins the 2nd Division there.

In other activity, the 38th Regiment begins a seventy-three mile advance to Chonju. At 0400, the 2nd Battalion departs Kuch'ang and leads the way across the mountains. The enemy raises some resistance along the route, but the regiment eliminates it and continues on course. The column reaches Chonju in the western plain of Korea at 1315, after being on the road for nine and one-half hours.

Once in Chonju, there is no time to relax. About 300 enemy defenders remain in the town. The 2nd Battalion shrinks the ranks of the N.K. 102nd and 104th Security Regiments as 170 prisoners are seized and about 100 additional Communists are killed. Following the skirmishes, the 2nd Battalion halts in Chonju; its vehicles have expended their fuel. The battalion informs a passing liaison plane of the situation, and division begins to deliver more gasoline.

In the 25th Division sector, the 27th Regiment departs Uiryong and attacks toward Chinju against minimal resistance. Also, TF Dolvin resumes its attack at dawn and makes progress throughout the morning. It establishes contact with contingents of the 2nd Division at about 1100.

Later, TF Dolvin approaches a bridge that is about to be blown. A passing liaison plane detects the enemy at work and alerts the TF. Colonel Dolvin speeds his tanks forward and they arrive just as the span is about to be blown. The enemy is interrupted by the clanging sounds of the tanks' machine guns, and the bridge is then secured intact. The seizure upsets the enemy's plans and permits the attack to continue.

Once across the bridge, TF Dolvin advances at a steady pace. It sprints about twenty miles per hour. By the middle of the afternoon, TF Dolvin pushes into Namwon and encounters contingents of the U.S. 24th Regiment and TF Matthews. TF Dolvin pauses there until slightly after midnight, before it pushes out toward Chonju.

In the meantime, TF Matthews is back on the hunt in an attempt to rescue additional U.S. captives. The task force advances to a river crossing below Namwon at about noon. One tank crosses the river without incident, but those trailing become stuck and the column stalls. Sergeant Raymond Reifers, in the lead tank, continues to advance and he penetrates Namwon unnoticed by the enemy. Apparently, the North Koreans had become preoccupied with a pair of F-84 jets that are striking the town. Reifers moves his tank forward as if accompanied by a regiment. The unexpected armor becomes a great stimulant to the enemy. The North Koreans caught on the streets break for safety. They scamper over fences, and jump from roof to roof, then haphazardly scatter in all directions.

The effort to escape prompts the enemy to abandon the American prisoners, although Sergeant Reifers' tank stands alone in the town while the column remains stalled at the river. Reifers attempts to react accordingly, but he is surprised as voices begin to yell: "Don't shoot! Americans!" And then, a gate flies open and Americans jam the street.

At about the same time, back at the river, the radio in Lieutenant Sawyer's tank bellows an urgent request for assistance from Reifers. He proclaims that the town is full of enemy troops, and that he has made contact with American captives. By this time, additional tanks cross the river and speed into town to encounter Reifer and 86 near-starved American soldiers. The remnant enemy troops in Namwon are eliminated. Sergeant Reifers is killed in action on 27 November of this year.

Later, at about 1515, Task Force Dolvin arrives in Namwon. In conjunction, TF Blair moves out and continues to attack toward Chongup. TF Matthews remains in Namwon until the following day.

In Air Force activity, the 7th Fighter Bomber Squadron arrives at Taegu from Itazuke, Japan. It is the first jet squadron to operate in Korea.

In other activity, the Air Force's first three jet reconnaissance planes (RB-45 Tornadoes) arrive in the Far East to participate in the conflict in Korea. Also, Lieutenant Ralph G. Hall (35th Fighter Bomber Squadron, 8th Fighter Bomber Group), flying an F-51 Mustang, destroys an unidentified enemy fighter plane parked at the Pyongyang airfield.

In Naval activity, a South Korean minesweeper, YMS-905, is damaged when it strikes an enemy mine off the east coast of Korea. Also, Admiral Turner Joy, commander, Naval Forces Far East, issues OpnO 17–50 regarding minesweeper operations off Korea.

Things have changed drastically since the termination of World War II, when there was an abundance of ships to handle minesweeping. Only twelve U.S. minesweepers are involved at this time, due to the critical shortage of such vessels. The Japanese supply nine vessels and the South Koreans provide three minesweepers, but the ships lack some of the essential equipment. Two of the U.S. vessels, the USS *Doyle* and the USS *Endicott,* are severely restricted by their large size and high-speed capacity.

Three other U.S. vessels, the *Incredible, Pirate* and *Pledge,* are also too large to function properly in the shallow Korean waters. The remaining U.S. vessels — *Chatterer, Kite, Merganser, Mockingbird, Osprey, Partridge* and the *Redhead*— get the primary duty of clearing the mines off Wonsan; these smaller minesweepers each contain wooden hulls and move at slow speeds. Despite their sluggishness, the vessels are tough and easily adapted to the tedious chore.

September 29   *In the X Corps area,* the Corps has requested that the 1st Marine Division provide a band and two honor guards for the ceremony in Seoul; however, the Marines had not brought their instruments from Japan. It is suggested that the Marines send them by air, but in the meantime, General MacArthur makes it clear that there will be no fanfare at the ceremony celebrating the liberation of Seoul.

At 1000, General MacArthur, having traveled from Japan, lands at Kimpo Airfield to preside over the restoration of a civilian government in Seoul. By the time MacArthur arrives, his path of advance into the city has been swept free of resistance, but the enemy had been active during the early morning hours. The 3rd Battalion, 1st Marines, is posted along the route and the 1st Battalion, 5th Marines, is deployed all around Government House.

With many people, including politicians, citizens and military representatives of the combat units, in attendance, MacArthur begins the ceremony at 1200. He unabashedly refers to God during his short speech, referring to "a merciful Providence" while he reestablishes Syngman Rhee's government. After his speech, MacArthur leads the audience in saying the Lord's Prayer. President Syngman Rhee addresses the American military personnel in the audience and remarks, "How can I ever explain to you my own underlying gratitude and that of the Korean people."

General MacArthur departs Seoul immediately following the simple ceremony. His plane takes off from Kimpo Airfield at 1335, to the great relief of the Marines assigned to protect MacArthur and the other dignitaries. The Marines are quite aware that all the mines had not been extricated, and they remain concerned about snipers still in the area.

U.S. Intelligence had estimated that Seoul had been defended by about 8,000 soldiers, and that another 5,000 were deployed in Yongdungp'o. In addition, about 7,000 reinforcements had arrived in the area after the invasion of Inchon. This gives the enemy about 20,000 troops, but another 10,000 to 13,000 are spread out between the Han River and Osan. Intelligence also suggests that about 10,000 other troops had been in the area, but either they were not thrown into the fighting or they arrived too late.

While in Korea, General MacArthur confers with General Almond (X Corps), General Stratemeyer (FEAF), General Walker (Eighth Army) and Admiral Joy (NFFE) with regards to the Wonsan Operation. During the conference, MacArthur specifies October 20 as the date the 1st Marine Division will land at Wonsan.

Later in the day, General Almond confers with division commanders and various staff members at X Corps headquarters in Ascom City, outside Inchon, to discuss the Wonsan Operation. It is decided that D-Day for the invasion will be tentatively scheduled for October 15. Almond's decision to invade on the 15th is founded on the assumption that Eighth Army will complete relief of X Corps by October 3. The Marines in attendance, including General Shepherd, feel strongly that the schedule laid out by Almond is not feasible, especially in view of the fact that the Marines are still deeply involved with terminating the ongoing Seoul operation.

— *Inchon-Seoul vicinity: In the X Corps area,* all units are informed that another amphibious invasion will probably be undertaken and that it will occur on the east coast of Korea.

In the 1st Marine Division zone, at 2000, OpnO 13–50 is issued. It sets forth directions for securing the captured capital. The order specifies that the attack continue eastward, while simultaneous reconnaissance patrols (in strength) probe north and northwest. In addition, the order stipulates that the 1st Marine Division relieve elements of the 7th Infantry Division posted north of the Han River, and that it seize defined blocking positions. In conjunction, the 1st Marines will deploy to the northeast, the 5th Marines to the northwest and the 7th Marines to the north, essentially forming a semi-circle around the capital. Also, the Marines receive responsibility for the area north of the Han River and west of the Pukhan River.

In the 1st Marines sector, the enemy mounts two counterattacks, each against the 2nd Battalion. A rifle platoon defending an outpost to the front of the MLR is struck at 0445, but the assault fails. Soon after, the enemy strikes the left flank of the 2nd Battalion, but here, too, the enemy is easily thwarted. Much of the fighting is close-quartered and enemy grenades inflict the bulk of Marine casualties. A contingent of Company E, 2nd Battalion, holding positions at a listening post in front of Hill 132, comes under attack, but the main body of the platoon gets a warning when a runner is sent back by PFC Stanley R. Christianson.

Christianson volunteers to hold the position despite the high odds that he would be killed. He attempts to forestall the attack to give his platoon time to prepare. The enemy contingent closes upon Christianson and seven of them fall before his position is overrun. He is awarded the Medal of Honor posthumously for his extraordinary courage and for his selfless sacrifice to save others. The Marines sustain four killed and 28 wounded. The Communists lose 48 killed.

In the 7th Marines sector, at about 0600, the North

Koreans strike against the positions of the 7th Marines, but the attack is quickly extinguished. Following the early action, the 7th Marines advances from its positions and gains the remainder of its assigned objectives by dusk.

In the 7th Infantry Division zone, the 2nd Battalion, 17th Regiment, operating in the southeast section of Seoul, enters its first battle and encounters a strong enemy force. The firefights continue beyond dusk, and the battalion sustains seventy-nine casualties. The enemy attempts to mount a new counterattack, but the guns of the 49th FABn enter the fight and commence a powerful bombardment that shatters the attack. The enemy losses during the engagement amount to more than 400.

In other activity, South Korean Marines secure Yosu on the south coast.

In the Eighth Army area, IX Corps, since its establishment, has been short of equipment and some personnel. Now corps has a mere two and one-half companies of trucks to maintain the supply lines of both the 2nd and 25th Divisions.

In the I Corps area, 1st Cavalry Division sector, 5th Cavalry zone, a small enemy convoy, composed of 9 Russian-made jeeps, heads north from Taejon transporting about fifty Communist troops. Company L, 5th Cavalry, bushwhacks the convoy and the survivors scatter.

In the 24th Division sector, headquarters transfers to Taejon; it bears responsibility for keeping the Army line of communications secure within its sector and back to the Naktong River. The 24th Division perimeter stretches about 100 miles: the 5th RCT is deployed near Kumch'on, the 24th Reconnaissance Company holds the Waegwan bridges; the 19th Regiment is deployed in Taejon and stretches to the Kum River, and the 21st Regiment extends southeast from Taejon to Yongdong.

In the IX Corps area, 2nd Division sector, the 2nd Battalion, 9th Regiment, receives its needed fuel. By 1530, the battalion is back on the attack. It drives to Nonsan and beyond to reach the Kum River at Kanggyong at 0300 on the 30th. At this time, the 2nd Division supply line extends more than 200 miles across rugged terrain and confining roads. The average time for a supply convoy to race from Miryang to the front lines is forty-eight hours.

In the 25th Division sector, TF Dolvin advances to Chonju, where it encounters contingents of the 38th Regiment and from there, the TF drives to the Kum River at Iri. In the meantime, Task Force Blair secures Chungup by noon, and then it advances to Iri, which it seizes during the evening. TF Matthews arrives at Iri from Namwon and joins TF Blair there.

In other activity, the 27th Regiment departs Chinju and moves north to Hamyang and Namwon, while it keeps the supply road open.

In the ROK Army area, on the east coast, the S.K. 3rd Division continues its vigorous pursuit of the retreating elements of the N.K. 5th Division. The town of Samch'ok is captured during the morning, but the division continues the drive and speeds toward Kangnung. In conjunction, a small plane flies over Samch'ok, and a KMAG G-3 officer deposits a message, which is picked up and then forwarded (during the afternoon) to Colonel Emmerich at Kangnung. The message orders the S.K. 3rd Division to attack across the 38th Parallel. The attack commences on the following day.

In Naval activity, the commander, Fleet Air Wing Japan, orders the use of planes for detecting and destroying mines in the waters off the west coast of Korea. The patrols operate during daylight. Also, the USS *Magpie* (AMS-25), while participating in a mine clearing operation, hits a mine and sinks off Pohang.

— In Japan: On this day, subsequent to the recapture of Seoul, the capital of the Republic of Korea, General MacArthur receives a message from President Truman: "I know I speak for the entire American people when I send you my warmest congratulations on the victory which has been achieved under your leadership in Korea. Few operations in military history can match either the delaying action where you traded space for time in which to build up your forces, or the brilliant maneuver [Marine amphibious landing] which has now resulted in the liberation of Seoul."

More praise for MacArthur and his command arrives from the Joint Chiefs of Staff. President Truman also sends praise to the American commanders of the Air Force, Army and Navy: Lt. Generals George Stratemeyer and Walton H. Walker, and Vice Admiral Charles T. Joy. Personal congratulations to the troops of all nations fighting under the colors of the United Nations are also dispatched by Truman.

Although the magnificent victory at Inchon has compressed the differences between MacArthur and Washington, they still exist. MacArthur believes firmly that the Communists will conquer Europe via Southeast Asia unless they are halted, and he would prefer more powerful forces in Southeast Asia. But Washington maintains that Europe must receive the bulk of U.S. troops to forestall a Soviet advance there. If this strategy is to continue, the Korean crisis must be held to a small-scale war.

In other activity, General MacArthur receives a response to his message to the JCS on the 27th. He receives a confidential letter from General George C. Marshall, which in essence gives him full authority to cross the 38th Parallel. President Truman has approved Marshall's letter to MacArthur.

In other activity, General MacArthur issues Operations Plan 9–50, which gives the 1st Marine Division priority for embarkation at Inchon. The Marines again are the amphibious assault portion of X Corps.

September 30 *In the X Corps area,* the Corps reports that 14,000 North Korean troops have been killed during the Inchon–Seoul operations, and that an additional 7,000 enemy troops have been captured. Estimates of enemy casualties inflicted by South Korean

Top: U.S. Army engineers construct a Bailey bridge atop a destroyed span near Chinju. *Bottom*: U.S. Army gun carriages. On the left is an M19 with twin .40-caliber guns, and on the right is an M16 that carries four .50-caliber machine guns.

U.S. Army Sheridan medium tank passes a knocked out Russian T-34.

troops are not available. Also, there is no exact count on destroyed enemy tanks, but the losses are estimated at 45 to 50 in the vicinity of Inchon–Seoul–Yongdung-p'o. Enemy losses at Suwon–Osan amount to about fifteen tanks. The U.S. Army (X Corps) has no tanks in action during the operation. The Marines lose no tanks to the enemy tank forces, but enemy ground forces cost the Marines several tanks.

In the X Corps sector, engineers, with the strong support of the FEAF Combat Cargo Command, complete the fabrication of a pontoon bridge across the Han River that permits traffic to cross; 3,034 vehicles cross into Seoul today, and crossings continue 24 hours a day

for many days. The Air Force flies the bridge in from Japan on C-119s, which make seventy-nine flights. The engineers are working on completing a second span across the river to open two-way traffic.

In the 1st Marine Division zone, General O.P. Smith is informed of the probable X Corps invasion of Wonsan. The 1st Marine Division assumes responsibility for the 32nd Regiment sector in Seoul, which permits the regiment to move back across the Han River to the south bank.

Also, the 1st Marine Division reports that it has inflicted 13,666 casualties upon the enemy during the Inchon–Seoul operation, and it also states that 4,792 enemy troops have been captured. The Marines report that they have destroyed or seized nineteen 45-mm antitank guns, 56 heavy machine guns, 337 light and sub-machine guns, and twenty-three 120-mm mortars, as well as 59 14.5 antitank rifles and 7,453 enemy rifles. The 1st Marine Division sustains the heaviest losses of X Corps: 366 killed, 49 who succumb to wounds, 2,029 wounded and six missing. Marine losses are most severe September 21-27 in Seoul, when 1,482 casualties are sustained; 285 of these occur on the 24th.

Division issues OpnO 14–50 at 1500; it designates the missions of the regiments.

In other activity, The 1st Marines (RCT-1) takes responsibility for the right flank, and it is to establish blocking positions in the heights from two to five miles northeast of the capital. The 5th Marines (RCT-5) is ordered to maintain a strong reconnaissance presence by dispatching a reinforced battalion to Suyuhyon to establish a blocking position while also protecting the division's left flank. The order also stipulates that the 5th Marines is to (upon order) commit one reinforced rifle company for Task Force Kumpo. The attachment units are 1st Battalion, 11th Marines; one battery, 50th AAA Battalion, USA; Company A, 1st Tank Battalion; Company A, 1st Engineer Battalion, and one Company of the 1st Motor Transport Battalion.

The 7th Marines (RCT-7) is to speed to the area near Uijongbu and secure blocking positions there. The attachment contingents are 3rd Battalion, 11th Marines; one battery, 50th AAA Battalion, USA; Company D, 1st Tank Battalion, and one company of South Korean Marines. The order directs that the KMC Regiment (minus the 1st and 3rd Battalions and one company of the 5th Battalion), augmented by one detachment of Air and Naval Gunfire Liaison Company, is to proceed east to the confluence of the Han and Pukhan Rivers. Once there, it is to secure blocking positions along the road that stretches from Seoul.

Also, Task Force Kumpo, when activated by Division, is to include one reinforced rifle company, 5th Marines; the 3rd KMC Battalion; Battery C, 50th AAA Battalion, USA; and, if necessary, a detachment of tanks.

In the 7th Infantry Division zone, the 7th Division reports that its 32nd Regiment has killed about 3,000 enemy troops and captured 1,203. The 17th and 31st Regiments each inflict several hundred casualties upon the North Koreans. The 7th Division sustains 572 battle casualties: 106 killed, 409 wounded and 57 MIA. These casualty figures include 166 South Korean troops who had been attached to the 7th Division.

In other activity, the 7th Division begins moving to Suwon and Ich'on, south and southeast respectively, to begin the laborious movement by land to Pusan. The division's tanks and heavy equipment will embark from Ich'on aboard ten LSTs that await the arrival of the 7th Division components.

In the Eighth Army, I Corps, area, 1st Cavalry Division sector, the 5th Cavalry discovers three locomotives and attached trains the enemy had concealed in tunnels.

In the 24th Division sector, the road bridge over the Naktong at Waegwan has been repaired and it begins to handle vehicular traffic. Engineers have used pile bents and a 100-feet triple single-panel Bailey bridge to stitch the 207-foot hole.

In the IX Corps area, 2nd Division sector, the regiments are deployed throughout the area from the Kum River and the area south of it. The 9th Regiment stands in the Koryong–Samga vicinity. The 23rd Regiment is deployed around Anui and the 38th Regiment holds positions in the vicinity of Chonju–Kanggyong.

In the 25th Division sector, TF Dolvin, subsequent to accomplishing its objectives, is disbanded at 1500. Since the initiation of its attack on September 26, TF Dolvin has sustained one officer and forty-five enlisted men wounded. In addition, three tanks have been lost to enemy mines. In contrast, TF Dolvin has killed about 350 enemy troops and captured 750 others. It has seized or destroyed 19 vehicles, 16 antitank guns and about 250 tons of ammunition.

In other activity, the 1st Battalion, 24th Regiment, captures Kunsan, a port city on the Kum River estuary, without incident at 1300.

In the ROK Army I Corps area, the S.K. 3rd Division continues ripping up the coastal road as it races north. The pace-setting advance outdistances all other attacking units, and it winds up at a point five miles short of the 38th Parallel. Some advance patrols cross the 38th Parallel this day.

In the ROK II Corps area, South Korean troops advance several miles north of Andong and inspect a tunnel that had been bombarded by Air Force planes. The tunnel, obviously struck by napalm, contains dead enemy troops at both ends. It is packed with supplies and equipment, including 76-mm guns, 120-mm mortars, five trucks and four jeeps.

South of Andong at Uisong, other S.K. troops capture about 100 tons of rice and a tremendous amount of equipment. The cache includes large numbers of tanks and vehicles, and huge quantities of ammunition. The enemy division had expended its fuel and was compelled to abandon the vehicles.

In Naval activity, the USS *Mansfield* (DD 728) strikes a mine off Changjon.

— In Japan: General MacArthur dispatches a message to the secretary of defense: "Unless and until the enemy capitulates, I regard all of Korea open for our military operations."

October 1 The commander-in-chief of the North Korean Forces receives a call for surrender from General MacArthur: "The early and total defeat and complete destruction of your armed forces and war-making potential is now inevitable. In order that the decision of the United Nations may be carried out with a minimum of further loss of life and destruction of property, I, as the United Nations' commander-in-chief, call upon you and the forces under your command, in whatever part of Korea situated, forthwith to lay down your arms and cease hostilities...."

The North Koreans are also informed that they

should free all POWs and civilian prisoners. The broadcast receives no response. Subsequently, on October 9, another surrender offer is delivered to the North Korean leader. In other activity, from September 1 until this day, the U.N. has collected about 30,000 enemy prisoners.

In the X Corps area, preliminary directions from GHQ, Far East Command, concerning the amphibious landing at Wonsan are delivered to Admiral Struble and General Almond; Joint TF 7 is re-established. Struble is renamed the commanding officer. The objectives of JTF 7 are: to maintain a naval blockade of Korea's east coast from Ch'ongjin southward; to board and transport X Corps to the Wonsan area and provide cover and support en route; to initiate the required pre–D-day Naval operations; to launch (on D-day) an amphibious assault and seize, occupy and defend a beachhead in the vicinity of Wonsan; and to provide naval gunfire, air and initial logistical support.

The North Koreans have maintained Wonsan as a naval base, but it was the Japanese who initially developed the city's naval capabilities. Also, off Wonsan, a helicopter attached to the USS *Rochester* discovers enemy mines while conducting a reconnaissance mission; 61 mines are spotted. Also, the USS *Missouri* participates in the bombardment of targets on the east coast of Korea.

In the 1st Marine Division zone, General O.P. Smith receives a memorandum directing him to submit a plan by Oct. 3 for loading the 1st Marine Division at Inchon for the Wonsan invasion; however, at present, no ships have been designated for the operation, thus making it impossible for Smith to provide the requested information at the required time.

In the 1st Marines zone, as scheduled, the Regiment deploys at its assigned blocking positions northeast of the capital, and the day passes without major incident. Nevertheless, several patrols encounter some light resistance.

In the 5th Marines sector, in the 2nd Battalion zone, patrols are dispatched along the Pyongyang Road, stretching to Munsan-ni and the Imjin River. At 0600 the 3rd Battalion, bolstered by a detachment of engineers, one tank platoon and one battery of artillery, drives toward Suyuhyon. Its rear is guarded by the 1st Battalion's Company C, which is to simultaneously protect the route of the returning vehicles. The column advances throughout the day, hindered primarily by two enemy roadblocks, but both are demolished. By dusk, the 3rd Battalion, 5th Marines (reinforced), reaches the heights just shy of the objective. An enemy counterattack is sprung on the following morning.

Meanwhile, the 2nd Battalion, 5th Marines' patrols scan their wide area for the enemy. Contact with the enemy is made at about 1030, when about 150 to 200 North Korean troops are detected. The firefight is brief, thanks in great part to the timely arrival of planes and an effective mortar bombardment. The enemy is quickly routed, leaving thirty dead troops on the field.

In the 7th Marines sector, the Regiment moves out early. By 0630, the battalions advance with the 3rd Battalion acting as vanguard while the 2nd Battalion trails in reserve. Meanwhile, anticipating an enemy ambush about halfway to the objective, Colonel Litzenberg dispatches the 1st Battalion, led by Lt. Colonel Raymond Davis, to take positions from which it can provide cover fire for the 3rd Battalion when it traverses a passageway that is susceptible to heavy fire from concealed enemy positions on the sheer slopes that dominate the pass.

The 1st Battalion deploys on both sides of the passageway and awaits the advancing 3rd Battalion. In the meantime, the 2nd Battalion becomes snarled when it encounters an enemy minefield. While the ground troops, tanks and artillery units are forced to halt, engineers immediately begin to eliminate the obstacles.

During the day's march, one 3rd Battalion patrol comes across a grisly scene — the bodies of thirty executed civilian Koreans, including some women and one child, all of whom have their hands bound behind their backs. According to a Communist prisoner, the victims are relatives of South Korean soldiers.

While Major Roach's 2nd Battalion struggles to clear the mines and resume the advance, the enemy and the 1st Battalion clash. As expected, the hills are infested with enemy troops. The accompanying artillery initiates a heavy series of barrages that strike both Marine battalions during the day. Aircraft arrive to pound the slopes to loosen resistance, but the enemy holds firmly. The Marines halt the advance for the night.

In conjunction, the 7th Marines are reinforced by the 3rd Battalion, 11th Marines (Artillery), Company D, 1st Tank Battalion, Company D, 1st Engineer Battalion and one company of Korean Marines (Company C).

In the Eighth Army area, covering the period from its entrance into the war until today, Eighth Army has sustained 24,172 casualties: 5,145 killed in action; 16,461 wounded in action, including 422 who die from their wounds; 42 reported captured and 2,164 missing in action.

In other activity, Army suffers from the lack of unloading facilities at Inchon, as the 1st Marine Division has priority due to the Wonsan operation. Also, Army is unable to handle more than one corps beyond the Han River, forcing the IX Corps to suspend its advance into North Korea until the logistics situation eases. The U.N. rail system extends only as far as the original Pusan Perimeter, unable to supply Eighth Army elements now stretched about 200 miles north of it at the Han River. A Herculean effort is undertaken to restore the rails, particularly those north of Waegwan.

In conjunction, Eighth Army begins to repair the rail bridges and the larger road bridges, while I Corps assumes responsibility for the remainder of the road bridges. South Korean troops repair the smaller bridges.

Advance elements of the Thailand Battalion arrive at Pusan, followed by the remainder on 7 November. Also, the weather is quickly changing and the U.S. and other U.N. troops lack sufficient winter clothing.

Eighth Army continues to overwork its vehicles to

Wounded troops aboard a transport plane en route from Korea to Japan are treated by a nurse.

resupply the advancing units. During September and through October, more than seventy-five percent of the Eighth Army vehicles operate on a round-the-clock basis. The practice continues into November. During the operation, the trucks of the 2nd and 25th Divisions are cannibalized to supply other units. The ab-

sence of rails makes the supply situation terrible. Truck drivers must be flown into Pusan or transported there by train to pick up vehicles and drive them north. The trip takes the trucks on a 400-mile journey over nasty highways.

In the I Corps area, the corps has logistical problems.

Some units are reduced to one day's supplies. Many tanks are operating in advanced areas with inadequate fuel. The tankers frequently go into action realizing they may not be able to sustain the attack into the following day.

In the 1st Cavalry Division sector, Colonel Mon Che Won, commanding officer 19th Regiment, N.K. 13th Division, tires of hiding near Tabu-dong and surrenders. The enemy division has been decimated, but some of its troops eventually escape to Pyonggang, dubbed the "Iron Triangle."

In the 24th Division area, the 24th Division advances along the Kumsan Road and captures much enemy equipment and ammunition, fifteen artillery pieces and seven working tanks.

In other activity, the North Koreans establish a formidable roadblock on the main Seoul Road in an effort to buy time to permit about 2,000 troops of the N.K. 6th Division to escape to the North. The enemy had abandoned its heavy weapons, near Sanch'ong (Chirye Mountains), but retains its machine guns and mortars. The blockade, about fifteen miles northwest of Kumch'on, holds for nearly ten hours.

In the IX Corps area, 25th Division sector, about 200 enemy troops are spotted northeast of Kumsan. A Mosquito aircraft drops a message to them instructing them to lay down their weapons and march to a nearby hill. The North Koreans follow the instructions and wait on the hill until patrols, guided by the plane, advance and capture them.

In the ROK I Corps area, two rifle companies of the S.K. 3rd Division shoot across the 38th Parallel just before noon. These riflemen encounter some opposition from entrenched enemy troops, but by the following day, both the Capital Division and the S.K. 3rd Division establish their respective command posts at Yangyang.

In the ROK II Corps area, although the enemy is on the retreat, some units have evaded the surging South Koreans and maintained cohesion in the mountains. One of these groups, composed of between 1,000 and 2000 troops, is isolated but not docile. The North Korean contingent launches an attack to break through the S.K. lines and escape northward. Slightly after midnight (October 1-2) the ROK II Corps headquarters in Wonju becomes the recipient of the assault.

The Communists overwhelm headquarters and ravage the town. Five American officers are among the dead. The Americans had either been attached to the corps or been in Wonju on liaison missions. The rampage continues until the morning of the 2nd. At its conclusion, between 1,000 and 2,000 civilians are massacred.

The North Korean 1st Division, which is retreating through Wonju and Inje, eventually reaches the vicinity of Pyonggang. By the latter part of October, about 2,000 troops assemble there. According to U.S. estimates, about 25,000 to 30,000 Communist troops escape to North Korea, but the vast majority of the force has been destroyed or captured. For all intents and purposes, the N.K. Army has been destroyed.

In Air Force activity, Lieutenant Hamilton B. Shawe, a pilot attached to the 8th Tactical Reconnaissance Squadron, executes a most dangerous mission. He flies solo to Wonsan, a distance of 425 miles, in an unarmed aircraft to photograph enemy positions there. The Communists score several hits upon his plane, but he is able to get important photographs and return safely to his base.

Also, during another encounter between Sabre jets and MiGs near Songchon, Lieutenant Raymond O. Barton, 334th Fighter-Interceptor Squadron, 4th Fighter-Interceptor Group, downs one MiG-15 during a morning mission.

In other activity, a pilot based on a carrier is reported down about 90 miles inside enemy territory. A rescue helicopter races to the scene. Lieutenant William B. Evans and two escort F-86s arrive at the spot between Kyomip'o and Pyongyang. Evans lands and rescues the pilot. All aircraft return safely, although Evans' helicopter had come under intense enemy fire.

— *In China:* Premier Chou En-lai, during a speech today, lets it be known that China is prepared to directly enter the Korean conflict. The premier states that China "will not tolerate foreign aggression and will not stand aside should the imperialists wantonly invade the territory of their neighbor."

— *In Japan:* U.S. troops and the sparse contingents of the other U.N. Allies have supported the South Korean Army's plight against the Communist invaders. By today, the tables have turned 180 degrees. The North Korean forces are being thrashed all across South Korea. The combination of the invasion at Inchon and the breakout from the Pusan Perimeter has dealt General MacArthur the success he needed to forestall the loss of South Korea to the Communists. U.S. troops who had been mauled and forced into humiliating retreat are now on the offense. The successful advance permits General MacArthur to harness some of his power.

Today, MacArthur directs the Air Force to abort its missions to destroy the remaining bridges, rails and roads below the 38th Parallel. He also orders the Air Force to suspend attacks against communication centers in the same area. General MacArthur ceases all attacks against primary installations in North Korea and furthermore, he strikes enemy air fields south of the 40th Parallel from the list of targets.

October 2   Several conferences are held between this day and October 4 concerning the Wonsan operation. Admiral Struble and staff officers decide to establish Advance JTF 7. The advance group — composed of 21 minesweepers, including 8 Japanese, 1 South Korean and 10 U.S. vessels — begins its clearing operation in Wonsan Harbor on the 10th.

In the X Corps area, responsibility for Kumpo peninsula is transferred from X Corps to the 1st Marine Division. (Both Kimpo and Kumpo are names used to designate the peninsula formed by the mouth of the Han River. Kimpo is the name of the airfield and Kumpo is the name of the principal town on the peninsula.)

Task Force Kumpo, composed of the 3rd Korean Marine Battalion, a unit of the 1st Signal Battalion, USMC, and C Battery, 50th AAA Battalion, USA, relieves elements of the 187th Airborne RCT and assumes responsibility for the operations there. However, no enemy activity is discovered on the peninsula after this day. During the 187th's watch, the unit had been plagued with a lack of artillery, compelling it to depend on naval gunfire and the spot teams led by Lieutenants Leo McMillan, USN, and John E. Dolan, 7th Marines. Both officers and their respective teams remain with TF Kumpo. The 187th Airborne RCT had protected the Marines' right flank as they advanced to Seoul.

In the 5th Marines sector, the enemy launches a company-sized assault against the Marines at 0230. It is met by tenacious machine gun fire and easily terminated. The Marines discover 67 enemy dead on the field at daybreak. At 0700, the march is resumed and without further incident, Suyuhyon is occupied.

In the 7th Marines sector, the N.K. 31st Regiment, 31st Division, still holds its bulwark positions in the heights along the Uijongbu Road, near Nuwon-ni, several miles south of Uijongbu. At 0630, the 1st and 3rd Battalions, commanded by Colonel Davis and Major Roach respectively, reinitiate the drive down the road to fracture the resolute enemy entrenchments on the slopes above the defile. Marine squadron VMF-312 planes swarm over the area throughout the day, plastering the slopes to aid the eviction of the entrenched enemy.

The 1st Battalion, commanded by Lt. Colonel Davis, advances on the left (east) of the defile, in conjunction with the 3rd Battalion, which drives forward on the right (west). The 3rd Battalion, commanded by Major Roach, punches its way to the midpoint of the passageway, but again, enemy minefields slow the progress of the tanks and force the engineers to resume the task of clearing the path while under incessant fire. Meanwhile, the enemy throws a roundhouse punch to break up the advance. The North Koreans launch a horrific barrage that includes artillery fire and mortars. These supplement the ongoing small arms fire hammering both of the advancing battalions.

The tanks of the 1st Platoon spring into action. They swivel their turrets toward two dingy huts that contain enemy troops. The guns roar and their thundering fire decimates the huts and kills about 35 North Korean troops. During the heated exchange, the enemy manages to thread the needle by firing directly through the 105-mm gun tube of a dozer tank. The shot wounds two Marine crewmen.

The 1st Battalion, also bolstered by planes, continues its dogged advance. The battalion presses forward and darts across the stream east of the passageway and then lunges into the nearby heights. The battalion gains only about three hundred yards at day's end.

In the ROK Army Headquarters area, I Corps sector, the South Koreans continue to advance beyond the 38th Parallel. Divisional Headquarters is established at Yangyang about eight miles north of the parallel by both the Capital and S.K. 3rd Divisions.

North Korean officers and enlisted men who surrendered at the 38th Parallel under U.N. guards.

Elements of the ROK 3rd Division at the 38th Parallel.

Western press representatives announce the crossing of the border into North Korea, but official news is not forthcoming until the following day. A U.S. Air Force plane scours the area north of the 38th Parallel in the vicinity of Hwach'on and Kumhwa. The pilot reports spotting many small groups of N.K. troops and estimates a combined total about 5,000.

In Air Force activity, the 8th TRS Squadron arrives at Taegu form Japan to become the Air Force's initial day reconnaissance squadron to operate from a base in Korea.

In other activity, a contingent of twenty-two B-29s strikes a Communist military training complex located in Nanam and devastates it. Also, a contingent of F-86s attached to the 336th Fighter-Interceptor Squadron, 4th Fighter-Interceptor Group, clash with MiGs near Kunu-ri. One of the enemy planes is downed by Lieutenant Loyd J. Thompson.

— *In the United Nations:* The Soviets offer a plan to order a cease fire in Korea. The Russian proposal also calls for the withdrawal of all foreign troops from Korea.

— *In Japan:* General MacArthur issues U.N. Command Operations Order 2, the order concerning the imminent attack into North Korea. It stipulates specific instructions concerning U.N. operations above the 38th Parallel, and it clarifies the precise mission of X Corps and its plan of movement.

X Corps is to revert to GHQ reserve when Eighth Army moves through it, while advancing through Seoul. Also, the 1st Marine Division and X Corps headquarters are to embark at Inchon. The 7th Infantry Division and the majority of X Corps troops are to move to Pusan and

embark there. MacArthur concludes that the congestion at the port of Inchon, combined with the lousy tides, will definitely hinder the mission. He decides that some of the force will have to embark at Pusan to ensure that the operation remains on schedule. On the following day, Eighth Army issues its operation order to blueprint its portion of the attack into North Korea.

October 3 *Inchon-Seoul vicinity:* X Corps orders the 1st Marine Division to begin moving to an assembly area at Inchon to prepare to embark for Wonsan. The town of Wonsan, located along the southwest tip of Yonghung Bay, is much more accessible and the indigenous tides are more easily conquerable than those at Inchon. The port, considered one of the finest natural harbors in Korea, is strategically located about 80 miles north of the 38th Parallel.

By 6 October, the 1st, 5th and 11th Marines are in position at Inchon. The 7th Marines arrives later. The 1st and 7th Marines are scheduled to assault Wonsan. Unlike Inchon, the invasion force will face neither unruly currents nor nasty seawalls blanketed by fog, thereby ensuring the landing craft a quick trek to the beaches.

In the 1st Marine Division zone, the 1st and 5th Marine Regiments maintain their positions, but continue to send out patrols. The commandant, General Clifton Cates, arrives by helicopter at Division headquarters. His party includes Generals Edwin Pollock and Clayton Jerome. After receiving a briefing, General Cates departs by helicopter to observe the sectors of the 1st and 5th Marines. Afterward, Cates takes a jeep to the front lines of the 7th Marines to watch the Regiment hammer its way to the objective.

A USMC F7F Tigercat at Kimpo Airfield.

In the 7th Marines sector, the attack to seize the heights above the defile and to gain Uijongbu resumes. Roach's 3rd Battalion pushes along the west side of the road, while the 1st Battalion, under Davis, drives along the east side, with each afforded heavy air and tank support. The armor throws its full weight into the battle and slams the enemy with relentless firepower, expending 167 rounds of 90-mm shells and about 20,000 machine gun shells to bolster the attacks. The supporting air attacks by VMF-312, although effective, are costly.

An unending string of low-level sorties blasts the North Korean–held slopes. Enemy small arms fire knocks out one plane, piloted by First Lieutenant Robert Crocker, who dies shortly after the crash. Another pilot, Major Charles McLean, is also shot down. He lands his plane on friendly terrain and survives.

During the day's fighting, the planes of VMF-312 spot an enemy column of vehicles and immediately take it under fire. The swift action decimates seven vehicles, but one truck escapes destruction. The attackers gain ground and both battalions surge to the high ground on opposite sides of the road. To add more momentum, Colonel Litzenberg commits Major Webb D. Sawyer's 2nd Battalion, 7th Marines. It speeds through the passageway, aware that the 1st and 3rd Battalions dominate the east and west respectively.

The attacking Marines welcome the buffer in the heights, which provides them with extra stamina to burst through the remaining obstacles. The attack accelerates further when the 2nd Battalion discovers that the enemy artillery positions and supply centers have been deserted. The 2nd Battalion storms down the highway heading straight for the objective, fully aware that the regiment has bludgeoned the resistance. Two damaged enemy tanks are captured during the assault, but seven tanks escape.

Meanwhile, the Marine planes have also destroyed four additional supporting tanks. Three battalions of the N.K. 31st Regiment, one artillery battalion, and contingents of the N.K. 17th Division and the Seoul Division had staunchly blocked the 7th Marines. Nevertheless, subsequent to three brutal days of grueling combat, Colonel Litzenberg's RCT-7, the freshest regiment in the division, prevails. Today's advance of about three miles through strenuous terrain crushes the resistance.

At 1700 the 2nd Battalion, 7th Marines, under Major Webb Sawyer, enters the abandoned town and takes uncontested control of Uijongbu, which is reduced to charred debris by the air assaults. The advance also severs the enemy's communications between the areas east and west of the captured town. The victory for the Marines' newest regiment also provides X Corps with a vital blocking position along its final phase line. But the victory is not without pain. The regiment sustains 13 killed and 111 wounded during the three-day fight for the town.

The 7th Marines occupy the heights north of the prize and establish a line around the town as a night perimeter. The combat in the vicinity of Uijongbu, during the 2nd-3rd, is the final organized resistance raised against the 1st Marine Division during the Inchon–Seoul operations. From this point on, the Marines hold their blocking positions, but continue to

Marine Corsairs at Kimpo Airfield.

dispatch patrols to the front and along the flank. Orders arrive on October 5 that direct the Marine regiments to begin staging in Inchon.

In the Eighth Army area, Eighth Army issues its operation plan for the attack into North Korea. I Corps is ordered to seize a line north of the Imjin River near the 38th Parallel. The order stipulates that the minimum force to be committed is one division. The IX Corps is to relieve the I Corps, then I Corps is to drive north. The advance is to be spearheaded by the 1st Cavalry Division. In conjunction, the flanks are to be protected by the 24th Division and the S.K. 1st Division.

In related activity, the ROK Army is ordered to field a new division (the 11th) by October 5. The S.K. 11th Division is to support IX Corps during the operations south of the 38th Parallel. Also, ROK Army is directed to transfer its I Corps to terrain on the east coast, between Chumunjin-up and Yongp'o. Its II Corps is to move to Central Korea and deploy between Ch'unch'on and Uijongbu. Both S.K. corps are then to prepare for the northward attack.

In other activity, the 3rd Battalion, Royal Australian Regiment, arrives at Kumch'on to join the British Brigade. Upon the arrival of the Australian Regiment, the British 27th Brigade becomes known as the 27th British Commonwealth Brigade. On October 5, most of the British Brigade will be flown to Kimpo Airfield, where it becomes part of the S.K. I Corps operations in the vicinity of the 38th Parallel.

In ROK Army Headquarters area, I Corps sector, the S.K. 3rd Division maintains its quick paced advance and gains an average of about 15 miles a day, despite formidable opposition raised by the surviving elements of the N.K. 5th Division. Some enemy groups are bypassed during the northward march. These stragglers begin to harass the rear supply columns of the S.K. 3rd Division. Other contingents of the N.K. 5th Division continue to defend the routes of advance as they retreat. Mortar fire and heavy 76-mm antitank guns also pound the South Koreans.

— In the United Nations: The Indian delegate to the U.N., Sir Benegal Rau, makes it known that India is against sending U.N. troops across the 38th Parallel. In conjunction, Chinese government officials have informed India's ambassador to China that the Chinese will enter the war if U.N. troops enter North Korea.

— In Japan: General MacArthur makes the first official statement concerning the U.N. crossing of the 38th Parallel.

October 4–10 1950 *In Naval activity,* Admiral Doyle gathers an array of vessels off Inchon to accommodate the landing force for the Wonsan operation. The ships include some from the Military Sea Transport Service and LSTs, the latter manned by Japanese sailors. Transport Squadron One arrives on the 8th, bringing the complement to 71 vessels. The force is composed of one AGC (amphibious force flagship); eight APAs (assault transports); two APs (transports); ten AKAs (assault cargo ships); five LSDs (landing ship, dock); 36 LSTs (landing ship, tank); three LSUs (landing ship, utility) and one LSM (landing ship, medium). The Naval force also includes six commercial cargo ships ("Victory" and C-2 types).

In other Naval activity, Task Force 77 reports that its carrier planes, for the 13-day period covering the Inchon attack, had flown 3,330 sorties. Also, the commander, Naval Forces Far East (COMNAVFE) reports that during the past month, patrols had detected and more than 65 mines, including floating

and moored, in the waters off Korea. COMNAVFE orders the bombardment (air and naval surface) of the areas around Chinnampo and Haeju.

October 4   At Wonsan, during the darkened hours, the Communists have been working tirelessly to lay an impenetrable minefield in the channel and on the beaches. Subsequent to the arrival of U.S. X Corps troops, it becomes known that thirty Russians had supervised the entire operation until today. The Russians evacuate the town due to the imminent approach of U.S. and S.K. troops.

Some of the first Chinese Communists captured by U.N. forces in Korea.

In the X Corps area, the corps is less than jubilant when Far East Air Forces and the Fifth Air Force, pursuant to an order of July 8, take control of all Marine squadrons at Kimpo Airfield. Nonetheless, the Marines sustain no substantive losses, as the FEAF orders the 1st Marine Air Wing to continue to support the X Corps.

In other activity, General Almond issues corps order OpnO-4, which details the plan of operation for the Wonsan mission and specifies the missions of subordinate units. The plan directs the 1st Marine Division to seize a base of operations by initiating an amphibious assault to secure the airport. In conjunction, the 7th Division and the 92nd and 96th FABns receive orders to embark from Pusan and land at Wonsan (upon orders). In the meantime, the 7th Division is directed to attack west toward Pyongyang and link up with the advancing Eighth Army there.

In other activity, the fuel situation at Kimpo eases during October, subsequent to the completion of a pipeline that carries aviation fuel from Inchon to the airfield.

In the 1st Marine Division zone, the 1st Cavalry Division passes through the lines of the 5th Marines northwest of Seoul as it moves toward Kaesong. Also, the S.K. II Corps begins to assemble in the sector of the 7th Marines, in the vicinity of Uijongbu.

In the Eighth Army area, Army specifies which route the 7th Division (X Corps) is to use to advance from Inchon and Suwon to Pusan. It is to advance through Ch'ungju, Hamch'ang, Kumch'on, Taegu and Kyongju. The troops are directed to board trains at Taegu to carry them on the last phase of the 350-mile journey. From Taegu, the trucks are to return to the departure areas and duplicate the trip with other troops.

In the IX Corps area, IX Corps is scheduled to relieve I Corps, but it is also designated the responsibility to continue reducing the remaining enemy resistance in South Korea. It is also under orders to keep clear the line of communications among Seoul, Suwon, Taejon, Taegu and Pusan. The South Korean police are to assist IX Corps with the operation to finish off the North Koreans in South Korea.

In the ROK Army Headquarters area, the S.K. 3rd Division, trailed by the Capital Division, continues to advance, disregarding its own dire circumstances. Many of the troops have no shoes. Undaunted, the advance drives straight over the rocky, mountainous terrain. En route, some of the Capital Division units are diverted into the Diamond Mountains.

In Air Force activity, Far East Air Forces assumes control of all land-based aircraft in Korea, including USMC units. With the recent gains in Korea and the expectation of gaining enemy airfields, Fifth Air Force halts the majority of its raids on fields below the 40th Parallel.

In yet other activity, a South African Air Force contingent, the 2d South African Fighter Squadron, arrives and is attached to Far East Air Forces.

— *In Japan:* During the early morning hours an urgent telegram for Ambassador Sebald arrives at the embassy from Washington. The message documents a conversation between the Indian ambassador to China and Chou En-lai, whereby Chou En-lai convincingly suggests that if U.N. troops cross the 38th Parallel, Chinese combat troops will join the fight. At this point, it has already been determined that Chinese forces are involved and have been since August. This has been confirmed by antiaircraft fire originating on the Chinese side of the Yalu River in Manchuria. Active Chinese participation has also been irrefutably verified by the capture of Chinese soldiers.

October 5   Admiral Struble reinitiates JTF-7, again utilizing vessels from his Seventh Fleet. The units are: TF-95 (Advance Force), commanded by Rear Admiral Allen E. Smith; TG-95.2 (Covering and Support), commanded by Rear Admiral Charles Hartman; TG-95.6 (Minesweeping), commanded by Captain Richard Spofford; TF-90 (Attack Force), commanded by Rear Admiral James Doyle; TF-79 (Logistical Support Force), commanded by Captain Bernard Austin; TF-77 (Fast Carrier Force), commanded by Rear Admiral Edward Ewen; TG-96.8 (Escort Carrier Group), commanded by Rear Admiral Richard Ruble; TG-96.2 (Patrol and Reconnaissance), commanded by Rear Admiral George Henderson; and TG-70.1 (Flagship Group), commanded by Captain Irving T. Duke. Admiral Struble's flag will fly aboard the recently arrived battleship USS *Missouri.*

Pursuant to Struble's order, the Fast Carrier Force and the Patrol Reconnaissance Force initiate search and attack missions prior to the landing of the ground forces at Wonsan. The cruisers, destroyers and minesweepers of the Advance Force will also be operating off Wonsan. These combined forces will coordinate their efforts to lessen enemy resistance and seize control of the seas off the objective.

Inchon–Seoul vicinity: *In the X Corps area, 1st Marine Division zone,* as directed by OpnO 15–50, the final order issued by the 1st Marine Division during the Inchon Operation, the 5th Marines culminates its dogged 20 days on the fields of battle. It is to begin staging in Inchon at 1700. The exhausted regiment moves back across the Han River and returns to Inchon, where it prepares to move against Wonsan. In conjunction, the 11th Marines is scheduled to begin its staging at 1700 on the 6th, followed by the 1st Marines, prior to darkness on 6th. The 7th Marines' orders stipulate that it is to join the other regiments in Inchon during the afternoon of the 7th. The Korean Marine Regiment is to arrive in Inchon prior to darkness on the 7th.

In the 7th Infantry Division zone, General Almond, apparently unsatisfied with Colonel Ovenshine's methods of command during the fighting below Suwon, relieves him of command of the 31st Regiment.

Division begins its move toward Pusan at 0350. The 3rd Battalion, 31st Regiment, takes the lead. At about 0750, the 32nd Regiment begins to advance through

Inchon. The 32nd Regiment had protected the Marines' left flank during the advance against Seoul. The 17th Regiment holds in place until October 8 to maintain a blocking position until relieved. The division's tanks move to Pusan by sea.

In the Eighth Army area, Army issues the order authorizing the crossing of the 38th Parallel, but the date for the attack is not publicized.

In other activity, the rail bridge at Waegwan is repaired and traffic begins to move across the Naktong River. Subsequent to some preparatory work, engineers persevere for seven days to fix the 165-foot breach in the span.

In the I Corps area, the 1st Cavalry pushes north from Seoul to seize an assembly area for the I Corps. Company I, 5th Cavalry, reaches Munsan-ni on the north bank of the Imjin River during the evening.

In the IX Corps area, Corps opens its command post at Taejon. The 2nd Division bears responsibility for the terrain west and southwest of Taejon, and the 25th Division will defend the area south and east of the city, as well as Taejon proper. The area of operation for the division encompasses 6,500 square miles of terrain, nearly all of it in the mountains. The enemy, much of which has been bypassed, remains in the high ground, and the 25th Division concentrates much of its activity against guerrillas. In conjunction, the S.K. 11th Division is attached to IX Corps to assist corps in the rear areas of its zone.

In the ROK Army Headquarters area, II Corps sector, Corps prepares to attack across the 38th Parallel on the following day.

October 6   The 3rd Logistical Command (USN) assumes responsibility for all unloading operations at Inchon. X Corps uses its muscle to pull strings — it requests that all unloading unrelated to the X Corps mission be suspended to prevent the ongoing operation (Wonsan) from running behind schedule. It is estimated that unless X Corps retains total use of the port facilities, the operation would run six to twenty days behind schedule.

In the X Corps area, 1st Marine Division sector, the 1st Marines departs its positions near Uijongbu and moves to Inchon to join the 5th Marines. Along the outskirts of Inchon where the Marines had established a cemetery, responsibility for it is transferred to the United Nations. A stirring ceremony includes an invocation by Chaplain R.M. Schwyhart (1st Marine Division). Following the prayers, General Almond, USA, gives his remarks and then lays a wreath on the grave of an unknown soldier. Following this, the graves of a Marine, an Army soldier and an ROK trooper receive similar wreaths by General O.P. Smith, General Barr, USA, and S.K. Colonel Lee, respectively. Taps blows and erect riflemen fire volleys over the graves of their fallen brothers. The ceremony ends with the playing of the "Star Spangled Banner" and the Korean national anthem.

In other activity, the Attack Force–Landing Force obtains the required intelligence and maps to enable staff officers to plan for the invasion of Wonsan, but the arrival is not timely. It soon becomes obvious that the tentative invasion date (October 15) must be postponed. Nevertheless, General O.P. Smith orders the 1st Marine Division to embark on the 8th. The initial Landing Force contingents and accompanying weaponry will prematurely be placed aboard ships to await the conclusions of the planners with regard to the expected enemy resistance at Wonsan.

In the 7th Division sector, the 7th Division continues moving toward Pusan, but remnant enemy forces raise havoc with elements of the 2nd Battalion, 31st Regiment. At 0200, the North Koreans spring an ambush from positions in the mountains near Mun'gyong and inflict nine casualties.

In the Eighth Army area, I Corps sector, 1st Cavalry Division zone, the advance to secure the assembly area is maintained.

In the 24th Division zone, Division focuses on the terrain around Seoul.

In the ROK Army Headquarters area, II Corps sector, the S.K. 6th Division pushes out from its positions in the vicinity of Chonchon and drives across the 38th Parallel toward Hwach'on, which is fiercely defended by the remnants of the N.K. 9th Division. Several days of bitter combat ensue. In conjunction, ROK warships receive permission to proceed as far north as necessary along the east coast of Korea to support the ROK ground troops.

In Air Force activity, Kimpo Airfield, under the jurisdiction of the Marine Corps since its recapture, is transferred to the U.S. Air Force. In other activity, a contingent of eighteen B-29s strike the arsenal located in Kan-ni in North Korea. Also, the Air Force initiates a new interdiction blueprint that halts its attacks on the bridges located south of Pyongyang and Wonsan.

October 7   Admiral Doyle, commanding officer of the JTF-7 Attack Force, suggests October 20 as the earliest date on which the Wonsan assault forces could meet for the purpose of invading Wonsan. Admirals Joy and Struble agree with Doyle. The recommendation is then forwarded to General MacArthur, who accepts the tentative date for D-day, but he recommends that everything possible should be done to attempt to jump off earlier. Necessary transport vessels for the invasion have arrived late, and they lack the promised supplies. Also contributing to the delay is the fact that Eighth Army's relief of X Corps has run four days behind schedule.

The carrier USS *Leyte Gulf* (CV 32) arrives on this day from the Atlantic to join TF-77. Also, Marines are being withdrawn from north of Seoul to participate in Wonsan landings. Elements of 1st Marine Division commence embarking in assault shipping at Inchon for Wonsan operations.

In the X Corps area, Corps relinquishes responsibility for the Inchon-Seoul area to Eighth Army at 1200, when elements of Eighth Army relieve the remaining

The USS *Cimarron*, a fuel tanker, refuels the carrier USS *Leyte Gulf* off Korea, while the USS *Henderson* in the background stands watch.

troops of the 7th Marines at Uijongbu. X Corps then reverts to GHQ reserve, as stipulated in prior orders. The 7th Marines move to Inchon to rejoin the division there. In other activity, the 31st and 32nd Regiments begin reaching Pusan.

In the 1st Marine Division sector, the 7th Marines departs Uijongbu to join its division at Inchon. During the early morning hours, the 1st Marine Division command post departs Seoul and moves to an area slightly north of Ascom City. The Marine Corps, having concluded one of the most daring and important amphibious invasions of its history, successfully ends the Seoul–Inchon operation, and without incident. At 0935, General O.P. Smith, acting upon orders (Corps OpnO 5), reports to Admiral Doyle to assume responsibility as landing force commander for the expected invasion of Wonsan.

The 1st Marine Division casualties for the entire Inchon-Seoul operation stands at 366 Marines killed and 49 who die of their wounds. In addition, 2,029 men are wounded and 6 others are listed as missing in action. Marine Corps records indicate that the 1st Marine Division accounts for the destruction of 44 enemy tanks (the figure is later adjusted to 38 due to duplicated claims).

At Kimpo Airfield, squadrons of the 1st Marine Aircraft Wing remain in action for two additional days, despite the relief of the ground Marines. The five Marine squadrons, in action since 7 September, terminate operations on October 7, having flown 2,774 sorties. The bulk of the missions during the thirty-three day span consisted of close support for the ground units. Marine aviation losses are 11 planes shot down at a cost of six pilots killed, 1 crewman killed and two pilots wounded.

Also, the Flying Angels of VMO-6 buzzed in and out of the furious battlefields to rescue downed pilots and evacuate wounded ground troops. These helicopters and observation planes flew 643 flights within a period of 515 hours. The crews extricated 12 downed pilots from behind enemy lines, and in addition, they evacuated 179 seriously wounded troops to receive medical aid at hospitals at sea and on shore.

Subsequent to the seizure of Seoul, General MacArthur, in a report to the United Nations, emphasizes the dedicated effort to prostrate the enemy strength. He states:

Events of the past two weeks have been decisive.... Caught between our northern and southern forces, both of which are completely self sustaining because of our absolute air and naval supremacy, the enemy is thoroughly shattered through disruption of his logistical support and our combined combat activities.... The prompt action of our two forces is dramatically symbolic of this collapse.... A successful frontal attack and envelopment has completely changed the tide of battle in South Korea. The backbone of the North Korean Army has been broken and their scattered forces are being liquidated or driven north with material losses in equipment and men captured.

In the Eighth Army area, Army prepares to move its headquarters from Taegu to Seoul. The new headquarters opens on October 12. In other activity, Army informs General Milburn of I Corps and the ROK Army chief of staff that the attack to seize Pyongyang is imminent.

The 3rd Logistical Command based at Inchon is assigned to Army and its key mission is to maintain the logistical support to sustain the drive into North Korea. However, Eighth Army attaches the 3rd Logistical Command to the 2nd Logistical Command, which is at Pusan. From Pusan, the 2nd Logistical Command maintains its operation to shuttle supplies forward by use of trucks and trains. It is the rails that play the dominant role in moving Army supplies, relegating the trucks and air deliveries to emergency shipments out of Pusan. Also, engineers complete laying a second pontoon bridge across the Han. On the following day, two-way traffic resumes in Seoul.

In the I Corps sector, 1st Cavalry Division zone, the ongoing operation to secure an assembly area continues. The 16th Reconnaissance Company advances into Kaesong. Later, during the night, contingents of the 1st Battalion, 8th Cavalry, enter Kaesong. In conjunction, probing patrols cross the 38th Parallel during the latter part of the afternoon.

In the IX Corps area, 25th Division sector, a large enemy force composed of about 400 soldiers is detected. The 1st Battalion, 35th Regiment, plasters the column with devastating artillery fire. Nearly eighty percent of the North Koreans are killed. Also, during the anti-guerrilla activity of the 25th Division, the 3rd Battalion, 35th Regiment, captures 549 prisoners (October 7–8). The 25th Division, during October, is heavily involved with anti-guerrilla operations within its vast perimeter, which extends for about 6,500 square-miles of mountainous terrain.

In the ROK Army Headquarters area, I Corps sector, the S.K. 8th Division crosses the 38th Parallel and begins its northward attack toward the "Iron Triangle."

In the ROK II Corps sector, vicious combat continues near Hwach'on, between two defending regiments of the N.K. 5th Division and the advancing S.K. 6th Division.

In Air Force activity, planes drop food rations to a large group of about 150 POWs who escaped from the Communists as they headed north.

— *In Japan:* General Hickey receives a call from General Frank Allen (asst. commander, 1st Cavalry Div.); Allen, inquiring for General Walker, requests a date for A-day (crossing the 38th Parallel) and he receives the response: "You're a-Day will be at such time as you see it ready." General Allen then informs General Hickey that Eighth Army is nearly ready to attack. In conjunction, Eighth Army, subsequent to relieving X Corps, deploys along the 38th Parallel. Elements of the 1st Cavalry will cross on the 9th.

October 8

In anticipation of a premature seizure of Wonsan, General MacArthur has devised a supplementary plan to incorporate a landing at Hungnam, about 50 miles north of Wonsan. But, the modified plan of CinCFE Plan 9–50, issued this day, is not flawless. If implemented, Eighth Army's mission remains identical, but X Corps would be required to sever the enemy communications north of Wonsan and eliminate the resistance there. In conjunction, the landing at Hungnam by the 7th Infantry Division would greatly hinder its ability to quickly seize Pyongyang by overland march, due to the distance involved. In addition, the usual shortages of landing craft make it implausible for the 7th Division to debark at Wonsan while the Marines are striking Hungnam.

If two separate landings occur, the U.S. Navy's overburdened minesweepers will be overwhelmed by the task of clearing mines from both sites, but the option planners are not yet fully aware of the impending complications. Admirals Joy and Doyle, at their positions in Japan and Korea, respectively, concur that there is not enough time to change the mission of X Corps, but Admiral Joy's attempts to change MacArthur's mind are unsuccessful.

In related activity, Admiral Turner Joy directs Admiral Doyle and General O.P. Smith to implement his OpnPlan 113–50.

In Naval activity, Task Group 95.6, commanded by Captain Richard Spofford, converges off Sasebo. It will initiate action to clear the mines from the waters off Wonsan prior to the appearance of the giant 250-ship flotilla that will transport the 1st Marine Division and other elements of X Corps to the objective. Captain Spofford's task group departs Japan on the 10th.

In the X Corps area, the 2nd Logistical Command is ordered to provide enough supplies of all classes for fifteen days for each of the 25,000 troops boarding ships at Pusan. All troops boarding at Inchon are to be provided ten days of Class II and IV supplies. Fifteen days of re-supplies are to be delivered to Wonsan on October 28, to ensure the operation continues unhindered. To meet the stiff requirements, the logistics personnel are compelled to draw much of the supplies from

Eighth Army's source, Japan Logistical Command. The logistics personnel are unfamiliar with the requirements of the individual units with regard to Class II items, including winter clothing and post exchange comfort items. At Inchon, the loading of bulk cargo for the Wonsan mission begins. The operation, completed by October 16, is overseen by George C. Stewart, commanding officer of 3rd Logistical Command.

The 5th Marines, commanded by Colonel Murray, begins boarding ships. The 1st Battalion boards the USS *Bayfield*, while the 2nd and 3rd Battalions board the vessels *George Clymer* and *Bexar*, respectively. By this time, Eighth Army is beyond the 38th Parallel and maintaining its northern drive.

In other activity, the 7th Division command post at Anyang-ni is closed. A new CP is established at Pusan.

A view of the terrain at Kaesong. A U.S. soldier in the foreground leans over at communications equipment.

Also, X Corps orders the 7th Division to complete its loading operation at Pusan by October 17.

In the Eighth Army area, additional United Nations troops are now arriving in Korea. Although it is beginning to seem as if their presence might not be necessary, in light of the ongoing destruction of the North Korean Armed Forces, these troops still must become familiar with U.S. equipment and weaponry. General Walker orders the 2nd Logistical Command to establish a U.N. Reception Center at Taegu University, once the EUSAK departs from it. The center is also to provide clothing and equipment to the new arrivals. The maximum number of troops expected to be receiving training at any one time is 6,200 men.

In the I Corps area, 1st Cavalry Division sector, the advance to secure the assembly area from which to launch the northward attack continues. By the end of the day, contingents of the 7th and 8th Cavalries complete the mission. Ground is secured near Kaesong, in close proximity to the 38th Parallel. Some contingents are within range of enemy small arms fire. During the evening, more probing patrols venture across the 38th Parallel.

General Gay issues the order to attack on the following morning. Eighth Army anticipates heavy resistance, once it crashes across the 38th Parallel. Intelligence estimates have concluded that as many as six newly trained divisions are ready to join the North Korean forces that had raised opposition at Seoul.

In other activity, the 7th Cavalry receives orders to advance to the Yesong River to locate crossing sites and to eliminate any remaining North Korean troops discovered southwest of Kaesong. The 7th Cavalry lacks bridging equipment, making the crossing especially difficult. All available bridging is being used at Munsan-ni to carry the primary attack force across the Imjin River there. In conjunction, the I&R Platoon locates the bridge. The span is damaged, but still capable of carrying ground troops. The platoon also discovers enemy presence. The North Koreans hold positions extending from the southern end of the peninsula on the opposite bank (west) to a point about one-half mile northeast of the bridge.

Colonel Clainos, commander 1st Battalion, accompanies one Company A platoon to the river and makes contact with the I&R Platoon. Clainos' contingent, similarly to the I&R Platoon, comes under enemy fire. The unexpected news concerning the bridge ignites quick reaction. Colonel William Harris, commander 7th Cavalry, orders the bridge seized, but General Gay is skeptical and fears the enemy has set a trap on the crossing site. Colonel Harris and his S-3, Captain Webel, eventually convince Gay to permit an attack on the following day.

The regiment had been informed by the divisional G-4 that gasoline and some ammunition could not be provided to sustain the drive. Colonel Harris and Captain Webel had improvised and sent an officer, Captain Arthur Westburg, to Inchon to seek help. The port commander, Brigadier General George Stewart, and

the 3rd Logistical Command take the challenge and provide thirteen LCVs, which arrive at the 7th Cavalry crossing site at the Yesong River the afternoon of the 10th.

In the IX Corps sector, the 25th Division continues searching for guerrillas, but these contingents continue to wreak havoc on unprotected South Korean villages and some S.K. police stations. The guerrillas, allegedly instructed by Kim Chaek, commander, North Korean Front Headquarters, have stretched their hit-and-run tactics way down the peninsula. In particular, they seek out U.N. trains and communication wires for destruction.

In the ROK Army Headquarters area, Army reorganizes and expands. It activates the 1st Guerrilla Group, which is composed of the 1st, 2nd, 3rd, 4th and 5th Battalions, and it reactivates the S.K. 5th Division at Taegu.

In the ROK I Corps sector, the S.K. 7th Division begins to cross the 38th Parallel to the right of the S.K. 8th Division on or about this day. It, too, drives toward the "Iron Triangle."

In the ROK II Corps sector, the S.K. 6th Division overcomes three days of stiff resistance and drives into Hwach'on during the latter part of the afternoon. Two enemy battalions retreat northwest after being driven from the town. Following the seizure, the 6th S.K. Division lunges toward Ch'orwon and Kumwha.

In Air Force activity, two pilots in F-80s on a mission near the Yalu River stray northeast across the border into Russia and inadvertently strafe a Soviet airfield in the vicinity of Vladivostok. In reaction, the group commander is reassigned to FEAF headquarters and the pilots receive a court martial. Also, the Air Force reinitiates Razon bomb missions in conjunction with the arrival of better radio-guided bombs from the States.

In other activity, the 162d TRS arrives at Taegu from Itazuke, Japan. It is the first night reconnaissance squadron to be based in Korea.

October 9 Admiral Struble issues his operation plan, which blueprints the JTF-7 organization. It is listed as follows: (1) 90—Attack Force, Rear Admiral James Doyle; (2) 95—Advance Force, Rear Admiral Allan E. Smith; (3) 95.2—Covering and Support Group, Rear Admiral Charles Hartman; (4) 95.6—Minesweeping Group, Captain Richard Spofford; (5) 92—X Corps, Major General Edward Almond; (6) 96.2—Patrol and Reconnaissance Group, Rear Admiral George Henderson; (7) 96.8—Escort Carrier Group, Rear Admiral Richard Ruble; (8) 77—Fast Carrier Force, Rear Admiral Edward Ewen; (9) 70.1—Flagship Group (USS *Missouri*), Captain Irving T. Duke; (10) 79—Logistics Support, Captain Bernard L. Austin.

In the X Corps area, the loading activity at Inchon is not a longshoreman's delight and there are many reasons, including a tremendous shortage of loading berths. The port contains only seven berths capable of loading beached LSTs or landing craft, and these can be used only during high tide. Furthermore, the staging area is scant and Inchon has only one pier from where vehicles can be loaded into LCMs. The process becomes one of great improvisation. The Logistical Cargo Command personnel load many of the vehicles onto the top decks of LSTs, which then transport the equipment out to the ships in the harbor. At that point, cranes transfer the cargo to the APAs and AKAs. Other equipment is similarly loaded, unloaded and reloaded again, as the dilemma seems never-ending. In related activity, some X Corps troops begin boarding ship this day.

In the X Corps area, 1st Marine Division sector, General O.P. Smith is informed that the landing site for the Marines is about to be changed. Meanwhile, Admiral Joy maintains his argument (with MacArthur) that the proposed modified plans are not feasible. On the 10th, MacArthur relents and the original plan to land the entire X Corps at Wonsan is agreed upon.

In the 7th Division sector, the enemy springs another deadly ambush on the Division in the same general area (in the mountains outside Mun'gyong) as the ambush of the previous day. At 0230, the divisional headquarters column is attacked as it advances through a pass several miles northwest of the town. Six troops are killed by machine gun fire and several vehicles are destroyed.

During the afternoon, contingents of the 1st Battalion, 17th Regiment, secure the pass above Mun'gyong and it remains in the high ground for several days to assure that no further incidents occur.

In the Eighth Army area, I Corps sector, armored contingents of the 1st Cavalry Division spearhead the I Corps attack across the 38th Parallel to capture Sariwon and Pyongyang. At 0900, General Gay gives the word to launch the attack. The strategy calls for the 8th Cavalry to act as vanguard and drive straight along the primary highway toward Kumch'on. Meanwhile the 5th Cavalry attempts a rope trick, swinging east and then swinging west in a looping motion designed to lasso the enemy troops south of Kumch'on.

In the meantime, the 7th Cavalry is to ford the Yesong River and drive north along the road toward Hanp'o-ri, situated about 6 miles north of Kumch'on, beside the Yesong River at a point where the primary Pyongyang Highway crosses over it. General Gay has calculated that the sweeps of the 5th and 8th Cavalries will stampede many enemy troops into the clutches of the 7th Cavalry. Nonetheless, General Gay is aware that the mission to cross the Yesong River will be extremely difficult, due to the lack of sufficient support. He is depending on the 5th and 8th Cavalries' attacks to ensure success of the drive.

The attack is launched and the 8th Cavalry soon encounters opposition. Enemy mines block the road in frequent intervals, causing the advance to continually stall waiting for engineers to clear the road.

Company E is struck by heavy mortar and automatic weapons fire, which pins it in a deadly crossfire and inflicts many casualties. One trooper, PFC Robert H. Young, is repeatedly wounded while he holds his ground and returns fire. He kills five enemy troops before sustaining yet another wound. Tanks rush forward to assist the beleaguered platoon, and Young, still refusing medical treatment, directs the

A pause in the action. U.S. troops take a break to consume C-rations.

tanks' fire. The tanks knock out three enemy guns. Young then begins to aid several other wounded men, but a mortar shell bursts and he is again struck. The fatally wounded Young insists that the other wounded soldiers be evacuated before himself. PFC Young receives the Medal of Honor posthumously for his extraordinary actions. The 8th Cavalry overcomes the obstacles and maintains its drive toward Kumch'on.

Meanwhile, the 5th Cavalry becomes slowed but reaches the 38th Parallel at 1930. The regiment commences its attack on the following morning. At 1500, in the midst of a three-hour artillery and mortar bombardment against the enemy-held west bank, one platoon of Company C moves across the bridge and encounters small arms fire. The unit sustains several casualties, but seizes a hold on the west bank. Shortly thereafter, engineers attached to Company B initiate repairs on the bridge while the remainder of Company C, charges across the span and secures a hill to the right.

All the while, enemy guns remain active and pound the troops as they cross. Once the entire battalion completes the crossing, the U.S. barrage is adjusted whereby the fire in the vicinity of the bridge is terminated. The 1st Battalion sustains 78 casualties during the crossing. The heaviest toll is suffered by Company C, which sustains six men killed and thirty-six wounded.

By dark, the enemy is thinking counterattack. The North Koreans commence their assault to dislodge the 1st Battalion. In turn, Colonel Harris orders the 2nd Battalion to speed up its crossing to bolster the 1st Battalion. However, the enemy guns are still ringing the bridge. Slightly before midnight, Lt. Colonel Gilmon Huff leads his 2nd Battalion to the west bank and reaches a point about 100 yards west of the bridge and on the south flank of Clainos' 1st Battalion. Company G, 2nd Battalion, spearheads the attack. It drives west along the Paekch'on Road and is soon struck by a devastating enemy counterattack.

The 2nd Battalion becomes temporarily stunned, but Colonel Huff maintains his composure and the battalion rebounds splendidly despite the lack of heavy weapons. The night-long fight continues into the following morning. Although Huff is wounded early in the battle, he continues to command until he relinquishes it to his executive officer. The fierce contest remains relentless, but when dawn (10th) rises over the horizon there is no doubt as to the victor. The enemy is vanquished and the 2nd Battalion holds the high ground southeast of the bridge, which assures that the regiment will make further progress.

In the ROK Army area, the S.K. 3rd Division and the Capital Division converge on the southern fringes of Wonsan after having advanced about 110 air-miles north of the 38th Parallel. The S.K. 3rd Division has driven up the coastal road, and the Capital Division has advanced along the Wonsan–Iron Triangle Road. The latter captures six enemy tanks and 5,000 Russian rifles as it gains the ground. In addition, about 500 submachine guns, 4 artillery pieces, 11 mortars and 1 boxcar full of medical supplies are among the seized enemy equipment during the day's march.

However, the enemy still has some awesome firepower in its arsenal. Contingents of the N.K. 24th Mechanized Artillery Brigade, naval amphibious troops of the N.K. 945th Regiment and some other miscellaneous naval units engage the advancing South Koreans at Wonsan. By the following day, troops of the Capital Division and the S.K. 3rd Division penetrate the enemy lines and enter the city.

— In Japan: General MacArthur again urges the North Koreans to surrender. He addresses a message to the "The Premier, Government of North Korea." As with his announcement on the 1st, the North Koreans ignore the suggestion. Ambassador Sebald, speaking with Colonel Laurence Bunker, an aide to MacArthur, expresses his concerns about the unorthodox method of the general, addressing the surrender directly to the political leaders of an unrecognized government. Bunker worries that it could cause ramifications in Washington. Nonetheless, the Communists show no interest and no official response is forthcoming.

October 10   *In the X Corps area,* at Inchon, General O.P. Smith establishes his command post on the USS *Mount McKinley.* He issues OpnO 16–50, which culminates the planning at Inchon regarding the 1st Marine Division's participation at Wonsan. The chosen points of attack are beaches Blue and Yellow on the eastern shore of Kalma peninsula. The order specifies the particulars of the Wonsan assault, and it includes the blueprint of the duties expected of the subordinate units. Later in the day, an alternate plan is issued that directs (upon orders) the Marines to initiate an administrative landing on Red Beach, situated north of Wonsan, rather than the initial landing sites on Kalma peninsula.

The 1st and 3rd Battalions, 1st Marines, board LSTs and await orders to land. It will be sixteen days aboard the overcrowded ships before these Marines get to refamiliarize themselves with the ground. Once ashore, they are to secure ten objectives within the projected sweeping arc of the beachhead, and each is located in the high ground. The 5th Marines is to land and form west of the town to await instructions. The Korean 3rd and 5th Marine Battalions, attached to the 7th and 1st Marines respectively, are to land behind the U.S. Marines.

In the meantime, the S.K. 3rd and Capital Divisions advance rapidly. Just after 0800, the South Koreans, who have punched their way overland, drive into Wonsan. By the latter part of the following day, the port city is secure, and its nearby airfield is fully controlled. These seizures render the invasion of Wonsan unnecessary.

In other activity, the 7th Division artillery units depart Inchon and complete the operation by 1700. It is the final major component to leave the town. Off Wonsan, a helicopter swoops over the channel and discovers that the thirty-fathom channel is saturated with mines. The plan to sweep the channel here is aborted. The new designated target area is the 100-fathom curve in the Russian Hydropac Channel that passes between Yo-do and the Hwangto-do Islands. Without delay, the minesweepers begin to vacuum the harbor. By the 12th, the ships clear twenty-four miles to secure the channel to within 10 miles of the inner harbor.

In the Eighth Army area, following seventeen tedious days of work by the engineers, Army reopens the 200-mile stretch of rails that runs between the Naktong and Han Rivers. Rail traffic begins to cross the Han and roll into Seoul during the latter part of October.

In the I Corps area, 1st Cavalry Division sector, the 5th Cavalry commences its attack. The regiment crosses the 38th Parallel and seizes the nearby heights to permit progress along the highway. The 1st Battalion drives forward, but about fifteen miles northeast of Kaesong, the enemy controls a large ridge line with three fortified knobs (Hills 174, 175 and 179). The stiff resistance raised there causes the 1st Battalion to halt its advance for the night.

In the 7th Cavalry zone, the 3rd Battalion prepares to cross the Yesong River to join the other two battalions. The required supplies (500 tons) needed to sustain the attack arrive by LCVs from Inchon. Meanwhile, by noon, the 2nd Battalion completes the defeat of the enemy counterattack that had begun on the previous night. During the afternoon the 2nd Battalion secures Paekch'on and the heights north of it.

In the IX Corps area, Eighth Army Ranger Company is attached to IX Corps; it hooks up with the 25th Division Reconnaissance Company to add punch to the anti-guerrilla missions that are operating northeast of Taejon in the vicinity of Poun.

In the ROK Army Headquarters area, I Corps sector, fighting erupts in enemy-held Wonsan when elements of the Capital Division and the S.K. 3rd Division each push troops into the city. The corps commander, Brigadier General Kim Baik Yil, determines that both divisions had simultaneously entered Wonsan at 0600 and that the city was secured by both units at 1000. However, the enemy has yet to be vanquished and heavy fighting continues throughout the day. Colonel Emmerich is with the 23rd Regiment when it enters the city just before noon.

By about this time, the enemy has ceased its morning-long artillery bombardment and has pulled most of its guns from the city to relocate them in the heights northwest of Wonsan. Despite the continuing shelling by the Communists, the South Koreans seize the airfield on the peninsula east of the city. In the meantime, the battle for control of Wonsan continues without pause. Blazing firefights permeate the city's streets until dusk. The contest then moves to another phase. The heavy street fighting subsides until the following day, but a feverish skirmish erupts for control of the airfield. An enemy armored force closes against it and blasts everything in sight. Nearly all buildings and hangars are destroyed.

In the ROK II Corps area, elements of the S.K. 6th Division reach the "Iron Triangle," the defensive triangular-shaped enemy line located between twenty to thirty miles north of the 38th Parallel in the mountainous east central portion of Korea. It contains a key rail and road communications center that links the east and west coasts of Korea. The Triangle area, with Pyongyang at its northernmost point and supported at the eastern base by Kumhwa and Ch'orwon at the western base, is also the junction that maintains the communication network that runs south through Central South Korea. The ROKs intend to compress the enemy within it and force its collapse. Contingents of the 16th Regiment encounter and defeat an enemy force near Ch'orwon. The 16th Regiment convincingly turns back successive heavy attacks, which forces the enemy to retreat. Later, contingents of the S.K. 16th Regiment penetrate Ch'orwon.

In Air Force activity, a crew aboard a 3d ARS H-5 craft while in flight successfully administers blood plasma to a wounded pilot that they had rescued.

In Naval activity, TG-95.6 arrives off Wonsan to initiate mine-clearing operations. The big guns of the cruiser *Rochester* and the destroyers *Collett, Maddox, Swenson* and *Thomas* are operating in the vicinity of the minesweepers. A helicopter from the USS *Rochester* again spots enormous amounts of enemy mines. By the latter part of the afternoon, the minesweepers clear a 3,000-yard channel that extends from the 100-fathom curve to the thirty-fathom line, giving the Navy high expectations that the job might be concluded sooner than expected. However, five more strings of mines are detected, dousing the enthusiasm. The discoveries seem to verify the intelligence reports that stated Russian assistance had been given to the North Korean Communists.

Apparently, the Russians began helping the Reds at Wonsan, either during the latter part of July or the first days of August. The North Koreans, utilizing sampans, junks and barges, combined with Russian know-how, spread about 2,000 mines in the sea approaches to Wonsan.

— In Japan: General MacArthur orders that UN Operations Plan 2 be placed into effect, superseding all other tentative plans. In other activity, personnel monitoring the various radio broadcasts pick up a broadcast originating in Pyongyang. The speaker is Kim Il Sung, and he is rejecting MacArthur's call to surrender.

October 11 X Corps closes its on-shore command post and transfers it to the USS *Mount McKinley*. In other activity, other X Corps troops begin to move by land to Pusan. Engineers, medical personnel, ordnance troops, and quartermaster, chemical and signal units are included. In conjunction, during the seven days of moving X Corps to Pusan, the vehicles transport 13,422 troops and 1,460 tons of supplies and equipment. The 52nd Truck Battalion and 7th Division vehicles handle the task.

Inchon vicinity: In the 1st Marine Division sector, Colonel Murray, CO, 5th Marines (reserve regiment for Wonsan), establishes his command post aboard the USS *Bayfield.* Embarkation of 5th Marines is concluded. In conjunction, elements of the 1st and 7th Marines (reserve and administrative components) board their vessels early; however, the four assault battalions remain onshore until the 13th, awaiting available LSTs. In the meantime, South Korean forces take Wonsan. This prompts the scheduled air support for the invasion to be canceled. Elements of the 1st Marine Air Wing arrive at the Wonsan airfield on the 13th.

In the 7th Division sector, the 27th Regiment, 25th Division (Eighth Army IX Corps) relieves the 1st Battalion, 17th Regiment, 7th Division in the mountains near Mun'gyong. Also, about 450 soldiers (7th Division) are airlifted from Kimpo Airfield to Pusan.

In the Eighth Army area, 1st Cavalry Division sector, the 5th Cavalry reinitiates its attack to clear the hills northeast of Kaesong. The 1st Battalion, stopped on the previous day, is bolstered by the 2nd Battalion to expedite the elimination of the obstacles. At Hill 174, Company C advances against a strong barrage of small arms fire. One soldier jumps into an enemy position, thinking it to be unoccupied, but concealed enemy troops are there to greet him. Lieutenant Samuel S. Coursen jumps to aid the beleaguered soldier who becomes wounded but escapes. Coursen engages the enemy in vicious and bloody hand-to-hand combat. He saves the wounded soldier but loses his life.

Later, when the company recovers Coursen's body, seven deceased North Koreans lie beside him and a few of them had obviously succumbed to Coursen's rifle butt; their skulls had been smashed. Lieutenant Coursen, for his heroism in the face of the enemy, receives the Medal of Honor posthumously. The three knobs and the ridge fall to the 5th Cavalry during the afternoon.

In the 7th Cavalry sector, the 3rd Battalion crosses the Yesong River and joins the other two battalions there, which now places all three regiments on the west bank of the river and above the 38th Parallel. The 8th Cavalry maintains its slow-paced advance toward Kumch'on and dislodges enemy mines along the road as it moves.

In other activity, the 27th British Commonwealth Brigade, accompanied by a contingent of tanks (Company B, 6th Med. Tank Bn.), crosses the Imjin River and traces the steps of the 5th Cavalry. The British move through the mountains and head northwest to execute an envelopment operation at Kumch'on, but the roads on the maps are inaccurate. An aerial observer had provided Gay with the inaccurate information concerning the roads. The road used by the British deadends in the mountains.

The British, with their usual stiff upper lip, backtrack and wind down the road, which is ill-suited for anything larger than a cart. They select another route and reinitiate the drive to Kumch'on, but it, too, leads nowhere, and the British get lost. Undaunted, they dis-

cover yet another road and take it, hoping to arrive at Kumch'on, but the effort is futile. The contingent remains lost in the mountainous forest and misses the entire operation at Kumch'on.

In the S.K. 1st Division sector, at dawn, the Division departs Korangp'o and crosses the Imjin River. The South Koreans, operating east of the 1st Cavalry Division, drive northwest along a highway that funnels into the road used by the 5th Cavalry.

In the ROK Army Headquarters area, I Corps sector, at Wonsan, vicious combat is reinitiated on the streets of the city as the South Koreans continue to purge the enemy. Once the city is secured, the attack moves beyond. By dusk the 3rd S.K. Division, which had carried the bulk of the attack, advances north about one mile. The Capital Division has supported the mission to seize the city. Generals Walker and Partridge arrive at the airfield to inspect it. Later, General Partridge directs the Combat Cargo Command to bring in the supplies on the following day.

In the ROK II Corps sector, the S.K. 8th Division and the 7th Regiment, S.K. 6th Division, close on Pyongyang.

In Naval activity, planes attached to TF 77 attack North Korean vessels in the waters off Songjin, Wonsan and north of Hungham. Other targets of the carrier planes include railroads, vehicles, and supply depots in the vicinity of Songjin.

— *In Japan:* General MacArthur sends a radio message to General Walker informing him that Wonsan Airfield is to be utilized for land-based planes, which will be under the command of X Corps. It adds that the S.K. I Corps will be detached from Eighth Army and attached to X Corps upon the latter's landing at Wonsan.

October 12
In Naval activity, minesweeping operations continue off Wonsan, while other elements of JTF 7 bombard enemy positions along the east coast. The warships of TG 95.2 concentrate their fire on Songjin and Tanchon. The USS *Missouri* pounds the marshaling yards of Tanchon. The cruisers *Ceylon, Helena* and *Worcester* focus their fire on Chongjin. Captain Spofford attempts to streamline the minesweeping operation. He requests assistance from the carriers. Thirty-nine aircraft attached to the carriers *Leyte Gulf* and *Philippine Sea* arrive and drop about fifty tons of 1,000-pound bombs in the Russian Channel, but to no avail. The high-percussion explosions fail to detonate the mines. Similar efforts had been undertaken during World War II, and those experiments concluded with identical results.

Later, three minesweepers proceed through the targeted area, which had just been bombed. At 1209, the USS *Pirate* (AM 275), while sweeping approaches to Wonsan, strikes an unexploded mine off Yo-do Island and sinks. Within a short while, at 1215, the USS *Pledge* (AM–277) hits a mine and it, too, sinks. Rescue operations get underway immediately, but enemy shore batteries remain cogent and hinder the missions. Both minesweepers sustain heavy casualties; 12 men are killed and one wounded man succumbs to his wounds. Exact numbers of wounded are not known, but the figure is estimated to be about 87. During the rescue operation, a third minesweeper, the USS *Incredible,* comes under severe fire. Still, it rescues 27 sailors before it bolts toward safer waters.

In the meantime, the mines remain a serious problem. Captain Spofford deduces that depth charges might be the solution, prompting him to call for more naval craft. This improvised method also fails and proves only that the mines must be destroyed the old fashioned way, one at a time. The flying boats (*Mariners* and *Sunderlands*) resume the task of detecting and demolishing the mines with .50-caliber machine gun fire. Navy innovation soon eases the burdensome task. It implements the use of hydrographic office charts. The planes spot the targets on charts and drop them onto the minesweepers to give the crews the exact locations of hundreds of floating death traps.

In the Eighth Army area, advance elements of the 1st Turkish Armed Forces Command arrive at Pusan. The remainder of the brigade arrives on the 17th.

In the 1st Cavalry Division sector, the 5th Cavalry continues its advance. During the afternoon, the enemy raises fierce resistance at an intersection along the highway. In the meantime, the S.K. 1st Division, driving from the southeast, arrives at the crossroads and bolsters the cavalry. The U.S. commander, Colonel Crombez, and the S.K. 1st Division commander confer. It is decided that the U.S. troops will control the road until the 5th Cavalry pivots at a point about five miles farther north to drive down a lateral path toward Kumch'on. The S.K. 1st Division, supported by tanks of Company C, 6th Medium Tank Battalion, is scheduled to trail the cavalry until it swings off the road. At that point, the tanks are to continue their advance using the main road to Sibyon-ni. From Sibyon-ni, the S.K. 1st Division is to turn northwest and drive toward Pyongyang.

In the 7th Cavalry sector, the 3rd Battalion secures the railroad and road bridges at Hanp'o-ri, and it seizes control of the road junction there. Friendly aircraft erroneously strafe the town and inflict several casualties. The captured objectives prove to be strategic positions that enable the 3rd Battalion to tightly close the northern escape routes from Kumch'on. About 1,000 North Koreans remain isolated in the town.

After darkness falls, the 2nd Battalion arrives at Hanp'o-ri to join the 3rd Battalion. During the night, 11 enemy vehicles, with their lights on, approach the 7th Cavalry blockade, manned by one platoon of Company L. Four of the vehicles are transporting ammunition and it becomes evident as each explodes. The excursion costs the Communists about 50 men killed, and another 50 are captured, including a mortally wounded regimental commander.

A captured document reveals that the N.K. 19th and 27th Divisions plan to break out of the cordon around Kumch'on during the night of the 14th. A captured officer, prior to his demise, informs the Americans that some of the enemy force has been instructed to depart Kumch'on, and head to Namch'onjom, about fifteen miles farther north.

The battleship USS *Missouri,* operating on the east coast of Korea, bombards Ch'ongjin on 12 October.

At the 7th Cavalry crossing site along the Yesong River, a contingent of I Corps' engineers constructs a pontoon ferry capable of handling tanks. Company C, 70th Tank Battalion, moves across the river and supports the assault.

In the 8th Cavalry sector, the regiment continues to attack north, but upon reaching the halfway point from the objective, it is intercepted by a strong enemy force. The Communists commit antiaircraft guns, self-propelled guns and tanks to jackhammer the 8th Cavalry, but the cavalry calls for air strikes. Sixteen planes arrive and lambaste the enemy positions. Artillery fire is also committed, but the enemy holds steadfastly. Again, the regiment halts its advance for the day. During the heavy exchange, Lt. Colonel Robert W. Kane, the 1st Battalion commander, receives a serious wound and is evacuated.

In the 24th Division sector, several groups of the N.K. 43rd Division are trapped below P'aekch'on. The groups bypass the town and attempt to flee north to evade elements of the 21st Regiment. One of these enemy contingents ambushes a 7th Cavalry unit on the following day.

Pusan: The 7th Divisional artillery and the 1st Battalion, 17th Regiment, arrive in Pusan to terminate the divisional transfer from the Ich'on area to Pusan. The units prepare for the Wonsan operation.

In the ROK Army Headquarters area, I Corps sector, Wonsan is controlled by the S.K. 3rd Division, which remains in the area for the next week to maintain security until X Corps troops arrive. Twenty-two aircraft, attached to the Transport Cargo Command, arrive at Wonsan Airfield and deliver about 131 tons of supplies required to sustain the South Korean offensive. In other activity, the Capital Division drives farther north as it heads toward Hamhung and the port at Hungnam.

In the ROK II Corps, elements of the S.K. 6th Division advance about twenty miles and establish contact with the S.K. Capital Division, which is advancing from Wonsan.

In Air Force activity, in conjunction with the recent capture of Wonsan by ROK forces, planes from Far East Air Force Combat Cargo Command arrive there to deliver military equipment and supplies. Planes laden with supplies also land at Kimpo Airfield.

October 13   *In Inchon:* LSTs, having completed ferrying operations off Inchon, arrive to receive the assault battalions of the 1st and 7th Marines. The boarding operation is completed during the early hours of the 15th. Major General Field Harris, CG 1st Marine Aircraft Wing and Tactical Air Command X Corps, arrives on the east coast at the Wonsan Airfield to inspect the facility. He concludes that conditions are acceptable and that operations should be initiated immediately. By the following day Marine aviation units begin to arrive.

In the Eighth Army area, 1st Cavalry Division sector, the 7th Cavalry maintains its roadblock north of Kumch'on, in conjunction with the 5th and 8th Cavalries,

which are pressing against the enemy from the south and east respectively to squeeze the Communists at Kumch'on.

In the 5th Cavalry sector, the regiment grinds forward, hindered throughout the day by minefields. Nevertheless, the 5th Cavalry overcomes the mines and continues the march. Less than ten miles from Kumch'on, it engages and scatters several hundred enemy troops. By dusk, the 5th Cavalry encroaches the objective and at midnight, it reinitiates the attackand drives from the east to strangle Kumch'on. The forward thrust of the 2nd Battalion overwhelms an enemy force in front of the town. The Americans are to drive into Kumch'on and secure its northern sector. In the meantime, the trailing 3rd Battalion plows into the southern sector of town and secures it.

In the 8th Cavalry sector, the regiment encounters fierce resistance as it grinds along the main road. A huge artillery barrage strikes the enemy to loosen resistance and B-17s are scheduled to also pulverize the area, but the air strikes are aborted due to the close proximity of the U.S. troops to the target area. The Communists then launch several counterattacks to hold the 8th Cavalry at bay and buy time to evacuate Kumch'on. During one blistering attack, armor moves under the cover of morning mist and drives into the positions of Company B's tanks, and within the direct sights of the tank commanded by Sergeant Drewery.

From a distance of fifty yards, Drewery's gunner commences firing, but the T-34 maintains its speed. A second shot strikes the T-34 when it reaches a point twenty yards away, but still it rambles forward. Drewery's tank is then rammed by the enemy tank and they become entangled, but the U.S. tank reverses gears and pulls free. Immediately thereafter, from a distance of a mere two or three yards, the T-34 receives another punishing blow that shatters its turret and sets it afire. Still, the T-34 refuses to halt. Rather, like a bloodied bull, it again plows into Drewery's tank. Finally a fourth round strikes the killing blow.

In related activity, Company B, 70th Tank Battalion, has a good day of hunting. It kills another six T-34s and loses none. Ground troops account for the destruction of one additional enemy tank. Despite the successes, the Americans are unable to break through the enemy resistance. While the 8th Cavalry is forestalled, the Reds attempt to evacuate Kumch'on, but they run directly into the 7th Cavalry.

In the 7th Cavalry sector, a large enemy convoy of trucks and carts accompanied by about 1,000 troops moves north from Kumch'on. All goes well until the column reaches the bridge at Hanp'o-ri, where it is intercepted by the 7th Cavalry and U.S. aircraft. The enemy is relentlessly pounded and the convoy is shredded. About 500 Communists are killed and 201 additional enemy troops are captured, but several hundred more troops evade death or capture and flee northeast into the hills.

In other activity, the 1st Battalion, 7th Cavalry, advances north from P'aekch'on. The trailing part of the

Major General Field Harris (Commander, 1st Marine Aircraft Wing) stands with a captured Russian-made burp gun.

column is snarled by an enemy ambush. The North Koreans slam the contingent, which includes some of Battery A, 77th FABn, and Company B, 8th Engineer Combat Battalion. One trooper sprints back to P'aekch'on to inform the 3rd Battalion, 21st Regiment, of the disaster. Colonel Stephens (21st Regimental Commander) is at the command post of the 1st Battalion. He reacts immediately. Reinforcements speed to extricate the beleaguered cavalrymen. But time is of the essence, and apparently the trapped Americans offer little resistance, causing devastating results.

The reinforcements arrive at the site, thrash the enemy and capture thirty-six troops. The ambush costs the lives of twenty-nine Americans and eight South Koreans. Also, 30 Americans and 8 South Koreans are wounded. The Communists destroy four trucks and damage 14 others.

During the evening, a supply convoy of the 2nd Battalion, 7th Cavalry, advances down the highway, and it, too, is caught by an enemy ambush. The officer and 11 troops are captured. Five of the enlisted men and the officer manage to escape.

In the ROK Army area, the S.K. 1st Division secures Sibyon-ni, a strategic crossroads sector northeast of Kaesong. Meanwhile, the S.K. 7th Division arrives at Pyongyang from Kumhwa.

October 14 Two enemy planes manage to penetrate and strike the harbor at Inchon and the airfield at Kimpo. The planes remain unidentified, but it is thought they had arrived from a North Korean town, Sinuiju, on the border with China.

In the X Corps sector, at Pusan, work crews begin to load the supplies aboard ships for the 7th Division's Wonsan operation. The troops begin to board on the 16th, and the entire operation is completed on the 17th.

In other activity, General Almond flies to Wonsan to confer with the S.K. I Corps commander and inform him of the unfolding developments regarding his corps, which will come under Almond's jurisdiction, and it will be affected by the newest directive, which stipulates that X Corps makes an administrative landing. Once ashore, X Corps is to initiate a speedy westward advance to hook up with Eighth Army. The drive is scheduled to move along the Wonsan–Pyongyang axis.

In the 1st Marine Division area, General O.P. Smith, in accordance with X Corps orders, activates his alternate plan and orders an administrative landing on Red Beach. The Marines are ordered to seize an objective northeast of Pyongyang.

Meanwhile, Marine aviators take advantage of the South Korean seizure of Wonsan. Marine Fighter Squadron VMF-312 arrives at Wonsan from Kimpo. In addition, R5Ds (transport planes) deliver 210 men of the advance units of Headquarters Squadron Hedron-12, Service Squadron SMS-12, and VMF(N)-513, the all-weather night fighter squadron.

VMF(N)-513 initiates missions to deliver bombs and rockets to Wonsan while naval transports embark from Kobe, Japan, and transport critical cargo for MAG-12. The captured airbase is further augmented, as planes attached to Combat Cargo Command arrive to begin ferrying the crucial aviation fuel required to keep the show moving until the sea blockade is broken.

In conjunction, the two Marine squadrons, operating from Wonsan, remain dependent upon airlifts until the ships can safely enter port. In the meantime, the support crews are heavily burdened. Only one jeep and eight trailers are available to transfer the bombs. And MAG-12 is presented with a new quandary due to the change in orders for the Marines to execute an administrative landing rather than an assault landing. The new circumstances place MAG-12 under the control of Far East Air Forces, which operates under totally different procedures not indigenous to Marine Corps close-air support tactics.

Nonetheless, the Marine aviators try to conform with the new directives, including the requirement that all scheduled missions be received by Headquarters (Fifth Air Force in Seoul) by 1800 on the previous day. Time restrictions make it impossible for the Marines in Wonsan to receive clearance in a timely manner, but a meeting is soon called, and General Partridge (Fifth AF) and General Harris (USMC) agree on a pragmatic solution. Partridge gives Harris verbal permission to plan and execute missions while awaiting permission from Headquarters. The agreement works satisfactorily, and later, during November, General Harris receives permission in writing from Fifth Air Force.

In the Eighth Army area, I Corps sector, the North Korean Army, which had earlier slashed through the U.N. forces with little effort, no longer bears any resemblance to its initial characterization of being near-invincible. The Communists are in complete disarray and the North Korean Army is facing total annihilation. Enemy lines of resistance, standing between the 38th Parallel and the North Korean capital, have vanished.

In the 1st Cavalry sector, Colonel Crombez, commanding officer, 5th Cavalry, arrives in Kumch'on at 0830. Crombez orders the 1st Battalion to remain and mop up the town. Crombez directs the 2nd Battalion to drive north and hook up with the 7th Cavalry at Hanp'o-ri, and he orders the 3rd Battalion to move south on the Kaesong Road, to link with the 8th Cavalry.

— *In North Korea:* Premier Kim Il Sung, the leader and commander in chief, North Korea, and Pak Hon Yong, the chief of Supreme Political Bureau, issue a blanket order to all troops of the N.K. People's Army. The order rationalizes the reasons for the defeat of the North Korean Army and details tough measures to be instituted to insure discipline within the remaining ranks. The measures include the summary executions of "agitators" and "deserters." The pointed command: "Do not retreat one step further. Now we have no space in which to fall back."

North Korean division commanders and regimental commanders are also directed to organize (by the 15th) what Kim Il Sung refers to as the Supervising Army, to be composed of troops who had distinguished themselves on the battlefield.

At about this time, Chinese Communist troops begin to enter Korea to aid the North Koreans. Their movement is confined to the darkened hours to avoid detection by aircraft. Eventually, the troops disperse in the heights about 50 air-miles south of the Yalu, amidst the mountains. The line of deployment stretches west from Huich'on and extends about sixty air-miles to skirt through Onjung, and from there to Unsan. By about the 20th, the Chinese units, scattered east to west along this route, are the 38th, 40th and 39th Armies. Two additional armies are hidden in reserve.

In essence, the Eighth Army and the ROK II Corps will face fifteen separate Chinese Divisions, excluding the Chinese 125th Division, which will be engaged with the S.K. 7th Division, below Ch'osan. Also, before the end of October, the Chinese 50th and 60th Armies enter Korea to further bolster Chinese strength.

The Chinese 42nd Army, composed of the 124th, 125th and 126th Divisions, departs T'ung-hua in southern Manchuria by train for Korea. Subsequent to arriving at Chi-an, across the Yalu from Manp'ojin, the 124th Division is the first unit to ford the river. Two days later the 124th Division, trailed by the other two divisions, marches southeast toward Hagaru-ri. It encounters and engages ROK troops and shortly it will meet X Corps, U.S. Marines.

October 15

Admiral Doyle, commander, Amphibious Group One, issues OpnO 16-50, which calls for an assault landing at Wonsan. It is in contrast to the scheduled administrative landing about to be executed; however, for the U.S. Navy, the movement of troops from ship to shore remains identical, regardless of the type of landing.

On October 24, division dispatches instructions canceling OpnOs 16 and 17, and it directs an administrative landing on Kalma peninsula, as ordered by CTF 90. The dispatch is sent at 1450.

In the X Corps area, the remnants of the N.K. 7th Division, which had escaped from South Korea, begin to reassemble above the 38th Parallel, in the Inje-Yanggu vicinity. It has been reported that its commanding general had been killed during fighting near Kumch'on while the division was fleeing north.

In other activity, the Fifth Air Force headquarters transfers from Japan to Seoul. The recent victories in Korea permit the Air Force to again base planes on Korean soil, enabling Fifth Air Force to get maximum time over targets. The bombers and fighters will also be afforded heavier bomb-loads and they will have the ability to plunge deeper into North Korea.

Also, near Seoul, a group of guerrillas attacks a radio relay station less than five miles from the capital building. Guerrilla activity is ongoing behind U.N. lines, and the raids stretch as far south as Pusan.

In other Air Force activity, Chinese Communist anti-aircraft artillery downs an F-51 while it is on a mission at the Yalu River in the vicinity of Sinuiju.

In yet other activity, Fifth Air Force in Korea establishes headquarters in Seoul.

In the 1st Marine Division area, the U.S. Navy LSTs receive the final elements of the 1st and 7th Marines, which concludes the embarkation process. The Division had originally expected a speedy westward advance following the landing at Wonsan; therefore, each RCT is equipped with sixteen trucks, all laden with supplies.

Sixteen additional trailers and three truck companies are also committed to the attacking regiments, to enable them to have ammo dumps extended well to the front. By the latter part of the day, the landing craft sail for the objective, and by evening, the majority of the transports also depart.

The USS *Mount McKinley* and USS *Bayfield* embark on the 17th. The landing force and accompanying X Corps troops that depart Inchon number 1,902 officers and 28,287 enlisted men. Of these, 1,461 officers and 23,938 men are mustered on the rolls of the 1st

A U.S. Sheridan medium M4A3 tank moves back down a hill following its support for an infantry attack against enemy positions.

Marine Division. Further breakdown of the numbers are: Marine officers 1,119; Marine enlisted 20,597; Navy officers 153; Navy enlisted 1,002; USA and KMC officers attached, 189; and USA and KMC enlisted attached, 2,339.

In other activity, MAG-12 initiates operations from Wonsan. These sorties continue until November 9. There are some early restrictions due to the airfield's lack of lighting. VMF(N)-513 is unable to conduct night missions until the latter part of October, but it does operate during daylight hours, along with VMF-312 and the two fighter squadrons that fly from the carriers. Refueling is not an easy task either, as the ground crews are compelled to hand-roll the 50-gallon drums of fuel from the depot to the airfield one mile away.

In the Eighth Army area, General Walker shows signs of dissatisfaction with the pace of the advance.

In the I Corps sector, General Milburn, mirroring Walker's sentiments, attempts to speed the attack. He orders the 24th Division to pivot and then spring an attack from the left (west) of the 1st Cavalry and capture Sariwon. The Division is to then attack north into the capital (Pyongyang).

In the 1st Cavalry Division sector, heavy rainstorms begin to strike the area. The inclement weather neutralizes the progress of some units of the cavalry, particularly the 5th Regiment. Nonetheless, General Gay continues to push the advance. Gay orders the British Commonwealth Brigade to take positions to the rear of the 7th Cavalry and prepare to push through it to seize Sariwon.

In the 7th Cavalry zone, the regiment reaches positions near Namch'onjom, but it awaits the cessation of an air strike, which begins at 0700, before launching its assault. The 2nd Battalion, bolstered by artillery, drives against staunch defenses. It hammers the enemy, but in turn, the defenders raise tenacious resistance. By noon, the 2nd Battalion reduces the resistance, storms into the town, and secures it. Captured prisoners state that the morning bombardment had devastated the command post of the N.K. 19th Division and killed the division's chief of staff. The battle for Namch'onjom costs the 2nd Battalion 10 troops killed and thirty wounded.

In the ROK Army area, the S.K. 1st Division, operating to the right of the 1st Cavalry Division, advances to the vicinity of Miu-dong, about 12 miles northeast of Namch'onjom, and once there, it encounters a large enemy force. The North Koreans, about regimental strength, are accompanied by artillery and six tanks, but the South Koreans are bolstered by U.S. Air Force planes. The South Korean infantry drives through the high ground while their supporting tanks grind forward on the road. The advance closes toward Suan.

In Naval activity, U.S. naval vessels converge on the Wonsan area to support and protect the minesweeping operations and amphibious landings. The approaches to Wonsan are protected by the destroyers and the USS *Missouri* (BB 63), USS *Helena* (CA 75), USS *Toledo* (CA 133), and the USS *Manchester* (CA 83).

— *Wake Island:* President Truman arrives at Wake Island in the Pacific to confer with General MacArthur, who has flown in from Japan. It is an apparent attempt to clarify misunderstandings between the commander-in-chief and the commanding general, as well as to scrutinize the battle plans for winning in Korea. The meeting ends amicably, but differences of opinion on how to conduct the war will re-emerge. The friction between the general and his commander-in-chief shows no signs of easing. However, at present, it is common belief that the war in Korea is about to be terminated, and in accordance with this premise, agreements are reached during this meeting to alter troop movements to meet the changing situation.

MacArthur is of the opinion that Russia is unable to muster forces soon enough to change the situation in Korea before winter, and he believes that Chinese intervention is, at best, a remote possibility. However, the possibility of Communist intervention is not totally discarded by him, or by Washington. MacArthur remains convinced that the hostilities will cease by Thanksgiving Day and that Eighth Army should return to Japan by Christmas. He also believes that X Corps can retain stability within a united Korea until peace is fully restored. General MacArthur receives a Distinguished Service Medal (his fifth) from President Truman.

The Department of the Army and the commander-in-chief, Far East, have agreed to embark the U.S. 2nd Division to the States or to Europe. Other participants at the Wake Island meeting include Frank Pace (secretary of Army), General Omar Bradley, Admiral Arthur Radford (CinCPacFlt), General Courtney Whitney, Assistant Secretary of State Dean Rusk and Secretary of State Averell Harriman.

October 16   Elements of the Chinese 124th (CCF) Division cross the Yalu River into North Korea on or about this day, but they are not discovered. The units are later identified by prisoners. During the following ten days, elements of the two regiments move south and deploy near the Chosin Reservoir.

In the X Corps area, 1st Marine Division sector, Wonsan begins to bustle with activity. Marine Fighter Squadrons VMF-214 and 323 arrive off Wonsan from Sasebo, Japan, to begin operations from the decks of the *Sicily* and the *Badoeng Strait.* The Marine pilots initiate sorties on the following day. During the latter part of the afternoon, Amphibious Group One and the LSTs, transporting the tractor group, embark from Inchon. These ships will be followed by the main attack force, which departs on the following day. VMO-6 remains under the operational control of the 1st Marine Division, but it is controlled administratively by MAG-12. Elements of VMO-6 (still at Kimpo) begin to arrive at Wonsan on the 23rd.

In other activity, the 7th Division Advance Command Post is established aboard the USS *Eldorado.* It will be some time before it is transferred to shore. Wonsan harbor is saturated with enemy mines, causing a two-week postponement of the convoys' arrival at the objective.

Lt. Colonel William J. McCaffrey (deputy chief of staff, X Corps) and the X Corps advance command post depart Kimpo Airfield by plane and arrive at Wonsan. McCaffrey immediately makes contact with the commander of the offshore minesweeping operation and with the ROK I Corps. Once contact is established with the South Koreans, McCaffrey's group initiates the task of discovering who had laid the minefields and, if possible, determining where the remaining mines are stored.

ROK intelligence makes contact with a Korean civilian who had worked in the mine storage area. The civilian leads a detachment to the place where the mines had been assembled. He also informs the party about the captain of a sampan who assisted with the dispersion of the mines. The meek Korean civilian and the other informer disclose that Russian troops had overseen the operation. Thirty-two small boats and their crews had placed about 3,000 mines in the waters off Wonsan and on the beaches.

In related activity, South Korean troops have discovered and moved about 1,000 20-pound box-mines to a location at the northern sector of the harbor. Six S.K. troops, including one officer, move about 200 yards away from the stacked explosives and seemingly decide to celebrate. The officer fires into the cache and the explosion that follows shatters nerves and windows for several miles around. The six soldiers are killed in the blast.

Also, General Almond is directed to have X Corps attack west. The advance is to drive along the Wonsan–Pyongyang axis, but these orders are modified on the following day.

In the Eighth Army area, Army anticipates the imminent fall of Pyongyang and establishes Task Force Indianhead, commanded by Lt. Colonel Ralph Foster (Asst. CoS for G-2, 2nd Division). The force is composed of Company K, 38th Regiment, a contingent of demolition engineers, a detachment of 82nd AAA Battalion automatic weapons vehicles and 6 tanks attached to Company C, 72nd Medium Tank Battalion. A group of counterintelligence troops also joins the mission. The task force moves into Pyongyang with the 1st Cavalry and seizes particular government buildings and some foreign countries' compounds to gather intelligence.

Once the city is secured, Army utilizes supplies that had been airlifted from Kimpo Airfield in Inchon and from Ashiya Airbase in Japan. This cargo sustains the attack and alleviates some pressure, as the trucks are being worn down into wrecks from the non-stop use.

In the I Corps area, General Milburn informs General Gay (1st Cavalry) and General Church (24th Division) that the division, which is first to reach Sariwon, will be the division that spearheads the attack into Pyongyang. There is already plenty of competitiveness between divisions and the individual units, and it is not necessarily always friendly, as the troops are becoming increasingly edgy.

In the 1st Cavalry Division sector, 7th Cavalry zone, the 3rd Battalion, commanded by Colonel Lynch, drives from Namch'onjom. By noon it advances 17 miles and secures Sohung. In the meantime, the 1st Battalion, commanded by Colonel Clainos, passes through the captured town and swings north to prepare to take Hwang-ju on the following day.

Meanwhile, the 3rd Battalion holds the prize and with Company F, it establishes roadblocks south of Sohung. Colonel Harris issues orders to shoot at all targets spotted in front of the perimeter after dusk. Harris' 7th Cavalry is aware that the British will be passing through on the following morning, but no other friendly troops are due in the area. Colonel Harris transfers his headquarters to Sohung and he arrives there during the latter part of the afternoon.

In other activity, the road at Namch'onjom becomes clogged. The 5th Cavalry, the 19th Regiment (24th Division) and the British Commonwealth Brigade converge there and create a log-jam. The vehicles are nearly immobilized.

In the 24th Division zone, the 21st Regiment, commanded by Colonel Stephens, advances toward Sariwon and closes on Haeju, against enemy resistance. General Church has ordered the 19th Regiment to speed its advance, but it trails the 5th Cavalry on the highway and becomes part of a massive traffic jam.

In the ROK Army area, Army activates the ROK III Corps, which is delegated responsibility of retaining the security of the ROK-held terrain south of the Seoul–Chunchon–Inje–Yangyang line. It is to eliminate the remnant enemy groups, including guerrillas. The ROK III Corps is composed of the S.K. 5th and 11th Divisions.

The S.K. 1st Division, commanded by General Paik, overcomes the opposition and drives into Suan. Now standing about forty miles from Pyongyang, General Paik decides that his tactics are "No stop." Paik intends to drive straight into the North Korean Capital. His troops still lack transportation and many are shoeless. Nonetheless, the South Koreans race far ahead of the U.S. motorized columns.

October 17   By this time, the North Koreans have concluded that it would be futile to prepare a steadfast defense at Pyongyang, and that such a plan would most probably cause the annihilation of the remaining North Korean troops. In conjunction, four South Korean divisions are rapidly racing toward the capital. The British contingent (27th Commonwealth Brigade) of the U.S. I Corps and the Americans are also closing fast.

MacArthur's initial flanking operation of Wonsan by X Corps is executed by the ROKs prior to the landing of X Corps. MacArthur informs General Almond that if Eighth Army takes Pyongyang prior to X Corps' landing, X Corps is to alter its plans and attack north. By the 19th, the final order is received by Almond and it directs the attack to move north.

In other activity, about 300 American soldiers, crammed aboard two enemy trains at Pyongyang, are taken north. During September, when the Communists marched them from Seoul to Pyongyang, the captives numbered about 370 men. The death-trains move slowly, as the tracks along the way must frequently be repaired, and travel during daylight hours is especially dangerous due to U.S. planes. During the repair stops, some of the captive GIs manage to escape into the woods; however, many more do not survive the ordeal. About five to six soldiers die each day during the cruel voyage due to either starvation or dysentery. Their bodies are removed from the trains by the Communists and left to rot in the woods.

In the X Corps area, the 1st Marine Division embarks from Inchon aboard the warships of JTF 7's Attack Force (including TF-90). At 0800, the armada heads for the Yellow Sea to begin the 830-mile voyage to Wonsan on Korea's east coast.

In the 7th Division sector, the loading operation at Pusan is concluded. Men and equipment are set for embarkation. Corps troops begin boarding the ships on the 19th.

In the Eighth Army area, Army has concluded that the combined effective force of the N.K. 17th and 32nd Divisions at Pyongyang stands at about 8,000 troops, and Eighth Army is convinced that the enemy will raise only token resistance to permit the bulk of its troops to cross the Ch'ongch'on River to flee north. The river is about 65 miles from the Yalu, and it flows northeast to southwest, similarly to the Yalu. General Walker directs the 1st Cavalry to spearhead the attack into the North Korean capital. Its attached British Brigade had entered Sariwon before the 24th Division.

In the I Corps area, 1st Cavalry Division sector, General Gay, upon receiving word from Army that his division is to make the attack against Pyongyang, delegates the furthest unit (7th Cavalry) to initiate the attack on the morning of the 18th.

In the 7th Cavalry zone, Captain Arthur Truxes, Jr., commanding Company F, holds the roadblock south of Sohung. At about 0300, his troops spot some movement. Pursuant to orders, Company F commences fire; however, the approaching force is a contingent of the 5th Cavalry. The unnecessary firefight costs the 5th Cavalry seven wounded before the two American units discover the error.

Testimony shows that opinions differ on some of the details of the firefight. Captain Webel (7th Cavalry S-3) states that he informed the 5th Cavalry liaison officer of the orders to shoot, and that he asked him to go to the 5th Cavalry to relay the information. The officer apparently remains in the 7th Cavalry sector during the night. Captain Truxes is killed; therefore, his account of the incident is never ascertained.

General Gay replaces Colonel William Harris with Colonel James Woolnough as commanding officer, 7th Cavalry. Harris, infuriated with the disciplinary action, returns to Seoul. Later, Gay alleges that Harris was merely sent back for R&R.

In other activity, as scheduled for the morning, the British 27th Commonwealth Brigade moves through the 7th Cavalry positions at Sohung. The unit, equipped with U.S. tanks, drives tenaciously along the main road toward Sariwon. The advance is spearheaded by a platoon of Company A, Argyll 1st Battalion, which travels aboard the tanks. Soon the 7th Cavalry, spearheaded by the 1st Battalion, also drives west toward Sariwon, but it takes a roundabout route to Hwangju to strike against the primary road (Pyongyang Road) north of Sariwon. Russian tanks, seemingly abandoned for lack of fuel, line the road and there is also much human debris. North Korean troops await an opportunity to surrender. But, farther down the road, about four miles short of the objective, other enemy troops establish resistance.

Brigadier General Frank A. Allen (asst. 1st Cavalry commanding officer) is accompanying the British. He immediately orders the tanks to rake an orchard to eliminate the opposition there. A spotter plane pinpoints the enemy positions to aid the effort. As the tanks begin to fire, some North Koreans bolt from the orchard, abandon their weapons and sprint to the opposite side of the ridge line.

The tanks then oversee the British as they romp through the orchard, confiscate 10 machine guns and clear it of any remaining Communists. Forty Communists are killed and some others are captured. After passing an abandoned battery of antitank guns in the pass, the British roll into Sariwon. The skirmish costs the British one man killed and several wounded.

Meanwhile, the 7th Cavalry treks along the slim path toward its objective. At about 1600, General Gay flies over the regiment at Hwangju and drops instructions that direct one battalion to divert southward at Hwangju and join with the British on the primary road to help eliminate or capture a large concentration of enemy troops spotted there. After a brief meeting, the commanders determine that the 1st Battalion (Colonel Clainos) will move to join the British and the 2nd Battalion (Colonel Callaway) will remain in Hwangju.

Almost immediately after swinging south and driving down the Sariwon–Pyongyang Road, the 1st Battalion captures a contingent of enemy cavalry and about thirty horses. The 1st Battalion then resumes its advance, but it retains its vehicles rather than switching to the horses. It has been rumored that one of the saddles becomes an ornament for Colonel Clainos' jeep.

Shortly thereafter, the 7th Cavalry's 1st Battalion encounters more of the enemy and a skirmish erupts. A South Korean interpreter, despite being wounded, advances to the enemy positions and falsely tells them that they are firing upon Russian troops. The enemy is successfully duped and it walks into the hands of the 7th Cavalry. Several of the North Koreans become frustrated and resist, but the episode is brief. A squad leader punches one of the resisters and knocks him into a ditch.

Unknown to the cavalrymen, this unusual daylight capture is being observed by several hundred other enemy troops from their positions in the nearby heights. In a little while, the eastern side of the slope begins raining enemy troops who swarm toward the battalion to surrender. The enemy on the west side continues to fire at the 1st Battalion until dusk. Nonetheless, during the evening, about 1,700 enemy troops, including 13 female nurses, surrender to Colonel Clainos' 1st Battalion. Clainos establishes contact with the Australians by radio at 1800.

Later, at 2230, he informs them that he is about to move through the pass to enter the Australian lines. Meanwhile, at about 1700, the Australian 3rd Battalion passes through Sariwon and drives 5 additional miles to close on Hwangju, where the enemy is entrenched in the hills. The Australians halt their advance and prepare to launch an attack on the following morning.

During the day, there are many cases of mistaken identity. In one instance, the enemy believes the British are Russian and in another instance, U.N. troops inadvertently accept enemy troops as South Korean troops.

A contingent of British reconnaissance troops encounters an enemy truck that is heading north into Sariwon. The Communists break through to the town, but unable to exit, the vehicle reverses course and runs back into the British. About twenty Reds are killed during the second encounter. Another high-spirited fight erupts when the Communists stumble upon the British, begin to call them "comrade" and hand out cigarettes before they realize the troops are British. A close-quartered battle erupts.

In yet another incident, Lieutenant Robin Fairrey, a British mortar officer, walks around a corner and finds himself in the middle of a group of enemy troops. He bellows, "Rusky! Rusky!" and the North Koreans remain fooled. He briskly walks to safety.

During another peculiar encounter, south of Sariwon, a contingent of the Australian 3rd Battalion spots a large enemy force as it approaches a roadblock and prepares for a heated struggle. At the same time, Major I.B. Ferguson jumps upon a tank and begins to call for the enemy to surrender. Erroneously, he informs them that they are surrounded. Surprisingly, they capitulate and the Australians rake in 1,982 prisoners. After this incident, the Australians prepare to launch an attack on the following day, but the troops on the line receive yet another surprise.

At 2300, the pass that leads toward Sariwon becomes illuminated. The convoy transporting the 1st Battalion, 7th Cavalry, is moving south on the highway and it advances through the pass with all the vehicles' headlights beaming brightly. The entourage of accompanying prisoners is highly visible and at midnight, when the column reaches the Australian lines, the Australians are buzzing. Colonel Clainos notes that one Australian soldier quips to another, "Here we are all set for a coordinated attack in the morning and the bloody Yanks come in at midnight from the north, with their lights burning, and bringing the whole damned north Korean Army as prisoners."

In the 24th Division sector, the advance moves up the west coast to the left of the Kaesong–Sariwon–Pyongyang axis. The 19th Regiment closes on Sariwon, but at 1700 orders arrive that instruct it to halt its attack, as the town had already been secured.

Meanwhile, Colonel Stephens' 21st Regiment encounters stiff resistance at Haeju, but it continues to hammer the 300 defenders and overwhelm them. The town is secure before evening.

In the ROK Army area, a contingent of South Korean troops eliminates the enemy shore batteries that had been firing upon the minesweepers in the Russian Channel off Wonsan. With Wonsan under control, the S.K. forces also secure the peninsulas and islands that dominate the Wonsan harbor approaches. Although the shore guns are liquidated, the channel remains filled with mines. The Capital Division secures Hamhung, Hungnam and Yonpo Airfield. The S.K. 3rd Division has one regiment en route to Hamhung, and two other regiments are at Wonsan and Kojo.

In other activity, the S.K. 1st Division advances from the southeast and reaches a point about 15 miles from the North Korean capital, Pyongyang. To the right from the east, the S.K. 7th Division also closes against Pyongyang.

Meanwhile, in the central mountains, the S.K. 6th Division drives from the northeast and nears Yangdok, about fifty air-miles from the objective. The S.K. 8th Division is also in the central mountains near Yangdok. It closes on the Pyongyang–Wonsan Road, from where it is to swing west and drive to the city.

In Air Force activity, Far East Air Force initiates flights to recently captured Sinmak, less than fifty miles from the Communist capital of Pyongyang. The planes deliver food rations and fuel. Then the aircraft evacuate wounded troops and transport them to Kimpo Airfield.

— *In the United States:* President Truman, back in San Francisco from Wake Island, gives General MacArthur high accolades: "It is fortunate for the world that we had the right man for this purpose, a man who is a very great soldier." The president notes that the only reason for being in Korea "is to establish peace and independence. We seek no territory or special privilege — the only victory we seek is the victory of peace."

Also, the president mentions the Soviet Union's incessant military buildup in Asia and Europe, which he then proclaims is threatening world peace. Truman states emphatically: "The free men of the world have but one choice if they are to remain free. They must oppose strength with strength.... We hate war, but we love our liberties. We will not see them destroyed."

— *In Japan:* General MacArthur issues UNC Operations Order 4 that removes the restriction specified in the previous order issued on September 27 forbidding troops (other than South Korean) from advancing beyond a line extending from Ch'ongju on the west to Hamhung on the east coast. The new line is drawn along an axis thirty to forty miles south of the Manchurian border with North Korea. The order will be confirmed in a distributed message on the 19th. Also, the previous orders restricting Fifth Air Force planes from flying closer than fifty miles from the North

Korean border, at the Yalu River, are somewhat relaxed to give the pilots some slack.

October 18

In Naval activity, minesweeping operations continue off Wonsan as the Navy chisels out a safe channel that leads to the harbor. A successful conclusion seems near until a Japanese vessel (JMS-14) strikes a mine and plummets to the bottom. The tragedy sobers the optimism.

In the Eighth Army area, the principal body (5,192 troops) of the 1st Turkish Armed Forces Command, which had arrived at Pusan on the previous day, comes ashore. The Turkish Brigade then moves to Taegu to begin training at the newly established U.N. Reception Center (UNRC). The Turkish Brigade is fully equipped with the exception of certain weapons, which must be provided by the Americans.

In the 1st Cavalry Division sector, the morale of the troops skyrockets when erroneous rumors spread through the ranks. The false notions imply that once Pyongyang falls, the mission of the Americans is terminated and the U.S. troops will embark for Japan, in time to eat dinner there on Thanksgiving Day.

In the 7th Cavalry zone, the Regiment resumes its attack at dawn. The 3rd Battalion, following its tedious night march to reach Hwangju, jumps off and bolts across a small stream at Hwangju. From there, it advances toward the objective, Pyongyang. Initially, the enemy raises nominal resistance to harass the battalion, but later, when the 3rd Battalion encroaches the high ground slightly south of the midway point at Hukkyo-ri, the stakes get raised. Communist gunners begin to pour extremely heavy fire into the ranks. The resistance includes high-velocity guns, 120-mm mortars, several entrenched T-34 tanks and a heavily mined road.

The U.S. troops are bolstered by planes and twenty tanks attached to Company C, 70th Tank Bn. Enemy small arms fire, which is also tenacious, brings down one of the attacking aircraft. The enemy force, composed of about 800 troops, holds its ground firmly and greatly hinders progress. General Gay becomes impatient with the headway of the assault. Consequently, during the middle of the afternoon, he directs the 7th Cavalry commander, Colonel Woolnough (temporarily replacing Colonel Harris), to commit the remaining two battalions. To speed up the advance, they are each to flank the enemy-dominated ridges. Colonel Webel urges General Gay to cancel the order, claiming that the ridge is nearly secured and that the reinforcements are not needed. Nevertheless Gay, after being informed by Woolnough that the mission is in progress, decides to let the order stand.

In the meantime, the 1st and 2nd Battalions advance toward the enemy flanks and the attack continues throughout the night. Also, General Gay tells Colonel Woolnough that the 5th Cavalry is to pass through the 7th Cavalry on the morning of the 19th to resume the assault. After this conversation, Gay departs and locates Colonel Crombez and his 5th Cavalry, which is still scattered along the lousy road that is more suitable for donkeys or oxen rather than cavalrymen. Crombez is informed that his regiment will spearhead the following day's attack.

The 5th Cavalry Regiment, trailing the 7th Cavalry, completes its march through the mountains and reaches Hwangju at 2300. The 7th Cavalry remains deeply disappointed with General Gay. The 7th had spearheaded the drive from Seoul, but it is now being denied the opportunity to take Pyongyang.

In the ROK Army area, two South Korean warships strike mines in the channel off Wonsan. A minesweeper sinks and the other vessel sustains damage.

In other activity, the S.K. 1st Division rapidly advances toward Pyongyang, far ahead of the American drive, but when it reaches a point about ten miles from the city, resistance intensifies. The combination of the accelerated opposition and a heavy concentration of mines prevents great progress. The South Koreans advance only about two miles. The contest outside Pyongyang continues throughout the night and into the following morning, all the while under a dreary rainstorm.

The leading elements of the 1st Cavalry Division stand about 30 miles from the city; however, the cavalry is not encountering heavy resistance. *In Air Force activity,* during a mission, an RB-29 reconnaissance plane's crew spots about 75 fighter planes on the ground at the airfield in Antung, China, across the Yalu River along the border with North Korea. The presence of the enemy aircraft suggests an imminent entry by China into the war.

October 19

In Naval activity, the risky minesweeping operation off Wonsan sustains another devastating blow when the S.K. minesweeper YMS-516 is rocked by a thunderous explosion as it passes through a supposedly clear sector of the channel. The area had been swept, but the enemy had also spread magnetic mines. These were implanted with time devices that permit as many as 12 vessels to pass safely before detonation.

In other activity, the USS *Mount McKinley* arrives off Wonsan. Admiral Doyle, General Almond and other X Corps staff set up a conference with Admiral Struble aboard the USS *Missouri.* Struble thinks it will take three additional days to clear the remaining magnetic mines from the channel. He states that no landing will occur until all the magnetic mines are eliminated from the channel.

The UNC Operations Order 4, issued by MacArthur on the 17th, is confirmed today. The new line of operations for the U.N. troops (other than South Korean) runs from Sonch'on and extends through Koindong–P'yongwon–P'ungsan and beyond until it terminates at Songjin on the east coast. The new line remains within the original guidelines of the original JCS directive of September 27, which is still in effect. It is about 100 miles from the Soviet Union.

The directives still permit only South Korean troops

to operate in the provinces that border the Yalu River and neighboring Communist China. Soon after, on the 24th, General MacArthur again changes the parameters of the operation in North Korea. This directive creates an even larger gap between Eight Army and X Corps.

In the X Corps area, following his meeting with Admiral Struble aboard the *Missouri,* General Almond decides to move to Wonsan on the following day.

In the 1st Marine Division area, although it cannot be found in the official government records, the Marines aboard ships in the Yellow Sea, slightly beyond the Wonsan Channel, initiate what becomes known as Operation Yo-yo. The Marines, who had originally been scheduled to storm the beaches on the 20th, find themselves in a most uncomfortable position on the eve of their landing. Rather than facing D-Day and enemy resistance, the Marines face Z-day, as in zany.

At about 1700, the colossal 250-vessel armada, which is steaming north, suddenly spins on a dime and swings around, then heads south toward Pusan. The rumors begin as murmurs, but then, they accelerate into great exhortation as the floating procession begins its southward course. The sounds of the Marines bellow across the decks: "War's over!" "They're taking us back to Pusan for embarkation to the States." Nevertheless, if the Marines feel the surge of magnanimous surprise, they are in for another bombshell when dawn arrives on the following day.

In the Eighth Army area, the forward distribution center for Army is at Kaesong. It requires about 200 trucks to transport the supplies from there to the forward positions, and most units are more than 100 miles north of Kaesong. The vehicles move food, gasoline and other supplies to small depots located about fifty miles north of Seoul.

The 187th Airborne Regiment at Kimpo Airfield in Inchon prepares to parachute into North Korea on the following day. These airborne troops have been held in GHQ Reserve and did not participate in Eighth Army's attack across the 38th Parallel.

In the 1st Cavalry Division sector, 5th Cavalry zone, Colonel Paul Clifford's 2nd Battalion, having received little sleep, departs Hwangju at 0500. The battalion reaches the 7th Cavalry lines at Hukkyo-ri, toward the tail end of a battle in which the enemy has been repulsed by the 7th Cavalry. Three tanks roar into the area and stop suddenly. The tankers open their hatches and begin conversing with each other in close proximity to three 5th Cavalrymen, who realize that the tanks are hostile. One trooper, in obvious slang, yells to the team leader, "Them ain't GIs, them are gooks." The bazooka team leader chimes in: "Let's shoot the S.O.B.s." Their marksmanship is superior to their use of the King's English. The three enemy tanks are destroyed.

Soon after, Company F, commanded by Lieutenant James H. Bell, pushes off with the added support of one platoon of engineers, a section of heavy machine guns and five tanks. The attacking unit is further bolstered by aircraft.

Company F is hardly out of the gate when a jet plane attempts to lend support and nearly causes a disaster. While the column passes by the first burning tank, the jet dives and fires a rocket that knocks Lieutenant Bell out of action by the concussion. Following the near-mishap, Company F picks up its pace and grinds forward. At 1102, the vanguard reaches the southern fringes of Pyongyang, where it pauses briefly at the Mujinch'on River, a tributary of the Taedong River. The advance troops wait while mortar fire is brought to bear on the enemy positions on the opposite side of the twenty-yard-wide river. The defenses include three antitank guns, which are zeroed in on the road bridge. After about one-half hour of effective fire, the guns become docile as the defenders abandon the positions.

Following the elimination of the enemy fire, Company F enters the city. The drive had been shepherded by Fifth Air Force aircraft. The official Army records, from an aerial observer's report, indicate that Company F enters Pyongyang at 1102, but Lieutenant Bell estimates that his unit breached the city at about 1330. Pyongyang is located along the Taedong River, about 40 miles from its confluence with the Yellow Sea. The sector of the city north of the Taedong contains the primary government buildings.

South of the river, an industrial suburb area has been established. Bell's orders direct him to swing west and secure the two railroad bridges (Pusan–Seoul–Mukden Railroad) situated about two miles downstream from the primary road bridge. Particular factories there are also listed as targets. Bell is directed to establish a bridgehead on the north bank of the river. When Lieutenant Bell reaches the south bank of the river, he discovers that each of the three-span railroad bridges contain only one span intact. Using the eastern span, which he considers sturdier, Bell orders a detachment to remain at the southern end to guard the tanks, while he leads the remainder of the company to secure an island in the river. An enemy contingent operating on the north bank destroys a section of the bridge there.

During the afternoon, Company F secures the island. Later it is relieved by the 3rd Battalion, 5th Cavalry. In the meantime, the remainder of the 2nd Battalion crosses the Mujinch'on River and swings right to secure the primary bridge (the sole remaining intact bridge at Pyongyang), that spans the Taedong River. Before contingents of Companies E and G reach the objective, the North Koreans detonate the middle span. The 2nd Battalion, 5th Cavalry, commanded by Colonel John Clifford, then continues northeast to find a new crossing site. Soon after, a contingent locates a stream and discovers that the S.K. 15th Regiment had already crossed there. The South Koreans, familiar with the area, knew the exact location of the crossing site.

In the 7th Cavalry sector, at dawn, the two battalions that had flanked the enemy positions in the high ground in front of Hukkyo-ri on the previous day discover that the enemy has abandoned their ridge positions.

In other activity, the North Koreans launch an

A contingent of ROKs (S.K. 7th Division) engage in a firefight with Communists in Pyongyang on 19 October.

unsuccessful early morning attack against the 7th Cavalry perimeter at Hukkyo-ri.

In the ROK Army area, IX Corps sector, S.K. 1st Division zone, fighting from the previous night continues even after dawn. The division grinds through tough op-

position and gains another two hard-fought miles. Following about one or two hours of tenacious battle, the South Koreans mount an attack supported by tanks of Company C, 6th Tank Battalion. The thrust of the tanks blows a giant hole in the defenses near Kojo-dong.

The S.K. (ROK) YMS-516 is destroyed after striking a mine on 19 October off Wonsan.

Afterward, the armor converge on both flanks and pulverize the North Korean positions. Machine guns, some other weapons and enemy troops are blown into particles. The tanks account for about 300 deceased Communists.

Meanwhile, elements of the S.K. 2nd Battalion, 12th Regiment, 1st Division, maintain their advance and slightly before 1100, the units reach the Taedong River. The regiment deploys northeast of the road bridge along the south bank of the river.

As the 1st Cavalry Division pounds its way into Pyongyang, the S.K. 1st Division drills through the city's defenses northeast of the lines of the 1st Cavalry. The ROKS advance along the Sibyon-ni–Pyongyang Road. By dusk, most of the S.K. 1st Division enters Pyongyang.

The records of the U.S. tank unit (Company C, 6th Med. Tank Bn.) that accompanies the South Koreans indicate that its tanks enter the southern fringes of the city at 1245. Soon after, tanks of Company D drive into the city via the identical route. The tanks of Company C swing north to support the S.K. 11th Regiment, which is assaulting the main airfield. It is secure by 1440.

Earlier in the day, other South Korean contingents had seized a smaller airfield. In addition, the 8th Regiment, S.K. 7th Division, enters Pyongyang from the east. At 1700, Kim Il Sung University in the northeast sector of the city is secure.

October 20 General MacArthur has been keeping the 187th Airborne Regiment at Kimpo while he prepares to unleash it to conduct a dangerous operation. It is expected to rescue American POWs suspected of being held captive on North Korean trains that are being sent farther north. The mission is executed on this day. The airdrop is supplemented by seventy-four tons of equipment, which is also dropped. This is the first time heavy equipment is airdropped in combat, and it is also the initial use of C-19s in a combat parachute operation. The paratroopers will be followed to earth by such items as 90-mm towed antitank guns, 105-mm howitzers, jeeps and a mobile radio transmission set. In conjunction, seven 105-mm howitzers of the 674th FABn and 1,125 shells are also dropped. Six of the guns survive in operable condition, and only about ten percent of the shells are damaged and fortunately, none explode upon impact.

In what is considered a usual practice for MacArthur, he and Generals Stratemeyer, Whitney and Wright have flown from Japan to observe the parachutists. At 0230, during a torrential downpour, the paratroopers fall out for an early reveille. The soaked troops are treated to breakfast before they move to the airstrip to await a change in the weather. At about noon, conditions improve and the flying warriors board their aircraft. About 2,800 men of the airborne unit cram into 113 planes to execute the first combat troop airdrop since World War II.

About 1,200 more paratroopers will follow on succeeding days. The total weight of the dropped equipment amounts to more than 600 tons. The C-19s and the C-47s, of the 314th and 21st Troop Carrier Squadrons respectively, are scheduled to make two primary drops at positions about 30 miles north of Pyongyang.

Prior to the arrival of the paratroopers, fighter planes fly over the target areas to bomb and strafe the terrain. The commanding officer, Colonel Frank Bowen, Jr., is aboard the lead aircraft, which is airborne at 1200. Once the remaining planes are in the air and assembled, they head toward Sukch'on and Sunchon, to intercept the targeted train.

At about 1400, Colonel Bowen and 1,470 troops (1st Bn., Regimental Headquarters and Headquarters Company, medical personnel, engineers and service troops) jump from their planes over Drop Zone William southeast of Sukch'on. They encounter only some sniper fire. Twenty-five troops are accidentally injured during this jump. One group misses the drop zone by about one and one-half miles. One man is killed by enemy fire while he is descending.

The airborne troops of the 1st Battalion quickly seize Hill 97 east of Sukch'on and Hill 104 to the north. Simultaneously they secure the town.

The terrain to the immediate north of the town must also be seized to provide the paratroopers domination of the primary road that runs north of Sukch'on. It is cleared on the following day. Colonel Bowen establishes his command post on Hill 97 and a roadblock is established near Hill 104. The 3rd Battalion, commanded by Colonel Delbert E. Munson, also lands in Drop Zone William, but it moves south and establishes roadblocks below the town at the highway and at the railroad.

By 1700, its objectives are seized without any casualties. In turn, the enemy loses five troops killed and forty-two others captured. Trailing the first air-drop, at 1420, the 2nd Battalion, commanded by Col. William J. Boyle, jumps to begin its descent and lands in Drop Zone Easy, about 2 miles southwest of Sunchon, against no opposition. However, 20 paratroopers are injured during the jump.

Following a quick assembly, the battalion quickly moves out and seizes all of its objectives by dusk. Roadblocks are established south and west of the town and manned by two companies, while another company moves to Sunchon and makes contact with the S.K. 6th Division. The South Koreans are advancing from the southeast, en route to the Ch'ongch'on River.

Once all the paratroopers hit the ground, the entourage of brass departs the area for Pyongyang, where MacArthur makes some comments to the waiting press. MacArthur claims that the airborne operation has caught the enemy by complete surprise and that about 30,000 enemy troops have been clamped between the paratroopers in the north and the claws of both the 1st Cavalry Division and the S.K. 1st Division, which are closing from the south. In addition, MacArthur claims

that either the demise or capture of the trapped enemy is at hand.

While at Sunchon, the 2nd Battalion does not encounter much difficulty, as the S.K. 6th Division secures most of the town and the immediate vicinity. The successful operation does sever two key enemy escape routes that lead to Manchuria. One of the two trains transporting the American POWs into the northernmost areas of North Korea pauses in a tunnel northwest of Sunchon. During the evening, while the train is still halted, the Communists massacre the GIs (*See also* **October 21,** *1st Cavalry sector.*)

In the X Corps sector, Admiral Struble had decided on the previous day not to take unnecessary risks by landing Marines at Wonsan on this day. His decision was probably influenced by the lack of pressure, due to the earlier seizure of the town by South Korean troops and their subsequent advance to positions beyond the North Korean capital. General MacArthur and Admiral Joy concur with the decision. General Almond departs the USS *Missouri* by helicopter and arrives at Wonsan Airfield, where he assumes command of the X Corps troops in the area, north and east of the Taebaek Range. Most of the X Corps is still at sea.

In the 1st Marine Division area, Marines aboard the ships of the armada are again surprised as the flotilla makes another seagoing "about face." The flotilla reinitiates its northward course and sails back toward Wonsan. The perplexed Marines and accompanying X Corps troops don't realize their short respite was based on military strategy rather than the cessation of hostilities.

Meanwhile, the assault troops mark time aboard ship as they prepare for the landing. The troops reach the pinnacle of grumbling, one of the other things Marines are best known for besides fighting. The warships cruise northward, but after 12 hours and without notice, the vessels again suddenly swirl and retrace the southern course, giving the landing force another quick dose of mixed emotions. The armada takes on an aura of mystery, and the Marines, seemingly on a string, dub the cruise to nowhere Operation YO YO.

The troops suffer from a variety of ailments due to the crowded conditions and prolonged duration of the unusual pattern, which automatically reverses course every twelve hours. Operation YO YO creates much more than boredom and anxiety. The transports and LSTs, anticipating a brief cruise, are ill-equipped for the arduous trek and unexpected complications emerge. Smallpox breaks out on the *Bayfield* and everyone aboard receives urgent vaccinations. Other medical emergencies such as dysentery and various stomach troubles take a high toll. The *Marine Phoenix,* a heavily laden transport, is plagued with illness, despite all necessary medical precautions. The sick list soars to 750 men during the revolving north-south excursion, which continues until the 25th.

In the Eighth Army area, the Communists remove most of the American captives from Pyongyang prior to the arrival of U.N. troops; however, some POWs are saved.

Troops of the 187th Airborne Regiment board a C-119 at Kimpo airfield on 20 October. One of the paratroopers carrying full gear gets help from two others to make it inside the aircraft.

Twenty Americans either escape from the enemy or are rescued when the city falls. Subsequent to the seizure of Pyongyang, General Milburn orders the I Corps to resume the attack and advance to the MacArthur Line, a point about 35 miles south of the Yalu River.

In the 1st Cavalry Division sector, the 5th Cavalry deploys in the southern fringes of Pyongyang. The 7th Cavalry will hold at Chinnamp'o, the city's port, and the 8th Cavalry stretches out in the northern suburbs. Subsequent to the fall of the city, the 7th Cavalry moves to Chinnamp'o, arriving there after a forced night march on October 22.

Part of the airborne operation on 20 October, when 113 planes fill the skies over the Sukch'on–Sunchon region and drop about 2,800 men of the 187th Airborne RCT.

In the 5th Cavalry sector, engineers' assault boats arrive to carry the 3rd Battalion, 5th Cavalry, across the Taedong River to the north bank. The attached 3rd Battalion, 7th Cavalry, also fords the river, and by noon, the troops are being received by the resounding clang of church bells rather than enemy artillery. The Christian churches ring their bells in unison as these Americans enter Pyongyang.

In other activity, pursuant to orders of October 16, TF Indianhead, which acquires its name from the patch of the 2nd Division, secures the bulk of its objectives in Pyongyang and in the process discovers much intelligence from within the seized buildings and captured compounds. The documents include both military and political information. The pertinent items are transferred to a special detachment from GHQ Far East Command, which carries them by plane back to Tokyo.

In the 8th Cavalry zone, TF Rodgers, commanded by Lt. Colonel William M. Rodgers and composed of the 1st Battalion, 8th Cavalry, and one company of tanks (70th Tank Bn.), departs Pyongyang to establish contact with the 187th RCT (Airborne) at Sunchon. En route, the task force discovers five Americans who escaped from their captors. TF Rodgers arrives at its objective on the following morning.

In the 24th Division sector, pursuant to orders from I Corps, the 24th Division, spearheaded by the 27th British Commonwealth Brigade, advances toward the Yalu River with instructions to halt at the MacArthur Line.

In the ROK Army area, the S.K. 1st Division drives into the center of Pyongyang and effortlessly seizes the Administrative Center, as the defenders exhibit no desire to fight, and in fact, abandon their positions. Soon

Top: LSTs unload cargo at Wonsan. *Bottom*: U.S. Navy frogmen engage in a mine clearing operation at a landing beach near Wonsan.

after, at 1000, the South Koreans declare the entire city secure.

In other activity, the S.K. 1st Division, attached to I Corps, and the 6th and 8th S.K. Divisions (ROK II Corps) are poised to join the I Corps attack.

October 21   General MacArthur arrives by air at Pyongyang Airfield to meet with Generals Walker and Stratemeyer. While there, MacArthur reviews Company F, 5th Cavalry, the first U.S. unit to enter the North Korean capital. The 5th Cavalry, which arrived in Korea on July 18, less than 100 days ago, receives a request from General MacArthur. He asks that all troops of the Company (nearly 200 men) that initially landed in Korea step forward. Five cavalrymen advance, and of these, three are wounded.

In other activity, General Almond attempts to get one Marine regiment to immediately land at Kojo-dong to relieve elements of the S.K. 3rd Division, but Admiral Struble (CO, JTF 7) responds in the negative, still refusing to permit the Marines to pass through the channel due to the minefields.

Also, General O.P. Smith, USMC, receives a message from Admiral Joy informing him that at the close of hostilities (anticipated to be in the near future), Joy will recommend that the 1st Marine Division be returned to the U.S., with the exception of one RCT, which would be deployed in Japan.

In the Eighth Army area, the airborne operation in North Korea continues. The 1st Battalion, 187th Regiment, commanded by Colonel Arthur H. Wilson, pushes north and captures the strategic ground north of Sukch'on, which gives the battalion domination of the highway there, but there is yet another string of hills that sit north of the 1st Battalion at Sukch'on, and it, too, must be reduced. Later in the day, contingents of the 1st Battalion encounter elements of the 2nd Battalion, 187th Regiment, at Sunchon, linking the two battalions.

At 0900, the 3rd Battalion, divided into two combat teams, begins to move from its roadblock position. It drives toward Pyongyang. Company I and Company K advance south along the railroad and highway respectively. At about 1300, Company I reaches Op'a-ri, where an enemy contingent estimated at battalion strength springs an attack. The muscle of 40-mm guns and 120-mm mortars is thrown at the advancing Americans, who tenaciously engage the enemy for about two and one-half hours of nasty combat. However, the overwhelming numerical strength weighs in heavily. The enemy overruns two platoons of Company I. The commander of the besieged unit, having ninety men unaccounted for, orders a withdrawal toward the west to grasp more tenable positions at Hill 281.

Meanwhile, PFC Richard G. Wilson (medic, Co. I, 187th Airborne Regiment), attempts to save some wounded troops by totally disregarding his own safety. Wilson moves about the casualties while the contingent continues its desperate attempt to extricate itself from the ambush. Wilson is convinced that he has retrieved all the wounded, but as the unit withdraws, he moves back into the line of fire to save one more soldier who originally was thought to be dead. Wilson reaches the wounded man, but he lacks a weapon and comes under heavy fire. When the unit retakes the ground, Wilson is found next to the body of the other soldier. Wilson is riddled with bullets and in a position that exhibited his intent of shielding the wounded trooper. PFC Wilson receives the Medal of Honor posthumously for his extraordinary valor and courage in the face of the enemy.

Fortunately for outnumbered Company I, the enemy chooses to disengage and retire to their entrenched positions in the heights around Op'a-ri. Meanwhile, the other U.S. column, Company K, moves south along the highway and it, too, encounters about one enemy battalion. Slightly north of Yongyu, the two opposing forces clash, but in this case, the smaller unit, Company K, fends off the Communists. Following a fierce firefight, the enemy breaks off the engagement and moves to positions south of O'pa-ri. Company K resumes its advance along the highway to Yongju and deploys slightly north of it at Hill 163.

Company K, at Hill 163 and Company I, at O'pari, are separated by about three miles. The airborne regiment in its entirety is deployed between Pyongyang and Suk'chon. The enemy is stretched along a chain of hills that lean from the southeast to the northwest and are straddled between Pyongyang and the Ch'ongch'on River. The positions are defended by about 2,500 troops of the N.K. 239th Regiment, the final unit to depart Pyongyang. Its mission is to hold the rear against the advancing I Corps, Eighth Army. Suddenly the situation is reversed on the North Koreans, who find themselves in an unenviable position of having their positions being pounded from the rear.

At about midnight, the enemy launches a northward attack to penetrate the U.S. lines and flee the trap, but the endeavor does not end successfully. Initially, the attack penetrates the command post of Company K at Hill 163. The company commander becomes wounded twice, but he gives no quarter and lunges directly at a Communist attacker and seizes his burp gun. Immediately thereafter, Captain Claude Josey collapses from his wounds. The company executive officer is also wounded during the brief confrontation, but ultimately the North Koreans are either wiped out or driven back.

More attacks are launched. The first one commences just after midnight (21st-22nd). A Company K contingent again resists tenaciously, but the unit holding the roadblock at Hill 163 spends its entire complement of ammunition and is compelled to abandon its positions. At 0400 the enemy ignites another assault against Company K. By 0545 the North Koreans smash into another unit, but this time they stumble into the battalion command post of Company L, a fresh unit. The enemy is met with smothering fire that inflicts heavy casualties upon the attackers. Nevertheless, the North Koreans refuse to relent. They reinitiate the attack and cause some concern among the airborne contingent. A quick call is placed, urgently requesting immediate support, and reinforcements rush to the scene. Company L continues to withstand the thrust of about 300 attackers while headquarters halts the progress of about 450 charging enemy troops.

A contingent of the advancing I Corps is also close at hand. The attached British Commonwealth Brigade remains about two miles away at day's end.

In the I Corps area, 1st Cavalry Division sector, 8th Cavalry zone, TF Rodgers arrives at Sunchon at 0900 and makes contact with the 2nd Battalion, 187th RCT (Airborne). The linkage is observed by Generals Gay and Frank A. Allen, both of whom are flying overhead in an L-5 plane. The aircraft returns to Pyongyang and General Allen moves back to Sunchon by jeep. He arrives there at about noon and soon after a Korean civilian is brought into the command post of the 2nd Battalion (Airborne) to give details of a slaughter of GIs. The Korean tells how the Communists had recently killed American soldiers in a railroad tunnel about five air-miles northwest of Sunch'on.

General Allen, his aide and two correspondents move to the site of the massacre, taking the civilian with them. Along the way, Allen pauses momentarily at the command post of the S.K. 6th Division and picks up a South Korean colonel to accompany him on the mission. At about 1500, the team reaches the tunnel just beyond Myonguch'am. The S.K. colonel climbs the hill from the road and walks into the railroad tunnel to verify the story.

Seven dead GIs lie near the track, but their causes of death appear to have been either starvation or disease. The bodies are emaciated and several of the seven corpses have obviously aged wounds. By now General Allen and the others in the party also enter the tunnel. The S.K. colonel moves through the tunnel and emerges at the other end and then, he spots five more dead GIs at the top of a ridge. At about the same time, a seriously wounded GI moves from his hiding place and is rescued. The soldier, PFC Valdor John, is overwhelmed by the sight of the friendly troops, and when he is given General Allen's coat to make him warm, he proclaims that he is "too dirty to wear it."

PFC Valdor John is the sole survivor of his group of eighteen. The other seventeen American soldiers, each executed by bullets, lie in a blood-filled gully. One correspondent who is present walks away, sickened by the sight, only to stroll directly into another group of massacred Americans. Fifteen more executed GIs lie dead, each holding an empty rice dish in his hands, apparently expecting food from the Communists, not death. And yet another group of 34 massacred GIs are found nearby, bringing the total of executed American soldiers at this site to sixty-six, not including the seven thought to have died from other causes.

In addition to PFC Valdor John, twenty-two other Americans are rescued, and of these, two men die during the night. The remaining survivors are carefully transported back to Pyongyang by S.K. troops, and from there they are airlifted to Japan for treatment. The bodies of those killed are taken back for burial. These troops had been the POWs that the airborne had been dispatched to rescue. Information gathered by the survivors details the excruciating journey they endured on the trains that departed Pyongyang on the 17th.

In the 24th Division sector, the British Brigade departs Pyongyang at noon and drives north along the road toward Sukch'on, where contingents of the airborne regiment are deployed. Unknown to the British, when they halt for the night, they are close to the beleaguered airborne troops who are heavily engaged. The heavy fire can be heard and it appears to be about three miles farther north. The Commonwealth troops join the fight at dawn.

— *In North Korea:* The Communists make a radio broadcast proclaiming that Sinuiju, situated on the south bank of the Yalu River across from An-tung, China, is the new capital for Kim Il Sung's government; however, the surging U.N. advance will force the Communists to relocate in the mountains at Kanggye, where the terrain is perfectly suited for guerrilla tactics. It was in this general area (Kanggye–Manp'ojin) where the Koreans had based their operations against the Japanese occupation during World War II.

In Air Force activity, A C-47 aircraft operating in the vicinity uses a loudspeaker rather than bullets to convince about 500 enemy troops to surrender.

In other activity, Combat Cargo Command initiates the use of helicopters to evacuate wounded from Pyongyang. Fifth Air Force supports the 187th Airborne operation to intercept and rescue American POWs. Air Force helicopters (H-5s of the 3d ARS) evacuated about 35 paratroopers in what becomes the initial mission of helicopters in support of an airborne operation. In addition, 7 former POWs are also evacuated.

— *In Japan:* Continuing to speak with optimism, General MacArthur reiterates his praise of the previous day's airborne operation and notes that the "War is definitely coming to an end shortly." However, it is determined that the surprise airdrop is unable to isolate any large enemy units, nor any high-ranking North Korean officers. Information gathered from civilians explains that the chief N.K. officials had departed Pyongyang on October 12 and moved toward Manp'ojin at the Yalu River. Contrasting intelligence indicates that the N.K. government officials had evacuated the capital and moved to the mountains at Kanggye, about twenty air-miles from Manp'ojin.

October 22

In the X Corps area, 1st Marine Division sector, General O.P. Smith, USMC, issues a new plan to conform with the proposed X Corps boundaries. The Marines will deploy in the far southern portion of the corps zone (according to plan). X Corps is to extend from the Chongsanjangsi–Songjin line. Marine reconnaissance units come ashore on the 24th or 25th to select assembly areas, but the effort proves to be of no value, as General MacArthur, on the 25th, cancels the restrictions and orders the forces to proceed to the Manchurian and Soviet borders.

Information reaches General Smith that a dispatch (for the purpose of planning) had been delivered to X Corps indicating that the Americans would leave an occupation force in Korea, comprised of about one division. It also said that the X Corps commander would become commander of the forces. At this time, it is still thought that the final destruction of the enemy is close at hand.

In the Eighth Army area, At Pyongyang, Colonel Collier (Eighth Army staff) establishes Advance Eighth Army Headquarters in the building recently evacuated by North Korean Premier Kim Il Sung. Kim Il Sung had departed in hasty fashion, but a large portrait of Stalin still hangs on the wall.

The 3rd Battalion, 187th RCT (Airborne), continues to battle the N.K. 239th Regiment while it awaits reinforcements. In conjunction, the 24th Division continues to close fast. The spearhead unit is the British Brigade.

In other activity, General Walker now believes that the U.N. forces have more ammunition than will be required to complete the destruction of the North Korean Army and terminate the war. Walker asks General MacArthur to authorize re-routing any additional ships that are transporting bulk-loaded ammunition en route to Korea; Walker wants to divert them to Japan. MacArthur concurs and he initiates action that intercepts six ships transporting 105-mm, 155-mm and Air Force bombs. The vessels are diverted to either Hawaii or back to the States.

A primitive road several miles south of Sunchon. Note the one-way sign on the solitary tree.

The commanding officer, Japan Logistical Command, Major General Walter Weible, requests that the commanding general, San Francisco Port of Embarkation, take action to abort fulfilling all pending requisitions for ammunition (pertaining to ground troops). The request also asks that all loaded ships remaining in port be unloaded. The aura of victory is overtaking all levels of the U.S. Armed Forces in the Far East at this time, and many of the troops expect to be departing Korea in the near future.

In the I Corps area, Company C, 6th Medium Tank Battalion, is designated Task Force Elephant. It departs Pyongyang and shoots through Sunchon to reach the railroad at Kujang-dong to intercept any enemy trains that arrive there. The objective is reached at 2200. From Sunchon, the task force, trailed by the S.K. 1st Division, moves west toward Kunu-ri, sometimes referred to as Kaech'on, in the Ch'ongch'on valley. En route, forty American GIs who escaped from the death trains are rescued by the South Koreans. The ROKs immediately transport them back to Pyongyang.

In the 1st Cavalry Division sector, The 7th Cavalry arrives at Chinnamp'o, thirty-five miles southwest of Pyongyang and is assigned the task to hold the port city.

In the 24th Division sector, the Argyll 1st Battalion moves out at dawn to relieve the pressure against the 3rd Battalion, 187 RCT. It moves into Yongju. Then the Australian 3rd Battalion, commanded by Lt. Colonel Charles Green, passes through its lines and initiates the advance. Company C, commanded by Captain A.P. Denness, takes the point. Bolstered by the tanks of Company D, 89th Tank Battalion, the contingent moves quickly, but slightly north of the town, the column approaches an apple orchard on both sides of the highway. The apples trees are permeated with enemy troops. The North Koreans commence fire from the orchard, and the Australians spring from their perches aboard the U.S. tanks and bolt into the orchard to shred the enemy in a brutal close-quartered battle.

One of the Australians, described as a rather large man with red hair, dives into an entrenchment and ignites a lightning-quick squabble. When the noise subsides and the battle ends, only the Australian trooper emerges from the trench, looking much different than when he entered it. His uniform is splintered and blood is running from his hands, caused by innumerable cuts. Eight deceased North Koreans remain in the foxhole.

In the meantime, more enemy fire erupts from another cluster of enemy troops. Colonel Green dispatches another company to meet this threat that emerges from the heights to the right of the highway. A third company sprints to the ground that lies left of the highway to bolster Company C. Green then leads his headquarters contingent directly into the orchard, and they, too, become heavily engaged.

Meanwhile, the enemy commits mortars to supplement its automatic weapons and rifle units. Undaunted, the Australians penetrate deeper into the bush, pressing their rifles and bayonets into as many of the enemy as possible. Grenades are also used as the Americans'

cousins punch their way through the enemy defenses. Green's small headquarters contingent is struck by a strong force, but it is quickly cut down to size. Thirty-four North Koreans are killed and the Australians sustain only three wounded. The Australians whack the enemy and send the survivors into flight.

The close-quartered battle costs the enemy a total of about 270 troops killed, and the Aussies collect an additional 200 prisoners during the morning confrontation. The Australian Battalion sustains about seven wounded and none killed.

Following the battle in the apple orchard, the Middlesex Battalion moves through the lines of the Australian 3rd Battalion and supported by tanks, it advances.

At 1100, the Middlesex Battalion establishes a link with the 187th RCT (Airborne). In conjunction, the 187th Regiment's 3rd Battalion had scored success against the enemy at Yongyu. The 3rd Battalion, 187th RCT, reports that the enemy it faced had sustained 805 killed and 681 others captured. The combined thrust of the Americans and the Commonwealth Brigade has nearly wiped out the N.K. 239th Regiment.

Later, during the afternoon, the 3rd Battalion, 187th RCT, moves back to Sukch'on, trailed by the British Brigade. Once there, the British Commonwealth Brigade relieves the 187th RCT (Airborne). The British then push on toward Sinanju. During the evening, some 24th Division forward elements arrive in an assembly area north of Pyongyang and assume control of the British 27th Commonwealth Brigade, the 90th FABn, and the 89th Tank Battalion.

In the ROK area, enemy guerrilla forces continue to operate behind Eighth Army lines. On this day, a South Korean force, composed of more than fifty soldiers and police, are driven from the Hwach'on Dam, located north of Wonju in central Korea above the 38th Parallel. The guerrillas unlock the valves and by the following day, the Pukhan River rises by several feet. It causes damage downstream. S.K. troops recapture the dam on the 25th.

In the ROK II Corps area, the S.K. 6th Division continues its rapid advance and begins to close against Kunu-ri, about 45 air miles north of Pyongyang.

October 23 *In Naval activity,* the USS *Mount McKinley* ventures into the inner harbor of Wonsan, a signal that the minesweeping operation is finally nearing its welcome conclusion. Admiral Doyle directs the fleet to arrive on the 25th. The order terminates the dubious Operation YO YO, to the relief of the men aboard the ships. The transport group is to enter first, trailed by the tractor group.

In the X Corps area, the Advanced Group JTF 7 reports that the channel leading into Wonsan is secure to Blue-Yellow Beach, but the report also indicates that the beach area must still be cleared.

In the 1st Marine Division area, two helicopters (VMO-6), piloted by Captain Wallace Blatt and Lieutenant Chester Ward, arrive at Wonsan from Kimpo.

The bulk of the remainder of the squadron is en route by LST, but one Echelon unit, commanded by Captain Victor Armstrong, temporarily remains at Kimpo to assist in the evacuation of wounded men of the 187th Airborne Task Force, which is engaged in the vicinity of Sukch'on. Fifth Air Force has requested the aid of the Marine helicopters.

In the Eighth Army area, General Walker assumes personal command of the Advance Eighth Army Headquarters. He informs General Coulter that IX Corps will be relieved by the ROK III Corps no later than November 10, thereby freeing IX Corps to drive into North Korea.

At Kunu-ri, two GIs who escaped from the Communists straggle into the lines of Task Force Elephant, but again, many more are not so lucky. Later during the afternoon, a South Korean sergeant (S.K. 6th Division) discovers the bodies of twenty-eight additional American soldiers (POWs) along the railroad tracks about four miles north of Kujang-dong. Three other soldiers are found alive.

In the Airborne zone, the 187th RCT departs the Sukch'on–Sunchon area and returns to Pyongyang, but it does not use the main road, which is reserved for the British Brigade and the 24th Division. Since October 20, when the 187th Combat Team began its operation, it has achieved excellent success. The unit captured 3,818 enemy troops while ravaging the N.K. 239th Regiment. The operation costs the Airborne Regiment 111 casualties, but of these, sixty-five are jump injuries.

Colonel Bowen, the 187th Regimental Combat Team commander, will be promoted to brigadier general. Colonel George H. Gerhart, the regimental executive officer, becomes the CO of the 187th Airborne Regiment. Also, Colonel William J. Boyle, the 2nd Battalion, 187th RCT, commander, will be replaced by Colonel John P. Connor. Colonel Munson, wounded during the operation, returns to take command of the 3rd Battalion, 187th, after he recuperates.

In the I Corps area, 1st Cavalry Division sector, General Gay appoints Colonel Marcel B. Crombez, commanding officer, 5th Cavalry Regiment, to the position of civil assistance officer for the city of Pyongyang. Crombez is familiar with Korea and its citizens. Colonel Harold K. Johnson (previously CO, 3rd Battalion, 8th Cavalry) succeeds Colonel Crombez as the CO of the 5th Cavalry until December 14.

In other activity, during the morning, the S.K. 1st Division, operating to the rear of the 1st Cavalry Division, departs Kunu-ri and advances down the Ch'ongch'on valley, which is much larger than most of the valleys in Korea. Its width ranges between three and twenty miles. When the column nears Anju, its supporting tanks (Company D) capture one enemy T-34 and knock out two other T-34s and two self-propelled guns. Once the enemy armor is reduced to scrap, the force resumes its advance and leaps forward to reach the wooden bridge at the river several miles northeast of the town. Just before noon, one platoon of tanks commandeers the bridge and gains access over

the Ch'ongch'on River. Between this day and the 24th, the S.K. 1st Division crosses the Ch'ongch'on River at Anju and at several other seized crossing sites.

In the meantime, another contingent of tanks continues moving farther downstream to Sinanju and discovers it abandoned by the enemy. The bridges there are out. Without fanfare, repair to the Anju bridges begins. By the following morning, vehicular traffic begins to cross the Ch'ongch'on River.

The Ch'ongch'on and its tributaries, the Kuryong and Taeryong Rivers, each flowing from the north, mold the final dominant water barrier in the Eighth Army field of operations south of the North Korean border. The Ch'ongch'on River will prescribe the greater part of Eighth Army's tactics and troop deployment strategies in the latter part of October through November.

In the 24th Division sector, the British Brigade arrives from Sukch'on at Sianju, several hours after the arrival of the tanks that are supporting the S.K. 1st Division. The British contingent also seizes an airstrip about five miles southeast of the town. Meanwhile, the 24th Division, pursuant to orders, concludes its twelve-mile northward advance from the Pyongyang vicinity to Sunan.

The Division has not arrived in time to rescue General Dean. As reported by Korean civilians, General Dean had indeed been at Sunan and from there shifted farther north before the arrival of the Americans. Up to this time, Dean's fate had been unknown.

In the ROK Army area, ROK I Corps, on or about this day, elements of the Chinese XIII Army Group arrive in the vicinity of Sudong. The 370th Regiment is the first unit to arrive, followed by the 371st and 372nd Regiments that come into the area during the next few days. The Chinese have apparently crossed the Yalu River near Manp'ojin on about the 14th or 16th.

In the ROK II Corps area, the S.K. 6th and 8th Divisions, operating on the U.N. right in conjunction with the advance of I Corps (on the left), advance swiftly despite the mountainous terrain. The S.K. 6th Division whacks its way through the mountains and has seized two enemy trains near Kunu-ri. Eighth enemy tanks are aboard one of the trains. The S.K. 6th Division surges forward, and near Kujang-dong, another bonus is found, fifty boxcars, each crammed with ammunition. The S.K. 6th Division encounters stiff resistance outside of Huich'on. Nonetheless, the South Koreans drive from the south and overwhelm the enemy force, estimated to be regimental strength. During the night (23rd), they drive into Huich'on and seize supplies and equipment, including twenty T-34 tanks, each in need of only slight repairs. From Huich'on, the division swings west and advances toward Onjong, located about ten air-miles northeast of Unsan. Meanwhile, the S.K. 8th Division reaches Tokch'on at midnight (23rd-24th) and from there, it pivots north and grinds toward Kujang-dong at the Ch'ongch'on River.

In Air Force activity, planes attached to Combat Cargo Command for the fourth consecutive day deliver supplies, ammunition and equipment to the paratroopers. The Flying Boxcars (C-47s), in the four-day period, have dropped about 600 tons of supplies in addition to the 4,000 paratroopers of the 187th Regimental Combat Team.

October 24　Off Wonsan, a conference is held aboard the USS *Missouri* to decide when to debark the Marines. Admirals Struble and Doyle and General Almond conclude that the Marines will debark at Yellow and Blue Beaches, as originally designed by Marine Division OpnO 16–50. The landing is scheduled for the morning of the 26th. It is also decided at the meeting that the minesweepers, subsequent to securing the inner harbor at Wonsan, would proceed to Hungnam and clear the channels there.

Apparently, the task becomes much more difficult and more dangerous than anticipated. The inner harbor area is not fully secured by the minesweepers until November 4. Wonsan is to be utilized as a supply base. In conjunction, the Hungnam mine-clearing operation, required to support X Corps in northeast Korea, is equally hazardous.

Also, VMF-312, while operating out of Wonsan, detects a plump enemy column tramping along a road about 39 miles south of the airfield. The pilots dive and attack, spewing relentless fire upon the estimated 800-man contingent. The pounding is incessant and registers hit after hit, while the Communists seek refuge from the hell-fire, but there is little chance for escape and no entrenchments to offer shelter. The planes dive in near-overlapping layers and ravage the enemy columns with cogent fire that decimates the ranks. The fire disperses the remnants and speeds their retreat.

In other activity, while the Marines at sea fare badly aboard the crammed ships, several special guests, including "Thanks For The Memories" Bob Hope and the USO, arrive at Wonsan by air to entertain the troops. Hope's entourage beats the Marines to Wonsan, and much of his humor during the USO show is pointed to the seafaring Marines.

In other activity, Marine pilots report coming under fire from positions in Manchuria.

In the Eighth Army area, Eighth Army contingents cross the Ch'ongch'on River, penetrating the sole remaining primary river standing between Eighth Army and the Chinese border. It has been about four weeks since the seizure of Seoul. Subsequent to the breakout at the Pusan Perimeter, Eighth Army has driven 160 air-miles north of Seoul, seized the Communist capital at Pyongyang and played a key role in ravaging the remaining North Korean fighting units. Eighth Army has undergone a remarkable transformation since the invasion of Inchon less than six weeks ago. The combined thrust of Eighth Army and the ROK forces have catapulted the front lines 300 miles northward to enter the enemy's back yard and place them close to the Yalu River and China.

In other activity, advance contingents of the Netherlands Battalion and the British 29th Brigade arrive in Korea.

In the I Corps area, 1st Cavalry Division sector, at Anju, the S.K. 1st Division completes its crossing of the Ch'onch'on River. The ROKS move northeast to seize Unsan. Trucks begin to roll across the repaired bridges at 0900. The tanks of the 6th Medium Tank Battalion discover a crossing site east of the bridge and ford the river there.

In the 24th Division sector, The 1st Battalion, British Middlesex Regiment, boards assault boats and crosses the Ch'ongch'on River at Sinanju. The primary Pyongyang Road crosses the river there and leads west and northwest to Sinuiju, on the coast at the North Korean border. The remainder of the Commonwealth Brigade and its vehicles wait until nightfall to cross over the bridge at Anju. In conjunction, engineers continue to repair and prepare the terrible roads for carrying the bulk of Eighth Army's logistical support units, a prerequisite if the attack to the Manchurian border is to be sustained.

In the ROK Army area, I Corps sector, the I Corps has been driving swiftly through the mountains in the eastern sector of Korea, and with its capture of Wonsan, X Corps's debarkation there is switched from an amphibious invasion to an administrative landing.

In the ROK II Corps area, the South Korean 6th and 8th Divisions continue to make progress. The S.K. 6th Division, having pocketed Huich'on on the previous night, drives toward Ch'osan at the Yalu River, about sixty air-miles away. This fast-paced drive places the unit far in advance of all other divisions, including the Americans. The march heads west, but then the division swings north to reach its objective. During the night, the 7th Regiment moves through Onjong, then pivots and races north to catch up with its forward battalion. Ch'osan stands at the Yalu about fifty air-miles away.

— *In Japan:* In Korea, the advance forces of the U.N. command are crossing the Ch'ongch'on River. General MacArthur issues a new order to his commanders in Korea, which removes the previous restrictions on the northward advance to the Yalu. He directs all participating units to implement maximum force and drive to the Yalu River. In reaction, the JCS send a memorandum to MacArthur, stipulating that his order is in direct conflict with the initial orders of September 27 concerning the U.N. advance, but the message does not countermand MacArthur's order. It merely requests an explanation. MacArthur responds to the JCS on the following day.

October 25　*In the X Corps area,* Corps issues OI (Operation Instructions) 13, but a copy of it does not reach General O.P. Smith until the 27th. The Marines' area of operations stretches fifty miles wide and runs 300 miles north to south.

In the 1st Marine Division area, finally, after seven trying days of cruising up and down the Yellow Sea, the transports move into Wonsan harbor and drop anchor to the jubilation of the 1st Marine Division, which is anxious to set foot on ground. But, the approaches are not totally secured until the latter part of the afternoon, which causes many of the Marines to be treated to yet another day of Navy hospitality (and some seasickness). The main body debarks on the following day.

During the evening, five LSTs arrive at the beach (Kalma peninsula). Contingents of Combat Service Group, Engineer and Shore Party, debark. Advance elements have been ashore for about nine days, and they have used Korean laborers to prepare for the landing.

Tonight, Shore Party Group C, commanded by Major George A. Smith, takes responsibility for Yellow Beach. Shore Party Group B, commanded by Major Henry Brzezinski, takes control of Blue Beach. The task of debarking X Corps is hefty and many of the heavy-laden amphibious craft are unable to pass through the shallow water. The shore parties fabricate ramps, composed of sand-filled rice bags, which stretch about thirty feet into the water.

X Corps directs the 1st Marine Division to relieve the South Korean units at the Chosin and Fusen Reservoirs and to deploy one RCT where it can focus on the Hamhung area, about 50–60 air-miles south of the reservoirs. In other activity, reconnaissance units, which had cleared the channel during the past several days, have selected various assembly areas for the Marine regiments. One of the locations is the Saint Benedict Abbey, near Wonsan, which had been selected for the 7th Marines to give the unit a good jump-off spot for its drive north.

In the Eighth Army area, toward the latter part of October, the Far East Command has altered the ratio of South Korean troops assigned to U.S. divisions. The previous figure of 100 men per company is lowered to twenty-five per company. The new procedure releases several thousand South Korean troops for reassignment to the South Korean Army.

In other activity, Army is informed of the capture of a Chinese soldier and the probability that tens of thousands of Chinese soldiers are now positioned to block the northward advance.

In the I Corps area, at 1600, Corps circulates its orders calling for the advance to the Yalu River. The attached S.K. 1st Division is to continue the mission of destroying the remaining North Korean troops in the sector. However, the Chinese have already crossed the Yalu and as the order is being published, they are already on the attack against U.N. forces.

In other activity, S.K. General Paik, the 1st Division commander, is informed about the intervention of the Chinese while he is attending a celebration in Pyongyang. He rushes back to his command post at Yongbyon, and soon after, he moves forward to inspect the enemy dead. His conclusions make it irrefutable that the force is Chinese, and he so informs General Milburn, I Corps Commander. Paik had previously served with the Japanese Manchurian Army during World War II, where he became knowledgeable of the Chinese.

In the 24th Division sector, the British 27th Commonwealth Brigade maintains its advance throughout the day. Later, during the evening, the unit crosses the Taeryong River, at Pakch'on. Once on the west bank of the river, the British progress is slowed by opposition.

In the ROK Army area, the S.K. 9th Division, composed of the 28th, 29th and 30th Regiments, each containing two battalions, is established today. By the end of the month, additional forces will be attached to become the 3rd Battalions of the respective regiments of the newly activated 9th Division.

The S.K. 1st Division continues its advance. It has units spread out on the road that runs between the Ch'ongch'on River and Unsan. The 15th Regiment, spearheaded by tanks of Company D, 6th Medium Tank Battalion, advances without incident to Unsan, about fifteen air-miles north. The forward contingent of the column passes through the town and continues the advance. The column gains about one and one-half additional miles and is about to cross a bridge when suddenly it is struck by a storm of enemy mortar fire.

The South Korean troops spread out and engage the enemy, estimated to be about 300 Chinese. After a short while, the South Koreans capture one Chinese soldier, the first Chinese troop to be seized. The soldier informs his captors that 10,000 Chinese are dispersed in the hills north and northwest of Unsan, and he also states that another 10,000 Chinese Communists are deployed east of the town. Apparently, Chinese 39th Army units are on the move against Unsan. The South Koreans continue to battle the Chinese throughout the afternoon.

The TACP controller has been under constant fire and unable to establish communications with the Mosquito plane in the area, but eventually the hook-up is made. Shortly thereafter, news of the arrival of large numbers of Chinese troops is sped to Eighth Army. The captive is taken to Pyongyang and interrogated there on the following day.

In the meantime, the S.K. 12th Regiment, the second unit in the advancing column, reaches Unsan, but it swings west. It also encounters Chinese troops soon after it exits the town. Fighting erupts at the enemy roadblock. The trailing 11th Regiment halts short of the town and establishes a night perimeter. The battle north of Unsan continues tenaciously throughout the day and into the night.

In the ROK I Corps area, The S.K. 3rd Division and the Capital Division advance north, the former toward Changjin Reservoir and the latter along the coastal road. Elements of the S.K. 3rd Division reach two hydroelectric plants of the Changjin Reservoir, the midway point from the reservoir. After dark a prisoner is taken who states that he is from the 5th Regiment, Chinese 8th Army. Also, south of the Changjin Reservoir, elements of the Chinese 124th Division, 42nd Army, engage contingents of the S.K. 26th Regiment. It is the 42nd Army that will soon engage the 1st Marine Division in the vicinity of Sudong. This entire day has been exceptionally cold, and during the early morning hours of the following day, the troops will witness the first snowfall of the season.

In the ROK II Corps area, the S.K. 6th Division

maintains its quick advance during the morning, but it pauses at Kojang about eight air- miles from Ch'osan. The ROKs prepare to attack Ch'osan on the following day. Also, the 3rd Battalion, 2nd Regiment, S.K. 6th Division, composed of about 750 troops, departs Onjong and drives northwest toward Pukchin. A KMAG advisor, Lieutenant Glen C. Jones, is with the battalion. It advances about eight miles and encounters enemy fire. The South Koreans are about to find out first-hand that the Chinese have entered the war.

South Korean troops jump from the vehicles to eliminate the obstacle, thought to be remnant North Korean troops, but the foe is the Chinese 40th Army and the ROKs have entered a deadly trap. The Communist Chinese nearly wipe out the battalion. Only about 400 ROKs evade death or capture and are able to make it back to Onjong. Stragglers move back into the town during the afternoon. Lieutenant Glen Jones is captured and dies in a Communist prison camp.

When troops at Onjong hear about the encounter with the Chinese, the 2nd Battalion, 2nd Regiment, S.K. 6th Division, speeds to support the 3rd Battalion. En route, it detects enemy movement in the heights to the north. Patrols are immediately dispatched, and during the mission, the troops capture another Chinese soldier. The Communist captive bears even more bad news. He in-

An ROK minesweeper hits a mine off Wonsan.

forms the South Koreans that the Chinese have been implanted in the hills around Pukchin since October 17, waiting for the U.N. forces. Soon after, as elements of the battalion advance farther along the road, another Chinese soldier (seriously wounded) is captured.

The Chinese stake out the approaching 2nd Battalion and isolate it, but the South Koreans extricate themselves from the trap and make it back to rejoin the 1st Battalion and regimental headquarters in Onjong. In the meantime, the S.K. 8th Division arrives at Kujang-dong during the night (25th-26th). On the following day, it swings north and marches up the Ch'ongch'on Valley to hook up with the S.K. 6th Division at Huich'on.

In Air Force activity, Far East Air Force, which initiated the use of B-29s against enemy targets the previous June, on this day suspends combat flights for its B-29s. The bombers have run out of lucrative targets. In other activity, restrictions on close-air support missions near the Yalu River are removed. This action frees pilots and permits the fighters to increase their fields of attack as far north as the border with China. Also, Combat Cargo Command on this day delivers 1,767 tons of equipment to various locations within Korea to set a new record for deliveries on a single day.

— ***In the United States:*** The Department of the Army informs General MacArthur that the scheduled transfer (October and November) of enlisted reserve corps troops from the States to the Far East is to be canceled, but the dispatch of 17,000 NCOs will proceed as scheduled.

— ***In Japan:*** General MacArthur, responding to the message from the JCS on the previous day, informs the JCS that the new directive ordering the advance to the northernmost border of Korea is of "military necessity." MacArthur also explains that the South Koreans are incapable of carrying the mission by themselves, and he believes he has enough leeway in the present directives to issue the order extending the area of advance. General MacArthur also informs the JCS that the entire matter of the advance to the Yalu had been covered at the Wake Island Conference.

Fifth Air Force is authorized to fly certain missions up to the Yalu River to afford ground troops close support, but the planes are forbidden to bomb any targets within five miles of the border. Nonetheless, missions that encroach the Manchurian border continue to come under close scrutiny and must be overseen by a tactical air control party or a Mosquito observer.

October 26 *In the X Corps area,* at the first glimpse of daylight, the transports off Wonsan are especially animated as the Marines clog the decks and begin their long-awaited descent to the landing craft. Thirty-nine waves are set to hit the beaches in an administrative landing on what has finally become D-Day, dubbed "Doyle Day" by General Almond. At 0730, tanks (1st Tank BN., USMC), adapted with deep water apparatus, burst from the bellies of LSUs, crash through the waves and come to rest on the beach.

At about the same time, the 1st Amphibian Tractor Battalion moves onto the beachhead to deliver men and supplies. The seemingly unending line of landing craft continues to pour men and equipment onto the beaches. At 0900, the 1st and 3rd Battalions, 1st Marines, sprint from LSTs and land on Yellow Beach, while headquarters (1st Marines), aboard the USS *Noble,* arrives on other landing craft. Colonel Puller's 2nd Battalion (Reserve), 1st Marines, remains aboard ship until the 28th. The rifle units of the 1st Battalion, 1st Marines, depart at 1200 by train for Kojo, a little seaport town about forty miles down the coast. It remains unscathed by the hostilities.

Another train, carrying reinforcements and supplies, will depart for Kojo on the following day. Upon arrival at Kojo, the 1st Battalion, 1st Marines, begin to replace the South Korean troops and take responsibility for the supply depot. Unknown to Lt. Colonel Hawkins, the supplies have dwindled as the South Koreans have expended nearly everything in the depot. By 1700, the 3rd Battalion, 1st Marines, establishes its night positions near Wonsan.

In other activity, Colonel Puller is informed by General O.P. Smith that he has been selected for promotion to brigadier general.

While the 1st Marines are landing, advance contingents of the 5th Marines (Reserve) begin landing at 0800 on Yellow and Blue Beaches; however, the majority of the regiment (minus 2nd Battalion and some reconnaissance units) comes ashore on the following day.

The 7th Marines lands on Blue Beach and then advances north of Wonsan to assemble around Saint Benedict's Abbey, which was recently ravaged by the Communists during their retreat. Colonel Litzenberg establishes his command post there at 1300.

Also, the 2nd Battalion, 11th Marines, and some reconnaissance units of the regiment land on this day, but the majority of the artillery regiment debarks on the 27th. The remainder of the 11th Marines comes ashore on the following day. Later, during the night, two Marines are instantly killed when they attempt to pick up booby-trapped firewood on the beach. These are the only Marine casualties to occur on D-Day.

According to its schedule, Combat Service Group establishes its Class I, III, and V Depots, but other supplies (Class II and IV) arrive on the beach. This causes an enormous mix-up, which hinders the operation. About 1,500 to 2,000 Korean laborers are hired daily to untangle the supplies and issue them to the various units.

In the ROK area, the S.K. Capital Division, holding positions north of Hungnam, continues to drive northward utilizing three regimental combats teams, including a motorized cavalry regiment dubbed "The Flying Regiment" by General Almond. This cavalry unit speeds toward the border, supported by a tactical air control team of the 7th Division and by an LST that supplies it from sea. The cavalry drives northeast toward Songjin. Also, the 1st Regiment, Capital Division, advances toward P'ungsan.

An LVT, followed by an LCT, moves to the beach at Wonsan on 26 October. A C-54 in the right background is making its landing approach.

In the Eighth Army area, Army intelligence officers interrogate a recently captured Chinese prisoner at Pyongyang. He speaks no Korean, nor Japanese. Throughout the day, more information concerning the Chinese intervention pours into headquarters. It is concluded that the Chinese troops have been dispatched to assist the North Koreans to defend the border approaches. Intelligence also determines that "there is no indication of open intervention on the part of Chinese Communist forces in Korea."

Nevertheless, North of Unsan, the S.K. 1st Division remains entangled with Chinese forces and their presence is further confirmed when thirty dead Chinese troops are discovered. The S.K. 12th Regiment repels the Chinese west of Unsan and surrenders no ground. The 11th Regiment advances to bolster the 12th Regiment, but the Chinese envelop the rear and the S.K. 11th Regiment withdraws to eliminate the enemy unit that is cutting the main supply road south of Unsan. Unfortunately, the 11th Regiment fails to reduce the enemy force. Instead, it is shoved north to the fringes of Unsan.

Meanwhile, during the morning, the S.K. 15th Regiment is also forced to give some ground. It pulls back to more tenable positions. Lt. Colonel John S. Grow-

den, 6th Medium Tank Battalion, commanding officer, moves to prevent his armor from becoming jeopardized. Growdon orders Company D's tanks to retire and redeploy in the heights southeast of the town.

Also, the U.S. 10th Antiaircraft Artillery Group receives information concerning the new threat; it prepares for a possible withdrawal. At present, the U.S. 17th FABn, 10th AAG, and two companies of the 6th Medium Tank Battalion are supporting the S.K. 1st Division. According to S.K. intelligence, about one Chinese division is in action against the S.K. 1st Division.

In the ROK II Corps area, the S.K. 6th Division remains in position at Kojang, but it dispatches a reconnaissance patrol into Ch'osan. The reconnaissance unit, accompanied by Major Harry Fleming (KMAG advisor, S.K. 7th Regiment), advances into the town and observes enemy troops reaching the sanctuary of Manchuria by streaming across a small footbridge that spans the Yalu. The patrol establishes some machine gun positions to intercept the enemy column, but alters the line of fire to prevent the guns from firing into China.

In the meantime, the town is combed for enemy remnants before the patrol returns to Kojang. A small contingent is left behind to protect the artillery and hold the town until the following day, when the S.K. 7th Regiment is expected to arrive. A strange precedent is set by the reconnaissance patrol. On the 24th, General MacArthur authorized all U.N. units to drive to the Yalu. This patrol is the first unit to reach the river and it is also the final Eighth Army unit to advance to the Yalu.

In other activity, the S.K. 8th Division advances up the Ch'ongch'on valley en route to Huich'on to join the S.K. 6th Division. Also, at 0300 the Communists strike the South Korean positions at Onjong. The South Koreans attempt to flee, but officers halt the troops at the southeastern fringes of the town and restore order. Three KMAG advisors are with the regiment when the attack commences. The Communists pierce the lines at 0600, and the South Korean 2nd Regiment begins to abandon its lines and retreat. The regiment becomes disorganized.

The survivors move about three miles east and encounter a Chinese roadblock. Rather than fight their way through it, the South Koreans flee into the hills. Two American advisors escape, but a third, Captain Paul V. Liles, is captured by the Communists. About 2,700 troops of the regiment make it back to Ch'ongch'on, out of an initial force of 3,100 troops.

In other activity, the 10th Regiment, S.K. 6th Division (less one Battalion), and the 19th Regiment, S.K. 8th Division, are at Huich'on when the Chinese encounter the S.K. 2nd Regiment. The ROK II Corps' commanding officer, Major General Yu Jae Hung, orders the 1st Battalion, 10th Regiment, to remain in Huich'on while the other troops attack to reclaim the abandoned vehicles and weapons of the 2nd Regiment. The force moves west and reaches the general area on the 28th.

In other activity, the S.K. 7th Regiment, 6th Division, is deployed around Kojang. It prepares an attack for the following morning to occupy Ch'osan, but it is informed of the devastation of the 2nd Regiment by the Chinese and ordered to withdraw to rejoin the division. The order cannot be executed. Major Fleming (KMAG advisor) responds to the orders by informing ROK 6th Division that the regiment lacks ammunition, gasoline and food. Fleming requests an airdrop, but it does not arrive until 1100 on the 28th. By this time, the Chinese 38th Army has bolstered the Chinese 40th Army against the S.K. 6th and 8th Divisions at Onjong and Huich'on. The enemy then drives the ROK II Corps back to Kunu-ri.

October 27 *In the X Corps area,* the 1st Marine Division closes its command post on the USS *Mount McKinley* at 1000, and reopens it in a crusty Russian barracks about one mile north of Wonsan. General O.P. Smith receives his operational instructions (issued on 25th). The Marines are to secure the Wonsan beaches, relieve the South Koreans in the area and proceed north to the border with Manchuria. The instructions also direct the Marines to guard the Wonsan–Kojo–Majonni area, while dispatching patrols on all roads that head west in the zone of operations.

In addition, the Marines receive two orders; commit one engineering company to assist the South Koreans with repairs along the Yonghung–Hamhung railroad, and prepare a battalion landing team for debarkation at Chongjin, upon orders.

In other activity, the remainder of Colonel James Brower's 11th Marines (Artillery) debarks at Wonsan. The 2nd Battalion, which had debarked on the previous day, is assigned to the 1st Marines at 1715. The 1st and 3rd Battalions, 11th Marines, remain in assembly and await orders. The ongoing operation to unload supplies continues under difficult circumstances. Many of the landing craft, laden with heavy cargo, are unable to move into the beaches, compelling shore party personnel to fabricate piers that stretch about thirty feet from shore. Some other vessels get hung up on a nuisance sandbar and must be towed.

At Kojo, the South Korean troops, having been relieved on the previous day by elements of the 1st Battalion, 1st Marines, head north. Today, a second train departs Wonsan at 1330 to deliver reinforcements and supplies for the 1st Battalion, 1st Marines, at Kojo. The train arrives late in the afternoon following an uneventful trip. In addition, a convoy composed of vehicles from the 1st Battalion, the Motor Transport Battalion and Battery F, 2nd Battalion, 11th Marines, arrives from Wonsan. The convoy is further bolstered by the 1st Platoon, Company C, 1st Engineer Battalion, and a contingent of Company D, 1st Medical Battalion.

The area around Kojo remains tranquil throughout the day, but only on the surface. The South Koreans confer with Lt. Colonel Jack Hawkins concerning the perimeter that extends along a coastal plain for a distance of about 5,000 yards (diameter) and encompasses the terrain from the bay to a cluster of slight hills. Marines assume responsibility for the perimeter.

The Marines have been informed by the South Koreans that the enemy has confined its activity to sporadic raids to commandeer rice. Nevertheless, the 1st Battalion, commanded by Lt. Colonel Hawkins, takes extra precautions to secure the perimeter, including the vulnerable supply depot at the rail station, which is poorly positioned just south of Kojo on dangerously low ground. The depot is susceptible to attack from every point.

The bulk of the regiment deploys west of Kojo. However, Company B, commanded by Captain Wesley Noren, deploys south and southwest of Kojo atop several lumps of high ground amid the rice paddies. Extending east to west, the 1st Platoon holds the east slope of Hill 109, the 3rd Platoon takes positions in high ground south and west of the 1st Platoon, and the 2nd Platoon deploys on Hill 185. Company C holds positions about one and one-half mile north of Company B. The 2nd, 3rd and 1st Platoons, respectively, spread out from west to east. About 250 yards east of Company C, two platoons of Company A hold the ground. Its 3rd Platoon spreads out on the crest of Hill 117.

Colonel Hawkins establishes his command post

north of Company A's positions. The mortar platoon (4.2" mortars), commanded by Lieutenant Kaufer, shares the slope with Hawkins' command post. While the Marines are establishing their positions, the valley southwest of Kojo becomes flooded with refugees who are attempting to reach the port. Darkness arrives and prevents the Marines from inspecting the refugees to weed out enemy infiltrators, but Colonel Hawkins funnels them toward the peninsula northeast of Kojo to keep them isolated until morning.

However, it becomes apparent that some Communist troops have infiltrated the march to the sea. At about 1600, hostile fire strikes a detachment of Marines as they lay wire near Hill 185, and at about 1800, near Hill 109, enemy fire strikes a small detachment of Marines while they attempt to repair a stalled vehicle. The vehicles are abandoned.

At about 1900, another detachment comes under fire, but it retrieves the stranded vehicles. Aside from the minor skirmishes, the day passes without any obvious signs of organized resistance, but once darkness arrives, signs of the enemy emerge. The Marines also become acquainted with Korean cold weather. The heat of summer has faded and the first frost appears. The foxholes spaced around the perimeter of Company B each contain two men. One man attempts to get warm and rest while the other keeps vigil with his rifle.

Suddenly, the calm is shattered when the enemy launches simultaneous attacks against opposite ends of Company B's positions. Soon an equally devastating thrust is thrown against Company C.

These well-organized assaults are sprung from grenade-throwing distance in lightning-quick fashion. During the engagement, the enemy attempts to be cunning by using English. The soldiers bellow: "Come this way.... Don't shoot! We're friends." Shouts of warning fly from the foxholes, nearly in cadence with the explosion of the hostile projectiles. The tranquility is gone and the frost is forgotten as the Marines defend their positions. The 1st Platoon, Company B, holding the eastern slope of Hill 109, is struck quickly and the position is overrun. Seven Marines are slain before they get out of their sleeping bags.

At about the same time, the command post and the 3rd Platoon come under severe attack at several locations. In response, Marines launch mortars, including 60-mm and 81s, which closely pass over the defenders' heads to rivet the paths of the attackers. The mortars seal the entranceway and hold the line for the 3rd Platoon, but the pressure against the 1st Platoon continues to build. Once the tenacious skirmish winds down it becomes clear that the 3rd Platoon and the command post has held.

Later, the enemy mounts another fierce attack to dislodge Company B. Meanwhile, back on Hill 109, the enemy utilizes blaring whistles and brilliant flares as it methodically pounds the 1st platoon's positions. About 160 Communists attack and isolate an outpost position and overwhelm a squad deployed on the right flank.

All the while, the slugfest in the perimeter of Company C continues. The enemy, having gained positions about ten feet from the perimeter, lunges against the Marines' positions. The contingent pierces the lines, gains ground and isolates about twenty Marines. However, they persist, and eventually their actions throughout the night reunite them with their unit.

Although Company C is pushed back, it is only temporary. The troops soon recover the momentum and regain the advantage. And afterwards, for the remainder of the night, they repel every enemy attack. Although the horrendous night-long combat does isolate Companies B and C from the remainder of the battalion, the mortars incessantly pound the approaches and contribute greatly to keep the situation stabilized. Undaunted, the Communists continue to press the attacks.

At 2215, beleaguered Company B is the recipient of a repeat performance. The Reds again pound against the positions of the 3rd Platoon, led by Sergeant Matthew Monk, on the heights to the south and west of the tenuous positions of the 1st Platoon. The 3rd Platoon, bolstered by mortars and machine gun fire, slashes the attackers and thwarts the assault. However, the enemy, despite incurring severe casualties, presses relentlessly.

Meanwhile, the 1st Platoon (Company B) is shoved from its positions on the eastern slopes of Hill 109. When the unit withdraws, thirty troops are missing. Sergeant Clayton Roberts makes the extrication possible by singlehandedly holding the ground and covering the evacuation with a light machine gun. The 1st Platoon evades annihilation, but Clayton is encircled and slain. And the donnybrook continues within the positions of the 3rd Platoon, which is struck by another multi-pronged assault. Its left rear and front are simultaneously stung heavily.

Finally, at 2350, when it becomes inevitable that the positions are untenable, Captain Noren, CO, Company B, requests permission from battalion to pull back. Without hesitation, permission is granted. The three platoons are ordered to converge at a point where the railroad tracks meet the dike. At about midnight, while Companies B and C are exchanging heavy blows with the Reds, artillery (Fox Battery) arrives in the vicinity of Kojo and establishes positions northeast of the town on the beach by about 0200. The three beleaguered platoons, each exhibiting heavy discipline, maneuver to the point of convergence.

By 0215, the 2nd Platoon, having fought its way from Hill 185, is the last to arrive at the dike. Here the three Company B platoons regroup. Captain Noren, lacking an operative radio, instinctively forms a defensive circle that covers both sides of the railroad tracks at a point just south of Chonchon to thwart an anticipated attack.

Noren's instincts prove true, but in the meantime, the artillery of Fox Battery prepares for fire. Noren's men combine spare parts and reactivate a radio, extending their chances of survival. The Reds strike from the east and from the west; however, Company B returns heated fire and firmly holds the line. By about 0300, radio contact is established between Noren and the mortar units, which provides the mortarmen man-made night vision. Under the guidance of Captain Noren, an avalanche of 61-mm fire disperses the enemy attack. Simultaneously, they deliver sheets of 81-mm mortar fire into Chonchon-ni.

By 0330, the Communists disengage and retire northward toward Kojo. One Marine is killed and six are wounded in the engagement. By about 0400, Fox Battery artillery registers, but its guns remain still. The battlefield known as Company B's area has become silent, and it remains quiet until dawn.

In the 7th Division sector, like the 1st Marine Division, the 7th Division has been stuck aboard ship and float-ing off Pusan for ten days. On this day, it receives or-ders and departs for Iwon, about 150 miles north of Wonsan. The initial plan of attack called for X Corps to drive west from Wonsan, but the situation has dras-tically changed and the attack will advance north toward the N.K. border at the Yalu River.

The 17th RCT, commanded by Colonel Herbert B. Powell, is scheduled to spearhead the landing at Iwon, and this causes logistics problems. The 17th RCT, which could encounter resistance at the new objective, unloads its equipment from the transports and reloads it on LSTs to enable it to overcome opposition on the beach. Seven LSTs, transporting the 17th RCT, leave Pusan, but in the meantime, South Korean troops pressing north by land have already secured the town. They continue the advance.

In the Eighth Army, 1st Cavalry sector, the attached S.K. 1st Division receives assistance. C-119s arrive from Ashiya Airbase, Japan, and deliver tanks of the 6th Medium Tank Bn. and fresh ammunition for the how-itzers of the U.S. support units. The S.K. 12th and 15th Regiments launch an assault and make some progress north and west of Unsan, while the 11th Regiment fights to secure the ground south of the town. The 11th Reg-iment secures the highway, then during the afternoon, it reports that the Chinese have withdrawn heading northwest.

In the 24th Division sector, the British launch an at-tack from their positions at the Taeryong River. The 1st Battalion, Middlesex Regiment, bolstered by ar-tillery, gains about three miles, but then it encounters fierce opposition. Artillery and air strikes are ordered to support the advance and the added muscle nets ten T-34s and two self-propelled guns destroyed. The tena-cious enemy resistance convinces the British Brigade commander, Brigadier General Coad, that daylight ad-vances will cease and that intense combat is imminent. Coad reverts to a different type formation, better suited to meet heavy opposition.

In the ROK I Corps area, The S.K. 3rd Division con-tinues to drive toward the Changjin Reservoir, but the resistance is becoming increasingly rigid.

In Air Force activity, planes (B-26s) attached to the 452nd Bomber Group are launched on their initial combat mission in Korea. The unit had been recently activated in the States.

October 28   On this day, the North Koreans again move General William Dean. He is taken in se-crecy to Manchuria and kept from being seen by any-one, even the Chinese. In a memoir written later, Gen-eral Dean recalls that the numerous flies in Manchuria are not bothered by the cold; "They just move indoors." He notes that during his captivity near Pyongyang he killed thousands of flies in one day.

In the X Corps area, 1st Marine Division sector, Divi-sion orders direct RCT-5 (minus 2nd Bn.), under the temporary control of RCT-1, to bear responsibility for Munchon and Yonghung, and Company A, 1st Tank Battalion (attached to 5th Marines), receives responsi-bility for the three primary roads that converge on the MSR from the west.

In the 1st Battalion, 1st Marines sector, the early morn-ing hours remain hectic, but the bulk of enemy activ-ity has subsided. At 0418, the 1st Battalion gets word by radio to the 7th Marines concerning the situation at Kojo, but communication remains poor. The 7th Marines, in turn, informs 1st Marines, which finally gets information to the 1st Marine Division. Compa-nies B and C, 1st Battalion, 1st Marines, each are greeted at dawn with a silent perimeter, but the Communists launch an assault against Hill 117, defended by Company A. One platoon, led by Lieutenant John Sword, repulses the assault.

Meanwhile, Company B reinitiates its withdrawal from Hill 109, slowed somewhat by the evacuation of its wounded. Marines attached to Company A help carry the wounded through the deep and muddy rice paddies coated by a slim layer of ice. The operation en-sues without incident, but suddenly, a contingent of enemy troops emerges from Kojo and heads west. The Marines do not pause to determine whether the Reds are moving to attack or trying to escape. Rather, the artillery, joined by the weaponry of Companies A and B, commence firing and kill about 75 of the estimated 200 Communists. The survivors scatter into the heights west of the town, hotly pursued by a contingent of C Company. Planes of VMF(N)-513 arrive at about 1035 to further terrorize the retreating enemy. Despite con-tinuing poor communications between the aircraft and the forward air controller, the planes swoop in low and deliver a powerful dose of fire.

At 1238, a report received at division headquarters de-scribes the ordeal of the 1st Battalion: "Received deter-mined attack from south north and west from sunset to sunrise by large enemy force. Estimated from 1,000 to 1,200 ... civilian reports indicate possibly 3,000 enemy this immediate area. Have suffered 9 kia, 39 wia, 34 mia, probably dead. Two positions overrun during night. If this position is to be held, a regiment is re-quired ... request immediate instructions. Send all avail-able helicopters for wounded."

Instantly, a decision is made to hold Kojo. Orders are drawn to dispatch Colonel Puller's 1st Marines and a reinforcing battalion. And to bolster the one offshore destroyer, a second destroyer is requested to be sent to Kojo. In addition to one hospital ship for casualties, an

LST is also requested to transport the tanks, which had been unable to make the land trip due to poor roads and bridges. The LST 883 embarks with the tanks, but the vessel gets snagged by a sandbar and is unable to reach the area until the following day. Helicopters are also dispatched to Kojo to evacuate wounded.

During the day, things brighten somewhat when seventeen Marines, listed as missing, make it to their lines safely. Several more are rescued later. By the 29th, accurate casualty figures become known.

The 1st Battalion continues to assess the situation, and all intelligence points to a heavy attack, expected to be launched after dark. Fresh reports arrive at division at 1415 and 1840, each delivering urgent information. The first dispatch mentions the possibility of 7,000 enemy troops of the N.K. 5th Division being near Tongchon. The second report, which arrives over the radio, indicates more dire news. It exclaims that the enemy is on all sides, except the sea, and that no reinforcements have arrived. Nevertheless, the 1st Marines hold the perimeter.

At 2230, reinforcements arrive on the first train to enter the area. But since 1000, there has been no action. A second train with reinforcements arrives within several hours. With the arrival of Colonel Sutter's 2nd Battalion, 1st Marines, and its supporting units, the 1st Battalion rests easier. The 2nd Battalion reinforcements establish night positions at Hill 117 and bunk with the 1st Battalion. Puller informs Division that the situation is well, and that no further artillery should be required.

Meanwhile, the Navy keeps the pressure on Kojo, initially with one destroyer, the USS *Hank,* and then with two when the USS *English* arrives and begins to plaster the town. Both vessels remain offshore throughout the night. The USS *Wantuck,* transporting medical personnel, rushes to the area, and VMO-6 dispatches six helicopters to the 1st Battalion positions. To keep the lid on the enemy, Marine Corps' planes pummel Tongchon throughout the day, reducing it to ashes.

In other activity, at 0800, division issues OpnO 18–50, which designates the tasks of the regiments. The 1st Marine Division is delegated to cover 15,000 square miles. It is imperative to deploy troops at Majon-ni, situated along the Imjin River and at a key road junction that spins east to Wonsan, west to Pyongyang and south to Seoul. The 1st Marines is to relieve the South Korean troops in the vicinity of Wonsan–Kojo–Majon-ni, establish blocking positions and dispatch patrols. The situation at Kojo creates some problems at Wonsan; the 2nd Battalion is required to move out of Wonsan to support the 1st Battalion.

Since the departure of the 3rd Battalion to Majon-ni to relieve South Korean troops there, no other 1st Marine units are available to patrol the roads or establish blocking positions at Anbyon. To remedy the situation, the 2nd Battalion, 5th Marines, and the 5th Korean Marine Battalion are attached to the 1st Marines and assigned the responsibility for patrol and blocking positions. The 1st Marines also receive additional muscle with the availability of the 1st Amphibious Tractor Battalion, Company B, 1st Armored Amphibian Tractor Battalion, and the 1st Shore Party Battalion. Each of these units can be utilized to protect the airfield and Wonsan harbor area.

The 1st Marines is to prepare to activate a battalion landing team for Chongjin. The 3rd Battalion, 1st Marines (reinforced), commanded by Lt. Colonel Thomas Ridge, arrives at Majon-ni at 1600 to relieve elements of the 26th S.K. Regiment. The ROKs are transported to Wonsan in the vehicles that had brought the 3rd Battalion.

The 3rd Battalion's mission is to establish defensive positions, keep the 28-mile highway to Wonsan open, dispatch patrols and prevent the enemy from using the roads there. The battalion is composed of the three rifle companies, headquarters and service (H&S) company and weapons companies, but it is bolstered by Battery D, 2nd Battalion, 11th Marines, 3rd Platoon, Company C, 1st Engineer Battalion, contingents of ANGLICO, 1st Signal Battalion, Company D, 1st Medical Battalion and H&S Company, 1st Marines.

Although there are extra troops, the area is rough and the dominating ground is far from the town. Ridge and his S-3, Major Joseph Thompson, decide that company outposts will be established only during daylight hours and that the battalion perimeter, with a circumference of 3,370 yards, will be heavily patrolled to maintain control of the three key highways. Colonel Ridge's command post is established in the local schoolhouse. The responsibility for the three roadblocks falls to Major Edwin H. Simmons' weapons company. Along with containing the enemy, Simmons' troops also bear responsibility for sorting out the Communist troops that pose as civilians.

In the meantime, the 5th Marines is to deploy to the rear of the 7th Marines (in the vicinity of the Hamhung–Chosin Reservoir Road), relieve contingents of the South Korean Army at the Fusen Reservoir and establish roadblocks. The 7th Marines is to relieve contingents of the S.K. I Corps along the Hamhung–Chosin Reservoir Road. Once the relief is complete, it is to push elements to the northern edge of the reservoir and to Changjin.

From these points, the 7th Marines is to prepare to drive to the northern border of Korea. This is a monumental and punishing task. The roads, except the key coastal route, are primitive mountain paths unsuitable for tanks or heavy vehicles. The 11th Marines (reinforced and minus detachments) is to assemble near Hamhung and await orders. Also, The 1st Marine Division gets its full complement of combat troops ashore by the end of this day.

In the ROK area, Capital Division sector, the S.K. Cavalry Regiment overcomes fierce resistance and seizes Songjin, 100 miles northeast of Hungnam. Also, the S.K. 1st Regiment, driving inland, encroaches P'ungsan at about the midway point from the Korean-Manchurian border along the Iwon–Sinch'ang-ni–Hyesanjin Road. Meanwhile, the ROK 18th Regiment advances toward the Pujon Reservoir.

In the Eighth Army area, reports about the Chinese units in Korea and their probable numbers continue coming into headquarters, but the information is not considered totally accurate. Nonetheless, General Walker and his staff become acutely aware of Chinese advances north of the Ch'ongch'on River. The original information extracted from prisoners and gathered from the field causes Eighth Army to modify its conclusions.

In other activity, the rails that lead to Seoul are opened, permitting trains to cross the Han River and reach the city, but by now, Eighth Army is beyond the capital. Some advance elements have reached points about 200 miles north of the Imjin River at Chonchon. However, the rails extend only into Munsan-ni at the south bank of the Imjin River.

In the 1st Cavalry sector, the attached S.K. 1st Division has forestalled an enemy rout in its sector. The skirmishing around Unsan subsides; however, the South Koreans capture two more Chinese troops. The drastic changes in the situation alarm General Walker. He orders the 1st Cavalry Division to relinquish its security mission at Pyongyang, immediately advance to Unsan, then pass through the S.K. 1st Division to launch an assault toward the Yalu River. General Gay orders the 8th Cavalry to spearhead the attack. It will depart Pyongyang on the following morning.

In the 24th Division sector, the British Brigade drives fifteen miles and reaches positions about three miles from Ch'ongju, then halts for the night and prepares to attack on the following morning.

In the 5th Regiment zone, the Regiment, trailing the British, crosses the Ch'ongch'on River, becoming the first 24th Division unit to cross it. The 5th Regiment pushes farther and crosses the Taeryong River. Then, from positions above P'akch'on and on the right of the British units, it drives north toward Taech'on.

In the ROK Army area, I Corps sector, South Korean contingents (S.K. 3rd Division) sustain heavy casualties as they drive against fierce enemy resistance near Sudong.

In the ROK II Corps sector, the S.K. 19th Regiment, 6th Division, and the S.K. 10th Regiment, S.K. 8th Division, each minus one battalion, reach the area of Onjong, the point where the 2nd Regiment had previously broken ranks and run. Neither makes any further progress. Both regiments have a minor enemy encounter on the 29th.

In other activity, the S.K. 7th Regiment, 6th Division, receives supplies by airdrop and prepares to withdraw south.

In Air Force activity, a recently captured airfield at Sinanju along the mouth of the Ch'ongch'on River is utilized by C-47s to evacuate wounded. The airfield, about forty miles north of Pyongyang, becomes the northernmost field used by the U.S. Air Force.

October 29 *In the X Corps area,* OpnO 18–50, issued by 1st Marine Division on the previous day, is altered. The 1st Battalion, S.K. Marines, is attached to

the 5th Marines and the 5th Battalion, Korean Marines, is attached to the 1st Marines. The security of Munchon and Yonghung, thirteen and thirty-two miles north of Wonsan, respectively, is delegated to the 5th Marines, bolstered by Company A, 1st Tank Battalion.

In the 1st Marines area, helicopters in support of ground troops initiate reconnaissance missions. Several Marines isolated by the previous fighting are rescued by Lieutenant George Farish's patrols. During the afternoon, the undisturbed bodies of twelve Marines are discovered when a patrol led by Captain Noren (Company B) arrives back at its previous positions near Hill 109. Later, Noren's detachment probes farther south and encounters enemy fire originating in the ruins of Tongchon. Marine planes arrive to assist. Twenty Communist troops hurriedly flee their positions; however, there is little chance of escape. Noren's patrol, bolstered by machine guns, shreds the enemy force and kills 16.

In other activity, patrols of Companies D and F enter Kojo and see first-hand the devastation inflicted by planes and naval surface vessel guns. No enemy presence is found. Nor does Company E's patrol encounter any enemy activity as it scours the terrain west of the town. General Craig and General Almond arrive at Kojo on this day and they conclude that the situation is stable.

Meanwhile, LST 883 arrives at Kojo, but it runs aground and must be nudged by a tug. Its cargo, ten tanks of Company C, 1st Tank Battalion, is no longer required and the LST returns to Wonsan. The bodies of nineteen Marines and seventeen enemy prisoners are brought aboard. Pilots of VMO-6 rush seven seriously wounded Marines from Kojo to a hospital transport vessel moored off Wonsan, and twenty-four other wounded are transported from Kojo to Wonsan. Marine casualties for the mission are 23 killed, 47 wounded and four missing in action. The estimates of Communist casualties are 250 killed and an indeterminable number of wounded. Marine patrols count 165 enemy dead and capture 85 men.

At Majon-ni, Ridge's 3rd Battalion maintains control of the roads. Civilians are halted and questioned at blockage points to weed out enemy troops. Today, 24 POWs are seized. This operation continues for seventeen days, and the average number of prisoners taken is 82 per day. A supply convoy arrives to supplement the 3rd Battalion, but it is the last one to safely make the trip for one week.

In related activity, 3rd Battalion patrols detect no enemy activity along the roads to Wonsan, Pyongyang, or Seoul. As a precaution, Major Simmons' weapons company continues to plaster suspected enemy positions, and the effort is coordinated with planes capable of spotting enemy targets and calling in air strikes. These missions, during the first four days, discover no enemy activity. However, prisoner interrogation sessions confirm the presence of the battered 15th N.K. Division and its components, including the 45th, 48th and 50th Regiments. The enemy division, commanded by Major General Pak Sun Chol, has been moving north from Seoul under orders to initiate guerrilla activity in the Imjin Valley and attempt to dominate the area. Intelligence, based on prisoner information, estimates that about 11,000 enemy troops are in the area.

In the 7th Marines sector, the Regiment, having only received some of its winter gear, departs Wonsan by overland route for Hamhung and completes the trek by the 31st. The 7th Marines is scheduled to be the vanguard for the advance to the northern border of North Korea. The full amount of cold-weather gear is received by the 7th Marines when they reach Koto-ri.

In the 7th Division sector, the 17th RCT, commanded by Colonel Herbert B. Powell, lands at Iwon without incident. The remainder of the Division follows later. The entire Division, except for the majority of its tanks, is ashore by November 8. Minesweeping operations prior to the landing reveal no mines. The 7th Division is also scheduled to drive to the northern border of Korea.

This day, the 1st Battalion, the 49th FABn, and Company A, 13th Engineer Battalion, move fifty miles from the beachhead and deploy at Cho-ri, from where the 7th Division is to begin its drive to the town of Hyesanjin at the border with Manchuria. The ROK I Corps, already on the move, is far ahead of other X Corps troops. The 3rd Infantry Division, due to arrive in Korea about November 8, is to relieve the 1st Marines units deployed south of Hamhung, and then the Marines are to advance to the Yalu.

In the Eighth Army area, the emergence of the Chinese Communists into the conflict and the near instant destruction of the ROK II Corps cause grave concern, and the rising number of confusing reports filtering into headquarters makes matters worse. General Walker releases the S.K. 7th Division from U.S. I Corps and attaches it to the faltering ROK II Corps, which is sustaining terrible routs by the Chinese. Army also directs the ROK II Corps to deploy the S.K. 8th Division north of the Ch'ongch'on River to establish defensive positions that stretch eastward from Yongbyon to Kujang-dong. From there, the S.K. 7th Division is to pick up the defensive line and string out to the south toward Tokch'on.

In the I Corps area, 1st Cavalry Division sector, the 8th Cavalry advances from Pyongyang and reaches Anju at the Ch'ongch'on River. It establishes a night perimeter at Yongsan-dong during the evening.

In the S.K. 1st Division sector, an attack is launched at dawn, but it is repulsed by the Communist Chinese. Fifth Air Force planes arrive to bolster the attack, but still the Chinese remain well-entrenched and raise resolute resistance. Due to the near destruction of the ROK II Corps, the S.K. 1st Division has become a key player in holding off the Chinese on the northern extension of the U.N. line. However, the S.K. 1st Division and the 24th Division, the nearest Eighth Army contingent to the west, are separated by fifteen miles.

In the 24th Division sector, the British initiate an attack to seize Ch'ongju; the Australian 3rd Battalion supported by some aerial assistance advances. Mean-

while, an observation plane spots enemy tanks and supporting North Korean troops. Air Force aircraft arrive and decimate four T-34s. The Australians (Argylls) then press forward and seize the pass and the ridges in front of the objective. At about 2200, the North Koreans launch a counterattack. They commit tanks and employ self-propelled guns. The Australians, indifferent to the danger, move up bazooka teams, and shortly thereafter, three additional T-34s are destroyed. Accompanying U.S. tanks join in and pour their fire into the enemy ranks. Enemy fire during the skirmish slays nine Australians and wounds thirty others. On the following day, the Australians move into Ch'ongju.

In the 5th Regiment zone, the Regiment, commanded by Colonel Throckmorton, drives closer to Taech'on and encounters strong North Korean resistance. Planes quickly arrive to support the advance. The combination of ground force and air power knocks out the resistance, giving the 5th Regiment control of Taech'on. Nine enemy tanks and four self-propelled guns are destroyed in the heated skirmish.

Eighty-nine prisoners are seized and of these, two are Chinese, but no Chinese units had engaged the 5th Regiment at Taech'on. The two Chinese POWs, apparently stragglers, are the first Chinese captured by American troops. From Taech'on, the 5th RCT drives northwest toward Kusong against a defending force of about 5,000 to 6,000 North Korean troops.

In the ROK Army area, I Corps sector, more tenacious fighting occurs near a Changjin Reservoir hydroelectric plant, located about thirty miles inland from Hungnam. The close-quartered engagement takes a toll on the South Koreans and a rapidly depleting supply of grenades adds to the problem. During the brutal struggle, sixteen additional Chinese are taken prisoner. They inform their captors that the Chinese 370th Regiment, 124th Division, 42nd Army, is deployed slightly north of the reservoir, and that the remainder of the division is at Hagaru, at the southern fringe of Changjin Reservoir. General Almond is informed of the Chinese POWs by S.K. General Suk Won Kim.

Also, sixty North Korean troops are captured by the S.K. 26th Regiment. Ironically, most of the enemy's mortars, machine guns, and Thompson submachine guns are U.S. issue, which had apparently been previously captured from the Nationalist Chinese. Also, the Chinese 124th Division, facing nasty mountainous terrain, has advanced into North Korea without transporting its artillery. The division's heaviest weapons are 82-mm mortars.

In the ROK II Corps area, the Chinese cut off the attacking units of the S.K. 19th and 10th Regiments and badly whip them. The ROKs lose all three of their artillery batteries and every vehicle in the column. The S.K. 7th Regiment, 6th Division, begins withdrawing from Kojang to reach the remainder of the division, but time has withered away and the Chinese wait in ambush. Almost immediately after the column gets underway, it encounters a roadblock, but this regiment attempts to fight its way through. Air support arrives to neutralize the enemy's power and it forestalls disaster. However, at dusk, when the fighter plane support ceases, the regiment is overwhelmed. Still, many South Korean troops hold their positions and tenaciously resist throughout the night. During the dark of night, many others vanish into the hills.

By dawn the South Koreans are thoroughly beaten. According to a document captured later, in March 1951, it seems as if only one battalion of the Chinese 373rd Regiment, 125th Division, had engaged and destroyed the S.K. 7th Regiment. Major Fleming, the only American to survive the battle, is wounded fifteen times and captured. Major Fleming survives his imprisonment by the Communists and is among the POWs exchanged in 1953. The other survivors, about 875 troops of an original number of 3,552, evade capture or death and make it back to Kunu-ri to rejoin the division. The regimental commander, Colonel Lim Bu Taik, and two of his battalion commanders escape, but the other S.K. staff officers and KMAG advisors are killed or captured.

October 30   *In the X Corps area,* at headquarters in Wonsan, General Almond briefs General Barr, 7th Division commander. Almond makes it clear that the 7th Division will drive to Hyesanjin on the Yalu River, while the Marines advance to the border via Chinhung-ni, Koto-ri and Hagaru. The 3rd Infantry Division is to assume responsibility for the rear. General Almond, pointing to the map and referring to the surge to the border, optimistically states: "When we have cleared all this out, the ROKs will take over, and we will pull our Divisions out of Korea." Major Henry J. Woessner, (S-3, 7th Marines) attends a portion of the briefing. Woessner makes a reconnaissance flight over the route of advance. (*See also, In the 7th Marines sector,* this date.)

In the 1st Marine Division sector, at Kojo, the division continues to maintain outposts across its front and probing patrols. During the past several days, Marines have recovered various pieces of equipment that had been abandoned earlier. Much to their surprise, nearly all the equipment is still operable. Relief contingents arrive at Kojo on the following day.

In other activity, engineers under 1st Lieutenant Leroy Duffy continue working to complete an OY landing strip along the eastern perimeter, but the effort is tedious because the valley, which contains a rugged cliff, is not suitable for accommodating planes.

In the 7th Marines sector, Major Henry Woessner takes an aerial surveillance flight aboard an Air Force plane and scrutinizes the expected route along which the 7th Marines will advance. The reconnaissance flight discovers no enemy forces, but it does reveal much rugged terrain that stretches along the MSR. Woessner informs Colonel Litzenberg of the various dangers that lurk along the route in the vicinity of Hamhung–Hagaru.

Litzenberg then calls a briefing meeting to inform the officers and NCOs of what might occur because of their actions. He states that they might be initiating the opening battle of World War III. And Litzenberg then emphasizes the point to his 7th Marines. "We can expect to meet Chinese Communist troops, and it is important that we win the first battle. The results of that battle will reverberate around the world, and we want to make sure that the outcome has an adverse effect in Moscow as well as Peiping."

In the ROK I Corps area, the elements of the S.K. Capital Division drive to positions just south of the Pujon Reservoir.

In other activity, along the coastal road, the S.K. Cavalry Regiment continues its advance. In its path stands an enemy force of about one battalion strength. The enemy contingent retires and heads north toward Kilchu, an inland town that is out of range of the U.S. naval surface gun fire. South Koreans give pursuit.

In the Eighth Army area, Army continues making progress, but logistically the situation is still poor. The railroad lines lack the distance to maintain pace with the rapid advance of the ground troops. In some instances, such as with the 24th Division, the trucks remain the beasts of burden. Their trips begin at the termination point of the divisional rail lines at Yongdungp'o south of the Han River and must move northward more than 200 miles, much of it along primitive paths, to reach and supply the units at Pakch'on. The unsung heroes of the motor pool are the mechanics who have kept the vehicles rolling nonstop for the past two months.

In the 1st Cavalry sector, the 5th Cavalry arrives at Yongsan-dong from Pyongyang. The regiment, commanded by Lt. Colonel Harold K. Johnson, is directed to guard the rear of the 8th Cavalry, which has now advanced to Unsan to relieve the pressure from the S.K. 1st Division.

In the 8th Cavalry zone, the 1st Battalion arrives at Unsan during the afternoon. Its commanding officer, Major John Millikin, meets with KMAG officers attached to the 12th Regiment, 1st S.K. Division, to discuss the situation. Millikin is informed of the condition of the divisional line, which is under tremendous strain. The line stands 800 yards north of Unsan but is being driven back by the surge of the Chinese.

Company C, 99th FABn, advances to bolster the 3rd Battalion, 8th Cavalry. Also, the enemy is beginning to set large fires in the mountains, seemingly to create hovering smoke to conceal Communist troop movement in the area. The 8th Cavalry relieves the S.K. 12th Regiment on the following day.

In the 24th Division sector, the Australian 3rd Battalion (Argylls), having defeated the defending enemy force outside the town, enters Ch'ongju. During the evening, the North Koreans bombard the town with an artillery barrage. The 3rd Battalion headquarters area becomes the recipient of six high velocity shells. One projectile, of the six that strike near headquarters, soars over the crest of a hill, smashes into a tree and detonates close to the commanding officer's tent. Although many troops are nearby, only one man is wounded, but it is fatal. One shell fragment plunges into Colonel Green's stomach. Green is rushed to Anju for emergency treatment, but he succumbs in three days. Lt. Colonel I.B. Ferguson succeeds Colonel Green as commanding officer, 3rd Australian Battalion. One other British officer, Major Reith, is killed by either enemy tank or artillery fire.

In other activity, British Brigadier General Coad informs General Church that the Commonwealth Brigade at Ch'ongju is extremely tired. He requests that a U.S. regiment leap-frog ahead of it. General Church orders the 21st Regiment to pass through the British Brigade and take the point. By dusk, the 21st Regiment passes through the British lines and advances north, observing many houses in Ch'ongju that are burning under the brightness of the autumn moon.

In the 5th Regiment zone, Throckmorton's 5th RCT continues to grind forward toward Kusong against stiff opposition, which includes tanks and self-propelled guns. Planes arrive to blast the enemy positions and provide support for the advance.

In the ROK I Corps area, General Almond arrives at Hamhung to speak with Chinese POWs held at the command post of General Kim Suk Won. The prisoners state that most of the troops in their parent unit, the 124th Chinese Division, had initially been in Chiang Kai-shek's Nationalist Army when it surrendered to the Communists during the Chinese Civil War that followed the close of World War II. General Almond informs General MacArthur of the presence of Chinese troops in northeast Korea.

In other activity, three battalions of the 1st Antiguerrilla Group are assigned to the newly activated S.K. 9th Division. One battalion is attached to each regiment as its 3rd Battalion.

October 31 U.S. aircraft are intercepted by Russian-made MiG-15s near Sinuiju, but these propeller driven craft engage and knock out several of the Communist jets. This is the first encounter between U.S. planes and MiGs, but it is not determined whether the enemy planes are piloted by North Koreans or by a possible "volunteer air force."

In other activity, ships attached to CTF-90 move to Moji, Japan, to begin to transport the 3rd Infantry Division to Korea. The first contingents of the 65th RCT arrive on November 5. Also, ComNavFE dissolves JTF-7. In conjunction, TG-95.2 Support and Covering Group now comes under the jurisdiction of CTF-90, commanded by Admiral Doyle.

In the 1st Marine Division area, Lt. General Lemuel Shepherd, Jr. arrives at Wonsan and meets with Admiral Struble, General O.P. Smith and General Almond at X Corps headquarters. It is ascertained at this meeting that Communist Chinese soldiers had been captured by South Korean troops near Hamhung. Information is also being gathered by the 1st Cavalry Division, since it is encountering Chinese troops in Western Korea.

Shepherd takes a helicopter to Kojo to make an aerial inspection of the perimeter. At 1430, the LST 973 arrives at Kojo and debarks the 5th Battalion, KMC

Regiment. On the following day, U.S. Marines begin moving to Wonsan.

Also, General Smith orders Colonel Murray, CO, 5th Marines, to dispatch one battalion to Chigyong, eight miles southwest of Hamhung. The 1st Battalion, 5th Marines, moves out, but one company is diverted and instructed to relieve a contingent of the 7th Marines at the advance supply point at Yonpo Airfield, about five miles southwest of Hungnam. The 1st Tank Battalion (minus Company C, attached to 1st Marines) departs for Munchon. Its Company A is already there.

The components of the 11th Marines, excluding the battalions attached to the RCTs, are deployed at Munpyong, about five miles northwest of Wonsan.

In the 7th Marines sector, a small patrol composed of three jeeps moves out on a reconnaissance mission to aid the upcoming advance. The contingent, led by Captain Myron Wilcox, stops at the ROK 26th Regiment's command post. When the patrol reports back, it informs headquarters that it encountered one Chinese prisoner at the ROK 3rd Division lines. Actually, the South Korean 26th Regiment has captured sixteen Chinese prisoners to date. The 7th Marines are scheduled to relieve the South Korean 3rd Division at Sudong on November 2.

In other activity, a patrol composed of five jeeps and twenty men moves toward Chigyong, but it encounters no enemy presence. Colonel Litzenberg believes he will be engaging Chinese forces soon. On the following day, he again sends out patrols.

In the 7th Division area, the 1st Battalion, 17th Regiment, and headquarters depart Cho-ri and move 70 miles to P'ungsan, about the mid-point between the landing site at Iwon and the ultimate objective, Hyesanjin. The journey is relatively quiet, as the 1st Regiment, S.K. Capital Division, has already advanced there, clearing the resistance as it moved.

In the Eighth Army area, General Walker gives General Milburn, I Corps commander, a verbal order to continue the attacks of the 24th Division within the limits of the fluid situation in the vicinity of Unsan, but some contingents penetrate farther than anticipated. These over-stretched units are quickly ordered to pull back.

In the 1st Cavalry Division sector, General Gay establishes his divisional command post at Yongsan, about twelve miles south of Unsan.

In the 8th Cavalry sector, the 2nd and 3rd Battalions relieve the 12th Regiment, S.K. 1st Division. Another South Korean unit, the 2nd Battalion, had been attacked during the night and forced to surrender more than one mile. But this battalion insists on regaining the ground before being relieved.

Later, General Milburn, I Corps commander, confers at the 8th Cavalry command post. It is agreed that the S.K. 2nd Battalion is stable. On the following day, it attacks to re-secure the lost ground.

In the 24th Division sector, the 21st Regiment continues its advance that began October 30 from Ch'ongju. The column moves cautiously along the eerie route.

Despite lack of sleep, the regiment still maintains alertness at 0200 as it reaches a point several miles west of Kwaksan.

Suddenly, dark shadows begin to come alive. Nearly 500 enemy troops concealed in the heights spring an ambush. The surprisingly bright illumination spotlights seven tanks that lurk along the road. At about the same time, the enemy infantry pours out menacing fire that rivets the column, and in concert, the point tank, standing about 300 yards away, spews a string of fire toward the 2nd Battalion. Soon the other T-34s commence firing. The roar of incoming fire galvanizes the troops, who instantly return heavy fire.

Unending strings of flying orange shells catapult from the posted T-34s to deliver the thunderclap from many angles, all converging near the American armor. Undaunted, the U.S. tanks immediately unleash their fire power. An avalanche of fire begins to spin directly toward the origin of the gun flashes to transform the ambush into a spectacular duel between nocturnal fireballs. But when the guns silence, it is the Communists who have been bushwhacked.

Most of the sheets of fire that swarmed into the area had failed to hit the mark and the few shells that struck the U.S. armor harmlessly bounced off without exploding, similarly to what happened to TF Smith when its ammo ineffectively bounced off the T-34s when the U.S. first encountered them back in July. Lt. Colonel Charles Smith, commanding officer of the 3rd Battalion, 21st Regiment, was the commander of Task Force Smith during that lopsided July battle.

The fighting remains heavy throughout the night, but at dawn's first light, the enemy is vanquished and the heights are free of North Koreans, as they have abandoned their positions and equipment. Five enemy tanks, seven antitank guns and one self-propelled gun have been reduced to twisted, charred metal. In addition, fifty dead North Koreans remain at the scene of the failed ambush.

The 21st Regiment resumes its march following the early morning battle and encounters only sporadic, minimal opposition. The 1st Battalion jumps ahead of the 2nd Battalion and leads the way. By noon on the following day, Lt. Col. Charles B. Smith's contingent reaches Chonggo-dong.

In the 5th Regiment zone, the 5th RCT forces the collapse of the defenders at Kusong and secures it slightly after noon. The combat team resumes its attack on the following day.

In the ROK I Corps area, General Almond again visits Hamhung and finds that seven more Chinese soldiers have been taken prisoner. They provide information that one more Chinese division is deployed near the Changjin Reservoir.

In the ROK II Corps area, the Chinese launch attacks against the ROK II Corps' defensive line, and pound against the positions north and east of Kunu-ri. The incessant attack cracks through the lines of the S.K. 16th Regiment, 8th Division, at a point near its boundary with the S.K. 1st Division. One battalion collapses

and runs for the hills. The Chinese Communists also hammer the S.K. 7th Division's lines south of the Ch'ongch'on River.

November 1   Marine Corps planes initiate nightly strikes against Sinuiju at the mouth of the Yalu River. These raids ignite incessant fires, but according to reports from the pilots, enemy vehicle traffic continues to flow south through the town. Pilots of VMF(N)-542, on a nightly basis, detect convoys that originate in Antung, Manchuria. The air-strikes continue until November 9 and all intelligence information is passed to Division G-2 Officers.

In the 1st Marine Division zone, the assistant division commander, General Craig, inspects the area at Hungnam where division headquarters will be located after it moves from Wonsan on November 4. While there, Craig is taken to see a ghastly scene, the bodies of about 200 civilians. The North Koreans had killed them and left them lying along a knob in a perfectly straight line.

In the 1st Marines zone, the 3rd Battalion, 1st Marines, maintains its roadblocks and patrols at Majon-ni, but no enemy activity is detected. Lt. Colonel Ridge, concerned about resupply problems, requests a practice air-drop. The operation is a success and Ridge's instincts prove correct. On the following day a supply convoy is attacked and forced to return to Wonsan.

In other activity, the 2nd Battalion, 1st Marines, remains at Kojo. Also, the 2nd Battalion, 5th Marines, at Anbyon, awaits relief by Korean units. Marines receive word of the heavy losses incurred by the 1st Cavalry Division while engaged against Chinese forces, but their orders are not altered. The 7th Marines is still to drive to the border with Manchuria and the initial objective remains Koto-ri, about twenty-three miles north of Majon-dong.

In the 7th Marines zone, the regiment is transported by truck to an assembly area between Oro-ri and Majon-dong. A patrol composed of twenty-one jeeps moves to the vicinity of Huksu-ri, about 45 miles northwest of Hamhung, to search for Chinese. The convoy halts about 4,500 yards in front of the town and establishes a night perimeter.

During the night, fire is exchanged sporadically with North Korean guerrillas; however, the patrol reports that no contact is made with Chinese forces. The 1st Battalion, 7th Marines, probes about four miles north and reaches the area of the ROK positions above Majon-dong. During the latter part of the afternoon, the 7th Marines establish a secure and stiff night perimeter.

The 7th Marines is bolstered by the 3rd Battalion, 11th Marines, commanded by Major Francis Parry; Company D, 1st Engineer Battalion, commanded by Captain Byron Turner; the 1st Motor Transport Battalion, commanded by Lieutenant Colonel Olin Beall; and the Division Reconnaissance Company, commanded by 1st Lieutenant Ralph Crossman. The 7th Marines is augmented by Company E, 1st Medical Battalion, commanded by Lt. Commander Charles K. Halloway,

Top: 11th Marines artillery (105-mm howitzers) in action. *Bottom*: 11th Marines artillery crew.

USN; contingents of the division military police company; and components of the 1st Signal and 1st Service Battalion.

When the 7th Marines advances to the border, its entire left flank will be exposed, with the exception of the division reconnaissance company, which is scheduled to be relieved by RCT-1 shortly.

In the 7th Division zone, the division contains 18,837 men, which places it at nearly full strength, and an attached complement of 7,804 South Koreans. At P'ungsan the North Koreans engage the 1st Regiment, S.K. Capital Division, a couple of miles north of the town. The recently arrived 1st Battalion, 17th Regiment, U.S. 7th Division, receives its baptism under fire when it joins in the battle to help the ROKs turn back the heavy assault. The commanding officer, Colonel Powell, orders his 17th Regiment to prepare to attack at 0800 on the following day to eliminate the remaining resistance, but the North Koreans have other plans of their own.

In the Eighth Army area, headquarters is not taking too seriously the ongoing infusion of Chinese troops into the battle; many of the incoming reports that give specifics concerning Chinese troops are disregarded. The U.S. 2nd Division has thoughts of being shipped back to Japan due to the anticipated termination of the war, but those dreams are shattered. The Division is attached by Army to the I Corps and ordered to make a snappy assembly at Sunchon and be prepared to move out to cover a newly created gap between Army and the ROK II Corps.

Eighth Army now faces a new threat. Its right flank is unprotected since the thrashing of the ROK II Corps. The Chinese have crossed the Ch'ongch'on River and are threading the gap. In addition, the Chinese jeopardize the center of Eighth Army's lines at Unsan, where the S.K. 1st Division is attempting to hold the line. With the arrival of the 8th Cavalry at Unsan, the line of deployment will be: the 8th Cavalry, north, west and south of the town; and the S.K. 1st Division northeast, east and southeast of Unsan.

In the I Corps area, during the afternoon, General Milburn receives a call from General Walker, who informs him that the ROK II Corps has disintegrated and is no longer considered a cohesive fighting unit, thereby leaving U.S. I Corps' right flank bare. Milburn is directed to take protective measures and to assume control of any ROK units that move into I Corps' area. Milburn immediately dispatches a contingent of troops, commanded by General Rinaldo Van Brunt, to hold the line. His force, principally composed of engineers and ordnance troops, moves to positions on the Kunuri–Anju Road, southwest of Kunu-ri to defend the right flank and the pontoon bridges that span the Ch'ongch'on River.

In the 1st Cavalry Division sector, General Gay, concerned with the stretched out deployment of his 1st Cavalry Division, requests permission from I Corps to move the 7th Cavalry from its tenuous positions near Ch'ongch'on to Yongsan-dong, and he requests that the 8th Cavalry withdraw a few miles from Unsan. His requests are denied. Gay also is disturbed because the 3rd Battalion, 5th Cavalry is dangerously over-extended at the corps' eastern boundary.

At Yongsan-dong during the afternoon, General Gay and General Charles Palmer (1st Cavalry Artillery Commander) scrutinize the conversations that are buzzing across the artillery radios when an aerial observer recounts the bizarre activity in his view. The observer, guiding the fire of the 82nd FABn, explains that two separate enemy columns moving southeast along the paths near Myongdang-dong and Yonghung-dong continue to advance, despite being pummeled by artillery shells. Both enemy columns remain oblivious to the bombardment. General Palmer takes the radio and orders the 99th FABn to lend its guns to the fight to intensify the heat.

In the 5th Cavalry sector, Lt. Colonel Harold K. Johnson prepares to dispatch the 3rd Battalion to the boundary line with the S.K. ROK II Corps to support the collapsing lines there. The regiment is to advance east at 1230. At about noon, the 8th Cavalry executive officer, Lt. Colonel Hallet Edson, arrives at Johnsons' Headquarters and explains that throngs of civilian refugees are pouring into the middle of the area that separates the 5th and 8th Cavalry Regiments. He reports that the civilians speak of seeing huge numbers of Chinese troops driving from the west and closing on the immediate rear of the Korean civilians. This places the enemy near the Nammyon River at its confluence with the Camels' Head Bend of the Kuryong River, a tributary of the Ch'ongch'on.

The information is an unwelcome reality. Colonel Johnson, ordered to protect the rear of the 8th Cavalry, dispatches a patrol of the 1st Battalion to confirm the story. The platoon speeds to the scene and validates the information. The Chinese are located at positions less than five air-miles from the 8th Cavalry lines at Unsan. About 2,000 Chinese are in a valley about nine miles southwest of Unsan and another large group, composed of about 3,000 troops, is at Obong-san, about six miles southwest of Unsan.

In the meantime, Johnson accompanies the 3rd Battalion to its objective about six miles northeast of Yongbyon. Johnson orders the battalion to deploy in a set of low hills near the Yongbyon–Kujang-dong Road to meet any threat coming from the east. Johnson and the 3rd Battalion commander venture farther east to get a handle on the situation. Soon after, they encounter troops of the ROK II Corps. The South Koreans are totally disorganized and in full retreat, oblivious even to the moving vehicles.

Johnson returns to his command post (5th Cavalry) at Yongsan-dong during the evening and receives intelligence gathered by the 1st Battalion's platoon. The Chinese were detected at Turtle Head Bend along the Kuryong River and they are close to the 8th Cavalry lines. The 1st Battalion commander, in response to the information, rushes reinforcements (Companies A and B) to bolster the platoon.

Johnson dispatches Company C (in response to request from 1st Battalion commander) to speed north to further augment the force. However, while Company C is en route, the Communists strike and dislodge Company B. Four mortars and other equipment are abandoned. Company B is then directed to withdraw and dig in near the newly established positions of Company C. The enemy roadblock at Turtle Head Bend thwarts the two U.S. rifle companies, despite their air support throughout the day.

The situation continues to deteriorate as enemy troops now hold entrenched positions on three sides of the 8th Cavalry Regiment. Its only buffer is to the east, defended by the S.K. 15th Regiment. The 2nd Battalion, which had sustained heavy resistance on the previous day, reinitiates its drive. It arrives in the 1st Battalion, 8th Cavalry, zone during the early morning hours of November 2 to aid the battle-weary troops there.

In the 8th Cavalry zone, the 2nd and 3rd Battalions are in place, having relieved contingents of the S.K. 12th Regiment on the previous day near Unsan, but the 1st Battalion remains in a defensive stance to the rear of the 2nd Battalion, S.K. 12th Regiment, awaiting the ROKs to retake lost terrain from the Chinese.

In the S.K. 1st Division sector, the 2nd Battalion, 12th Regiment, supported by tanks (6th Med. Tank Bn.) makes minor gains, but the Chinese are not easily moved. Company B, 1st Battalion, 8th Cavalry, initiates an attack to support the S.K. 2nd Battalion. Supported by tanks of Company B, 70th Tank Battalion, the unit drives north shadowing the west bank of the Samt'an River. The added weight of B Company's tanks succeed in reducing the pressure on the S.K. Regiment. The attack regains about one-half mile by noon. Nonetheless, three U.S. tanks sustain damage during the fight, and the afternoon wears down the determination of the S.K. 12th Regiment. Fierce enemy mortar fire halts further advance by the tanks.

The S.K. battalion commander, who on the previous day insisted on regaining the ground, now informs the cavalry that if it is not relieved by 1600, the positions will be abandoned. In response to the S.K. ultimatum, Colonel Raymond Palmer rejects the idea and forbids any U.S. advance, while the Chinese continue their intensive artillery attack. Nevertheless, the 1st Battalion relieves the South Koreans at 1600 by necessity. The South Koreans abandon their positions and retreat through the American lines. However, the 1st Battalion, 8th Cavalry, remains in place and simultaneously relieves the ROKs. All the while, the heights on the east side of the river become more crowded as legions of Chinese troops move along the ridge.

Meanwhile, the S.K. 11th Regiment, 1st Division, is deployed near the ROK II Corps boundary. An enemy column advances toward the regiment and it is detected less than ten miles southwest of Unsan. Planes and artillery strike the column before it can inflict damage. About 100 horses and an indeterminable number of enemy troops are killed. Later, during the afternoon,

other enemy columns are spotted in the same general area and also in the area northeast of Unsan. Again planes arrive to hammer twenty-nine troop-laden vehicles. About two miles away, the S.K. 15th Regiment is heavily engaged east of the river, then Chinese on the ridge begin to approach its lines.

The 8th Cavalry is deployed in a half-moon type perimeter. Its 1st Battalion stands one mile northwest of Unsan on the west bank of the river and slightly below the village of MaeBong-dong. The 2nd and 3rd Battalions continue the east-west line, which leans southwest and slides over a mountain to a point several miles west of Unsan. There it cuts across the east-west road that leads out of Unsan before it swerves southeast to the Yongsan-dong–Yongbyon Road, three miles southeast of Unsan. The enemy plows through the South Koreans.

By 1700, the 8th Cavalry comes under attack. By dusk, the Americans face the enemy on three separate sides, north, south and west. The initial assault is supported by new weaponry, truck-mounted Russian-made rockets. Major Millikin's 1st Battalion sustains the assault and is aided by artillery, which zeroes in on the enemy rocket trucks. Effective fire forces the enemy to withdraw their rockets. Prior to the withdrawal, the enemy's attack had hit an ammunition truck parked near the battalion headquarters.

The 1st Battalion controls the Samt'an River's northern approaches by dark, but its left flank is fragile. At some points, troops are insufficient to stretch to the primary ridge that moves into Unsan. Contact in this area between the 1st and 2nd Battalions is possible only by patrols. The main ridge is manned, but only with outposts of both battalions.

Following the initial attack at 1700, the enemy renews its assault at 1930 and again pounds the 1st Battalion, but this new assault also hammers the entire line and ruptures the right flank, which withdraws about 400 yards.

Meanwhile, a platoon of engineers and the heavy mortar company rush to help hold the line. The troops defending the left flank pull back about 200 yards to tighten the line. The 1st Battalion then holds against vicious attacks.

The Communist Chinese discover holes on the primary ridge, and at about 2100, they begin funneling through to descend upon the rear of the 2nd Battalion. Shortly thereafter, all hell begins to break loose. Both battalions are fully engulfed in battle, and to the east, the South Koreans are heavily engaged.

Northeast of Unsan, the tank contingent guarding the bridge over the Samt'an River discovers large numbers of enemy troops on the opposite bank. This new threat imperils the 1st Battalion's positions north of Unsan. Major Millikin sends an officer across the river to attempt to locate the mortarmen who had been supporting the ROKs, but his jeep comes under fire, which forces him to scurry back.

By about 2300, the S.K. 15th Regiment collapses. While the Communists to the east barrel past the 1st

Battalion positions, Millikin orders all 1st Battalion trains and non-combat vehicles to move back through Unsan and converge on the road fork south of the town. Lt. Colonel William Walton gives a similar order and the 2nd Battalion also begins withdrawing its vehicles. By 2300, each battalion had paid high prices and lost some ground during the close-quartered fighting. From the road fork, the vehicles of both battalions move southeast and reach Ipsok. To make matters worse, the 1st Battalion is nearly out of ammunition, and the reserve stores are close to exhaustion, too.

Unknown to the 1st and 2nd Battalions, a meeting had been held at I Corps headquarters at 2000 to deal with the deteriorating circumstances in the South Korean II Corps sector. This is the second meeting on the subject this day. The meeting concludes with an order going out to the 8th Cavalry to withdraw and for the Corps to take a defensive posture. However, the news of the enemy progress in the 8th Cavalry zone is still not known at I Corps Headquarters.

Slightly after midnight, General Gay returns to his headquarters and is told of the disastrous news at Unsan. The orders to withdraw arrive at Colonel Palmer's headquarters at about 2300. At midnight, the 8th Cavalry attempts to withdraw, but easier said than done. Colonel Palmer orders Colonel Edson, the 8th Cavalry Regimental executive officer, to oversee the operation.

Elements of the 3rd Battalion deploy to defend the exit route at the south fork near Unsan. Edson and Captain Rene Guiraud (Regimental S-2) and a contingent of the I&R Platoon travel to the junction to coordinate the regiment's withdrawal. By about midnight, Captain Filmore McAbee (3rd Battalion S-3) and one platoon of Company I, 3rd Battalion, move to the junction to guard the approaches from the north. Soon after, the four tanks of the 1st Platoon arrive, followed by two tanks of the 2nd Platoon (70th Tank Battalion) to bolster the road fork positions. Upon arrival of the 2nd Platoon's tanks, the 1st platoon of tanks crosses the Kuryong River to cover the withdrawal from there. The regiment's trains pass through safely, as do those of the 1st and 2nd Battalions.

North of Unsan, the beleaguered 1st Battalion remains under severe pressure, and the supporting tanks (Company B, 70th Tank Battalion) on the right flank at the bridge northeast of the town are equally endangered. They have been compelled to withdraw to the road fork at the northeast tip of Unsan. The tanks attempt to hold the fork to permit the 1st Battalion to extricate itself. One platoon each from Companies A and B act as rear guards, while the companies, including Company D, retreat to the fork.

Meanwhile, the enemy has heavily penetrated Unsan. Major Millikin arrives at the north road fork slightly before Companies A and B, which arrive at about 0030 November 2. Enemy fire originating in Unsan inflicts more casualties, which prompts Millikin to divert the troops. He directs them to skirt around the eastern side of the town and proceed to the road fork

south of Unsan, then hold in place until he arrives. In the meantime, two tanks and several Company D mortar vehicles have arrived at the northeast road fork.

Other tanks have entered Unsan. They are engaged against the enemy in an attempt to fight their way to the southern road fork. Four tanks of the 1st Platoon, Company B, break through, but the course remains much rougher for the remaining tanks and the mortar vehicles.

At about 0045, two more tanks and the mortar vehicles attempt to break through and get the wounded to safety. Burning debris blocks passage at a turn. The first tank maneuvers around the fiery truck, but then it gets bogged down in a crater. Quickly, the Communists rake the stalled tank with shells while blowing the tracks on the remaining tank. The other vehicles also are pummeled. Apparently, all the wounded aboard the mortar vehicles are lost. Of the ten tanker crewmen, two are killed, including the tank commander of the stalled tank. Five others are wounded.

Meanwhile, the scattered 2nd Battalion lacked good communications when the order to withdraw had been issued. Company H, the only unit in contact with Lt. Colonel Walton, is given the instructions with orders to pass on the word to the other units. There is still contact between the rifle companies. Millikin had told Walton that he would try to keep control of Unsan until the 2nd Battalion had withdrawn. Some of the 2nd Battalion will break out, but much of it will be cut off, unable to reach the road fork. Walton reaches the roadblock and from there he leads 103 troops to Ipsok, arriving the following morning. The situation near and in Unsan continues worsening.

By about 0100, Millikin is greeted by stragglers from the ROK 15th Regiment and troops of various units, including Company C, but Chinese soldiers also arrive north of the town at the road fork. The Americans evacuate the area in small groups and try to make it to the southern fork. Another contingent, Company H, 2nd Battalion, meets Millikin and his small group at about 0200 as they take a circuitous route to the fork south of Unsan. This group reaches the destination, but the scene is ugly and permeated with abandoned equipment. The enemy is closing fast and the south road fork is now under small arms fire.

Millikin encounters Major Robert Ormond, 3rd battalion commander, and one platoon of infantry from Company I at the roadblock. Ormond informs Millikin that no new orders have arrived and that the 3rd Battalion had been instructed to cover the withdrawal of the 1st and 2nd Battalions. Ormond departs to begin to withdraw his 3rd Battalion. Millikin uses the radio of the lone operable tank at the south roadblock to try to contact other units, but he is able only to communicate with another tank. It is at the Kuryong River and engaged.

Millikin and the troops with him attempt to break through the blockage by following the remaining tank at the fork, but enemy fire thwarts the effort. Millikin's contingent bolts from the area in tiny groups that head south. Millikin and the men ford the Kuryong River and reach Ipsok on the morning of the 2nd. Contingents that are moving to the rear of Millikin had not reached the south road fork. And west of the blockage, the Chinese had brought other units to a sputtering halt. Battery A, 99th FABn and the 3rd Platoon, Company B, 70th Tank Battalion, are stopped less than one mile from the fork.

Almost immediately the road becomes jammed as vehicles are deserted. The tanks then become paralyzed; the crews are forced to destroy the weapons and abandon their armor. Most of the infantry (primarily 2nd Battalion) and the tankers make a dash for the heights, but some manage to reach the south road fork. In conjunction, the stragglers spread out. Some reach the positions of the 3rd Battalion on the following morning and others stumble into the lines of the ROK troops at Ipsok.

In the 3rd Battalion area, south of Unsan, the enemy has been quiet to this point. By about 0130, the supporting artillery components (99th FABn units) of the 3rd Battalion begin passing through the fork. In the 3rd Battalion zone, things have been tranquil during the day. The battalion command post is several air-miles south of Unsan and slightly north of the Nammyon River. Northwest of the headquarters, along a ridge line atop a stream, Companies I and K are deployed. The perimeter is further protected by a platoon of tanks (Company B, 70th Tank Battalion) dispersed on either side of the road north of the river. And elements of Company M guard the bridge to the rear.

By midnight (1st-2nd) Major Ormond informs his commanders that the withdrawal is imminent. Soon, Companies I and K receive orders to pull back to the command post; Company L, stretched out west in the heights along the south side of the river, is ordered to protect the withdrawal.

At 0115, the first units, Battery B, 99th FABn, and battalion headquarters move north and pass the south road fork without incident. At about 0230, Captain Bolt, commanding officer, Battery C, pauses to speak with Colonel Edson at the road fork and Edson assures him that everything is under control and that the artillery should proceed. Bolt's convoy, composed of twenty vehicles, moves out toward the Kuryong River. The second vehicle misses a turn and it goes unnoticed momentarily by Captain Bolt, but then he orders his jeep to halt to await the column. In the meantime, the vehicle that missed the turn is forced to reverse and the mishap clogs the road.

Suddenly, Bolt spots some troops moving toward his stalled jeep, and at first glance, they appear to be retreating 8th Cavalrymen. However, when shots ring out, it becomes apparent they are enemy troops. The jeep roars off, but when it rounds a curve about twenty Chinese troops are to its front stretched along the road. Chinese fire rings out, but Bolt returns fire with his submachine gun and the ambush is thwarted when the enemy scatters. The jeep keeps moving with Bolt's gun blazing and it breaks through several more small groups

of enemy troops and finally makes contact with the convoy, which is now Battery B and four tanks (1st Platoon Company B, 70th Tank Battalion).

Bolt directs one of the tanks to return down the road and fire upon the enemy, but the tanker states that he has expended his ammunition. At about the same time, Bolt's jeep vanishes around the curve, another U.S. vehicle comes under fire at the road fork and its driver loses control of the vehicle, causing it to tumble over and block the highway. All attempts by a tank to push it aside are futile, and the tank becomes disabled. It is abandoned after its weapons are demolished. The last vehicle to pass the roadblock is Bolt's jeep.

For the remainder of the troops at the roadblock south of Unsan, the nightmare continues to become more grim. Colonel Edson attempts to raise resistance to break out, but to no avail. There is no group of soldiers who band together to strike back. Several officers collect troops who have abandoned their vehicles, but while the officers attempt to gather more, the others stream for safety. In the meantime, Major Ormond had spoken with Major Millikin at the roadblock and then moved back to his headquarters to complete the withdrawal. He departs only moments before the Chinese command the area at the roadblock, which makes his withdrawal difficult. Unable to move north, Ormond chooses a circuitous route and orders some tanks to guard the withdrawal. A tanker, Sergeant Elmer L. Miller, sets out to probe for a crossing site for the tanks, but he is forced back.

Before 0300, the vehicles are positioned nose to tail awaiting orders, but again, grave mistakes are made and pandemonium occurs. The Company M squads at the bridge south of headquarters observe a contingent of troops encroaching the Nammyon River bridge, and assume they are South Korean. The troops pass over the bridge and advance toward the command post without incident, but then a Chinese bugle blares to ignite a gruesome surprise assault on the CP. Chinese converge from all directions, but the Americans believe it to be a North Korean attack.

Major Ormond and Captain McAbee leave their headquarters to gauge the depth of the assault. Ormond moves toward Company L at the river but he becomes wounded and left unattended for the night. McAbee heads for the bridge to the south, but he also is wounded. Undaunted, McAbee attempts to reach the command post and encounters several Chinese, which he eliminates with his carbine. Then, McAbee stumbles upon about thirty more Chinese troops who are trying to destroy a tank; again he fires his carbine until all his ammunition is expended. Having sustained a great loss of blood, McAbee reinitiates his bid to return to the command post. It is a harrowing trek. He brushes with the enemy several more times, and even though they have him in their reach, he works his way out of the crisis.

Meanwhile, small arms fire intensifies and grenades are flying in every direction. All the while, the shrill sounds of whistles and giant speakers in the distance bellow the amplified sounds of stampeding horses. The Chinese also blare taps. During the swift attack, the Chinese toss explosive charges into the vehicles, setting many afire. The Americans are caught flat-footed and some are still bleary eyed in their foxholes and trenches, still awaiting the order to board the vehicles. Bloody hand-to-hand fighting is the order of the day, but the enemy holds the advantage. Many of the troops near headquarters are thrashed and stabbed to death by bayonets.

The morbid sight of slaughtered soldiers is not easily cloaked under the brightness of the moon, nor are the grim expressions on the faces of the surviving fighting men. The enemy continues to press forward, hoping to annihilate those at the command post. The chaplain, Father (Major) Emil Kapaun, ventures outside to check things out and spots Captain McAbee as he struggles to reach the CP. Father Kapaun rescues him, and then someone else is yelling for help. Major Moriarity, the battalion executive officer, rushes to the aid of another officer (Battalion S-4), who is wrapped up on the ground with a Communist. Moriarity kills the enemy troop with his pistol and he eliminates one other enemy soldier in the vicinity.

Later, Moriarity spots a group of U.S. infantry positioned around Sergeant Elmer Miller's tank. As he moves to the tank, the enemy begins to sling mortars that land dangerously close to the armor. Moriarity gathers the men and leads them south to ford the stream. Along the way, they encounter and destroy an enemy contingent at the stream. Moriarity and the troops then head southeast toward friendly lines, picking up stragglers as they move.

In the meantime, at about the same time headquarters had been struck, the Chinese also pour fire into the 3rd Battalion lines. The tanks, still posted near the road south of the command post, are struck hard. Sergeant Miller, who had gone to seek a crossing, creeps back to his tank to join the defenders. Again at close-range, Miller uses his pistol. One of the tanks is damaged and then it blows. The remaining three tanks pull back to the road and successfully hold back the enemy. The tank fire prevents them from fording the stream from the south.

Company L, southwest of the command post along the stream, also receives heavy attacks. Nonetheless, Company L fights tenaciously and completes its previous orders to reel into the command post. Company K attempts to make it to the battalion zone and is struck by an ambush that inflicts heavy losses on one platoon and its command group. However, the remainder of the company reaches headquarters and augments the defenses there. The three tanks band tightly together and the nearby infantry help galvanize the resistance.

At the command post, the small group of defenders throws back the Chinese and holds until dawn, but the cost is high. Enemy grenades slay three soldiers who had manned the machine gun at the command post, and of the twenty or so troops who defended the position, only five remain alive at dawn.

In the 24th Division sector, elements of the Chinese 66th Army engage contingents of the 19th Regiment in small firefights near Kusong.

Meanwhile, the 1st Battalion continues to set the pace for the 21st Regiment. It reaches the fringes of Chonggo-dong by noon, which places the regiment within eighteen air-miles from the Yalu River. The troops of the 21st Regiment are anxious to proceed to the border; however, orders have filtered down from I Corps that direct the regiment to halt and establish strong defensive positions at Chonggo-dong.

The order delivered by Colonel Stephens stuns the troops, but they are not fully aware of the rapid changes dictating the battle plans. During the afternoon, the 1st Battalion is struck by a grueling counterattack. A North Korean infantry force, composed of about 500 troops and augmented by seven tanks, attacks the lines of the 1st battalion to ignite a fury-filled battle. The U.S. artillery and the ground troops propel a hurricane of fire toward the attackers, while the tanks of Company A, 6th Medium Tank Battalion, gallop toward the enemy armor to instigate a deadly joust. The opposing tanks begin to bludgeon each other. The tanks slug it out and pound each other with incessant fire for about one-half hour. The tanks' guns subside after the seventh T-34 is decimated.

Meanwhile, the curtain of fire raised by the 1st Battalion and the accompanying guns of the artillery repulse the infantry and inflict about 100 casualties. Two of Captain Jack G. Moss' tanks receive some minor damage. This action becomes the Eighth Army's northernmost battle for the duration of the conflict and Lt. Colonel Charles B. Smith's 1st Battalion, 21st Regiment, is the engaging unit. TF Smith, which had fought the initial battle against the North Koreans during early July, was commanded by Colonel Smith and the task force included elements of the 21st Regiment.

In the 5th Regimental zone, the regiment reinitiates its attack. The column advances several miles north of the town and runs into a formidable enemy roadblock. Undaunted, the RCT rams against it and pulverizes the defenses. The enemy loses between 300 and 400 troops. In addition, six anti-tank guns, eight howitzers (76-mm), five machine guns and eight mortars are destroyed. Two self-propelled guns are also decimated.

Once the road junction is secured, forward elements of the regiment push north and reach positions about ten miles beyond the town. At about noon, a liaison plane flies over Kusong and drops an urgent message instructing the regiment to halt where it stands. The 5th Regiment's reaction is the same as the 21st Regiment's; the disappointment of the troops is conspicuous.

Toward the end of the night, at about 2300, orders arrive from division directing the regiment to pull back to the Ch'ongch'on River at once. The 21st Regiment receives the same instructions and during the night (Nov. 1-2), both regiments retire to the river, still perplexed by the turn of events.

In the ROK II Corps area, the S.K. 15th Regiment comes under severe attack during the day and during the

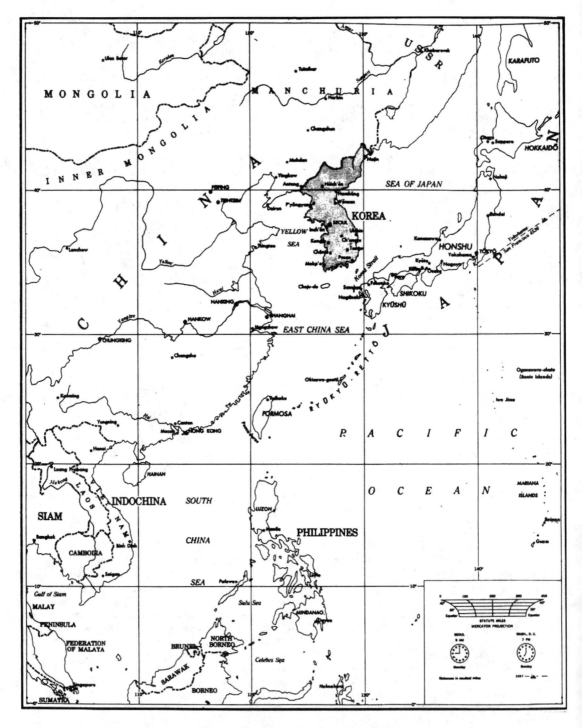

The Pacific, November–December 1950.

battle, it captures some equipment including two 57-mm recoilless rifles and two other automatic rifles. Each weapon is marked conspicuously with Chinese identification.

By 1900, the supporting U.S. artillery unit, the 10th AAA Group, is ordered to prepare to pull back. At about 2030, the fire center controlling the guns is shut down, and within another hour, the unit moves back. The vehicles head south with their lights out.

In the meantime, the struggling South Koreans still

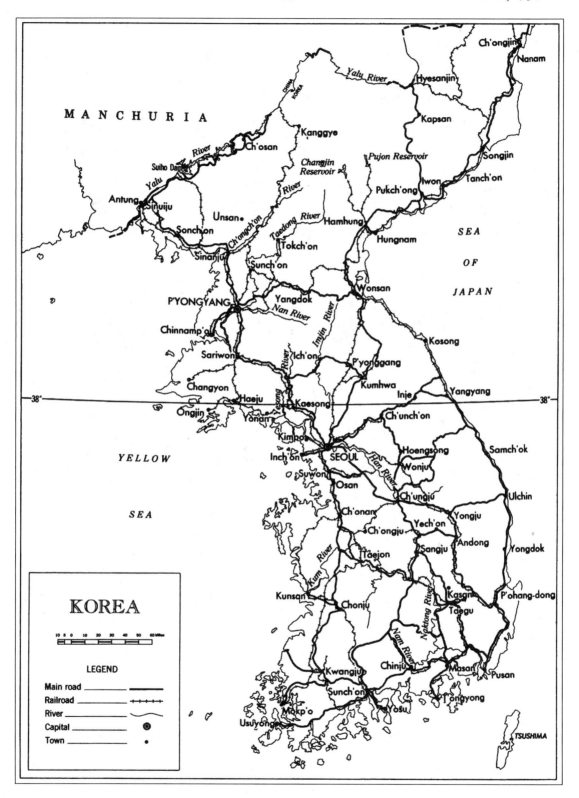

Map of Korea, November–December 1950.

Leaflets are loaded into a bomb-type cluster adapter (M16M1) in Japan on 1 November. The leaflets are afterward dropped in North Korea to persuade North Koreans to surrender.

have some artillery support as the more mobile 90-mm guns of the 78th AAA maintain fire for one or two more hours, until orders arrive from corps that mandate a pull-back. By midnight (1st-2nd), the South Koreans have been decimated and shortly thereafter, the ROK 15th Regiment is rendered unfit for battle. Nearly the entire regiment is killed or captured. The collapse of the regiment gives the Chinese an easier route toward the 8th Cavalry. The regiment's equipment is totally written off, and the losses include four liaison aircraft, used to assist the 6th Tank Battalion and the 9th FABN. The planes are destroyed on the ground by U.S. aircraft to prevent capture.

In other activity, Chinese Communist units continue to smash against the South Koreans. Below the Ch'ongch'on River, the S.K. 7th Division has been shoved back to the vicinity of Won-ni. The gigantic Chinese Communist pressure jolts the ROK II Corps into positions that have the line facing east, but this opens a huge hole between its left flank and Eighth Army.

General Milburn arrives at ROK Headquarters and discovers that it is moving to Sunchon. Milburn is informed that communication with the various units has been lost. The ROK commander believes he has three battalions of the S.K. 7th Division still able to fight. Milburn orders the South Koreans to hold Kunu-ri and he informs them that a contingent of U.S. troops is en route to strengthen the defense.

In Air Force activity, a group of American planes, including one B-26, is attacked over North Korea by a band of three Yaks. One of the enemy planes is downed by the B-25 and the other two are shot down by two F-81 fighters. Also, a contingent of six MiGs, later on this same day, attack a group of F-51 Mustangs and a T-6 in the vicinity of the Yalu River, but the U.S. sustains no losses.

— *In the United States:* President Truman is temporarily residing in the Blair House. He survives an assassination attempt there on this day when two Puerto Rican nationalists spring their attack, but one is killed and the other is apprehended before the president can be harmed.

November 2 The U.N. Command believes about 16,500 Chinese are now in Korea and that about 450,000 more remain in Manchuria, close to the Yalu River.

In the X Corps area, General Almond relocates his command post farther north at Hamhung. The remainder of his headquarters arrives on the 10th. On the 14th, the USS *Mount McKinley* arrives off Hungnam. Admiral Doyle and his staff can now coordinate with General Almond.

In the 1st Marine Division sector, Corps directs the 2nd Battalion, 1st Marines to depart its positions near Kojo and return to Wonsan. The departure, which occurs this day, causes the X Corps boundary to be adjusted. It is moved 70 miles farther south. In conjunction, the Korean Marine Regiment, recently detached from the 1st Marine Division, is directed to assume responsibility for the Corps' zone south of the 39th Parallel.

In other activity, the 2nd Battalion, 5th Marines, positioned at Anbyon, about eight miles southeast of Wonsan, is relieved by Korean contingents. The 2nd Battalion departs by trucks to return to its regiment, which is stationed farther north. Also, following completion of mine-sweeping operations, the port facilities at Wonsan become operative today. During the next nine days, the Combat Service Group moves nearly 4,000 tons of ammunition by rail from Wonsan to Hamhung.

At Majon-ni, 3rd Battalion, 1st Marines' patrols continue, but the enemy's inactivity ceases. A motorized patrol of Company H ventures south from the village along a slim road and hits an ambush site after traveling about five miles. Enemy fire pours down from each

side of the heights and creates massive problems for the patrol when the vehicles stall. Marines attempt to set up their mortars and machine guns to return fire, but their positions are poor, and the enemy is concealed, which causes casualties to climb. A desperate message is sent by radio to headquarters: "We've been hit. Send help. Send help."

Soon after, enemy fire takes out the radio. Two men defy the fire and race their jeep back to headquarters to get reinforcements. They arrive safely, but one of the tires had been blown by an enemy shell. Two rifle companies and other Marines with 81-mm mortars rush to rescue the besieged patrol. One man in the relief force, PFC Jack Golden, transporting a heavy machine gun, ascends to a position atop the enemy.

Meanwhile, communications between Majon-ni and Wonsan remain terrible, which causes a delay in getting air support to the imperiled patrol. Major Simmons convinces a pilot of an OY to take him to the battle scene, from where he can observe the positions. Marine Corsairs then arrive to assist and the enemy is forced from the heights. Rescue operations continue and the seriously wounded are evacuated by helicopters. One Marine dies during the night, but the other wounded are evacuated by three helicopter flights.

In related activity, a 3rd Battalion, 1st Marines' supply convoy, escorted by a rifle platoon of Company G, departs Wonsan en route for Majon-ni. It is ambushed about seven miles outside of Wonsan. A withering storm of enemy fire strikes the column. The first two trucks escape harm and continue to move, but the third vehicle, transporting diesel fuel and C-3 explosives, bursts into flames. The two lead trucks encounter an impassable road and turn back. About the time they reach the ambush site, the other vehicles are attempting to turn around. During the dangerous maneuver, enemy fire continues to thrash the area. Two trucks fail to safely navigate the narrow road and are lost.

In the meantime, reinforcements race to the area and three Corsairs attached to VMF-312 arrive and drive off several hundred enemy troops. Riflemen aboard six trucks and five tanks, including a dozer tank, safely rescue the imperiled convoy and return it to Wonsan. Nine Marines are killed and fifteen are wounded during the ambush. Nonetheless, the 1st Marines at Majon-ni desperately need the ammunition. Lt. Colonel Ridge requests delivery by air and within several hours, C-47s of the Air Force soar overhead and deliver more than 150 parachutes, each carrying supplies to the Majon-ni perimeter. Colonel Puller, concerned that his Marines would require more supplies and ammunition, schedules another truck convoy for November 4.

In the 5th Marines sector, the Regiment prepares to move to Hamhung. The 1st Marines hold responsibility for the MSR as far north as Munchon and the road from there to Chigyong. Also, a distance of about 54 miles is to be guarded by the Special Operations Company, USA, and some Korean agents. The 2nd Battalion, 5th Marines, departs today after being released from the 1st Marines.

An LST unloads equipment at Iwon, about 180 miles north of Pyongyang. Elements of the U.S. 7th Division gather nearby on the beach.

In the 7th Marines sector, the 1st Battalion, 7th Marines, commanded by Lt. Colonel Raymond G. Davis, departs its assembly area and moves toward Majon-dong. It is closely followed by the 2nd Battalion, commanded by Major Webb D. Sawyer. The columns are accompanied by VMF-312's Corsairs that

are on scene to aid reconnaissance and provide close-air support. The columns receive some long-range fire from Chinese units and incur a few casualties.

The 2nd Battalion takes responsibility for the heights on both sides of the MSR, despite being the trailing battalion. The artillery also is involved. Batteries G and

North Korean POWs at Wonsan.

H are pushed to the front before noon. Battery I, also of the 3rd Battalion, 11th Marines, commences firing at about noon with the initial barrage. The artillery executes 26 missions during the day.

During the afternoon, Company D, 2nd Battalion, 7th Marines, begins to climb the eastern slopes of Hill 698 to relieve the South Koreans that are unable to secure and hold the summit. Once the ROKs see the Marines, they abandon their positions and seek positions in the rear. Colonel Litzenberg continues to get his regiment organized to meet any threat in the valley.

By about 1630, the regiment completes a 1,300-yard advance. The troops are susceptible to coming under fire from any direction. Litzenberg has directed that the columns be restricted to a minimum of 4,000 yards and a maximum of 6,000 yards, to ensure that either close-artillery or inter-battalion infantry support can be utilized to fend off any opposing force. Colonel Litzenberg remains concerned about potential dangers that could emerge. He directs Colonel Roach to take a reconnaissance flight by helicopter to scrutinize the Sudong valley, which abuts the smaller valley that the 7th Marines have occupied. Roach takes the excursion flight to the area below Oro-ri during the afternoon, but no Chinese presence is detected.

In the meantime, the 2nd Battalion pushes two Company D platoons ahead. They drive up the steep slope, against what starts as sporadic fire and culminates with mediocre fire from the summit. The attacking platoons are ordered to pause while calls for air strikes are made. The planes appear within several minutes and the suspected positions are blasted. Despite an open field of about fifty yards, the Marines inch forward and sustain casualties while they climb. The Marines finally take the summit, but enemy troops remain in well-concealed positions, and they continue their fire against the exhausted Marines. Captain Milton Hull, concerned about the condition of his Marines after the stiff ascent, and their ability to hold the summit, orders them to pull back and take positions on the eastern slope. Meanwhile, Hull calls for support fire to keep heat on the enemy, but it never arrives. Company D, 2nd Battalion, holds its positions despite the lack of artillery fire. Company E moves to relieve Company D.

At 2200, Company E passes through D Company and establishes a night perimeter at positions on a plateau that lies about 150 yards from the crest. Back in the valley earlier in the day, aircraft had plastered the heights to provide some security for the regiment. The Corsairs of VMF-312 and VMF(N)-513 continue their support missions; the former executes twelve missions and the latter contributes several additional sorties. At about 1700, three Marines are wounded when an enemy shell strikes the regimental command post.

By dusk, the regiment begins to forge a night perimeter. While Company D is committed on the eastern slope of Hill 698, Company A, commanded by Captain David Banks, digs in along the right side of the MSR. Its three platoons stretch across Hill 532 to a spindle of Hill 727, and from there the line swerves and flows backward to cover the left flank. The line is bolstered by a 3.5 rocket squad, deployed to intercept any advancing armor. Mortars are placed in the vicinity of the company command post.

Lieutenant Colonel Davis establishes his command post to the rear of Company A; it is protected by one platoon of Company C and a battalion of 81-mm mortars. Opposite Company A, to the left of the MSR, C Company establishes its line on the northeastern slopes of Hill 698. In the process of moving into position, the company receives some luck.

The opposition raised against Company D hinders the movement of C Company until dark, but the Chinese who have kept a constant vigil on Marine movement fail to detect the deployment of Company D. To further tighten the perimeter, one platoon of Company B and headquarters deploy close by and to the rear of Company A on a spindle of Hill 698. The remaining two platoons of Company B also deploy to the rear of Company A, but on the lower portion of Hill 727.

The 2nd Battalion maneuvers to strengthen its perimeter, while its Company D and E are engaged on the slopes of Hill 698. Company D remains on the lower portion once it is relieved by E Company. Company F strings out along the precipitous Hill 727. The 2nd Battalion command post is established in a small glen just under the positions of Company F. The CP is bolstered by contingents of the 7th Marines antitank company and some 4.2 mortar units.

To close the loop, the 3rd Battalion, 7th Marines, commanded by Major Maurice Roach, deploys in such a way as to create a backup perimeter. Opposing ridges separated by the MSR are occupied by Companies I and H on the right and left respectively. Both companies are linked from the south by Company G, which stretches across the valley and holds the regiment's southernmost point, from where it is poised to guard the regiment's trains and the command post of Colonel Litzenberg.

As the latter part of the day approaches, still there are no significant signs of concentrated Chinese presence. The perimeter does, however, receive sporadic incoming mortar rounds. Later, toward midnight, the Chinese Communists make their presence known. Unknown to the 7th Marines, who are expecting some Chinese, there are two regiments lurking nearby. The 1st Battalion, 7th Marines, reports at about 2300 that enemy forces are attacking its right flank, defended by Company A. The pressure is actually a probing movement.

During the night fighting, an enemy contingent at-tacks the positions of Company B, 1st Battalion. Sergeant Archie Van Winkle takes the initiative. He races across the ground for about 40 yards, through an onslaught of heavy fire, to regroup the command. Then he leads an attack despite having been wounded during his jaunt. Sergeant Van Winkle is hit again with a grievous wound to the chest. The others provide some momentary help, but Van Winkle refuses evacuation, choosing instead to continue leading his beleaguered platoon. He shouts orders until he falls into unconsciousness. His extraordinary heroism inspires the platoon further. They continue the fight and repulse the assault.

Sergeant Van Winkle is awarded the Medal of Honor posthumously for his tremendous courage and leadership in the face of a superior numbered enemy force. Van Winkle is the first Marine reservist to receive the medal. Twelve other Marine reservists will receive it as well.

Subsequent to the probing attacks, at 2400 (2nd-3rd), a heavier assault begins.

In related activity, the 1st Marine Division's reconnaissance company moves toward Huksu-ri to probe for Chinese presence and returns to the valley on the following day to assist against the Chinese attacks in the 7th Marines sector. (*See also*, **November 3**, *In the 7th Marines zone*.)

In the Army's Special Operations Company area, enemy guerrillas strike the MSR. A call is placed for support and the Marine 1st Tank Battalion speeds a patrol to the area west of Munchon. The guerrillas are driven off by the Marines. The U.S. Army contingent loses some equipment and one man is wounded.

In the 7th Division sector, at P'ungsan, the 1st Battalion, 17th Regiment, prepares to jump off and initiate an attack at 0800; however, in the meantime, the North Koreans launch an assault at 0700. The enemy strikes against the Americans and ROK lines with the strength of about one regiment to ignite a day-long slugfest.

As the fighting ensues, other elements of the regiment arrive to bolster the 1st Battalion. By the latter part of the day, all but one company arrives. By day's end, the 1st Regiment, Capital Division, is relieved by elements of the 17th Regiment. The ROKs depart the area and join the Capital Division, which is driving along the coastal road.

At the beachhead at Iwon, the debarkation continues, hindered by the weather. The unexpected slow pace keeps many vehicles from coming ashore.

In the ROK I Corps area, at Kilchu, a town situated twenty miles north of Songjin and almost fifteen air-miles from the coast, has become fortified by North Koreans who have moved north and out of the range of the U.S. Navy's big guns. Prior to dawn, the cavalry regiment, South Korean Capital Division, attacks to eliminate the opposition. Stiff resistance repels the attack, but the cavalry unit is bolstered by the 1st S.K. Regiment. Still the town holds. The fighting remains fierce throughout the day. It continues on the following day.

In the Eighth Army area, the recent entrance of Chinese troops into the Korean conflict has imperiled I Corps. Steps are being taken to prevent it from being trapped above the Ch'ongch'on River. There is a constant flurry of activity, including a steady flow of new orders being issued throughout the day, all centered around getting the corps to more tenable positions to hold the river line.

The I Corps is to funnel through the Anju–Pakch'on areas. The U.S. 19th Regiment, 24th Division, and the British Brigade (27th Commonwealth) will form a galvanized bridgehead on the north side of the Ch'ongch'on to defend the ford crossings of the tanks and the bridges that span the Ch'ongch'on and Taeryong Rivers. The line must hold if the allied offensive is to regain any momentum. However, a huge five-mile hole lies between the lines of 19th Regiment's left flank and the British Brigade. At Anju, the 3rd Engineer Combat Battalion resumes its role as an Infantry unit and defends the bridges there.

In the I Corps area, 1st Cavalry Division sector, 5th Cavalry zone, contingents are rushing to the aid of the cavalrymen near Unsan. The 2nd Battalion, 5th Cavalry, drives to positions north of Unsan and reaches there at 0400. The 1st Battalion, 8th Cavalry, had held these positions on the previous day, until forced out by the Chinese. At dawn, Colonel Johnson's 5th Cavalry reinitiates its mission to rescue the beleaguered 3rd Battalion, 8th Cavalry's survivors, still at the battalion command post, south of Unsan. The 1st and 2nd Battalion, on the left and right sides of the road respectively, are to drive forward and seize the enemy-controlled ridge to their front and create a gap to permit the 3rd Battalion to surge through and extricate the trapped 8th Cavalrymen.

The 3rd Battalion, 5th Cavalry, released for this duty during the morning, speeds to the area. Its attack will be bolstered by tanks. General Gay authorizes the commitment of the 1st Battalion, 7th Cavalry, to support the attack of the 5th Cavalry. It is to drive toward the left flank of the Chinese and pound the flank in conjunction with the 5th Cavalry's frontal assault. The attack, also supported by air strikes, commences, but anticipated light artillery is not brought up to support the assault. Apparently, corps or even higher sources do not authorize their movement. Consequently, the assault force is augmented by a mere two 155-mm howitzers. The spearhead fails to gain its objective. Both assault companies fall short of the goal. Elements of the 7th Cavalry needed to strike the Chinese left flank never reach the battle area.

Following some afternoon air strikes, the 2nd Battalion drives against the enemy-held positions, but the hefty air strikes are deemed ineffective. The battalion is unable to gain ground. However, the attack does cost the 2nd Battalion heavy casualties. By 1500, another grim decision is made. General Milburn tells General Gay that the 1st Cavalry Division is to abort the attack and retreat, which leaves the feisty survivors of the 3rd Battalion, 8th Cavalry, to the mercy of the enemy.

Just before dark a liaison plane flies over the positions of the trapped cavalrymen and deposits an order from General Gay, which instructs the survivors to withdraw after dusk. The message fails to instruct the isolated troops on how they are to transport the wounded through the lines of the Chinese. General Gay claims that his order to have the 5th Cavalry retreat and leave the 3rd Battalion, 8th Cavalry, alone is the most difficult decision he was ever called upon to make. The failed attack costs the 5th Cavalry about 350 casualties and of those, about 250 of these are sustained by the 2nd Battalion.

In the 8th Cavalry zone, many troops of the 8th Cavalry, including those with Major Millikin, have made it to Ipsok from the vicinity of Unsan during the night. Millikin's group had crossed the river before dawn and arrived at Ipsok at about 0800.

Millikin discovers his trains there and about 200 1st Battalion troops (mainly men of Companies A and B) who had been among the first to evacuate Unsan. Four tanks (Company B, 70th Tank Battalion), five artillery pieces and the greatest part of the battalion headquarters, which departed the area the night before, reaches Ipsok, but nearly half of the 1st Battalion's heavy weapons and mortars have been lost. Also, more 1st Battalion troops filter into Ipsok to give Millikin a more accurate picture of the disaster. The 1st Battalion casualty list, including all brackets, stands at about 15 officers and 250 enlisted men.

At dawn the survivors of the 3rd Battalion near Unsan still hold the command post. The Chinese have been driven off. However, enemy mortars continue to rain on the Americans, which compels them to keep their heads low.

About one hour after first light of dawn, U.S. planes arrive overhead and initiate day-long strikes to keep the Chinese at bay. During the lull in the ground combat, the survivors seek out the wounded and assess the damage. Major Ormond is located, but he has been severely wounded. It is also determined that the other 3rd Battalion staff officers are either wounded or missing. Just over 200 men, including six officers, remain able to fight. About 170 wounded soldiers are rounded up within 500 yards of the besieged 200-yard perimeter and brought to safety.

Attempts to reinforce and resupply the embattled troops unfold. A helicopter tries to land to evacuate the seriously wounded troops, but enemy fire hits the aircraft and the crew departs without landing. However, twenty-one critically wounded are flown out of Ipsok by helicopters. In the meantime, some medicine is air-dropped. And, a pilot in a Mosquito plane helps build morale by informing the exhausted troops that a 5th Cavalry relief column is at the road fork north of Unsan, a position held the previous night by the 1st Battalion, 8th Cavalry.

As previously mentioned, the attack fails. Subsequent to the order to withdraw the 1st Cavalry Division, word does reach the trapped troops. A plane soars overhead and delivers orders to withdraw by their own methods.

Nevertheless, the 8th Cavalry survivors near the command post area choose to ignore the order. They remain in place to fight or die. The tiny perimeter is now much smaller, and the command post (where 50–60 wounded are held) is about 150 yards outside the lines. Only two machine guns remain there to defend it. The tankers and infantrymen brace for a tough night as the last of the planes depart the area.

The Chinese strike up the band, the bugles and the whistles and everything else they can muster. Heavy artillery shells ring the spartan perimeter and Sergeant Elmer Miller, who thinks the shells are from mortars, moves his tanks outside the area in an attempt to add a slight safety net for the infantry, but to no avail. The bombardment continues to intensify. The infantry, undaunted by the full-scale barrages and full of obstinacy, continue to forestall disaster. All of the tanks are hit by shells, and one is set afire. One of the crew is killed trying to extinguish the flames.

Miller speaks with the infantry over his radio and it is agreed that the tanks, which are extremely low on fuel and lack sufficient ammunition, are of no more value to the trapped soldiers. The tanks head southwest, but within several miles, they are abandoned. Miller and several of the tankers eventually reach friendly lines.

In the meantime, the wounded at the perimeter begin to outnumber the able-bodied troops. Major Ormond, seriously wounded during the opening moments of the initial Chinese attack (November 1), still refuses treatment until all the other casualties are tended.

Relentlessly, the Chinese maintain the pressure. They mount six major night attacks against the perimeter. But the Americans refuse to capitulate. The Americans fire bazooka shells to ignite their own vehicles to provide some nocturnal illumination. Nonetheless, the Chinese come in hordes, wave after wave, and charge across an open field. During the fighting, about fifty men of the 2nd Battalion that had been isolated in the heights during the day race to the perimeter to give it added strength.

Meanwhile, the Chinese eliminate the machine guns at the old command post and overrun it. They capture about fifteen walking wounded, but permit between 30–45 seriously wounded troops to remain. Both Captain McAbee and Chaplain Kapaun are among those seized and taken to the Nammyon River area. At dawn, the defenders still hold the ground and Chinese dead are piled in layers. Still, no relief force is en route, but a three-man patrol reaches the besieged unit.

In the ROK area, having anticipated relief by the 7th Marines, the South Koreans have pulled back from their forward positions at Sudong and redeployed about four miles south of the village at a valley junction. At 0600, the South Koreans are struck by an enemy force comprising about two platoons. The enemy attack subsides after about one-half hour. Later, elements of the 7th Marines approach. The South Koreans pull up stakes and stream toward the rear.

In other activity, within the Iron Triangle, near P'y-onggang, about 1,000 Communist guerrillas attack a work train, but the ambush backfires. A 200-man contingent of the S.K. 17th Regiment is aboard as an armed guard. The regimental unit repels the attackers, kills about 40 and captures 23 others. Upon interrogation, the captives reveal that about 4,000 guerrillas are in the area to strike all trains that attempt to reach Wonsan. To meet the threat, the whole 27th S.K. Regiment moves to the area and later, it is bolstered by units of the U.S. 25th Division.

In Air Force activity, Far East Air Forces launches an RB-45 Tornado jet, which becomes its first reconnaissance mission of the war.

November 3 1950–January 24 1951. THIRD DESIGNATED CAMPAIGN: CHINESE COMMUNIST FORCES (CCF) INTERVENTION.

November 3   In the X Corps area, 1st Marine Division sector, the Division accelerates its march to the north, which mandates that the Wonsan-Hungnam MSR be securely held. The 1st Marines and contingents of the 1st Tank Battalion guard the route from Wonsan to a northward point about fifteen miles distant. In conjunction, the 1st Battalion, 5th Marines, protect the route from Hamhung south to Chigyong.

A 54-mile gap remains nearly totally undefended. The area stretching from Chigyong to Munchon is protected only by Special Operations Company, USA, and some patrols of Korean Counter Intelligence units. Both of these outfits are under X Corps control.

In the 1st Marine Division sector, 1st Marines zone, at Kojo, the 2nd Battalion, 1st Marines, initiates its overland march to Wonsan. En route, information arrives that informs Colonel Sutter that Korean bandits, unaligned with either side, have blown the rail line at Anbyon. Colonel Sutter halts the march at Anbyon and he stops two small convoys (a train and a truck convoy), which had also departed Kojo. Another small contingent of the battalion also pauses for the night at Anbyon.

In the 5th Marines zone, the regiment has been scouring the routes that lead to the Fusen Reservoir, which is located east of the 7th Marines operations, without incident.

In the 7th Marines zone, the Chinese had initiated small actions against the perimeter of Company A, 1st Battalion, at 2300, on the previous night. Around midnight (3rd–4th), the pressure begins to intensify as the Chinese 370th and 371st Regiments move to shred the 7th Marines. The 372nd Regiment, Chinese 124th Division, establishes a defensive perimeter in the vicinity of Chinhung-ni, less than five miles north of Sudong. The 2nd Battalion, 7th Marines, reports two enemy battalions on its left flank. The enemy fire continues to increase during the first hour, and by 0100, the Chinese that had silently navigated the ridge lines are poised to launch a full-scale assault against the left and right flanks.

At the sound of blaring bugles, the illumination of

U.S. troops fire a 3.5 rocket launcher (M20) into the heights against Communist positions on 3 November.

flares, and the howling of shrill whistles, two battalions of the Chinese 371st Regiment sprint down the slopes and plow into 1st and 2nd Battalion perimeters. Companies A and F on the east and Company B on the west are struck. However, on Hill 698, Company C encounters no activity along its lines. The Chinese, who brandish grenades and submachine guns, show no signs of timidity. They descend the slopes with total disregard

to the Marines' return fire. Close-quartered fighting erupts in the heights, and at times, the enemy detects holes in the line. When this opportunity arises, the Chinese bolt straight down to the lowest reaches of the slopes and gain positions within the Marine perimeter to carve a wedge between the battalions.

During the fighting, an enemy tank moves down the MSR and effortlessly passes a roadblock when the guards believe it to be friendly. Soon after, a T-34 comes to a halt just to the front of Company A's command post. At about the same time that a sergeant yells "tank!" as a warning, the T-34 commences fire, which prompts the Marines to scramble for safer positions from which to return fire. But the tank roars back onto the road and speeds south toward the 1st Battalion, 7th Marines' command post, then halts and bangs out some more shells. Nevertheless, the tank fire overshoots and instead strikes the heights to the rear of the CP. Nearby Marines return fire, but the rockets and recoilless rifles do not stop the tank.

The tank retires while under fire and moves back to the highway and comes within firing range of Company A's roadblock. This time the Marines are prepared. Their 3.5-inch rockets commence fire and the tank is hit by at least one shell, but the only apparent damage is that the sandbags that insulate the turret are set ablaze. However, the armor also sustains some inconspicuous damage. The simmering tank instantly gets off a round from about point-blank range. The solitary shell strikes a solid devastating blow that takes a very high toll on the antitank crew, and nearly wipes it out. The enemy tank then disengages and moves back toward its lines, visible because of bouncing sparks and a trail of flame that vanishes once the tank rounds the bend; it is abandoned on the following day. This loss brings the number of available enemy tanks down to four.

Nonetheless, the destruction of the tank does not provide a reprieve for the Marines in the heights. Instead, the enemy, dressed in sneakers, continues to creep and leap upon the Americans. Company A, now perilously deployed and heavily outnumbered, continues to sustain high casualties, while its 1st and 2nd Platoons attempt to throw back simultaneous assaults that press from three separate directions. The combat expands from the heights and breaks out in the lower ground at the MSR. The 3rd Platoon, deployed at the beginning of the spur, absorbs elements of the other two hard-hit platoons that had been forced back.

Meanwhile, enemy infiltration prevents some of the troops from completing the pull-back. Those troops join with Company B, but here, too, enemy pressure causes problems. The Communists tighten a vise on two of Company B's platoons and compel both to move to the low ground. In turn, the remaining platoon is also forced to pull back. But, the enemy's occupation of Company B's ground is temporary. A do-or-die counterattack retakes the ground.

In the meantime, west of the MSR, other contingents of Company B remain engaged in hotly contested skirmishes to the rear and on the left flank against Chinese forces that bypass Company C on Hill 698. Reinforcements are committed to the battle to thwart the attacks. The 1st Battalion reserve, Company B's 2nd Platoon, moves to fill the gap on the left flank, but there, too, the enemy infiltration curtails the aid. Enemy troops stretched along the river bed flood the MSR with fire that severs the relief route and halts the reserves before they can cross the MSR.

Still, in the heights and also besieged by infiltrating Chinese, Companies E and F, 2nd Battalion, 7th Marines, maintain their steadfastness, giving no ground. The Chinese numbers continue to multiply in all areas. By now, enemy contingents have bee-lined from the heights and grabbed positions along the MSR. Other components are poised to inundate the valley and overwhelm the command posts of the AT Company, as well as both the 1st and 2nd Battalion CPs. Chinese who spotted even small gaps along the flanks of Companies E and F in the heights have gnawed their way to dominant ground at the principal curve in the MSR. The maneuver splits the route between the 1st and 2nd Battalions. The main defending force at the curve is Battery I, but it occupies low ground and remains unaware that about one company of Chinese troops has circumvented the Marine positions in the heights above it and has settled in for the kill.

Meanwhile, more Communist troops flood the valley. The advance overpowers the positions of the 4.2-inch mortar sections of the 7th Marines; one mortar tube is captured. The darkness factor does not favor the Marines. They realize that the Chinese have struck in force, but the total damage to the perimeters will not be understood until the break of dawn, when it is discovered that enemy forces hold ground that is unmistakably within the Marine perimeter in the valley that lies south of Sudong. During the course of the confusing night fighting, the mortars and the howitzers of Batteries G and H bombard suspected enemy positions, but much is blind fire that probably scores little damage. The defenders trying to hold Hills 698 and 727, as well as the valley, eagerly await the rising sun and the imminent arrival of Marine Corsairs. The Chinese have pushed, shoved, and thrown everything they have available to dislodge the 7th Marines, but to no avail.

At the break of dawn, despite the intense pressure and the rising rate of casualties, the 7th Marines still hold. Colonel Litzenberg prepares to rectify a bad situation, particularly the weaknesses along his right flank. His tattered and exhausted regiment prepares to retake the ground and evict the Chinese. The end of the suppressing darkness brings mixed blessings. The enemy seems to be herded in batches amidst and above the Marines. They had successfully conducted an elaborate and unrestrained night-long attacking maneuver, which has them positioned to either celebrate the demise of the 7th Marines or at least act as a human guillotine to decapitate many of its components.

The newly discovered irregular alignment of the enemy regiments seems to present an immense challenge to Litzenberg's strategy. Unwilling to capitulate to the odds against some of his isolated units, Litzenberg utilizes his unexpected defensive stand to regroup.

The Marines' artillery, mortars, heavy machine guns and infantry fire in unison. As expected, Corsairs arrive to stitch the ridges with steel seams. The planes of VMF-312 remain on scene. They scorch the squatted enemy formations that lie upon the naked ridges, but they also form a deadly sky-chain that delivers enormous sheets of fire toward Chinese artillery, trucks and an assortment of other vehicles. At 0910, VMF-312 is joined by four planes of VMF(N)-513. Together, they further shatter the stability of the enemy. Meanwhile, the ground Marines struggle to hook up with Battery I at the key road bend along the MSR.

By 1100, the Chinese are dispersed and Battery I is again able to hold tenable positions. The battery joins the other artillery units' action by catapulting its supply of shells into the enemy lines. In addition, the 7th Marines continue to kill off infiltrators that remain within the respective sectors of the 1st and 2nd Battalions. The Chinese continue to raise tough opposition during the day, but now the Marines' firepower is far superior to that of the diminishing Chinese still in the valley.

The 1st Battalion puts its heavy machine guns to work. By noon, the low ground is under Marine control. And by late afternoon, more concentrated action evicts the Chinese from the valley. The Chinese attempt to depart the valley by heading north, walking astride the railroad tracks. The 1st Battalion's weapons company rivets the column with machine gun shells that ravage the ranks. The daylight retreat greatly increases enemy casualties. Six hundred and sixty-two enemy bodies are counted when the din of battle subsides.

Nevertheless, other Chinese units are simultaneously engaged against the Marines in the 2nd Battalion sector. The enemy still holds ground in the heights on a spur of Hill 727, above the MSR at its dominant curve. Consequently, some contingents of the 2nd Battalion remain isolated.

To ensure availability of sufficient ammunition, Colonel Litzenberg requests that planes deliver supplies to his forward contingents. Company D, deployed at the base of Hill 698 and south of the roadblock, is ordered to cross the river and eliminate the blockage. Contingents of Company E advance up the slope against opposition.

By about 0800, the 2nd Platoon, led by Lieutenant John Yancy, gains positions about 50 yards from the summit, which is defended only by one Chinese soldier. Atop the summit, the defenders show no signs of relinquishing control. The 3rd Platoon, commanded by Lieutenant Robert Bey, moves through the 2nd Platoon and charges toward the crest, but an avalanche of grenades tumbles down the slope and forces the 3rd Platoon to halt its attack.

At about 1400, planes arrive to plaster the top of the mass and clear the way to the crest. Company E drives to the peak and discovers its 40 defenders, all of whom are deceased. In the meantime, the roadblock at the curve still exists. Company D's attempt to take out the enemy on the spur of Hill 727 hits obstacles. Passage through the valley had gone well, but at the water's edge, enemy fire bars a crossing. Company D improvises. It swings left to new positions near the slope of Hill 698. From there, the Marines face Chinese on the opposite side of the MSR.

During the operation, Litzenberg again improvises. He directs Lieutenant Delong, executive officer, AT Company, to advance with a 75-mm recoilless rifle to join the fire of the planes and the ongoing artillery barrage that are pounding the obstacle. At about this time, the division's reconnaissance company returns from a night patrol and forms near Litzenberg's command post. It, too, joins the battle, and fires upon the enemy from the rear. These reconnaissance troops climb into the heights atop the enemy positions, then they move north along the ridgeline to attack.

All the while, Company D continues to destroy the remaining resistance on Hill 698 while it drives toward the blockage. The ground troops continue to receive support from the air and artillery, a combination that takes a high toll on the defenders and prompts them to abandon the roadblock.

Company D, subsequent to terminating the resistance on Hill 698, awaits the cessation of two air strikes, then it mounts a stiff charge. In the meantime, the Chinese head for safer positions. The reconnaissance company's troops spot the retreating Chinese as they scurry across open ground. Immediately, they call for air strikes to annihilate them, but the response is negative, as Captain Hull's Marines are too close, and in fact, directly in the target area.

The MSR is re-secured by 1810; however, the enemy does raise two counterattacks to oust Company D. Both assaults fail. Twenty-eight dead Chinese are counted at the roadblock. With the route again open, Marine supply convoys begin again to roll north from the regimental CP at about dusk to bolster the 1st and 2nd Battalions and to bring out the wounded. About 100 casualties are transported back to either the division hospital or to Hungnam, to receive treatment at the 121st Army Evacuation Hospital.

The Chinese resort to long-range harassment fire and a spattering of some light contact through the night of the 3rd-4th. Nevertheless, Marine artillery and mortars negate the enemy's efforts. The sporadic night contacts are deemed to be either Chinese patrols or Communist stragglers, not full-size contingents.

The fighting initiated on November 2 continues through November 4, and in the process, the ranks of both attacking enemy regiments are greatly thinned. The 371st Regiment's 1st and 3rd Battalions sustain a combined loss of about five companies and the 370th Regiment's 3rd Battalion incurs the loss of about two companies. The dead count in the 370th Regiment's field of attack stands at 793.

Subsequent to the battering the two enemy regiments have received at the hands of the 7th Marines, they move back to the lines of the 372nd Regiment to defend against the expected advance of the 7th Marines.

In addition, planes spot various enemy columns while they hurriedly move in the area south of the Chosin Reservoir. The reports estimate about three convoys that travel in groups of about 15 to 20 trucks in a column. Litzenberg absorbs the information and prepares to encounter more opposition on the following day.

North of Chinhung-ni, elements of the 124th Chinese Division entrench themselves on gargantuan Hills 891 and 987. These dominant masses overlook the MSR at a point about two miles north of the town. The Chinese are unable to accommodate the remaining four tanks of the 344th N.K. Tank Regiment because the narrow roads will not permit passage of armor.

Meanwhile, relative calm settles in for the night and the 7th Marines' perimeter, which had been unnaturally altered on the previous day, is restored. One difference is that east of the roadblock, the heights are now possessed by Company D. At dawn, probing patrols will penetrate farther north to set the tone for the advance.

In the 7th Division area, At Iwon, the 3rd Battalion, 31st Infantry Regiment, debarks. The remainder of the regiment comes ashore on the following day. Its mission will be to advance and deploy west of the 17th Regiment on its left flank in the vicinity of P'ungsan.

In other activity, the 17th Regiment at P'ungsan requests an airdrop of ammunition and supplies.

In the Eighth Army area, 1st Cavalry Division sector, the dwindling number of survivors, 3rd Battalion, 8th Cavalry, receive no reprieve. The Chinese continue to hammer the defenders, but the Americans exhibit a fighting spirit. Early in the day, a three-man detachment moves to the old command post to get rations to the wounded. The patrol is told that the Chinese had been there and taken prisoners.

The enemy attacks continue throughout the day, but the Americans again hold and throw the Chinese back. The defenders continue to rack up heavy casualties against the Chinese, but they attack in legions. The cavalry's ammunition is quickly depleting and no air support is available, but the Americans borrow from the Chinese. After each attack, the troops slither out of their holes and retrieve ammunition and weapons from the piles of dead Chinese that lie close to their positions. The Americans keep the weapons but return the ammunition on each succeeding attack.

The Chinese inch closer, but the 8th Cavalry retains its honor and still controls the perimeter. The number of Communist buglers that have been silenced is unknown, but the blaring noise continues through the night. At dawn (4th), having repelled all assaults, the cavalrymen maintain their positions. The 8th Cavalry reports that it is about 55 percent under strength. Division consensus considers the regiment unfit for combat until it receives replacement troops and becomes re-supplied.

In the British 27th Commonwealth Brigade zone, pursuant to orders, the Brigade has moved from Taech'on. It deploys near Pakch'on to build a defense at the northwest junction of the bridgehead. Chinese Communist troops move into Taech'on soon after the British depart. The British have had some slight skirmishes at Taech'on and several enemy troops desert and enter British lines. The deserters are Chinese, and upon inspection of enemy dead near Taech'on, it is discovered that they are attired in superb fur boots.

In the 24th Division sector, the 19th Regiment moves from its positions and redeploys northeast of Anju; from left to right, the 1st, 2nd and 3rd Battalions stretch from the Ch'ongch'on River to the Kuryong River. Meanwhile, the 5th RCT deploys to the rear of the ROK II Corps, less than five miles northeast of Kunu-ri. The South Korean 7th Division holds Hill 622, about three miles northeast of the town.

In the 2nd Division sector, the 9th Regiment is deployed south of Kunu-ri and delegated with responsibility for guarding the road to Sunchon.

In the ROK II Corps area, after the redeployment of the 19th Regiment, 24th Division, the S.K. 1st Division disengages its fight with the enemy at positions northeast of the Americans. Afterwards, the ROKs withdraw through the U.S. positions and cross the Ch'ongch'on. The maneuver by the South Koreans is complete by the following day.

The S.K. 7th Division's 3rd and 5th Regiments are stationed on the most strategic terrain at Kunu-ri, Hill 622. It is a huge mountain that lies several miles northeast of the town. The 8th Regiment, 7th S.K. Division, is posted east of Kunu-ri and held in reserve. Hill 622 controls the town and Ch'ongch'on Valley, through which flows the rails and communication lines. The U.S. 5th RCT is stationed to the immediate rear of the S.K. 7th Division.

November 4   U.N. minesweepers conclude the minesweeping operation to clear the inner harbor at Wonsan. Still, mines remain in the channel. The minesweepers move to Hungnam to secure a thirty-two mile channel and also to sweep the inner harbor.

In the X Corps area, Special Operations Company, USA, operating between Chigyong and Munchon, informs corps that it has spotted huge numbers of North Koreans as they descend into the area west of their positions. Also, Corps informs the 1st Marine Division that mounted guerrillas had struck Kowan about fifteen miles north of Munchon and fired upon the railway police.

In the 1st Marine Division area, the command post is relocated from Wonsan to Hungnam in coordination with the assignments that direct the 5th and 7th Marines to initiate missions in the north. The 2nd Battalion, 5th Marines, which has been under the operational control of the 1st Marines while performing patrol details for the 1st Marines, is included in this movement. The 2nd Battalion, 1st Marines, and two accompanying convoys arrive at Wonsan from Anbyon.

General O.P. Smith arrives at Hungnam by helicopter and establishes the command post at 1100. At 2130, a train transporting 160 officers and men of headquarters also arrives from Wonsan. Enemy guerrilla fire strikes the train while it is en route, but no casualties are sustained. A defensive perimeter is established to fortify the CP. Two outposts and eight machine gun positions are spread about to guard all probable approach routes. Unknown to the Marines at the command post, three nearby connected caves house about

250 tons of high explosives. This dangerous material is not discovered for about one week. A detachment of sixteen Marines guards it until it can be removed from the caves and detonated.

In other activity, Division issues OpnO 10–50; it directs the 1st Battalion, 1st Marines, to prepare to move to Chonjin, located 220 air-miles from Wonsan; however, the order is rescinded by X Corps on November 9.

In the 1st Marines sector, At 1440, a heavily guarded thirty-four supply vehicle convoy departs Wonsan for Manjon-ni. A light observation plane is airborne and two Corsairs are available to bolster the column, but no forward air controller makes the trip. Instead, a tactical air control party, placed toward the rear of the convoy, receives the information from the OY and transfers it to the VMF-312 Corsairs. Company A, reinforced by one platoon of Company C, engineers, a mortar section and a contingent of recoilless rifles, provides ground security for the convoy.

The engineers act as vanguard to clear the path of obstacles. The column encounters four unprotected enemy roadblocks. Engineers effortlessly plug the craters to speed progress, but the next obstacle is heavily fortified by troops in the heights that spring an ambush on the engineers. About eight miles out, a wall of fire cascades down from the high ground on both sides of the primitive road. Vehicles stall and clog the path, which hinders the advance of the riflemen. The engineers take cover near their vehicles and return effective fire to forestall disaster.

In the meantime, the Corsairs arrive to assist, but the effort falls short due to the lack of the forward air controller and the approach of dusk.

The convoy's commanding officer, Captain Barrow, attempts a return to Wonsan rather than risk unnecessary casualties in the darkness. The vehicles reverse direction through a series of harrowing turns on a dangerous road, where one false move could plunge a vehicle several hundred feet into the valley. Long-range artillery fire accelerates and it prompts Barrow to order the convoy to proceed without lights.

The besieged convoy makes it back, but along the route, one vehicle misses a turn and shoots off the path. Fortuitously, the truck, transporting twenty Marines, lands on a rare road shoulder and no fatalities occur. Other Marines pull the men to safety. Captain Barrow's force sustains eight men killed and sixteen injured. The convoy loses five vehicles. Barrow's reinforced Company A retraces the route on the following morning.

Colonel Puller informs Barrow that the failure of the mission was due to the late start and the absence of a TAC, not his decision in the field.

In the 5th Marines zone, the 5th Marines detaches its 1st Battalion to divisional control. In addition, its 3rd Battalion deploys near Oro-ri, while the 2nd Battalion moves toward the Sinhung Valley to relieve the S.K. 18th Regiment. The 2nd Battalion effect the relief at about 1145, at positions about five miles north and

fifteen miles east of the 7th Marines. Lt. Colonel Roise's 2nd Battalion is given the task of guarding the Sinhung corridor while assessing the enemy's positions and related strength. The 2nd Battalion is to inspect particular northerly paths to the Chosin and Fusen Reservoirs. Patrols will be initiated on the following day.

In the 7th Marines sector, at about dawn, elements of the 1st Battalion advance through the valley floor and move toward Sudong. They reach the fringes of the town without incident, and then return to the perimeter, again without encountering resistance. Colonel Litzenberg directs the 2nd Battalion to hold in place in the heights on Hills 698 and 727, to provide cover fire for the advance. At about 0800, the column moves out, spearheaded by the 1st Platoon's reconnaissance company. The reconnaissance company moves swiftly in jeeps. Soon after, the 2nd and 3rd Platoons begin to move through the heights above the town, while the 1st Platoon enters the supposedly unoccupied town. At a point midway through the town, the lead jeeps swing around a turn and stun some lingering Chinese troops. A heated fire-fight erupts, but thirty minutes later, three Chinese are killed and twenty others are taken prisoner. Meanwhile, the 7th Marines maintains its advance as it shadows the reconnaissance company.

Following the interruption at Sudong, the 2nd Platoon replaces the 1st Platoon as vanguard. Later, the column reinitiates its drive toward Chinhung-ni, while the 1st Battalion, 7th Marines, moves out from its positions south of Sudong and follows the route taken through the lowlands by the reconnaissance company.

At the next objective, Chinhung-ni, there is a railroad connecting point that services Funchilin Pass with cable cars. The rail lines straddle the west side of the river, opposite the highway, and the tracks enter the town by way of a bridge that crosses over a medium stream.

At Samgo station, slightly beyond the town, a small contingent of Chinese soldiers are posted, but they seem not to notice the approaching jeeps of the reconnaissance company that are clearly visible on the highway on the opposite bank. Neither do the Marines detect the presence of the four T-34s lying in wait along their approach route, but suspicions are soon raised when conspicuous enemy tank tracks are discovered at a point about 2,000 yards in front of Chinhung-ni. Word of the tracks is sent back, but orders from Lt. Colonel Davis instruct the reconnaissance platoon to advance.

The 2nd Platoon moves directly past the first Communist tank as it reaches the road that enters the town. The vanguard continues for a short distance, and at that point, the Marines glance across the river and spot the Chinese on the opposite bank, yet they fail to detect yet a second tank that is perilously close to them. The Marines fire upon the enemy ground troops, prompting the Chinese to hurriedly disperse, but not before many of them succumb to the effective fire.

During the brief exchange, Lieutenant Sharon and his troops notice a strange pile of brush, which conceals the second tank. There are no visible signs of it being occupied. Sharon and two other Marines board the tank and suddenly the periscope begins to turn. Staff Sergeant Twohey and Corporal McDermott both move into action. McDermott breaks the glass, while Twohey quickly deposits a grenade into the tank. Sharon, Twohey and McDermott fly from the tank to take cover just as it detonates.

The grenade damages but does not kill the tank, which suddenly bolts forward. Twohey re-boards the cantankerous vehicle and makes another grenade deposit. In quick motion, the grenade is flipped into the periscope. Afterwards, a huge bang terminates any further movement by the tank. Smoke emerges from the charred armor, but to be sure, more devastation is thrust upon the tank. Other troops, including the recoilless rifles and Company C's 3.5-inch rocket crews, begin to catch up with the vanguard. The recoilless rifles and rockets blast the tank to ensure its demise.

In the meantime, the first tank remains tranquil, but at the burst of fire, a third tank springs from its cover, a thatched hut that collapses as the tank roars out. The enemy tank appears as the nearby valley becomes consumed with advancing vehicles and Marines. The tank's turret points toward the column and prepares to unleash its 81-mm shells.

A forward air observer, Lieutenant Elledge, radios for air support while the recoilless rifles and rockets again commence fire. The tank is hit, but not fatally. It advances farther and comes under attack from the air. One of the planes dives and delivers a killing blow with two 5-inch rockets that strike the mark and instantly decimate the armor. Both VMF-312 and VMF(N)-513 provide close-support missions. It is not determined which outfit scores the kill.

Following the destruction of the second tank, Lieutenant Sharon and the reconnaissance Marines move forward, but prudently, in expectation of more trouble. And they find it. The landscape is again unnaturally bulging. A fourth tank is detected, nestled just to their front and nudged alongside a hill.

Meanwhile, the trailing Marines continue to advance, and at about the same time Sharon spots the fourth tank, the initial tank is discovered by other Marines. Tank number one, back near Chinhung-ni, finds itself in the middle of the advancing Marine column. The recoilless rifles and the rockets hammer it with fire. The crew decides to abandon the tank and surrender.

In the meantime, the final tank comes under attack by Sharon's men, who ford the stream and close on the armor. But before a shot is fired, the crew, which is outside and to the rear of the tank, capitulates without a struggle. The surrender culminates the demise of the 344th N.K. Tank Regiment. The abandoned tank is not spared. The recoilless rifles and rockets destroy it.

All the while, the trailing elements continue to arrive at Chinhung-ni. The 7th Marines gains about 6,000 yards by the middle of the afternoon and at that point, Colonel Litzenberg prepares to form his perimeter. By 1600, the 1st Battalion begins to dig in tightly. Recon-

naissance company patrols are dispatched into Funchilin Pass to probe enemy strength and confirm earlier reports of enemy troops across the canyon from Hill 987 on Hill 891. The units are to penetrate about 2,000 yards and establish an outpost on Hill 891's southern tip.

The Reconnaissance company's 3rd Platoon, led by Lt. Charles Puckett, takes the point as the column rolls about one mile deep into the pass and reaches a point where the road swerves to the east and obstinate Hill 987 bulges on the west. The precarious highway moves dead east for about 1,000 yards before it makes a deep curve, and then ascends on a coinciding route that heads back toward the initial point of the curve, but just before the point, it again changes direction and leads north, astride the granite-like slopes of Hill 891. The road challenges all vehicles, with or without accompanying opposition. The patrol proceeds with prudence and expects danger at any moment.

At about 1630, immediately after rounding the steep curve, the Communists commence firing. To the left, across the abyss, shells descend from Hill 987. From the front on the slopes of Hill 891, more fire is poured upon the lead vehicles. To the right, a Chinese patrol operating on the serpentine highway joins the attack. The riveting fire halts the patrol and compels it to remain pinned to the ground with no alternative except to await help.

Finally, through the combined aid of Marine aircraft and darkness, the besieged patrol is able to extricate itself and return to the perimeter. Enemy fire inflicts fatalities. Two men are killed and five others are wounded. Also, the two lead jeeps are destroyed.

The remainder of the night is calm for the 7th Marines. During the tranquility, Colonel Litzenberg establishes the blueprint for the following day's advance. The Marine night fighters of VMF(N)-513 receive little sleep. They execute sorties to bombard and strafe enemy convoys in the vicinity of the Chosin Reservoir to lessen resistance for the following day.

Also, during the day, an enemy contingent attacks Company A, 1st Battalion, 7th Marines, at its positions on Hill 532. The contingent, led by Sergeant James L. Poynter, repels the assault, despite initially being surrounded. Poynter spots three enemy machine guns being brought against his diminutive command. He bolts from his position, knocks out two of the crews and then eliminates the third gun, but in the process, Poynter is mortally wounded. His actions save the platoon, which is able to extricate itself from encirclement and deploy in more favorable positions. Sergeant Poynter is awarded the Medal of Honor posthumously for his extraordinary heroism under fire.

In other activity, the 2nd Battalion, 7th Marines, deployed to afford cover fire for the day's offensive, engages the enemy at a strategic position near Hills 698 and 727. Company E receives the task of taking the elevation, which has already survived five assaults by other U.N. units, including Marines. Corporal Lee H. Phillips leads the attack and begins to ascend the nearly un-ascendable hill. When the detachment makes it up the rocky cliff, its numbers have been cut to five, with the others all wounded along the way. Nevertheless, Phillips' command charges against the strongpoints and eliminates all but one; however, his command is again thinned, down to three men. Undaunted, Phillips continues the ascent to eliminate the lone surviving obstacle.

The position is seized by the Marines, but shortly thereafter, a larger enemy force counterattacks. The attack is repulsed; however, Corporal Phillips is killed. He is awarded the Medal of Honor posthumously for his extraordinary heroism and leadership in the face of a hostile force.

In the 7th Infantry Division zone, the tardiness of the unloading operation at Iwon beachhead has created pressure on the 17th Regiment at P'ungsan. The regiment on the previous day had requested an airdrop with particular emphasis on the delivery of 4.2-inch, 60-mm and 81-mm mortar ammunition to ensure it has enough weaponry and supplies to meet any threat that might arise. The items are dropped this day.

In other activity, patrols discover that the enemy to their front has vanished. Expecting no resistance, the 17th Regiment advances, feeling the chill of the 2-degree weather, to the Ungi River without incident.

At Iwon, the 31st Regiment completes its debarkation and begins to initiate its movement to the high ground at the Pujon Reservoir, where it will deploy west of the 17th Regiment to guard the left flank. It, too, will soon experience the Korean winter in the mountains.

The 32nd Regiment begins to debark, then it advances southwest along the coast, and after passing Hamhung, it pivots and heads northeast to deploy at Tangp'ang-ni, from where it will stage to participate in the upcoming offensive.

In the ROK I Corps area, heavy fighting continues at Kilchu as elements of the S.K. Capital Division reinitiate the battle to seize the town. The contest continues into the following day.

In the Eighth Army area, 1st Cavalry Division sector, the survivors of the 8th Cavalry (south of Unsan) now number about 450 men; however, of these, about 250 troops are wounded and unable to fight. Realizing that circumstances are not going to be altered for the better, it is decided that those still able should attempt to break for safety. A small 4-man probing contingent, composed of two officers and two enlisted men, squirm out of the perimeter and creep to the old command post, then, after a brief pause, the group safely makes it to the river and beyond to a village, unoccupied except for several wounded Chinese.

Lieutenants Walter Mayo and George Peterson remain at the village to check out the crossing site, while the enlisted men, at about 1430, return to the 3rd Battalion perimeter to bring out the remaining officers and troops. Captain George McDonald (2nd Battalion), Captain William McClain (Company E), Lieutenant Paul Bromser (Company L) and the other healthy troops begin to head east and barely in the nick of time.

Just after they move out, the Chinese carpet the perimeter with white phosphorous shells, obviously preparation fire for yet another assault. As the able-bodied troops depart, reportedly there are no tears from the wounded. In fact, they remain steadfast and encourage those leaving to hurry back with reinforcements. Captain Clarence Anderson, battalion surgeon, elects to remain behind with his wounded.

The 200 evacuees continue moving throughout the night, disregarding their weariness and the inclement weather that deteriorates further when a rainstorm moves over the area. The column swings from its eastward direction and moves northeast, and then it swings southward. By the following morning, the column still has not been spotted by the Chinese.

Major Ormond is taken prisoner, but he succumbs from his wounds. Later, it is reported that he had been buried near Unsan. The chaplain, Father Kapaun, dies in a Communist prison in 1951. Captain Filmore McAbee and the surgeon, Captain Anderson, survive captivity and return to the U.S.A. during the POW exchange after hostilities end.

At Anju, endless columns of refugees flood across the Ch'ongch'on River heading south.

In the 24th Division sector, the U.S. and British contingents that hold the line north of the Ch'ongch'on River to protect the retreat of the I Corps receive a strong attack. About 1,000 Chinese soldiers skirt across the Kuryong River and strike the rear of the 1st Battalion, 19th Regiment. The effect is devastating. The Chinese interrupt a radio operator while he is informing headquarters of the attack and abruptly terminate the transmission. Soon after, and without any genuine resistance, evident by the lack of casualties, the Chinese have overrun the positions and the regiment abandons its positions hastily.

Reinforcements rush to the scene, but the 1st Battalion almost in its entirety bolts eastward across the Kuryong and the Ch'ongch'on Rivers. Its equipment is abandoned; however, some equipment and vehicles are self-destroyed. The reinforcements, composed of contingents of the 3rd Battalion, make no headway. The remainder of the battalion enters the fight, but still the Chinese hold the road.

At about the same time, Chinese pound against the defenses of the 5th RCT south of the river. The alarms ring loudly at divisional headquarters and General Church attempts to forestall total disaster. Church directs General Garrison Davidson to take command of all 24th Division troops north of the Ch'ongch'on. By about noon, Davidson reaches the 19th Regimental command post and takes command of TF Davidson and in addition, he is directed to co-ordinate the activity of the British troops at the bridgehead. However, the enemy presses forward at full-throttle. At some points, the night attacks further pierce the lines of the 19th Regiment.

By mid-afternoon, General Church orders the 21st Regiment to await darkness, then ford the Ch'ongch'on to prepare to attack on the following day to push the

Chinese back. British defenders on the western portion of the Ch'ongch'on bridgehead receive a slight reprieve, but only until dawn on the 5th.

Across from Pakch'on, on the west bank of the Taeryong River, the Australian 3rd Battalion and the bulk of the British Argyll 1st Battalion are deeply dug in at their positions. The Middlesex Regiment and Company A of the Argylls are posted in and around Pakch'on. These British Commonwealth units are bolstered by the guns of the 1st Cavalry's 61st FABn, which are deployed less than three miles south of the town.

In addition to the attacks against the defenses at Kunu-ri and the western sector of the Ch'ongch'on bridgehead, the Chinese have dispatched other contingents east with orders to bypass Pakch'on and close toward the U.S. artillery positions to eliminate the guns and, simultaneously, sever the road to the rear of the British. The mission succeeds. By dawn November 5, the enemy is poised for the attack.

In the 5th RCT zone, the enemy crashes through the defenses of the South Koreans on Hill 622 and plows into the American defenses south of the Ch'ongch'on near Kunu-ri. The progress threatens the right flank of Eighth Army. The Chinese elements are components of the 38th Army and estimated to be about division strength.

Initially, the 5th RCT surrenders about 1,000 yards, but it quickly bounces back. The vicious fighting at times is close-quartered, with tenacious hand-to-hand fighting. Chinese machine guns enter the fight and rip into the ranks. Lieutenant Morgan Hansel disregards his own safety and singlehandedly charges numerous enemy emplacements to prevent the annihilation of one platoon of Company C. The courageous action of Hansel results in the loss of his life. But, the regiment thwarts the attacks and holds Kunu-ri.

In the ROK II Corps area, Chinese forces close against Hill 622 and the powerful surge plows into the S.K. 3rd Regiment and drives it back toward U.S. lines. The retreating South Koreans are halted and by Captain Hubert Ellis, who dispatches the unit back toward the hill. In addition, the 8th Regiment is taken out of reserves and committed.

Heavy see-saw fighting continues on the mountain throughout the day, but by dusk, the Chinese are driven back and the South Koreans control the strategic northwest ridge.

In Air Force activity, while Eighth Army comes under heavy pressure, B-26s arrive to provide close-air support. The air strikes in the vicinity of Chongju kill about 500 of the enemy.

November 5   *In the X Corps area, 1st Marine Division sector, 1st Marines zone,* Captain Barrow again leads his convoy toward Majon-ni. It departs Wonsan at 0830, which should provide plenty of daylight if the Communists intend to spring another ambush. Barrow also changes the rules. Anticipating that the enemy will hear the noisy lead vehicles, he sends out his infantry with orders to alternate the platoons, but main-

tain a pace that keeps them at least 1,000 yards in front of the vehicles. The modified plan produces excellent results.

Apparently, the enemy is resting and having breakfast while awaiting the roar of the vehicles when the Americans unexpectedly arrive. The vanguard platoon, led by 2nd Lieutenant Donald R. Jones, silently rounds a curve near the scene of the previous day's fighting and discovers an early morning picnic with about seventy participants. Without warning, the platoon riflemen open fire. The threat that had lurked is instantly terminated. Some of the contingent escape, but fifty-one of the Communists succumb and three others are taken prisoner. The Marines sustain no casualties, nor do they sustain any for the remainder of the trip.

The convoy passes the ambush scene unhindered by the enemy corpses and rolls into Manjon-ni just after lunch without further incident. The supply-laden trucks are greeted jubilantly by the 3rd Battalion defenders; Army Intelligence has informed them that the enemy has planned to attack the perimeter at 0100 on the 6th.

With the arrival of the ammunition and supplies, coupled with Barrow's reinforced Company A, 1st Battalion, 1st Marines, the 3rd Battalion initiates a search mission to discover the suspected 2,000–3,000 enemy troops expected to launch the attack. A strong force composed of Companies G and I, bolstered by a contingent of weapons company, advances about six miles along the Pyongyang Road to the suspected objective.

Except for some distant sniper fire, the convoy encounters no resistance. Eighty-one enemy troops are encountered, but they choose to surrender without any prompting. Although it had not been necessary, the convoy was further buffered by artillery units in Manjon-ni. Nevertheless, Army Intelligence reports prove true. The Communists initiate an attack during the early morning of November 6.

In the 5th Marines sector, in the Sinhung Valley, the 2nd Battalion initiates reconnaissance patrols composed of about squad strength. Additionally, reinforced combat patrols are dispatched to augment the inspection of the routes that lead to the reservoirs. These patrols continue until November 9. Ultimately, the patrols discover that all southern routes to the Fusen and Chosin Reservoirs are not fitted for military traffic. However, the road that leads northeast from Sinhung is capable of sustaining traffic to the sector of the 7th Division and beyond to the Manchurian border. Lieutenant Colonel Roise's 2nd Battalion begins making contact with U.S. Army patrols on November 7.

In the 7th Marines sector, the memory of the ambush on the previous day is fresh in the minds of the regiment as it plans to advance. Mortars and the artillery of the 3rd Battalion, 11th Marines, are to remain in positions south of Sudong, from where they can catapult support fire if opposition emerges from the heights in Funchilin Pass.

At 0700, the 1st Platoon's reconnaissance company

retraces the steps of the patrol that had gotten snagged on the previous day. It drives down the highway, guarding the right flank in concert with the 1st Battalion, also designated to protect the right flank. The 2nd Battalion trails the lead 1st Battalion, but it is to pass through and take the lead to initiate the attack to secure the pass. However, the enemy remains tightly concealed and within impregnable positions, awaiting the arrival of the vanguard.

At the same place Lieutenant Puckett's 3rd Platoon had been bushwhacked, the Chinese catch the 1st Platoon, led by Lt. Hargett. It, too, is unable to advance, nor is it able to immediately retire. But within minutes, support fire arrives to cool the slopes. The artillery crashes down on the enemy positions and the planes of VMF-312 arrive on scene to blister the heights. During the enfilade, the 1st Platoon pulls back to avoid the friendly fire.

In the meantime, the 3rd Battalion, commanded by Major Roach, departs at 0800 to clear the obstacles. Company I drives toward Hill 987, while Company G, commanded by Captain Thomas Cooney, advances toward equally obstinate Hill 891. The enemy raises walls of fire that strike both companies as they reach the vicious bend in the road. The intense fire

Chinese POWs.

Two captured Russian-built 76-mm self-propelled guns.

A U.S. infantryman has a .30-caliber Browning automatic rifle (M1918A2) at an assembly area.

essentially severs the highway and forces the Marines of Company G to hold where they stand. The Marines return fire as effectively as possible. Captain Cooney is wounded twice during the day's fighting.

Meanwhile, from about 1000 until the end of the day, the engagement leans toward the action of the planes, artillery and mortars that support the Marines against the long-range mortars of the enemy. During the course of the day's combat, General O.P. Smith pinpoints Koto-ri as the initial target, but the task becomes unattainable. The day-long ground skirmishes remain nearly stationary with no measurable gains.

During the incessant bombardments, one of the enemy troops decides to call it a day. He jumps from his position and surrenders to Marines. Following his capture, the Chinese soldier outlines the positions of his comrades. The Americans zero in on the two battalions on Hills 891 and 987 and the enemy battalion held in reserve on a knob between Hill 987 and 1304.

The huge amount of firepower dispensed by the Americans keeps the enemy at bay and scores much destruction to men and equipment. Although the Chinese in the heights sustain heavy losses and have watched many of their guns fall prey to the American air and artillery barrages, they maintain control of their positions when the fighting subsides at the fall of darkness.

In the meantime, Marine pilots from VMF-312 pound enemy positions throughout the day to disrupt convoys running between Chinhung-ni and the Chosin Reservoir. Twenty-one trucks are decimated. During the raids, the pilots report that the ridges are infested with Chinese. They also report that the air strikes have greatly diminished their numbers.

The planes of VMF(N)-513 execute 37 sorties that consume 90 hours of close-support missions. The roving aircraft blast an array of targets that stretch from Koto-ri to the reservoir at Haguru, and inflict more losses of men, equipment and vehicles upon the enemy.

Marine casualties for the day are extremely light, and due as much to the nasty terrain as well as enemy fire. It becomes apparent that the Marines will need another day to take their objective. Colonel Litzenberg establishes a night perimeter and prepares to reinitiate the attack on the morning of the 6th. The 3rd Battalion will lead the attack. As darkness settles, the area at the pass again becomes peaceful and no enemy night-attack forms. Only a few minor encounters occur along the perimeter.

In the U.S. 3rd Infantry Division, the first units of the 3rd Division arrive at Wonsan. The 2nd Battalion, 65th RCT, debarks, followed by the remainder of the regiment. The operation is completed on November 18.

The 65th Regiment is the first of the 3rd Division units to join X Corps. When the Regiment embarked from Puerto Rico, its enlisted men were all Puerto Ricans, and 64 of the complement of 206 officers were also Puerto Rican. Now it is composed of Puerto Ricans, men from the Virgin Islands, Japanese-Americans and Americans. South Korean draftees also join the regiment.

In the ROK I Corps area, at Kilchu, following several days of fighting, the South Koreans encircle the town before dawn. The North Koreans continue to resist, but by noon, the town is captured by the S.K. 1st Regiment and the cavalry regiment. Corsairs attached to the 1st Marine Air Wing support the attacks and knock out two tanks and four pieces of artillery, and they also slay about 350 ground troops.

On the following day, when the toll is taken, the enemy has sustained 530 killed. The South Koreans lose 21 killed and 91 wounded. Upon questioning POWs, it is determined that Kilchu had been defended by elements of the N.K. 57th Brigade. In addition, the South Koreans capture nine 45-mm antitank guns.

In the Eighth Army area, Army proclaims that due to an "ambush," all arriving replacement troops would be assigned to the 1st Cavalry Division. The decision is mandated because of the mauling of the 8th Cavalry Regiment at Unsan. Casualty figures, thus far, are high; about 1,000 troops are listed as missing in action. However, stragglers continue to arrive within friendly lines and when the final census is taken, the losses total about 600 troops.

In the 1st Cavalry Division sector, the surviving men of the 8th Cavalry continue to head toward friendly lines. From their positions in the heights, they observe Chinese troops, including infantry and horse cavalry, that are moving on a road below them. Undetected, the Americans continue to move through the hills toward Ipsok.

In the 24th Division sector, Colonel Throckmorton's 5th RCT has repelled the Chinese attacks of the previous day. Kunu-ri remains safe.

In the 19th Regimental zone, the previous day's fighting at the bridgehead has cost the 1st Battalion some ground, but this day the 2nd and 3rd Battalions, 21st Regiment, are thrown into the fight and the ground is regained. Nevertheless, the Chinese continue to infiltrate in great numbers and they then combine with North Korean forces. The Chinese 355th Regiment (119th Division), the Chinese 358th Regiment (120th Division) and one N.K. regiment oppose the U.S. 19th Regiment.

After dark, the Chinese and North Koreans launch an attack that crashes against the entire front and lasts through the night of the 5th-6th. Vicious combat erupts in every sector and artillery fire is called upon to assist the outnumbered ground troops. The 1st and 3rd Battalions successfully hold their ground; however, the Chinese hit the 2nd Battalion on Hill 123 especially hard. The attacks strike the front and rear of the line to gain surprise against Companies E and G. Hill 123, on the right flank of Eighth Army and less than five miles above the Ch'ongch'on River, overlooks the village of Ch'ongch'on.

Apparently, some Chinese discover the communication wires of Company E and trace them to the rear of the command post. One trooper, Corporal Mitchell Red Cloud, Jr., Company E, is the first to be greeted by the Chinese. Red Cloud, positioned on the tip of the ridge where a path heads to the command post, spots the enemy. He clasps his BAR, bolts to his feet and unleashes devastating fire that rips into the Chinese at point-blank range. Return fire cuts Red Cloud down, but he refuses medical treatment; rather, he struggles to his feet, clamps his arm around a tree and resumes fire that kills more Chinese. Enemy fire finally inflicts a mortal wound, but Red Cloud's valiant actions buy some desperately needed time.

Another Company E BARman, Corporal Joseph Balboni, spots Chinese troops that encroach his position. Balboni, from a distance of about seventy-five feet, intercepts the Communists and rains fire upon them. Again, they maintain the advance despite the wall of fire. Balboni refuses to yield; he remains steadfastly in place and maintains his incessant fire until enemy fire kills him.

The Communists, seemingly disregarding their high losses, continue to attack and finally penetrate the battalion lines. The Chinese overrun much of the area. Many men of Company E are still asleep when the enemy strikes from the rear. The Chinese slaughter some with shots to the back of the head and others are killed while still in their sleeping bags. The tenacious enemy pressure forces the 2nd Battalion to pull back.

By 0300, it has surrendered about 1,000 yards. For the next several hours, the 2nd Battalion struggles to retain control of its new line, but it holds. At about dawn, the Chinese disengage and the eastern bridgehead remains intact.

The 1st Battalion, 19th Regiment, which had been routed on November 4, has received new equipment. During the night (5th-6th) it moves back across the Ch'ongch'on River to the north bank.

Corporal Red Cloud receives the Medal of Honor posthumously for his extraordinary courage in the face of the enemy. Corporal Balboni, credited with the death of seventeen Communist troops subsequently discovered to the front of his corpse, receives the Distinguished Service Cross posthumously.

In the British zone, at the western sector of the bridgehead along the Ch'ongch'on River, the Chinese strike against the U.S. 61st FABn, which is deployed to the rear of the British perimeter. The attack is geared to include the destruction of a strategic bridge and to ensure the annihilation of the artillery battalion. Suddenly, shells arcing from the east rain upon the artillery positions. The artillerymen react positively. The gun crewmen and every other available man circles the tightened perimeter to form a solid wall of fire, including that of automatic weapons. The British are informed of the ongoing assault, and they immediately rush reinforcements to the aid of the Americans.

Planes appear to hammer the attackers throughout the day and into the night. Company A, Argylls, speeds to the area. Slightly afterward, the Australian 3rd Battalion receives orders to withdraw from its positions on the west side of the Taeryong River and redeploy east of the river. From a quickly tightened line, the artillery batteries prepare for the brunt of an attack. Battery C becomes the recipient of the harshest fire. Its commander, Captain Howard Moore, shifts one howitzer to meet the threat. From point-blank range, a raging storm of fire streams eastward into the advancing troop formation and causes the enemy-occupied rice paddy to turn blood-red.

Within about forty-five minutes, another howitzer redirects its withering fire against a new line of attackers. And, to further hinder the advancing Communists, an aerial observer guides the fire of yet another battery toward the charging Chinese. The artillerymen maintain their discipline and exhibit no signs of abandoning their positions, despite the incoming firestorm of mortar fire and small arms fire. Nevertheless, the Chinese continue their relentless assault. Initially, the attackers comprise only about one battalion, but the entire assault force climbs to the strength of an entire division during the attempt to decimate the British Brigade and the 61st FABn, 1st Cavalry Division.

More air power arrives to pound the attacking Chinese and help forestall the isolation of the Commonwealth brigade. The Chinese continue to inundate the area. Accurate fire saves the bridge, which an enemy demolition team attacks. One enemy soldier is slain within twenty yards of the objective.

The besieged artillerymen fend off the onslaught, but the attack takes a toll. One howitzer, six vehicles and some other equipment are destroyed; however, loss of life is less than anticipated. By 0900, the 61st Artillery Battalion has sustained thirty-five wounded and two dead. Battery C sustains some fatalities and eighteen wounded.

At about the same time, two tanks pull into Battery C's line to stiffen the resistance. Outside the meager perimeter, enemy dead continue to pile up. British reinforcements, Company A, Argyll, and some additional tanks also arrive at the perimeter.

Meanwhile, the remainder of the Argyll Battalion receives instructions to withdraw to the east bank of the Taeryong River. Following a quick regrouping, Company A, Argylls, drives against a menacing hill about two miles below Pakch'on. The British seize the objective, but an enemy counterattack regains the heights. During the afternoon, the Australian 3rd Battalion, which has moved through the zone of the Argylls, attacks to dislodge the Chinese on the hill in front of Pakch'on. It's a bloody close-quartered assault that includes bayonets. The Australians retake the ground, but the cost is high; twelve troops are slain and 64 men are wounded.

The determined artillerymen and the equally heroic actions of the reinforcements have held the perimeter, but there are simply too many enemy troops against it. During and after the attack, the Pakch'on bridgehead is relinquished. With the Australian assault, the Middlesex 1st Battalion drives south to open the road.

Meanwhile, the U.S. artillery units and the remainder of the brigade retire south under heavy fire toward the Ch'ongch'on River. The Australians trace the steps of the British Brigade and enter the new perimeter

about 4,000 to 6,000 yards north of the Ch'ongch'on. It is built along a chain of hills on both sides of the Pakch'on Road.

The Chinese await dusk, then upon the signal of the bugle launch another attack. The assault strikes the farthest extension of the perimeter, which is defended by the exhausted Australians. Two greatly outnumbered companies give some ground; however, the powerful thrust fails to knock out the Australians. Following about four hours of incessant fighting, the battle begins to subside, and when the sun rises on the 6th, the Australians watch the enemy retire northward through a valley.

In Air Force activity, Bomber Command initiates incendiary bomb strikes against selected North Korean cities and towns. A contingent of twenty-one B-29s attached to the 19th Bomber Group strike Kanggye and drop 170 tons of fire bombs. The strike devastates the town, which is located less than 20 miles from the border with China.

— In Japan: General MacArthur dispatches a crucial report to the United Nations, which includes the particulars of Chinese participation in Korea. He enumerates the complications developing because of their involvement. MacArthur has become concerned about the heavy infusion of Chinese soldiers and their equipment into Korea. He orders the Air Force to bomb the Yalu River bridges on the Korean side of the river to halt or at least lessen the abundance of ground forces entering Korea.

The orders go out, but word reaches Washington, and the JCS immediately countermand the order. MacArthur argues vehemently that the destruction of the bridges is necessary and he implores the intervention of President Truman. Also, General Willoughby's intelligence summary makes it clear that the Chinese have the potential to commence a full-scale counteroffensive.

November 6

The 65th RCT (minus one battalion), subsequent to landing at Wonsan, is directed to relieve contingents of the 96th FABn at Yonghung. The artillery unit had only recently been deployed there. The other regimental battalion had been given a temporary assignment with the 1st Marine Division and is operating at Majon-ni. At Yonghung, the artillerymen come under attack during the early morning hours and lose some equipment and ammunition to the enemy. The 2nd Battalion, 65th RCT, which arrives later during the afternoon, will be attacked on the 7th.

In Naval activity, Task Group 95.6 initiates minesweeping operations in the vicinity of Hungnam.

In the X Corps area, 1st Marine Division sector, mine-clearing operations postpone troop movement by water from Wonsan to Hamhung. The disruption compels Division to increase rail movements. During the afternoon, one train that departs Hamhung is halted at Yonghung at 1700 due to reports of guerrilla activity.

The first two trains that depart Wonson complete the journey, but at dusk, a third train, protected by 38 enlisted Marines and one lieutenant attached to the 1st Amphibious Tractor Battalion, encounters difficulty. It is halted at Kowon due to a break along the tracks. Korean guerrillas take advantage of the darkness and strike the stalled train, firing from all sides. The surprised Marines feel the bullets as they rip through the wooden walls and drop to the floor. Soon after, grenades are tossed into the car and they kill eight men and wound two others. The other twenty-nine Marines take positions about two hundred yards from the damaged train and engage the guerrillas. Six men sustain wounds. The Marines then break off the firefight and make it to the lines of the 96th Field Artillery Battalion.

On the following day, at about 1400, a fourth supply train is forced to stop south of Kowon because of a break in the rails due to sabotage. The Marine guard advances to examine the scene and comes upon the devastation of the previous day. The bodies are found and one ammunition car remains in flames. The damage is too bad to easily repair. Train service is postponed until 9 November.

Also, the 1st Marine Engineering Battalion receives orders to improve the main supply route to enable tanks to reach Koto-ri.

In the 1st Marines zone, at 0100, the expected time of an enemy attack, the perimeter at Majon-ni remains quiet. Nevertheless, the Marines keep a deep-seated vigil. Army Intelligence information proves true. At 0130, conspicuous alarms go off. Booby traps explode in cadence with sudden illumination created by trip-wire flares. Despite the blasts and instant lighting, no enemy is seen. The engagement remains at long-distance, as the North Koreans fail to openly attack.

At about 0500, in a thick fog, the battalion outpost, located within the Company H zone, is attacked. Marine wiremen, artillerymen and mortarmen raise stiff resistance, but lack of ammunition compels them to pull back. Briefly, the enemy takes the abandoned outpost; however, the moment the fog dissipates, H&S Marines, led by Captain Thomas McCarthy, retake the position. Corsairs arrive overhead to totally terminate the skirmish at 0730, as the Communists head for the heights. The Marines sustain two wounded during the fighting.

In other activity, Company A, which had brought in supplies on the previous day, heads back for Wonsan and retraces the steps through "Ambush Alley." The convoy transports unusual cargo, 619 Communist prisoners who are jammed into the vehicles to be transferred to a stockade. Following the return of Company A, Colonel Puller dispatches the 2nd Battalion to Munchon-ni, but there are only sufficient vehicles to carry one rifle company. In addition, the convoy must travel the treacherous Majon-ni Road to reach the village, which sits near the crown of the highest pass within Ambush Alley.

Less than five miles out, the convoy is ambushed. As the final vehicle enters a curved portion of the road, a steady stream of boulders cascades from the heights to

block passage. The trucks stall, leaving the troops no options. To their right stand huge slopes, and to the immediate left, there is a perpendicular drop. Meanwhile, heavy enemy fire rings down from the high ground. Company E's riflemen jump from the vehicles and begin to return the fire, but the enemy positions are well concealed.

Rather than remain trapped, the Marines attack to clear the roadblock, manned by about 200 enemy troops. They burst through the enemy positions, but the attack is costly. The Marines sustain eight men killed and thirty-eight wounded. Six truck drivers are also wounded. Captain Charles Frederick, the Company E commander, and four other officers are also wounded. The most seriously wounded are evacuated by helicopter and the others are returned to Wonsan once Able Company arrives on scene.

As the passage is cleared, the Marines count sixty-one enemy dead on the field. About 300 boxes of small arms cartridges and fifty containers of 120-mm shells are discovered and destroyed during the operation. By 1600, the balance of the 2nd Battalion, 1st Marines, under Colonel Sutter, and Company A converge on the roadblock from different directions. Company A then transports the wounded and its entourage of prisoners to Wonsan without incident.

Meanwhile, as scheduled, Colonel Sutter's force moves to Munchon-ni.

In the 5th Marines zone, patrols continue to inspect the routes near the Chosin and Fusen Reservoirs.

In the 7th Marines sector, Colonel Roach's 3rd Battalion prepares to attack through Funchilin Pass. Company I reinitiates its drive to secure Hill 987. Company G supplies support-cover fire to the troops of Company H as it drives against the southeastern slopes of Hill 891. The craggy terrain causes horrendous problems. Company H begins its advance at 0800, but it takes about seven hours to reach the jump-off point, the high ground slightly above Company G.

In the meantime, Company I grinds forward only about 300 yards, but in the process it throws back a counterattack and continues to fend off fire from the heights above the MSR.

Prior to H Company's attack, two Corsairs pound the enemy positions in conjunction with barrages by the artillery and mortars. At about 1615, two platoons of Company H drive down the slopes and reform in the vicinity of the sharp curve in the road to strike from the southeast and secure Hill 891. When the ascent to the summit begins, the two platoons use separate but parallel paths, each destructive to the assault troops because of the precipitousness of the slope and the dogged soil.

The Chinese raise resistance against one of the platoons, but the other encounters no opposition. The unopposed platoon, operating on the right, makes it to a point where the two paths converge just below the crest. Meanwhile, the hard-pressed platoon, led by Lieutenant Minard Newton, joins with Lieutenant Robert Dale Reem's men. Lieutenant Harris, Company

H commander, who had climbed the slope with Newton's platoon, now directs Newton to lead Reem to the crest where they will divide. Reem is to swerve to the right and Newton to the left to overwhelm the opposition. The Chinese react determinedly by initiating a counterattack, in concert with a wave of grenades to annihilate Newton's force. One man, Sergeant Foster, singlehandedly charges to interrupt the assault. His actions cost his life when he surges to the summit, but he inspires the other Marines to break up the attack.

Meanwhile, on the left, Lieutenant Reem's group remains engaged in close-quartered fighting. Reem calls his squad leaders together to finalize the assault to gain the right portion of the crest, but an enemy grenade is flipped into their area. Reem blankets the grenade with his body and sacrifices his life to spare the other nearby Marines. Following the death of Reem, Sergeant Anthony Ricardi assumes command of the platoon.

By this time, it is dusk and Company H is overtired from the tedious climb and the incessant battle. Lieutenant Harris, at about 1800, informs the battalion commander, Major Roach, of the condition of his men. He reports eight casualties, including two dead. The platoons are running low on ammunition.

Colonel Litzenberg, upon notification of the situation, orders Roach to withdraw the attacking platoons. Aware of remaining Chinese strength, support fire is commenced to provide an umbrella during the descent to the friendly lines of the 7th Marines.

As the sun disappears, the enemy apparently decides to vacate the area. The darkness brings tranquility throughout the night and at dawn, there still are no visible signs of the enemy. The Chinese 124th Division had met and engaged the 7th Marines, but it had sustained heavy casualties. Colonel Litzenberg, who had informed his Marines of the importance of victory over the Chinese in the first battle, had not been disappointed.

Lieutenant Robert Dale Reem, Company H, 3rd Battalion, who had been killed during the fighting, is awarded the Medal of Honor posthumously for his extraordinary heroism in the face of hostile enemy fire.

In the ROK I Corps area, the Capital Division holds Kilchu; however, reports indicate that more enemy forces, about six to seven battalions, have departed Ch'ongjin, advancing southward on the coastal road. The armor-supported column will encounter the South Koreans on November 12.

In addition to the advancing enemy, the South Koreans face more hardship; another brutal touch of Korean winter is also en route. By the 16th, the temperature will be 16 degrees below zero.

In the Eighth Army area, the Chinese maintain predawn strikes against Kunu-ri and the Pakch'on bridgehead, but these are the final major confrontations that occur during the first phase of Chinese participation in the conflict. Observers in aircraft detect great numbers of Chinese as they travel north throughout the daylight hours. Eighth Army has sustained twelve days of terrific battle against the Chinese, but the Ch'ongch'on bridgehead has held.

In the 1st Cavalry Division sector, the remnants of the 8th Cavalry continue to evade the Chinese as they move south. The troops realize they are close to safety once they see the U.S. artillery in action, but before reaching the lines, the Chinese detect them and in a flash they are surrounded. With little time to spare, another quick decision is made. Rather than surrender, the group will splinter itself into small detachments to attempt a break out from the trap.

The fighting 8th Cavalrymen run out of luck. The Chinese decimate the groups and by about 1600, the 3rd Battalion, 8th Cavalry, no longer remains an organized fighting force. Nearly all its remaining troops are either captured or killed during the fighting and breakout at Yongbyon.

Aside from some stragglers who rejoin later, fewer than 200 enlisted men and ten officers of the 3rd Battalion escape to rejoin the 8th Cavalry Regiment. Initially, more than 1,000 men of the 8th Cavalry are unaccounted for, but during the next few weeks, some troops make it to U.S. lines.

Tanks that patrol the area continue to encounter and rescue Americans who were wounded during the fighting at Unsan, some of whom have been hidden and cared for by friendly Koreans. Later, it is determined that 8th Cavalry losses at Unsan totaled about 600 troops. The Communists eventually make it known that they captured between 200 and 300 of those troops at Unsan.

In the 24th Division sector, 19th Regimental zone, the Chinese attacks of the previous night have been thrown back. But, the hole between the bulk of the regiment and the 2nd Battalion to its left remains open. Slightly after dawn, the 1st Battalion, 19th Regiment, launches an assault and seals the gap. Subsequently, the 19th Regiment starts rebuilding its initial lines along the eastern bridgehead.

In the 2nd Division zone, a patrol of Company M, 23rd Regiment, led by Lieutenant Doric A. Ball and assisted by a local Korean chief of police, uncovers a large enemy arms-manufacturing center less than ten miles northeast of Kangdong in an abandoned lead mine. The underground location, in proximity to P'yongyang, is out of reach of U.S. bombing raids. It was the bombing strikes that compelled the North Koreans to transfer the facility from its above ground location to the cave.

The facility, known as Arsenal No. 65, is split into nineteen big rooms and utilizes offices, storage sections, and manufacturing. The underground complex also contains an auditorium and about 400 lathes that were manufactured in America, England and the Soviet Union. These machines had given the enemy the ability to make burp guns and 120-mm mortars.

In the 25th Division zone, a 27th Regimental patrol composed of the I&R Platoon, Company L, and Battery C, 8th Field Artillery Battalion, is ambushed by guerrillas as it moves between Kumch'on and Sibyonni. Reinforcements speed to the scene and reach it by midnight, but the enemy had vanished, taking captives with them. The relief force rescues the wounded survivors and it rounds up several others who had been missing.

Later, on the 9th, another contingent discovers a shallow grave that contains the bodies of 15 men of the 8th FABn. According to an account by a survivor, the Communists interrogated one of the captured men, Lieutenant Harold G. Parris, who gave them only his name, rank and serial number. The other captives followed suit and consequently, the Communists executed them.

In other activity, a Communist force composed of about 1,000 troops controls the town of Ich'on. During the previous week, the North Koreans had attacked a field hospital in Ich'on and massacred the wounded and the hospital personnel.

On the following day, the 27th Infantry and the S.K. 17th Regiment, attacking from the southwest and east respectively, strike against the town and drive the enemy out.

In the British sector near the Ch'ongch'on River, dawn arrives and the new line has held against fierce enemy attack. The enemy disengages and begins moving north. The enemy attacks of the previous day and night against the bridgehead cost the Chinese high casualties without the luxury of destroying the defending elements. According to British estimates, the Chinese sustain between 600 to 1,000 casualties due to air attacks and lose about 300 troops to ground fire.

— In Japan: General MacArthur receives his answer from Washington concerning the bombing of the Yalu Bridges. As requested, Truman had been brought into the decision-making process. The JCS inform MacArthur that he now has permission to bomb the bridges, but he is forbidden to strike the dams and power plants on the Yalu. MacArthur is further restricted by instructions not to violate Manchurian air space, nor to strike any targets in Manchuria.

Enemy planes blow across the border, strike targets at will, then shoot back across the Yalu, aware that U.S. planes are forbidden to pursue. This practice remains in effect for the duration and presents the enemy with an extraordinary advantage. Nonetheless, during the course of the war, U.S. planes shoot down the enemy at a ratio of fourteen to one despite the restrictions.

November 7
By today, pursuant to the recent FEC directives concerning the number of South Koreans serving with U.S. Divisions, 8,272 ROK troops have been detached and transferred back to ROK control. Several thousand additional South Korean soldiers are close to being released from U.S. units.

In other activity, the S.K. 2nd Division, which had been decimated during the early days of the conflict, is re-established this day. It is initially composed of two regiments, the 17th and the 38th, but within a week a third will be attached.

In the X Corps area, at Yonghung at about 0300 the recently arrived 65th RCT, 3rd Division, is attacked by guerrillas. The combat team sustains six killed and fourteen wounded. The guerrilla elements, composed of between 500 and 800 men, also strike the 96th FABn and contingents of the 4th Signal Battalion, USA.

A Marine tank of Company D, 1st Tank Battalion, and one M-29 ("Weasel") move to the besieged troops to evacuate the wounded. An Amtrac platoon, assigned to guard the empty train that had been stalled since the previous day, also aids the evacuation mission. At 1400, the train is permitted to move to Wonsan, but about two miles down the track, the engine and six cars derail while passing a split in the rails. The accident costs one man killed and 14 injured.

Also, General O.P. Smith meets with General Almond at Wonsan. General Almond decides to slow the pace of the troops that are sprinting to the border. General Smith suggests that the priority ground to hold is Hamhung, Hungham and Wonsan. Almond is inclined to add Hagaru, but he concurs with Smith that the other three should get the most attention. It is decided that Wonsan supply trains will run only during daylight hours and that the complement of guards will be increased from 38 to 58 men.

The 65th RCT, the 96th FABn, and the S.K. 26th Regiment are temporarily assigned to the 1st Marine Division. Their responsibilities are to protect primary points and bridges. The South Koreans are to push the North Koreans toward the 65th RCT at Yonghung, but the mission never gets initiated. During their short tenure under Marine control, the S.K. units carry out security duties along the MSR.

In the 1st Marine Division sector, following forty-eight hours of intense fighting, the Marines compel the Chinese Communists to cease making contact against Marine units and begin to retreat northward.

In the 5th Marines zone, patrols of Lt. Colonel Roise's 2nd Battalion encounter patrols attached to the U.S. Army units in the vicinity of the Fusen Reservoir.

In other activity, the 1st Battalion's Companies A and B, led by Major Merlin Olson (executive officer), move toward Huksu-ri, an obstinate road junction west of Oro-ri. No enemy activity is discovered, but the Marines encounter an enemy force on the following day.

In the 7th Marines zone, the unit, composed of a force that includes 34 percent reservists, defeat the Communists after heavy fighting at and around Sudong. The 7th Marines is the first U.S. unit to defeat the Communist Chinese in battle.

The Chinese 124th Division has abandoned the area during the previous night after several days of battling the Marines near Sudong. This disengagement by the enemy provides the Marines easy access to the southern slopes of Hills 891 and 987, both of which, the Marines discover, are unoccupied, while they climb to the crest of Hill 891 against no resistance. The 7th Marines personnel ponder the absence of the Chinese, but they continue to search. The Marines realign their forces along the MSR and simultaneously dispatch patrols, but no enemy encounters occur.

In the Eighth Army area, a small group of Canadians, composed of 345 troops, arrives at Pusan to prepare for the arrival of the main body of 10,000 volunteers, but because it appears that the war is nearly at an end, the Canadians send only one battalion and hold the remainder in Canada.

At Pakch'on, aircraft strike the enemy positions and inflict heavy damage to components of the re-created N.K. 105th Armored Division. It loses six tanks, forty-five vehicles and several armored cars. The N.K. armor had been committed to aid the Chinese, who are traveling light, but the Fifth Air Force has more or less canceled its importance by decimating most of its equipment before it can advance to the scene of battle. However, some armor arrives at several of the skirmishes.

— *In Japan:* During a general headquarters meeting, General Willoughby gives a brief but detailed evaluation of Chinese units operating in North Korea. Based on additional intelligence, he specifies that individual reserve contingents are still in Manchuria, but they are nudging close to the Yalu River. During the meeting, Ambassador Sebald asks Willoughby if the information on "units and locations" was accurate. Willoughby responds: "Affirmative."

November 8 *In the 1st Marine Division area,* at Majon-ni, the Communists bolster their forces to about 250 troops. They maneuver toward the rear of an outpost defended by two squads of Company H's Second Platoon, 1st Marines. To forestall encirclement of the squads and prevent further jeopardy, a Company I platoon and the remaining two platoons of Company H move out to engage the enemy. Supported by artillery fire and mortars, the enemy force is quickly dispersed, but not before sustaining heavy losses of about 100 troops. The Marines lose one man killed and ten wounded during the clean out operation.

In the 1st Marines sector at Wonsan, it is reported that aircraft have spotted some small enemy vessels. Colonel Puller is then informed that there have been two unidentified explosions. The level of concern at headquarters begins to rise as more information arrives. It states that the enemy is launching an amphibious landing north of Wonsan. Supposedly, the force is being transported by between 500 and 1,000 boats. An armored patrol attached to Company C, 1st Tank Battalion, speeds to the suspected target area, but no enemy is sighted.

In the 5th Marines zone, a skirmish develops when an enemy force is encountered short of the objective of Companies A and B. Orders arrive, which direct them to disengage and return to regimental lines. Headquarters has received word that a force of about 2,000 North Koreans is en route to the MSR. The 5th Marines are being reeled in to meet this potential threat.

Meanwhile, Company D, reinforced, moves to a valley northwest of Sinhung and advances to within ten miles east of Koto-ri. During the overnight mission, a sleeping Chinese trooper is snagged and brought back to headquarters. Upon interrogation, the prisoner claims that he is attached to the Chinese 126th Division and he informs the Marines that China is prepared to throw twenty-four Divisions into the conflict.

In the 7th Marines sector, just as on the previous day near Sudong, patrols search in vain for Chinese Communists, while the remainder of the regiment advances along the MSR. At about 1200, a group of fifteen volunteers, attached to the 2nd Battalion and led by Lieutenant William Goggin, probes through the ragged, mountainous area west of the MSR. The patrol engages Chinese in one firefight. Lieutenant Goggin sustains a superficial wound, but no other Marines are hurt. The platoon reaches the plateau at the Chosin Reservoir at about 1400 on the 9th, finding no visible signs of the enemy at Koto-ri.

In other activity, General Almond arrives in the 7th Marines sector. Upon being informed of the actions of Captain Cooney at Hill 891, now dubbed "How Hill," General Almond awards him a Silver Star, despite not having authentic citations with him. The general simply attaches a note to Cooney's uniform, complete with his signature, attesting to the award.

In the 7th Division zone, the landing operation at Iwon is completed. When the debarking operation is completed, 28,995 troops, 5,994 vehicles and about 30,116 short-tons of supplies will have been brought ashore.

In other activity, the 31st Regiment, en route to the Pujon Reservoir, encounters Chinese opposition a little more than ten miles from the southern end of the Pujon Reservoir on the eastern slopes of Paeksan, a huge peak that rises to a height of 7,700 feet. This, the initial battle for the 7th Division, begins during the early afternoon in bitter cold weather and terminates prior to dusk. The Chinese unit, later found to be the Chinese 376th Regiment, 126th Division, sustains about fifty killed prior to its disengagement. Also, a patrol encounters a U.S. Marine patrol about halfway between Hamhung and the Pujon Reservoir, initiating the first contact between the 7th Division and the 1st Marine Division in northeast Korea.

In Air Force activity, about seventy B-29s, supported by fighter planes, initiate the first bomber attack against the Yalu River bridges and other targets at Sinuiju. The planes execute the largest incendiary strike of the war.

Russian MiGs arrive to intercept and drive off the U.S. planes to protect the rail and highway connection that links China and Korea. This clash ignites the first air duel between jet planes. A U.S. Air Force F-80, piloted by Lieutenant Russell J. Brown (16th Interceptor Fighter Squadron), knocks out a MiG-15, which plummets to the earth in flames. Brown's elimination of the Soviet-made MiG-15 over Sinuiju gives him the first jet air-to-air kill in Korea. The name and nationality of the downed Communist pilot remains unknown to the West.

The air raids against the border bridges continue until the end of November, but pursuit of enemy planes terminates at the Yalu.

In the X Corps area, some small enemy vessels are sighted by aircraft.

November 9 *In the X Corps area, 1st Marine Division sector, 1st Marines zone,* again the supply trains begin to roll at Wonsan. Since the hold-up on the rails, about 95 cars have accumulated in the yards.

In the 5th Marines zone, the Regiment is ordered to deploy along the MSR that leads to the Chosin Reservoir. Colonel Murray directs the 1st Battalion to defend it at Majon-dong, and he instructs the 3rd Battalion to spread out near Chinhung-ni. Some complications develop on the following day and cause the mission to extend into two days before it is completed.

In the 7th Marines zone, Lieutenant Goggins' patrol reaches the vicinity of the Chosin Reservoir at 1400. Finding Koto-ri unoccupied by the enemy, Goggin informs Colonel Litzenberg of the situation, then he leads the patrol back to the lines of the regiment's 3rd Battalion near Sudong. There is relative quiet within the lines throughout the night.

In other activity, Lt. Colonel Randolph Lockwood relieves Major Webb Sawyer as commanding officer, 2nd Battalion, 7th Marines. Sawyer becomes executive officer on the 10th. He succeeds Major Roland Carey.

In the Eighth Army area, 25th Division zone of the Iron Triangle, at Ch'orwon, a defending force of 800 South Korean police is struck and driven out by a 1,400-man contingent of the N.K. 4th Division's 18th Regiment.

In the 7th Infantry Division zone, the 7th Reconnaissance Company, 7th Infantry Division, pushes to Sillyong, which is east of P'ungsan, and deploys to safeguard the power facility located there.

In Air Force activity, Sergeant Harry J. Levene (Lavine), a gunner aboard a B-29 (RB-29, 91st Strategic Reconnaissance Squadron), downs a MiG-15 during an air engagement. Levene receives credit for the first kill of a jet during the war. The B-29 becomes damaged during the attack, but it makes it back to Japan. The plane makes a crash landing in which five of the crew die.

November 10 A convoy of supplies and the 3rd Korean Marine Corps Battalion arrives at Majon-ni to fortify the area against increasing numbers of enemy troops. The Korean Marines deploy in the sector vacated by Company I, 1st Marines, which had recently departed for Wonsan.

In the afternoon, enemy troop concentrations are discovered less than five miles from Majon-ni by an observation plane of VMO-6. Remedies are quickly sought. Through the assistance of aerial observers, the force of about 300 troops is scattered by effective artillery fire. Also, Intelligence informs the 1st Marines that an attack against the perimeter by the N.K. 45th Regiment should be expected during the night of the 11th-12th.

In the X Corps area, 1st Marine Division zone, the Marines gain six miles in the Changjin Reservoir area on this day.

In the 5th Marines' zone, an enemy force ambushes a Company C, 1st Battalion, patrol. The patrol is extricated on the following day by an attack by the battalion.

In the 7th Marines zone, the 1st Battalion begins its march at 0830. It passes through the 3rd Battalion lines and exits the Funchilin Pass, then occupies Koto-ri at about 1000. There is little contact with the enemy for the next several days; however, the Marines, now entrenched in the mountains of northeastern Korea, create a defensive perimeter around the village. A new terror enters the perimeter and the Marines are unprepared for it. Another frigid Korean winter arrives with devastating results: casualties due to the unexpected cold.

In the 3rd Division sector, an advance contingent of the 3rd Division establishes a tactical command post at Wonsan. Elements begin to arrive on the following day.

In the Eighth Army area, 25th Division zone, a 500-man unit of the 5th Regiment, N.K. 4th Division, moves into and occupies the town of Yonch'on, which lies about ten miles south of Ch'orwon, a town seized by the North Koreans on the previous day. Later, elements of the 25th Division's 24th Regiment attacks to regain the town, but the Communists repulse it. After dusk, the North Koreans strike hard. They spring a fierce ambush outside the Ch'orwon, which inflicts devastating damage and loss of life against Company A, 24th Regiment, and the I&R Platoon.

On the following day, the 24th Regiment resumes its attack and secures Yonch'on. The North Koreans also attack P'yonggang, defended by the S.K. 17th Regiment. The heat of battle rages incessantly throughout the day and by dawn on the 11th, the South Koreans become isolated.

In Air Force activity, a contingent of B-29s attached to the 30th Bomber Group comes under attack by MiG-15s near the Yalu River. One of the planes is shot down, the first B-29 lost to the enemy. The crew is able to parachute; however, they are in enemy territory when they land. The crew is captured and imprisoned.

In other activity, the recently arrived 437th TCW (Troop Carrier Wing) initiates its airlifts on this day to deliver cargo to Korea.

November 11 *In Naval activity,* the USS *Buck* (DD 761) and the USS *Thompson* (DE 203) collide (at 39° 13′ N, 129° 32′ E). Both vessels sustain some damage.

In the X Corps sector, OpnO 6 directs an advance to the border with Manchuria. The 1st Marine Division is to establish blocking positions to the west in the villages of Huksu-ri and Yudam-ni, but it is to still continue its northern drive to the border. Corps issues OpnO 6 at 2400. The S.K. I Corps and the 1st Marine Division are to advance on the left and right respectively. The 7th Infantry Division is to proceed up the middle. The 3rd Infantry Division is to relieve contingents of the 1st Marine Division, then assume responsibility for the Wonsan-Hamhung vicinity. The S.K.

26th Regiment, attached to the 3rd Division, will assist. The Marines are to establish blocking positions at Huksu-ri and Yudam-ni. The rear of the corps' sector is held by elements of the 1st KMC Regiment, deployed south and west of Kojo. The various forces are widespread and resupply will be difficult, but the feeling remains that the Chinese will not pour into the conflict.

In the 1st Marine Division area, the Marine zone of operations at the Yalu is about 40 miles wide. Two roads that branch off from the Changjin area approach it; one terminates at Huchanggangu and the other ends at Singalpajin. From there, the 7th Division zone leads east to Hyesanjin, then leans sharply north before turning east again toward Hapsu.

The South Korean I Corps picks up at the Hapsu–Chuchonhujang area. It is to march north along the coastal route to secure Chongjin. *In the 1st Marines sector,* near Majon-ni, the 1st Marines continue to prepare for an anticipated attack against the perimeter.

In the 5th Marines zone, the 1st Battalion launches an assault to rescue a patrol of Company C, which had been trapped since the previous day. Following the successful mission, the battalion departs for Majon-dong.

In the 7th Marines zone, at Koto-ri, Company C encounters an enemy force. The company reports four killed and four wounded, while inflicting forty casualties upon the enemy.

In other activity, Lt. Colonel William Harris (son of Major General Field Harris) succeeds Lt. Colonel Roach as CO, 3rd Battalion. Roach had become Battalion S4 on the 10th.

In the 7th Infantry Division zone, X Corps directs Division to prepare to continue its northward drive. Kapsan, below Hyesanjin, and the south shore of the Pujon Reservoir are to be secured by the 17th and 32nd Regiments, respectively. The 31st Regiment is to drive forward on the left of the 17th Regiment, then advance to the border at Hyesanjin on the Yalu.

In the 3rd Division zone, the 15th Regiment begins to debark at Wonsan. It is followed by the 7th Regiment, which completes the operation on November 17. The mission of the 3rd Division is to relieve the 1st Marine troops deployed in the vicinity of Wonsan and those stationed south of Hamhung.

Additionally, the 7th Division is to control the primary highways in the southern portion of X Corps zone, eliminate any guerrilla activity and maintain the security of the Hungnam coastal strip. It is a Herculean task, as the area handed over to it is ninety by thirty-five miles. Four regimental combat teams are established, each having separate missions and separate sectors.

Colonel John S. Guthrie commands the 7th RCT, which is held in reserve, with responsibility for controlling the area near the coast from Chong-dong to Hungnam. The 10th FABn will support the 7th RCT. Colonel Dennis M. Moore commands the 15th RCT, which assumes responsibility for the security of Wonsan and the area south and west of it, including the

Wonsan–Majon-ni–Tongyang Road; it is supported by the 39th FABn. The 65th RCT, commanded by Colonel William W. Harris, takes responsibility for the division's west central zone, north of the positions of the 15th RCT, which includes the Yonghung–Hadongsan-ni Road, the primary highway that leads into the regimental sector from the coast. It is supported by the 58th Armored Artillery Battalion (Self-propelled guns) and by Company C, 64th Heavy Tank Battalion.

The fourth RCT, the ROK 26th Regiment, commanded by Colonel Rhee Chi Suh, is augmented by Battery A, 96th FABn. The ROKs are directed to control the area west of Hamhung, the northern portion of the division zone. The combat team will also patrol the area of X Corps to the boundary with Eighth Army.

In the ROK area, the 3rd Korean Marine Corps Battalion lands at Wonsan with orders to move westward and establish a blocking position near Tongyang.

In the Eighth Army area, 25th Division zone, the 24th Regiment successfully regains Yonch'on from elements of the N.K. 4th Division, but the victory brings little joy. Upon regaining the ground, the unit reaches the site of the ambush that occurred on the previous night and discovers the corpses of thirty-eight U.S. soldiers. All the vehicles had been torched.

In other activity, the elements of the S.K. 17th Regiment, surrounded at P'yonggang and still embattled with elements of the N.K. 4th Division, refuse to capitulate. The accompanying KMAG advisor, Major Robert B. Holt, sends out a radio call for help, requesting the 3rd Battalion, posted at Ich'on, to attack eastward and break the encirclement of the 1st and 2nd Battalions. Major Holt also requests and receives an airdrop of ammunition, to ensure the besieged units can survive until the reinforcements arrive and arrangements are made to pick him up.

A Mosquito observation plane lands and soon after, Holt directs the arriving aircraft to enable the planes to strike with accuracy. The enemy continues its quest to eliminate the South Koreans, but in vain. Finally, having sustained heavy casualties, due in great part to effective air strikes, the Communists pull out during the night of the 11th-12th. However, on the 13th, again the North Koreans attack to seize P'yonggang.

— *In Japan:* General MacArthur, apparently still anticipating a successful mission, suggests that X Corps offers assistance to Eighth Army to speed its march to the Yalu. MacArthur's request is delivered to X Corps by General Wright, G-3 of Far East Command. General Almond will reply on 15 November.

November 12   *In the X Corps area,* X Corps issues OpnO 6; it stipulates that the 3rd Division is to relieve contingents of the 1st Marines. The 3rd Division would then be responsible for the security of the X Corps' left flank, but it is also to plan to launch a westward attack.

Meanwhile, the 1st Marines is to prepare to move north. Also, planes attached to carriers strike a Yalu River border town, Hyesanjin. These air strikes thoroughly damage the area and destroy the military facility there. A warehouse and barracks are set afire and destroyed. When elements of the 7th Division reach it on the twentieth, they observe a town in ruins.

In the 1st Marine Division sector, General O.P. Smith, commanding general, 1st Marine Division, issues FragO at 2130. It directs the seizure of Hagaru and it orders the 5th Marines to dispatch a battalion to Koto-ri.

In the 1st Marines zone, at 0130, the Communists initiate an attack against the perimeter at Majon-ni. It fails to deliver any genuine punch. Several small probing attacks strike the lines, and these are followed by a weak attack against the Korean Marines. The Communists seem intimidated once they encounter a minefield that lies close to the perimeter. The lagging attacks cease by 0600, to end the final engagement at Majon-ni, when the enemy disengages and pulls back. Casualties for friendly forces are two men killed and six wounded.

Later, in retrospect, General Ruffner, CoS, X Corps, states that the "Marines had done a masterful job at Majon-ni." Ruffner adds that he believed the Marines broke up the remaining North Korean units that otherwise would have created much trouble at Wonsan.

Following the disengagement at Majon-ni, the N.K. 15th Division concentrates on guerrilla operations in the Imjin Valley. At Majon-ni, the American and Korean Marines are to be relieved on the following day.

At Wonsan, a large U.S. Army convoy that includes thirty-six Marine supply vehicles departs for Majon-ni at 1030. The 1st Battalion, 13th Regiment, 3rd Division, is the relief unit. The convoy proceeds past the Marine outposts held by elements of the 2nd Battalion, 1st Marines, but soon after, a damaged bridge and several craters halt progress. Enemy guerrillas open fire and pound the convoy. The action kills two soldiers and wounds three more. A jeep and two supply vehicles are also lost.

The delay postpones the arrival of the Army contingents at Majon-ni until the following day. Lt. Colonel Robert Blanchard directs his 1st Battalion, 15th Regiment, to establish a defensive perimeter while repairs are completed.

In the 7th Marines zone, there is no contact with the enemy at Koto-ri, but the Marines do spot Chinese forces. On the following day, the 7th Marines will set out for Hagaru.

In the 3rd Division sector, the North Koreans initiate roadblocks along the main supply routes and launch ambushes at various points to hinder the division's progress. These clashes continue until the end of the month and at times, inflict heavy casualties. The 15th RCT sustains the heaviest casualties and at times great losses of equipment, while operating west of Wonsan, between Majon-ni and Tongyang. It appears as if the North Koreans are acting in concert with the Chinese troops that have entered Korea.

In the ROK I Corps area, a huge clash occurs when a large force of enemy armor and supporting infantry encounter and engage elements of the S.K. Capital Division at a point along the coastal road near Orang-ch'on, about thirty miles north of Kilchu. The contest rages at a feverish pace under poor weather conditions. The nasty weather prevents the arrival of supporting planes and the scene is out of range for the guns of U.S. Navy destroyers. But, the heavy guns of the cruisers can hit the mark. The USS *Rochester* sails to a point from which its firepower can join the battle, but still the ROKs are compelled to fall back under the pressure. On the following day, the two antagonists resume the fight.

November 13   *In the X Corps area, 1st Marine Division zone,* Division issues OpnO 21–50. It directs the 1st Marines to secure Huksu-ri, while the 5th Marines deploy to guard the MSR and simultaneously prepare to pass through the 7th Marines at Haguru, from where it will move to Changjin, about forty miles north. The 7th Marines are to capture Hagaru and await orders to move against Yudam-ni. The division reconnaissance company is to operate on the right flank, in the Soyang-ni–Sinhung Valley, and extend as far as the division's eastern boundary.

In the 1st Marines zone, relief troops, the 1st Battalion, 15th Regiment, 3rd Division, arrive at 1530 and begin to assume responsibility for the Majon-ni area. The 1st Marines prepares to move to Wonsan and departs at 1015 on the following day.

In the 5th Marines zone, the 2nd Battalion begins to depart the Sinhung Valley en route to relieve the 7th Marines at Koto-ri. The battalion, under Colonel Roise, had encountered little opposition during the mission. Nevertheless, it has captured thirteen prisoners, including one Chinese trooper.

In the 7th Marines zone, the regiment departs for Haguru once contingents of the 5th Marines arrive at Koto-ri to relieve them. Additional relief elements of the 2nd Battalion, 5th Marines, continue to arrive through the following day. Through verbal orders from the divisional commander, the 7th Marines is to establish blocking positions at Toktong Pass, midway between Hagaru and Yudam-ni, until more reinforcements arrive. The regiment will encounter about 150–200 enemy troops, bolstered by machine guns, near the pass. Air power and artillery is called upon to assist and afterward the enemy is scattered.

General O.P. Smith remains concerned about full-scale Chinese intervention. At Koto-ri, an OY (observation plane) airstrip is completed this day. At Hagaru, the necessary equipment to fabricate an airstrip will require much heavier equipment. Lt. Colonel Partridge, CO, 1st Engineering Battalion, will be responsible for the project. A sturdy road will have to be constructed to enable the heavy equipment and armor to be transferred to Hagaru.

In the ROK Army area, the S.K. 32nd Regiment is activated at Seoul and attached to the recently reestablished S.K. 2nd Division.

In the ROK I Corps area, at Orang-ch'on in the S.K. Capital Division sector, the North Koreans continue to drive against the S.K. lines. Later in the day, after the weather clears somewhat, Corsairs arrive and join the fight to blast the enemy positions. Armor spread about a snow-filled battlefield feels the sting of the planes. Two tanks are destroyed; one is damaged and another disengages and retires hurriedly through six inches of snow to avoid the firepower of the airstrike. The enemy has pushed the 18th Regiment back across a stream, but it still has some tenacity and will again engage on the following day. The 1st S.K. Regiment loses no ground.

In the 7th Infantry Division zone, the 17th Regiment, acting upon Corps' orders, sets up to launch an attack against the enemy at the Ungi River. It is scheduled to cross the frigid waters on the following morning, disperse the enemy and reconstruct the bridge that had been destroyed by the enemy. In preparation for the crossing, Colonel Powell directs South Korean troops to fabricate a floating footbridge by laying planks between empty oil drums. This mission, initiated by the 2nd Battalion, gets underway, but the North Koreans seriously disrupt the plans of the 3rd Battalion. Later this day, during the night of the 13th-14th, the enemy operating upstream opens the floodgates of the dams in the area and the results are disastrous.

In the Eighth Army area, 25th Division zone at P'yonggang, the S.K. 17th Regiment, which has repelled enemy attacks on the 11th-12th, is again struck. After dark, elements of the N.K. 4th Division launch an assault that strikes both the town and the airport, but again, the South Koreans repel the attacks. Fighting lasts into the late morning hours of the 14th. For their unsuccessful effort, the Communists lose 141 killed and 20 taken prisoner. The S.K. 17th Regiment sustains 11 troops killed and 23 wounded.

Nevertheless, the guerrilla activity in this area will not recede. Once the U.S. 25th Division pulls out to prepare for its part in the upcoming offensive, scheduled for November 24, the South Koreans face even more pressure.

November 14   *In the X Corps area, 1st Marine Division sector, 1st Marines zone,* seventeen days of operating at Majon-ni ceases for the 1st Marines. Having been received by Army contingents of the 3rd Division, the Marine contingents depart for Wonsan. The mission accounts for 1,395 prisoners, the majority of whom have voluntarily surrendered. The Marines sustain 16 killed in action, four of whom die of their wounds, and 45 wounded. Marine estimates of enemy casualties at Majon-ni are 525 killed, but numbers of their wounded are unknown. Regarding the main supply route, Marine casualties amount to nine killed and eighty-one wounded while guarding convoys as they moved through Ambush Alley.

In other activity, at 1820, 1st Battalion, 1st Marines, arrives by train at Chigyong from Wonsan. Other elements follow by truck convoy. Also, the ROK 3rd Korean Marine Corps Battalion arrives at Majon-ni from Wonsan, then it advances about twelve air-miles and establishes a roadblock near Tongyang, along the north-

south road, where it crosses the Wonsan–P'yonggang Road.

In the 7th Marines zone, Hagaru is seized without incident at 1400. *In the ROK I Corps area,* heavy fighting continues at Orang-ch'on for the fourth day and the enemy continues to hammer the Capital Division, but the South Koreans dish out equal punishment. Nonetheless, the pressure forces the Cavalry Regiment and the 1st Regiment to pull back and give ground. The South Koreans are saved from more disastrous results by continuing close-air support that stops the North Koreans from a full-scale breakthrough.

The combined hammering by the ROKs and the support fire of the Navy and aircraft finally deflate the enemy's staying power. This day, the planes take out another three tanks, two self-propelled guns and twelve trucks. By the following day, the 18th Regiment, S.K. Capital Division, resumes its advance.

In related activity, thirty B-29s deliver 40,000 incendiary bombs to the vicinity of Hoeryong, along the Tumen River at the Manchurian border. The Korean town is located about 100 miles southwest of Vladivostok.

In the 7th Infantry Division zone, in below zero weather, the 17th Regiment launches its assault to cross the Ungi River. The 2nd Battalion fords the river by use of a recently constructed floating footbridge, but the enemy has complicated the operation by flooding the river with water from an upstream dam, which brings the water level to about waist high to hinder the crossing of the 3rd Battalion. Crossing without the footbridge causes instant casualties among the troops who attempt to cross the freezing cold water. Those who crossed had to immediately return, but then their clothes had to be cut from their bodies. The endeavor costs 1 man killed, six wounded and another eighteen with frostbite. The battalion is forced to postpone the crossing and use the footbridge later.

The rapidly sinking temperatures also hinder the operation of the vehicles and compel the regiment on the following day to urgently request special supplies to keep the gasoline from freezing. The needed item is an alcohol-based antifreeze that can be mixed with the gas. The enemy fire aimed at the regiment is from a great distance and off-target.

In the Eighth Army area, the road blockage established by the 3rd Korean Marine Battalion lies on the Army boundary line that separates it from X Corps.

In Air Force activity, B-29s again bomb the bridges at Sinuiju along the Yalu River, but the mission is interrupted when fifteen MiGs attack. Two of the B-29s are damaged, but all return to their base.

In other activity, a band of MiGs attack a four-plane formation of B-29s in the vicinity of Sinuiju. The planes attached to the 371st Bombardment Squadron, 307th Bombardment Group (M), engage the enemy. A tailgunner aboard one of the closing planes attempts to take out a MiG, but his firing range is outside the gunner's range. Sergeant Richard W. Fisher, aboard the same aircraft as the central fire controller, finds the MiG

A Corsair on the ice covered deck of the USS *Badoeng Strait* on 14 November 1950.

within his sights. Fisher commences fire and holds the trigger down until a huge cloud of black smoke is spotted, and then he pours more fire into the plane until it begins to fall from the air to crash.

— *In the United States:* Captain Leonard A. Miller becomes the first Marine to be assigned to helicopter training at Quantico.

— *In Japan:* In Tokyo, General MacArthur and Ambassador Sebald discuss the Korean strategy from MacArthur's point of view. MacArthur specifies that he intends to decimate the Yalu River bridges, thereby severing supply routes and cutting off enemy forces between the Yalu and the U.N. forces. Air Force and ground forces will devastate all fortified obstacles in these sectors as they drive the enemy across the Yalu, but he indicates that specific instructions will halt the U.N. troops at the Yalu.

Ambassador Sebald later states that General MacArthur believes if the offensive fails, the only viable alternative would be to make air strikes against strategic enemy targets in Manchuria. Lt. General Stratemeyer, commander, Far East Air Forces, during a later conversation with Ambassador Sebald, states that he "could flatten China with his airpower if authorized to do so."

Stratemeyer's opinion is not an isolated one among the military commanders. However, some Washington politicians and the United Nations members feel otherwise. They seem intimidated by the thought of Russia and China combining their forces.

November 15 *In the X Corps area,* General Almond responds to MacArthur's letter of 11 November. He seeks permission to continue the northern attack, but to also initiate an attack west of the Chosin Reservoir.

Meanwhile, MacArthur, prior to Almond's letter reaching him, decides to instructs Almond by radio, to devise an attack plan (alternate to OpnO 6) to move his attack westward to seize Chanjin and sever the Chinese main supply route, the Manpojin–Kanggye–Huich'on Road and rail line. This changes the mission, as CinCFE had during the latter part of October called for a drive to the border. The X Corps report indicates that the enemy's stiff challenge to Eighth Army's drive prompted the change in plans.

In the 1st Marine Division sector, General O.P. Smith dispatches a letter to the commandant, General Clifton B. Cates. It indicates his opposing view to the ongoing optimism regarding the U.N. war efforts in Korea. Smith and his staff anticipate the probability of Chinese intervention on a large scale and initiate preparations for such an event. Smith emphasizes the eighty-mile gap between the Eighth Army and the Marines. He also states:

Someone in high authority will have to make up his mind as to what is our goal. My mission is still to advance to the border. The Eighth Army will not attack until the 20th. Manifestly, we should not push on without regard to Eighth Army. We would simply get further out on a limb.... I believe a winter campaign in the mountains of North Korea is too much to ask of the American Soldier or Marine, and I doubt the feasibility of supplying troops in this area during the winter or providing for the evacuation of sick and wounded.

Smith's letter contains other thoughts and concerns, including his "wide open left flank" and the deployment of one Marine Division scattered along a single mountain road from Hamhung to the border, a distance of about 120 air miles.

Later on, during 1956, General Almond comments on General Smith's letter. He states: "I am mindful of the skepticism of General Smith in all of the supply plans that X Corps conceived and I sympathize with his viewpoint very thoroughly. However, in my mind there was always the assistance to be gained by air supply either drop or landing them and the counterpart of that, the evacuation to be expected by plane from the air field that we were to build."

In the 1st Marines zone, the 3rd Battalion, 15th Infantry, completes its relief of the 2nd Battalion, 1st Marines, which had been deployed to block the enemy at Ambush Alley. Company D, 2nd Battalion, 1st Marines, deployed to the rear of Wonsan, is also relieved by Army forces. The 2nd Battalion, 1st Marines, prepares to move seventy miles to Chigyong. Problems with the rails have also hindered a quick move.

In the 5th Marines zone, the 2nd Battalion is perched at Koto-ri. The 3rd Battalion is at Chinhung-ni, supported by Battery K, 4th Battalion, 11th Marines, a detachment of 1st Service Battalion and Company B (minus 3rd Platoon), 1st Engineer Battalion. In addition, the 1st Battalion and Company D, 1st Tank Battalion, is deployed at Majon-dong.

In the 7th Marines zone, the regiment stands at Hagaru, the entrance to the Chosin Reservoir. General Edward Craig, assistant division commander, arrives at Hagaru. He believes it should be the Marines' forward base.

In the 11th Marines zone, Lt. Colonel Harvey Feehan assumes command of the 1st Battalion, 11th Marines. He relieves Lt. Colonel Ransom M. Wood, who had commanded the battalion since its arrival in Korea on 2 August.

In the 7th Infantry Division sector, because of the severe weather conditions, division requests 500 oil-burning stoves, 250 squad tents and special fuel. Also, the 1st Battalion, 17th Regiment, fords the Ungi River and deploys to the left of the 2nd Battalion, which had preceded it. Each makes only minimal gains during the day. Also, a 3rd Battalion patrol advances to the eastern side of the Pujon Reservoir.

In the ROK I Corps area, following hard fighting against a large enemy force, the S.K. 18th Regiment,

Capital Division, reinitiates its advance toward the border.

In Naval activity, the U.S. Navy initiates minesweeping operations in the vicinity of Songjin.

November 16   An Army tugboat, towing a crane barge, strikes a mine at the entrance of the Wonsan harbor and disaster ensues. The vessel sinks and only ten men out of about forty troops survive.

In the X Corps area, General Almond, in response to MacArthur's directive to devise an alternate plan of attack, directs his staff to produce a blueprint. The initial plan is given a negative by Almond, but a second plan is developed during the next four days. He accepts it, but makes some modifications. The third draft is then taken to Tokyo to be presented to General Headquarters.

In the 1st Marine Division sector, the mine clearing operation at Hungnam is complete. The port is opened.

In the 1st Marines zone, the 2nd Battalion, 1st Marines, departs Wonsan by rail and moves towards Chigyong. The 2nd Battalion, 1st Marines, departs on the following day.

In the 7th Marines sector, the regiment occupies Hagaru and discovers a new enemy, the weather. The temperature at Hagaru stands at four degrees below zero, indicating a vicious premature beginning of winter. Generals O.P. Smith and Field Harris arrive to inspect the area. General Harris, commander 1st Marine Aircraft Wing and Tactical Air Command, X Corps, had been asked by Almond to check out the site. Almond wants an airstrip long enough to handle R4Ds to enable evacuation and resupply missions to be carried out. A suitable site is discovered south of the village.

In the 7th Infantry Division sector, the 17th Regiment, across the Ungi River, advances about eight miles, in marked contrast to the slow gains of the past several days. Information reported by observation planes reveals that the enemy units are separating into small contingents and retiring in the direction of Kapsan, the objective of both the 17th and the 32nd Regiments. Also, a patrol of the 3rd Battalion, 31st Infantry, moves from its positions east of the reservoir to reconnoiter the northern side of the Pujon Reservoir. The contingent discovers and engages about 200 Chinese troops. Following a short firefight, the Chinese retire.

In Naval activity, the USS *St. Paul* (CA 73) joins in the operations with Fast Carrier Task Force (TF 77) at Kyojo Wan. Also, the USS *Rochester* (CA 124) arrives off Songjin to bolster Cruiser Division 5.

November 17   *In the X Corps area, 1st Marine Division sector,* at Wonsan, the 3rd Battalion, 1st Marines, departs for Chigyong. The final components of RCT-1 also depart. The 1st Tank Battalion's headquarters and service companies begin operating at Soyang-ni, about eight miles northwest of Hamhung. The route from Chinhung-ni to Koto-ri still is unable to carry M-26 tanks, but engineers continue to expand the width of the curves along the one-way road.

In the 5th Marines zone, pursuant to Division OpnO

A contingent of the recently arrived Thai Battalion is inspected by a U.S. Army officer and a Thai officer on 17 November at Taegu.

U.S. Marine riflemen in vicinity of Yudam-ni.

22–50, issued at 0800, the regiment receives instructions for its imminent advance east of the Chosin Reservoir. The 5th Marines is to pass a minimum of one battalion through the 7th Marines at Hagaru and advance about seven miles up the east side of the reservoir to secure Sinhung-ni, northeast of Hagaru. Then, upon orders, the 5th Marines is to capture a key road junction about twenty miles north of Hagaru at Kyolmul-ni.

Lt. Colonel John W. Stevens II replaces Lt. Colonel George R. Newton as commanding officer, 1st Battalion, 5th Marines.

In the 7th Marines zone, today's Division OpnO 22–50 presents the regiment with multiple missions. It is to post at least one battalion to guard the division's left flank between Hagaru and Yudam-ni. It also is to relieve contingents of the 5th Marines and assume responsibility for the MSR in its area, between Chinhung-ni, Hagaru and Koto-ri.

The division reconnaissance company holds responsibility for the left flank of the MSR, near

Majon-dong, while the 11th Marines deploys its 4th Battalion in the same vicinity awaiting orders to advance north.

In the ROK I Corps area, the Capital Division continues its march, but the pace has slowed, due in part to the enemy, but equally due to the temperature, which has sunk way below zero. These troops have not been properly equipped to deal with the elements. Most have only fatigues, inadequate shoes and one blanket per man in addition to a U.S. winter overcoat.

This day, an LST arrives at Songjin, bringing 26,000 South Korean winter uniforms. Other supplies are en route. Another LST departs Pusan transporting winter shoes, socks, field jackets and other necessary items of clothing.

Also, a report that details fighting between the evening of the 14th through today lists the North Korean casualties at 1,753 killed and 105 captured. It also reports the seizure of 101 burp guns, 62 light machine guns, four rapid-fire guns and 649 rifles.

In related activity, the USS *St. Paul* is en route to throw its weight into the advance. Also, the S.K. 3rd Division, on the advance along the coastal road, is nudging toward the Capital Division. The 23rd Regiment departs Songjin en route to Hapsu.

In Naval activity, operations to clear the harbors of Hungnam, Chinnamp'o, Inchon and Kusan are complete. The harbors are safe and prepared to accept shipping.

November 18 *In the X Corps area,* the debarkation of the U.S. 3rd Infantry Division, commanded by Major General Robert H. Soule, at Wonsan is completed this day. Its arrival brings X Corps to its full strength of major units. X Corps now consists of the 1st Marine Division, the 3rd and 7th Infantry Divisions and the ROK I Corps. Each is assigned a zone, but the area for each is massive.

The 65th Regiment, 3rd Division, establishes its perimeter, but a huge gap that contains the Paeksan Pass, which reaches a height of 5,600 feet, exists between it and the S.K. 26th Regiment, posted to the north. Attempts are initiated by Company B, 65th Regiment, to establish contact with the South Koreans. Between today and November 22, two separate engagements develop between the Communists and Company B, but the Americans cannot penetrate the pass. And there are no roads capable of handling vehicles in the northern part of the 3rd Division sector.

In other activity, X Corps requests and receives permission to use the S.K. 26th Regiment to seize Huksu-ri. Subsequently, the 1st Marines are to relieve the Koreans, but these orders change on November 21.

In the 1st Marine Division area, at Majon-dong, Lt. Colonel Harry Milne, CO, 1st Tank Battalion, has recently established a provisional tank platoon composed of two Sherman (M4A3) tanks attached to Headquarters Company and four Company D dozer-tanks. The improvised tank platoon departs for Hagaru and arrives without encountering any resistance. Thanks to

the opening of the road to Hagaru to heavy traffic, the engineers begin constructing the airstrip.

In the 1st Marines sector, the regiment, still hindered by poor rail and truck transportation, is behind schedule in its attempt to reach Chigyong. The final contingents are still en route. However, the mission is still to march westward to secure Huksu-ri. In the meantime, the S.K. 26th Regiment departs Chigyong during the early morning hours of the 19th to seize Huksu-ri.

In the 7th Infantry Division sector, patrols of the 31st Regiment spread out on both sides of the Pujon Reservoir.

In the ROK I Corps area, the S.K. 22nd Regiment, 3rd S.K. Division, departs Kilchu and advances toward Hapsu, the same objective as that which elements of the S.K. Capital Division are driving toward. Both divisions of I Corps are receiving supplies from six Korean LSTs.

In Naval activity, planes attached to Fast Carrier Task Force (TF 77) encounters a group of Russian MiG-15s. An engagement ensues and the Soviets lose one plane; five others sustain damage. The F9Fs sustain no losses.

November 19 *In the X Corps area, 1st Marine Division zone,* five huge dozers arrive to assist the engineers of Company D at Hagaru. The engineers must create the airstrip from a piece of earth that stands like solid rock in a frozen wasteland. The runway is to be 3,200 feet, some shorter than what the engineers' manuals dictate, but the engineers hope it can suffice.

Also, a supply regulating station is established at Hagaru to permit a resupply operation to function. Previously, the supply depots had been handled by the 1st Service and 1st Ordnance Battalions at Hamhung. The port operation at Hamhung is the responsibility of the 2nd Engineer Special Brigade, USA. Korean laborers are also employed.

Trains depart Hungnam for Chinhung-ni once the Marines put the line back into activity. The 1st Service Battalion gets the job. Korean civilians operate the trains. Once at Chinhung-ni, the trains are unloaded and from there the supplies are trucked to Hagaru.

The newly unfolding operations expect large casualties. The divisional hospital, expanded to 400 beds, remains at Hungnam, staffed by Companies A and B, 1st Medical Battalion, and H&S personnel. The 1st, 5th and 7th Marines receive Companies D, C and E, 1st Medical Battalion, respectively. Soon after, division anticipates the need of a hospital scenario at Hagaru. It is decided that in an emergency, medical detachments will be airlifted from Hungnam. To further bolster the operations, the hospital ship USS *Consolation* will embark from Wonsan and take a position off Hungnam. In addition, heated rail cars will be emplaced to handle the transporting of casualties along the 35-mile stretch of narrow gauge tracks from Chinhung-ni.

In other activity, the 1st Motor Transport Battalion (minus detachments) comes under the control of the 1st Supply Regulating Detachment at Hagaru, which increases the productivity of supply movement for the Marines. Transportation units have been overwhelmed since the Wonsan landing. The 7th Motor Transport Battalion had earlier been moved to the operational control of X Corps, which forces the 1st Mountain Battalion to be attached to the 7th RCT.

In the U.S. 3rd Division zone, one great difficulty, because of the lack of roads, is the task of supplying the S.K. 26th Regiment, which is deployed on the opposite side of Paeksan Pass. In addition to the nasty terrain, intelligence estimates that of around 25,000 North Korean guerrilla fighters operating in its zone, most are within about a ten-mile radius of the ominous pass.

In the 7th Division sector, the 1st Battalion, 17th Regiment, following a strongly coordinated assault supported by artillery and tanks, seizes Kapsan. North Korean troops, defending from their foxholes, are mismatched against the roving tanks that roll through as if passing anthills. In addition, other enemy infantry, deployed in trenches and pillboxes, receive a hurricane of fire compliments of the guns of the 15th AAA Artillery Battalion. The enemy troops quickly bolt from their positions to escape the firestorm, but combined effective fire slays them as they run.

Subsequently, under the identical support fire, the 1st Battalion crosses the river and secures the town by 1030. After the capture, it advances, trailed later by the 2nd and 3rd Battalions, and by evening, it stands about 23 miles from Hyesanjin along the headwaters of the Yalu River. The regimental command post is established in Kapsan for the night.

On the following day, the regiment closes against the Yalu. In the 31st Regimental sector, both the east and west sides of the Pujon Reservoir are patrolled without incident. By the 20th, the regiment begins to move to terrain near the Cho-ri–P'ungsan Road to the rear of the 17th Regiment.

In the ROK I Corps area, the USS *St. Paul* is on scene and its guns bolster the ROK Capital Division's advance. Also, the weather is sufficiently clear to permit aircraft to shadow the advance. This day, planes destroy two tanks and two artillery pieces. Intelligence determines that the opposing force engaged with the Capital Division at Orang-ch'on is the N.K. 507th Brigade and one Regiment of the N.K. 41st Division, which combined total about 6,000 troops. On the following day, the Capital Division bolts across the Orang-ch'on River and reinitiates its drive toward Ch'ongjin.

In Air Force activity, Musan, North Korea, is attacked by a group of fifty B-26s (light bombers), initiating the first massive strike by light bombers during the Korean War. The planes drop incendiary bombs on the military barracks in the town, located along the Tumen River at the border with Communist China.

November 20

In the X Corps area, 1st Marine Division sector, the British 41st Independent Commando, Royal Marines, arrives at Hungnam to serve with the U.S. Marines. The unit, commanded by British Lieutenant Colonel Douglas B. Drysdale, is composed of 14 officers and 221 enlisted men. It had been in Japan attached to ComNavFE and had requested to serve with the American Marines.

General O.P. Smith, during conversations with Admiral Doyle in the beginning of November, had consummated the agreement to have the British join the 1st Marine Division. General Smith will utilize the troops, who are greatly skilled in reconnaissance, to guard the left flank of the Marines' advance. The British contingent suffers from the lack of transportation and is scheduled to move to Hagaru on the 28th, in conjunction with the transfer of the division CP to Hagaru.

In the 3rd Division sector, in Majon-ni, the 1st Battalion, 15th Regiment, which had relieved the Marines on the 13th, is struck by an enemy assault during the night and the fighting continues into the early morning hours of the 21st. The enemy force, composed of about two hundred troops, is repulsed; however, at a point, it succeeds in breaking through the perimeter line.

In the 7th Infantry Division sector, in freezing cold weather and along ice-covered roads, the 17th Regiment reinitiates its march to the border at Hyesanjin. The 1st Battalion acts as vanguard, trailed by the 3rd and 2nd Battalions. The columns tread slowly for nineteen miles as the troops cautiously walk along the treacherous mountain roads. They encounter only sporadic light opposition, raised by small enemy contingents. The march terminates several miles from the objective and establishes a night perimeter.

Also, upon orders of General David Barr, the 31st and 32nd Regiments advance to the vicinity of P'ungsan–Kapsan to take positions behind the 17th Regiment; however; contingents are left behind to keep secure the mountain passes that lead east.

South Korean troops arrive at about midnight on the 20th-21st to relieve Company I, 32nd Regiment, at Sillyong on the divisional right front, but mistaken identity by both parties ignites a firefight. The skirmish ends quickly, but five South Koreans are wounded.

In related activity, U.S. Air Force planes arrive on this day to drop food and gasoline to the 7th Division at Kapsan.

In the ROK I Corps area, having tended its wounded following the vicious struggle of the previous week, the Capital Division crosses the Orang-ch'on River en route to seize the big industrial facilities at Ch'ongjin, about thirty miles north. Once there, the unit will be only 65 air-miles (southwest) from the Siberian border.

In the Eighth Army area, intelligence estimates that the Chinese build-ups are emerging in Korea, as well as in Manchuria. Nevertheless, headquarters in Tokyo remains convinced that the Chinese will not intervene in great strength.

— *In Japan:* General MacArthur receives a U.N. directive indicating that only minimum sized units will advance to the boundary of Korea and Manchuria. The order also states that no U.N. troops are permitted to leave or enter Korea by use of the Manchurian or Soviet borders. The directive insists that the international border be "meticulously preserved." The general belief is that the advance is occupational and will not incite confrontation with the Chinese.

November 21   *In the X Corps area,* the U.S. 7th Division reaches the Manchurian border. The pending massive Chinese Communist assault is still unexpected. Up to this point, the Chinese remain intertwined with North Korean units under the guise of volunteers. X Corps informs the 1st Marine Division that the 1st Marines are relieved of responsibility for Huksu-ri, which is now placed under the 3rd Division, with its modified boundary.

General Almond receives a request from Major General Robert H. Soule, 3rd Division, who wants Almond to realign the existing boundary between the 3rd Division and the 1st Marine Division. By modifying the line and extending the 3rd's perimeter northward by only several miles, it would give the division access to the Huksu-ri–Sach'ang-ni Road and provide an easier method of resupplying the S.K. 26th Regiment. Soule receives an affirmative response on the following day.

In Majon-ni, a patrol composed of two officers and 91 men of the 1st Battalion, 15th Regiment, moves westward by vehicles to make contact with the 3rd Battalion, Korean Marines, holding the roadblock at Tongyang. At about the halfway point, while the convoy passes through an eight-mile gorge, disaster strikes. The column drives directly into an ambush, which costs the unit 28 men killed and the loss of nearly its entire complement of vehicles and heavy weapons. The Communists mine the roads to impede the U.S. movement between Majon-ni and the South Korean Marines at Tongyang. With Majon-ni imperiled, reinforcements are rushed to bolster it. One company of infantry from the 2nd Battalion, accompanied by a contingent of tanks, speed to the perimeter.

In the 7th Infantry Division sector, the 17th Regiment enters and occupies Hyesanjin without incident by 1000. In addition to Colonel Powell, commanding officer of the 17th Regiment, Generals Almond and General Barr enter the town with the leading contingents and they observe the remnants of the objective, which had been heavily struck by carrier-based planes on the 13th to bring about near-total destruction.

Word of the occupation of Hyesanjin by the 7th Division reaches General MacArthur, who dispatches a message to X Corps commander General Ned Almond: "Heartiest congratulations, Ned, and tell Dave Barr that he hit the jackpot." General Almond, on the following day, sends his congratulations.

At this time, the Yalu is nearly totally frozen. Only

A contingent of the 17th Regiment, U.S. 7th Division, in the desolate village of Hyesanjin at the Manchurian border on 21 November.

Troops of the 17th Regiment, U.S. 7th Division, move through the snow at Hyesanjin at the Manchurian border with China on 21 November.

about a six-foot-wide channel remains open and within days, the entire river will be frozen over. As troops stare across the Yalu, they see Chinese guarding the opposing banks and an unscathed village on the Manchurian side several hundred yards upstream. The close proximity of CCF soldiers immediately raises concerns of the troops about the probability of China's entry into the conflict. Still, there is no official word on any imminent threat of a major attack by the Chinese. The troops are preparing for Thanksgiving and a hot meal featuring turkey.

November 22   *In the X Corps area,* Corps directs the 3rd Infantry Division to establish blocking positions at Yudam-ni. In other activity, the boundary separating the 1st Marine Division and the 3rd Infantry Division is changed to move the Huksu-ri–Sach'ang-ni Road into the 3rd Division's zone. In conjunction, the 26th S.K. Regiment receives orders from the 3rd Division to establish positions at Huksu-ri and Sach'ang-ni. Following several successful skirmishes, including one at Sach'ang-ni that costs the enemy more than 100 killed or captured, the order is carried out. Soon after, the South Koreans again initiate attacks northward and westward, gaining several miles beyond Sach'ang-ni.

General Almond offers his optimistic congratulations to the 7th Division for its success in reaching the border at Hyesanjin: "The fact that only twenty days ago this division landed amphibiously over the beaches at Iwon and advanced 200 miles over tortuous mountain terrain and fought successfully against a determined foe in subzero weather will be recorded in history as an outstanding military achievement."

In the 1st Marine Division sector, General Smith will begin to step up the advance now that he can utilize the 1st Marines to occupy rear positions on the MSR and dispatch the forward two regiments and the accompanying British contingent.

In the 7th Division sector, despite frigid weather conditions and primitive mountain roads, elements of the 17th Regiment advance to Hyesanjin at the Yalu River and become the first American unit to reach the border. It is also the only U.S. component to reach the border. News of this mission arrives throughout X Corps by the following day. The fact that no Chinese opposition is encountered expands the optimism of the troops and makes for a happy Thanksgiving.

The 32nd Regiment at Kapsan prepares to drive to Singalpajin to deploy to the left of the 17th Regiment, which is at Hyesanjin. Task Force Kingston, commanded by 2nd Lieutenant Robert C. Kingston, advances without incident to Samsu and enters it by the middle of the afternoon. Later, the remainder of the 3rd Battalion (minus Company I) arrives there. It and the nearby 32nd Regiment are to hook up, but as the 17th Regiment initiates an attack, North Korean resistance prevents the hook-up. North Korean opposition continues to hinder the 17th Regiment in this area for the next week.

In Majon-ni, a patrol supported by armor heads toward Tongyang to again attempt to establish contact with the ROK Marines, but it is compelled to abort the mission because the Communists had spent the night destroying the road and laying mines along the route. This action totally isolates the 3rd Korean Marine Battalion at its roadblock positions and places the South Koreans in great jeopardy. Their only sure source of supplies from this point on will be by airdrop.

November 23   *In the X Corps area,* it is Thursday, Thanksgiving Day, the eve of the U.N. offensive scheduled to be carried out primarily by U.S. troops. Most of the men believe they will be home by Christmas. The day's festive menu throughout the various X Corps units, as prescribed by Corps, is shrimp cocktail, roast turkey, cranberry sauce and candied sweet potatoes. For dessert, the samplings include fruit salad, fruit cake, mince pie and coffee. This menu had been

distributed from Corps to subordinate commands on 18 November.

In the 1st Marine Division sector, Division OpnO 2350 is issued at 0800. RCT 1 is to relieve contingents of the 7th Marines near Hagaru and Koto-ri and it is to guard the MSR at Chinhung-ni, Hagaru and Koto-ri. The 5th Marines is to capture Kyolmul-ni, which lies

X Corps troops enjoy Thanksgiving dinner at Hamhung.

about twenty miles north of Hagaru. In addition, the 5th RCT is to prepare to advance northwest to the village to seize Toksil-li. From there, upon orders, the RCT is to prepare to move northeast about fifteen additional miles to secure Tuan-di.

The 7th Marines is to march to Yudam-ni, secure it and maintain one battalion there. Additionally, the OpnO directs the Royal Marines to advance on the left flank, as far as fifteen miles west of Koto-ri. The combined force of division reconnaissance troops and the British might be in a position to discover and destroy Chinese forces that have been undiscovered by regular infantry patrols. The 1st Tank Battalion is ordered to guard the main supply route near Majon-dong and Soyang-ni. The 1st Engineer Battalion is ordered to augment Division operations, but to primarily focus on the airstrip at Hagaru and the upkeep of the MSR.

In the 1st Marines zone, the regiment still suffers from lack of adequate transportation vehicles. The 1st Battalion, using 11th Marines' trucks, arrives at Chinhung-ni and relieves the 3rd Battalion, 5th Marines.

In the 7th Marines zone, pursuant to OpnO 23–50, the Regiment advances to seize Yudam-ni. The 1st Battalion acts as vanguard. It will miss its Thanksgiving dinner. The route is sporadically blocked with a variety of minor obstacles, including abandoned roadblocks that contain cunningly placed booby-traps. The regiment also encounters several detachments of enemy troops, but they, too, are overcome.

In Majon-ni, for the third time in as many days, a contingent of the 15th Regiment moves out to establish contact with the South Korean Marines at Tongyang, but the contingent is also forced to first repair holes and clear mines along the way. The South Korean Marines have been directed to dispatch a contingent to hook up with the advancing Americans. Initially, all goes well as the convoy advances, even through the site of the recent ambush. However, once it advances about two miles beyond the ambush site, the Communists, from concealed positions, again strike.

The patrol returns fire against the force of about 300 troops and during the heated skirmish, the South Koreans arrive from the opposite direction to partially foil the ambush. Nevertheless, the Communists continue to pound the positions of both the Americans and the South Koreans. Sixteen men of the regimental patrol sustain wounds and three others are missing in action.

At about this time, the patrol and the Korean Marines break off the fight and retire to their respective lines. On the 25th, yet another attempt will be made to unclog the Communist blockage.

In the South Korean 3rd Division sector, a contingent of the S.K. 26th Regiment, operating near Sach'ang-ni along the highway that leads south from Yudam-ni and the west shore of the Changjin Reservoir, captures 26 Chinese soldiers.

In the U.S. 7th Division sector, elements of the 7th Division occupy Hyesanjin on the Yalu River. At Samsu, North Korean contingents continue to raise opposition against the 32nd Regiment, preventing Task Force

Kingston from advancing to Singalpajin. Also, as of this day, casualties due to the extreme weather have skyrocketed. The 31st Regiment has sustained 83 frostbite cases and 53 of these are evacuated. The divisional cases of frostbite stand at 142.

In other activity, a downed pilot, stranded about eighty miles behind enemy lines near Kanggye, comes close to being captured, but a helicopter crew risks its own safety to rescue the pilot. Just as the helicopter reaches the position, the pilot shoots a flare into the air. Enemy fire commences immediately, but the helicopter lands and one man, Sergeant James K. Bryson, leaps from the helicopter and brings the injured pilot to the aircraft. The crew takes off with Communist troops about two feet from their helicopter. Although the helicopter sustains hits, it makes it back to friendly lines at Sinanju.

In Naval activity, the East Coast Blockade and Patrol Task Group (TG-95.2) comes under the operational control of United Nations Blockading and Escort Task Force (TF-95).

November 24   The Eighth Army offensive begins at 0800. General MacArthur dispatches a special message to the U.N.: "The United Nations' massive compression in North Korea against the new Red Armies operating there is now approaching its decisive effort.... If successful this should for all practical purposes end the war[,] restore peace and unity to Korea, enable the prompt withdrawal of U.N. military forces, and permit the complete assumption by the Korean people and nation of full sovereignty and international equality. It is that for which we fight."

By this time, MacArthur's intelligence units and his troops in the field have determined that Chinese Communist contingents have been infiltrating North Korea. General MacArthur flies to Korea to oversee the initiation of the planned offensive. On the following day, Communist forces swarm against Eighth Army's western positions and follow this attack with another gigantic assault on the 28th, against the 1st Marine Division positions to the east near the Chosin River.

In other activity, X Corps G-3 Lt. Colonel Chiles delivers X Corps OpnPlan 8, Draft 3 to Headquarters in Tokyo. It is approved at United Nations Headquarters, but with some alteration. The proposed boundary separating X Corps and Eighth Army is moved farther south and into the 1st Marine Division sector.

Eighth Army and the X Corps, under Generals Walker and Almond respectively, begin the final attack to gain the remainder of terrain between the UN forces and the northern border of Korea at the Yalu River. The carriers of Task Force 77 support the offensive. The Eighth Army and X Corps operate independently.

According to calculations the Americans, along with the South Koreans and other allies, expect to encounter nearly 50,000 Chinese and North Korean troops as they advance the final 100 miles that stand between them and northern border of Korea, where it primarily meets the Yalu River and Manchuria; however, at the northeastern border, for a short distance, it meets with Soviet territory.

At this time it is thought that the conflict would be terminated by Christmas Day. General Walker, as of the previous day, maintains logistical control of General Almond's X Corps, which had arrived in Korea during the previous September; however, X Corps operates as a totally separate command.

In the Eighth Army area, I Corps sector, General Frank W. Milburn orders his two divisions to advance west and northwest toward Chongju and Taech'on, but he retains the British Brigade to keep it in reserve. The 21st Regiment, 24th Division, operating on the left, moves out with a supporting complement of tanks, then along Route 1 toward Chongju, just under twenty miles away. On the corps' right, two regiments of the ROK 1st Division move against Taech'on, but they lack a good road and are forced to advance along both sides of the Taeryong River. En route, the force encounters some enemy resistance, but it is still able to reach a point less than five miles from its objective by nightfall.

The Chinese launch a stiff counterattack that lasts through the night of 24th-25th and terminates at about dawn. Some South Korean units on the right (east bank of the Taeryong) are driven back about two miles; however, those on the west bank maintain their positions.

In the IX Corps sector, the 2nd Division, under General Laurence B. Keiser, stands about three miles in front of the 25th Division, and essentially, it stays in place when the offensive begins. Nonetheless, General Keiser, in an effort to prevent any penetration of its west flank, directs the 9th and 38th Regiments to adjust their positions by making a small forward jump to the lower bank of the Paengnyong River, a tributary of the Ch'ongch'on River.

In the meantime, General John B. Coulter orders the 25th Division, led by General William B. Kean and his second in command, Brigadier General Vennard Wilson, to advance north (left), towards Unsan. The 24th and 35th Regiments hold the right and left respectively, while Task Force Dolvin advances in the center. These I Corps troops move parallel to the Kuryong River. Enemy resistance is sporadic, which permits Task Force Dolvin to advance about seven miles.

Meanwhile, the 24th and 35th Regiments gain about four miles. During the advances, thirty weary troops of the 8th Cavalry are discovered by Task Force Dolvin. These troops, earlier captured at Unsan and subsequently released by the enemy, are suffering from wounds, frostbite or both.

In the ROK II Corps sector, the ROK 7th and 8th Divisions gain only about one mile and at some points, much less, particularly when the forces encounter two battalions of Chinese infantry. Nevertheless, the ROK 3rd Regiment, 7th Division, is able to gain additional ground. It reaches the Paengnyong River and makes contact with the U.S. 38th Regiment, 2nd Division (I Corps).

In the X Corps area, 1st Marine Division sector, 1st Marines zone, the 2nd Battalion and 1st Marines Headquarters initiate the relief of the 2nd Battalion, 5th Marines, at Koto-ri. The operation is completed on the following day.

In the 5th Marines sector, each of the three battalions is now operating east of the Chosin Reservoir. General Smith remains concerned about the situation and carefully watches the advance, while awaiting the supplies to increase at Hagaru.

In the 7th Marines zone, the advance toward Yudam-ni continues. The 1st Battalion pauses to celebrate Thanksgiving a day late; they savor their turkey dinner. They do not realize this will be the last hot meal for seventeen days.

In the 3rd Division zone, at Sach'ang-ni, the S.K. 26th Regiment holds its positions in the vicinity of Paeksan Pass. It is to be relieved on the following day by elements of the U.S. 7th Infantry Regiment.

In other activity, there has been a large Communist buildup in this area. Contingents of the Chinese 125th Division have been here for several weeks in expectation of a U.N. advance.

At Samsu, Task Force Kingston (32nd Regiment) still is unable to break through to hook up with the 17th Regiment at Singalpajin.

In the Eighth Army area, at 1000, the offensive begins. MacArthur is flying overhead to observe the units as they advance against no resistance. Various components across the wide front gain between 4,000 and 16,000 yards. There has been guerrilla activity in Eighth Army's area (west coastal area) during November, but it has been at a lower level than that which has been unfolding in the central and northeast sectors of Korea. Nevertheless, Eighth Army patrols continue their activity to discover enemy presence. The area north and east of Pyongyang contains many deposits of enemy supplies that have been concealed in abandoned mine shafts, caves and tunnels.

In Air Force activity, Far East Air Forces and Fifth Air Force strike enemy targets. B-29s for the former hit the Yalu River bridges and for the latter, fighters execute close-air support mission. The Eighth Army offensive continues in conjunction with the air strikes. Also, planes attached to Combat Cargo Command fly missions to drop ammunition to the front lines.

November 25
A contingent of C-47s, attached to the Greek Royal Hellenic Air Force arrives in theater and is attached to Far East Air Forces.

In the X Corps area, Corps issues OpnO 7. It is tailored to conform with the plan presented to Tokyo on the 24th. Basically it directs the Corps to supply more assistance to the ongoing Eighth Army offensive. The attack, primarily carried out by the Marines, 3rd and 7th Infantry Divisions and the S.K. I Corps, is to commence at 0800 on 27 November.

The 1st Marine Division is to advance to the Yalu and seize Mupyong-ni en route. The 3rd Division is to establish and maintain contact with Eighth Army's right flank, while simultaneously guarding the left flank of X Corps. In addition, upon order, the overtaxed 3rd

MANCHURIA

Ch'ongjin

Hyesanjin

Kanggye

Kusong

Suho-Bong

Yudam-ni

Changjin
Reservoir

Sinuiju

Unsan

Chonsen R.

Tokchon

Hamhung

Chongju

Hungnam

Sinanju

Sukchon

SEA

Anju

Tonson

PYONGYANG

OF JAPAN

38°   38°

Kaesong

Ch'unch'on

SEOUL

Samch'ok

Inch'on

Wonju

Suwon

Han R.

YELLOW

Chongju

SEA

Taejon

Kunsan

Taegu

Sangau

Pusan

SITUATION
25 NOVEMBER 1950

▬ ▬ ▬   APPROXIMATE FRONT

Tsushima I.

0   50
      MILES

Division is to bolster the 1st Marine Division while it guards the airfield and harbor at Wonsan. Meanwhile, it is to seek and destroy any enemy guerrilla units operating in its sector.

The 7th Division is directed to launch its assault from the east side of the Chosin Reservoir and advance to the Yalu River. The 7th Division is also to cooperate with the S.K. I Corps and secure the terrain in the vicinity of Pungsan. According to the directive, the S.K. I Corps is to depart the areas of Hapsu and Chongjin and move to the border while eliminating the enemy within its sector.

A briefing occurs at 1000. General Smith is informed that his division will now form the northern arm of the pincer movement rather than launch the attack east of the Chosin Reservoir. In conjunction, the 7th Division will attack from east of the reservoir to reach the Yalu River.

In related activity, the 1st Battalion, 7th Infantry relieves the S.K. 26th Regiment at Sach'ang-ni.

In the 1st Marine Division zone, the boundary changes now thrust the Marine lines across Korea to the area north of Eighth Army. The path for advance leads west about fifty-five miles and stretches from Yudam-ni to Mupyong-ni. The rear boundary of the Marines has also moved north, to a point slightly south of Hagaru, listed as 3rd Division responsibility. However, General O.P. Smith, aware that the 3rd Division is too overstretched to provide enough troops, requests permission to deploy garrisons at Koto-ri and Chinhung-ni. The response is affirmative. Now the 3rd Division retains responsibility for the security of the MSR leading south from Sudong to Hamhung. The attack remains scheduled for the 27th, with the 1st Marine Division acting as vanguard.

In the 5th Marines sector, two tanks accompany a platoon-strength patrol that reaches the area near the end of the Chosin Reservoir. It encounters some enemy troops and a brief fight ensues. The chase nets one prisoner and five killed. In addition, the Marines destroy an abandoned 75-mm gun. Neither this patrol, nor any others, including a helicopter reconnaissance flight, uncover any large numbers of enemy troops. In addition, subsequent to relief by elements of the 32nd Regiment, the 5th Marines prepares to move against Mupyong-ni.

In the 7th Marines zone, Yudam-ni is seized by the 1st Battalion, which encounters paltry resistance. The 3rd Battalion, 7th Marines, contingents of the 3rd Battalion, 11th Marines, and regimental headquarters arrive later.

In the 7th Division zone, the 1st Battalion, 32nd Regiment, begins the relief of the 5th Marines, thus terminating Marine activity in the area east of the Chosin Reservoir at 1200. The Army battalion remains under temporary operational control of the 1st Marine Division. By noon on the following day, all elements of the 5th Marines are to be relieved.

In the ROK I Corps area, elements of the Capital Division reach Ch'ongjin. The advance is preceded by a

thunderous bombardment of naval gunfire, which permits the ROKs to more easily encircle the objective. During the evening, the 1st Regiment slips to a point about five miles north of the town, while the 18th Regiment deploys along the southern fringes. Meanwhile, the ROK Cavalry Regiment moves to the western tip of the town and captures the airfield. An attack to seize Ch'ongjin is planned for the following day.

In the Eighth Army area, I Corps sector, the 21st Infantry Regiment, 24th Division, enters Chongju without incident, while the 19th Regiment continues to move towards Napchongjong. This seizure places the 24th Division on the Eighth Army first phase line.

In other activity, the Corps is struck, as part of an ongoing Chinese offensive, by contingents of the 50th and 66th Armies.

In the 1st ROK Division zone, the Chinese continue to raise heavy resistance near Taech'on, which prevents the South Koreans from gaining the town. Following day-long opposition, the objective remains three miles beyond their reach. Nevertheless, the Division is deployed in close proximity to the U.S. 24th Division.

In the IX Corps sector, the 38th Infantry, 2nd Division, remains in place at Paengnyong, while the 9th Regiment moves through the Ch'ongch'on Valley and gains about two miles. Later, the 2nd Division establishes night positions along its fifteen-mile perimeter that stretches across the Ch'ongch'on Valley.

A contingent of the 38th Regiment holds positions north of Kunu-ri and east of the Ch'ongch'on River. Its line extends southeastward towards the lower bank of the Paengnyong River. The 2nd and 3rd Battalions, 38th Regiment, are deployed on a line that extends parallel to the south bank of the Paengnyong River to the zone of the ROK II Corps.

On the left side of the perimeter, the 9th Regiment is deployed in line with the 38th Regiment, but a wide gap of about one-half mile stands between them. The 2nd and 3rd Battalions, minus one company of the 2nd Battalion (38th Regiment), hold the line on the opposing side of the river, with each company in separate positions along a series of ridges. The 23rd Infantry is deployed in the vicinity of Kunu-ri, but a contingent composed of headquarters, the 1st Battalion and one tank company is stretched out across the valley highway at the lower bank of the Ch'ongch'on River, just to the rear of the 9th Regiment.

In the meantime, the Chinese XIII Army Group, commanded by General Li Tien-yu, initiates its offensive, with the heaviest thrust unfolding against the IX Corps; however, other contingents will strike the I Corps and the ROK II Corps. In the 2nd Division zone, the Chinese commit elements of the 39th and 40th Armies to launch two regiments against the forward 9th Regiment positions, while another regiment drives against the middle of the 38th Regiment at Paengnyong.

The 2nd Battalion, deployed in the high ground, is not assaulted, but the 3rd Battalion sustains a heavy hit and as the fighting continues through the night, the regiment is compelled to give some ground. Meanwhile, other Chinese troops funnel through the gaps between the separate company positions of the 3rd Battalion and plunge ahead into the lines of the 1st Battalion, 23rd Regiment, as well as the 61st Field Artillery Battalion.

The artillery contingent, a unit of the 1st Cavalry Division attached to the 2nd Division, is severely struck. The commanding officer of Battery A is among those slain. The entire unit begins a hasty retreat. But Battery A leads the way, as it abandons its weapons and vehicles. The routed Americans scatter with a few moving east, but the Chinese pursue the main group, which is speeding southward right into the positions of Colonel Freeman's 23rd Regiment. The 23rd also sustains a heavy attack, but despite the initial confusion caused by retreating troops and heavy Chinese fire, the assault is repelled. The Chinese retire to Chinaman's Hat, a mountain northeast of the 23rd Regiment. They will return later.

Meanwhile, another Chinese regiment plows into the 1st Battalion, 9th Infantry, in a double strike. While some of the regiment hits the front, another column moves through the gap between the 9th Regiment and the 38th Regiment, which gives the Communists positions from which to lunge forward into the rear of the 1st Battalion, 9th Regiment. The momentum blows through the lines and tramples over the command post and the medical aid station. The Chinese continue moving and make their way to Chinaman's Hat to hook up with the regiment that preceded them.

Prior to dawn, the Chinese bolt from the mountain positions and again strike Colonel Freeman's lines, on the right flank east of the valley road. The Chinese force a small collapse on the flank, but Freeman modifies his positions and his troops repulse the assault. By dawn, the enemy returns once again to Chinaman's Hat.

In the 38th Regimental zone, the evening remains quiet, but toward midnight, yet another Chinese regiment that had eased through the half-mile gap between the 9th and 38th Regiments launches an attack that pounds against Company A, which is deployed north of the Paengnyong River. Simultaneously, the same regiment strikes against the regimental boundary positions of the 2nd and 3rd Battalions on the opposing bank of the river. These assaults jackhammer Companies F and L, but they are unable to gain ground. Both companies hold steadfastly. The enemy maintains the attacks for about three hours, but at 0230, after the apparent realization of having sustained heavy casualties, the Chinese disengage. Nonetheless, at about 0500, the attack is reinitiated.

Meanwhile, isolated Company A, 1st Battalion, 38th Regiment, becomes encircled. The remainder of the 1st Battalion initiates a counterattack to regain lost ground. The attack is executed just before dawn when the battalion jumps off and drives east into the west flank of the Chinese, who had earlier penetrated the middle of the regiment's lines. Shortly thereafter, the enemy is driven off and the perimeter is realigned to its former positions.

In the 25th Division sector, resistance is encountered as the columns move towards Unsan. The bulk of the fire is from long-range artillery and machine gun fire; however, some small arms fire meets the advance. Nevertheless, the division gains about two miles as it pushes along the left bank of the Kuryong River, reaching a point about one day's march from Unsan, when it establishes night positions.

Later, the Chinese (39th and 40th Armies) strike, but in less force than that used against the 2nd Division. The brunt of the assault hits Task Force Dolvin's lines on the east side of the Kuryong River, where they also control two hills in their most forward positions. The fighting lasts throughout the night of the 25th-26th. Eventually the Chinese push the Americans from one of the hills.

In the S.K. II Corps area, the Chinese Communists strike hard against the Koreans at Tokchon, located about seventy miles southwest of Yudam-ni, a point that the 7th Marines are preparing to move toward. The South Koreans are slugged back by contingents of the 38th and 42nd Armies, but the episode is not sufficiently bad to warrant changes in the attack plan. However, the Chinese will again strike on the following day.

Meanwhile, the S.K. 16th Regiment, ROK 8th Division, assigned to the east flank of the corps (and Eighth Army), engages enemy troops east of Yongdong-ni. The enemy assault, which includes horse-cavalry troops, succeeds in driving the regiment back about two miles. Despite the regimental setback, the corps' gains seem in line with General Walker's plans to maintain the offensive. Nevertheless, the threat against the II Corps endangers the nearby 2nd U.S. Division and the right flank of Eighth Army.

In Majon-ni, using a full-strength attack, the 1st Battalion, 15th ROK Regiment, drives from Majon-ni and the South Korean Marines advance from Tongyang to converge upon the Communist force that holds the ground separating the two contingents. The combined power of the two forces overwhelms the enemy and clears the passageway from Majon-ni to Tongyang. The victory costs the Communists about 150 killed and the loss of a huge amount of ammunition and four 120-mm mortars. Although the enemy is dispersed, they continue to operate in the area for the duration of the conflict.

November 26   The S.K. 1st Division captures an important enemy document that specifies how the Chinese appraise the fighting ability of their American opponents. After the Chinese 39th Army drove the U.N. forces from the vicinity of Unsan, the Chinese 66th Army Headquarters issued a memorandum (on November 20) based on the resistance raised by the 8th Cavalry Regiment. The memo states the potency of the U.S. mortars and artillery and emphasizes the terrific transportation network. It also underscores the accuracy of air strikes and long-range artillery. However, the Chinese depiction of American soldiers, once cut off, is not very positive:

They abandon all their heavy weapons and play possum.... Their infantrymen are weak, afraid to die, and haven't the courage to attack or defend. They depend on their planes, tanks and artillery. At the same time, they are afraid of our fire power. They will cringe when if on the advance, they hear firing ... they specialize in day fighting. They are not familiar with night fighting or hand to hand combat.... If defeated, they have no orderly formation. Without the use of their mortars, they become completely lost.... At Unsan, they were surrounded for several days, yet they did nothing. They are afraid when the rear is cut off. When transportation comes to a standstill, the infantry loses the will to fight.

The document also states the goals of the Chinese against the Americans in the future; the terms include avoiding highways and level terrain to evade the fire of tanks and artillery and night attacks: "As a main objective, one of the units must fight its way rapidly around the enemy and cut off their rear.... Small leading patrol groups attack and then sound the bugle. A large number will at that time follow in column."

The Chinese XIII Army Group will maintain its offensive and attack throughout the night of the 26th into the 27th, hitting most points except the Eighth Army west flank.

In the X Corps area, 1st Marine Division sector, Division issues OpnO 24–50 at 0800. It orders the attack, which is to commence at 0800 on the following day. General O.P. Smith moves by helicopter from Hungnam to Yudam-ni, and he cautiously observes the MSR en route. Among the units spotted south of Chinhung-ni, are the 1st Tank Battalion less the Provisional Armored Platoon at Hagaru and Company D's 2nd Platoon at Chinhung-ni.

Upon returning to Hungnam, General Smith is informed that the Communists have scored greatly against the S.K. II Corps, which had been thrashed, endangering the right flank. This unexpected setback imperils both the U.S. 2nd Division and the Turkish Brigade, exposing them to a flank attack. No enemy activity is discovered during the day and the night remains especially frigid, but inactive.

In the 1st Marines zone, the vehicles previously used to transport the 1st and 2nd Battalions to their new positions have returned to Chigyong. They transport the 3rd Battalion, 1st Marines (minus George Company and elements of a weapons company), to Hagaru to relieve the 2nd Battalion, 7th Marines. Company G has remained at Chigyong due to lack of trucks.

When the attack is launched on the 27th, the 1st Marines is to remain in divisional reserve to guard the MSR, Chinhung-ni, Hagaru and Koto-ri. Hagaru, located at the base of the Chosin Reservoir, contains the Marines' sole airstrip and it is not yet completed. Nonetheless, Hagaru must hold or there is no way to regroup the scattered division. The responsibility for Hagaru, surely a huge task, lies solely with Lt. Colonel Ridge's 3rd Battalion.

In the 5th Marines zone, the 5th Marines prepares to pass through the 7th Marines on the 27th by 0800, and from there move to seize the road junction at Yongnim-dong, about twenty-seven miles west of Yudam-ni. The 2nd Battalion, 5th Marines, completes its move from the reservoir to Yudam-ni by evening.

The town, surrounded by five huge ridges, is located in the middle of a giant valley. These massive ridges, each with large numbers of nasty peaks, dangerous spurs and spooky draws, exhibit a natural blueprint for disaster. The ridges are named North, Northwest, South, Southeast and Southwest. The difficult terrain, matched with abominable weather, guarantees a grueling mission. Today's temperature plunges to zero degrees. On the 27th, the weather in Korea reaches a temperature of 20 degrees below zero.

The 2nd Battalion receives orders to seize a pass west of Yudam-ni. The attack will be assisted by the 7th Marines, which will drive forward along two ridgelines.

In the 7th Marines zone, the regiment is to guard the MSR from Yudam-ni to Sinhung-ni, which lies about seven miles west of Hagaru. The Division Reconnaissance Company is to act in conjunction with the 7th Marines and operate north of Yudam-ni. The British Royal Marines unit will operate southwest of Yudam-ni to guard the Division's left flank. The 7th Regiment is deployed on four of the five ridges that encircle Yudam-ni. Companies D and E, attached to 1st Battalion, are deployed on North Ridge. The 1st Battalion stands on both South and Southeast Ridges, while the 3rd Battalion is deployed on Southwest Ridge. These positions give the 7th Marines the heights that dominate the attack route of the 5th Marines.

A patrol composed of a rifle platoon of Company A, 1st Battalion, moves into an ambush site and comes under fire from point-blank range. Lieutenant Frank N. Mitchell maintains discipline, then bolts to the front of his command, takes over an automatic weapon and returns fire.

Mitchell gets volunteers to gather the wounded, despite the confusion of the darkness. The Marines move into the enemy terrain to conduct the search. With the litter bearers to his rear, Mitchell carries the fight to the enemy. Afterwards, the platoon is able to extricate itself, while Mitchell, already repeatedly wounded, provides cover fire. He is slain while holding the line to enable his troops to withdraw. Lieutenant Mitchell is awarded the Medal of Honor posthumously for his extraordinary bravery and leadership while under enemy fire.

Later this day, the 5th Marines receives a new objective, a pass about ten miles west of Yudam-ni. Contingents of the 7th Marines will grind forward along Northwest and Southwest Ridges to protect the 5th Marines' flank.

At 2200, the regimental officers confer on the individual missions. The 3rd Battalion is to penetrate deeper along Southwest Ridge on the 27th, but it is also assigned the task of securing an objective on the opposite side of the MSR. It is to take Hill 1403, on Northwest Ridge, to enable it to provide sufficient support for the 5th Marines. Companies D and E are assigned responsibility for running patrols along the west coast of the reservoir and on North Ridge. The 1st Battalion is to scour South and Southeast Ridges with patrols while focusing on the routes along the low ground. The primary road to Hagaru stretches through the valley between huge hills.

In other activity, the Regiment announces that it has captured three Chinese soldiers, attached to the Chinese 60th Division. Intelligence officers have discovered from the captives that the Chinese 58th, 59th and 60th Divisions had arrived in the vicinity of Yudam-ni on the 20th. This brings the total of identified Communist Chinese units in northeast Korea to six divisions. Nevertheless, it is still thought that the Chinese probably will not attack in strength. Rather, it is thought that a westward withdrawal will be executed. The Marines anticipate an engagement with the Chinese in the mountains west of Yudam-ni.

In the 11th Marines area, the units deployed in the vicinity of Yudam-ni are to contribute support to the attacking elements.

In the ROK I Corps area, Ch'ongjin is attacked and captured by the S.K. Capital Division. Following the victory, the ROKs prepare to pivot and initiate a northward attack that will push the force inland along the highway and railroad toward Hoeryong, which is located at the border with Manchuria.

In the Eighth Army area, reports regarding the losses inflicted upon the ROK II Corps pour into headquarters during the day. General Walker, informed that his right flank now consists of the 38th Regiment, 25th Division, moves feverishly to rearrange his defenses. By day's end, General Walker is informed that the estimate of about 54,000 Chinese troops in the area is inaccurate. The new estimate by Intelligence is more than 100,000 troops.

The Chinese XIII Army Group, under General Li Tien-yu, continues its offensive. During the course of this day and into the following day, the greater part of the Eighth Army sector comes under assault.

In the I Corps area, the situation is comparatively calm, but General Milburn remains concerned about the Chinese threat as I Corps, like the other Corps, is at less than full strength and General Walker is also utilizing I Corps forces to strengthen other units that face imminent threat by the enemy.

In other activity, General Hobart Gay is ordered by General Walker to redeploy his 1st Cavalry Division to meet what appears to be a serious threat by the Chinese, due to the collapse of the ROK II Corps this day. The cavalry makes preparations to depart from its positions at Kunu-ri and Sukch'on on the following day to establish new positions at the village of Sunchon and protect the approaches from the east. The 187th Airborne RCT, augmented by the Philippine 10th Battalion Combat Team, will take over the protection of supply depots at Kunu-ri and Sukch'on.

In other activity, the British 27th Brigade is directed by General Walker to redeploy with the IX Corps to bolster its forces in place of the reserve Turkish Brigade, which is en route to Tokch'on. Although the Eighth Army offensive is essentially at a standstill, the 24th Division is deployed along Route 1 and poised for an advance to the Yalu River, but this attack, despite anticipation of slight resistance, is aborted for fear of the division overextending itself and becoming isolated with no means to launch a relief force.

General Church then orders the 5th Regimental Combat Team to establish positions to the right of his two regiments that are extended along Route 1. Church assumes that this deployment will fill the hole between the ROK 1st Division and the 24th Division's positions. The ROK 1st Division is operating on the corps' right and has advanced along the banks of the Taeryong River to the vicinity of Taech'on. Although the Koreans had advanced beyond the 24th Division, the Chinese continue to raise fierce resistance.

In the meantime, General Su Ching-huai, commander of the Chinese 66th Army, awaits dusk before he orders his force to drive down the east bank of the Taeryong River. Once properly positioned, the Chinese spring an attack against both sides of the river and strike the 11th and 12th S.K. Regiments on the east and west sides respectively.

The South Koreans on the east side are driven back, and on the west bank the 12th also loses ground, but it is able to recapture the terrain by dawn on the 27th. Nonetheless, the Chinese maintain the pressure on the 27th and the enemy progress is beginning to seriously threaten the 24th U.S. Division, which is stationed on the west side of the Taeryong River.

In the IX Corps sector, General Walker directs General John B. Coulter to use his reserve, the Turkish brigade, to recapture Tokch'on, which had been lost by the ROK II Corps. Tokch'on gives the Chinese a path towards the rear of Eighth Army, but if it is seized, the Turks would hold the ground and be near the 2nd Division northwest of the village. The assault is set for the following morning and if successful it will give Eighth Army control of the Tokch'on–Kunu-ri Road, an attack route from the west to Kunu-ri.

In the meantime, General Coulter dispatches the 1st Battalion and he will later order the 2nd Battalion to move out with both units expected to be at Wawon by dawn on the following day.

In the 2nd Division zone, in the Ch'ongh'on Valley, the 9th Regiment, led by Colonel Charles Sloane, redeploys in the heights above the upper bank of the Ch'ongch'on River. Due to losses within the 3rd Battalion during the previous night's combat, the regiment is bolstered by the 2nd Engineering Combat Battalion (minus Company C).

Meanwhile, General Keiser makes other adjustments. The 1st and 2nd Battalion, 23rd Regiment, advance and redeploy below Chinaman's Hat, the latter taking positions alongside the 61st Field Artillery Battalion. The artillerymen had, by this time, returned to their positions of the previous night and reclaimed some of the abandoned weaponry lost, prior to pulling back and establishing new lines near the other two artillery battalions deployed under the 27th Regiment. General Keiser directs his final reserve unit, the 3rd Battalion, 27th Regiment, to deploy to the rear of the 27th Regiment. It stretches out in the vicinity of Kujang-dong on a highway east of the town that is used to resupply the 38th Regiment.

A contingent of Company C, 1st Battalion, 27th Regiment, led by Sergeant John A. Pittman, volunteers to attack and regain a previously lost strategic position. The detachment encounters heavy fire. A grenade lands in the midst of the patrol and Pittman throws his body upon it to take the full impact. He survives and the others are saved from harm. When medics reach him, he immediately asks how many of his men had been wounded from the blast. The answer was none. Sergeant Pittman becomes a recipient of the Medal of Honor for his intrepid actions and selfless sacrifice to save others.

In the 38th Regiment zone, at Paengnyong, Colonel Peploe is working on his defenses, but his command had sustained very heavy casualties on the previous day. Company G stands at about sixty troops and Company A had been devastated after being caught in a trap. There is no enemy activity during the early part of this day; however, Peploe's lines, north of the supply road, seem to be in the direct route of the enemy, which at this time is mauling the S.K. II Corps. Once informed of the inability of the South Koreans to hold the line, he deduces that the 38th Regiment might well become the right flank of the Eighth Army if the II Corps falls.

As the day progresses, the Chinese on Chinaman's Hat prepare for yet another assault. After dusk, they descend from the mountain and execute a two-pronged attack against Colonel Freeman's 23rd Regiment, and later, just before midnight, they pound against the middle of Colonel Sloane's 9th Regiment. During the first assault, the enemy forces Freeman to abandon his command post. Shortly thereafter, just prior to midnight, Freeman commits Company F and headquarters personnel from the 2nd and 3rd Battalions as well as the regimental headquarters company. The attack regains the command post, but the Chinese who still dominate the heights east of the Ch'ongch'on River unleash a hurricane of fire that again forces Freeman to abandon the positions.

Rather than risk unnecessary casualties, Colonel Freeman postpones any further activity until daylight. In the meantime, the 9th Regiment, posted on the ground east of the Ch'ongch'on River, remains vigilant during the night, which passes without enemy activity, but as midnight nears, the middle of the line suddenly comes under a severe attack. The 2nd Battalion returns fire, but the pressure continues to mount. The enemy, bolstered by mortars, recoilless rifles and 3.5 rocket-launchers, evicts the weary battalion and drives it to the bank of the river.

The battle continues, but after awhile, the 2nd Battalion is compelled to escape to the east bank, leaving some of its weapons behind. The regimental commander, Colonel Sloane, calls in artillery support to cover the retreat and it apparently deters enemy pursuit across the river. Consequently, the 2nd Battalion escapes; however, the ordeal squeezes the unit of its operational ability for the time being.

In the 23rd Regiment's zone, the night passes without any major combat. Despite the routing of the 2nd Battalion, 9th Regiment, the Chinese choose not to ford the river into the 9th Regiment's zone on the east bank.

In the 38th Regiment sector, which lies in and around Somin-dong to the right of the 9th and 23rd Regiments, elements of the Chinese 40th Army launch attacks just after darkness overcomes the area.

The first assault is sprung against Company C while it is en route to the east side of the perimeter to reestablish the positions previously held by Company G. The enemy, driving from the northwest, encircles Company C, but only with a contingent of the force. Other troops in the attack force continue moving and strike the middle of the perimeter hammering against Companies F and L. The heavy penetration causes problems throughout the lines and some companies are compelled to give ground. The Chinese continue to pour troops into the area and it is determined that about two divisions are involved between this contest in the 38th Regimental zone and the nearby ROK II Corps sector.

During the engagement, many of the American units get splintered and wind up in different companies. As the night-attack intensifies, Colonel Peploe calls upon the S.K. 3rd Regiment to assist. It had already retired from the ROK II Corps perimeter. All the while, Peploe struggles with the dilemma of reorganizing his scattered units while he gets help from the 2nd Reconnaissance Company, which holds the line on the Kujang-dong Road in an effort to halt the South Koreans who are hurriedly retiring. The 38th Regiment is forced to pull back on two sides, the east and north. Nevertheless, the regiment continues to engage the enemy all through the night and into the following day.

In the 25th Division sector, General Kean aborts plans to reinitiate the advance of the 25th Division. Instead, he prepares for a potential attack by the Chinese. Task Force Dolvin, which had been struck during the previous day, and the 1st Battalion, 24th Infantry Regiment, are enjoined as Task Force Wilson. However, the ranger company, which had been attached to the 1st Battalion and had recently withdrawn from the front, is not part of the new task force, which is to be commanded by General Vennard Wilson.

Kean's deduction that the Chinese would attack proves to be accurate. Slightly after 1200, while a two-company contingent of the 24th Regiment is attempting to retrieve supplies that had been dropped by planes, are caught in a trap by the enemy. The remainder of the regiment under Colonel John Corley is not involved in a rescue, but the greater number of the troops slip away and make it to the lines of the 2nd Division.

In the meantime, Task Force Wilson is bolstered by the 2nd Battalion, 27th Regiment, which establishes positions to its rear. The 24th Regiment, minus the contingent that had been encircled, is augmented by the remainder of the 27th Regiment, the latter having been held in reserve.

Later in the day, the reports of the near disintegration of the ROK II Corps' resistance is authenticated. Peploe is compelled to again realign his forces. The 38th Regiment establishes a new line beginning with the 2nd Battalion, which holds the ground above the highway to Kujang-dong. The other units in the regiment extend eastward to the town of Somin-dong and from there, the regiment stretches through the heights west of the road leading to Tokch'on. These drastic redeployment maneuvers are in place by about 1800, but still the weakened regiment is unable to form a large perimeter. Consequently, the right flank of Eighth Army, specifically, the 38th Regiment, is confined to a small perimeter, leaving open paths for attack from the northeast. And adding to the dilemma, there is also a huge threat to the rear of Eighth Army.

In the S.K. II Corps area, the Chinese reinitiate the attack that causes the Korean II Corps to collapse under the extreme pressure. The inability to withstand the assault causes the Eighth Army offensive to ostensibly stall prior to the commencement of the 1st Marine Division jump-off on the 27th.

During the previous night, much of the South Korean corps came under heavy attack when an enemy regiment pounded its way through the 16th ROK Regiment, while other forces clamped down on the ROK 7th Division. By 0800 this day, the corps is being shredded at various points all across the perimeter. The enemy pressure compels the east flank to collapse. Its defenders, the 21st Regiment, abandons its positions and heads for Yongdong-ni and another, the 10th Regiment, begins retiring to the same location.

The west flank, defended by the ROK 3rd Regiment, for the time being remains unscathed, but only until dusk. Then the Chinese push some of the regiment from its sector into the lines of the U.S. 38th Infantry. Throughout the day, the Chinese continue to plow through other South Korean lines. An enemy regiment pushes against an unsteady 7th ROK Division and effortlessly causes its 5th and 8th Regiments to hastily retire. Lacking the support of these two regiments, the 3rd regiment soon departs the area and speeds towards the lines of the U.S. IX Corps.

Other Chinese troops are able to bolt from the corps' frontal positions and advance to Tokch'on, ten miles inside the perimeter. This unexpected action isolates the 2nd Regiment, ROK 6th Division, which had been held in reserve in the village. The South Koreans are unable to regroup. General Yu's repeated attempts to galvanize some type of resistance fails. The Chinese continue to topple the resistance and overrun additional terrain as troops that had come in from the northeast take the towns of Yongdong-ni and Maengsan.

In Air Force activity, light bombers (B-26s) under the guidance of tactical air control party (TACP) initiate their first night close-air support missions. Sixty-seven planes attached to the 3rd Bomber Group strike targets along the Eighth Army's bomb-line. Nonetheless, the massive bombing runs do not halt the Communist pressure in northwestern Korea against Eighth Army or in the X Corps zone in northeast Korea.

Lieutenant John W. Enyart, while on a reconnaissance mission in the area around Tokch'on, receives a message on the radio about a ground observer and his contingent that the Communists had encircled. Enyart, despite being in an unarmed plane, moves through extremely heavy fire, lands on a primitive airstrip and rescues the controller, then he returns to pick up another of the contingent, but by the time he returns, the Communists control the strip.

— *In Japan:* Reports indicating nearly a 100 percent increase in the estimated number of Chinese troops in Korea reach the Far East Command. Nonetheless, despite the fact that 100,000 Chinese troops are facing Eighth Army, the information does not bring the Intelligence section to disagree with Eighth Army that the Chinese will initiate a major offensive. Rather, both General Willoughby in Japan and Walker in Korea think the enemy will rely on defense and counterattack. Eighth Army still concludes that its offensive, although stalled, will soon be reinitiated and if the Chinese take the offensive in the valley, their effort will only stall the drive to the Yalu. These conclusions regarding the U.N. offensive are dispatched by Headquarters to Washington.

November 27 *In X Corps area, 1st Marine Division sector, 1st Marines zone,* Hagaru, defended by the 3rd Battalion, is under threat by the Chinese. Lt. Colonel Ridge, after scanning the terrain, realizes that his battalion is insufficiently strong to withstand a major assault, due to the length of the perimeter that extends about four miles. And this only includes protection of the two reverse slopes. Other areas would have to be covered by supporting fire. To add to the uncertainty, while the Marines anticipate an assault from either the hill east of the town or a draw that heads into the southwest end, the Chinese could yet find another approach. The Chinese who control the heights around the town can observe the Marines as they fortify their positions.

Also, a convoy (Headquarters Battalion) arrives at Hagaru to set up the divisional command post. While the Marines must evaluate the time and estimated strength of an assault, they are also under the gun to check a large amount of Korean civilians who are moving into the town. The refugees had been halted and searched at a roadblock, and then escorted to the local police station for interrogation. The day passes without an enemy attack being launched.

In the 5th Marines zone, the 2nd Battalion, 5th Marines, drives down the highway leading from Yudam-ni to seize its objectives. Company H moves to Toktong Pass. The battalion is supported by the guns of Battery H, 3rd Battalion, 11th Marines, which remains in Hagaru. The carved, undersize highway slithers along the valley and passes between the gargantuan walls of Southwest and Northwest Ridges. The vanguard, Company F, commanded by Captain Uel Peters, advances toward the first objective, an elongated knob on Northwest Ridge. This frozen, rock-hard spur lies about 500 yards across a ravine from Hill 1403.

At about 0935, Chinese that hold positions on the knob commence long-range fire that strikes the Marines just as they approach the entry to the ravine. Meanwhile, an overhead spotter plane from VMO-6 detects enemy troops entrenched along the entire front. Company F pauses to reassess its situation. In the meantime, engineers speed to the front to demolish undefended roadblocks that are scattered along the MSR. Nine such obstacles are unblocked. Company D, 2nd Battalion, advances down the MSR, while Company F moves along slopes and passes through the 7th Marines on Hill 1403. It too comes under heavy fire as it approaches the mouth of the ravine. Mortar units and recoilless rifles return fire against the slopes of the knob.

By 1015, the guns of the 1st Battalion, 11th Marines, begin to hammer the slopes and the barrage eases the resistance. At 1115, planes of VMF-312 jolt the slopes with heavy strikes, then Companies F and G resume the attack. Company F's 1st Platoon, led by Lieutenant Gerald McLaughlin, plows toward the knob's north flank. It is bolstered by cover fire from the remainder of the company from positions on Hill 1403. The combined strength of the air strike, mortars and artillery that pummels enemy positions prompts many of them to flee westward from the knob. The northern portion of the knob is seized by the 1st Platoon by 1300. Three Chinese are captured.

Following the collapse of the northern half, the southern half of the knob above the road is attacked. The 2nd Platoon, led by Lieutenant Donald Krabbe, moves through the 1st Platoon, and afterwards, it encounters heavy machine gun fire as it advances. The menacing fire originates on another peak that lies about 1,000 yards to the west. While the advance continues in the heights, Company D grinds forward along the road. It reaches a bend in the road effortlessly, then drives toward a valley road junction several hundred yards in the distance.

Meanwhile, the Chinese have constructed layers of defensive positions in the heights of the eastern slopes of Sakkat Mountain to stall the advance. The Chinese commence firing upon Company D. The blanket of fire compels Colonel Roise to terminate the attack. At 1440, Company D is directed to establish a defensive perimeter by extending across the MSR on a spur of Southwest Ridge. Fox Company is directed to establish positions on Northwest Ridge. The key attack gains 1,500 yards with the successful seizure of the intended objective. Nevertheless, the attack is unable to gain the additional several miles targeted by the advance. The lack of further success turns into a blessing. Further

gains would have caused the Marines to become totally encircled.

In other activity, the 1st Battalion, 5th Marines, arrives from its positions east of the reservoir to Yudam-ni subsequent to dusk and establishes positions in the valley. The 3rd Battalion, 5th Marines, under Lt. Colonel Taplett, which had been on the east coast of the reservoir, arrives at North Ridge at about noon. The troops deploy on an unoccupied spur that flows to Hill 1384.

In the 7th Marines zone, the sun begins to rise at Yudam-ni, but it beams no heat. The scene at Yudam-ni at daybreak is bleak. Near-frozen men gather close to the fires to thaw their rations and de-ice their weapons for the dogged day that awaits them. The 5th Marines launch the primary assault. The 7th Marines remain high in the hills. Companies G and H, 3rd Battalion, on Southwest Ridge move out at 0815. Company H, commanded by Captain Leroy Cooke, seizes Hill 1403 without incident. Cooke had become company commander on November 12. Lieutenant H. Harris reverted to executive officer.

Initially, Company G, commanded by Captain Thomas Cooney, also makes good progress. It swiftly gains about 1,200 yards and secures Hill 1426, a dominating peak on Southwest Ridge, by 0845. The advance encounters no opposition. However, the Chinese lurk in the distance. Cooney's Marines resume the advance, but resistance rises almost immediately, as another ridge about 500 yards distant is layered with Chinese.

In other activity, a contingent of the 1st Service Battalion arrives to institute a system of resupply and to build a divisional depot. Rations are down to about three days' supply, but a convoy requested by the 7th Marines arrives well after dark. Additionally, Lt. Colonel Beall, CO, 1st Motor Transport Battalion, commands a night convoy from Yudam-ni to Hagaru. Beall anticipates a return trip on the 28th with additional supplies to ease the situation. He takes all 5th and 7th Marines' organic vehicles except between 40 and 50 trucks. Although the Chinese have heavily infiltrated the area, the trucks reach Hagaru unmolested; however, there is no return trip.

Also, four M-4 tanks (Provisional Tank Platoon) depart from Hagaru for Yudam-ni, but all return after each slides off the road. Later, one M-26 succeeds in making it to Yudam-ni before the Chinese sever the road to prevent any others from arriving.

The 3rd Battalion, 7th Marines, experiences difficulty during the afternoon. Company G pushes forward to occupy a peak of Hill 1426 by 1500. The advance is costly. During the fighting, Captain Cooney heads to the rear to bring up reinforcements, but he sustains a mortal wound. Captain Eric Haars becomes commanding officer, G Company, on 27 November.

Similar to the 5th Marines' predicament, the heavy fire originating on Sakkat Mountain hinders progress. Company G is compelled to withdraw from the crest. Company I, 3rd Battalion, speeds from its positions in the heights above Yudam-ni to bolster the efforts of Company G. At about 1230, Company B, 1st Battalion, 7th Marines, diverts from its patrol duties in the valley between South and Southwest Ridges. It climbs to the sound of the guns in the high ground to offer its firepower. Chinese fire clamps the advancing company with a ring of fire, prompting Company C to lunge forward from its positions at Yudam-ni.

During an attack against Company E, 2nd Battalion, 7th Marines, on the night of the 27th-28th, an enemy grenade is thrown into the midst of some Marines during a heated battle in which the platoon leader had been wounded. The assistant leader, Staff Sergeant Robert S. Kennemore, is directing the return fire when the grenade lands in the vicinity of a machine gun position. Kennemore immediately moves to it and places one leg upon the grenade to take the brunt of the blast. His actions save a machine gun squad and the gun. Kennemore survives the blast and his Marines drive the enemy from their positions. Sergeant Kennemore becomes a recipient of the Medal of Honor for his heroism and leadership against a superior enemy force.

Still, the Chinese hold the dominating ground. In addition, while elements of three battalions (2/5, 1/7 and 3/7) slug it out on Southwest Ridge, more complications develop. A patrol of Company D, 2nd Battalion, 7th Marines, encounters heavy resistance on the west coast of the reservoir at positions about 400 yards from Yudam-ni. Marine planes provide support and quell the machine guns positioned north and northeast on North Ridge. At 1645, the patrol disengages and extricates itself, but some casualties are sustained.

By day's end, the battalion gains include about 1,200 yards on the crest of Southwest Ridge. About 2,000 yards is gained with Company H's seizure of Hill 1403, which is in concert with the primary assault launched by the 5th Marines. The advance of Company H gains about 1,500 yards.

In the meantime, Company F, 2nd Battalion, departs Hagaru at 1200 en route to heights at the midpoint of Toktong Pass about seven miles distant.

In other activity, Colonel Litzenberg dispatches his S-4, Major Maurice Roach, to Hagaru to procure ammunition, petroleum items and rations. Litzenberg requests five truckloads of each item. Toward the latter part of the day, the trucks arrive at Yudam-ni. These are the final truckloads of supplies to reach the perimeter.

In the Eighth Army area, I Corps sector, 1st Cavalry Division zone, orders arrive from General Walker directing the 1st Cavalry Division to join the IX Corps. It moves out on the following day for Pukch'ang-ni to join with the S.K. 6th Division to form a defensive line to protect Sunch'on from a Chinese assault.

In the Turkish Brigade zone, the advance from Wawon, ordered by General Walker on the previous day, begins during the morning. The unit, having no battle experience, is supported by one tank platoon (72nd Tank Battalion) to bolster the attempt to seize Tokch'on.

In the meantime, a large enemy force advances westward from the objective, Tokch'on. When the information reaches headquarters, the Turkish Brigade is contacted and ordered to abort its attack. The brigade, led by General Tahsin Yasici, at about noon, begins to retrace its steps; however, rather than pull back to positions about seven miles east of Wawon, the order is misinterpreted and the Turks redeploy along the Kunu-ri road just outside of Wawon.

In the 24th Division zone, Division remains west of the Taeryong River, but the progress of the enemy forces General Church to make some quick adjustments to avoid being isolated. He directs the 21st Regiment at Chongju to depart for Napch'ongjong, while the 19th Regiment advances from the latter to Pakch'on, which lies at about the middle of the corps sector on the east side of the river.

The Chinese 66th Army, which is advancing on the east side of the river against the ROK 1st Division, causes peril for the 24th Division. General Milburn, the I Corps commander, is set to order the 24th Division and the S.K. 12th Regiment to pull back about five miles on the following day to be positioned in conjunction with the S.K. 1st Division, which has given up ground.

In other activity, the 25th Division (IX Corps) is directed by General Walker to transfer to the I Corps.

In the ROK 1st Division zone, the Chinese 66th Army maintains its advance. The defending ROK units on the east bank of the Taeryong River are unable to withstand the pressure. Consequently, the enemy gains about five miles. The Chinese are able to deeply penetrate and also jeopardize the 25th Division (IX Corps).

In the IX Corps area, 2nd Division sector, General Keiser begins to take steps to realign his perimeter into a more compact line along the Ch'ongch'on river in an effort to thwart the Chinese, who are on the offensive. The new line is to be established on the following day.

In the 9th Regimental zone, the 2nd Battalion attempts to regroup at Kujang-dong after having been pushed across the Ch'ongch'on River during the early morning hours. Due to the excessive shortage of manpower, the regimental commander, Colonel Sloane, is forced to redeploy the unit, despite its lack of equipment (having lost it the previous night). Nonetheless, the left flank badly needs some protection; Sloane dispatches the 2nd Battalion back across the river to form a defensive line. The beleaguered battalion is needed particularly because of the 25th Division's withdrawal back to Ipson. By dusk, the 2nd Battalion completes its move and establishes the far left positions of the regiment.

In related activity, subsequent to darkness, the Chinese again strike along the 2nd Division perimeter. The 1st Battalion, 9th Regiment, along with the 2nd Engineering Battalion hold positions on the west side of the Ch'ongch'on River, but a Chinese attack forces both units to abandon their positions and ford the river. Meanwhile, other regiments on the east side of the river also come under a stiff attack. The Chinese offensive jeopardizes the entire 2nd Division, particularly its flanks.

In the 23rd Regimental zone, at first sunlight the 1st and 2nd Battalions, 23rd Regiment, advance toward the regimental command post, which had been relinquished to the enemy during the early morning hours after a battle that had begun just before midnight.

In the 38th Regimental zone, Colonel Peploe, having sustained some setbacks the previous night, decides to withdraw somewhat to concentrate on the middle of the regiment's positions, whereby they can consolidate and maintain dominance over the Kujang-dong Road. The regiment stretches out along a two-mile perimeter between Kujang-dong and Somin-dong.

After dark, the Chinese engage the 9th Regiment on the west side of the Ch'ongch'on River and they also unleash a stinging assault against the 38th Regiment along its perimeter on the west side of the river. Enemy units plow into the lines from both the east and the north. The regiment is unable to withstand the overwhelming numerical strength and is compelled to retire towards Kujang-dong. The regiment continues raising resistance into the following day.

In the 25th Division sector, elements of the Chinese 39th and 40th Armies continue their offensive. Other units of these armies also pound the 2nd Division perimeter. The Chinese drive from the north during the early morning hours and hammer the 35th Regiment and Task Force Wilson in the middle and on the left respectively. The main outposts and Task Force Wilson get stung at about 0300, and within one hour, the main body sustains a major assault. The Chinese 117th Division drills against the perimeter line and with the support of mortars and machine gun fire, some indentations are made, but the line holds and the enemy sustains high casualties.

By 0800, with their casualty list rapidly climbing toward 400 killed, the Chinese abort the attack. In the meantime, Task Force Wilson on the east side of the Kuryong River engages the 115th and 116th Chinese Divisions. Initially, the enemy vanguard strikes, but soon the task force sustains an attack by both regiments. At this point, reinforcements drawn from the divisional reserve are committed to bolster Task Force Wilson; however, as the 2nd Battalion, 27th Regiment, prepares to advance, it comes under attack by elements that had succeeded in penetrating sufficiently to arrive in the rear of the task force.

Meanwhile, other enemy units attached to the same group strike about one mile behind the 2nd Battalion at Ipsok. There the artillerymen (8th FABn) gain enough time to fire at point-blank range before they retire to more tenable positions. This enfilade, supported by machine gun fire, buys enough time for the battalion to safely retire with all of its equipment. Following the evacuation, the 8th Field Artillery Battalion redeploys slightly less than five miles to the rear. Meanwhile, the 2nd Battalion, 27th Regiment, continues to exchange heavy fire with the Chinese and denies the enemy any gains. Nonetheless, the Chinese prevent the 2nd Battalion from getting to Task Force Wilson. Undaunted by the overwhelming force against it, TF Wilson maintains the positions.

Later, due to modifications along the line of the 25th Division by General Kean, the task force finally withdraws under the protective fire of the 27th Regiment (excluding 2nd Battalion) to rejoin the main body, which during the day had withdrawn about four miles and redrawn its perimeter. Company E, 27th Regiment, is to defend the task force's command post in the vicinity of Ipsok to prevent the enemy from using the darkness to penetrate. The company commander, Captain Reginald Desidario, accompanies a reconnaissance patrol and afterwards draws a defensive line. Soon after, the company comes under attack. Desidario is wounded, but he refuses evacuation and retains command.

Another attack follows and Desidario bolts from his position and charges the attackers, taking some down with his carbine and others with grenades, but again he is wounded, mortally. The remainder of his command continues the fight and repels the assault. Captain Desidario is awarded the Medal of Honor posthumously for his tremendous leadership and courage in the face of a superior enemy force.

In the meantime, the ROK 1st Division has regrouped at its new positions, essentially forming and covering the left flank of General Kean. The 25th Division, including its Task Force Wilson, completes its task prior to 1900, then it redeploys on an east to west line, which passes through Ipsok. Nonetheless, the Chinese 39th Army remains intent on maintaining its attack. Slightly before midnight, the intensity of the Chinese attack accelerates when the 39th and 66th Chinese Armies, operating from the west, advance on two fronts, south and southeast, with both expecting to converge on Yongsan-dong, a strategic village that lies between the Taeryong and Kuryong Rivers.

The attack forces stream towards the objective, which is to the rear of the ROK 1st Division and on the left of the 25th Division perimeter at Ipsok. The 39th Army elements drive along the west bank of the Kuryong and strike the 35th Infantry, 25th Division, while the 66th Army hammers the ROK 11th and 15th Regiments, which hold the left flank of the 25th's perimeter. The enemy attacks terminate about dawn; however, the Chinese are able to seize Yongsan-dong without the knowledge of the 35th Regiment.

Pursuant to orders by General Walker, the 25th Division is attached to the I Corps, to bolster it following the evaporation of the ROK II Corps. In its place, General Walker attaches the 1st Cavalry Division, under General Gay, to the IX Corps. General Coulter's perimeter on the east is lessened by the loss of the 25th, but with the addition of the 1st Cavalry Division, the perimeter is extended on the west.

The IX Corps is to receive one division of ROK II Corps troops or a combination of troops to establish a force equal to a division. The corps at this time is composed of the U.S. 2nd Division, the U.S. 1st Cavalry Division, the British 27th Brigade, the Turkish Brigade and an ROK II Corps division. The 1st Cavalry, at positions east of Sunchon and in the vicinity of Kujong-ni, advance to Pukch'ang-ni on the following day.

In the ROK II Corps area, confusion continues following the strong Chinese offensive that rolled through the area. General Yu focuses on regrouping scattered troops of both the ROK 7th and 8th Divisions; however, only disorganized groups have reached the vicinity of Pukch'ang-ni. Essentially, the entire corps is unfit for the field. The situation is so dangerous here that General Coulter is informed by General Walker that the S.K. II Corps sector is being placed under his responsibility.

In other activity, Sgt. Raymond N. Reifers, 25th Reconnaissance Company, is killed in action near Unsan, North Korea. Sgt. Reifers had entered Namwon with his tank on September 28 and liberated eighty-six American POWs by surprising the enemy and pushing them into a panic. (*See also,* **September 28,** *In the 25th Division sector.*)

In the 1st Marine Division zone, at dusk the regimental CPs of the 5th and 7th Marines are within Yudam-ni, supported by their respective headquarters contingents; however, the 7th Marines' antitank company remains at Hagaru. In addition, the headquarters elements of the 2nd Battalion, 7th Marines, and some sections of its weapons company also are at Hagaru. The majority of the artillery of the 11th Marines is at Yudam-ni, but only a few tanks are there in support of division. The 1st and 4th Battalions and Batteries G and I, 3rd Battalion, are on scene. Battery K, 4th Battalion, remains under the direction of the 1st Battalion until its parent arrives.

The 3rd Battalion is deployed below the slopes of Hill 1240 (North Ridge). Its 105s had provided support fire for the 7th Marines on the 26th and 27th. The 1st Battalion arrived earlier this day to provide support for the 5th Marines operating in the valley between South and Southwest Ridges. The 4th Battalion, 11th Marines arrives later in the day, but all three batteries will be in operation on the lowlands that separate South and Southeast Ridges by 2300.

South of the town near South and Southeast Ridges, along the lowlands, stand the howitzers, thirty 105-mm and eighteen 155-mm. To the north of these, the 75-mm recoilless rifles and the mortar companies of the 5th and 7th Marines are posted. Nevertheless, these artillery and mortar units lack stockpiles of extra ammunition. Enemy fire harasses the artillery positions throughout the day, but few casualties occur due to the marksmanship of the enemy. The units of the 5th and 7th Marines that are scattered amid the heights comprise ten rifle companies (all under full strength). Two battalions of the 5th Marines are posted near the town in the valley and two additional rifle companies of the 7th Marines hold extended and isolated positions along the MSR.

On North Ridge, Companies D and E, 2nd Battalion, 7th Marines, occupy Hills 1240 and 1282. The combined perimeter spans about one mile in width,

but a gap of about 500 yards exists between the two units. The flanks of both units are naked; however, the 2nd Battalion, 5th Marines' units stationed below in the valley can provide support. The 1st Battalion holds positions in the valley just below Hills 1240 and 1282. The 3rd Battalion's perimeter is established at the foundation of North Ridge, near Hill 1384. The 1st Battalion, 5th Marines, commanded by Lt. Colonel John W. Stevens II, and the 3rd Battalion, 5th Marines, commanded by Lt. Colonel Taplett, are in position to assist the 7th Marine units on Hills 1240 and 1282.

To the left of North Ridge stands Company H, 3rd Battalion, 5th Marines, which is dug in on the summit of Hill 1403, the terminal height of Northwest Ridge. Company E, 2nd Battalion, 5th Marines holds positions in the wide ravine to the left of Northwest Ridge and its line stretches along the left side of the ravine until it links with Company F. The latter unit had earlier captured its spur from the Chinese. Company F's left flank is above the road that separates the spur from Southwest Ridge.

Opposite Company F stands Company D, which is deployed on a slim finger of Southwest Ridge. Farther left stands the 3rd Battalion, 7th Marines' Companies G and I. These two units hold the summit of Southwest Ridge. Behind these units on the same hill mass to their left stands Company A, 1st Battalion, 7th Marines, which is deployed on Hill 1294, a terminal peak that towers above a wide valley that separates it from South Ridge. To hold the floor of the valley, one platoon of Company C, 1st Battalion, 7th Marines, deploys to protect the approaches to the Marine artillery to the rear.

On South Ridge, Company B, 1st Battalion, 7th Marines, is entrenched on the farthest point of the cone-shaped ridge that juts about 1,600 feet into the sky. The company's weapons are focused upon the deep and slim gorge that lies between South and Southeast Ridges.

Opposite South Ridge, Company C holds perilous positions on a finger of Southeast Ridge, which lies about five miles from Yudam-ni. The positions guard a narrow portion of the MSR at a point where it sharply swerves east about three miles from Yudam-ni valley and leads into Toktong Pass. Another unit is farther left and separated from Company C by two miles of rugged mountain terrain.

Company F, 2nd Battalion, 5th Marines, is deployed in Toktong Pass, which is equally dangerous ground with overextended positions. The mission of Company F is identical to that of Company C, 7th Marines, to protect the MSR between Hagaru and Yudam-ni.

After dusk, the Communist Chinese 9th Army Group, commanded by Sung Shin-lun, springs from its concealed positions in northeast Korea to conclude its mission. It expects to annihilate the 1st Marine Division. The Marines are aware of some Chinese presence, but the Communists have successfully concealed their overwhelming numbers by moving only at night. Now, the heretofore hidden hordes close against the Yudam-ni perimeter under cover of deep sable skies.

Twilight quickly fades, leaving not even a glimpse of moonlight on the village as the sun slips behind Sakkat Mountain at 1630. It had been a grueling, cold day; however, once the skies over Yudam-ni darken, the intolerable weather takes yet another turn for the worse. The frigid weather shows no mercy to either the troops or their equipment as the temperature in the pitch-dark village drops to twenty degrees below zero. The combination of bone chilling cold and eerie darkness stirs the imaginations of the guardians of the perimeter, each of whom look forward to a quiet night and the arrival of dawn.

The Marines' carbines and BARs are unreliable due to the extreme cold and in many cases the weapons fail to function at all. However, the M-1 rifles and the Browning machine guns split the difference between life and death for many of the Marines on the rugged ridges. The troops remain unaware that the stark silence is about to be shattered by a massive attack against their northwest arch, at North and Northwest Ridges. In synchronization with this powerful frontal blow by the Chinese 79th and 89th Divisions, another assault will be unleashed against the southern portion of the perimeter by the 59th Chinese Division. The Chinese 59th Division, having maneuvered to positions to the south, will launch its attack to sever the MSR between Yudam-ni and Hagaru at South Ridge and Toktong Pass.

Meanwhile, the Marines hold their positions and try to avoid frostbite. Just before midnight, the Chinese announce their presence with the flare of whistles, sirens and blaring bugles. Screaming infantrymen, donned in rubber sneaks, recklessly charge under the cover of machine gun fire. These three Chinese divisions crash against the 5th and 7th Marines to test the mettle of the two regiments.

The 5th and 7th Marines complain about the nasty weather, lack of sleep, cold food and just about everything else on this piece of frozen terrain, but as always, the grumbling ceases at the first sizzling sound of gunfire.

At about 2100 the pernicious trap set against Northwest Ridge is sprung by elements of two units of the Chinese 89th Division, the 266th and the 267th Regiments. About fifteen minutes earlier, Company I, 5th Marines, had come under fire at its positions on the slopes of Southwest Ridge by vanguard elements of the 237th Chinese Regiment. These sniper-type actions in the south continue sporadically while the attacks against North and Northwest Ridge unfold.

The Chinese initiate several diversionary probing raids. While the Communists continue to silently inch closer to the perimeter of the 5th and 7th Marines' positions on Northwest Ridge, one enemy patrol jabs at the roadblock manned by Company D, 5th Marines. A quick flurry of soaring grenades exchanged by the two sides and the skirmish terminates with the death of two Chinese. Mortars join the skirmish, which prompts an expeditious withdrawal by the enemy patrol. At about the same time, other enemy detachments poke annoyingly at Company F's perimeter on Northwest Ridge, but here, too, the contact is slick and quick. The enemy prods for a while, then disappears into the bleak darkness.

As the 2nd Battalion, 5th Marines, fends off the stinging actions against its mid-section, more enemy troops flood into the area. Northwest Ridge is permeated with Chinese troops, most within a couple hundred yards of the Marines, which sets up a deadly confrontation that threatens Companies E and F. Company H, 7th Marines, dug in on Hill 1403 to the north, is equally imperiled.

Suddenly, the piercing sounds of whistles blast and the Chinese bugles blare to signal the ominous charge into a blood-filled confrontation between two half-frozen forces. These shrill sounds infuse the defenders with a surge of adrenaline that prepares them for the imminent clash for survival. Meanwhile, more sinister sounds arrive when the thundering mortars streak through the bleak night air to plummet upon the Marine lines. This is followed by the roar of blazing submachine guns, coupled with the lightning crackle of grenades. Shortly thereafter, more vicious fire pours upon the Marine lines when the Chinese add some savage automatic weapons fire, which originates from positions all along Northwest Ridge. This massive unanticipated wave of hellish fury, devised to crack the nerves and destroy the 5th and 7th Marines, transforms Northwest Ridge into a cauldron of death.

By 2125, the mortars begin to strike the rear positions of Companies E and F. Shortly thereafter, the machine gun fire subsides, only to be replaced by another round of shrill whistles and bellowing yells of charging columns of Chinese troops who boldly encroach the steadfast Marine perimeter. Upon reaching grenade-throwing positions, the columns begin to flow into a ragged skirmish line. The Marines, initially surprised, now anxiously wait the signal to fire.

At nearly the same time, Company H, 7th Marines, deployed slightly north on Hill 1403, sustains a withering attack by these seemingly unending waves of enemy troops.

The machine gunners and riflemen of Companies E and F raise a solid wall of fire and create a horrid mountain of enemy dead all along their front, but for every enemy troop slain, seemingly, five or more appear. Eventually, the overwhelming numbers of Chinese force a crack in the thinly held gap. They flush through a point on the northern spur to expose the Marines' flanks with this jagged wedge. During this lightning-fast incident, Company F's right side is penetrated and the enemy forces back a portion of one platoon, threatening a breakthrough in the fragile draw.

Nearby, the 1st Platoon, Company E, stands at the fringe of the penetration where it forms a small but cohesive line of defense against the onslaught. A detachment from the 1st Platoon, Company E, led by Lieutenant Jack Nolan, and a section of light machine guns race to the front to sew up the hole and bolster the 1st Platoon. In addition, the 81-mm howitzers of the 2nd Battalion, 5th Marines, enter the fight and propel round after round into the enemy positions to lessen the pressure within the gap.

The battlefield psychology works and the barrage validates the laws of physics. A howitzer shell and an enemy soldier cannot occupy the same space. The iron injections strongly support Company E, and it holds firmly to forbid any further enemy penetration and encroachment to its rear. Unable to crack through Company E, the Chinese maintain their pressure against the rear positions of a defiant Company F.

Meanwhile, the 2nd Platoon, Company E, stretched thinly on the right front of the perimeter, scores a fortuitous round of shots. During the incessant donnybrook, its machine gun fire cascades upon a Korean hut and gains unexpected results. The succeeding explosion ignites a huge fire that propels spiraling arcs of flame into the ebony sky. At about 2215, the enemy assault reaches its pinnacle, but by 2230, when the hut becomes a huge bonfire, the attack nears its culmination. The immense illumination creates a gargantuan natural spotlight that dispenses imminent doom for the enemy. The hovering radiance pinpoints the precise locations of the Chinese troops as they tramp through the slim corridor.

Clusters of other enemy contingents dispersed along the adjoining slopes instantly discover that their concealed positions have been revealed. The Marines become jubilant, having discovered what appears to be the whole remains of the primary enemy assault force. A short while ago, while the attack was hitting high gear, Lt. Colonel Roise had been saddled with some pessimism based on the tremendous odds that faced his command. Roise had ordered H&S Company, 2nd Battalion, 5th Marines, to form a defense around the CP; however, the challenge has been met and the threat forestalled. As the Marines react to their new-found prize, the gloom dissipates and the CP remains unscathed. The scant number of Chinese who succeed in breaking through the lines ultimately encounters furious return fire. Their effort is futile and fatal. The Marines take complete advantage of the ongoing raging fire. Every available weapon is brought to bear on the Chinese that still remain alive in the grilled corridor. Marine fire hammers the shattered attackers. The ruthless force of arms shreds the columns and scorches the corridor and its opposing slopes.

The enfilade ends at 2400. At the conclusion, the grim result is that the primary attack force has been blown into oblivion. Nevertheless, the Communists still hold ground on the northern tip of the spur, which gives them tenable positions from which they can deliver a deluge of fire into the Marines' positions. In addition, Company F remains separated from Company E. Patrols are unable to re-establish contact with the isolated unit. Lt. Colonel Roise pushes Company D's reserve platoon to positions that fortify Company F's side of the perimeter to equalize what Company E had earlier done to plug the gap on its side. In essence, the reassignment keeps the defense in the gap more cohesive and forbids easy advance through the draw. The Communists, having sustained huge losses, abort further attempts to re-enter the draw.

In the meantime, at Company H, 7th Marines' isolated positions on Hill 1403, north of the 5th Marines' units, come under attack at 2135. They soon discover that the half-moon perimeter that stretches from the road to the crest of the hill is vulnerable to attack from all directions. The mission of the far-strung company is to safeguard the communications that link with Yudam-ni and the valley. Captain Cooke, the CO, posts his command post on the reverse slope.

Subsequent to a series of quick, stabbing raids lasting about thirty minutes, the Chinese mount a fierce frontal strike against the right side, held only by one platoon, led by Lieutenant Elmer Krieg. This powerful blow quickly rips through the front line of the outnumbered platoon. As the brittle right flank folds, communications also end between the platoon and the company command post. Lieutenant Krieg orders his troops to redeploy to the left to link with Lieutenant Paul Denny's platoon to form a tougher defense.

The Chinese maintain the pressure; however, the command post makes an urgent request for supporting fire to strengthen the line. The valley floor seemingly rises to a crescendo as the howitzers and mortars catapult shells toward the lost ground on the crest to subdue the enemy. Captain Cooke regroups his platoons and readies a counterattack. When the barrage lifts, Cooke leads a futile charge to regain the lost terrain from the newly entrenched Communists. The attack hits a solid wall of machine gun and small arms fire that terminates the charge and kills Captain Cooke, who had been at the point of the assault. Lieutenant James Mitchell assumes temporary command. Company H sustains heavy casualties, but the Chinese are unable to overrun its positions.

By about midnight, Lieutenant H.H. Harris climbs the hill to relieve Lieutenant Mitchell and discovers that Lieutenant Minard Newton is the sole unwounded company officer. Harris quickly redeploys Newton's platoon from the left flank to the right flank to give it more sturdiness. Newton's platoon counterattacks and recaptures some primary real estate to guarantee that the company locks its hold on the frozen hill, despite the high casualties sustained. During the fighting, a few troops wind up at Lt. Colonel Taplett's 3rd Battalion, 5th Marines' CP, at the foot of Southwest Ridge. They report that Chinese had overrun their mortar position on Hill 1403.

Despite high losses, the Chinese bring in more reinforcements to break the impasse. Following about two hours of quietness, the enemy again advances toward the perimeter and strikes Companies E and F, 5th Marines, and Company H, 7th Marines, with ferocious fire. In the infamous draw, about three hundred Chinese advance towards the center of the two-mile front, manned by Jaskilka's Company E. To the left, more Chinese close toward Company F. To the right, Company H, in the heights on Hill 1403, is struck along both flanks and the front.

Blazing fire meets the threats at all points. At Company E's positions on the floor of the draw, several hundred Chinese fly into the incessant machine gun fire; most die suddenly. Trailing columns note the grim scene in the bloody corridor and choose to stop short and take cover. Most of the remaining action in Company E's zone is long range; however, some sporadic close-range action occurs on the flanks.

In the meantime, about two hundred Chinese assault F Company. Company F sustains high casualties as it pours deadly fire into unending numbers of charging troops who plow into the center of the line. The enemy disregards their layers of dead as they tramp over them to break through. Eventually, two outnumbered machine gun positions are overwhelmed, but the company holds. Throughout the remainder of the night, Companies E and F hold their ground.

Back in the heights, Company H remains under tremendous siege for about one hour. Successive waves of Chinese also pound this perimeter, but Harris' command catapults round after round into the attackers, increasing the number of corpses on Hill 1403. The roadblock in the valley, defended by Sergeant William Vick (Company H, 7th Marines) also holds firmly and gives no ground. Nevertheless, the beleaguered company, out of touch with other units, is ordered by Lt. Harris to pull back at 0400 and redeploy to the rear of Company E, 5th Marines.

By about 0600, Company H successfully disengages and fights its way back, but the situation deteriorates as the enemy gains the heights of the key hill and with it, the means to strike the rear of the 2nd Battalion, 5th Marines. The 2nd Battalion is threatened with isolation and those Marines on North and Southwest Ridges face a threat to their flanks and rear. In addition, by break of dawn, the Chinese are able to scrutinize the positions of about two thousand Marines still deployed down in the hazardous valley.

While the elements of the Chinese 89th Division pound the Marines on Northwest Ridge, contingents of the Chinese 79th Division seek to wipe out two isolated companies of the 2nd Battalion, 7th Marines, at their lonely positions in the heights above Yudam-ni on North Ridge at Hills 1240 and 1282. These attacks simultaneously threaten the command posts of the 5th and 7th Marines in Yudam-ni. The Marines surmise that the village will become a target. Colonel Taplett redeploys his 3rd Battalion, 5th Marines. He directs it to switch from its compact assembly area north of the village to form a wide defensive perimeter in the same vicinity, to forestall any potential breakthrough from the slopes of Northwest Ridge.

Companies H and I dig in on Hill 1403 facing the ridge, while Company G spreads out at Southwest Ridge. Two platoons of Company G entrench themselves at the foundation of the ridge, while the third

platoon disperses among the slopes to establish an outpost there.

Meanwhile, Colonel Taplett establishes his 3rd Battalion, 5th Marines' CP in the low ground at the foundation of Northwest Ridge, between Hill 1282 and the knob of Hill 1384. Taplett learns that the spur of Hill 1384 is undefended. He dispatches one platoon of Company I, with orders to take positions about 300 yards up the slope. About 300 yards to the rear of Company I, a detachment of South Korean police manning machine guns holds a section of the spur that lies directly above the battalion CP.

The enemy elements had maneuvered over the spine of North Ridge to reach positions near the 2nd Battalion, 7th Marines. The 1st Battalion, 235th Chinese Regiment, is to overrun Hill 1240, but it receives no orders to capture Hill 1282. Inadvertently, while advancing in the bleak darkness, the enemy 1st Battalion climbs a knob that leads toward Hill 1282, still thinking it is the objective. Meanwhile, the 3rd Battalion, 236th Regiment, operating to the left of the 1st Battalion, 235th Regiment, moves toward its objective, unoccupied Hill 1167. However, the tactical error rolls into its ranks and causes the 3rd Battalion to end up at the foundation of the sheer slopes of Hill 1240.

The terrain is in sharp contrast to the shallow rolling slopes of Hill 1167. The confusion stalls the attack of the 3rd Battalion for a few hours, but the equally confused 1st Battalion, 235th Regiment, executes its attack at 2200. Convinced they are stalking a lone Marine platoon on Hill 1240, the Chinese launch their assault against Company E, commanded by Captain W.D. Phillips, positioned on Hill 1282 about 1,000 yards west of Hill 1240. The Chinese 1st and Special Duty Companies initiate probing raids with the resounding sounds of their sub machine gunners and grenadiers.

The Marines commence fire and drive the attacks back. Within about two hours, the Communists lunge against Hill 1240. At 2345, Company D, 2nd Battalion, informs headquarters of enemy infiltration on the hill. Both Company D and Company E prepare for the inevitable. All patrols interacting between the two companies are postponed. Two platoons of Company E plant themselves on the crest, while the remaining platoon, under Lieutenant Bey, deploys in the rear to the right of the line to hold a spur on the eastern side above Yudam-ni. Company D diligently denies the freezing temperature on Hill 1240 to bolster its positions.

At midnight, amidst the howling winds and darkened crevices on the crest, Chinese bugles bellow to signal the attack. Instantly, these clamors are joined by the screaming chants of the night-assault troops who charge the perimeter's northeastern bow. They advance headlong into an intrepid sheet of gunfire, provided by Lieutenant Yancey's platoon. Many of the chants cease as the attacking squads are ripped to pieces.

The Chinese attempt to sidestep the hurricane of fire by swerving eastward to break through, but here, too, the Chinese face disaster. Bey's platoon holds an iron grip on the jutting spur. His Marines fire incessantly and again thin the ranks of the Chinese. Undeterred, many more continue to charge, ignoring the layers of their dead comrades that are splattered along the ghastly perimeter. The remainder of the two attacking companies maintain their futile attack.

By about 0200, the Chinese have been ravaged by Company E and the assault to begins to fizzle. Company E takes high casualties but remains rigid. Machine gunners and riflemen, aided by the timely tossing of grenades, maintain the pressure. By about 0300, both enemy units are literally wiped out as fighting units, having sustained the loss of nearly every man. When the battle subsides, Hill 1282 remains in possession of battered Company E, 7th Marines.

The hill's frozen slopes become cluttered with more than 200 recently deceased Chinese of the 1st Battalion, 235th Chinese Regiment. Reinforcements are struggling to reach the embattled U.S. command, but in the meantime, the Chinese show no signs of relenting. In a short while, the 3rd Company, 1st Battalion, 235th Regiment, is thrown upon the fiery gauntlet to seize the obstinate crest. The scant force, the surviving troops of the first attack, are clamped into the unit, bringing the attack force to about 125 men.

Meanwhile, back at Hill 1240, on North Ridge, the probing raids also begin at about midnight when elements of the 3rd Battalion, 236th Chinese Regiment, explore the perimeter of Company D, 2nd Battalion, 7th Marines. These jabbing raids shift upward to a full-scale attack just after 0100. Within the first thirty minutes of the initial attacks, some Chinese bolt through the saddle between Hills 1240 and 1282. They occupy positions in the high ground, from where they commence fire upon the regimental (5th and 7th) command post in the village.

Actually, an outpost on Hill 1384 held by Company I, 3rd Battalion, 5th Marines, had received incoming fire prior to 2100, becoming the first unit to come under fire. It is this outpost that gets badgered at 0145, about thirty minutes after the battalion goes on full alert. Once the enemy commits to the assault, Colonel Murray redeploys the 1st Battalion in anticipation of a second assault. The 1st Battalion, 5th Marines, moves to positions to the rear of the 3rd Battalion, 5th Marines.

At 0100, the 1st Platoon, Company A, led by Lt. Nicholas Trapnell, begins to ascend the slippery slopes of Hill 1282 to bolster hard-hit Company E, but the trek takes longer than two hours. The abominable weather, having reached twenty degrees below zero, makes the task unbearable. Shortly thereafter, Company A's 3rd Platoon, commanded by Lieutenant Robert Snyder, makes the ascent, trailing the 1st Platoon.

In the meantime, at 0145, Company I's platoon on the spur of Hill 1384 reports that it is coming under increasingly heavy fire from the heights above. Soon after, reliable word is spread from Company H, 7th Marines, on Hill 1403 that Chinese are maneuvering around the hill to sever the MSR.

By dawn, Company H is forced to withdraw from the hill, leaving it to the enemy. Some of these troops make it to the lines of the 3rd Battalion, 7th Marines, while others reach the positions of the 2nd Battalion, 5th Marines. A short time later, at about 0218, Company I identifies enemy movement and commences firing to thwart a platoon-sized enemy contingent. The enemy unit retreats, but this incident is soon overshadowed by the advance of a larger force. Between one and two companies begin to flow down the slopes of Hill 1384. They sweep over the undersized Company I platoon and lunge nearly 300 yards toward the South Korean police. The Koreans, on the spur that overlooks the command post, dish out tenacious machine gun fire to momentarily halt the marauders, but the Korean platoon is unable to permanently hold. It is compelled to pull back, leaving the heights to the swarming enemy.

Down below in the draw, the CP becomes threatened. H&S and Weapons Companies return fire toward the heights, but the former is forced to pull back to the other side of the MSR. The Weapons Company, holding more tenable positions, holds its ground despite the avalanche of fire from above. All the while, the 3rd Battalion rifle companies remain unengaged. Nevertheless, the CP stands nearly naked in the draw since the pull back of H&S Company.

Taplett, informed of his precarious situation, chooses to remain in the tent to maintain contact with his rifle companies. The Chinese, apparently thinking the tent is unoccupied, fail to direct their fire upon it, leaving Taplett the opportunity to control his command. The battalion executive officer, Major John Canney, departs the tent, leaving the S-3, Major Thomas Durham, armed with only his pistol to guard Taplett. Canney moves to regroup H&S Company, but as he reaches the MSR, an enemy bullet kills him.

Outside the blackened CP tent, Taplett has one other guard, PFC Louis Swinson, whose radio has fallen prey to the elements. Swinson, poised with his rifle, keeps vigil on the approach routes to the CP. This harrowing incident, which lasts for about one hour, goes unnoticed by the battalion's three rifle companies posted about 300 yards away. Luckily, the Chinese make no genuine effort to storm the CP. Very few Chinese attempt to make the descent from the spur.

Back on Hill 1282, a second assault is thrown against Company E, 7th Marines while reinforcements are en route to the summit. The exhausted troops of Company E repeatedly throw back the attackers, but at high cost, including probable annihilation at any moment. Meanwhile, the 1st Platoon, Company A, reaches the bloody peak slightly after 0300 and takes positions with Lt. Bey's platoon on the spur that bolts out from the eastern side of the ridge. The platoon arrives prior to the full velocity of the Chinese thrust.

Subsequently, the haggard 3rd Platoon of Lieutenant Snyder arrives to reinforce the few survivors of the two besieged platoons. Snyder, unable to establish contact with the troops on the spur, directs his men to intertwine with the troops of E Company, but even more Chinese reach the crest to offset the arrival of reinforcements. The Oriental chants and screeching whistles increase the intensity, but now the sky bursts with illuminating flares and the profound reverberating sounds of multiple explosions that quiver the frozen earth. Brutal hand-to-hand combat and ferocious exchanges of grenades and gunfire erupt. The wild donnybrook inflicts horrifying numbers of casualties to both sides. The Marines' resources are quickly diminishing.

Eventually, the Communists drive a wicked spear between the defenders holding the crest and those on the equally perilous spur. By 0400, the summit is overrun by Chinese. They take over the command post on the peak and begin to speak in Chinese on the captured telephone. The summit takes on the appearance of a slaughterhouse as the surviving men of Company E attempt to circle the rhetorical wagons for a final stand. Like falling dominoes, the remaining able-bodied Marine officers become casualties during this desperate struggle.

During the regrouping, Lieutenant Yancy, a wounded platoon leader, is again struck, as is Lieutenant William Schrier of the mortar section. Lt. Leonard Clements, the other Company E platoon leader, sustains a wound. The company commander, Captain Phillips, continues throwing grenades at the encroaching enemy until he is slain. Immediately, Lieutenant Raymond Ball (executive officer) assumes command of Company E, but he, too, has sustained multiple wounds.

Yelling advice and encouragement from his prone position, Ball sustains several additional wounds that render him unconscious. He is rushed to the medics, but he succumbs. Recently arrived Lieutenant Snyder (3rd Platoon, Company A, 5th Marines) assumes command of the dwindling company and his battered platoon. The Chinese ignore their horrific casualty rate that has climbed to about 250, as opposed to the 150 sustained by the Marines on this contested Hill 1282, which now resembles a huge morgue.

By 0500, the Chinese control the crest, but they remain convinced that their effort has given them Hill 1240. The enemy wedge has widely separated the Marine defenders. Snyder's survivors have been pushed to the reverse slope. The contingent stands at about one-half rifle platoon from Company E and about six able-bodied men of his 3rd Platoon. The combined casualties of the two Company A Platoons, since their ascent to the summit, stands at about forty killed and wounded. To the left, the remainder of Company E's riflemen, led by Lt. Bey, and Lt. Trapnell's 1st Platoon, Company A, 5th Marines retains a precarious hold on the summit of the rugged southeastern spur directly above Yudam-ni.

Meanwhile, the Chinese have also made some substantial gains at Hill 1240 against Company D, 7th Marines which had brushed back the initial probing strikes. At about 0105, elements of the 3rd Battalion, 236th Chinese Regiment, uncork a full-blast assault against the perimeter, which ignites a furious slugfest. The enemy surge encounters a platoon led by Sergeant O.J. Reller when it slams into the northwestern sector,

and another platoon led by Lieutenant Seeburger that holds the eastern (right) side of the line.

Supporting machine gun sections hold the line to the front of Captain Hull's CP. Successive assaults are turned back by Reller's unit, but the Chinese intensify the effort and pour unending amounts of troops into the battle. By 0230, the enemy breaks through the line on the left. Full-throttled pressure bars Seeburger from moving to assist Reller's platoon. Lieutenant Webber, a machine gun platoon leader, attempts to stem the tide by rushing reinforcements, but the Chinese raise the pressure against the CP and compel Weber to abort the attempt. Heavy fighting continues without pause.

Nonetheless, by 0300, Captain Hull's CP is overwhelmed by Chinese. The remnants of the two platoons on the line and the reserve platoon, led by Lt. Anthony Sota, is directed by Captain Hull to form at the base of the hill. Hull, wounded but determined to hold the hill, regroups his troops and leads a counterattack to regain the lost ground. The assault stuns the Chinese and prompts them to give ground, but the weakened command finds itself in near untenable positions.

The Chinese mount an attack, pounding the diminutive contingent at three separate points. The Marines hold steadfastly as they simultaneously defend their front, right flank and the right side of their rear. The cost is high, but as dawn approaches and the company becomes compacted like a squad, the remaining sixteen able-bodied Marines still hold their positions.

However, the Chinese retain the heights to their front, the slopes to the rear and both flanks. The Communists' gains on Hill 1240, combined with the seizure of Hill 1282, add to the dilemma of holding Yudam-ni and preserving the firepower of the accompanying artillery units, especially the 3rd Battalion, under Major Parry, and Battery K, 4th Battalion. The former is deployed just under the slopes of 1240 and the latter stands at positions just under the southeastern spur of Hill 1282.

While the 5th and 7th Marines are engulfed in bitter combat at North and Northwest Ridges, other Chinese contingents begin to whack the defenders at South Ridge. Company B, 7th Marines, is heavily engaged with elements of the Chinese 59th Division at Hill 1419. By the arrival of dusk, the company has sustained serious casualties. Company C drives down the MSR and deploys across the road from Hill 1419 to support B Company. After the arrival of reinforcements, Company B brings out its wounded and returns to Yudam-ni with Lt. Colonel Davis, who had brought in Company C (only two rifle companies), commanded by Captain Morris. He establishes positions on Hill 1419. His two platoons deploy in a half-moon perimeter along the lower slopes of the eastern spur. The 60-mm mortar section is also within the perimeter. In the distance is the ominous crest.

At 0230 (28th), the slopes come alive with the usual notorious sounds of attacking Chinese. The right flank of the perimeter is heavily struck by large numbers of troops that spring from the heights. The defending platoon, commanded by Lieutenant Jack Chabek, sustains high casualties and the Chinese penetrate. The left flank then comes under a ferocious attack and the weakened platoon under Sergeant Earle Payne also is pummeled. One squad is deployed in higher ground, causing the platoon to partially collapse and be pushed back. This detachment becomes totally isolated and its fate remains unknown at dawn.

Captain Morris attempts to forestall disaster. He speeds reinforcements to both flanks, utilizing his headquarters and mortar personnel. The maneuver saves the command from being decimated. The Marines contend with the attacks until dawn, when the din of battle subsides and artillery fire is turned against the enemy positions. Nonetheless, enemy fire continues to rain down on the beleaguered unit from every direction. The circumstances remain dire, as the combat had destroyed the radio and racked up high casualties. The pinned-down command, which has sustained about forty casualties, also suffers from lack of air support due to the break-down of communications.

Meanwhile, the Chinese have gained control of the MSR leading south toward Toktong Pass and to the north toward Yudam-ni. Attempts to contact the missing squad from Sergeant Payne's platoon are futile. One man, Corporal Kiesling, voluntarily heads up the slope to locate it, but machine gun fire slays him. The daylight brings no solace to Company C. It becomes captive to the terrain while the enemy begins to encircle it. The only option is to tighten the perimeter and hold until relief arrives, but ammunition is running low. The besieged company regroups in hills east of the road.

Throughout the morning of the 28th, Captain Morris and his Marines await rescue. Meanwhile, they watch the Communists form a deadly circle around the diminutive perimeter.

In Fox Company's zone, Captain William Barber, 2nd Battalion, 7th Marines, deploys his unit midway through Toktong Pass, upon a sequestered hill just north of the MSR. The reinforced company, composed of 240 officers and men, also has heavy machine guns and 81-mm mortars. The machine guns are placed with the rifle platoons. The 1st Platoon, led by Lieutenant J. Dunne, and the 2nd Platoon, commanded by Lieutenant Elmer Peterson, take the right and left flanks respectively. With each leaning toward the MSR, the platoons string down the hill to fortify the 3rd platoon, under Lieutenant R. McCarthy, which holds the crest and stares northward. At the foundation of the hill, Barber establishes his headquarters. Between it and the flanking platoons, the reverse slope is held by headquarters company and a rocket section and these are hooked to the flanking platoons.

The night positions of Fox Company are under a full moon, which creates a mixed blessing, but the temperatures become extremely hostile, challenging the minds and numbing the bodies of the men. The area remains quiet throughout the night of the 27th and into the early part of the 28th, but concentration is difficult.

The exceptions to the silence are the convoys transporting the 1st Battalion, 5th Marines, and the 4th Battalion, 11th Marines, back to Yudam-ni and the empty vehicles of Lt. Colonel Beall that are en route to Hagaru. The 3rd Platoon stretches out along a hilltop position linked to the other two platoons, which lean down the slopes pointing toward the MSR. Each of the platoons is bolstered by machine gun units.

Fox Company's positions remain unchallenged during the night of the 27th; however, this situation changes drastically during the early morning hours of the 28th. Under a bright moon, the 3rd Platoon waits apprehensively in anticipation of an attack, but it is hindered by the extreme cold that dulls attentiveness. Lieutenant McCarthy zips through the positions a little after 0100 to make sure all are prepared for the inevitable. He emphasizes the need to maintain a constant vigil.

At about 0230, the Chinese announce their presence when a force estimated at about company strength plows into the positions of Company F. The enemy tries to open a gap between the lines of the 2nd and 3rd Platoons. The attack is met with ferocious fire that inflicts heavy casualties upon the enemy on the hills; however, the 3rd Platoon under McCarthy, holding the crest, is struck with an overwhelming blow that nearly eradicates two squads. Although McCarthy's command loses fifteen killed and nine wounded, eight survivors make it back to the reserve squad's positions.

Meanwhile, as the Chinese take this peak, the Marines steadfastly hold and otherwise prevent penetration, due in great part to the valor of several who refused to accept defeat. These men, PFC Robert F. Benson, Private Hector A. Cafferatta (2nd Platoon) and PFC Gerald J. Smith, supported by Smith's fire team, provide two enemy platoons with sudden death, eliminating these contingents in their entirety.

Private Cafferatta intentionally makes himself a target to draw fire away form the others. He leapfrogs along the lines, singlehandedly taking on the enemy as they arrive. Fifteen of them fall. He wounds many others during his atttempt to buy time for reinforcements to arrive. In one incident, at close quarters an enemy grenade is tossed near him and others. Cafferatta jumps into the gully, retrieves the grenade and tosses it back; however, just after it leaves his right hand, it detonates. He loses one finger and sustains other injuries to his hand and arm. He disregards the wounds and continues to battle the enemy. Later he is hit by a sniper's bullet and is finally forced to agree to evacuation. Private Cafferatta, for his extraordinary heroism under fire, becomes a recipient of the Medal of Honor.

Fox Company remains engulfed in combat throughout the frigid night. Apparently, the Chinese had expected to overrun two rifle platoons, but instead, these attackers bump into the main command post of Captain William Barber, which contains the mortars. Barber's troops fall back to more tenable positions, giving the enemy some running room, while the Marines climb higher to a cluster of trees that stand above an embankment along the MSR. The Chinese give pursuit and find themselves unable to climb the hill. On each attempt to ascend the embankment, Marine fire cuts them down. While they take measures to find safety behind the embankment, the Marines pull the pins on grenades and let them tumble directly upon the Chinese.

After concluding the Marine positions are impenetrable, the enemy attempts to retreat, but as they hit the open ground, Marine fire eliminates more of them. The Chinese attack finally is deemed over at 0630 on the 28th. About 100 dead Chinese are laid out to the front of the 1st Platoon and along the MSR at the foundation of the hill, while another 350 are in front of the 2nd and 3rd Platoon positions. These Marines sustain 20 killed and 54 wounded.

November 28 Intelligence reports reveal that the Chinese are heavily involved in Korea, something that had not been anticipated. General MacArthur sends additional information to the United Nations concerning new players in the fighting: "Enemy reactions developed in the course of our assault operations of the past four days disclose — continental armed forces in army, corps, and divisional organization of an aggregate strength is now arrayed against the United Nations forces in North Korea.... Heavy reinforcements are now concentrated within the privileged sanctuary north of the international boundary and constantly moving forward." Soon after Macarthur sends an alert: "We face an entirely new war."

Within several days, President Truman issues a statement that points the blame on the Soviets. Also, during the evening, General MacArthur summons Generals Walker and Almond to Tokyo to confer with them regarding the situation in Korea. Walker and Almond return to Korea during the following day.

In the X Corps area, 7th Division sector, following a week of heavy skirmishing with North Korean troops, Task Force Kingston, reinforced, commanded by 2nd Lt. Robert C. Kingston, finally breaks through and reaches Singalpajin. TF Drysdale arrived at Koto-ri, but instead of being used for reconnaissance as planned, circumstances compelled X Corps to slip it into the operations designed to bolster Hagaru. The 41st Independent Commando, Royal Marines, joins with U.S. Marines and Army contingents on the following day in an attempt to break through to Hagaru.

In the 1st Marine Division sector, General Oliver P. Smith arrives at Hagaru from Hungnam and officially establishes headquarters at 1100. Staff and intelligence officers fill him in on the situation, while plans continue for an assault. Agents operating in the field report back later in the day and inform headquarters that they have actually conversed with enemy officers and the Chinese boasted that they would seize Hagaru on this day, after dark. Meanwhile, Lt. General Edward M. Almond, USA, arrives at Hagaru to discuss strategy with General Smith.

In the 1st Marines sector, Lt. Colonel Ridge continues

to direct his 3rd Battalion, 1st Marines, to prepare for an imminent attack. The enemy has established positions that isolated Marine positions at Yudam-ni, Fox Hill, Hagaru and Koto-ri, preventing the Marines from maintaining contact with each other. Companies H and I protect the south and southwest sector of the line. George Company was to defend East Hill, but it has not yet reached the area. Other units, including Company D, 1st Engineer Battalion, and elements of the 2nd Battalion, 11th Marines, are deployed on the southeast part of the perimeter, which links How Company with East Hill. Lacking the manpower of George Company, East Hill had to be defended by troops from X Corps headquarters and a contingent of the 10th Engineer Battalion, USA. The area just north of East Hill is held by the Antitank Battalion (7th Marines).

The Chinese launch an attack on the following night.

In the 5th Marines zone, the 1st Battalion, 5th Marines, executes an attack to lessen the pressure in its zone. Company C, which had recently deployed to reinforce the 3rd Battalion, 5th Marines, to hold the line in the valley, comes under the jurisdiction of the 7th Marines to help stabilize the unsteady situation on Hills 1282 and 1240.

Two platoons under Captain Jack R. Jones during the early morning hours begin to climb Hill 1282 to support Company E, 7th Marines. Meanwhile, the other Company C platoon moves to Hill 1240 to bolster Company D, 7th Marines. As the contingent under Jones ascends the slope, many wounded Marines are descending and even from them, it is impossible to determine what is actually occurring at the crest in the darkness. Nonetheless, the platoons maintain the slow advance in the bitter cold.

By about 0430, enemy fire from the nearby crest alerts the Marines they are near the objective. Shortly thereafter, it becomes clear that the situation is grim. Company E has lost is positions and about twenty survivors are regrouping to attempt an attack to regain the lost ground. Captain Jones aligns his two platoons and joins the Company E survivors under Sergeant Daniel Murphy. Supported by mortars, the men launch their attack just after the crack of dawn to dislodge the 235th Chinese Regiment's 3rd Company, 1st Battalion.

In numbing cold, the Marines defy the onslaught of machine gun fire and a barrage of hand grenades. They lack artillery cover due to the close quarters of the opposing forces. And the skies are clear of planes; the Corsairs have not yet reached the target.

Nevertheless, the charge gains speed and overwhelms the enemy defenders. Of the fifty or so Chinese troops, only about five survive. Within a while, led by an officer who had survived the attack, another enemy platoon ascends the slope, only this time, the slope is dominated by Marines. Another Chinese platoon follows and it, too, is struck by riveting fire.

The Marines repulse attack after attack and finally the enemy company is reduced to seven survivors. The Chinese commander has one company remaining and it is down to one platoon. The Marines of Company C also greet this attack and it, too, amounts to nothing more than additional dead Chinese. Following the final attack by the remaining reserve squad, six of these Chinese remain standing.

The Chinese 1st Battalion, 235th Regiment, loses about 400 men, including nearly every one of the NCOs, platoon leaders and company commanders. Company C, 1st Battalion, 5th Marines, sustain 15 killed and 67 wounded. Company E, 2nd Battalion, 7th Marines, suffer about 120 casualties, including killed and wounded.

Following the early morning action the Marines attempt to rescue their wounded, some of whom are from Company E, still in their foxholes on the slope of Hill 1282. The operation succeeds despite heavy fire from enemy positions. By about noon, the Marines definitely maintain control of Hill 1282.

In the 2nd Battalion, 5th Marines zone, Lt. Colonel Roise's battalion at Northwest Ridge has been heavily involved against the Chinese. The enemy is able to gain some ground on the spur and it overruns two machine gun positions. However, the Marines succeed in repelling several major attacks in the draw and along the spur to the left of the 7th Marines' lines. The 5th Marines dominate in its area and the enemy dead continues to rise, but at about 0430, stragglers from Company H, 7th Marines, which had held Hill 1403, arrive at 5th Marines lines, which makes it clear that the Communists hold the hill and that communications with the remainder of the 5th Marines at Yudam-ni are also in jeopardy. At one point during the early morning hours, fifteen Chinese troops penetrate the positions of Company F and all are killed.

By about 0600, a counterattack executed by Company E succeeds in pushing out the Chinese and it regains the two machine guns that had earlier been seized. In the meantime, Company E, 5th Marines, takes the offensive and engages a large Chinese force on the spur, which is setting up an assault against the 2nd Battalion's right flank.

After the night's combat in Roise's zone, the weather inflicts more casualties than the enemy. The Chinese, however, suffer heavy casualties. Combined, Companies E and F sustain 60 casualties to the elements and seven killed. Also, 25 Marines are wounded. The Chinese sustain about 500 killed, but this figure does not include those killed at Hill 1403, as Company H had not made a body count.

The 5th Marines, under recent orders to launch an attack after dawn, abort the assault following an assessment that the area now contains too many Chinese troops. At about 1650, orders to officially stop the offensive arrive from General Oliver P. Smith's headquarters. The 5th Marines deploy to positions where they can cooperate with the 7th Marines. By 2000, the 2nd Battalion, 5th Marines, complete a movement from Northwest Ridge to Southwest Ridge.

In the meantime, Company I, 3rd Battalion, 5th Marines, relieves contingents of the 1st Battalion, 5th

Marines at Hill 1282 (North Ridge). Also, Companies G and H, 3rd Battalion, 5th Marines, establish positions from where they can guard the northwest approaches to Yudam-ni. The beleaguered troops at Hill 1240 are relieved by Company B, 1st Battalion, 5th Marines.

In the 7th Marines zone, at about 1015, Company A, 1st Battalion, acting as vanguard, moves out to rescue Companies C and F, both of which are trapped and surrounded at their positions along the MSR that heads to Hagaru. The remaining troops of the 1st Battalion, led by Lt. Colonel Davis, bring up the rear. They encounter heavy enemy resistance, particularly after they drive into the gorge between South and Southeast Ridges.

The unit manages to reach a point about one mile from the besieged companies just after 1500; however, after it ascends to the high ground, the Chinese effectively halt the column. Meanwhile, Davis directs Company B, to take a circuitous route and outflank the Chinese by advancing on the west side of the MSR to gain the heights. The operation, supported by mortar fire and planes, succeeds. Combined, the relief force drives the Chinese from their positions.

From the newly gained ground directly overlooking the positions of Company C, the force deploys in a half-moon position and points towards the MSR, forming a solid line of fire between the Chinese to the South and the once imperiled platoon. Although the trapped Marines of Company C have an umbrella of protection, Fox Company, which had been unable to extricate itself from the Toktong Pass, is still jeopardized when darkness overtakes the area.

Davis' relief force prepares to establish night positions, but Colonel Litzenberg concludes that to permit the 1st Battalion to remain in its dangerous positions could also endanger the 1st Battalion. Davis is ordered to return to Yudam-ni to eliminate any possibility of being surrounded in the gorge. Shortly after receiving the directive, Davis moves out. The unit brings Company C and its 46 wounded Marines along.

In the 2nd Battalion's zone, Company F remains in control of its positions; however, the Chinese night attacks have inflicted casualties that total 54 wounded.

After dawn, the Marines scrounge around the Chinese dead and seize many weapons, including American Thompson submachine guns and some Springfield rifles. Attempts to relieve Company F through the day are unsuccessful, but some air support by Australian planes eases the pressure for a while. In addition, Marine RFDs drop supplies, but the unit on Fox Hill sustains two casualties while it retrieves the supplies from the bottom of the hill. The unit remains surrounded and two separate rescue missions from Hagaru and Yudam-ni each fail to reach the lines. Fox Company prepares to hold the position. The situation on the hill remains tranquil through midnight, but during the early morning hours of the 29th, the Chinese attack.

In the 3rd Battalion, 7th Marines zone, a counterattack is initiated against Hill 1384. Company G commits two platoons while one remains in place at the outpost on Southwest Ridge. Both units move out simultaneously, push across the MSR and quickly rescue the imperiled command post of Lt. Colonel Taplett. Continuing, the Marines move into the draw and eliminate resistance, essentially ensuring the safety of the Weapons Platoon (3rd Battalion, 5th Marines) still stuck there.

From this point, the attacking platoons continue to advance through the stark darkness and reach the spur defended by about 25 Chinese. After evicting the defenders, the Marines claim the spur and soon after, the Korean police platoon, which had earlier abandoned the position, redeploy there. Once the ground is secured, the attack is halted to await sunrise.

Soon after, at the first glimpse of the sun, the attack is reinitiated by these two dogged platoons. To the amazement of the commanding officer, Colonel Taplett, the troops have clearly penetrated the enemy's lines and stand at the approach to the crest of Hill 1384. Taplett, aware that only the platoons of Lieutenants John Cahill and Dana Cashion are on the offensive, immediately orders the attack to cease. Nonetheless, these platoons have alleviated the enormous pressure on the other Marines in the valley west of Yudam-ni. The attack had also cleared a path for H Company, 7th Marines, which permits it to retire from imperiled positions and join with the 3rd Battalion, 5th Marines, at the slopes of Hill 1403 at Northwest Ridge. Following orders to retire, Cashion and Cahill return to the recently captured spur.

In Company D's zone, the unit holding Hill 1240 has been under attack by the 3rd Battalion, 236th Chinese Regiment, and it holds only a skimpy piece of the hill while defending against attacks from several sides. The 3rd Platoon, Company C, 5th Marines, had earlier advanced to support it, but the darkness and enemy resistance had impeded progress.

As the sun rises, it becomes obvious to the Marines on Hill 1282 that their counterparts on Hill 1240 are in trouble, but the distance of 1,000 yards is too much for an easy solution. With the light of the sun and the determination of Lieutenant Dawe's platoon, a hook-up finally occurs with Company D, 7th Marines. However, by this time, the situation is getting more grave, as the Chinese are massing on the reverse sides of Hills 1240 and 1282. The Marines are able to eliminate the enemy from Hill 1240, but they lack sufficient strength to hold off a major attack. All communications have ceased, which forbids Dawe's from informing Headquarters of the imminent assault and eliminates any possibility of artillery support.

At about 1100, the sirens blare and the Chinese send about two battalions against the diminutive force. Unable to totally withstand the attack, the Marines are compelled to pull back, but they hold again about 150 yards to the rear and refuse to budge. Dawe's shattered platoon and about sixteen survivors of Company D repel the remaining assaults. Relief finally arrives at about 1700. Company B, 5th Marines, arrives at Hill 1240 and discovers the high casualties it cost to hold the ground. Only about one-half of Dawe's platoon

still functions and most of Captain Hull's Company D has been lost to the casualty list.

In the Eighth Army area, prior to noon, due to the intensity of the enemy offensive, General Walker issues orders to the I Corps and the IX Corps to pull back from their respective positions to draw a new line of defenses at the Ch'ongch'on River. The redeployment operations begin at about noon, but the IX Corps is unable to complete the operation by the end of the day. As the day passes, General Walker learns of several situations in the Eighth Army sector that impede his plans, but still he is convinced that the re-initiation of the offensive will proceed in a short while.

Complications develop in the 1st Cavalry sector, the ROK II Corps sector and in both corps areas. Meanwhile, the onslaught of the Chinese XIII Army Group also continues to thwart plans. By day's end, it becomes crystal clear that the bridgehead at the Ch'ongch'on River will not be completed to ensure that the Chinese will be halted. Specifically, the ROK II Corps, already having been clobbered, is positioned to fold and Eighth Army's left flank is endangered. Throughout the day, reports both from the field and from the air, filter into headquarters and sound the alarm about large numbers of enemy troops moving southwest towards Sunch'on, while another huge force advances from two directions, east and northeast, against Kunu-ri.

In the I Corps area, the 24th Division establishes new positions without any major interference by the enemy; however, pursuant to orders from Eighth Army, the bulk of the division, except the 5th Regimental Combat Team (attached to Eighth Army), will move again on the following day to strengthen IX Corps.

In the 25th Division sector, the 25th Division has recently been transferred from IX Corps to I Corps. The division had come under assault during the latter part of the previous night by elements of the 39th Chinese Army. The fighting, which concentrated heavily upon the 35th Regiment, continued until sunrise. Task Force Wilson also sustains a severe assault by contingents of the Chinese 39th Army. The enemy pressure compels TF Wilson to pull back to the vicinity of Yongbyon, east of the Kuryong River. Subsequent to the termination of the attack, the 35th Regiment is ordered to move from its positions near Ipsok and advance to a point slightly less than five miles below the Kuryong River, from where it can guard the approach to Kunu-ri.

The 35th Regiment heads towards its objective, but en route, the unit is unaware that Yongsan-dong had fallen during the early morning hours and when it approaches the town, it is hit with heavy enemy fire. The 35th Regiment is able to return fire and eventually break through the trap, but much of its equipment is abandoned in the process. The regiment, led by Colonel Fisher, finally arrives at Yongbyon, where it regroups and deploys in a spot just northeast of the 27th Regiment.

In the meantime, the 27th Regiment redeploys in positions that lie to the right of TF Wilson. In conjunction, the enemy assault of the previous night had gained nearly five miles and in the process had pierced the lines between the Kuryong and Taeryong Rivers. The unexpected advance increases the danger to the entire I Corps.

In related activity, under orders of General Walker, General Milburn oversees the redeployment of his entire corps. The corps initiates a move to the Ch'ongch'on River, where it is to design a new bridgehead that extends from the mouth of the river to the village of Pakch'on, in conjunction with the IX Corps, also under orders to retire to a new line. The latter will deploy along the lower bank of the river at Pugwon and stretch out toward the southeast to the village of Taeul-li, which is near the boundary of the X Corps.

During the afternoon, the ROK 1st Division sets up as cover force by deploying its 11th and 15th Regiments, while the remaining regiment, the 12th, heads for the new line at the river. With the support of the ROKs, the 24th Division and the 25th Division retire to the new defensive line at the Ch'ongch'on River. During the operation, the Chinese 66th Army repeatedly attempts to eliminate the cover force, but the South Korean regiments repel the enemy attacks.

The 24th Division under General Church stretches out along the west side of the Taeryong River with its 21st Regiment and forms a half-moon between it and Route 1, a strategic highway. The remainder of the division establishes a perimeter on the east side of the Taeryong. The 25th Division under General Kean disengages and retires about two miles to positions near the Kuryong River (corps' right). In addition, Task Force Wilson is disbanded. Although the 24th Division's retirement had been simple, the 25th Division had been heavily engaged with elements of the Chinese 39th Army, making the operation much more complicated. Nonetheless, General Kean by the end of the day has his three regiments in place, following the two-mile southward march to the Kuryong River.

The 24th and 27th Regiments line up between the east bank of the Kuryong to the vicinity of the west bank of the Ch'ongch'on, near the village of Puwon. Consequently, the 25th forms a blocking position along the highway that leads from Yongbyon in the north to the Ch'ongch'on River, as well as the path to Kunu-ri.

Meanwhile, the two South Korean regiments that had covered the retreat are still in great jeopardy. General Paik orders the 11th and 15th Regiments to remain in place throughout the night rather than risk unnecessary casualties. Subsequent to dawn on the 29th, they are to join the main force at the new lines.

In other activity, as the day progresses, more modifications occur as General Walker becomes concerned that the Chinese, who are making large gains in the ROK II Corps area, might well cut off the rear of Eighth Army. He orders General Church to dispatch the greater part of his 24th Division to the IX Corps for deployment at Sunch'on. With only one regiment of the 24th scheduled to remain in I Corps area, Walker directs the British 29th Brigade to move up to Anju to bolster the I Corps.

In the IX Corps sector, 1st Cavalry Division zone, the 1st Cavalry Division under General Gay, like the other units in Eighth Army, receives new orders. Rather than retire to the newly drawn defensive line, the 1st Cavalry is directed to drive up the Sunchon Road to bolster the ROK 6th Division, posted near Pukch'ang-ni. General Gay, however, does not immediately initiate the advance. Instead, he awaits the arrival of the 5th Cavalry Regiment, which is en route from Kaech'on. Meanwhile, the 7th Cavalry holds in place at a point near Pukch'ang-ni, less than ten miles from the South Korean 6th Division. The 8th Cavalry remains at Sinch'ang-ni, leaving its objective, the primary lateral road between Songch'on and Pyongyang, open for the Chinese advance. The delay adds to the dilemma of Eighth Army. The Chinese launch large-scale attacks towards midnight (28th-29th).

In the meantime, the 5th Cavalry initiates its advance to division positions during the morning hours, but enemy resistance occurs soon after it departs the vicinity of Kaech'on. The vanguard, composed of the intelligence and reconnaissance platoon, is intercepted by Chinese who hold dominant positions in the heights near Samso-ri. The ambush succeeds in devastating the platoon, leaving only four troops, including the platoon sergeant, as survivors. Reinforcements trailing the advance unit arrive, but the enemy force, originally at about 100 troops, is now heavily increased. Heavy fighting continues as the 2nd Battalion bolts to both sides of the highway and into the respective heights to terminate the blockade, but Chinese fire prevents any progress.

The regiment is compelled to regroup and modify the route to evade the trap. Nevertheless, the 5th Cavalry, due to its circuitous route, does not arrive at Sunch'on until late in the night. Consequently, the ROK 6th Division receives no reinforcements and at least four enemy regiments are encroaching its positions. General Gay anticipates completing the movement on the following day.

In the 2nd Division zone, General Keiser oversees the redeployment of the division at Kujang-dong. The line stretches from a point about three miles west of the Ch'ongch'on River to a point that lies about four miles southeast of the river. Two regiments, the 23rd and 38th, hold on the left and right, respectively, with the 9th Regiment being held in reserve at two locations, Yongdam-ni below Kujang-dong and at Pugwon. The S.K. 3rd Regiment at this time is with the 38th U.S. Regiment.

The ongoing Chinese offensive causes more adjustments within Eighth Army. The IX Corps receives new orders this morning. The 2nd Division is to raise as much resistance as possible while the division pulls back to the new line, drawn for the division as the ground between Pugwan and Wawon, the latter being where the Turkish Brigade under General Tahsin Yasici is posted. The high number of vehicles causes the road to become too congested, slowing everything down until a quagmire develops. The attempt to simultaneously move the 9th, 23rd, and 38th Infantry Regiments as well as the ROK 3rd Regiment and armor paralyzes the Ch'ongch'on Road, particularly between Kujang-dong and Kunu-ri.

While the roads remain jammed, the Chinese continue their attacks. Units emerge from the east and the north against the 38th Regiment. Despite the confusion, Colonel Peploe modifies his plans and moves his 38th Regiment and the ROK 3rd Regiment westward toward Kujang-dong. And from there, Peploe pivots southward to the vicinity of Kunu-ri. He halts the movement at about 2000 to await daylight on the following day. In the meantime, the 23rd Regiment under Colonel Freeman moves in separate units with one battalion trailing Peploe's 38th Regiment and another following the 9th Regiment. The remaining battalion (1st), accompanied by the 72nd Tank Battalion, maintains the Division rear to cover the main body. The tanks are repeatedly forced to fight off Chinese units on the heels of the Division.

The 9th Regiment, led by Colonel Sloane, again fords the Ch'ongch'on River to the west side and drives southward to Pugwon, where it arrives about one hour before midnight. Colonel Sloane spreads out his regiment. He places the 1st Battalion along the west side of the river on the right and rear of the 24th Regiment, 25th Division. He directs his 2nd Battalion (9th Regiment) to establish positions above the town along the valley road. The 3rd Battalion takes positions in the heights just south of the village. Slightly farther to the rear, about two miles south of the village, the 1st and 2nd Battalions, 23rd Regiment, deploy and await orders to relieve the 9th Regiment.

Also, the 27th British Brigade, posted in the vicinity of Kunu-ri, is to redeploy about five miles south of Sunchon at Chasan, from where it will be poised to bolster either the 1st Cavalry Division or the 2nd Division, whichever becomes more threatened. General Keiser anticipates completing his redeployment at the crack of dawn, but the Chinese choose not to let the night pass quietly.

At about midnight, the bugles blare near the 2nd Battalion, 9th Regiment's positions below Pugwon, only a short while after it had arrived. Unfortunately for the 2nd Division defenders, the new lines are not yet set up and there is much confusion between the division and the Turkish Brigade assigned to it. While the 2nd Battalion comes under attack, the Turks at the opposite end of the line sustain an assault at about the same time. The Turks had, in the meantime, been under assault at Wawon by the Chinese 38th Army.

At about dusk, the Turks are out of radio contact with corps. They disengage and pull back several miles to regroup at Sinnim-ni, arriving there a few strokes before midnight. The Turkish Brigade had been totally unaware of its recent attachment to the 2nd Division, and although earlier it had communications with corps, at this time there is no contact with either the 2nd Division or corps. Nonetheless, the mix-up is costly. The brigade was ordered to be at Wawon and it does not become aware of its attachment to the 2nd Division until the latter part of this night.

With the Turkish Brigade absent at Wawon and the non-arrival of the 1st Cavalry Division in the ROK 6th Division zone, the Eighth Army situation becomes precarious, particularly when the Chinese also seize Pugwon in the valley. And the Turkish Brigade, which is regrouping at Sinnim-ni, again comes under attack in the early morning hours of the following day.

The Chinese mount a huge force along the road between Kunu-ri and Sunchon, which the 2nd Division uses as its supply road. Some of these enemy troops are dispatched to establish roadblocks in the I Corps sector, along a road that runs southeast from Anju to Sunchon. These enemy units, on the following day, attempt to ambush elements of the 24th Division as its units move toward Sunchon.

In the 25th Division sector, General Kean continues to rework his lines at Ipsok. In conjunction, the 25th Division is transferred to the I Corps. Also, the 1st Cavalry Division, commanded by General Gay, is transferred from I Corps to IX Corps.

In Air Force activity, U.S. troops encircled in the vicinity of the Changjin Reservoir by Chinese begin to receive supplies from planes of Combat Cargo Command. The air-drop resupply missions continue for two weeks.

In related activity, the 35th Fighter Interceptor Group based at Yonpo, North Korea, begin to fly close-air support sorties to bolster the beleaguered ground troops that are surrounded. B-26 light bombers, for the first time, with the added element of more accurate radar, are able to bomb within 1,000 yards of he front lines.

In other activity, a solitary small plane penetrates and bombs the airfield at Pyongyang. The raid inflicts damage on eleven P-51 Mustangs parked on the ground.

During the day's fighting, pilot Lieutenant William P. Dougherty (35th Fighter Bomber Squadron, 8th Fighter Bomber Group) strafes the airfield at Pyongyang and destroys a parked enemy fighter of undetermined make.

In Naval activity, due the enormous enemy pressure, all available aircraft are requested for Eighth Army and X Corps. TF-77, which has been concentrating its carrier planes on the Yalu River bridges, switch the priority to the ground forces to provide close-air support.

— *In Japan:* General MacArthur, following a conference with his staff and the field commanders in Korea, notifies the Joint Chiefs of Staff in Washington, D.C., that his command in Korea is preparing to cancel the offensive and take a defensive position. The Joint Chiefs concur; however, there is disagreement between them and MacArthur about the type of defensive lines to be established. MacArthur clings to the strategy of the ongoing separation of Eighth Army and X Corps under Generals Walker and Almond

Signs of a Korean winter at sea. A Navy crewman aboard the icy deck of the USS *Philippine Sea* turns the snow-covered propeller of an F4U Corsair fighter prior to its takeoff.

Top: An M41 (155-mm howitzer) in action near Pukch'on on the east coast of Korea. *Bottom*: A U.S. infantry contingent advances to rescue a convoy stalled under heavy enemy fire during U.N. withdrawal.

respectively. However, the Joint Chiefs are convinced that a line is required between Pyongyang and Wonsan, the latter on the east coast of Korea in the X Corps area.

The major concern of Washington is that the gap between the forces affords the Chinese an opportunity to drive a wedge between the two and outflank either or both. MacArthur contends that the purported line is neither supportable nor tenable, due in part to the lack of roads in the mountains that divide the I and IX Corps. He further contends that the available forces under him are insufficient to retain Pyongyang. Nonetheless, he receives no encouraging words from the Joint Chiefs regarding reinforcements.

November 29   *In the X Corps area, 1st Marine Division sector, 1st Marines zone,* the enemy had attacked at about 2230 on the 28th and struck the center of the line defended by Companies H and I. The Chinese had surrounded the command post; they stole clothing but chose not to penetrate further against the outnumbered Marines. They had gained East Hill soon after an ROK platoon gave way. Reinforcements from X Corps, composed of engineers and signalmen, arrive to bolster How Company. How Company and Item Company are able to regain the territory and the divisional command post remains intact. The defenders at East Hill were not bolstered with any infantry troops. The army engineers there lose 10 killed and 25 wounded. Of the ninety ROKs, some are killed and wounded, but most are missing.

By 0400 on this day, the Marines prevail and the Chinese attack fails to gain its objectives. The Marines initiate plans to counterattack at 0440 to restore the line and liquidate the resistance on East Hill. The Marines move out with artillery support at 0530 and within about one hour, the line is restored. In the meantime, the attack to regain East Hill is suspended until the early morning fog clears. By about 0930, Marine planes (VMF-312) arrive to deliver napalm on the enemy-held hill. The Marines, however, have no artillery or mortar support as they climb the slippery slopes against enemy fire and grenades. The tossed grenades pick up speed as they roll down the icy slopes. The Chinese still hold the hill at noon, but by that time reinforcements arrive. Nevertheless, the exhaustive trek to the hill by Able Company (1st Platoon), led by Lieutenant Nicholas A. Canzona, does not attack. Orders arrive to cancel it.

Headquarters had planned an attack from a point other than the southwestern slope, which is held by troops under Major Reginald R. Myers and his improvised unit. Myers, however, is later credited with preventing the Chinese from encircling Hagaru-ri. Myers becomes a recipient of the Medal of Honor for his heroism under fire.

Canzona, leading approximately twenty men, afterwards moves up the opposite slope, but his contingent, too, is pinned down and subjected to the same resistance as that sustained by Myers. As the night settles around the hill, the Chinese still control the summit.

In addition, George Company, 1st Marines, and British Commandos had not been able to break through from Koto-ri. The Chinese hold the heights outside Koto-ri and despite dogged fighting, dusk arrives and the advance stalls less than five miles outside Koto-ri. One hill had been seized, soon after the column departed and the second objective, Hill 1236, is seized after a heavy skirmish by the British and Marines.

At the third objective, Hill 1182, Captain Carl Sitter (George Company) is ordered by Colonel Drysdale to disengage after the attackers sustain unending heavy fire. After dark, an enemy grenade is tossed into a truck that holds elements of Company G. PFC William B. Baugh shouts a warning to the others in the vehicle, then to save lives, he blankets the grenade with his body to absorb the full impact of the blast. PFC Baugh is awarded the Medal of Honor for his selfless sacrifice above and beyond the call of duty.

The situation at Hagaru remains desperate and the column is ordered to continue the drive. Air cover vanishes at dusk, but the column advances. Later, it is ambushed. The Chinese destroy a truck in the middle of the convoy and block the road. Consequently, vehicles and personnel (including a reserve unit, Company B, 31st U.S. Infantry Regiment) in the rear of the destroyed truck become isolated.

Tanks rush from Koto-ri, but the hills cleaned out earlier are again held by Chinese, who impede the tanks' progress at Hill 1182 and Hill 1236. In the meantime, the column splinters into several groups, which also decreases the ability of the smaller groups to forestall overwhelming Chinese forces. Some of the troops at the rear are able to make it back to Koto-ri before midnight and some in the middle of the column get back by about 0230 on the following morning.

Those still defending the column, under Major John N. McLaughlin, USMC, include only about forty operable troops (British, Army and Marines) who begin to run out of ammunition. During the confrontation with the Chinese, more of the troops are able to escape. About one hundred infantry and one tank company punches through to Hagaru. The battle is known as the Fight in Hell Fire Valley.

At dusk, the lead elements of the column under Drysdale are unaware that the column had been cut off. Drysdale's British troops and the Americans reach the perimeter at Hagaru at about 1900, after fighting through more heavy enemy fire about 2,200 yards from Hagaru. British Lt. Colonel Douglas Drysdale had been wounded during the advance. Command passes to Captain Carl L. Sitter, Company G. The troops remain in reserve for the night, but on the following day, George Company is ordered to attack East Hill, which still jeopardizes Hagaru.

In conjunction, one contingent of twenty-two British Marines becomes isolated, but the fate of the men remains unknown until the breakout from Hagaru. On 7 December, the British Marines will be rescued. The precise casualties remain unknown; however, the estimated casualties are: 41st British

Commando, 18 killed or MIA and 43 wounded; George Company, 3rd Battalion, 1st Marines, 8 killed or MIA and 40 wounded; Company B, 31st U.S. Infantry, 100 killed or MIA; Divisional Headquarters Battalion, USMC, 25 killed or MIA and 25 wounded; 1st Signal Battalion, 4 killed or MIA and 2 wounded; 7th Motor Transport Battalion, 2 killed or MIA and 3 wounded; elements of Company B and Company D, USMC, 12 and 8 wounded respectively; and elements of Antitank Company, RCT-5, USMC, 1 wounded.

The Allied force also loses 75 vehicles. Captain Carl Sitter is awarded the Medal of Honor for his heroism, leadership and courage during the breakout. Captain Sitter, while carrying out his duties, also moved from foxhole to foxhole weeding out infiltrators. During the fighting, Sitter was wounded in the face, arms and chest, yet refused evacuation.

In the 7th Marines sector, Company F, 2nd Battalion, on Fox Hill comes under an enemy mortar attack at about 0215. Shortly thereafter, a force of less than fifty Chinese, having discovered what they believe to be a weak spot in the line, initiate a charge and manage to push the Marines back a short distance, but the Marines still hold firmly at that point. Rather than risk unnecessary casualties in the dark, they suspend further action, but once the sun rises, they bolt forward and drive the enemy from the hill. Once the regained positions are secured, the Marines, still entrapped, prepare for another long day while awaiting relief. Various colored parachutes gathered from the air-drops of the previous day are stretched out to provide the planes with a conspicuous spot for supplies to be delivered.

As expected, about mid-morning, supplies including ammunition are dropped and soon after a helicopter from VMO-6 lands and delivers fresh batteries for the radios. Chinese fire damages the helicopter, but its pilot, Lieutenant Floyd Englehardt, departs safely. No relief force is able to reach the beleaguered unit, but during the afternoon, more planes arrive to drop fresh ammunition. Despite the marker chutes, the deliveries sometimes miss the target and force the Marines to brave enemy fire to retrieve the desperately needed mortar shells. A patrol moves out to gather the stray ammo, but effective fire prevents it from making it back to the lines. Consequently, the ammunition and the patrol are stranded about 500 yards from the main body. Lieutenant Elmer Peterson, the leader of the detachment, sends the men back individually.

In the meantime, a relief force composed of Companies A (1st Battalion, 5th Marines), Company B (1st Battalion, 7th Marines) and G Company (3rd Battalion, 7th Marines), bolstered by mortars and a recoilless rifle detachment, set out to rescue the besieged unit, but shortly after it moves out at 0800, it encounters heavy resistance. Aircraft arrive to support the advance. The planes remain overhead, but after gaining about 4,500 yards, the ground troops are notified by the pilots flying cover that the Chinese hold strong positions on either side of the MSR and in the high ground. Headquarters at Yudam-ni is also notified of the situation.

The new crisis compels Colonel Litzenberg to modify his orders. Rather than rescue Fox Company and continue forward to open the route to Hagaru, Major Warren Morris is directed to abort the plan to move to Hagaru and confine his actions to extricating Fox Company. Nevertheless, the Chinese strength is far superior to the composite battalion under Morris. By about 1315, the orders are again modified and the rescue force is ordered to return to Yudma-ni due to the possibility of it, too, being surrounded. After dark, Captain Barber, Fox Company's commanding officer, dispatches another contingent and it succeeds in retrieving the supplies. All remains relatively quiet until the early morning hours of the following day.

In the 7th Infantry Division sector, Lieutenant Colonel Don C. Faith (TF Faith), deployed north of Sinhung-ni with his 1st Battalion, 32nd Infantry, above the perimeter of the 3rd Battalion, 31st Infantry Regiment, and the 1st Battalion, 57th Field Artillery Battalion, drive through enemy resistance to reach Sinhung-ni. During intense fighting on the night of the 27th-28th, the Chinese managed to separate the units and prevent a link-up. On the 28th, Marine close-air support maintains missions to keep the positions from being overrun. Chinese attacks are beaten back and afterwards, Colonel Faith drives southward to link with the forces at Sinhung-ni.

Nevertheless, the combined force remains greatly outnumbered and under threat of annihilation. Reinforcements (one company) from the 31st Infantry Regiment are dispatched (29th) to rescue the beleaguered force, but the Chinese hold greatly superior numbers. The relief force sustains heavy casualties and it is forced back. In addition, two of the supporting tanks are destroyed. Lieutenant Colonel Faith assumed command after the senior ranking officer was killed. Faith holds in place and receives supplies from air deliveries to forestall disaster. Later, on 1 December, the force attempts to drive through the resistance to reach Marine lines at Hagaru.

In the Eighth Army area, I Corps sector, 24th Division zone, General Church, acting on orders from Eighth Army, directs the division to advance from its lines on both sides of the Taeryong River to new positions closer to Sunchon. The movement begins at about noon and continues into the latter part of the night. The 19th Regiment leads the advance from Pakch'on, while the 21st Regiment is held up to await South Korean reinforcements to take over its positions on the I Corps' left. The 21st, under Colonel Richard W. Stephens, departs for the objective during the latter part of the afternoon. By the time the 19th Regimental Combat Team advances less than five miles beyond Anjou on a highway that leans southeast towards Sunchon, it is informed that the Chinese have erected at least two roadblocks. Colonel Moore directs part of his force to eliminate the blockages, while he takes the remainder on a circuitous route via Route 1 to the village.

Meanwhile, the contingent driving down the lateral road from Anju hits the first ambush at about 1400 and effortlessly drives the Chinese from their positions. Several additional miles down the road, more Chinese are encountered and they hold the heights near a reservoir. The regimental combat team utilizes its tanks and mortars while it requests air strikes. The combination of fire power quickly clears the heights of the enemy and permits easy passage towards Sunchon. Colonel Moore's force arrives slightly after dusk and the task force that had been directed to clear the blockage arrives prior to midnight. The 21st Regimental Combat Team under Colonel Stephens arrives afterwards. Both regiments are in place and prepared for action by the following morning.

In the 25th Division sector, around midnight (28th-29th), elements of the Chinese 40th Army move down the west side of the Ch'ongch'on River and strike the 24th Regiment, 25th Division. Subsequent to the assault, which succeeds in jolting and denting the regiment's right flank, the Chinese ford the river and join the Chinese forces that had captured Pugwon in the IX Corps sector. I Corps maintains its bridgehead, but later during the afternoon, orders arrive to retire to a new line, similarly to those orders that arrive at IX Corps. General Milburn is directed by General Walker to await dusk and then retire to a new line, but following this, the corps is to again move on the following morning to a line behind the Ch'ongch'on River.

The U.S. 25th Division under General Kean and the ROK 1st Division complete the initial phase of the operation prior to midnight (29th-30th). While the Chinese attack in the IX Corps sector, some elements move through a gap created when the 3rd Battalion, 23rd Regiment (IX Corps), retire from their positions on the Ch'ongch'on Road to rejoin the main body of the regiment. This enemy contingent drives into Kunu-ri and at about midnight, assaults the positions of the 3rd Battalion, 24th Regiment. It also prepares to move out to positions southwest of the village, where it is to establish a perimeter close to the 23rd Regiment (2nd Division, IX Corps) below the Kaech'on River.

The strength of the unexpected attack stuns the battalion, but it rallies and heavy fighting ensues. The battalion command post loses communications with regimental headquarters, but the battalion headquarters' troops are able to fight their way back to Colonel Corley's headquarters. Soon after he arranges for the Air Force to provide support, however, the three trapped companies are unable to break through the enemy line, which has come in from the east to positions in their rear.

In the IX Corps area, 1st Cavalry Division sector, the 7th Cavalry Regiment's positions along the Sunchon Road about seven miles below Walpo-ri become active early in the morning, due to retreating South Korean troops of the ROK 6th Division, which had been scattered by a Chinese attack just prior to dawn against its lines near Pukch'ang-ni. The 1st Cavalry Division had been expected to reinforce the 6th ROK Division on the previous day, but General Gay had delayed the advance. Nonetheless, as the South Korean troops and hordes of

Korean civilians race to the perimeter, it becomes apparent that the Chinese will soon be banging on the door.

The unending lines of civilians moving south are complicating the task of the 7th Cavalry in several ways, including the presence of enemy troops disguised as civilians within the crowds.

The 7th Cavalry troops bring some semblance of order by about 0630; however, at about the same time, the Chinese 125th Division that holds the heights above the cavalry positions commences firing. Fire is quickly returned by the cavalry. The contest ensues for about two hours and the added weight of artillery fire finally terminates the enemy enfilade. During the tenacious exchange, South Korean units continue to speed toward the friendly lines. One of these contingents gets severely rattled when its lead vehicle stalls and clogs the highway. Rather than clearing the path by ditching the truck, the South Koreans abandon their vehicles and weapons and sprint to the 7th Cavalry perimeter. Shortly thereafter, a seven-man contingent of the 1st Battalion moves out and retrieves sixteen vehicles and eight howitzers. Also, while the civilians flood the lines, some of the pretenders toss grenades and casualties occur. Seven troopers are wounded and one officer is killed.

After the fight ends, orders arrive from General Gay that direct 7th Cavalry to withdraw to a new line at Sinch'ang-ni, three miles to the rear. The cavalry along with the 6th ROK Division, without interference from the enemy, moves out during the afternoon. Once at the destination, the South Koreans deploy in the heights west of the village and the 7th Cavalry establishes positions above the village along the Sunchon Road along Eighth Army's right.

Following the deployment, the zone remains free of enemy attack until the latter part of the night, when the Chinese initiate an assault. At about 2230, the cavalry comes under heavy fire, including machine guns and mortars. The enemy infantry launches its attack about one-half hour later and it is intercepted by equally ferocious fire from the two advance battalions. The attack is repulsed, but about 150 Chinese penetrate a gap in the line and advance directly into the village of Sinch'ang-ni. The two forward battalions are each compelled to fend off attacks against their respective command posts.

Two tanks, accompanied by riflemen acquired from the reserve battalion, advance at about 0200 (30th) to eliminate the infiltrators. In less than one hour, the enemy retires. Prior to pulling back, the Chinese sustain a loss of 350 killed and 10 captured; however, the number of wounded is unknown. The 7th Cavalry sustains 38 killed, 107 wounded and 11 missing. It is reported, but not for certain, that the Chinese 37th Regiment, 125th Division, had initiated the attack.

In the 5th Cavalry zone, the 5th Cavalry deploys about two miles north of Sunchon along the Taedong River, which places the regiment to the left of the ROK 6th Division. All the while, the 8th Cavalry continues its trek from Sinch'ang-ni to Songch'on. The combined forces of the 1st Cavalry Division and the 6th ROK Division extend along what is known as the Sunchon–Sinch'ang-ni–Songch'on Line.

In the 2nd Division sector, in the Ch'ongch'on Valley near Kunu-ri, the tranquility of the night gets shattered at about midnight (28th-29th). The Chinese 40th Army, which has elements moving down both sides of the Ch'ongch'on River, initiates a full-scale assault that strikes units of the I Corps on the west side of the river, while elements operating on the east side hammer the 2nd Battalion, 9th Regiment (2nd Division). The 2nd Battalion raises resistance, but it is unable to repulse the attack. The Chinese push the battalion back and seize Pugwon. After dawn, the contingents that engaged the 25th Division (I Corps) on the opposite bank arrive at Pugwon. In conjunction, the 2nd and 3rd Battalions, 9th Regiment, retire to a line to the rear of the 23rd Regiment, which remains posted along the valley road below Pugwon. Meanwhile, the 1st Battalion, 9th Regiment, which is deployed with the 25th Division on the west side of the river, continues to support its 24th Regiment before finally returning to the main body toward the latter part of the night.

In other activity, during the early morning hours, the 2nd Division's command post below Kunu-ri is informed by some Turkish troops with a convoy transporting supplies to the Turkish Brigade that an enemy blocking force had been posted along the road north of Sunchon. Steps will be taken in an effort to eliminate the roadblock, but in the meantime, the relocation operation begins. A patrol of military police is dispatched to confirm the report and it proves accurate; however, one man is killed and several are wounded when the contingent encounters the roadblock in a pass in the vicinity of the village of Yongwon, less than five miles from the command post.

In the meantime, unknown to General Keiser, a platoon of American tanks, attached to the British 27th Brigade, encounters the blockage while it moves south on the highway, but it breaks through due to the enemy's inability to destroy the armor. Subsequently, a reconnaissance company supported by artillery attempts to eliminate the problem before noon, but the Chinese refuse to be dislodged. The 2nd Division dispatches yet another unit, Company C, 38th Regiment, supported by a contingent of tanks to augment the reconnaissance force already there, but the enemy force had been strengthened and still, the blockage remains intact.

By dusk, the operation is aborted and the contingents are ordered to return to the division's headquarters. In the meantime, the corps commander, General Coulter, once aware of the roadblock, orders the British Middlesex Battalion (reserve) to divert from its mission to clear some Chinese from Samso-ri and instead, advance towards the blocked pass. By dusk, the British are slightly more than five miles from the target. Plans are made for a joint attack on the following morning, with the Americans striking from the north and the British attacking from the south.

In the Turkish Brigade zone at Sinnim-ni, the right flank of the 2nd Division, an attack is launched by contingents of the Chinese 38th Army against the advance units of the brigade shortly after midnight. Communications, which had been poor on the previous day, show no improvement, and the lack of contact with brigade headquarters at Kaech'on adds to the dilemma of the brigade. Nonetheless, the three defending infantry battalions continue to battle the enemy until dawn.

Meanwhile, word gets back to headquarters only when the artillery battalion abandons its positions and retires to Kaech'on. General Yasici is told that the infantry units are encircled, but due to the darkness, he postpones sending reinforcements until first light. Slightly after dawn (29th), a relief force accompanied by one platoon of tanks (72nd Tank Battalion) speeds to the rescue. Without any interference from the Chinese, the infantry and the relief force return to headquarters.

In related activity, due to the fluid activities within the 2nd Division sector and the rising threat of the Chinese, General Keiser by about noon is again changing plans for his defensive line to meet the threat, which is expected to include a massive enemy assault along the entire Eighth Army line. Just off the northeast tip of Kaech'on, the right flank of the 2nd Division, the 38th Regiment establishes positions that extend along the Tokch'on–Kunu-ri Road toward a string of hills that run directly below Piho-san Ridge on the left. The S.K. 3rd Regiment deploys on the left in the heights while the 2nd and 3rd Battalions, 38rd Regiment, extend over to Kaech'on, which is held by the Turkish Brigade. And the 1st Battalion remains in place at a point about one mile east of Kunu-ri, where it had deployed the previous night.

West of the U.S. 38th Regiment's positions, General Keiser directs the 23rd Regiment to set up along the Ch'ongch'on Road between Kunu-ri and Pugwon. The 2nd Battalion takes the point position about two miles below Pugwon, while the 3rd Battalion takes up positions slightly north of Kunu-ri and the 1st Battalion redeploys slightly east of the 3rd Battalion, to protect yet another route to Kunu-ri.

In the meantime, the 9th Regiment continues to hold at its positions below Pugwon to the rear of the 23rd Regiment. The new 2nd Division line heavily depends on the Turkish Brigade at Kaech'on. Instructions are delivered to its commanding general to deploy his force in two places, the high ground at the southeast end of town near the 38th Regiment and within the terrain below the Kaech'on River from where the force can dominate a valley that contains a road from Sunchon. The Turks, however, prove unwilling to cover the terrain below the river and only about two companies move to the hill on the edges of the town. The main body of the brigade remains in the village, which causes a conspicuous weakening of the divisional right flank when only two battalions of the 23rd Regiment are posted below the river in position to attempt to block the passageway of the Chinese forces above the Kaech'on River.

While General Keiser prepares to design his new line and prior to receiving a new Eighth Army order to again withdraw, his perimeter comes under attack during the afternoon by elements of the Chinese 38th and 40th Armies. The Chinese skirt past the Turks at Kaech'on and a contingent of the 38th Army plows into the 3rd Battalion, 38th Infantry's right flank, shattering it from the sheer strength of the attack. Urgent requests for the Turks to reinforce are dispatched, but still they fail to respond and remain within the village.

Shortly thereafter, the Turks are greeted with a heavy artillery barrage that forces reaction. In conjunction with the incoming shells, Chinese troops emerge unscathed from a valley that lies southwest of the village. U.S. tanks in support of the Turks commence firing from their positions on the opposing bank of the Kaech'on River, but the Chinese relentlessly continue to advance toward some high ground about one mile behind and northwest of the village. Rather than initiate a counterattack, the Turks flee westward through a pass.

The Turks' abandonment of their positions further jeopardizes the 2nd and 3rd Battalion, 38th Regiment, the sole defenders along the road. In the meantime, the Chinese reach the hills northwest of the village and ascend to positions from which their fire can dominate the road leading toward Kunu-ri. All the while, the 2nd and 3rd Battalions, 38th Infantry, are heavily engaged with the advancing Chinese. Reinforcements composed of elements of the 1st Battalion mount trucks and speed eastward toward the embattled troops outside of Kaech'on; however, the convoy is brought to an abrupt halt when it encounters the Turkish Brigade racing westward on the same highway. The confusion brings all traffic to a halt. The retreating Turks prevent any further movement by the relief force. Consequently, the 1st Battalion, 38th Regiment, is directed by Colonel Peploe to abort the mission and withdraw to a position alongside the highway at a point about one mile east of Kunu-ri. Shortly afterward, he orders the 2nd and 3rd Battalions to disengage and make their way back to positions in the rear of the 1st Battalion.

While the 38th Regiment is attempting to redeploy, the Chinese are also striking the 3rd South Korean Regiment, which is posted in the hills slightly south of Piho-san Ridge. The Koreans withdraw to positions just behind the 3rd Battalion, 38th Regiment, and establish positions about one mile northeast of Kunu-ri, with its right flank linked close to the left flank of Peploe's 1st Battalion. The new line is designed to bolster the covering fire for troops retiring from the east; still the Chinese pressure continues to mount. Heavy fire rings down from the heights into the pass, essentially trapping Americans and Turks there. Only a few tanks and other vehicles transporting wounded are able to break out.

As the situation worsens, air power is called upon, but the Fifth Air Force is less than efficient with close-air support after dusk. Nevertheless, the Chinese are the recipients of a B-26 air strike and it does the trick with sufficient accuracy to terminate the Chinese fire.

Shortly after the cessation of the enemy fire and still in complete darkness, the 38th Regiment units in the pass and the Turks move out heading west towards Kunu-ri. The 38th Regiment is able to regroup at the new positions by about midnight, but the Turkish Brigade remains in a shambles with many of its officers unaccounted for and its units scattered in disorganized groups. Some troops still are in the pass and others are haphazardly located all along the road from the pass to Kunu-ri and beyond, as far as the 2nd Division headquarters more than five miles beyond Kunu-ri.

During the struggle in the pass, Chinese gains have continued to force Eighth Army to modify its plans and the 2nd Division is in the process of yet another withdrawal to positions farther beyond Kunu-ri, but the confusion in the pass hinders the movement. The 23rd Regiment under Colonel Freeman, presently deployed north of Kaech'on, pulls back to a line below the town and south of the Kaech'on River, under cover fire of the 38th Regiment and the ROK 3rd Regiment. Freeman also leaves his 3rd Battalion along the Ch'ongch'on valley road near Kunu-ri to ensure safe passage of the regiment. The retirement places Freeman's regiment, except for a contingent of riflemen and some supporting tanks, between the Kaech'on and the Ch'ongch'on Rivers. The 38th Regiment and the ROKs then pull back under cover of the riflemen of the 23rd Regiment and one platoon of tanks.

The Chinese interfere with the execution of the retirement; they strike the 3rd Battalion, 23rd Regiment, along the road, but the battalion disengages before midnight. It speeds toward the new perimeter, but one company and some tanks pause near the northern tip of Kunu-ri to cover the rear.

Later, at about midnight, the Chinese encroach the tanks (72nd Tank Battalion) and their supporting Company L. The rear guard raises tenacious resistance and repeatedly turns back the assaults. After the fourth attack is repelled, the tanks and the riflemen head for the main body's positions south of the river. Once the 3rd Battalion abandons its positions on the Ch'ongch'on Road, a hole develops that leads directly to what becomes, at this time, an undefended left flank of the 3rd Battalion, 24th Regiment (25th Division, I Corps).

Meanwhile, the 3rd ROK Regiment's 1st Battalion had also been struck with great force as it attempted to reach the lines of the 2nd Division. Here, too, the South Koreans battle with tenacity until they are able to disengage at about 0400 (30th). New orders from Eighth Army arrive at about 0100 on the 30th. The 2nd Division is to disengage at Kunu-ri and withdraw to the new line and redeploy at positions that extend southeastward between the villages of Sunchon and Songch'on. Once in place, the 2nd Division will be in close proximity to the 1st Cavalry Division, which is to deploy about six miles outside of Sunchon. The withdrawal is to take place on the following day (30th).

— *In Japan:* At a General Headquarters briefing, the mood is somber. The typhoon-like surge of the

Communists had ravaged the center and west portions of the Eighth Army right wing, decimating the South Korean II Corps as it advanced. The total collapse of the right wing creates great peril for the left wing. An instant pull back to the Ch'ongch'on River is initiated to avoid a second catastrophe. Reports on the previous day had announced that more than 200,000 enemy troops are involved with the powerful offensive. Some estimates project the amount to be nearer 300,000.

November 30 *In the X Corps area,* the 1st Air Delivery Platoon, domiciled at Wonsan Airfield, has been involved with responsibility for 141 replenishment missions that consisted of 864 man-hours of flight, and the delivery by parachute of about 377 tons of supplies. At Hagaru, General Almond concludes that it is not pragmatic to consolidate the forces in the vicinity of the Chosin Reservoir. Almond authorizes General Oliver Smith to destroy all equipment that might impede his withdrawal to Hamhung, but Smith informs Almond that all equipment will be necessary in order for the Marines to fight their way out and carry their wounded with them. At the conference it is also decided that Wonson is to be abandoned. The aircraft there was relocated at Yonpo by 1 December; however, during the transfer period, missions were maintained to provide support for the ground troops.

In the 1st Marine Division area, the situation in Yudam-ni remains calm; only some sporadic skirmishes with the Chinese occur. Nonetheless, the Marines again received little or no rest, as attacks had been anticipated.

In the 1st Marines sector, George Company, which had fought its way to Hararu-ri on the previous day, is heavily engaged at East Hill. Just before midnight, engineers of Able Company plow into the positions of George Company without pausing to give the password, "Abraham." The Communists were right on their tails, so they shouted the password and the response, yelling Abraham Lincoln. The hill is defended by the 1st Platoon of Baker Company engineers and the 3rd platoon of Able Company engineers as well as George Company's 2nd and 3rd platoons. Other units there include the 1st Platoon, Able Engineers under Lieutenant Canzona, a couple of tanks and elements of the 1st Service Battalion.

The enemy regiment arrives just behind the engineers and a donnybrook breaks out. George Company is overwhelmed and compelled to give ground and abandon their positions with the Communists Chinese giving pursuit. Toward the bottom of the hill, the elements from the 1st Service Battalion join the fight and the Chinese there are eliminated.

Meanwhile, the Chinese who gain the evacuated positions hold the ground, but with no friendly troops in the area, they are pounded with artillery and by tank fire. In addition, the enemy is struck by withering machine gun and mortar fire. The Army engineers who had been thrown into the positions as a makeshift defense prove themselves to be a credible fighting force,

which greatly assists in holding the line and preventing a breakthrough at the gap on the central and northwest slopes of East Hill.

The night fighting occurs under nasty conditions along extremely icy slopes. The British commandos that had arrived with the Marines remain in reserve during the initial fighting; however, following the losses sustained by George Company, the British Commando unit moves to secure the line and bolster the remaining George Company able bodied troops. A counterattack during daylight (1 December) retakes the lost ground and within a short while, air cover arrives to ensure it is not again threatened. George Company and the support units combined sustain about sixty casualties, including killed and wounded.

Also, at about midnight, the Communists strike in force against Item Company's positions. The attackers are shredded by the concentrated fire power. Several Chinese advance to the well-defended foxholes, only to be killed. Marine estimates place the enemy dead at between 500 to 750. Item Company, commanded by 1st Lieutenant Joseph R. Fisher, sustains 2 killed and 10 wounded.

In the 7th Marines zone, Fox Company maintains its hold on Fox Hill despite the lack of reinforcements and continuing frigid weather. The previous night had been calm, but at 0200, the Marines are greeted by a curious sounding Chinese soldier who pretends to pass himself off as an officer from the 11th Marines. Fox Company hears a plea that the Marines should surrender to the Chinese and in return they would be given clothes and fair treatment. The Marines, unable to see the benevolent messenger, greet him with illumination shells. Once the sky brightens, the Marines notice that the impostor is trailed by a large force of Chinese troops approaching from the south.

The Marines, having refused surrender and the new clothes, greet the attackers with hot steel as they maneuver across the valley. They unleash a furious enfilade of fire, including machine gun and mortars, which devastates the enemy assault. By dawn, it is clear that the Marines still own the hill and when the Corsairs soar overhead just after dawn, the success is validated. About three enemy companies are wiped out. Fox Company sustains none killed and only one Marine wounded.

In the Eighth Army area, toward the latter part of the previous night, General Walker had issued a general order directing all Eighth Army units to withdraw to a new line at a point about twenty miles south of Kunuri, in an effort to prevent any chance of being encircled by Chinese who are swiftly moving down from the north and the east against Kunu-ri. The new line is expected to galvanize Eighth Army's corps and tighten the defenses, which are expected to hold firmly about thirty miles above Pyongyang, near the villages of Sukch'on, Sunchon and Songch'on.

In the I Corps area, General Milburn, in compliance with Army orders, directs the withdrawal of corps to the new line.

In the 25th Division sector, at Kunu-ri, Companies I,

K and L, 3rd Battalion, 24th Regiment, remain under heavy fire from an attack that had begun at about midnight of the previous day. Their confined positions in Kunu-ri had received air support, but the blocking enemy force had been impenetrable. The three companies maintain their positions throughout the day until about 1630, when they succeed in breaking out of the trap. The engagement costs the battalion 1 killed, 30 wounded and 109 missing. Following the break out, the troops head for the regimental lines which Colonel Corley established about five miles southwest of Kunu-ri.

The remainder of the division had begun to retire to the new line at 0700, under the protection of the 5th Regimental Combat Team (24th Division) at Anju, near the Ch'ongch'on River. It will, later in the day, assemble outside Sunchon. The ROK 1st Division initiates its retirement at 0600 and heads for Sukch'on. By about 1800, the cover force receives instructions from General Milburn to abandon its positions and head for Yongyu; however, friendly troops are still coming through the area and Colonel Throckmorton decides to remain for their safety. Some of the retiring forces are attached to the 3rd Battalion, 24th Regiment, which had for awhile been cornered in Kunu-ri, but others include tank units of the 89th Tank Battalion and

An ice covered Marine convoy during the fighting withdrawal from the Chosin Reservoir.

troops from the 27th Regiment, 25th Division. Consequently, Throckmorton's combat team is unable to depart from the Ch'ongch'on River until the early morning hours of the following day.

In the IX Corps area, 2nd Division sector, during the early morning hours, the Division command post comes under fire by an enemy patrol that had overwhelmed a small contingent of military police posted on a nearby hill. The Division, however, is still preparing to withdraw south to its newly designated positions at Sunchon. The operation commences at 0330. The 2nd Battalion, 9th Regiment, trailed by the mortar company, leads the way from Kunu-ri, followed by the 3rd Battalion, 9th Regiment, and a contingent of tanks. The columns are expecting to eliminate a roadblock in a pass along the way, but at about 0630, the enemy initiates an attack north of the roadblock. The lead vehicles pull back, while infantry contingents prepare to clear the high ground of the enemy. The Chinese repel an attack launched by the 2nd Battalion and one company of the 3rd Battalion. Meanwhile, the remainder of the 3rd Battalion seeks to hit the Chinese from another direction, but as the enemy pulls back from this attack, yet another hill to the south commences fire and both battalions are brought to a halt.

The Chinese, having moved to expand the roadblock, had not been anticipated by the battalion, and the British Middlesex Battalion still remains south of the roadblock, unaware of the snag in the plan. The British wait in place for orders from the 2nd Division to attack from the south. Attempts are made by the 2nd Division to contact the British by radio, but without success. Also, on the north side of the blockage, the ROK 3rd Regiment is committed to the fight. In addition, urgent messages are sent to IX Corps headquarters requesting that it contact the British and instruct them to attack the blockage.

As this activity continues, the ROKs move up and relieve the 9th Regiment, which is stranded on the west side of the road, to permit the regiment to regroup and prepare to renew the attack. Tanks are then directed to crack the blockage and race to the British positions south of the pass. The tanks plow through intense fire and succeed in reaching the Middlesex Battalion.

By the time the tanks arrive, the British had already received the orders from IX Corps to attack, but the Chinese also stymie them. Some small gains are made by the South Korean 3rd Regiment, but it is a gain of less than one mile, despite being supported by air strikes and machine gun fire from accompanying tanks. The morning passes into afternoon and while General Keiser is still attempting to solve the problem and eliminate the roadblock, the Chinese are closing fast on Colonel Freeman's 23rd Regiment near Kunu-ri. The situation in the 23rd Regiment's positions make it clear that General Keiser can not use the roads used by I Corps to move south. He decides, based on his assumption that the Chinese have only small arms fire against them, to run the blockade.

All units and their vehicles are directed to form with the 38th Regiment taking the lead, while the 23rd Regimental Combat Team holds the rear. The lead tank breaks through to the British positions by 1400; however, it comes under severe fire from the heights and is forced to plow through two blockages, each composed of recently captured American vehicles. The tank rumbles along and pushes the vehicles out of its way, but the delay causes a domino effect throughout the convoy that stalls the entire line.

The arrival of the lead tank causes the British to send a premature message to Eighth Army headquarters proclaiming that the supply road between Kunu-ri and Sunchon had been cleared. Back on the MSR, the Chinese fire, including machine guns and mortars, rains down on the 38th Regiment and casualties rise rapidly while stalled and destroyed vehicles clog the roads further. Attempts are made to clear the highway and other troops try to rescue the wounded, but each time the convoy gets rolling, another stoppage develops. Eventually, the discipline of the regiment dissolves; however, all the while, fire is returned by the Americans as well as the South Koreans and the Turks that are attached to the convoy.

Meanwhile, the 9th Regiment, under Colonel Sloane, is moving down the road toward the pass and by now the enemy fire is much heavier, particularly at the pass. The 2nd Battalion and the regimental mortar company lead the way, while the 3rd Battalion remains farther back as protection against any Chinese coming in from the rear. While the lead troops of the 38th Regiment break through the pass at about 1500, the MSR and the pass begin to resemble a massive junkyard with trucks and other vehicles scattered about. The 9th Regiment contingents and some ROKs and Turkish troops hit the pass but, again, disabled vehicles create a major problem. The other trailing contingents — including the divisional headquarters unit, the 82nd Antiaircraft Artillery Automatic Weapons Battalion and the 1st Battalion, 9th Regiment — get squeezed between the vehicles and the incessant fire from the opposite sides of the pass. The length of the stalled units reaches back for at least two miles.

By about 1500–1530, General Keiser reaches the front of the blocked convoy at the pass. Shortly thereafter, air support is requested, but still, Keiser contemplates abandoning all vehicles in order to break out. However, the planes that arrive succeed in their attacks, flying dangerously low in the close quarters of the pass. Apparently, the planes come in at such low altitudes that they can clearly see the enemy groups in the heights above both sides of the pass. A combination of bombs, napalm and machine gun fire quells most of the enemy fire.

Meanwhile, tanks roar forward and begin to shove the debris off to the side to clear a path for the stranded convoy, which by about this time has been shortened. Colonel Freeman's 23rd Regimental Combat Team, holding up the rear, receives permission to take a different route around the roadblock, using instead the Kunu-ri–Sinanju–Sukch'on Road through the I Corps sector. Freeman, subsequent to receiving permission to use the alternate road, inquires of the 38th FAB and the rear elements of the 9th Regiment if they want to accompany his outfit, but they decide to remain in the rear of the main column. Freeman's force, including attachments, makes it to Sunch'on just before midnight.

In the meantime, darkness settles in and the fighter-bombers are forced to depart the area, but their efforts ease the pressure enough for the remainder of this section of the column to complete the run through the pass. Some enemy fire continues, but it is not sufficient to halt the column. Nonetheless, the final section of the column, including division engineers, the trailing units of the 9th Regiment and four artillery battalions, have yet to enter the pass. The lead unit is the 17th Field Artillery Battalion. It begins the trek after darkness falls and encounters no enemy fire, but when nearly out of harm's way, misfortune strikes as the unit attempts to cross a stream slightly west of the village of Karhyin-dong.

Suddenly, one of the 8-inch howitzers overturns and tumbles into a ditch. Rather than permitting it to fall into the hands of the enemy, one soldier moves into the ditch and disables it. Enemy troops in the village spot a light being used by the artillerymen and soon the area comes under mortar attack. Nevertheless, the battalion moves forward to the assembly area.

The 37th Field Artillery Battalion, trailing the 17th, also comes under fire, but it, too, makes its way through the pass to safety. The remaining units in the column advance toward the pass, but by now the Chinese have descended from the heights to positions extremely close to the highway. As the convoy jumps off, it comes under severe attack and the road becomes blocked by the damaged and destroyed vehicles. Some in the lead are able to penetrate the fire and continue, but for the remainder of the final segment of the column, it is a dead end. As the attack continues, the troops attempt to break out of the trap, leaving the equipment, weapons and vehicles; however, the Chinese had been closing in great strength, making it difficult for the stragglers to evade the Chinese and make it to Sunchon.

In related activity, November is an especially difficult for the 2nd Division, particularly after the 15th of the month, when 4,940 battle casualties are sustained, including 1,267 for the 9th Regiment, 1,075 for the 38th Regiment, 485 for the 23rd Regiment, and 1,461 for the 2nd Division Artillery. In addition, the 2nd Engineering Battalion sustains 561 casualties and the 72nd Tank Battalion suffers 19 casualties. Units that sustain lighter casualties are the 2nd MP Company, 13 casualties; 2nd Reconnaissance Company, 27 casualties; Divisional Headquarters Company, 15 casualties; Divisional Headquarters, 3 casualties; 2nd Signal Company, 10 casualties; and one other detachment suffers three casualties. Equipment losses for the division are also extremely high and include 64 pieces of artillery and more than one hundred trucks.

— In the United States: President Harry Truman makes another statement regarding Korea:

Recent developments in Korea confront the world with a serious crisis. The Chinese Communist leaders have sent their troops from Manchuria to launch a strong and well-organized attack against the United Nations forces in North Korea.... Because of the historic friendship between the people of the United States and China, it is particularly shocking to us that the Chinese are being forced into battle against our troops in the United Nations command.... If aggression is successful in Korea, we can expect it to spread through Asia and Europe to this hemisphere. We are fighting in Korea for our own national security and survival. This country is the keystone of the hopes of mankind.

December 1 Some U.S. forces and other U.N. troops continue to come under attack by enemy aircraft, which then quickly seek sanctuary across the border in Manchuria. In air action over Korea, the U.S. fighter pilots outfight the Soviet aircraft, including the superior MiGs, knocking them out at a ratio of fourteen to one. Rather than permit General MacArthur to authorize his forces to pursue across the Yalu River, the U.N., with the support of the U.S. State Department and the British Government, seeks to open peace negotiations with the Communists.

In other activity, Fifth Air Force designates the 1st Marine Air Wing as the unit to provide close-air support for X Corps. Also, the initial C-37 arrives at Nagaru-ri to evacuate X Corps casualties.

In the X Corps sector, 1st Marine Division zone, the 1st Marine Division and supporting elements have for several days come under attack. A battle that had started around midnight the previous night, at East Hill in the area covered by the 1st Marines, is concluded. Unknown to the Americans, the Chinese attacks had lessened due in great part to the enormous casualties that had been recently inflicted upon them by X Corps. High casualties were also sustained by some American units that had been in the area east of the Chosin Reservoir. Three beleaguered battalions and some ROK troops under Lieutenant Colonel Faith, isolated at Sinhung-ni and close to being wiped out, attempt to break out and fight through to Hagaru. Since the U.S. Army units came under heavy attack on the night of 27–28 November, more than six hundred casualties have been sustained. After destroying their howitzers and other equipment before they can be seized by the Communists, the column, under close air support of Marine pilots, moves out heading toward Hagaru.

Lt. Colonel Don Faith had been able to lead the column through one roadblock, but enemy fire again pins it down. Faith takes the point and leads an assault to demolish the obstacle. At a point about thirty yards from the roadblock, enemy fire rips into him and inflicts a mortal wound, but Faith refuses to quit. From his position, he directs the attack. Although Faith succumbs, his courage and leadership permits the beleaguered column to break through and reach safety. Lt. Colonel

Faith is awarded the Medal of Honor posthumously for his extraordinary heroism under fire. At the time Faith is killed, the column stands about five miles from Hagaru.

The remainder of the trek is extremely dangerous, particularly with all the wounded in the column, and the lack of command due to the high casualties among officers and NCOs. The survivors lose discipline. The column splinters into a confused group of individuals who each seek personal safety. Small parties band together and move forward. Somehow, most stragglers make it to the Marine perimeter by about dawn on the following day. About 670 of the survivors of TF Faith are inside the safety of the Marine perimeter.

At daybreak, Marines move out in search of other survivors and discover more than they can transport. A convoy of assorted vehicles and some sleds, led by Lieutenant Colonel Beall (1st Motor Transport Battalion), is gathered. The convoy moves through the lines to collect the remainder of the survivors of Task Force Faith. Three hundred and nineteen additional troops, most suffering from frostbite and other wounds, are rescued.

The Marines afterwards share some confounding news. As it turned out, the Chinese not only raised little opposition, but they in fact on several occasions assisted in the rescue. The three army battalions posted east of the reservoir sustain a casualty rate of about seventy-five percent during 27 November through 1 December.

Task Force Anderson departs Hagaru in search of more survivors, but Chinese resistance holds up the column. The commanding officer, Lieutenant Colonel Berry K. Anderson, receives orders to abort the mission and return to Hagaru.

Meanwhile, Lt. Colonel Beall maintains his search operation. The Marines cancel their operation when it is believed that all survivors had been saved. A total of 1,050 soldiers out of the original force of 2,500 are saved. The Marines also count more than three hundred dead in the abandoned vehicles of the task force. Three hundred and eighty-five of the survivors remain to participate in combat. The contingent is formed into a provisional battalion after being supplied with arms by the Marines. The casualties at Hagaru place additional problems on the force there. Calls are made for aircraft to attempt a landing on a makeshift airstrip, created upon the frozen ground.

At about 1430, a C-47 descends to pick up a group of the wounded. The wheels bounce upon the riveted airstrip and then, despite the ice and snow, comes to a stop to the amazement of many observers. Soon after, the anxiety accelerates as the plane moves to take off and, as if in the very last seconds, gains just enough momentum to lift off and clear the hills to the south. The engineers that had carved that airstrip out of the frozen ground under searchlights within sight of the enemy had gained time and foiled any attempt by the Chinese to annihilate the trapped force. Aircraft will continue to evacuate the wounded and provide the ground forces with supplies.

The situation remains grim, but the Marines at Yudam-ni refuse to capitulate. They prepare to fight their way back to Hungnam. The mood however, remains somber, as circumstances forbid the transportation of the dead, an everlasting creed of the Marine Corps; however, all wounded are evacuated or placed in the convoy. No others are transported. Every man in the column, except the seriously wounded, faces the elements during the forced march along the frozen terrain. The vehicles, other than those carrying supplies, are reserved for the anticipated wounded and for the wounded of Fox Company, 7th Marines. The bodies of eighty-five men had to be left behind. Chaplains accompanying the troops conduct services at the grave sites in the field cemetery at Yudam-ni.

The evacuation plan, as stated by General Oliver P. Smith, calls for the transportation of all the wounded and the equipment. However, several Chinese divisions are deployed to block passage. This day, the 1st Marine Division initiates its fighting withdrawal from Yudam-ni, which takes the Marines (and afterwards other troops, including U.S. Army, British and South Korean) along a 56-mile highway of death and devastation. The temperatures drop to well below zero as troops advance under a massive air cover operation. The heights are a non-ending set of obstacles, blanketed by Chinese troops. An improvised battalion, dubbed the "Damnation Battalion," had been formed on the previous day. The unit is composed of George Company (3rd Battalion, 7th Marines), Able Company (1st Battalion, 5th Marines) and the remaining able-bodied elements of Dog Company and Easy Company (2nd Battalion, 7th Marines). The unit quickly becomes galvanized and uses a green bandana as their signal of pride and cohesion. The improvised contingent is given responsibility for clearing and maintaining the shoulder of the heights during the advance of RCT-7. The unit also contains elements of the weapons companies of the 7th Marines and some communications troops, also of the 7th Marines. Major Maurice E. Roach is assigned as the commanding officer.

The against-all-odds maneuver begins at about the time when the 2nd Battalion, 5th Marines, relinquishes its hold on Hill 1282, which allows it to pull back somewhat to relieve the 3rd Battalion, 7th Marines, who hold the left portion of the line. Once relieved, the 7th Marines redeploy south of Yudam-ni astride the main supply route. Surprisingly, the Chinese offer little resistance to the maneuvers, validating the decision to unfold the plan during daylight to assure air cover. Meanwhile, the 1st and 3rd Battalions remain the sole units deployed north of Yudam-ni. The pull-back from hill 1282 is problematic during the final phase, as the Chinese move within close range of George Company. Grenades become the weapon of choice, by both the Marines and the clinging Chinese. The situation becomes grim; the Marines need air cover, but due to the intermingling of the forces, it is not feasible.

One officer, Lieutenant Daniel Green, comes up with a solution and it is soon tested. Corsairs arrive to attack, but they drop no munitions; rather, they fly over for effect and while the Chinese seek cover, the Marines speed away. Afterwards, the Corsairs again visit the slopes and deliver a lethal blow that is bolstered by mortars and artillery. George Company becomes the grand recipient of the strategy. The unit sustains no casualties during the withdrawal.

At Hill 1240, 1st Lieutenant John R. Hancock unfolds his own ruse. After acting as rear guard at the hill, Hancock requests no air cover to permit elements of the 1st Battalion, 5th Marines, to just slip away. No casualties are incurred, as the Chinese have no notice of the withdrawal.

The 3rd Battalion, 5th Marines, advances at 0900 against enemy-held Hill 1542, while How Company of the same battalion moves against Hill 1419 to blow a hole in the Chinese obstructions. Hill 1419 holds steadfastly. Reinforcements are committed to the fight and at about

1930, the Marines vanquish the enemy there. At this time, the temperature stands at sixteen degrees below zero. The Marines gain the starting point from where the 1st Battalion, 7th Marines, departs to reach Fox Hill.

At 2100, the 1st Battalion, 7th Marines, led by Lieutenant Colonel Davis, begins to slug its way through the snow to traverse the mountains, despite no rest throughout the day. The first enemy obstacle to their front is Hill 1520, but en route, the elements extract a high toll as the Marines plow forward, often falling along the frozen slopes. Two over-exhausted columns ascend the hill and following a harrowing climb, the enemy estimated at about platoon strength is eliminated. The Marines, after the victory, essentially collapse, ignorant of the enemy fire and the sub-zero temperatures, surely the latter poised to inflict fatalities. At 0300, the column finally halts its progress. Nevertheless, the officers remain concerned and double check

U.S. Artillery north of the 38th Parallel is in action against enemy positions.

Top: A wounded U.S. troop is placed into liaison plane that evacuates him to receive medical aid. *Bottom*: An F-80 Shooting Star.

the men to ensure they are still capable of comprehending the surroundings and the situation.

Meanwhile, the vanguard, Lieutenant Colonel Taplett's battalion (3rd Battalion, 5th Marines), moves out to clear the heights on the opposing sides of the MSR. The two attacking units intend to converge in the vicinity of Toktong Pass and Fox Hill. Taplett's force is able to advance nearly 1,500 yards after it jumps off about 1500, but at that point, heavy resistance is encountered by the Chinese on opposite sides of the road.

Company H and Company I peel off west and east respectively, then nudge forward yard by yard until about 1930, when the obstacles are eliminated.

Following the slight conquest Taplett orders a short pause, but by the aura of the deep darkness, it becomes clear that there will be little rest. Just before midnight the Marines again advance, unknowingly against the opposite slope where the 7th Marines were engaged. Chinese had permeated the heights above the MSR and it is How and Item Companies (5th Marines) that move out to clear them off the mountain. How Company advances against slight opposition, but in the case of Item Company, it is quite different, as the Chinese bring about massive resistance, including an attack against the column. George Company joins in the fight and is caught by terrible enemy fire. In the meantime, Item Company becomes isolated in the frozen wilderness as the night-long clash ensues. After dawn, the results become apparent. Company Item had been severed into only about the strength of two platoons, when the reserve company (George) moved through the lines.

During the night's vicious combat, Sergeant William G. Windrich's contingent (Company I) is suddenly struck by a tenacious counterattack. Windrich, aware that his positions are untenable, attacks rather than withdraws. His Marines charge the assault troops. They defy the incoming machine gun and mortar fire and press forward through a storm of withering fire and soon get pounded with grenades. Windrich continues the attack to break up the Communist force, but overwhelming fire prevents further progress. Windrich, badly wounded and having lost seven of his command, moves back to the positions of the company's main body to get volunteers, then returns to the scene to evacuate the wounded. Afterwards, the wounded are evacuated, but Windrich continues to ignore his head wound and maintains control of the survivors of his contingent.

The Communists launch another stiff attack against Windrich's flank and he again becomes wounded, yet still refuses evacuation. The wounds take a severe toll on Windrich, so much so that he is unable to stand. From a sitting position, he controls his defenses and his Marines, in turn, repel the assault to save the command. However, Sergeant Windrich is not alive to see the Communists vanquished. The combination of the bitter cold and massive loss of blood cause him to fall into unconsciousness and succumb. Sergeant Windrich is awarded the Medal of Honor for is extraordinary heroism and intrepid courage in the face of the enemy. Nevertheless, about three hundred and forty-two Chinese are also there and their fighting days had been terminated.

In the Eighth Army area, the Chinese offensive continues, but Eighth Army, which had for the most part completed its withdrawal to the new line about twenty miles below Kunu-ri, has paid an expensive price. It loses equipment, weapons and vehicles. Eighth Army units come under heavy attack at certain points along withdrawal routes, but the enemy does not pursue. The short reprieve brings no solace to General Walker, who remains convinced that the enemy is not too far off, and he anticipates new attacks against his lines. But even more importantly, he is concerned that the enemy might still outflank his forces or totally surround it.

Meanwhile, Walker's force is greatly weakened from the combat of the past couple of weeks and one unit, the 2nd Division, is too weakened to remain on the field. This day, General Keiser leads his 2nd Division to a village about ten miles below Pyongyang to regroup and rebuild its strength. The plight of the 2nd Division, the other casualties within Eighth Army and the potential

A contingent of the 1st Marine Division prepares for its fighting withdrawal from Yudam-ni, located slightly west of the Changjin Reservoir.

Top: **U.S. Marines on 1 December huddle against snow covered vehicles at Yudam-ni, awaiting orders to break out and move to Hagaru to join with other Marine forces there.** *Bottom*: **A Marine column moves from Yudam-ni to Hagaru en route to Hungnam.**

overwhelming strength of the Chinese moving in from the east present a major dilemma for Walker. If he remains at this new line, he risks being overrun. Plans are laid to again retire. The Eighth Army forward units remain about thirty miles above Pyongyang, but with the 2nd Division out of action, the remaining units, including the few reserves, lack the strength to defend against what now appears to be more than 150,000 troops within six separate Chinese armies and the accompanying North Korean troops and guerrillas.

Walker's reserve units are composed of the 187th Airborne Regimental Combat Team with its attached U.N. units, a battalion of troops from the Philippines and another from Thailand. Another reserve force is a recently arrived battalion from the Netherlands, which is just preparing for use in the field. In addition, the French have committed a battalion of troops, which arrive in Pusan this day.

In related activity, Eighth Army has no major encounters with the enemy, which permits headquarters to concentrate on building a series of defensive lines in their blueprint for the withdrawal.

In Air Force activity, F-86 fighters (4th Fighter Interceptor Wing) arrive in Japan aboard the USS *Cape Esperance.*

In other activity, Fifth Air Force Headquarters relocates in Seoul from Nagoya, Japan. The 314th Air Division receives responsibility for the air defenses of Japan.

Also, a contingent of six MiG-15s intercepts and engages a group of three B-29s in an aerial duel that lasts for about six minutes, the first extensive MiG attack since the breakout of the war. The B-29s are escorted by F-80s, but still, three of the B-29s sustain damage. At Pyongyang, planes of Combat Cargo Command evacuate about 1,500 wounded troops.

— *In the United States:* President Truman announces that the North Koreans have been supplied with weaponry by the Soviet Union; he also proclaims the Chinese are actively involved in the fighting: "As the United Nations forces continued to defeat the aggressors and continued to advance in their mission of liberation, Chinese Communists participation in the aggression became more blatant.... The only explanation is that these Chinese have been misled or forced into their reckless attack, an act which can only bring tragedy to themselves, to further the imperialistic designs of the Soviet Union."

The President notes that 53 nations are unified to halt the aggression and that in essence, the U.N. and each of these nations is under assault by the Communists. Meanwhile, General MacArthur is convinced that he must be permitted to use air power to strike across the Yalu against enemy positions in Manchuria to halt the offensive. The thought of retaliation across the Yalu causes trepidation within the United Nations, for fear it might trigger World War III.

— *In Japan:* The U.S. Navy commissions the Atsugi Naval Air Station.

December 2 *In the X Corps sector,* following a

night-long confrontation with both the Chinese and the elements, the 1st Marine Division remains on the offensive. Several obstacles had been overcome earlier in the day. (*See also,* **December 1**, 1950, *In the X Corps sector.*) At about dawn, the 1st Battalion, 7th Marines, moves closer to Fox Hill and prepares to strike nearby Hill 1653. Initially, as the contingent encroaches Fox Company positions, no communications occur, causing concern that friendly fire might strike the 7th

Marines. Several obstacles are seized and in the interim, radio contact is made with Fox Company.

Slightly before 1130, the initial elements of Baker Company enter Fox Company's lines. Soon after, the remainder of the battalion arrives. During the operation, a contingent moves back to get the wounded and during the operation, a Chinese sniper fatally wounds Lieutenant Peter A. Arrioli (MC), USN, the 7th Marines' surgeon. Fox Company (2nd Battalion, 7th Marines), commanded by Captain Barber, remains strong enough for the fights to come, but after five days of resisting the Chinese, it had sustained 26 killed, 3 missing and 89 wounded. Captain William B. Barber becomes a recipient of the Medal of Honor for his extraordinary leadership and courage during the period.

Also, in the 2nd Battalion, 5th Marines sector, the Chinese pound their rear-guard positions at Hill 1276 during the early hours of 2 December. Lieutenant Colonel Roise (2nd Battalion, 5th Marines) orders Fox Company to attack and regain some lost ground; however, upon gaining the crest of the hill, after dawn today following two other assaults, enemy fire from the reverse slope compels the contingent to pull back. Air cover arrives and pounds the Chinese positions at about 1000. The Chinese also lose troops when they abandon their positions and flee into the sights of Company D and G.

The struggle for control of Hill 1520 also continues. George Company, 3rd Battalion, 7th Marines, moves against it, bolstered by How Company and a composite force composed of the men of the 2nd Battalion, 7th Marines, now known as Dog-Easy Company. At 1200, the western slope falls to the Marines of George Company.

Meanwhile, the Chinese erect a roadblock along the MSR and detonate a bridge to halt the Marines. George Company descends from above the Chinese positions, while the others drive forward, augmented by air attacks that pummel the enemy positions. The blockage is eliminated; however, the blown bridge slows the advance until a modified route can be erected by engineers. Afterwards, the column continues its advance.

In the meantime, the 3rd Battalion, 7th Marines, comes under fierce attack by elements of the 79th Chinese Division at 0430. Item and George Companies remain heavily engaged until dawn, but it is Item Company that sustains the bulk of the attack at Hill 1542. The combined strength of both companies on this day is down to about two hundred troops. The Chinese report later that one hundred enemy troops (Item Company) were killed. No records of that time from the 7th Marines exist; however, estimates of the Marine Corps place the Item Company's actual casualties from the night's fighting at thirty to forty troops killed or wounded.

During the day's struggle of the 3rd Battalion, 7th Marines, attached Company Jig, a provisional platoon including artillerymen and riflemen — has engaged the Chinese in a furious fight near Yudam-ni when the Communists approach in uniforms of friendly troops. Sergeant James E. Johnson takes command of the platoon and directs its fire. When the platoon is ordered to seek better positions from which to defend, Johnson holds his position and provides cover fire. Sergeant Johnson is last seen by his troops resisting the onslaught despite his wounds in a violent exchange between him and the enemy. Johnson uses hand-to-hand combat and his grenades to buy time for his platoon. Sergeant Johnson is awarded the Medal of Honor posthumously for his extraordinary courage under fire and for his intrepid leadership in the face of an overwhelming superior enemy force.

In related activity, the withdrawal continues throughout the day. Meanwhile, Company H, 3rd Battalion, 5th Marines, advances on the right of Company G at Hill 520 against an obstacle to the front of it. The troops of Company H encounter fierce resistance, but later, after support from planes, the unit advances. After

Top: Elements of Eighth Army retire from Sunchon and move south toward Pyongyang. *Bottom*: Defenders at Hagaru airstrip fire 105 howitzer shells at the enemy, which has the airstrip encircled.

dusk, the objective is seized. The 3rd Battalion, 5th Marines, arrives within about 1,000 yards of Fox Hill at 0200 on 3 December.

The route of the division is tedious, but the Chinese are unable to halt its progress. In addition to the Chinese, the Marines continue to get pelted by an equally pernicious enemy, the weather. By dawn of 3 December, a new layer of fresh snow blankets the area.

In other activity, the 1st Battalion, 7th Marines, under Lt. Colonel Raymond G. Davis, following yet another sleepless night in the frigid Korean hills, maintains its advance to secure positions from which the battalion can relieve a beleaguered rifle company and secure a strategic mountain pass to ensure the Marines make it to Hungnam.

In the Eighth Army area, General Walker initiates a withdrawal from the Sukch'on–Sunchon–Songch'on Line, just having reached it after withdrawing from Kunu-ri. Pyongyang is to be evacuated and the new line is to be drawn below the village. The forward units remain about thirty miles above the village and at a point about ten miles below that, a cover force will set up to delay any Chinese forces that attempt to close on the retreating columns. The enemy, in the meantime, continues to close from the east to present General Walker with yet another problem, the possibility of the enemy getting into Pyongyang by swerving west and catching Eighth Army before it can pass through the town.

The operation moves into high gear as troops are sped southward into Pyongyang to retrieve the supplies, while other units rush toward the port of Chinnamp'o to extricate equipment and supplies still remaining there. Meanwhile, to protect the retreat, Walker dispatches contingents to guard the east flank from assault. Pontoon bridges that span the Taedong River are barred to civilian traffic and the 187th Airborne troops set up positions at each of the eight bridges to enforce the rule. Walker had received authorization from Far East Command to destroy all supplies and equipment that could not be brought out with army.

— *In Japan:* The carrier USS *Princeton* (CV 37) arrives at Sasebo from the U.S. From there, the *Princeton* will depart for Korean waters.

December 3   *In the X Corps area,* the 1st Marine Division and attached troops continue their drive to Hungnam. In the 3rd Battalion, 5th Marines, sector near Fox Hill, the composite company known as Dog-Easy Company is declared ineffective due to high casualties. Company G takes its place along the main supply route. The 3rd Battalion is accompanied by one tank and although the new coat of snow gives the appearance of a tranquil mountain area, the Marines are aware that the hills are still consumed with Chinese.

The 1st Battalion, 7th Marines, initiates a set of attacks against the enemy positions. The Chinese are startled and take no time to defend. Instead, they abandon their positions and inadvertently head straight towards another Marine contingent, the 3rd Battalion, 5th Marines, which is on the attack. As the disorganized Chinese battalion speeds southwest with the 1st Battalion, 7th Marines, in pursuit, the skies clear as planes arrive to strike other enemy positions at about the same time Lieutenant Colonel Taplett's 3rd Battalion, 5th Marines, is closing. The Chinese battalion's untimely encounter with the threesome power of two Marine battalions and the aircraft brings about its demise.

By 1030, the enemy battalion is annihilated. Soon after, by 1300, the Chinese had also been eliminated at Toktong Pass, which permits the linkup of the 1st Battalion, 7th Marines, and the 3rd Battalion, 5th Marines. The first phase of the break-out ends successfully, but at high costs. After the anticipated rendezvous at the pass, the 3rd Battalion, 5th Marines, with the convoy holding the wounded reinitiates the advance towards Hagaru along the route to Hungnam. Some of the less seriously wounded abandon the trucks to make room for the troops with major wounds and still, the vehicles are jammed.

The 1st Battalion, 7th Marines, which had defended the pass to permit the columns to pass safely, descends from the heights and joins the column to the rear of the 5th Marines. Marine observation planes (VMO-6) maintain a flying blanket overhead to forewarn the column of any enemy positions that might lurk along the road. Six separate Marine squadrons combine to fly one hundred and forty-five sorties.

The airborne Leathernecks fly low-level missions that at times bring their planes to dangerously low altitudes, but that type of cover flight has become common practice. The Marines are determined to win and to discredit the erroneous reports that for months had been emerging from the American press, which frequently accused the American troops as being weak and unable to handle the heavy burden of combat.

At about 1930, following the harrowing march through the snow and winds and the incessant fighting for more than one week, mostly without sleep of any length, the 1st Battalion, 7th Marines, calls a halt to the march. From a point about several hundred yards from the base at Hagaru, all the pain is discarded. Those able to walk gather into a tightly knit formation, then march straight into the camp. They had accomplished what few thought could be done and they did it as promised, carrying their wounded and their dead. Lt. Colonel Raymond G. Davis, commanding officer of the 1st Battalion, 7th Marines, receives the Medal of Honor for his extraordinary leadership during the treacherous march, which included the rescue of an encircled rifle company.

Nonetheless, more miles of treacherous terrain stand between them and Hungnam. A contingent of Royal Marines had moved out of Hagaru to cover the flanks, but for the most part, the Marine aviators had cleared most of the loitering Chinese out of the way. The 3rd Battalion, 5th Marines, and the 4th Battalion, 11th Marines, are the next units expected at Hagaru.

Top: U.S. Marines en route to Hungnam carry one of their wounded. The hills in background are held by the enemy. ***Bottom***: Marines move through frigid weather along frozen roads toward Hungnam.

Chinese opposition obstructs the progress of the column at about 0200 on 4 December.

In the Eighth Army area, preparations for a withdrawal from the Pyongyang area continue. Meanwhile, the Chinese withhold offensive action, but apparently they are making plans to close from several directions to snap a trap around Pyongyang. Reports of enemy activity to the east and southeast of the town are scrutinized. General Walker becomes more convinced that the enemy is poised to cut off the withdrawal routes

Top: **A transport plane, while taking off, passes over a Marine transport plane that burned after crashing on the improvised airstrip at Hagaru. The in-flight plane is evacuating seriously wounded who are unable to make the march to Hungnam.** *Bottom*: **Vehicles in line at a dock wait for evacuation at Hungnam.**

near Sin'gye. The orders to retreat are to be executed on the following day. The new and temporary line is to be at a point about fifteen miles below the village of Pyongyang, with a secondary plan that calls for preparations to move from there to another line that drops the troops on the east about thirty miles. In conjunction, those on the west will pull back about fifty miles.

— *In Japan*: General MacArthur informs Washing-ton that he requires reinforcements in large numbers in order to beat back the challenge of the Chinese who have involved themselves in Korea. Based on his calculations, MacArthur believes that without additional troops, he will have few options, and be compelled to offer resistance while his forces withdraw southward in an effort to avoid the total devastation of the U.N. forces in Korea.

U.S. Army engineers place sachel charges on a railroad bridge in the vicinity of Pyongyang as the U.S. prepares to abandon the area.

Chinese prisoners captured by U.S. Marines during fighting withdrawal in the Chosin Reservoir Campaign. Some of the Chinese are wearing canvas shoes (sneaks) and others rags, but some others are wearing U.S. boots. All of the Chinese are wearing quilted uniforms.

December 4   Along the main supply route, the remaining elements of the 1st Marine Division continue to advance toward Hagaru from Yudam-ni. During the march, the column comes under attack at about 0200, shortly after some of the vehicles transporting artillery run out of fuel. The units to the front, Company G and Company H (3rd Battalion, 5th marines), continue to advance, unaware of the problem. Chinese forces open fire on the convoy. Marines attached to the 4th Battalion, 11th Marines (truck drivers and artillery-men), repulse the assault and in a short while, more Marines arrive to bolster the stalled convoy.

The unexpected attack causes confusion and a few of the troops panic. Others restore calm. The 1st Battalion, 11th Marines, and Company A, 1st Battalion, 5th Marines, arrive and by that time, Lieutenant Colonel Taplett had also arrived at the ambush. The warrant officer with the pointed tongue, after moving around a bend, soon returns with a driver and an artillery piece in tow. Ground troops combine with artillerymen to eliminate the blockage, but in the midst of the darkness and confusion, the Chinese blow a bridge, further complicating the possibility of further progress.

By daylight, the artillery begins to pound the enemy positions from close range and the Chinese are also struck by air attacks. Again, the Marines advance and the Chinese sustain devastating losses, estimated at about one hundred and fifty troops. The remaining el-

ements arrive at Hagaru at 1400, bringing the first phase of the operation to a successful close.

Of the 1,500 casualties that arrive at Hagaru, about one third of them are suffering from frostbite. Four days of Hell and fourteen miles of damnation end for the 1st Marine Division, but still for the Marines and the supporting troops, including the British and South Koreans, it is still a long, long way to Hungnam.

The Marines are startled to learn, while at Hagaru, that there were doubts among the American press and public that they could extricate themselves from the Chinese trap. Despite the hardships endured, the Marines at Hagaru, with a few exceptions, remained fully confident that they would fight through the remaining Chinese and reach the coast at Hungnam. Some in the United States had prematurely written off the entire 1st Marine Division.

In the Eighth Army area, Eighth Army is to withdraw to the new line, which is to stretch from Kyomip'o along the lower bank of the Taedong River on the west to Koksan in a valley near the Yesong River. I Corps moves out to deploy in the vicinity of Kyomip'o by traveling along a route through Pyongyang. In the meantime, IX Corps is to move along Route 33 toward the eastern sector of Eighth Army near Koksan. The east flank of army is in the Yesong Valley defended by the ROK II Corps, and the arrival of the IX Corps is intended to augment the South Koreans and ease somewhat General Walker's concern for his east flank. The Chinese continue to remain inconspicuous.

In Air Force activity, a three-plane contingent of reconnaissance Tornadoes is attacked by MiGs. The enemy shoots down one of the planes in what becomes the first successful shoot down of a jet bomber in the history of air power.

In Naval activity, Far East Naval Forces arrive at Wonsan to evacuate the U.S. forces there. The USS *St. Paul* (CA 73) is delegated as the gun fire support coordinator

U.S. infantry troops (X Corps) south of Koto-ri work in the snow to fortify foxhole.

Conditions at Marine positions in Koto-ri during early December. The Marines are greeted by another snowstorm.

during the operation. Also, the United Nations Blockading and Escort Task Element (TE 95.1) provides naval surface gun fire and air support for Eighth Army forces that are stretched between Chinnampo and Inchon. The operation continues into the following day.

In other activity, Lieutenant Thomas Jerome Hudner, a pilot of Fighter Squadron 32, attached to the USS *Leyte Gulf* (CV-32), attempts to assist a downed pilot in the vicinity of the Chosin Reservoir. Hudner flies in circles to protect the other aviator. Soon after, Hudner decides to land in full view of the enemy to save the pilot, whose plane had caught fire with him trapped in the cockpit. Hudner attempts unsuccessfully to retrieve the pilot. Afterwards, and still in great danger, he calls for a helicopter, all the while in the view of the enemy. The helicopter arrives, but still the pilot could not be extricated. Lieutenant Hudner becomes a recipient of the Medal of Honor for his extraordinary heroism in the face of the enemy, with great risk to his own life in an attempt to save another pilot, above and beyond the call of duty.

— In Japan: General MacArthur receives a response from Washington regarding his recent request for reinforcements, but it is not what he had expected. General Joseph Lawton Collins, Army chief of staff, makes it clear in a meeting with MacArthur that no large number of troops will be committed at this time. Nonethe-

less, MacArthur is also informed by the Joint Chiefs of Staff, in Washington, that they were in agreement with him on the establishment of beachheads from which the troops could be evacuated if necessary. Collins remains in the region for a while and spends a few days in Korea to get an onsite perspective of the situation.

December 5   *In the X Corps area,* at Hagaru, the 1st Marine Division continues its operation to reach Hungnam. The Chinese for the fourth straight night do not initiate any offensive action against the American lines at Hagaru. On this day, 1,400 casualties remain at Hagaru, but by the end of the day, all are evacuated by air, to bring the total of air evacuations of wounded to 4,312 troops (1 December through 5 December). The casualties include 3,150 Marines, 1,137 U.S. Army and 25 British Royal Marines (Task Force Drysdale). X Corps figures differ slightly from Marine records, with X Corps totals amounting to 4, 207 for the identical time period.

The Marines and other forces at Hagaru get a short reprieve, as the arrivals from Yudam-ni require some rest. The next step of the advance to Koto-ri will commence on the following day. At 0800 on this day, OpnO 25–50 is issued. The General Order lays out the plan for the breakout, which is to commence on the following day at dawn.

There is no activity against the base today and it

U.S. Army engineers construct a treadway bridge across the Taedong River. The new bridge is built close to another bridge that is operational.

remains tranquil throughout the night, permitting the troops to prepare for the next jump-off without major interruption, other than the ungodly weather. Nonetheless, the Marines and the U.S. Army elements at Hagaru are aware that the Chinese, although concealed, are in the vicinity in overwhelming strength. Intelligence gathered from POWs indicate that seven complete divisions block the path and another two enemy divisions are also suspected of being nearby. The identified divisions are: CCF 58th, 59th, 60th, 76th, 79th, 80th and 89th. The other two thought to be in the path are the CCF 77th and 78th. The X Corps forces are composed of only three Marine Regimental Combat Teams, 5, 7 and 8.

In the Eighth Army area, U.N. forces evacuate Pyongyang, the North Korean capital. The Americans and the Allied units attached to Eighth Army continue to retire toward the new line about fifteen miles below the capital. During the morning, large portions of the city are set afire and troops attached to IX Corps work to destroy all equipment and supplies not scheduled for transport by the retiring forces. The rail yards are jammed and operations are underway to move out the wounded; however, there is a shortage of operable trains due to several reasons, including damage from previous Allied air strikes.

Prior to 0800, most sections of the city are afire and all pontoon bridges that span the Taedong River are blown by engineers. Lingering, although unseen, Chinese pressure forces a hurried retreat, which hinders the operation to destroy the equipment. There is a huge amount of supplies and too little time. Consequently, although nearly all units are beyond the city during the day, the quagmire at the rail yard prevents the evacua-

tion of about fifteen M-46 tanks that are parked atop flat cars.

At Chinnampo, the port has been active for the last several days in an effort to transport wounded and remove supplies and equipment. Like the activity at Pyongyang, the operations continue without interference from the Chinese. Eighth Army utilizes U.S. Naval vessels, Japanese commercial vessels and even Korean sailboats to help with the task. The forces there are loading equipment, but they also allow boarding throngs of civilians and captured enemy troops. It was, for a while, thought that the prisoners should be left at the port, but after discussions, it is decided that the retreating South Korean forces would probably liquidate them.

By about 1700, the final vessels embark under the protection of U.S. destroyers offshore and a nearby British aircraft carrier that had been posted in the Yellow Sea to provide air cover during this last day of the evacuation of Chinnampo. As at Pyongyaang, engineers detonate the explosives to ensure the port town is of little value to the enemy. In conjunction, the vessels head toward Inchon and Pusan, with the service troops and the supplies primarily going to the former and the wounded and POWs moving to the latter. Evacuation of Chinnampo and Inchon is handled by naval vessels of Amphibious Task Force (TF 90.1) and United Nations Blockading and Escort Task Force (TF 95).

In related activity, General Walker orders I Corps and IX Corps to dispatch patrols to attempt to locate the enemy positions, but neither makes any contact. The absence of any prisoners makes it difficult for the time being to guess the next move of the Chinese.

In Air Force activity, Combat Cargo Command

Two bridges that span the Taedong River, both blown by U.S. forces on 5 December.

continues the operation to supply the troops surrounded in northeastern Korea. The recently arrived Greek contingent of C-47s participates in the airlift.

During this day's operations, 3,925 wounded and sick troops are transported to Japan. Most of the men are lifted from the primitive airstrip at frozen Hararuri.

In other activity, the Air Force cancels its strikes against the Yalu River bridges. The extreme cold weather along the Korean–Manchurian border has temporarily made the bridges irrelevant; the rivers are totally frozen, which permits the Chinese to walk across.

— *In the United States:* The rift between General MacArthur and President Truman continues to intensify, as the president remains infuriated at certain public statements made by MacArthur. Truman, on this day, issues a directive relating to all American officials stationed overseas, including military leaders, that any public statements be in concurrence with U.S. policies and that no statements or communications are to made by these officials about foreign policy or military matters. This is particularly directed toward General MacArthur and essentially prohibits him from making statements to the press or the other media from the United States.

In conjunction, there is great division between Washington and MacArthur on the way the conflict in Korea is being handled. And MacArthur has been defending his methods and strategy against the accusations

that he is responsible for the failures of the U.N. Command to halt the Chinese.

December 6 General Collins, Army chief of staff, concludes a three-day stop in Korea. During his visit, he spent some time conferring with Generals Walker and Almond, the commanding officers of Eighth Army and X Corps, respectively. He returns to Japan to confer with General MacArthur. Collins gains the separate opinions of Walker and Almond. Walker believes Eighth Army must withdraw, while Almond is convinced his X Corps can draw a solid line at Hungnam and withstand the Chinese attacks. A strategy meeting will be held at Far East Headquarters on the following day to solidify a plan.

In the X Corps sector, 1st Marine Division zone, at dawn, the X Corps 1st Marine Division and attached units, again unmolested overnight by the Chinese, commence the breakout from Hagaru. RCT-1 is assigned to hold Koto-ri and Changhung. RCT-7 drives southward. It had been relieved on the previous day from its deployment along the Hagaru perimeter by RCT-5.

RCT-5 moves out against East Hill and from there it is to trail RCT-7 to protect the rear. The coordinated attacks of RCT-5 and the spearhead, RCT-7, receive air support at about 0700. The advance is to be protected by scores of planes at just about all times. The Marine squadrons at Yonpo average about 100 sorties a

day and other Marines aboard the *Badoeng Strait* fly another thirty-five sorties a day, while the U.S. Navy's carriers provided additional blanket coverage to the point
of nearly creating a traffic jam in the skies above the column. The carriers *Leyte Gulf, Valley Forge, Philippine
Sea* and *Princeton* are instructed to place the column on
the top priority list and each carrier is directed to commit no less than one hundred sorties a day. Other carriers, the *Bataan* and the *Sicily,* are closing on the area
and they too are to join in the protective umbrella.

In addition, the 11th Marines contribute non-stop
artillery support for both RCT-7 and RCT-5. In the
meantime, at Hagaru, during the night of 5–6 December, the artillery units continued to plaster the forward
routes with artillery shells that could not be transported. In addition to the Marines, the survivors of
Task Force Faith — numbering 385 troops and other
7th Infantry Division elements numbering slightly
more than 100 soldiers — are with the column. The soldiers, formed into a composite battalion, are under the
command of Lieutenant Colonel Anderson and attached to the 7th Marines.

Meanwhile, enemy-held East Hill, a Chinese stronghold since 29 November, falls to the Marines at about
1100, when the resistance vanishes. Upon occupying
the hill, about thirty Chinese troops that had died during the fighting are discovered. Following the seizure of
East Hill, the Marines move against another hill in the
near distance; however, the Chinese do not relinquish
it easily. Nevertheless, by 1430, the Marines secure the
objective. Soon after, the Chinese are preparing a counterattack, but the Marines commence a momentous
and what turns out to be a historical bombardment.

While elements of RCT-5 pummel the Chinese,
planes arrive and deliver more lethal punishment. Consequently, the Chinese that are snagged on a saddle
choose to capitulate. A Marine patrol of platoon size,
led by 1st Lieutenant George C. McNaughton, accepts
the surrender of 220 Chinese, a record seizure for the
1st Marine Division during the Reservoir Campaign.

Despite horrendous casualties, the Chinese continue
to strike against Marine positions at East Hill until
about midnight, but the casualties do not deter them.
Soon after, at about 0205 (7 December), the Chinese
launch yet another assault against RCT-5. The Chinese charge and get dropped. More waves follow and
again they are eliminated, but still, even more continue
to make futile charges. The Marines sustain casualties,
but the return fire decimates the attackers. Most of the
killing was observed due to the high volume of tracer
shells and the illuminating flares that spotlighted the
Chinese as they advanced.

By the time dawn arrives it becomes noticeable also
that the Chinese escape route coincided with the line
of fire of the Marines' artillery. One group of about
sixty Chinese had maneuvered directly into the gun
sights, resulting in the instant demise of the group. A
smaller contingent nearby, composed of about fifteen
troops, had immediately surrendered. As the Marines
of RCT-5 check the field after daylight, the estimated

figure of Chinese killed to the front of the 2nd Battalion, 5th Marines, stands at about 800 troops.

The 2nd Battalion, 5th Marines, sustains 13 killed
and 50 wounded. The 1st Battalion, 5th Marines, sustains 10 killed and 43 wounded. To the front of the 1st
Battalion are 260 Chinese, killed at Charlie Company's
lines. At Able Company, 200 killed Chinese are
counted.

While RCT-5 had engaged the enemy at East Hill for
nearly twenty-two hours, RCT-7 had continued its forward drive toward Koto-ri. The 7th Marines initially
seizes its first objective effortlessly when it catches a
small contingent asleep in the heights just outside
Tonae-ri, but soon after, the RCT encounters fierce resistance. The resistance is eventually overcome by about
noon, but again, within a short while, the Chinese hold
another blocking point. That, too, is reduced after
dogged fighting.

By dusk, RCT-7 stands at a point about 5,000 yards
below Hagaru. The opposition had been anticipated
and the order to continue to drive forward had always
been part of the planned offensive withdrawal. The 2nd
Battalion, 7th Marines, advances to what had become
known as Hell Fire Valley, but there, the enemy machine
gun position halts progress until just about midnight,
when U.S. Army tanks arrive to liquidate the blockage
and permit the drive to continue. However, the Chinese also had blown yet another bridge, once again
bringing the beleaguered column to a halt. The troops
of Company D make repairs that allow the march to resume. The column soon after comes across another
blown bridge and still, the Americans continue. After
a delay of about one additional hour, a bypass route is
used and the 7th Marines move along the final stretch
without opposition and enter Koto-ri.

The 3rd Battalion, 7th Marines, encounters opposition when its train is struck at about 2100, but Company G and Company I form a protective shield and repulse the attack, which had come from close range.
More trouble is encountered in the vicinity of Hell Fire
Valley.

At about 0200, elements of Company I, supported
by a contingent of tanks, eliminate the obstacle before
dawn. In the meantime, the 1st Battalion, which is advancing on the west side of the river and clearing the
heights, descends the hills and hooks up with the column, which enters Koto-ri at about 0700 (7 December). During the afternoon, the 7th Marines had pro-
gressed far enough to finally permit Division Train
Number 1 to depart Hagaru at about 1600. Enemy resistance is encountered but elements of the 3rd Battalion, 11th Marines (Batteries George and How) repulse
the attack. Afterwards, at a point about 3,500 yards
south of Hagaru, again the convoy is struck. The convoy stalls, but the Marines hold the ground and following a two-hour conflagration, the enemy disengages. Marine estimates place the number of troops
that fled the area at only about fifty. The remainder of
the force, numbering between 500 and 800, had either
been killed or wounded. Another part of the convoy, the

Top: U.S. Marines, accompanied by Marine tanks, move along frozen road from Koto-ri to Hamhung during breakout. *Bottom*: Chinese POWs captured by Marines during fighting withdrawal from Koto-ri to Hamhung.

division headquarters company, also faces tenacious opposition after it departs Hagaru. Most of the resistance occurs during the early morning hours of the following day.

Division Train Number 2 departs Hagaru after dark on 6 December. The initial units that abandon Hagaru arrive at Koto-ri in just under sixty hours; however, the latter parts of the column encounter more difficulty, which adds nearly twenty additional hours to the hazardous trip.

In addition to the normal day sorties by Marine pilots and the supporting planes from the U.S. Navy carriers, Marine Corps Night-Fighter Squadrons supply limited protection during the darkened hours. Also, for the first time in any conflict, a transport plane is used as a TADC (tactical air direction center). The Marines use the aircraft to continue effective close-air support during the breakout. An RSD is used as the airborne tactical command post. It remains in action for six days.

In the Eighth Army area, General Walker's new lines below Pyongyang stretch from Kyomip'o to Sin'gye with the I Corps deployed on the west, while the IX Corps leans from Yuli towards Sin'gye on the left, in close proximity to the ROK II Corps in the Yekong Valley. Although there remains great concern about the large amount of Chinese that had been in pursuit, still there is no major interference detected this day.

Walker, in the meantime, does get a fresh reminder that the Chinese are around, as reports arrive at headquarters notifying him that Chinese troops have been spotted at Pyongyang. Aircraft take note that hostile forces are also on the move at Chinnamp'o, the port city recently abandoned by Eighth Army. Meanwhile,

a 1st Cavalry Division contingent, composed of two battalions, in search of the Chinese, encounters and engages a North Korean force at Koksan in the Yesong Valley (ROK II Corps zone).

Adding to these anticipated reports, Walker also learns that the North Koreans and their guerrilla counterparts are advancing towards his positions and all indications point to them striking the rear and the east side of the line. Walker decides to retreat as planned to the next line, but still he is unaware of whether the Chinese are poised to strike his left flank. The Chinese, who seemed to be everywhere Eighth Army moved during the latter part of November, remain concealed. The absence of Chinese forces, at least from the sight of the Eighth Army, leads Walker to think that they might well have swerved away from his east flank in an attempt to slide between his force and that of the X Corps. This maneuver could give the enemy an open running field from which they could swarm into South Korea.

A single U.S. soldier with full gear during the withdrawal from Koto-ri to Hamhung. U.S. Army troops, ROKs and some British had been with the 1st Marine Division during the fighting withdrawal.

To counteract this possibility, Walker concludes that he must establish a blocking force (Line A), which will extend across the peninsula from the area near the mouth of the Yesong River to the Sea of Japan. Meanwhile, top level strategy talks will be held on the following day in Japan and Walker, pursuant to orders that emerge from the meeting, will alter the line.

In Air Force activity, a unit attached to the Strategic Air Command, the 27th Fighter Escort Wing (FEW) based at Bergstrom Air Force Base, Texas, initiates missions from Taegu, Korea. This is the first time the F-84 Thunder Jet fighters enter combat in Korea.

— *In the United States:* The Joint Chiefs of Staff forward to General MacArthur in Japan the directive of President Truman regarding public statements by U.S. officials and military leaders regarding U.S. policy. (*See also,* **December 5,** 1950.)

December 7 *In the X Corps sector,* at Hagaru, some Marine elements still remain, while the columns RCT-1, RCT-5 and RCT-7 continue to move towards Koto-ri. The front elements have already arrived, but the column in its entirety is stretched across about a twelve-mile run. Division Train Number 1 had not been able to depart Hagaru until 1600 on the

6th. During the ongoing breakout from Hagaru, the remaining elements of the 7th Marines had entered Koto-ri by about 0700 this day. The 2nd Battalion arrived on the previous night.

During the latter part of the morning, units of the battalion move out to provide cover for trailing elements of the 1st Marine Division. In addition to establishing positions at points between Hill 1182 and Koto-ri along the MSR, another mission is assigned to the 2nd Battalion. Information had been passed to the ground troops that a group of British Marines had been spotted by aircraft on 4 December. The pilots that spotted the British contingents noticed that the word "help" was imprinted in the snow. Other planes airdropped food and supplies to ensure that the troops could hold out until the help they requested could arrive. The men had become isolated while Task Force Drysdale was under attack on the night of 29–30 November. The 2nd Battalion retrieves the entire group of twenty-two British Marines.

By 1700, the remaining units of RCT 7 arrive at Koto-ri. In the meantime, the divisional trains had begun their departure on the previous day and while en route, stiff Chinese opposition continues to impede progress. Artillerymen and others, including clerks and headquarters personnel, act as infantry to defend the convoys.

Also, the Division Headquarters Company convoy, which had departed Hagaru late on the previous day, again encounters stiff opposition at about 0130. Marine Corps Night-Fighter squadrons arrive to provide some air cover, while the Marines attempt to beat back

the attack. The planes neutralize the Chinese until just prior to dawn. By that time, a contingent of about thirty Chinese close against the convoy, which also has a large contingent of Chinese POWs within the column. As the MPs continue to keep vigil on the prisoners, while defending against the attack, the prisoners come under intentional fire from the attacking enemy forces. The Chinese prisoners who had been contained along the road immediately attempt to break, which places them in the sights of the Chinese and the Marines. Of the 160 POWs, 137 are killed. The wounded POWs had been left at Hagaru.

Soon after the fierce exchange, the convoy reinitiates its advance and upon entering the vicinity of Pusong-ni, a brief firefight develops as a small contingent of enemy troops, concealed in houses in the village, are captured.

The convoy, after reaching Hell Fire Valley at about dawn, halts progress. At the time, there is no enemy resistance; however, the troops receive the grim task of surveying the field where many of the members of Task Force Drysdale had died. A detail attempts to identify the bodies of the headquarters personnel and MPs there, to provide information for the contingents that later will arrive to remove the bodies.

Afterwards, the convoy rolls into Koto-ri at about 1000. Other units follow and by about 2300, the only units not yet at Koto-ri are the contingents of the 2nd Battalion, 5th Marines, the rear guard. The final elements depart at slightly after noon, just ahead of the major explosion detonated by the engineers that destroyed the town and prevented the Chinese from

U.S. Marines halt at a bridge destroyed by Chinese Communists during the march to Humnang. Bridge sections are dropped by planes and Marine engineers secure a crossing.

An aerial view of the route taken by the 1st Marine Division from Koto-ri to Hamhung. The mountains are full of Chinese troops. The part of the bridge blown by the Chinese can be seen on the right.

acquiring any supplies or ammunition still in the village.

The Marines at Koto-ri prepare for the next phase of the breakout, which commences on the following day. Meanwhile, planes attached to Combat Cargo Command arrive to deliver food and supplies, and when they depart, they evacuate the wounded. In addition, eight C-119s drop bridge sections to the troops to provide a means to cross a treacherous gorge with a depth of 1,500 feet. This is the first bridge to be delivered by air in the history of warfare. The bridges arrive by parachute. Some sections are damaged and one section lands

Top: **The 27th Fighter Escort Wing (Bergstrom Air Force Base) introduces the F-84 Thunderjet into combat in Korea on 7 December.** *Bottom*: **Marine casualties (many from frostbite) in the vicinity of Changjin Reservoir wait to be evacuated for medical aid.**

within Chinese positions; however, the ingenuity of the engineers prevails and with some modifications, the engineers are prepared to erect the span. Still, the distance between the engineers at Koto-ri and where the bridge is to be erected stands several miles away.

Several Chinese strong points, including Hill 1328, a mass that stood south and southwest of the village and Hill 1081, another huge threat located a few miles north of the village, remain in the way. The drive to reduce the obstacles is scheduled for 8 December. Also, the operations at Yonpo Airfield are beginning to wind down. Marine Squadron VMF-214 returns to the USS

Sicily. VMF-214 had moved to Itami on December 4, but by about 15 December, the squadron will operate from the USS *Bataan*. In conjunction, the 1st Marine Air Wing is commanded by Major General Field Harris.

In the Eighth Army area, General Walker continues preparations to withdraw to the new line, Line A, to be established along the Haeju–Sin'gye–Inchon Line. The operation to pull back is to begin on the following day; however, new orders arrive from Far East Command and the plan will be modified.

Meanwhile, patrols continue to operate from both the

I and IX Corps in search of the location of the Chinese. The 1st Cavalry Division, which had engaged some North Koreans at the village of Koksan on the previous day, dispatches a contingent back to the village this day, but no enemy troops are encountered.

In Air Force activity, Far East Air Forces' B-29s bomb targets in the vicinity of the Changjin Reservoir to provide some relief to the Marines and attached units of X Corps, while they fight their way from Hagaru-ri amd Koto-ri (*see also, In the X Corps area,* this day.)

— *In Japan:* A major conference is held in Tokyo to deal with the deteriorating situation in Korea. The attendees include General MacArthur, Admirals Joy and Struble, General Stratemeyer (Air Force Far East Command), Lt. General Shepherd, USMC, and General Collins, Army Chief of Staff. The group discusses the various possibilities available to forestall disaster in Korea, based on all available information received from intelligence reports as well as the convictions of the commanders in the field.

At the conclusion of the meeting, based on what is and is not considered conceivable, a decision is made to rely basically on the blueprint provided by General Wright of G-3 (Staff Operations and Training). This strategy calls for the sea lift of X Corps at Hungnam, from where it can be transported to southeastern Korea to permit it to converge with Eighth Army to galvanize the strength of both units for a more solid block of resistance against the advancing Chinese armies, now estimated to number nearly 170,000 troops. A series of potential defensive lines are to be established, four of these above Seoul, with the defense of Seoul to be paramount; however, if the positions there become untenable, and only then, General Walker will be authorized

to relinquish it. The fourth and final line above Seoul is to run across the peninsula in its entirety, extending east to west from the coast to the Imjin River. The final lines are spaced between the South Korean capital, with the last one to be set up in the vicinity of Pusan.

In conjunction, MacArthur informs Generals Walker and Almond by radio that new orders concerning the general withdrawal will arrive on the following day.

December 8   General Walker receives new orders (Order Number 5) that establish the guidelines for the withdrawal of Eighth Army and the incorporation of X Corps into Army. MacArthur's order sets up nine specific lines of defense. Walker begins to implement the plan. He switches from his original line to the one designated by Far East Command. The new line (Line B) is nearly identical to Line A; however, as it stretches from east to west, according to MacArthur's directive, at Hwach'on the westward section swings southwest along the lower bank of the Imjin and Han Rivers, which shortens the line somewhat on that side, while it maintains the original eastward line from the village. The defense of Seoul is to be at this line. The various units are directed to initiate movement to their respective positions.

In the X Corps area, the Marines of the 1st Division and attached forces at Koto-ri begin to depart en route to the coast at Hungnam. The Chinese remain in the area in great numbers, yet Koto-ri has not come under a major attack since the night of 28–29 November. The town, however, remains surrounded and the breakout is not expected to be less difficult than the twelve miles the troops had already traveled from Hagaru. About ten thousand troops arrived at Koto-ri

Marine riflemen are deployed along an icy road to defend against an attack during the breakout from Koto-ri.

U.S. planes drop supplies to elements of 1st Marine Division at the Changjin Reservoir as it fights its way to Hungnam.

from Hagaru. The diminutive village, on 8 December, is crammed with more than 14,000 men, including the Marines and U.S. Army troops already there. The Marine garrison at Koto-ri amounts to 2,640 troops, bolstered by 1,535 U.S. Army troops and twenty-five British Royal Marine Commandos. The new arrivals from Hagaru include 9,046 Marines, 818 U.S. Army, 125 British Royal Marine Commandos and 25 ROK Police (attached to the 5th Marines).

While the operation unfolds at Koto-ri, engineers

Top: General O.P. Smith, commanding officer of the 1st Marine Division, pays a final tribute to the eighty-five Marines who remained at Yudam-ni. *Bottom*: Marine tanks awaiting the order to depart Koto-ri.

An armored column of 1st Marine Division prepares to move from Koto-ri on 8 December. A Pershing M26 is in foreground. The other tanks are Sherman M4s.

widen the airstrip to provide access for larger planes to transport the wounded; however, the 1st Marine Division still must fight through the enemy forces. All those not seriously wounded continue with the breakout column. In the meantime, the Chinese, pragmatic in their choices of direct attack against the Marines, continue to mount obstacles, including blowing bridges, but they mount no offensives against the main body of the 1st Marine Division at Koto-ri.

Daybreak on 8 December brings yet another obstacle

into the picture. A fresh snowstorm saturates the area. At 0800, the Marines press forward to take out the opposition in the vicinity of Funchilin Pass, which dominates the route to Hungnam. The heights north of the pass are held by the Chinese. RCT-7 (reinforced) drives south toward the hill mass at Hill 1328. Two objectives stand at the hill, one southwest of the village and the other south, known as Objectives A and B respectively, held by elements of the CCF 60th Division. After reducing both, the 7th Marines are to sprint forward to the next objective, slightly less than three miles from Koto-ri.

In the meantime, RCT-5 drives towards another obstacle, Hill 1457, known as Objective D, at a point about two and one-half miles south of the village. Simultaneously, the 1st Battalion, 1st Marines, head north from Chinhung-ni to reduce Hill 1081, while the remainder of RCT-1 (reinforced) holds fast at Koto-ri to defend the trains (convoy). In the 1st Battalion zone, Company A, led by Captain Barrow, moves to gain the summit of Hill 1181, while Company C, under Captain Wray, drives against its southwestern tip.

Meanwhile, Company B, commanded by Captain Noren, presses against the enemy on the southern slope of Hill 1181. Baker Company strikes with surprise and gains an enemy command post, where the Chinese had apparently been preparing breakfast. The rice continues to boil as the exchange ensues. Although the 1st Battalion had not yet been engaged in a major battle during the period at the reservoir, its skills had not been dulled. The defenders at the southern slope are killed, except for those who flee. Company B sustains 3 killed and 6 wounded. Company A also uses the snow and the element of surprise to take out the defenders on the summit. One nasty machine gun blocks passage for a short while, but it is eliminated and afterwards, the remaining defenders in the bunker are immediately wiped out or killed as they attempt to flee from the crest. About sixty Chinese are killed. Company A sustains 10 killed, primarily from the machine gun nest, and 11 wounded.

In the meantime, Company C holds at its objective on the southwestern tip of the mass, but Company A remains under pressure. At about midnight, the Chinese launch an attack against Company A, but it fails.

To the area south of Koto-ri, the Chinese raise tenacious resistance against RCT-7 and impede its progress. Despite using the reserves, Hill 1328 remains under Chinese control, while the 3rd Battalion regroups. The objective falls on the following day. Other elements of the 7th Marines, attacking in support of the 3rd Battalion, 7th Marines, encounter stiff resistance in the vicinity of Hill 1304. In conjunction, RCT-5, also attacking southward, seizes its initial objectives. The high ground near the northern entrance to Funchilin Pass is taken by the U.S. Army Provisional Battalion (attached to RCT-5) without opposition. From there, the provisional battalion jumps off and takes the ground at the northwestern tip of Hill 1457, against no opposition.

By 1330, the battalion secures its sector and holds for the remainder of the day. The 1st Battalion, 5th Marines, holds at Koto-ri until about noon and then moves against Hill 1457. While Company C drives up the slopes, it joins with elements of the Army Provisional Battalion, and the two contingents combine their strength to clear the hill while Company B seizes the heights and provides cover fire for Company C's assault. By mid-afternoon, the objective is seized and by dusk, night positions are established as Companies B and C form with the provisional troops.

Meanwhile, Company A establishes a separate perimeter along the main supply route. The rear positions are covered by the British Royal Marines, who deploy in the high ground to protect against enemy infiltration from the rear of the 1st Battalion, 5th Marines. Darkness and more frigid temperatures overtake the area and the day ends without reaching the blown bridge. Nonetheless, the Chinese still resist launching a major assault against the 1st Marine Division.

Although there had been no major setbacks, the most grim part of the day at Koto-ri came about when there was no means of transporting the dead that had been brought in or retrieved from the field along the route from Hagaru. One hundred Marines, soldiers and Royal Marine commandos are interred at Koto-ri on this day.

The area surrounding Koto-ri also continues to be the gathering place for Korean civilians, intent on moving through the Communists to reach Hungnam. The civilians are not permitted to enter the perimeter due to the infiltration of Communist troops; however, some medical assistance is offered to the civilians who had lost everything except what they carried with them. One small incident of joy occurs as U.S. Navy personnel assist two pregnant women who give birth. *In the Eighth Army area,* a new UN unit, the Greek Expedition Force, arrives in Korea. It will be attached to the U.S. 7th Cavalry.

December 9   *In the X Corps sector,* at Koto-ri, the breakout continues as the 1st Marine Division and its attached forces reinitiate the attacks to clear passage along the main supply route leading to Hungnam. North of Koto-ri, one obstacle still impedes progress, but as dawn emerges and the skies are clear, the Marines in the 1st Battalion, 1st Marines (RCT-1), are aware that air cover is en route. The Chinese raise heavy resistance, but the persistence of Company A prevails, despite the elements and the tenacity of the enemy. Company A, which had departed Koto-ri with 223 Marines at about 1500, take possession of the hill with a strength of 112 men.

At the instant of victory, the number is cut by one, as Staff Sergeant Ernest J. Umbaugh is killed. Umbaugh had led a heroic mission at the onset of the fight for the hill by charging with a squad to destroy a Chinese bunker with grenades to open the way to the summit.

The Marines of Company A, during the ascent to the crest, eliminate 550 Chinese defenders. Meanwhile,

Top: Marine Corps tanks shepherd the ground troops during the fighting withdrawal to Hungnam. *Bottom*: U.S. Navy and Marine Corps planes pound enemy positions in the mountains in front of a Marine column.

The 1st Marine Division on 9 December resumes its march to Hamhung after engineers repair a destroyed bridge. The bridge sections were air dropped, the first time in the history of warfare that a bridge was delivered by parachute.

Company B, also operating north of Koto-ri, takes its initial objective on the slopes without opposition. Company A's domination of the Funchilin Pass greatly improves the chances of success of the breakout. In the RCT-5 sector, the 1st Battalion maintains its positions at Hill 1457 (Objective C). The remainder of the RCT-5 makes final preparations to depart Koto-ri, scheduled for 10 December.

In RCT-7's sector, south of Koto-ri, the attack advances against the remnant resistance on Hill 1304. It is taken by Company A, led by Lieutenant Hovatter, while Company B, commanded by Lieutenant Taylor, drives to its next objective (Objective C) a nose above the main supply route, slightly more than two miles south of Koto-ri. RCT-7 maneuvers freely, as most Chinese defenders have vanished and those who pop up as conspicuous targets are very speedily disposed of by the air cover.

Company C, led by Captain Morris and bolstered by one platoon (Company B), encounters some resistance at the site of the blown bridge, but the ground is seized, which opens the way for the engineers to bridge the gap and provide the exit route to Hungnam. By 1530, the span is erected and in the process the engineers improvise with plywood to place panels on the treadways to allow passage of the tanks and the trucks. The bridge undergoes its stability test at 1800, when the first vehicles begin the descent. Trouble strikes early, as one of the vehicles, towing earth-moving equipment, col-

lapses one of the plywood panels. The mishap halts all traffic and unhinges the entire day's work. The Marines again improvise as Lieutenant Colonel Partridge assesses the damage and concludes that with some alterations, the span can be adjusted to handle the traffic, if the treadways get realigned at the furthest space possible, setting the planks at points to handle the jeeps as well as the M-26s. Subsequent to extricating the stalled equipment, the traffic stood ready and the first jeep barely passes over with no room to spare while its tires rub against the sides. Nonetheless, the span holds and the remaining traffic follows.

At about 0245 on the morning of 10 December, the vanguard of the 1st Battalion, 7th Marines, moves into Chinhung-ni, a position protected by the 3rd U.S. Infantry Division.

In other activity, Amphibious Task Force (TF 90) evacuates the 1st ROK Corps from Songjin.

In Air Force activity, Combat Cargo Command, following two straight weeks of supplying the trapped X Corps troops in northeastern Korea, ends the mission. The planes (C-119 and C-47s) of the participating units had executed 350 flights. During the operation, just under 5,000 sick and wounded troops are evacuated and the planes deliver 1,580 tons of supplies, including ammunition and equipment.

December 10 *In the X Corps area,* the 1st Marine Division and attached units continue their withdraw from Koto-ri to Hungnam. The convoy had encountered some difficulty en route, but after the delays, traffic reinitiated its movement against sporadic opposition. The lead elements in the convoy arrive at Chinhung-ni at about 0830, on the heels of the vanguard of the 1st Battalion, 7th Marines, which had arrived about 0400. Chinese remain in the area in concealed positions, including the village of Sudong, and other Chinese troops in large numbers are spotted east of Hill 1081 during the latter part of the morning.

Earlier, Company G, 3rd Battalion, 1st Marines, came under attack on Hill 1328 (Objective A), but the assault was repulsed. Once the enemy sightings are confirmed, a massive artillery bombardment is initiated and it is supported by air strikes, which when combined, overwhelm and destroy large numbers of Chinese in the valley as they move southward, oblivious to the horrific numbers of slain troops in their midst. Meanwhile, at about 1300, Company B, 1st Battalion, 1st Marines, pounds against a Chinese stronghold near the railroad, located north of where the 1st Battalion was deployed. With the support of air cover, the area is reduced.

Task Force Dog (3rd Infantry Division) is posted at Chinhung-ni and other U.S. Army units attached to the 65th Infantry Regiment are deployed in the vicinity of Sudong and Madjong-dong, in an effort to keep the main supply route clear. The division trains and the 5th and 7th Marines move through Sudong without incident; however, subsequent to darkness, the Chinese block passage just outside Sudong. Elements of the 65th Infantry Regiment reduce the obstacle. Afterward, it is assumed that the road is open; however, by midnight, the Chinese bolt from their positions in the village of Sudong and stun the convoy. The initial moments inflict casualties on some of the drivers. The trucks attached to RCT-1, caught in the unusual ambush, are set afire, causing great confusion within the ranks.

Lieutenant Colonel John U.D. Page, USA, and Marine PFC Marvin L. Wasson move to the midst of the confusion and restore order, simultaneously eliminating about twenty Chinese at the head of the stalled column. Page is killed in the exchange; PFC Wasson returns to the fray wounded. Another U.S. Army officer, Lieutenant Colonel Waldon C. Winston, takes command and leads a counterattack with troops of the 52nd Transportation Truck Battalion, USA, and Marines. Wasson ignores his injuries and takes out an entire house with several rounds from a 75-mm recoilless rifle. The inhabitants that make it outside are then liquidated by machine gun fire.

Wasson's determination and his actions impress Lieutenant Colonel Winston, who nicknames Wasson "The

The port at Hungnam is crammed with supplies that are being loaded in conjunction with the abandonment of the port city.

Some of the thousands of Chinese dead who tried to annihilate the 1st Marine Division during its march to Hungnam.

Spirit of 76." Lt. Colonel Page is awarded the Medal of Honor posthumously for his extraordinary heroism during the period 29 November–10 December.

Nevertheless, the MSR remains unpassable until dawn. The donnybrook had also cost RCT-1 nine vehicles and one armored personnel carrier. PFC Wasson, who had been wounded prior to destroying the enemy strong point, further aids the cause by pushing stalled vehicles off the road while their cargo of ammunition is exploding.

In the 3rd Battalion sector, 1st Marines zone, the battalion abandons its positions at the Hill 1328 mass south of Koto-ri at about 2100 and descends to join the column. A column of tanks trails the regimental column in a change of strategy to ensure that if a tank stalls, it will not halt the column. However, with the tanks in the rear, other difficulties emerge, as the armor is just ahead of throngs of civilians, interlaced with Chinese troops who pose as refugees.

The forty tanks are protected only by a Marine Corps reconnaissance company. Slowly and cautiously, the tankers maneuver the serpentine paths that are layered with ice. The reconnaissance troops guard the flanks with extra vigil on the trailing civilians. While the lead elements continue to advance, problems develop in the rear when one of the tanks becomes a victim of the weather. Its brakes freeze. Thirty-one of the tanks are unaffected, but the stalled tank and the eight behind it remain stranded about two thousand yards from the temporary bridge at the pass.

Pandemonium sets in when a small group of Chinese approaches the rear guard and pulls off a ruse, pretending to surrender, only to open fire from close-range amid the civilians. The platoon commander, Lieutenant Hargett, attempts to check out the Chinese, and as they open fire, his carbine misfires due to the weather. Meanwhile, the encounter at close-range also includes enemy burp guns and grenades. Hargett uses his carbine as a club and beats one of the Chinese to death, but in the process, he is wounded by grenade fragments. Corporal A.J. Amyotte, a BAR man, takes out the other four Chinese.

As the platoon withdraws, the last tank in the stalled column is abandoned to other Chinese troops and the next in line is also lost. As the reconnaissance troops move forward, they pass the other vacated tanks. Finally, the stalled tank is repaired and it and one other is salvaged. Both scurry toward the bridge.

During the fighting an explosion knocked one Marine, PFC McDermott, unconscious, and it is assumed by the others nearby that he had been killed. The crewmen of the last two tanks in the column are lost and in addition, the reconnaissance platoon sustains three men MIA and twelve wounded. Two of the missing are later reported as killed; however, McDermott later regains consciousness and manages to use a bypass of the blown bridge with the civilians. Later he rejoins his unit. Once the two tanks clear the bridge, the engineers there (believing all able Marines have made the break) blow the bridge. The column completes the last phase of the move from Koto-ri at 1300 on 11 December, when the final elements arrive.

Also, VMF-311, the initial USMC jet squadron to participate in combat sorties, begins its support of the ongoing withdrawal of X Corps. Twelve F9Fs arrive at Yonpo, from where the squadrons operate until 14 December; afterwards they operate from Pusan.

In the Eighth Army area, a naval convoy from Songsin debarks elements of the South Korean Capital Division to hold the perimeter at Seoul during the operation to evacuate the city.

December 11   General MacArthur arrives in Korea from Japan to observe firsthand the situation and to confer with Generals Walker and Almond, commanders of the Eighth Army and X Corps respectively.

U.S. army troops (X Corps) guard a pass about twelve miles north of Hamhung during the evacuation of the port city.

Top: A U.S. Army artillery contingent prepares to fire against enemy positions north of Hamhung. *Middle*: Tanks carrying ground troops move through a village in the vicinity of Kaesong, the former capital of North Korea, during the Eighth Army withdrawal toward Seoul. *Bottom*: Buildings burn at Sibyonni during the Eighth Army withdrawal toward Seoul.

X Corps in northeastern Korea becomes MacArthur's first stop. Following a conference with General Almond, he proceeds to General Walker's headquarters to hold a discussion on the Eighth Army plans to withdraw and on the importance of holding control of Seoul.

In the X Corps area, the final elements of the 1st Marine Division and attached units arrive in the Hamhung–Hungnam sector to conclude the breakout from Hagaru. The 1st Marine Division casualties, since it departed Koto-ri on 8 December, amount to 51 killed (24 die of wounds), 16 missing and 256 wounded. The 1st Marine Division, upon its arrival at Hungnam, had reversed the Chinese plans. The overwhelming forces thrown into the region to surround the Marines and annihilate the division failed. Instead, the 1st Marine Division fought its way along a sixty-mile route, and through the support of air cover, devastated the Chinese forces it encountered.

The fighting withdrawal of the 1st Marine Division, which was at the time unaware that it had been written off by many in the United States, evolves as the greatest achievement of a trapped American fighting force in the history of the United States. Between six and eight Chinese divisions were planted to wipe out the Marines and they failed, while sustaining overwhelming casualties that greatly impeded their ability to mount a full scale invasion against Hungnam. The Chinese up to this point have not yet attempted to collapse the perimeter, which is defended by contingents of the U.S. 3rd Division and the U.S. 7th Division.

Enemy attacks are anticipated from three separate directions: along the coast from the northeast, from the Changjin Reservoir area, and from a southern point at Wonsan. Chinese advances had essentially severed any possible route back to South Korea over land. The evacuation is scheduled by sea and as long as possible, from the airfield at Hungnam. General Almond's evacuation plan calls for the 1st Marine Division to depart first, followed by the 7th and 3rd Infantry Divisions. It becomes a challenging operation to protect the perimeter while abandoning Hungnam.

Also, the South Korean Marines (1st Korean Marine Corps Regiment), which had been attached to the U.S. 3rd Division, moves to the airfield at Yonpo, from where it will be evacuated by air. During the operation, air cover is provided by the Navy and Marine Corps and in addition, U.S. naval vessels offshore remain to provide protection if their guns are needed.

The Allied forces to be evacuated number more than 100,000 men and more than 18,000 vehicles. Endangered supplies weigh in at about 350,000 tons, placing a Herculean task upon Admiral Doyle. His transport group numbers about 125 ships, but the number is insufficient to handle the operation with only one visit to the port. Some vessels would be required to make additional trips to the port at Hungnam. The troops and the transports get additional protection as seven aircraft carriers move into the area to ensure nonstop air cover. The U.S. Navy also had moved one battleship, seven destroyers, two cruisers and several rocket ships into the area to form a line stretching from ten miles south of Hungnam to a point about ten miles north of the port.

December 12   *In the X Corps sector,* at Hungnam, the evacuation operation continues. By the following day, the 5th and 7th Marines begin to board the vessels.

In other activity, Brigadier General Edward A. Craig, assistant division commander, and an advance party are flown from Hungnam to Masan to prepare it for the arrival of the 1st Marine Division, which is to assemble there. Masan is located on the Bay of Masan about forty miles west of Pusan. The Marines are familiar with Masan, as it is where the 1st Provisional Marine Brigade assembled at the Bean Patch following the Battle of the Naktong during the previous August.

Also, Marine Corps reports that division casualties during the fighting at and after the Chosin Reservoir when the Marines broke out stands at between 3,000 and 3,300, including those missing in action.

In the Eighth Army area, Eighth Army establishes a defensive perimeter north of Seoul to protect the capital. I Corps had withdrawn into Hamhung–Hungnam perimeter. General Walker continues to work out the details of the withdrawal lines. With Line B now established above Seoul, the new addition, Line C, is prepared. It will be initiated along the lower bank of the Han River and extend northeast to the village of Hongch'on and from there it will lead eastward to Wonpo-ri. In addition, Line D is drawn about forty-five miles below Seoul, where it extends from the west coast running in a northeastwardly direction through several villages, including P'yongt'aek, Ansong and Wonju, before terminating at the east coast port of Wonpo-ri.

These two lines are to give Eighth Army a buffer zone if they are compelled to relinquish Seoul, but Walker also believes these lines to be mandatory, due to his perception that the ROKs, who will bear responsibility for a large part of Eighth Army's eastern line, will give way once attacked in strength, thereby jeopardizing the Eighth Army forces still above Seoul.

Meanwhile, with the Chinese now facing Eighth Army and X Corps in great strength, all possibilities must be considered. Walker directs Eighth Army units in the north to head south, while he orders ROK units northward toward Line B. During the operation, which continues until December 22, the Chinese remain inconspicuous and only some North Korean troops contest the withdrawals. However, both corps, I and IX, experience difficulty with the unending lines of refugees that trail the columns and clog the roads.

In conjunction, the U.S. 2nd Division continues to rebuild its strength, subsequent to the beating it took during the previous November. At this time it is unprepared for the field and is already below Seoul. Although the Chinese have yet to take the offensive, Walker has concluded that Seoul can he held only if the South Koreans don't fold, for if they do, much of Eighth Army will get caught above Seoul. However, Walker also

The march is over. Marines at Hungnam hurry aboard a U.S. Navy troopship, where they will receive some hot Navy food.

anticipates the IX Corps' arrival, which will bolster his line and give Eighth Army the ability to hold the capital.

— *In Japan:* The Anti-Submarine Hunter Killer Group (TG 96.7), composed of the USS *Bairoko* (CVE 115) and Destroyer Division 32, initiates exercises off eastern Hunshu. The force is bolstered by submarines attached to Submarine Group (CTG 96.9). Also, Command, East Coast Blockading and Patrol Task Group (CTG 95.2) (COMCRUDIV 5), establishes East Coast Korea Blockade Patrol Element (TE 95.22). TE-95.22 is subsequently renamed TG 95.5.

December 13   *In the X Corps sector,* the evacuation of Hungnam continues. At 1500, General Oliver P. Smith, USMC, attends the graveside services for the troops interred at the cemetery there and afterwards, he moves aboard the USS *Bayfield,* where he reestablishes his command post for the 1st Marine Division. Elements of the division continue to board, while the U.S. 3rd and 7th Infantry Divisions maintain the perimeter. No Chinese attacks are mounted against the city. While the evacuation continues, Marine planes at Yonpo continue to strike Chinese positions.

December 14   *In the X Corps sector,* USMC squadrons at Yonpo cease operations in conjunction with the final phase of the abandonment of Hungnam. The field there remains in operation to continue airlifting the wounded from the area. The Marine land-based fighters there move to Japan.

In Air Force activity, Combat Cargo Command initiates its abandonment of Yonpo Airfield near Hamhung in conjunction with the approach of Chinese units.

In other activity, the U.S. Air Force drops its initial Tarzon bomb, which is a 6-ton version of the Razon bomb.

— *In the United States:* In the United Nations, the General Assembly passes a resolution calling for a ceasefire in Korea. A contingent of representatives is selected to sit at a peace table with the leaders of the Communists. It is to be an enduring ordeal, as the Communists, when they do attend, are arrogant and unwilling to seek compromise. Rather, the Chinese Communists, under the wing of the Soviets, humiliate the Allies with a continuous string of unending obstacles as they maintain their quest to wrest South Korea from its liberty.

December 15   *In the X Corps sector,* the 1st Marine Division completes its boarding of vessels at Hungnam and embarks for Pusan. The Marines had arrived at Hungnam from Koto-ri on 11 December. Hungnam remains under the protection of the 3rd and 7th U.S. Infantry Divisions, which are also in the process of abandoning Hungnam. Some Marines remain there to assist with the final phases of the evacuation. The units include elements of the Air and Naval Gunfire Liaison Company and the 1st Amphibious Tractor Battalion.

By this time, the 1st Marine Air Wing has been redeployed at Japan, Pusan and aboard carriers. In conjunction, the initial naval gunfire support at Hungnam commences with night harassing missions, executed by the USS *St. Paul* (CA 73). Also, air control is transferred from 1st Marine Air Wing Tactical Air Direction Center to the USS *Mt. McKinley* (AGC 7). The wing's command post transfers to Itami Air Force Base, Japan.

The Marine fighter squadrons and VMO-6 (helicopters and light fixed wing planes) play a dominant

U.S. F-86 Sabre jets. The F-86 made its initial appearance (4th Fighter Interceptor Group, USAF) in Korea on 15 December 1950.

role in safely concluding the breakout. VMO-6, during the period 28 October to 15 December, executed 1,544 flights in support of the 1st Marine Division and at times, isolated Marine units had contact only with VMO-6.

Also, along the 3rd Division perimeter at Hungnam, Chinese forces mount attacks in the vicinity of Chigyong and Orori. The lines have already been thinned due to the loss of the 1st Korean Marine Corps Regiment, which had moved to Yonpo, from where it was to be airlifted to its new assembly area in South Korea. The 3rd Division anticipated pulling back to the next line on the following day; however, the probing enemy assaults prompt General Soule to pull back during the afternoon of 15 December.

In the Eighth Army area, General Walker orders the 1st Cavalry Division to advance to positions northeast of Seoul to establish a blockage in the event the Chinese attempt to move against the capital from the village of Chunchon.

Also, the bulk of army headquarters departs Seoul for Taegu. Meanwhile, Walker remains concerned about the forces west of Seoul, as their destiny depends greatly on the performance of the South Koreans along the eastern side of the line if an enemy attack commences. A small contingent of headquarters will remain in the capital.

In Air Force activity, the 4th Fighter Interceptor Group introduces the F-86 Sabrejet into its operations in Korea. Also, Far East Air Forces Bomber Command launches its initial mission on a new sector interdiction plan.

— *In the United States:* President Truman declares a state of national emergency.

December 16   *In the X Corps sector,* the Chinese press against the perimeter at Hungnam. They strike heavily against the north and west portions of the defensive line, defended by the U.S. 3rd Division. The probing action is carried out by elements of the Chinese 81st Division (Chinese 27th Army).

While the military commanders continue to control the evacuation of the port and forestall enemy penetration of the perimeter, other problems develop as Korean refugees in large numbers flood into the area. The

civilians create a huge problem, including the inevitability of enemy troops masquerading among the throngs entering the perimeter.

Simultaneously with the withdrawal of the combat troops, the defensive line continues to thin out. The U.S. 7th Division began its embarkation on 14 December, beginning with the 31st Infantry Regiment and other units that had been at the Chosin Reservoir with the Marines. Other units that followed included the 1st Battalion, 32nd Infantry Regiment, and the 57th Field Artillery Battalion. In the meantime, the remainder of the 32nd Infantry forms a part of the protective line. The ROK I Corps, relieved by the 32nd Infantry, withdraws from the line still held by elements of the 3rd and 7th Divisions at the Songch'on River.

In the 1st Marine Division zone, the Division command post is established at Masan. The 1st Marine Division is being placed into Eighth Army reserve from X Corps, effective 18 December. The transfer of all units, except VMO-6 and some smaller specialist units, from Hungnam to Masan will be completed by the following day.

General O.P. Smith is concerned about his Marines, particularly since they had struggled during the Chosin Reservoir operation, which took a high toll on their physical strength. General Smith, soon after arriving at Masan, informs the commander of Naval Force Far East, Admiral Joy, that the Marines had only enjoyed fresh food on three days since they had arrived in Korea. Admiral Joy reacts quickly by dispatching a refrigeration vessel, which arrives at Masan with 50,000 rations of turkey.

— *In the United States:* President Truman issues a Declaration of National Security (national emergency), attempting to inspire Americans during the crisis in Korea. He requests that they become even more neighborly and make whatever sacrifices are necessary for the welfare of the nation. Truman declares: "World conquest by Communist Imperialism is the goal of the forces of aggression that have been loosed upon the world."

December 17   At Hungnam, the ROK I Corps embarks for Samch'ok, where it is to redeploy as part of the defensive line of Eighth Army. Other units that

 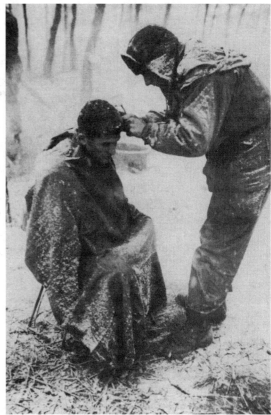

Left: Two U.S. soldiers transport items, including stove pipes, on their backs en route from Pyongyang to the 38th Parallel. *Right*: A. U.S. soldier gets a haircut during a blizzard.

U.S. troops (Eighth Army) erect barbed wire obstacles north of Seoul.

A U.S. Army tank keeps a vigil for the enemy while a contingent of Eighth Army soldiers digs foxholes as part of the defense of Seoul.

depart include the majority of troops attached to X Corps headquarters, which embark for Kyongju, where an advance command post is to be established. The 3rd Division elements in the vicinity of the Yonpo airfield prepare to withdraw to the next line of defense, in conjunction with the abandonment of the airfield. Another temporary airstrip in close proximity to the harbor is used to transport the remaining wounded.

In Air Force activity, a patrol composed of F-86 Sabre jets encounters a contingent of MiGs, the first time the Sabres spot MiGs. Lt. Colonel Bruce H. Hinton, 4th Fighter Interceptor Group, receives credit for the first kill of a MiG by a Sabre.

In other activity, Combat Cargo Command, which began to evacuate Yonpo Airfield on the 15th, completes the operation on this day. During the period December 14–17, the units evacuate 228 sick and wounded, and 3,891 other people. Also, the planes carry out 20,088 tons of cargo.

December 18 The 1st Marine Division, which sailed from Hungnam on 15 December, is assigned to Eighth Army. The orders from X Corps commander General Almond arrive at Masan at 2240. The Marines previously were assigned to X Corps. The Marines, after arriving in Pusan, had moved about 30 miles to Masan and assembled there while awaiting further orders. At Hungnam, the airfield at nearby Yonpo ceases operations. The final elements to depart are part of the Fifth Air Force. Marine squadrons based there had already moved to Pusan and to a base at Itami, Japan.

While in operation during the abandonment of

Hungnam, the transport planes there evacuated about 3,600 troops and managed to transport nearly two hundred vehicles. The airmen also evacuated several hundred civilians. Subsequent to the closing of Hamhung and the airfield at Yonpo, the U.S. Navy commences a thunderous ground shaking bombardment that plasters the entire front. Using a couple of cruisers, seven destroyers and several vessels that carry rockets, the Navy propels 34,000 shells and 12,800 rockets as a farewell to any Chinese troops observing the withdrawal. At the tail end of the shelling, the USS *Missouri* chimes in with the other ships with its guns bringing finality to the bombardment by contributing 162 16-inch shells.

Meanwhile, along the Hungnam perimeter, relief operations continue as elements of the 3rd Division take positions along the lower banks of the Songch'on River, while the 7th Division units there prepare to embark for Pusan. During the evacuation of Hungnam, the Chinese, this day intensify their attacks against the perimeter. The enemy contingents that launch the probing attacks are attached to the Chinese 79th Division; however, as the Chinese encroach, it is thought that two other divisions, the 80th and 81st, are also in close proximity. The attacks fail to inflict any severe damage to the lines, although some temporary gains are made against some isolated outposts.

Also, contingents of the ROK I Corps, transported by elements of Amphibious Task Force (TF 90), land without incident at Bukuko Ko in the vicinity of Samch'ok.

— In the United States: General Dwight D. Eisenhower is appointed supreme commander, Allied Powers, Europe (NATO).

December 19 *In the X Corps sector,* the remaining ground troops at the Hungnam perimeter pull back to the next line. The 3rd Division units initiate relief of the 17th and 32nd Regiments (7th Division). Meanwhile, enemy forces accelerate attacks against the perimeter as it shrinks. In addition to the presence of elements of the Chinese (CCF) 7th Army Group, North Korean units appear in the vicinity. All enemy incursions are turned back as the evacuation of Hungnam continues.

December 20 At Hungnam, the enemy probing attacks of the past few days subside. Large numbers of Chinese remain also in the vicinity of the Changin Reservoir, but there, too, the 1st Marine Division passed earlier without a major confrontation. Within the perimeter, General Almond relocates his headquarters (X Corps) from the city to the USS *Mt. McKinley* in the harbor. The remaining troops along the perimeter covering the withdrawal are placed under the command of General Soule.

The ROK I Corps, by this time, has been transported by sea from northeastern Korea to Pusan and in the vicinity of Samch'ok for its new assignment, attachment to Eighth Army. The operation to move the corps by sea places it in position to augment Eighth Army at its new line. The corps is attached to Army and then dispatched to its assigned position. It will complete the move within the next few days. Walker assigns the two divisions of ROK I Corps to the eastern end of the line.

Also, elements of the U.S. 7th Division, commanded by Major General David G. Barr, begin to embark for Pusan and complete the operation by the following day. Also, at K-9 airfield, where Marine Squadron VMF-311 operates alongside and under the jurisdiction of Fifth Air Force, seventeen officers and fifty-one enlisted men arrive. The new arrivals increase the squadron to a complement of twenty-seven pilots and ninety-five enlisted men. The task of the jets of VMF-311 is to seek and destroy Chinese troop formations that are gathering for an expected offensive.

In Naval activity, the USS *Bataan* (CVL 29) is detached from Fast Carrier Task Force (TF 77) and reassigned with Escort Carrier Group (TG 96.8). A short time later, the *Bataan* is again transferred. It joins Fast Carrier Task Force (TF 77) on December 24.

In Air Force activity, Operation CHRISTMAS KIDLIFT commences. The Air Force takes action to prevent Korean orphaned children from falling into the hands of the Communists. Twelve planes (C-54s) attached to the 61st TCG (Troop Carrier Group) evacuate 806 South Korean children from Kimpo, then transport them to Cheju-Do Island, a friendly-held location off the Korean coast.

December 21 The Chinese in the vicinity of Hungnam still do not mount a major assault against the perimeter as the evacuation continues. As on the previous day, there is no consequential activity by the enemy.

Meanwhile, the U.S. 7th Infantry Division continues boarding the evacuation vessels in the harbor. The remaining ground troops further shrink the perimeter under an umbrella of air cover.

December 22 By this date, the 1st Marine Division and the 7th Infantry Division have abandoned Hungnam, but the U.S. 3rd Division continues to hold the line against the enemy, which is closing at a slow pace. By the following day, the three regiments (7th, 15th and 65th) withdraw to their final line in preparation for evacuation. In the meantime, artillery units and other support contingents are boarding the evacuation transports. Despite the lack of a strong defensive line, the Chinese still initiate no major assaults. Nevertheless, some smaller scale assaults are launched against the line.

Engineers work tirelessly to ensure the imminent destruction of everything that cannot be evacuated from Hungnam. The 1st Marine Air Wing units that operated during the Hungnam redeployment operated from K-9 (VMF-311 Panther jets), an Air Force field near Pusan; and from Itazuke, Japan (VMF[N]-542 and VMF[N]513). The Corsair squadrons operated from the USS *Bataan,* a light carrier (VMF-212), the light carrier *Sicily* (VMF-214) and the light carrier *Badeong Strait* (VMF-323). In addition, VMO-6 operated from various Seventh Fleet ships during the evacuation of Hungnam.

In Air Force activity, the 4th Fighter Interceptor Wing employs a new tactic to level the playing field against the MiGs that have greater speed and can climb higher. The tactic consists of four flights of four Sabres, each arriving on target at separate elevations and at five minute intervals. The mission, led by Lt. Colonel John C. Myers (group commander), encounters a band of MiGs and a donnybrook erupts. The battle rages at elevations as high as 30,000 feet, but the opposing planes also badger each other at tree-top level in a hurricane of fire that lasts for about twenty minutes. Colonel Myers bags one MiG, his first during the Korean War. Added to his World War II score of 24, the hit gives him 25 air victories.

Five other MiGs are downed, including one by Lt. Colonel Glenn T. Eagleston, commander of the 334th Fighter Interceptor Squadron. Although it is Eagleston's first kill of the Korean War, he has 18.5 kills on his record from World War II. The others are downed by Captain James O. Roberts, 1st Lieutenant John Odiorne, 1st Lieutenant Arthur L. O'Connor and a U.S. Navy exchange pilot, Lt. Commander Paul E. Pugh.

Pugh claims a second kill on 30 December; however, Air Force records do not confirm the claim. The Americans also damage two other MiGs, one plane shot up by Captain James Jabara, who later becomes an ace. The Communists score one kill. They down a Sabre jet flown by Captain Lawrence V. Bach. It is the first Sabre jet lost. The downing of six enemy planes on a single day is the highest total for the month and the highest since June.

In other activity, Headquarters Fifth Air Force,

Eighth U.S. Army in Korea, and the Joint Operations Center relocate to Taegu from Seoul.

December 23

In the X Corps sector, at Hungnam, the X Corps perimeter guards shrink the perimeter to the final phase line. Although only the U.S. 3rd Division holds the line, still the Chinese and North Koreans fail to mount a major offensive. Some isolated fire strikes the perimeter, but no damage is incurred. This is the final day in which the enemy fires upon the troops at Hungnam.

In the Eighth Army area, the I Corps and the IX Corps by this time have reached their respective positions along the new line (B), above Seoul. Both corps are responsible for part of the western sector of the line, with I Corps deployed near the lower banks of the Han River and of the Imjin River. IX Corps takes responsibility for the sector covering Routes 3 and 33, in the vicinity of the 38th Parallel.

The South Koreans, with responsibility for the eastern part of the line, have encountered heavy resistance as they attempt to advance to their new positions. In addition, the ROKs lack sufficient vehicles to transport the troops. Nevertheless, the five South Korean divisions, three presently in central Korea and southern Korea and two others attached to the ROK II Corps, fail to reach their respective positions.

Walker, aware of the dilemma, reaches deep and brings up the ROK III Corps and two divisions of the ROK II Corps to fill the gap. The ROK III Corps takes positions along the middle of the eastern sector of the line, north of Chunchon and just under Line B, along the 38th Parallel. Their positions terminate near the IX Corps.

Meanwhile, the ROK II Corps, up from South Korea, plugs a gap along Route 24 to prevent the enemy from drilling through central Korea and the Hongch'on River valley to move from there toward the capital. ROK I Corps, recently arrived from X Corps area in northeastern Korea, has also been assigned responsibility along the line. By this day, its two divisions are deployed on the far end of the eastern line, where they establish blocking positions along the east coast road and at several strategic mountain paths. The addition of the seven South Korean divisions on the line provides General Walker some protection on the eastern side of the line; however, he continues to be concerned about their ability to withstand an enemy onslaught.

On 23 December, Lieutenant General Walton H. Walker is killed in a vehicular accident outside of Seoul. General Walker is succeeded by Lieutenant General Matthew Ridgway. In the interim, Major General Frank W. Milburn, I Corps' commanding officer, assumes temporary command of Eighth Army.

During the morning hours, General Walker's jeep after departing Seoul to check the situation at Uijongbu, about ten miles north of the capital, encountered a stalled column in the opposite lane heading south. While the driver attempted to pass the trucks, a vehicle being driven by a Korean civilian pulled out and while heading south, his truck wound up in the northbound lane. General Walker's driver made an attempt to evade the oncoming vehicle, but the truck and the jeep collided, causing Walker's jeep to roll over. Afterwards, General Walker and the others who had been thrown from the jeep were aided by the trailing vehicles in the column, but General Walker was declared dead at a nearby facility of the U.S. 24th Division.

In Air Force activity, A contingent of 11 U.S. troops and 20 ROKs, trapped about eight miles behind enemy lines, are rescued when three Air Force H-5 helicopters, protected by fighters, arrive and extricate them.

U.S. soldiers and ROKs board LCVPs at Hamhung while the evacuation of the port city continues.

Two soldiers (Eighth Army) in a company area eat their dinner under a Christmas tree. Other troops are in the background on either side of the tank.

In Naval activity, the USS *Charles S. Sperry* (DD 697) comes under fire from enemy shore guns while it is operating at Songjin. The vessel is hit several times.

December 24 The evacuation at Hungnam comes to a close without a major enemy assault. The perimeter remains unmolested by enemy fire. The remnant units withdraw toward the wharfs, while less than ten platoons remain deployed as rear guards. The U.S. Navy provides its guns for added incentive to the enemy to hold fast. Admiral Doyle's warships plaster an area that stretches inland for about one and one-half miles.

At about 1430, Army engineers and Naval underwater demolition units detonate the port, which contains a combination of four hundred tons of ammunition and dynamite, the latter frozen. The gigantic explosion also includes hundreds of barrels of oil and gasoline, as well as about five hundred thousand-pound bombs.

Despite the horrific circumstances of the evacuation of the entire X Corps, plagued by nature's elements as well as enemy forces, the operation concludes successfully. The X Corps, composed of 105,000 troops at Hungnam, is fully evacuated without the loss of a single man to enemy fire. After hearing of the successful operation, President Truman sends a message to General Almond and Admiral Joy, expressing his gratitude:

"This saving of our men in this isolated beachhead is the best Christmas present I have ever had."

As the final vessels depart, there is still quite a bit of high morale and a sense of sentimentality, as greetings of Merry Christmas are exchanged on this most memorable Christmas Eve. Only a short time ago, while the 1st Marine Division was en route to Hungnam, Christmas was on their minds. As reported by the Marine Corps, the optimistic message circulating through the ranks on one particular day had been: "Only fourteen more shooting days until Christmas."

After the capture of Chinese prisoners during the following year, the question of why the Chinese did not mount serious opposition at Hungnam began to be answered. Intelligence gathered showed that the high casualties inflicted upon the 9th CCF Army Group by the 1st Marine Division during its withdrawal from northeastern Korea forbid a full-scale offensive. The damage inflicted eliminated a force of three corps of four divisions each, militarily non-effective for a minimum of three months. Unintended consequences, from a Chinese point of view, included the inability of the Chinese to funnel those troops to attack Eighth Army. Major General Oliver P. Smith later said of the 1st Marine Division: "With the knowledge of the determination, professional competence, heroism,

U.S. Army engineers at Hungnam place explosives on a pier during the last stage of the evacuation of X Corps, 24 December.

devotion to duty and self sacrifice displayed by officers and men of this division, my feeling is one of humble pride. No division commander has ever been privileged to command a finer body of men."

At Masan, Christmas Eve becomes a big event. The battle-hardened Marines are especially thankful to be alive for Christmas. A group from the 5th Marines appears at division headquarters and sings Christmas carols.

In Air Force activity, during the evacuation of Hungnam, B-26s combine with the surface vessels to pound the enemy positions in front of the town, while the final ships at port embark.

Top: The USS *Begor* off Hungnam during final detonation on Christmas Eve. *Bottom*: U.S. Army engineers blow up the docks at Hungnam on Christmas Eve 1950.

In related activity, the 3rd Rescue Squadron (ARS) evacuates 35 former POWs from enemy held ground.

December 25   The Americans anticipate a major attack against its positions on Christmas Day; however, it does not occur. By this day, X Corps' evacua-

tion of North Korea is complete. All X Corps troops are either in South Korea or en route.

In other activity, the Communists cross the 38th Parallel and re-enter South Korea.

— In Japan: General Matthew Ridgway arrives in Tokyo from the United States en route to assume

A U.S. Eighth Army company bivouac area, complete with fresh snow.

command of Eighth Army in Korea at about midnight (25th-26th).

December 26   General Matthew Ridgway, the newly appointed successor to the late General Walker, arrives at Taegu at 1600 to take control of Eighth Army. General Ridgway starts off his tour with disappointment after discovering that his staff (formerly Walker's staff) is so far in the rear.

In the Eighth Army area, the North Koreans at about this time initiate actions against defenses along the eastern section of the line near Chunchon. The ROK III Corps is unable to halt the advance and within several days, the enemy advances from the Hwach'on Reservoir and penetrates the ROK 8th Division lines, gaining about one mile. At about the same time, another replenished North Korean force moves towards the southwest against the ROK 9th Division (ROK I Corps) and penetrates there to initiate an advance that reaches a point below Chunchon by 30 December. The latter threat poses the most danger, as the enemy establishes a roadblock more than twenty miles south of Chunchon.

— In Japan: At 0930 General Ridgway meets with General MacArthur in MacArthur's office in the Dai Ichi Building in Tokyo. The only other person in the meeting is Major General Doyle O. Hickey. MacArthur explains to Ridgway that according to previous information from General Walker, the Chinese always avoid the roads and attack with terrific fire power during the night hours. The discussion also involved MacArthur's belief that an attack against China by forces already in Formosa (Taiwan) would ease the pressure against Korea, but that Washington opposes such action.

Ridgway subsequently notes that General MacArthur displayed no animosity towards Washington for the decision to prohibit the attack. Ridgway also inquired of MacArthur if he had permission to launch an attack. McArthur's response: "The Eighth Army is yours Matt.

Do with it what you want." After the private meeting, Ridgway confers with the chiefs of all the General Headquarters general staff and two others, Vice Admiral C. Turner Joy (Naval Forces, Far East) and Lt. General George E. Stratemeyer (Far East Air Forces). By about noon, Ridgway departs for Korea.

December 27   General Matthew Ridgway, subsequent to the untimely accidental death of Lt. General Walton H. Walker, assumes direct command of the U.S. Eighth Army. Ridgway is flown to Seoul, where he convenes a meeting with his staff and others there before departing to visit each division and corps to acquire first-hand information on the situation among the troops. One area is not on the list, the ROK Capitol Division sector in eastern Korea, as it is not thought to be under threat.

At Seoul, General Ridgway confers with Generals Milburn (I Corps) and Coulter. Ridgway arrived at Kimpo Airfield on a B-17 Flying Fortress, which followed a circuitous route from Japan and maintained a very low altitude to give Ridgway a good opportunity to observe the layout of the land prior to meeting with the Eighth Army officers (IX Corps) regarding the defensive positions at Seoul.

Ridgway directs the generals to establish a line above Seoul and to select specific contingents to control the heights in the event the Chinese launch an attack. Two divisions will be assigned to the bridgehead there. Nevertheless, precautions are taken to protect the Han River bridges below the city in the event evacuation becomes necessary. General Ridgway anticipates an imminent assault.

In the meantime, he is informed of North Korean activity along the eastern line at Chunchon. U.S. contingents are sped to hot spots to defend against penetration. The 2nd Division is ordered to deploy north of Ch'ungju at Wonju. Ridgway is aware that the 2nd

Division had been hit hard recently at Ch'ongch'on, but his grave concern about an attack against a weak right flank compels him to push the 2nd to the limit rather than risk disaster.

Another of Ridgway's concerns is the defensive lines. He requests 30,000 civilian volunteers. By the following day, President Syngman Rhee provides 10,000 and within two additional days, Ridgway has 30,000. The Korean laborers using picks and shovels construct two defensive lines to bolster the defenses against Chinese attack. The line dug to the north is to act as a halting block, but the line south of the Han River is to become the final line, one which is to be held at all costs.

Also, General Ridgway is unimpressed with many of the Eighth Army unit commanders. Rules change immediately, as officers are directed to be at the front with the troops and if they have paper work to complete, it is to be done at night. Ridgway also concludes that the fighting men still have no answer to two basic questions, "Why are we here?" and "What are we fighting for?"

General Ridgway, this same night, pens a response. The message explains that the real estate is unimportant and he explains that the "issues are whether the power of Western Civilization, as God has permitted it to flower in our beloved lands, shall defy and defeat Communism...." He closes: "It has become and it continues to be, a fight for freedom, for our own survival, in an honorable, independent national existence."

In the X Corps area, the U.S. 7th Division, which had abandoned Hungnam on 20–21 December, redeploys at Yongch'on.

December 28

The North Koreans continue to launch attacks against the ROK positions in the ROK II Corps sector. The attack initiated from Inje above the 38th Parallel on 26 December and the penetration continues towards Hongch'on. At this time, General Ridgway continues to assess the situation by visiting the various defensive positions. Ridgway becomes concerned, not of the courage of the units, rather, of the spirit. Ridgway later describes his impressions, stating that at the time, "Eighth Army was bewildered." Ridgway focuses on rebuilding a fighting spirit in his troops.

Eighth Army is taking steps to prevent a breakthrough to the capital at Seoul. The X Corps is still completing its withdrawal from Hungnam after a prolonged fight and is not yet ready for offensive action. Some elements of X Corps have not yet debarked at Pusan.

In the 1st Marine Division zone at Masan, the Marines continue to train and rebuild their skills. At this time, they remain about two hundred miles from the front. The trek to the front, when called, will not include a lot of new vehicles. Only abandoned vehicles are replaced. Unfortunately, the Marines, upon fighting their way from the Chosin Reservoir, brought out their equipment. Now while the other units that lost or abandoned their vehicles in the field receive new replacements, the Marines must use their bullet-riddled trucks.

Also, General O.P. Smith receives word that he is to journey to Kyongju on 30 December to participate in a X Corps conference. The 1st Marine Division on 27 December was returned to X Corps from Eighth Army reserve.

In Naval activity, Fast Carrier Task Force (TF 77) reinitiates its operations off the east coast of Korea. The task force provides close-air support for the Eighth Army elements on the left flank and the carrier planes also strike enemy targets.

— *In Japan:* The first Bell helicopters arrive from the States. They are scheduled to be delivered to the Marine observation squadron in Korea. The Marines have initiated and completed the first "piggy-back" delivery of aircraft that had been flown around one-third of the world in RSDs.

British tanks that had been withdrawn from the 38th Parallel enter Seoul.

Top: A military convoy crosses the Han River at Seoul. A blown bridge is in the background. *Bottom*: A Sherman medium tank transports U.S. soldiers to positions north of Seoul to establish a defensive line.

December 29   General Ridgway continues his tour of Eighth Army positions. I Corps holds the ground westward at Kanghwa Island with the 8213th Army Unit, a ranger company. Heading eastward, the Turkish Brigade is deployed at the Han River estuary on the Kimpo peninsula between the Rangers and the 25th Division, which is posted near Route 1, along the lower bank on the Imjin River. The eastern sector (I Corps' right) is manned by the ROK 1st Division, which is stretched along the Imjin as far east as Route 33, at the Wonson–Seoul Corridor. The I Corps reserve, the British 29th Brigade, holds positions on the outskirts of Seoul.

In the IX Corps sector, which stretches along the 38th Parallel in the Wonsan–Seoul corridor, the ROK 6th

Division holds the left along Route 33, with the U.S. 24th Division to its right (west) at Route 3. At Uijongbu in the vicinity of the junction of Routes 3 and 33, the British 27th Brigade is deployed as reserve. According to intelligence reports, the main attack is anticipated to directly strike at the junction of where the British are deployed in reserve. The 7th Cavalry Division (reserve) is posted along the Chunchon–Seoul Road. The cavalry is reinforced with a Filipino battalion and a contingent of Greeks (Expeditionary Force).

The ROK II Corps is posted at the westward end of the defenses at the 38th Parallel, astride the ROK III Corps. In addition, the ROK I Corps is deployed along Eighth Army's right in extremely nasty terrain, with the ROK 9th Division in the mountains there, and beyond the slopes, the Capital Division is posted along the coastal road near Yangyang, at the far eastern terminus of the line.

The enemy had moved across the 38th Parallel, beyond the ROK III's line, and it slipped through a gap in the ROK II lines.

In other activity, on this day, Major General Robert B. McClure directs the 23rd Infantry Regiment, 2nd Division, and a French contingent to move to Wonju to check a North Korean force. However, the remainder of the division will move there and the 23rd is ordered to Hongch'on. Also, General Ridgway orders the operation at Pusan to accelerate to quicken the debarking of the U.S. 3rd Division at Pusan.

Other steps taken by Ridgway include stringent orders for his commanders. Divisional commanding officers are to be deployed with their battalions at the front and respective corps commanders are directed to be with whichever of their regiments is the most heavily engaged.

In Air Force activity, RF-51 planes initiate tactical reconnaissance missions from Taegu. The RF-51s have a longer operating range than the RF-80s that had been used before the new arrivals.

In Naval activity, the USS *Rochester* (CA 124) arrives at Inchon. The carrier begins operations there as Amphibious Task Element (TE 90.12).

December 30

A plane transporting the body of Lt. General Walton Walker departs Haneda Airfield to return the fallen general to the United States. As the year comes to an end, the new Eighth Army commander, General Ridgway, completes a quick sweep of the Eighth Army area that over several days gives him on overview of the situation.

Ridgway had concluded that an offensive was not possible. The recent clashes with the enemy had drained morale and the X Corps, including the 1st Marine Division, had just undergone a period of intense combat and was recuperating as temporary reserves. At this time, no accurate estimates of numbers or positions of the enemy is known; however, it is thought that six separate armies of the Chinese XIII Army Group are poised from where they can strike the Eighth Army lines. Defensive steps are taken to block suspected approach routes of the enemy.

The 2nd Division had, on the 27th, received orders to move to Wonju from Ch'ungju, to draw a line protecting an approach route from the northeast. Ridgway left little time for the X Corps to catch its breath. He directed X Corps to speed up its reassembly as portions of the 3rd Division were still in the process of debarking at Pusan. Nonetheless, it will be a while before X Corps in its entirety is redeployed for combat.

In the meantime, on the following day, the 1st Marine Division and the 3rd Infantry are assigned to army reserve. Also, the 23rd Regiment, 2nd Division, moves toward Hongch'on, about twenty-five miles north of Wonju; however, the recent North Korean progress through the ROK sector places strong points in the path. The Communists establish a road bock in front of Hongch'on. At this time, the ROK 27th Regiment holds Hongch'on. The South Koreans and the U.S. 23rd Regiment combine efforts to eliminate the obstacle.

In other activity, the U.S. 3rd Division, after completing unloading at Pusan, moves to a location south of Kyongju.

In the 1st Marine Division zone at Masan, General O.P. Smith and a small party is flown from Masan to Kyongju to attend a conference at X Corps headquarters. General Smith is informed that the 1st Marine Division is to redeploy above Taegu at Pohang-dong and prepare to operate in that region about sixty-five miles north of Pusan. However, on the following day, circumstances change and the division receives new instructions.

December 31, 1950–January 1, 1951

As the Communist offensive begins, the Eighth Army order of battle is:

I Corps: From left to right, northeast of Seoul — Turkish Brigade, U.S. 25th Division and ROK 1st Division. Also, the British 29th Brigade stands in reserve.

IX Corps: From left to right north of Seoul — ROK 6th Division and U.S. 24th Division. The 1st Cavalry Division and the British 27th Brigade are in corps reserve.

ROK III Corps: From left to right along central front — ROK 2nd, 5th and 8th Divisions. The ROK 7th Division stands in reserve.

ROK II Corps: The ROK 3rd Division stands at the east-central front.

ROK I Corps: From left to right — The ROK 9th and Capital Divisions along the eastern front.

X Corps: The U.S. 2nd and 7th Divisions at Wonju and Chungju respectively hold positions from which the ROKs on the Eighth Army's central and eastern front can be supported.

Eighth Army Reserve: 187th Airborne RCT at Suwon region with the Thailand Battalion attached; the U.S. 3rd Division at Kyongju; the Canadian Battalion at Miryang; and the New Zealand FABn at Pusan. The 1st Marine Division on this day receives orders transferring it from X Corps and placing it back in Eighth Army reserve.

The total number of U.N. forces in Korea at the start of the New Year stands at 444,336 troops.

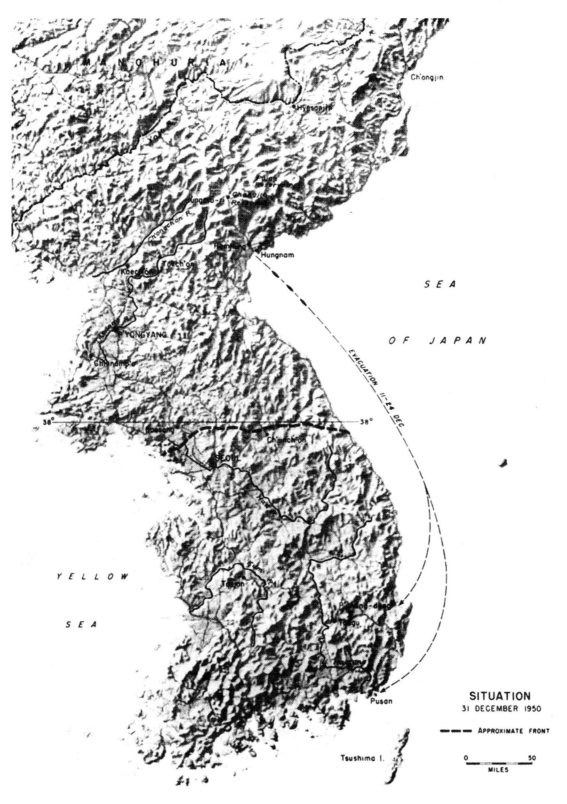

SITUATION
31 DECEMBER 1950

▬ ▬ ▬ APPROXIMATE FRONT

0   50
MILES

December 31 The Communist Chinese Third Phase Offensive is launched. The enemy force includes at least seven Chinese armies, supported also by the NK I and V Corps. The attack force is estimated at about 174,000 Chinese and 60,000 North Koreans. The number of Communists either in Korea or in Manchuria, poised to enter Korea, is 740,000 troops.

In the area north of Seoul, the 2nd Division continues to form in the vicinity of Wonju to neutralize an ongoing North Korean offensive. The 23rd Regiment advances above Wonju against the North Koreans in front of Hongch'on. In the meantime, the ROK 27th Regiment closes on the roadblock from Hongch'on, assisted also by the ROK 5th Regiment. Progress is made against the obstacle, but it is not totally eliminated.

In related activity, the X Corps' U.S. 7th Division dispatches elements to Chech'on, below Wonju, in an attempt to lay the foundation for a supply system along Route 29. The remainder of the division is to follow and to coordinate with the 2nd Division. Other steps in the works include the two reserve X Corps divisions, the 1st Marine Division and the 3rd Infantry Division. The Marines, as soon as possible, are to depart Masan and deploy in the region known as Youngch'on–Kyongju–Pohang-dong.

Meanwhile, the 3rd Infantry Division, once prepared, is to redeploy south of Seoul, in the P'yongt'aek–Ansong region. General Ridgway's instincts regarding a full-scale attack prove correct. The arc (Bridgehead Line) above Seoul becomes threatened. The earlier North Korean attacks that slipped through the ROK defenses northwest of Hongch'on on the 26th are now being bolstered by Chinese forces, which penetrate the main line of the ROK and advance from the northeast towards Tokchong, through the center above Tokchong and Kap'yong farther west.

Meanwhile, the Chinese attacks, which had started on the previous day, strike against the I and IX Corps lines, but the U.S. 25th Division does not come under assault and the U.S. 24th Division is met with only light enemy probing attacks. By about midnight, the Chinese attacks intensify against the ROK 1st and 6th Divisions of the I and IX Corps, respectively. As the New Year begins, the combined Chinese–North Korean force pushes towards Seoul.

In the 1st Marine Division zone at Masan, the Division is again placed under the jurisdiction of Eighth Army, following only four days with X Corps. The Marines are directed to continue training and rebuilding until advised to move to the Ulchin–Yongju–Yechon axis or to assume responsibility for the primary defensive line. Nevertheless, in less than one hour, new orders arrive instructing the Marines to move to the Pohang–Andong region to halt any enemy intrusions there.

1951

January 1 *In the Eighth Army area,* a major Communist offensive begins at midnight (December 31–January 1) and crashes into both the I Corps and the IX Corps perimeters. All units, except the U.S. 25th Division and the Turkish Brigade (extreme left) and the ROK Capital Division on the east coast, are struck. The attack is launched by elements of the Chinese 38th and 39th Armies, while other Communist forces crash against the ROK III Corps positions. Combined, the attacks stretch across a front of about forty-five miles in an attempt to collapse resistance along the 38th Parallel and then converge upon Seoul.

The Chinese offensive follows an earlier offensive initiated by North Korean units on 26 December. The Chinese intervention during the Chosin Reservoir Campaign threw large forces into the war unexpectedly; however, despite the huge amount of enemy troops engaged, the 1st Marine Division extricated itself at great cost to the Chinese. This offensive also involved a large force, initially about three divisions,

with others in reserve. The United States, however, is not caught by surprise and General Ridgway has taken steps to ensure that the mistakes of the initial invasion of June 1950 and the later Chinese intervention does not cause the eviction of the UN from Korea.

By dawn, the enemy makes progress against the ROK 1st Division. The ROK 12th Regiment is driven from its lines by the Chinese 116th Division. The gap is opened as the 11th and 15th ROK Regiments are unable to hold and they too fall back. Nearby, the ROK 6th Division is hit by elements of the 113th Division and elements of the 116th Division, but it only loses some ground and remains fixed. A U.S. artillery unit, Battery C, 9th Field Artillery Battalion, nearly gets wiped out after the collapse of the ROK 12th Regiment. The artillery troops attempt to reach American lines after the ROK unit flees, but they get snagged in an ambush. The troops relinquish four guns but escape capture or death.

In the meantime, General Ridgway is heading north while observing large numbers of vehicles crammed with ROK troops moving southward. Ridgway's attempt to halt the traffic is fruitless. Upon reaching the front, it turns out better than expected, as most of the 1st and 6th Division had not retreated. During the melee, the U.S. 24th Division is hit hard, but it holds, while the U.S. 25th Division receives only nominal opposition and also remains in place. Rather than risk unnecessary casualties, a counterattack is ruled out by Ridgway and the planned disciplined withdrawal is ordered.

In the I Corps sector, the South Koreans are to pull back to reassigned positions at Line C, while the U.S. contingents are directed to move back to the Seoul bridgehead, which arcs around the capital. The withdrawal includes the American Rangers and the Turkish troops from Kanghwa Island and the Kimpo peninsula. Prior to the evacuation, which begins during the afternoon, there was some confusion. General Milburn had intended to hold in place at the bridgehead, but that order is countermanded by Ridgway, who is prepared to conserve his forces by evacuating Seoul if necessary. During the evacuation, the ROK 1st Division is to hold in place until dawn on 2 January to act as rear guard.

The Chinese launch several attacks against the South Korean lines, but afterwards, the area remains quiet until about midnight. The South Koreans during the afternoon assaults withdraw southwestwardly several miles, but it is disciplined. In the IX Corps sector, the 24th Division is able to withdraw without great opposition. The Division, reinforced by the 7th Regiment, 1st Cavalry, arrives at the bridgehead line and with the cavalry deploys on the left. In the meantime, the ROK 6th Division encounters heavy opposition as it moves back from Line B. The South Korean division under General Chang Kuk reaches Tokchong too late to pass through easily, as the Chinese arrive there first, and compel the ROK 6th Division to take a circuitous route. The opposition creates havoc by causing the units to become separated. A U.S. convoy waits at a designated point to gather the division and transport it to the new line of defense; however, at dawn on the following day, only about four battalions arrive.

In related activity, the ground troops receive no coordinated air-ground support due to an explosion of requests that nearly strangle the system. Nonetheless, about 300 U.S.-U.N. fighter bombers (FEAF) are to strike enemy formations and other targets. Marine squadrons attached to Admiral Ruble's carriers about eighty miles south of Inchon participate in the attacks. VMF-323 strikes an enemy position at a village south of Imjin, while another group strikes enemy positions in front of the central sector of the line. Also, Marine Squadron VMF-212 strikes the enemy along the coastal highway on the east coast during the morning and later pounds enemy positions in the vicinity south of the Hwach'on

Reservoir. Afterwards, VMF-212 is ordered to the west coast to support the other two squadrons operating there.

January 2 *In the Eighth Army area,* I and IX Corps withdrew on the previous day to preassigned positions as the Chinese continued to advance. General Ridgway directs the 92nd and 96th FABns (supporting X Corps) to dispatch contingents of their 155-mm howitzers to head north to Seoul to bolster the I and IX Corps' artillery. The new perimeter is manned by 10 regiments and more than 250 artillery pieces.

In the I Corps sector, the perimeter is held by the Turkish Brigade, 24th U.S. Infantry (Colonel John T. Corley), 35th Infantry (Colonel Gerald C. Kelleher), British Brigade (Brigadier Brodie), and elements of the ROK 1st Division, with the 27th Infantry (Colonel John H. Michaelis) in reserve.

The 1st ROK Division, which remains in place, comes under new attacks at about midnight (1st-2nd) and the clashes continue until dawn. At that time, upon orders, the South Koreans withdraw to Pongilch'on. By midnight on the 2nd, the 1st ROK Division is in place, below Seoul along the Han River.

In the IX Corps sector, the perimeter is defended by the 19th Infantry (Colonal Ned D. Moore), 21st Infantry (Colonel Richard D. Stephens), 5th Infantry (Colonel John L. Throckmorton) and the British Commonwealth Brigade (Brigadier Basil A. Coad). In addition, the 7th Cavalry (Colonel William A. Harris) and the attached Greek contingent are in reserve.

It becomes apparent that the ROK 6th Division encounters difficulty after initiating its withdrawal. A convoy waits just outside Seoul to pick up the troops to transport them to the new positions, but most of the division is still en route and in small groups. The Chinese had cut off the escape route on the previous day. The other units, including the 24th Division and the attached 7th Regiment, 1st Cavalry, had arrived the previous night. Troops of the ROK 6th Division continue to arrive during the day, but by the following morning, still only about one-half of the division makes it to Seoul. Communications between the ROK units and General Ridgway's headquarters remains poor.

In the ROK II sector, the ROK 3rd Division is withdrawing toward Hongch'on. On the following day, the division will be assigned to the ROK I Corps and deployed in the mountains in the west near the Capital Division.

In the X Corps sector, General Ned Almond begins to establish his command post at Wonju. The 2nd Division (General Robert B. McClure) and 7th Infantry Division (Major General Claude B. Ferenbaugh) re-enter the fight to thwart the Chinese offensive. It assumes responsibility for three additional ROK Divisions in a newly created corps zone, between the IX

Corps and the ROK III Corps. General Ridgway confers with Syngman Rhee to inform him of his dissatisfaction with the performance of the ROKs, then travels to the area held by the 23rd RCT and confers with Colonel Paul Freeman at the front and explains the necessity of preventing the Communists from seizing Wonju.

In related activity, the 2nd Division's 23rd RCT, supported by the French Battalion, attacks north of Hoengsong, while the 38th Regiment, supported by the Dutch Battalion, advances to positions to the rear of the 23rd RCT.

Meanwhile, in the zone of the 23rd Regiment, Company E, positions on a hill manned by a platoon commanded by Sergeant Junior D. Edwards come under a fierce attack. The platoon is forced to abandon the hill. Edwards, afterward, singlehandedly attacks the enemy position. Grenades evict the enemy, but soon after, they return and again, Edwards moves to liquidate the obstacle. He charges and succeeds in destroying the gun and its crew, but in the process, yet another enemy machine gun opens fire. Undaunted, Sergeant Edwards attacks the third position and destroys it; however, the enemy fire inflicts a fatal wound. Although Edwards is killed, his force is able to continue the counterattack and regain the lost hill. Sergeant Edwards is awarded the Medal of Honor posthumously for his enormous courage under fire.

In the ROK III Corps sector, the Communists also drive against the ROK 5th Division. By this time, elements of four separate Chinese armies are on the attack, the 38th, 39th 40th and 66th. One other, the 50th, is within range of striking UN positions. And yet another, the 542nd Army, stands at Kumhwa.

Also, the X Corps moves up to the front and deploys at positions between the IX Corps and the ROK III Corps.

In Air Force activity, in line with the reversals of Eighth Army and the recent evacuations of Pyongyang, where the 8th and 18th Fighter Bomber Groups had been operating, and the subsequent abandonment of Seoul, the 4th Fighter Interceptor Group completes its evacuation of Kimpo Airfield. The final Sabre jet of the 4th FIG departs on this day for Japan. After dusk, while enemy fire strikes the airfield, the remaining ground troops and pilots of the 4th FIG depart on a C-54. Meanwhile, other aircraft, including F-80C–equipped 51st Fighter Interceptor Squadron and the RF-51-Ds of the TRS, still remain. On the following day, the 3rd, the pilots launch one last raid prior to their departure from Kimpo.

January 3   Three Chinese armies now threaten Seoul with their nine divisions and another strong force composed of two additional divisions is nearby, waiting to push forward. General Ridgway directs the X Corps to deploy and assume responsibility for part of Line C (south bank of the Han River). Five divisions are to hold the positions in the vicinity of Route 29. The U.S. 2nd and 7th Divisions and the ROK 2nd, 5th and 8th Divisions spread out in an effort to prevent the enemy from attacking from the vicinity of Chunchon.

In conjunction, the 1st Marine Division had been detached from X Corps, following the breakout from the Chosin Reservoir during mid December 1950. The Marine division at that time was attached to Eighth Army as reserve in the vicinity of Masan. While General Almond's X Corps deploys, the ROK III Corps is to stretch eastward across the mountains towards the ROK I Corps sector. The ROK 3rd Division in the western part of Korea is ordered to move eastward and deploy in the ROK I Corps area near the Capital Division.

At this time, despite the redeployment maneuvers, a large gap exists between the U.S. 2nd Division and the ROK Capital Division. While Eighth Army attempts to shore up the defenses, the Communists increase the tenacity of the attacks. By 0300, the I Corps comes under fierce attacks as the Chinese plow into the 25th Division on the corps' left. While the enemy there continue to funnel into the corps lines from Route 1, other units moving along route 33 pound the British positions on the 25th Division right.

In a sector held by the British 29th Brigade, the lines explode at about 0730, when the Northumberland Fusiliers on the right are struck heavily and forced to pull back. Shortly afterwards, the Royal Ulster Rifles holding the left of the perimeter are pounded and two of the rifle companies are overwhelmed. Despite the setbacks, armor and infantry mount a counterattack and during the afternoon, following a brutal hand-to-hand fight, the Chinese are halted and pushed back. However, the British sustain about 300 casualties. In conjunction, the British Brigade had been a fresh unit and until this day, not engaged in a major fight. The commander of the Royal Ulster Rifles, Major C.A. H.B. Blake, is among the fatalities.

In the IX Corps sector, during the early morning hours the area remains calm, but at about 0500, the U.S. 24th Division comes under attack. The initial thrust against the 21st Infantry Regiment causes only slight problems and the attacks are repulsed later in the morning. However, the 19th Regiment encounters much stiffer opposition and the 2nd Battalion is unable to hold its ground. After surrendering some terrain, the 2nd Battalion, bolstered by armor and air support, is able to regain the lost ground during the afternoon. Nonetheless, General Ridgway, aware of the great numbers of enemy troops threatening the bridgehead, decides to abandon the bridgehead line and redeploy his forces below Seoul.

In addition to the pressure being mounted by the Chinese, the North Koreans who had penetrated the lines in the east as they drove from Inje are now closing with two corps, composed of more than ten divisions. In the eastern sector, the ROK divisions are still in the midst of a withdrawal and many of the units remain unaccounted for, as communications remain sporadic. Information acquired is not helpful to the situation at Seoul. Reports have the ROK 2nd Division in

On 3 January 1951, portions of Seoul are afire, while the S.K. government officials and U.N. forces again abandon the capital.

A view of traffic on the Hongch'on–Wonju Road on 3 January 1951.

peril with two regiments encircled by the enemy and the other devastated, its strength reduced by more than sixty percent.

In the ROK III Corps sector, the units are still gathering and the C Line is unprotected. About one hour after noon, the order is given to prepare to evacuate Seoul. The abandonment includes evacuating Kimpo airfield and Inchon. General Ridgway insists that all civilian traffic be halted at the bridge at 1500. He places General Palmer as commander of 1st Cavalry Division in charge of the bridge operation, with orders to halt all non-military traffic with use of arms if necessary. However, the Korean civilians cooperate fully, despite their imminent danger at the hands of the Communists.

The I Corps under General Milburn withdraws from the Seoul bridgehead at 1600 without incident; however, Chinese elements are within striking range. Contingents of the Chinese 39th and 50th Armies stand just beyond the Seoul bridgehead. For most units, the withdrawal moves smoothly, but the British 29th Brigade, which holds the rear, comes under attack. Its rear guard encounters fierce opposition slightly before midnight and part of the Royal Ulster Rifles, along with a contingent of tanks, becomes entrapped. Some are able to drive through the enemy encirclement, but about two hundred and fifty troops or more are killed or captured. About ten tanks are also lost. The main body of the British Brigade moves across the Han River by 0330 on 4 January. The IX Corps initiates its withdrawal at about noon, although the official order was not executed until 1300.

The whole maneuver is completed without incident, with the final elements crossing the M2 bridge east of Seoul by 0200 on 4 January. The engineers attempt to take the bridge down, but many components are either frozen or jammed. Consequently, at about 0730 on 4 January the bridge is blown.

The 5th RCT, 7th Cavalry, and the British 27th Brigade abandon their positions by moving through I Corps sector and crossing over the bridge there and again, without any contact with the enemy. All units cross the bridge by 0900 on 4 January. The Turkish Brigade deploys at Kimpo Airfield and the 187th Airborne RCT deploys at Suwon Airfield, under orders to be prepared to launch an attack towards Ichon and Wonju on a moment's notice.

In the X Corps sector, advance elements of the 7th Division arrive at Wonju in search of positions to deploy for defense. The corps command post had been established at Wonju on the previous day.

In Air Force activity, Far East Air Forces Bomber Command joins the attack to bomb Pyongyang. The strike force, composed of more than sixty B-29s, delivers 650 tons of incendiary bombs against the enemy there.

In related activity, Far East Air Forces executes 958 combat sorties, which sets a one-day record.

— In the United States: The Joint Chiefs of Staff authorize the Marine Corps to add three fighter squadrons to its force, which will bring its number of fighter squadrons to twenty-one.

— In Japan: General MacArthur responds to the Joint Chiefs of Staff regarding their recent communication informing MacArthur that Korea was not a place where a major war should be fought. There is great concern that the U.S. might be forced to evacuate

Korea, but the decision had been to remain in Korea if possible. When MacArthur was informed on 30 December 1950, the fateful line was drawn at a point about half the distance between Seoul and Pusan. If the Communists are able to push the U.S. that far, orders to abandon Korea are to be forthcoming.

MacArthur informs the Joint Chiefs that he has no schedule for evacuation and at present, it isn't necessary. MacArthur suggests a naval blockade of China and air attacks against China's defense manufacturing. The suggestions of MacArthur are not accepted in Washington.

January 4 *In the Eighth Army area,* Fragmentary Operations Plan 20 is issued as an order, which calls for a withdrawal to Line D (extending from the west coast at P'yongt'aek to Samch'ok, on the east coast. General Ridgway had not anticipated such a quick withdrawal; however, intelligence reveals that Communist forces have been converging at points between Suwon and Wonju, creating a threat based on the possibility that the enemy might be able to penetrate between the I and IX Corps forces and the X Corps units at Wonju. The move is initiated during the evening and is completed by 7 January.

The final elements of U.N. troops depart Inchon aboard an LST on 4 January.

Top: Engineers prepare to blow a rail bridge across the Han River at Seoul on 4 January 1951. *Bottom*: The rail bridge over the Han after it was demolished.

In conjunction, the 7th Division is establishing positions in the vicinity of Wonju. The process is accelerated to strengthen the line there, while the 23rd and 38th Regiments, 2nd Division, pull back on their offensive posture to form a defense at Wonju.

In other activity, at 0900 at a meeting in the command post of the U.S. 27th Infantry Regiment, a rescue of the entrapped British regiment is discussed, but British Brigadier General Brodie concludes that too many other lives would be lost in the attempt

Top: The pontoon bridge across the frozen Han River, used to evacuate Seoul. After the final U.N. elements cross on 4 January, the bridge is blown. *Bottom*: The pontoon bridge across the Han River at Seoul as it blows.

and it is ruled out. Some of the rear guard troops who had been trapped on the previous day successfully fight their way out, but many are lost. (*See also,* **January 3,** 1951.)

The bridges in the I Corps and IX Corps areas are either dismantled or destroyed. Elements of Company K, 27th Infantry Regiment, tear down the remaining bridge over the Han and become the final unit to depart Seoul. The other forces had completed the evacuation by slightly after 1300. During the evacuation, there was no inadvertent interference from civilian refugees. All civilians had, on the previous day, been prohibited from using the roads and bridges to ensure that Communist infiltrators could not intermingle.

Following the demolition of the bridges, Company K crosses the Han by walking across the frozen river. Within a short time after the evacuation of Seoul, advance Chinese troops enter the city. Soon after, while observed by a small ROK reconnaissance patrol, the North Korean flag is raised in the city.

General Ridgway, although in Korea as Eighth Army commander for only about nine days, remains unconcerned about the ability of his forces to repel the Chinese, but his plan calls for doing it on his timetable. His grave concerns are focused upon some of the upper level officers who don't share his enthusiasm or his determination to galvanize his troops. Each step backwards had been anticipated and new innovation directed by Ridgway already is bearing fruit. He has demanded that all wounded and dead be brought out and not left to the enemy and he has ordered all units to resist fiercely. Essentially, Ridgway is attempting to eradicate what is known as "bugging out."

The withdrawals have not yet been completed, but Ridgway is prepared to again give ground rather than lose high casualties unnecessarily. The I and IX Corps redeploy above Suwon. In conjunction, the U.S. 3rd Division (under Major General Robert H. Soule), in Eighth Army reserve, is attached to I Corps. The 187th Airborne RCT (Brigadier General Frank S. Bowen Jr.) is placed under the operational control of IX Corps and directed to deploy east of Suwon to form a blocking defense to thwart an advance from the area near Ichon and Yoju.

In Air Force activity, most planes and their crews had abandoned Kimpo Airfield by the 2nd, but some still operated there on the 3rd. Despite the evacuation and the fact the Seoul is being taken, a C-119 transport lands at Kimpo to evacuate any troops that might still be there.

In other activity, Captain Charles F. Wright, a B-26 pilot, while on a bombing mission in the vicinity of Sunchon, destroys a few enemy structures and more than ten vehicles. Afterwards, he turns his rockets and his remaining two bombs on a train he spots. The locomotive manages to escape destruction and progress into a village. Undaunted, Wright dives to an elevation just above the trees and passes with his lights on under intense enemy ground fire. The locomotive is illumi-

nated by Wright's lights and it is destroyed. The enemy ground fire fails to down Wright's plane. He returns to his base unharmed.

January 5 Eighth Army continues to withdraw toward Line D. The withdrawal works in contrast to Ridgway's orders of fighting while pulling back. There is little contact with the enemy. During the pullback, a wide hole develops on the east flank as the IX Corps abandons its positions. Probing patrols of the enemy force in the vicinity of Yongdungp'o encroach the positions of the ROK 1st Division, but fortuitously, the gap is not discovered. At Suwon, the situation becomes confusing as refugees create congestion and block the rails there.

In Air Force activity, Pyongyang, which came under a heavy air strike on 3 January, is again struck when 59 B-29s plaster the city with 672 tons of incendiary bombs.

In other activity, the 18th Fighter Bomb Group executes its final missions from Suwon. The structures at the airfield are destroyed by U.S. ground troops before they abandon it.

In Naval activity, the redeployment by sea of the troops from Inchon to Taech'on continues. The operation is completed by 12 January.

January 6 *In the Eighth Army area,* Eighth Army continues its withdrawal, but the pull-back is accomplished without any attempts to maintain contact with the enemy to inflict losses and forestall progress. By this time the enemy is moving south of Seoul. The I Corps and the IX Corps complete the withdrawal by the following day. Also, during the morning of 6 January, the enemy strikes the ROK 3rd Battalion, 11th Regiment (ROK 1st Division), but the attack is repulsed by about noon. Later, during the night of 6–7 January, two divisions of the North Korean V Corps advance towards Wonju and by dawn, both units are in position to launch attacks.

In related activity, the North Korean II Corps advances subsequent to dusk. The NK 2nd and 9th Divisions move out from the vicinity of Hongch'on en route to the area northeast of Wonju, while the North Korean 10th Division sets out from its positions at Chunchon and advances through the mountains, which are undefended, toward Wonju. The 10th Division, under orders to avoid contact, inadvertently makes contact with elements of the ROK 7th Division during its advance on the 8th, but the minor skirmishes quickly cease. However, the North Koreans bump into the U.S. 7th Division on 9 January and heavy fighting erupts.

In Air Force activity, Combat Cargo Command completes its resupply mission to sustain the 2nd Division, which is heavily engaged with the enemy. During the operation, which lasted several days, 21 C-47s attached to a Troop Carrier Squadron land at Wonju and deliver 115 tons of cargo, while C-119s, attached to the 314th TCG, air drop 460 tons of supplies and ammunition to the 2nd Division.

An Air Force C-119 Flying Boxcar passes over some nasty terrain during January to drop supplies to ground troops.

January 7 The carrier HMS *Theseus*, commanded by British Admiral Andrewes, arrives back in waters off the west coast of Korea to resumes air patrols and provide naval air support in that region.

In the Eighth Army area, in conjunction with the recent withdrawal, Eighth Army initiates reconnaissance patrols to re-establish contact with the Chinese Communist forces. Eighth Army is unable to impress General Ridgway, who is determined to change the general attitude with the ranks. By this time, Eighth Army has surrendered Seoul, but it has not inflicted any genuine damage to the Chinese during the offensive that had begun at the start of the new year.

Meanwhile, Eighth Army has been pushed back more than fifty air-miles. The I Corps and IX Corps complete the withdrawal to Line D, which stretches west from the vicinity of P'yongt'aek, then eastward toward Changhowan-ni and from there northeast to the Han River. Strong words are pointed towards Generals Milburn and Coulter, I Corps and IX Corps commanders respectively, from General Ridgway, who becomes infuriated after learning that the withdrawal from Seoul had no contact with the enemy. Earlier, Ridgway had ordered both to make contact and inflict casualties while pulling back. No U.S. troops engaged any enemy forces since the abandonment of Seoul. The government buildings, hotels and other structures had been blown by explosives to prevent them from being used by the Communists.

In addition to Line D, for the I and IX Corps, the line extends eastward toward the coast in the ROK I and III Corps sectors, but still a large gap remains undefended in the eastern sector. General Ridgway had altered the original Line D in those sectors on 5 January. He moved the line about forty-five miles lower to Samch'ok on the coast. The mountains east of Route 29 are

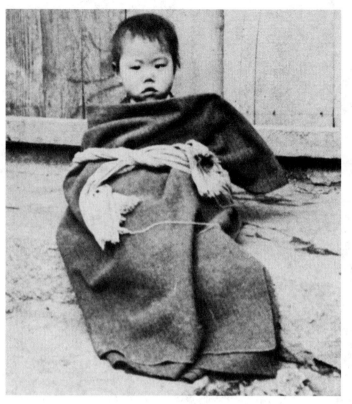

A well bundled South Korean child waits for his parents to gain passage on a vessel set to depart Inchon.

undefended. Both the I Corps and the IX Corps are directed to begin strong patrols to search for and engage the enemy. The 27th Infantry Regiment (Wolfhound Regiment) of the I Corps, pushes north from P'yongt'aek and heads toward Osan, but encounters no enemy forces. The regiment, led by Colonel John H. Michaelis, is supported by tanks of the 89th Tank Battalion (Colonel Thomas Dolvin) and the 89th and 90th FABns (Colonels Gus Terry and James Sanden respectively).

In addition, an IX Corps patrol moves toward Inchon and encounters only small enemy detachments. Other patrols on the western front encounter no enemy forces.

Also, in coordination with the evacuation of Seoul, Inchon had to be abandoned. The evacuation of Inchon is completed this day by the Western Deployment Group commanded by Admiral Thackrey. The U.S. Navy successfully evacuates about 5,000 troops, 2,000 vehicles and about 70,000 tons of supplies. The remaining supplies are destroyed by engineers under Eighth Army engineer Colonel (later brigadier general) Pascal (Pat) N. Strong.

In the X Corps sector, steps are taken to provide a defense in the event that the Communists exploit the hole to initiate a thrust along Route 29. The part of the road from Chech'on that stretches southward to Andong be-

comes the responsibility of the 7th Infantry Division and elements of the U.S. 2nd Infantry Division. At Chech'on the 17th Infantry Regiment (7th Division, X Corps) and the 9th Infantry Regiment (2nd Division, X Corps), bolstered by one battalion of the 23rd Regiment (2nd Division, X Corps), hold the line.

In the western sector of the X Corps area, the line extends from the vicinity of Wonju and moves southwestwardly to the perimeter of the IX Corps at the Han River. The main body of the U.S. 2nd Division stands at Wonju. The X Corps commander, General Almond, continues to bring back cohesion in the ROK 2nd, 5th and 8th Divisions as they continue to straggle into the lines from the mountains north of Line D and east of Wonju.

The ROK 5th Division deploys in the west alongside the ROK 8th Division, which is placed in the center. Meanwhile, the beleaguered ROK 2nd Division, at the time only containing slightly more than 3,000 troops, is assigned as X Corps reserve.

At 0500, the North Koreans strike Wonju. They approach without being noticed as they walk with the unending throngs of civilians who are fleeing. After passing through checkpoints, the guerrillas reach two separate command posts of the 2nd Division and commence firing. Units of the 2nd Division react swiftly and more than 100 of the North Koreans are captured. Nonetheless, attacks are launched against the main defenses, but they, too, are repulsed.

At about the same time, elements of the North Korean 12th Division strike from the west against the 10th Regiment of the ROK 8th Division. The ROKs there are unable to stem the tide. As pressure mounts, the 2nd Division commander, General McClure, unable to contact General Almond, pulls out of Wonju, with the intent to maintain the high ground just south of the town. However, the pull back moves to positions farther back and below the village, where the 23rd Regiment redeploys.

In the meantime, the 38th Regiment withdraws even further, to Mich'on, about seven miles from Wonju.

— In Japan: The issue of abandoning Korea remains unsettled, as Washington and General MacArthur are still communicating without results. General Ridgway informs MacArthur that no evacuation of Korea should take place if it would leave the South Korean forces alone to face the Chinese and North Koreans. Ridgway repeats the message on the following day. During this period of indecision, rumors continue to fly among the units that the UN forces are going to abandon Korea and no one in high command is able to give any definitive answers to quell them.

January 8 *In the Eighth Army area,* General Ridgway establishes two new lines, E and F, as the discussions about whether the UN forces, primarily the U.S., will abandon Korea. Line E is established about twenty-five miles below Line D, while Line F is drawn about sixty-five miles to the rear of Line D. The next line, known as the Raider Line, forms a semi-circle about twenty miles to the front of Seoul and the final line of defense is the Peter Line (previously Pusan Line).

General O.P. Smith, USMC, is called to Taegu to meet with General Ridgway. They discuss the possibility of attaching one Marine RCT to X Corps, but Ridgway does not insist. General Smith, reluctant to again serve with Almond (since his experience from the previous year), returns to Masan to discuss the subject; however, shortly after he returns, the idea is scrapped. A new plan is offered, suggesting the entire Division move to prepare to defend the MSR in the Andong and Kyongju region. On 10 January, the 1st Marine Division departs Masan for Pohang.

In the I Corps sector, a 3rd Division contingent (1st Battalion, 15th Regiment) is ordered to head north. The patrol moves toward Ansong and encounters strong opposition near the village, but initial progress is uninhibited and the artillery had not been able to maintain the pace. By the following day, the battalion, which is imperiled, requests authorization to pull back from its positions more than twenty miles ahead of the main body.

In the X Corps sector, General Almond becomes distressed after being informed how far the 2nd Division commanded by Major General Robert B. McClure had moved from Wonju. One battalion of the 23rd Regiment, 2nd Division, is dispatched at dawn to secure Wonju and its airstrip, while the remainder of the regiment secures the heights on the fringes of the town. At about noon, elements of the 2nd Battalion encounter some North Koreans near Hill 247, but the small group is easily scattered.

Soon after, despite the time of day, the contingent, Company K, discovers yet other North Koreans, and they are asleep. The soldiers bolt from the their naps and head for the hills to signal the arrival of the Americans. During the skirmish, about two hundred North Koreans are killed. However, in the meantime, other enemy contingents numbering at about regimental strength close from two sides, compelling the 2nd Battalion to pull back to positions just beyond Hill 247. Wonju remains under North Korean control.

In related activity, the ROK 10th Regiment is struck by the North Korean 12th Division. The South Koreans are driven back to Mich'on, which creates more problems, including the opening of a hole on the flank of the 23rd Regiment. Consequently, the 2nd Battalion is ordered back to its initial positions to guard the flank.

In Air Force activity, TF-77 is compelled to abort its close-air support missions for X Corps due to blizzard conditions in Korea. The Fifth Air Force takes the task and launches B29s (Superfortresses), which remain unaffected by the weather. The planes strike Kimpo Airfield outside of Seoul to prevent it use by the Communists.

January 9 General Ridgway arrives by plane at Masan to confer with General O.P. Smith, his staff officers and regimental commanders of the 1st Marine Division. Ridgway underscores the need for reconnaissance and a quick engagement with the enemy once the division moves to the MSR at Yongch'on under Eighth Army control, unattached to any corps.

In the Eighth Army area, X Corps sector, another attempt is made to clear the North Koreans from Wonju. The town is strategically located at a point considered a key to holding domination over central Korea. A 2nd Division contingent, Task Force Skeldon, composed of the 2nd Battalion, 23rd Infantry, and the 2nd Battalion, 38th Infantry, advances during a snowstorm at 1000. As the column approaches Hill 247, unprotected by air cover, the North Koreans holding the high ground commence fire and hold up the column. The task force is unable to ascend the hill due to enemy fire, but the unit holds there throughout the day. The task force establishes night positions and afterwards it is reinforced by a French battalion.

In related activity, the ROK 8th Division again comes under heavy attack and for a while, the 2nd Division's rear is threatened, but the South Koreans hold firmly.

In other activity, the North Korean 10th Division (NK II Corps) is intercepted by elements of the U.S. 7th Division at a spot east of Route 29 near Chech'on. The unit, the NK 27th Regiment, is shredded. About 500 North Koreans are killed. Fourteen others are captured and the information gathered is extremely important. The POWs inform their captors of the blueprint of the offensive and they detail the objectives, initially Tanyang and afterward Taegu.

Also, the 7th Division begins to arrive in the X Corps sector. The 17th Infantry Regiment led by Colonel Herbert B. Powell is the first to complete the trek through the treacherous icy mountain roads. Soon after, Powell is promoted and he is replaced by Colonel William "Bill" (Buffalo Bill) Quinn. The 32nd Infantry Regiment, led by Colonel Charles Beauchamp, trails closely behind. In conjunction, the 31st Regiment (John A. Gavin) remains in reserve as it continues to rebound from its heavy losses during the previous year at the Chosin Reservoir.

In the ROK III Corps sector, the ROK 9th Division arrives at Chongson. The ROK 7th Division had arrived at Yongwol on the previous day. General Ridgway bolsters the corps by placing the ROK 3rd Division (ROK I Corps), also near Yongwol, under General Yu Jai Heung, the new III Corps commander. By the following day, the ROK units are deployed at positions from where they are able to block the N.K. II Corps' advance, expected to come from the heights east of Route 29. General Ridgway, determined to hold the ground, also dispatches the 187th Airborne Regimental Combat

Team to the X Corps sector. And in yet another move, Ridgway directs the 1st Marine Division, at this time, Eighth Army reserve, to move from Masan to the Pohang-dong–Kyongju–Yongch'on region.

Meanwhile, some North Korean units had advanced to points beyond Route 60 between Yongwol and Chech'on and orders are given by Ridgway to liquidate all of them.

January 10 *In the Eighth Army area,* General Ridgway receives the plans for the evacuation of Korea from General MacArthur, in the event such a move

Elements of the U.S. 2nd Division move slowly along an icy mountain pass road south of Wonju on 10 January.

becomes necessary. The blueprint includes the evacuation of the South Korean Army and nearly 140,000 POWs, composed of just over six hundred Chinese and the remainder, North Koreans.

In the X Corps sector, the 23rd Infantry Regiment (2nd Division), continues for the third successive day to secure Wonju. The attacking force, lacking air support, is also pressed by the temperature, which dips as low as 25 degrees below zero, while the troops plod through deep snow. At Hill 247, the regiment advances toward the town against heavy opposition. Due to new snow storms, no air cover is available. The attack stalls by about noon. The regiment fortifies its positions and continues to withstand attacks throughout the day.

The intensity of the enemy assaults subsides somewhat following darkness, but the enemy is unable to dislodge the Americans, who dig in on the hill mass. The attacks are costly for the North Koreans. Colonel Paul Freeman's estimate of enemy dead or wounded is about 2,000.

In the 1st Marines zone at Masan, OpnO 2–51 is issued in conjunction with OpnO 1–51 of the previous day. The order authorizes the Division's movement to Yongch'on by road and water, to be in position to plug the gap where the enemy had penetrated the ROK III Corps on the 2nd Division's right. At 0545, the vanguard of RCT-1 departs overland for the Pohang–Andong region.

The 1st Marine Division has replenished much of its equipment, but the division remains nearly 1,900 men short of its full complement. The shortage of Marines has been a concern of General O.P. Smith, but the Marine Corps and Navy speed the gears and scramble to fill the ranks. Marines are snatched from security detachments in Japan, the Philippines and other Pacific stations, while others are gathered at Camp LeJeune and Camp Pendleton. By 21 January, 1,000 replacements have joined the division and another 799 aboard the *General Darby* are about to debark at Pusan. The task of finding and relocating nearly 1,800 Marines and getting them to the 1st Marine Division had been a remarkable achievement and exhibited the extraordinary cooperation of the Air Force, Navy and Marines.

In Air Force activity, the inclement weather over Korea again forces Fifth Air Force to cancel close-air support missions. Again, Far East Air Forces launches some sorties, but it is the lowest amount since July of the previous year.

In other activity, Brigadier General James E. Briggs, USAF, becomes commanding officer of Far East Air Forces Bomber Command. He succeeds General Emmett O'Donnell. Beginning with this change of command, Strategic Air Command initiates a practice that changes commanders of the Bomber Command every four months. The change is brought about to permit various officers to receive wartime experience.

— In the United States: George C. Marshall, the secretary of state, asks Congress to authorize the draft of 18-year-old males through legislation.

January 11 The weather remains nasty, but improves slightly. Far East Air Forces and Fifth Air Force are able to resume air strikes against enemy positions in support of the ground troops.

In the Eighth Army area, X Corps sector, the 23rd Regiment under Colonel Paul Freeman continues to withstand attacks by North Koreans at Hill 247 and again, the regiment holds steadfastly and inflicts high casualties upon the enemy. The regiment receives reinforcements when additional elements of the French Battalion arrive. More support arrives when the skies clear at about noon, permitting planes to help liquidate more of the attackers attached to the North Korean V Corps.

In the 1st Marines zone at Masan, the LSTs 898 and 914 embark with elements of the Tank Ordnance, Engineer and Service Battalions, as part of the operation to relocate the 1st Marine Division to the Pohang–Andong region. The operation is completed by 17 January.

January 12 General William Dean, a captive with the North Koreans, is moved in secrecy from Manpo to Kanggye. At this time, the Americans still have no word on the fate of Dean since his disappearance during the previous June. There has been no word on whether he had died or been captured.

In the Eighth Army area, IX Corps sector, General Church dispatches a contingent of the 24th Division to Yoju.

In the X Corps sector, outside Wonju, the North Koreans again attack the 2nd Division's 23rd Regiment at Hill 247, but still, the Americans and the attached elements of the French battalion remain fixed at their positions. The North Koreans again are unsuccessful and they sustain high casualties. Nevertheless, the weather takes a high toll on the defenders; frostbite, trenchfoot and other ailments strike the 2nd Division. Although the enemy is unable to dislodge the Americans at Hill 247, the North Koreans still control Wonju.

In Air Force activity, Wonju, now controlled by the Communists, comes under attack by B-29s attached to the 98th Bomber Group. Ten planes carry out the attack, which deposits 500-pound bombs that are timed to detonate in the air and spread the fragments over large areas. The new experiment works well and hinders the enemy's progress. In another new tactic, the Air Force introduces Shoran (a short-range navigation system) on its B-26s to improve the precision of the bomb runs.

January 13 *In the Eighth Army area, X Corps sector,* the 2nd Division continues to work to secure Wonju. At Hill 247, the North Koreans again attack the positions of the 23rd Regiment, but the assaults are much less in strength than those launched over the past several days. The final attacks to dislodge the regiment cease during the morning. The overall progress of the 2nd Division is unsatisfactory to the corps commander, General Almond. He requests and receives authorization to relieve General Robert McClure.

In Air Force activity, Far East Air Forces launches a mission to destroy an enemy controlled bridge at Kanggye.

The plane drops a Tarzon 6-ton radio guided bomb and it is the first effective mission that uses the bomb. It scores a direct hit on the center span and knocks out nearly 60 feet of the span. The bombing is witnessed by General William Dean, who is being held nearby at a place about ten miles north of Pyongyang. Dean maintains his sanity by keeping up with mathematics, including square roots, and he keeps a tally on the flies he kills. On one day, he kills 2,866, and he has to hand the results over to a North Korean officer. In his memoirs, he recalled that he would watch a guard who slept with his mouth open and the flies would enter and exit the guard's mouth at will.

January 14 *In the Eighth Army area, the X Corps sector,* the 2nd Division commander, Major General Robert L. McClure, is relieved. He is succeeded by Major General Clark L. Ruffner. McClure had only been in command for about one month. Historians give various reasons for his dismissal — some say political reasons, due to his differences with Almond, and others claim incompetence.

Upon McClure's relief, General Collins appoints him commander of the 6th Division back in the States at Fort Ord, but the damage is done and McClure's career is essentially over. He retires the following year. The assistant division commander, General George Stewart, is also a new appointment.

In other activity, elements of the 2nd Division continue trying to secure Wonju. The 23rd Regiment at Hill 247 is no longer under attack by the North Korean V Corps. The ROK 8th Division also receives a reprieve, as the North Korean V Corps ceases all activity against it as well as the area south of Wonju. The N.K. V Corps, under General Pang, has sustained extremely high casualties and its supplies and ammunition are extremely low.

Intelligence recently gathered from captives of the N.K. II Corps' 10th Division prompts General Ridgway to switch priorities. Rather than seizing Wonju, the focus moves to Tanyang, an objective of the N.K. II Corps offensive. The ROK 8th Division at Chech'on is redeployed at Tanyang. In conjunction, the 2nd Division deploys along a twenty-two mile section from Chech'on to the Han River, which covers the gap created in the western part of the sector with the redeployment of the ROK 8th Division.

In Air Force activity, elements of the 4th Fighter Interceptor Wing and the 27th Fighter Escort Group are ordered back to Korea from Japan. The units move to Taegu. The initial mission is air-to-ground bombing. After about 150 sorties, the F-86A Sabre jets of the 4th Interceptor Squadron return to their normal missions, without complaints from the pilots. Also, missions by the F-84E Thunderjets are not a fair match for the MiGs; however, the pilots do more than hold their own.

In Naval activity, a frigate, the *Prasae* of Thailand, which had grounded on 7 January, is destroyed by friendly naval gunfire from vessels of the East Coast Blockading and Patrol Task Group (TG 95.2).

January 15 General Collins, USA, and General Hoyt S. Vandenberg arrive in Korea to confer with General MacArthur and inform him of the president's views regarding the evacuation plans. MacArthur is told to stall as long as possible to protect Eighth Army and that in addition to evacuating the ROK Army, all South Korean government officials and the entire SK Police Force is to also be evacuated. After the conference, Collins and Vandenberg move to Korea to confer with General Ridgway at Taegu. General Collins, afterward, speaks to the press in an effort to quell rumors with regard to the possibility of abandoning Korea. He states: "As of now, we are going to stay and fight."

In the Eighth Army area, since 1 December of the previous year to this day, Eighth Army has been compelled to relinquish about 200 miles. It is the largest surrender of ground in such a short period in the history of the United States. The results have devastated morale; however, General Ridgway remains convinced that the leadership problems, as well as the discipline of Eighth Army, can be restored to transform the troops into a victorious army. An exception is the 1st Marine Division. Ridgway concurs with General O.P. Smith that the Marines, despite a horrendous 13-day fighting withdrawal at the Chosin Reservoir, have high morale and that they have lost none of their fighting ability.

In the I Corps sector, patrols continue, but little contact is made with the enemy. At this time, a North Korean offensive is ongoing, but it is not making any gains. Meanwhile, intelligence gathered suggests that Chinese forces are moving southward below Seoul. General Ridgway orders Eighth Army to initiate strong reconnaissance missions in the western sector. The I Corps is ordered to dispatch a contingent, including tanks and infantry (27th Regiment, 25th Division), artillery and engineers to Line D, in the Suwan–Osan region. The mission is called Operation WOLFHOUND. Marine squadron VMF-212 (CVE *Bataan*) and land-based Air Force planes support the advance and a battalion from the U.S. 3rd Division protects its right flank. The situation in the IX Corps sector is identical to that of the I Corps area.

In the IX Corps sector, General Coulter orders the ROK 6th Division to deploy in the vicinity of Kumyangjang-ni to protect the eastern part of Eighth Army's positions.

In related activity, elements of the 15th Regiment, U.S. 3rd Division, bolstered by a contingent of tanks, also moves along the identical route, but along Route 20 it encounters heavy resistance that prevents the unit from reaching Suwon. The opposition against the 3rd Division is the only resistance encountered by Operation WOLFHOUND. Despite no resistance, progress is slow due to the conditions of the roads and bridges, many of which have been badly damaged. The main body of the 27th Regiment (25th Division), reinforced, halts for the day near Osan. The force includes the 89th Tank Battalion, 8th Field Artillery Battalion, Battery B, 90th Field Artillery Battalion, 65th Engineer Battalion, 25th Reconnaissance Company, elements of the

25th Signal Company and two tactical air control contingents. The 1st Battalion, 27th Regiment, and its accompanying tanks halt progress in the vicinity of Paranjang near the coast.

In the X Corps sector, North Korean forces continue to close against Tanyang and Chech'on. The X Corps remains active and frequent patrols are dispatched in search of the enemy. The North Korean 10th Division, which received a pounding earlier by the U.S. 7th Division, continues to act as vanguard of the North Korean II Corps. The regiment is heading for Andong. The weather remains nasty and it is also taking a toll on the Communist forces as they advance. At times, temperatures drop to more than twenty degrees below zero.

— *In Japan:* An advance detachment of Marine Air Group 33 arrives at Bofu to initiate work on an airfield that had been rejected for use by the Air Force. On the following day, Seabees arrive to begin the heavy construction. The Navy initially declines the field, claiming it could not furnish the money for an Air Force field to be used temporarily by the Marines. However, the Air Force agrees to pay for the steel planking on the runways and the Navy agrees.

In conjunction, in Korea, repairs are being made on K-1 field, but until both airfields are operational, the only Marine squadron in combat is VMF-212, which operates from the carrier USS *Bataan.*

January 16 Marine Fighter Squadron VMF-311, which has been experiencing mechanical and other problems, is grounded. The jets had been operating, but not adequately. VMF-311 is the solitary Marine jet squadron in Korea. Marine Fighter Squadrons 323 and 214, aboard the USS *Badoeng Strait* (CVE 116) and the USS *Sicily* (CVE 118) move to Itami, Japan.

In the Eighth Army area, I Corps sector, two separate columns of the 27th Regiment arrive at Suwon from Routes 1 and 39. By early afternoon, no opposition is encountered except for a few Chinese stragglers. The units executing Operation WOLFHOUND are ordered to retire to the Chinwi River.

In conjunction, a small company-sized contingent moves towards Suwon to clear it of any enemy. No enemy forces are spotted along the southwestern fringes of the town, but after moving onto Route 1, the contingent is attacked by Chinese troops. A firefight ensues for about one-half hour. Afterwards, the unit moves on as air cover arrives to strike the enemy positions. Chinese troop formations near Suwon and Kumyangjang signal alarms within Eighth Army. Rather than risk a penetration that might get Communist troops to the rear of the 27th Regiment and the 89th FABn, both units are ordered to redeploy below Osan. The plan anticipates pursuit by the Chinese; however, the enemy does not advance.

In the X Corps sector, strong patrols maintain a presence and sporadic encounters with the enemy cut into the manpower. The Communists' resupply system is poor and as time elapses, the combination of casualties (due to weather and X Corps resistance) and ammunition shortages work against the N.K. II Corps and in the favor of X Corps.

In the 1st Marines zone in the Pohang–Andong region, the division command post is established at Sinhung.

January 17 *In the Eighth Army area, X Corps sector,* the North Korean V Corps is unable to knock out the 23rd Regiment below Wonju and sustains high casualties in the process. It withdraws from the region and redeploys in the vicinity of Hoengsong. In the meantime, the N.K. II Corps continues its advance, but progress is sluggish. The X Corps troops continue to punish the columns, which are also badgered by the inclement weather. To make the North Koreans' journey even more difficult, General Almond had earlier ordered the destruction of all structures that might be used by the Communists to avoid the freezing temperatures.

In Naval activity, the USS *Bataan* (CVL 29), along with Destroyer Division 72, arrives and relieves the HMS *Theseus* and accompanying destroyers. The armada assumes responsibility as Carrier Task Element (TE 95.11).

In Air Force activity, a contingent of F-86s attached to the 4th Fighter Interceptor Group initiates operations at Taegu. The Sabre jets execute their initial fighter bomber sorties in air-to-ground missions. The planes carry out close-air support missions, but they also execute reconnaissance missions. The pilots of the Sabres remain concerned about the advantage of the MiGs and continue to request heavier ammunition. The consensus is that the only sure way for a MiG to be knocked out is to maneuver to its rear and kill it from close range. Consequently, a miss from close range also places the Sabre pilot in additional danger. The MiGs operate in the area which is in close proximity to their bases, which usually places them at a higher elevation with the option of choosing when to attack.

In other activity, due to a shortage (only three remain in the theater) of radio guided bombs, Far East Air Forces suspends Tarzon bombing missions. The few available bombs are retained in the event they are needed for an emergency. In conjunction, between this day and the following day, Combat Cargo Command executes 109 sorties by C-119s to maintain a steady drop of supplies and ammunition to the front lines.

— *In Japan:* General Collins, subsequent to his visit along with General Vandenberg, USAF, to Korea, returns to Japan. The short tour invigorated their outlook on the situation in Korea and it convinced them General Ridgway had things under control. Ridgway's positive outlook and their personal observations present a different picture than that which is held by General MacArthur, who only about one week ago believed Korea to be untenable. After finding morale and attitudes higher than previously thought, General Collins focuses on the weaknesses of Eighth Army and concludes that the most vulnerable point is within the X Corps sector at Wonju.

January 18 *In the Eighth Army area, X Corps sector,* patrols continue to search for North Korean forces, but on this day, no complete contingents are encountered. The opposition is confined to small groups, signifying the effectiveness of the X Corps patrols.

In the 1st Marine Division sector, the Marines move out from the Pohang-dong–Andong–Yongdok region on a search and destroy mission against the North Korean guerrillas and the N.K. 10th Division. The defensive perimeter includes the town of Pohang, about 65 miles north of Pusan, along the western shore of Yongil Man, a bay within the defensive perimeter, about five miles above the command post at Sinhung. Pohang contains two jetties with ten feet of water alongside to provide a place for landing craft to debark troops and equipment. The line swings out from Pohang to Yongch'on and then begins to circle through Uihung, Ulsong and Andong, from where it swings back towards the coast at Yongok, north of Pohang.

The primary task of the Marines is to keep the 75 mile stretch of the MSR from Pohang to Andong clear. However, the new sector assigned to the 1st Marine Division encompasses 1,600 square miles, much of which is mountainous terrain. By this date, the N.K. 10th Division is within several miles of Andong and intelligence has ascertained that guerrilla operations are ongoing as far west as Tanyang and as far south as Taejon, which threatens the MSR of the I Corps. Nevertheless, the Marines search much terrain; however, up to this point, there is only sporadic contact with any considerable enemy forces.

In one instance on this day, a patrol of the 3rd Battalion, 1st Marines, comes upon a group of N.K. troops east of Andong, but the soldiers flee with Marines in pursuit. Most escape, but three are captured and identified as members of the N.K. 27th Infantry, 25th Division, which had been devastated during the Inchon operation of the previous September. Subsequent to its rehabilitation, the division, now led by Major General Lee Ban Nam, is engaged in guerrilla operations. With the capture of the three enemy troops, the enemy division, which had been concealing its location, has been discovered. Consequently, the mission is terminated before a strike could be launched against the rear of X Corps.

January 19 *In the Eighth Army area,* by this time, at least five enemy divisions are operating against Eight Army; however, there is no cohesiveness and the offensive that began on 7 January has lost all its tenacity. General Ridgway, meanwhile, continues to strengthen his foundation, while he prepares to launch a strong counteroffensive. The North Korean II Corps is no longer in a position to inflict much damage. The N.K. 2nd, 9th, 27th and 31st Divisions each have sustained heavy casualties and the commander, General Hyon Choe, is about to order a withdrawal. Choe's 10th Division near Andong is also close to collapse.

In the X Corps sector, a patrol from the 38th Regiment discovers that Wonju is not heavily defended.

Once General Almond is informed of the slim defenses, he instructs the 2nd Division to retake the town. The 9th Infantry Regiment is selected for the task. The 2nd Battalion is transformed into a task force with supporting elements that include Company E, 38th Infantry, a contingent of tanks, and a unit of the 15th FABn. The task force, led by Colonel Cesidio V. Barberis, bumps into some stiff resistance. Following a fierce fight with the frequent use of grenades and bayonets, the enemy is vanquished and the objective is gained. Following the seizure, patrols of the 1st and 2nd Battalions probe to the north, northeast and northwest. A large North Korean force is detected at Hoengsong, but the troops withdraw under fire and the patrol briefly enters the town before returning to Wonju.

In Air Force activity, Far East Air Forces begins a campaign to try to stem the flow of enemy supplies and reinforcements from reaching the front lines. The air campaign, which continues for three weeks, is carried out by fighters, light bombers and medium bombers.

In Naval activity, the USS *Leyte Gulf* (CV 32), attached to Fast Carrier Task Force (TF 77), completes its tour. It is detached and soon after, on 26 January, it departs for the United States. Also, Escort Task Group (TG 95.5) is activated, which bolsters the United Nations Blockading and Escort Force (TF 95) with seven additional frigates.

In other activity, a contingent of the Underwater Demolition Team (UDT 1) is spotted by an enemy patrol while it is engaged in a surveying mission on the west coast of Korea. The unit, attached to the USS *Horace A. Bass* (APD 124), sustains 2 killed, 5 wounded.

January 20 General MacArthur arrives in Korea from Japan to confer with General Ridgway at Taegu; however, he also meets with the press and states that the UN intends to remain in Korea and will not be ousted by the Communists. He emphasizes that they will remain as long as the UN intends them to stay. The visit seems out of the ordinary, as the offensive ordered by Ridgway had already begun. Nevertheless, MacArthur's staff states that his visit was to personally give his approval for the action.

In the Eighth Army area, General Almond is directed by General Ridgway to initiate infantry patrols, bolstered by armor, and dispatch them into the area along the Yonju–Wonju Line to intercept enemy units that attempt to seal off the region. In addition, the patrols are designed to prevent the North Koreans from launching operations south of the line. The patrols are in conjunction with the reconnaissance operations initiated by Ridgway on 15 January.

It had recently been concluded that the Communists had decreased the numbers of their forward units along the P'yongt'aek–Samch'ok Line and Ridgway intends to take advantage. The respective corps commanders are directed to initiate brief but vicious attacks to intimidate the enemy and throw them off balance to prevent them from launching a new attack.

In Air Force activity, after an absence of several weeks,

MiG-15s are again spotted in the skies by U.S. F84s. This is the first time the MiG-15s encounter the F-84s. No losses are reported.

In Naval activity, Amphibious Task Force (TF 90) initiates an operation to transfer Communist prisoners from South Korea to the island of Joje-do and to transport civilian refugees to the island of Oheju-Do.

January 21   General Ridgway issues a statement that stipulates his considered opinion on why the troops are in Korea, an apparent response to the questions that have been lingering since the start of the conflict, "Why are we here?" and "What are we fighting for?" He says: "In the final analysis, the issue now joined right here in Korea is whether Communism or individual freedom shall prevail; whether the flight of fear-driven people we have witnessed here shall be checked, or shall at some future time, however distant, engulf our own loved ones in all its misery and despair. Those are the things for which we fight...."

In the Eighth Army area, 1st Marine Division sector, the Marines continue to search for guerrillas, but still, the enemy remains evasive.

Also, the 1st Korean Marine Corps Regiment is attached to the 1st Marine Division. The four battalions of the regiment are directed to depart Chinhae for Pohang. Some are carried by LSTs and others move overland by convoy. A regimental command post is established at Yongdok, along the coast, north of Pohang.

In the IX Corps sector, a contingent (one battalion) of the 24th Division, bolstered by artillery, deploys at Ich'on.

In Air Force activity, a force of 12 MiG-15s attack U.S. planes this day and the superior numbered enemy force is able to down one RF-80 and one F-84 Shooting Star. An MiG-15 is downed by Lt. Colonel William E. Bertram, commanding officer, 523rd Fighter Bomber Squadron, 27th Fighter Escort Group. Bertram receives credit for the first victory by a USAF F-84 Thunderjet over an MiG-15.

In conjunction, this is the first major battle between the Chinese pilots and the Americans. The Chinese, between combat losses and accidents, primarily the latter, are compelled to seek more training. The Chinese 4th Air Division is withdrawn from its base at Antung and Russian pilots assume responsibility in the area known as MiG Alley.

January 22   Marine Squadron VMF(N)-513, which had arrived from Japan to replace VMF-311 jet squadron, executes its initial combat mission from K-9 field. Squadron VMF(N)-513 had been based at Itazuke, Japan, until transferred to replace the jets at Pusan, which had engineering problems.

In the Eighth Army area, IX Corps sector, a unit (TF Johnson) under Colonel Harold K. Johnson is formed for a one-day advance. Task Force Johnson is composed of the 70th Tank Battalion (Henry Zeien) and the 3rd Battalion, 8th Cavalry (1st Cavalry Division), reinforced with a company of 8th Cavalry's heavy mortar company. On the right, the task force is supported by the

2nd Battalion, 5th Infantry, and on the left by elements of the 7th Infantry.

Another contingent, the 1st Battalion, 35th Regiment, 25th Division, advances with tanks of the 89th Tank Battalion in support and heads towards Suwon as a feint to divert attention from the main attack. The task force moves out at 0530. It advances northward to a point about five miles east of Kumyangjang-ni. No enemy forces are encountered en route to Yangji-ri, indicating no organized opposition below Route 20; however, resistance is later met in the high ground above the town.

One part of the force moves east toward Och'on-ni, against no opposition. The other group moves west and encounters slight opposition, which is repelled by an air strike. En route back to friendly lines, the identical unit encounters another small enemy force and drives it away. The clash costs the task force two killed and five wounded; but the enemy loses fifteen killed. Air strikes kill an estimated fifty additional enemy troops.

In conjunction, the 7th Infantry seizes Kumyangjang, while the 2nd Battalion, 5th Infantry, advances toward Ich'on, where the Communists are engaged with an Australian patrol. The 5th Infantry contingent moves against the enemy and afterward moves into Ich'on.

Also, the 35th Regiment is able to make exceptional progress. It reaches and retakes Osan, which provides the 25th Division with strong positions slightly beyond the town, which they use to establish roadblocks. The 35th Regiment is out front, with the 24th Infantry south of it. Farther to the rear, a British contingent is deployed on Line D.

The entire operation had been executed for purposes of encountering and killing the enemy while gathering intelligence. TF Johnson had encountered few enemy troops; however, the operation is deemed a success for several reasons, including the new spirit of the troops, but most importantly for confirming that neither the I Corps or IX Corps fronts are under any serious threat from the Communists.

In the X Corps sector, little contact is made with the North Koreans.

In the 1st Marine Division sector, the situation is identical. The Marines' clearing operation continues for more than two weeks, but without any intense contact with the enemy. On this day, a patrol of the 1st Battalion, 1st Marines, discovers a guerrilla contingent attempting to conceal itself southeast of Andong, in the vicinity of Mukkye-dong. The Marines sustain no casualties during the engagement. The Communists vanish into the darkness.

   — In Japan: The airfield at Bofu is prepared to begin operations. Lieutenant Colonel Paul J. Fontana, USMC, establishes the MAG-33 command post.

January 23   *In the Eighth Army area,* General Henry I. Hodes, chief of staff to General Ridgway, directs General Almond to ensure that X Corps maintains contact with the IX Corps at Yoju to keep the

A contingent of the 25th Division is en route to Osan on 23 January 1951.

pressure on the enemy and prevent them from operating south of the Yoju–Wonju Road. The directive is in conjunction with an offensive that is ordered by Ridgway, scheduled to be executed on 25 January.

In other activity, the NK 10th Division (NK II Corps) is ordered by the corps commander, General Choe, to cease its offensive and attempt to retire toward P'yongch'ang. The order is issued with a stipulation that if the division is unable to backtrack, due to the X Corps' blocking its path northward and the 1st Marine Division scouring the area below, the unit is to initiate guerrilla tactics. The beleaguered North Koreans begin to move northward, faced with the task of evading both X Corps patrols and the Marines.

On the following day, the remainder of the enemy corps also initiates a retreat. Also, intelligence reports that the majority of the enemy forces are located in the area below Seoul near Route 20 and farther north and east along the Han River.

In related activity, VMF-212, aboard the light carrier USS *Bataan,* is the only Marine squadron operating at this time. While scouring the west coast and providing cover for the 1st Marine Division since the 16th, the squadron detects Chinese forces entrenched along the coast as far back as sixty miles from the lines. The discovery indicates that the enemy has learned lessons from Inchon, and exposes their apprehension about the Marines' ability to execute amphibious landings.

Three of the planes had been hit by small arms fire on the third day of operations and one of the planes, piloted by Captain Russell G. Patterson, Jr., was downed. Patterson crashed behind enemy lines; however, a daring helicopter rescue saved his life. One other pilot, Lieutenant Alfred J. Ward, was shot down and killed on the following day.

Marine Squadron VMF-312 is able this day to begin missions against Seoul from its refurbished field at Bofu, Japan.

In Air Force activity, a force composed of thirty-three F-84s (27th Fighter Escort Wing) based at Taegu strike enemy-held Sinuiju. The planes arrive in three flights, two that attack and a third that provides cover. Prior to the bombing run, eight planes strafe the field before MiG pilots at Antung can react, keeping the MiGs from gaining an advantage of holding the high altitude. Consequently, the air battles are fought primarily at elevations of about 20,000 feet. The MiGs arrive from across the Yalu River to intercept the F-84s. A huge air battle erupts and continues unabated for about thirty minutes. The F-84 ThunderJets knock three of the MiGs from the sky and sustain no losses. Two of the MiGs are downed by First Lieutenant Jacob Kratt, Jr., in less than two minutes.

In other activity, a group composed of about forty F-80s, attached to the 49th Fighter Bomber Group, attack the antiaircraft positions at Pyongyang, while an accompanying force of twenty-one B-29s bomb the airfield there. Captain Allen McGuire and Captain William W. Slaughter, also of the 27th FEW, each claimed a MiG during the battle of Sinuiju. In addition, three probable kills are claimed by the 27th. However, only three kills are listed in the Air Force official records of 1988. McGuire's claim is not among those. Also, four other MiGs are damaged. The U.S. sustains no losses.

January 24 *In the Eighth Army area,* General Partridge, acting as pilot, and General Ridgway initiate a reconnaissance flight. After two hours, the pair discover no large enemy formations in front of the I Corps, headquartered at Ch'onan. After the flight, Ridgway concludes that his forces will be able to take ground and hold what they have when an offensive begins on the following day.

In other activity, the North Korean II Corps ceases its unsuccessful offensive and begins its withdrawal towards P'yongchang. The offensive had begun on 7 January and four divisions (2nd, 9th, 27th and 31st) had sustained more than about a fifty percent casualty rate, including those caused by the weather. In addition, the N.K. 10th Division, which had advanced farther south toward Andong, also sustains extremely high casualties.

Meanwhile, Eighth Army prepares for an offensive (Operation THUNDERBOLT), scheduled to commence on the following day.

In the 1st Marine Division sector, Communist guerrillas that had been attempting to operate in the zones of the 1st and 5th Marines on this day venture southeast into the zone of the 7th Marines. During the afternoon, the positions of Company A and the 1st Battalion command post at Topyong-dong come under mortar fire.

In Naval activity, Rear Admiral I.N. Kiland (COMPHIBPAC) relieves Rear Admiral J. H. Doyle, commander Amphibious Group I, of the operational command of Amphibious Forces, Far East (TF 90).

Also, Marine Corsairs remain in the air over two downed pilots to protect them until a rescue helicopter arrives.

— *In Japan:* The 1st Marine Air Wing increases activity at Bofu airfield. General Field Harris establishes his headquarters. Shortly thereafter, VMF-214 and VMF-323 arrive from Itami, Japan, to join with VMF 312, which had commenced operations on the previous day.

January 25–April 21 1951.
FOURTH DESIGNATED CAMPAIGN:
FIRST U.N. COUNTEROFFENSIVE

January 25 At K-9 field near Pusan, VMF(N)-513, which has been flying in support of Eighth Army, gets its first request to support the 1st Marine Division ground forces in the Pohang region.

In the Eighth Army area, Eighth Army initiates its offensive (Operation THUNDERBOLT), an attack executed by the I and IX Corps, to drive to the Han River. Both I and IX Corps had on the previous night established positions about five miles above Line D. Each

corps is to commit one division, augmented by armor and with the stipulation of bolstering the force with an ROK regiment if required. X Corps is directed to protect the right flank, while it initiates some diversionary attacks north of the Yoju–Wonju Road. The cruiser USS *St. Paul,* some destroyers and the British cruiser HMS *Ceylon* remain offshore to support the offensive, which is also bolstered by the artillery of the 64th, 90th and 159th FABns along with the guns of the Turkish Artillery Regiment and the British 45th Artillery Regiment.

In the I Corps sector, the 25th Division advances with the 3rd Division covering the west flank. The Recon Company (25th Division), supported by the 3rd Division Recon Company on the far left, advances up the west coast road toward Suwon, while on the right, the 35th Regiment advances in two columns. One contingent moves up the Osan–Suwon Road, while the other drives northward from Paranjang, also toward Suwon. The 24th Infantry Regiment trails the 35th, to maintain control of the Paranjang Road. To its right, the Turkish Brigade moves northeastwardly toward Kumyangjang. Only the Turkish contingent operating east of Osan encounters heavy opposition. By day's end, the 35th Regiment advances to Osan and deploys in positions to encircle it; however, the enemy makes no attempt to counterattack; rather, it abandons the place, except for a rear guard. Meanwhile the 27th Infantry Regiment (reserve) moves to Osan.

In the IX Corps sector, the 1st Cavalry Division drives north in two columns. The 8th Cavalry (Colonel William A. Harris) moves along Route 55 on the right, while the 7th Cavalry (Colonel Harold Johnson) operates on the left and rolls up Route 13. Neither corps encounters any heavy resistance. During the advance of the 7th Cavalry, elements of the 24th Division reinforce the attack force. Initially, the support unit (2nd Battalion, 5th Regiment) holds at positions between Ichon and Yogu to await orders to join the attack. By the afternoon, the 8th Cavalry advances to the Suwon–Wonju Road, where it encounters some opposition, but it is overcome.

In the meantime, the 7th Cavalry, reinforced by the 2nd Battalion, 5th Infantry Regiment, advances to Ich'on. The 5th Cavalry (Colonel Marcel Crombez) remains in reserve. The U.S. Navy, at the request of General Ridgway, increases its patrols along the west coast to protect the left flank. On the following day, the offensive of the I Corps advances towards the second phase line out of the five lines identified earlier by General Ridgway.

In the 1st Marine Division sector, one day following a mortar attack, the command post of the 1st Battalion, 7th Marines, is attacked by a contingent of about 100 guerrillas. The Communists lose seven killed after an exchange that lasts about one and one-half hours.

In the 7th Marines zone, the 3rd Battalion, supported by a contingent of National Police, engage the enemy in the Chiso-dong area. Initially, nine of the enemy are killed, but as the battalion moves to take Chiso-dong, the resistance holds and the battalion is forced to halt for the night.

In the meantime, artillery continues to pound the enemy positions. Marine squadrons VMF(N)-513 and VMF-323 receive calls to support the attack, but due to the inability to communicate with the forward air controller, the sorties are not effective.

In Air Force activity, Far East Air Forces makes some changes. Combat Cargo Command, a provisional unit, is succeeded by the 315th Air Division (Combat Cargo). The 315th Air Division does not come under Fifth Air Force with regard to administrative and logistical support; rather is comes under the direct jurisdiction of Far East Air Forces.

In other activity, in conjunction with Eighth Army's operation to regain territory, including the port of Inchon and the airfield at Suwon, a force of sixty-eight C-119s support the offensive. Between this day and 7 February, the aircraft deliver by air-drop 1,162 tons of supplies and ammunition to the troops at Chunju, south of the Han River.

— *In Japan:* Marine Squadron VMF(N)-542 receives orders at Itazuke to support the Eighth Army advance. The F7F pilots of the squadron are directed to make the long flight of about 200 miles and after arriving, maintain non-stop patrols near the Han River to ensure the Communists cannot retire across the frozen river unobserved. The Marine aviators pound enemy formations and convoys; however, they report no large numbers of enemy troops attempting to retire across the river. While in support of the advance, the squadron gets tapped to spot targets for the U.S. and British cruisers that are bombarding Inchon.

January 26　Marine Squadron VMF(N)-513 executes forty-nine combat missions between this day and 31 January. The missions include 110 sorties, but of these, only ten are in support of the 1st Marine Division.

In the Eighth Army area, I Corps sector, the 25th Division moves toward the 2nd phase line against light opposition. By 1300, the airfield at Suwon and the town itself is occupied by elements of the 35th Regiment. Later, General Ridgway arrives at Suwon and discovers a town in ruins. At Kumyangjang, Chinese defenders raise fierce resistance against the Turkish Brigade. Fighting continues throughout the day until about 1930, when the Turks finally reduce the resistance. The Turks fight fiercely and gain a strategic hill just outside the town; however, most enemy deaths had been caused by artillery bombardments.

In the IX Corps sector, the 1st Cavalry Division encounters heavy resistance in the high ground above Yangji-ri, where Task Force Johnson had met heavy resistance on 23 January. The 8th Cavalry is unable to dislodge the opposition and sustains 28 killed and 141 wounded while it is encircled, until elements of the 7th Cavalry speed to reinforce it. The 7th Cavalry strikes from two separate directions to relieve the 8th Cavalry from its jeopardy. The cavalry is unable to advance to the second phase line. Meanwhile, the 7th Cavalry is ordered to shift east to defend the first phase line that stands slightly outside Ich'on. Following the lackluster performance of the 8th Cavalry, it is replaced by the 5th Cavalry. The 8th Cavalry is placed in reserve at Kumyangjang.

In other activity, Major General Blackshear M. Bryan becomes commander of the 24th Division. He succeeds General Church, who is transferred to the U.S. to become commandant of the Infantry School at Fort Benning, Georgia. It is a standard policy to relieve officers and to have them contribute their combat experience to training in the States and Church's transfer is part of that procedure. Also, by the end of the month, General Barr, the commanding officer of the U.S. 7th Division (X Corps), will be named commandant of the Armor School at Fort Knox, Kentucky. He will be succeeded by Major General Claude B. Ferenbaugh.

In the 1st Marine Division sector, the Marines continue to maintain patrols in search of an elusive enemy. The guerrillas do not hold the confidence of the Korean civilians and often when spotted by the villagers, the information is passed onto the Marines. In addition, the North Korean guerrillas are not properly equipped nor supplied to carry out an extensive guerrilla operation. The Marines, although not often calling for VMF squadrons for support on this type of mission, depend on VMO-6 to aid in the search for the Communists. The OY observation planes scour the hills and once an enemy contingent is spotted, helicopters are used to keep the Marines supplied while they give pursuit.

In the 1st Marines zone, TF Puller, led by Colonel Lewis B. Puller, is dispatched to Chongja-dong, less than ten miles northeast of Uisong, in a rapid response to a Korean police report that several hundred enemy troops had taken the village. Artillery plasters the village prior to a planned assault set for 1500. Company A enters the village, but discovers no enemy, only an abandoned village. In conjunction, on this same day, Colonel Puller is promoted to brigadier general. Colonel Francis M. McAlister succeeds him as commander, RCT 1.

In the 7th Marines zone, the attack from the previous day is reinitiated to advance one more mile to seize Chiso-dong. Artillery and more effective air strikes support the Marines against the defending force of about 400 troops. Chiso-dong falls to the Marines by 1530. The air strikes led by VMF-323 (Captain Don H. Fisher and VMF(N)-513 (Captain Floyd K. Fulton) are the first flights to succeed with air to ground cooperation since the Chosin Reservoir Campaign of the previous year.

In other activity, the 2nd Battalion, 7th Marines, seize Hapton-ni, about eight miles southeast of Topyong-dong. The Communists, after being evicted, mount a failed counterattack and for the day's action, sustain 161 casualties, either killed or captured.

In Air Force activity, Far East Air Forces improves its communications in the Korea Theater. On this day, it

Top: A plane in the distance (top right center) descends during a close-air support mission to bolster the 1st Cavalry Division near Ich'on on 26 January. *Bottom*: A convoy (96th FABn) crawls its way along an icy highway in the mountains to reach 1st Cavalry Division positions.

launches its initial C-47 "control aircraft." The plane contains sufficient communications equipment to ensure its ability to maintain communications by radio with all T-6 Mosquitoes, with its tactical air control parties, and with the Tactical Air Control Center.

Also, a contingent of planes attached to the 27th Fighter Escort Wing at Taegu encounters enemy aircraft in the vicinity of MiG Alley. One MiG is lost, shot down by First Lieutenant Jacob Kratt, Jr., who received his first victory on 3 January. This is his final aerial victory of the conflict.

In other activity, at about this time, some in command

remain fearful regarding the Eighth Army offensive, prompting General Partridge to direct a large number of his Fifth Air Force units to depart for Japan until the success of the offensive becomes clearer. The 49th Fighter Bomber Wing, 27th Fighter Escort Wing and the 4th Fighter Interceptor Wing are among those outfits ordered to Japan. Nevertheless, the doubts about General Ridgway's success soon vanish, as Eighth Army sends the Communists into retreat. Consequently, the 334th Squadron will be reordered back to Korea.

In Naval activity, Communist shore batteries at Inchon commence firing against the USS *St. Paul* (CA 7).

January 27 At airfield K-1, outside Pusan, Colonel Boelcer C. Batteton, USMC, establishes the MAG-12 command post, but the runway remains incomplete for about two additional weeks. In the meantime, the Marine squadrons of MAG-12 continue operating out of nearby K-9 airfield.

In the Eighth Army area, I and IX Corps sectors, Chinese resistance remains light, but progress remains very slow due primarily to an intensified search for the enemy.

In the I Corps sector, the 35th Regiment (25th Division) advances less than three miles beyond Suwon. In the meantime, the Turkish Brigade advances to a point between Suwon and Kumyangjang-ni. Also, the S.K. 3rd Division enters the fight today. Initially, a reconnaissance force advances, but afterwards, the division launches a heavy attack.

In the IX Corps sector, the Chinese continue to mount heavy resistance from their positions in the high ground slightly above Yang-ri, where the 8th Cavalry has been stalled since the previous day. The 5th Cavalry takes the offensive. It leap-frogs over the 8th Cavalry and drives against the stronghold to the west, killing several hundred Chinese during its drive to Kumyangjang-ni.

At Hill 312, the fighting is ferocious, as both sides pound against each other in close-quartered hand-to-hand combat. After reducing the obstacle and reaching the town, the 5th Cavalry advances slightly more than one additional mile along Route 17 to reach the first phase line. In the meantime, the 7th Cavalry Regiment remains at its positions in the vicinity of Ich'on.

Intelligence gathered from captured Chinese points to only one army in the immediate area, the 50th Chinese Army. From that information and other intelligence, Ridgway discerns that the bulk of the resistance is forming near the Han River and it is suspected that the forces include the six armies of the Chinese XIII Army Group and the North Korean I Corps. Ridgway's attack plan is modified to strengthen the attack of the I Corps. He informs General Milburn to include the 3rd Division in the next attack. To reinforce the 3rd Division, General Milburn attaches the Turkish Brigade.

In the X Corps sector, subsequent to the N.K. II Corps' pull-out from P'yongch'ang, a U.S. contingent composed of infantry and artillery advances to positions from which an artillery barrage is commenced to destroy the town.

— In the United States: The Marine Corps decides to appoint about 500 master sergeants, warrant officers and commissioned warrant officers to the rank of temporary second lieutenant to bolster the Marine Corps leadership during the ongoing Korean conflict.

January 28 By this date, all Marine tactical squadrons are in action for the first time since the previous December. The great majority of flights originating at Bofu in Japan and K-9 at Pusan are diverted from reconnaissance missions to support the ground troops.

In the Eighth Army area, General Ridgway commits the 3rd Division (I Corps) and 24th Division (IX Corps) to the attack. The move by Ridgway drains the reserve down to two units, the British 27th Brigade and the Commonwealth Brigade in the I and IX Corps respectively. Nonetheless, Ridgway is convinced his force is fully prepared to remain on the offensive and be more than a match for the enemy.

In the I Corps sector, elements of the 3rd Division drive northward toward Kumyangjang against sporadic resistance. In the early morning hours of the following day, the Chinese launch an attack against the perimeter. The 25th Division continues its advance toward the Han River. Elements reach a point about two miles from phase line three, the half-way point from the river, and eliminates resistance as it moves. One contingent of the 35th Regiment, 25th Division, enters Suwon.

Marine Squadron VMF-312, out of Bofu, Japan, receives a message that enemy troops north of the Suwon had concealed themselves in a small village. Through the direction of a Mosquito plane, the Marines plaster the suspected location and destroy about forty structures.

In the IX Corps sector, 1st Cavalry Division zone, the advance continues and it, too, receives resistance above Yangji-ri. The 5th Cavalry halts at the 2nd phase line and the 7th Cavalry ends its day about two miles below the line. The assaults against the 7th Cavalry had come from a new unit, the 112th Division, 38th Army. Intelligence gathered from captured troops indicates that the division had just been sent south to intercept the IX Corps.

At about this time, Colonel Harold Johnson, 7th Cavalry, moves to I Corps to become G-3. He is replaced as 7th Cavalry commander by Colonel Pete Clainos, who had been the commanding officer of the 1st Battalion, 7th Cavalry.

The 24th Division, commanded by Major General Blackshear M. Bryan, advances on the right of the 1st Cavalry Division. It moves through the area above Ich'on and Yoju, where the Han River takes a sharp turn in a southeastwardly direction. The 5th and 19th Regiments, led by Colonels Throckmorton and Kinney respectively, drive north toward the Han River, while the reserve 21st Regiment remains in the rear in the area around Yoju, also along the Han.

Top brass at the front lines north of Suwon on 28 January. Major General Courtney Whitney is second from left; Lt. General Matthew B. Ridgway has a grenade hanging from his left shoulder, commander Eighth Army General MacArthur is on the far right and General Kean, the commanding officer of the 25th Division, is in the background to the rear of MacArthur.

January 29   *In the Eighth Army area,* Operation WOLFHOUND continues. The I Corps and IX Corps each receive opposition and in some instances, land mines are encountered, but the mines are unsophisticated and poorly placed. By this time, the Chinese have committed additional units and the U.S. corps, based on information gained from POWs, move against five Chinese divisions and one NK division. The 148th, 149th and 150th of the 50th Army stand in the path of the I Corps' 3rd and 25th Divisions. The 112th and 113th Divisions (38th Army) oppose IX Corps' 1st Cavalry Division. In addition, the North Korean 8th Division opposes the Turkish Brigade and the 35th Regiment (I Corps).

In the I Corps sector, during the early morning hours, the Chinese strike hard against the 3rd Division positions near Kumyangjang and inflict heavy casualties upon the 65th Regiment; however, at dawn, the positions remain under American control.

In the IX Corps sector, on the right, elements of the 24th Division and of the 2nd Division (X Corps) form a motorized patrol and advance from Yoju, east of the Han River, towards a set of enemy-dug tunnels, but Chinese there cut the patrol off. Planes arrive to relieve the besieged troops. Reinforcements arrive about 0330 on 30 January. The patrol, composed of forty-five troops, sustains five dead, twenty-nine wounded and five missing and presumed captured.

In the 1st Cavalry sector, the Chinese raise fierce resistance against the 5th and 7th Cavalry Regiments on the left and right respectively, north of the Suwon–Wonju Road.

In the 1st Marine Division sector, a report of a large North Korean force spotted in the vicinity of Chachondong is received at the 5th Marines. A force is mounted to find and destroy the enemy; however, no contact is made. Additional information given to the Marines by South Korean police indicate that the guerrillas are planning to invade the village to confiscate food.

In other activity, the 1st Korean Marine Corps Regiment, recently attached to the 1st Marine Division, establishes a command post at Yongdok, which is in the area covered by the 7th and 5th Marines. The South Koreans receive a new sector, F, which is created out of sectors C and D, held by the 7th and 5th Marines respectively. Their section of responsibility stretches along the Yongdok–Andong Road and includes the villages of Pongdok, Chaegok-tong and Chinandong. The 1st Battalion is assigned the western portion of Sector F, while the 1st Battalion deploys in the central sector and the 2nd Battalion is assigned the eastern portion of the sector.

In conjunction, the 5th Battalion is attached to the 1st Marines and directed to deploy and patrol in the area around Andong. The regiment does not have a 4th Regiment due to the fact that the Korean word for 4th and death is identical and by the Koreans "4th" is considered a word associated with bad luck.

In the X Corps sector, a strong patrol of the 23rd Regiment, which had been dispatched towards Chipyong to divert attention from the main thrust, Operation THUNDERBOLT, meets with a patrol from the 21st Regiment that had departed Yonju. The combined force of slightly less than sixty men, including four officers, proceeds by jeeps towards Chipyong. The contingent is shadowed by an observation plane, but they encounter no enemy forces. Several miles from Chipyong, the patrol halts near the village of Sinchon to reconnoiter the double rail tunnels (Twin Tunnels) there. As they encroach the tunnels on foot, the enemy in the heights commence fire and the ambush proves deadly. Some are immediately killed during the melee and some others are seized. The remainder scurries up a hill to establish a desperate line of defense.

All the while, the liaison plane is urgently sending word back to headquarters. Soon after, while the patrol fights off attempts to annihilate it, Company F, 2nd Battalion, 23rd Regiment, speeds to the ambush site. Although under heavy fire since about noon, the beleaguered patrol remains tenacious throughout the afternoon and is still holding steadfastly at dusk when the reinforcements arrive. The troops of Company F mount an attack, clear the heights of the Chinese,

The infantry advances one step at a time. A soldier using an A-frame advances alone, with two jeeps to his rear and a truck moving up on his right.

and extricate the survivors of the patrol, which includes 37 wounded.

In Naval activity, TF 77 initiates action against bridges located along the east coast of Korea.

January 30   *In the Eighth Army area,* Operation THUNDERBOLT, which commenced on 25 January, continues against more solid resistance. The I Corps and the IX Corps each attach a South Korean regiment to augment the strength of the respective advances. In the IX Corps sector, the 24th Division pushes out the right. Heavy resistance is raised by the Chinese and it continues into the following day. General Ridgway orders the I and IX Corps to direct the final units at Line D to depart and advance to hold the ground that had been seized. In addition to resistance by the Chinese, the North Koreans are congregating east of Route 29.

In the IX Corps sector, 1st Cavalry Division zone, the Chinese attack the Greek Battalion at Hill 381. The struggle for control of the hill continues throughout the night and often includes close-quartered fighting. Some of the Greeks, at times, expend their ammunition, but they switch to knives and rifle butts rather than surrender the crest. The Chinese disengage by dawn after sustaining heavy casualties.

In other activity, in the 5th Cavalry zone, 1st Lieutenant Robert M. McGovern, Company A, leads a platoon against an enemy stronghold in the vicinity of Kumyangjang-ni. When the platoon reaches a point on the slope about 75 yards from the bunker, heavy fire pounds the assault and McGovern becomes wounded; however, he refuses to quit. The attack continues, despite the storm of enemy fire and the addition of grenades. The grenades for the most part are tossed back into the enemy positions, but still, casualties climb from the devastating fire. McGovern spots the machine gun that is holding up the attack. He charges it, but when he is within about ten feet of the nest, the ripping fire knocks his carbine from his hands.

Still, McGovern advances. Singlehandedly, he takes on the enemy using his pistol and grenades. Seven of the enemy are killed by his actions, but in the process, McGovern's wounds are fatal. He succumbs after eliminating the obstacle. His troops, however, with fixed bayonets, continue the attack and ascend to the crest, throwing grenades as they attack. The enemy abandons the hill. Lieutenant McGovern becomes a recipient of the Medal of Honor, posthumously for his heroism and leadership under fire.

In the 24th Division zone, Company E, 5th Regiment, launches an attack against enemy-held Hill 256, which has been retained by the enemy despite several attempts to dislodge them. A platoon led by 1st Lieutenant Carl H. Dodd acts as vanguard, but it is quickly halted ny intense fire including mortar and artillery, which originates from concealed positions. Dodd, ignores the small arms fire and the bombardment to attempt to reorganize his paralyzed platoon, and then, still oblivious to his own safety, he singlehandedly bolts towards an obstinate gun position. Dodd eliminates

the machine gun and its crew. His actions inspire the remainder of his command. They fly forward with fixed bayonets and an abundance of grenades. The swift and sudden thrust of the platoon takes the enemy positions one by one as they plod forward. The initial obstacles fall and then Dodd again reorganizes his men to take the grand prize, Hill 256.

At a point about 200 yards from the hill, Dodd again singlehandedly takes on a machine gun nest and destroys it and the crew. The advance continues with Dodd at the point. The troops move through a pea-soup fog, with their bayonets fixed and yet more grenades. The advance vanquishes the enemy on 31 January and Hill 256 is seized. Lieutenant Dodd becomes a recipient of the Medal of Honor for his extraordinary leadership and bravery in the face of a superior enemy force.

In the 1st Marine Division sector, the Marines await a raid by North Korean guerrillas, expected to hit Chachon-dong in the 5th Marines zone. The Marines had been informed of the raid and had on the previous night set up an ambush by concealing themselves throughout the village. Nevertheless, at dawn, the enemy fails to arrive.

In the X Corps sector, following the ambush near the Twin Tunnels at Sinchon on the previous day, it becomes apparent that the Chinese control Chipyong. General Ridgway, once informed of the incident, takes immediate steps to counter the Chinese. He orders General Almond to establish positions to protect Eighth Army from an attack through the Han River Valley. X Corps is directed to block any potential flow of enemy forces from the Twin Tunnels. The task is given to the 23rd Regiment.

In Air Force activity, supplies arrive by planes at the airfield at Suwon, which had been captured on the 28th. C-54s attached to the 61st TCG (Troop Carrier Group), the first U.S. planes to land since the field's capture, bring 270 tons of supplies to fuel the Eighth Army advance.

In Naval activity, the Blockading and Escort Force (CTF 95) initiates a bombardment of Kosong and Kasong. The operation includes minesweeping as part of the mission designed to act as a diversion landing on the east coast of Korea. On the following day, warships of Amphibious Task Force (TF 90), including the USS *Montague* (AKA 98) and USS *Seminole* (AKA 105), continue the deception by feinting a landing in an attempt to confuse the enemy ground forces.

January 31   Major General Bryant E. Moore assumes control of the U.S. IX Corps. He succeeds General Major General Milburn, who had been transferred to I Corps to replace General Coulter. Coulter's transfer is not related in any way to his service in the field and in fact he is promoted to lieutenant general.

In other activity, the I Corps and the IX Corps continue to encounter heavy resistance during Operation THUNDERBOLT. The I Corps, after a dogged advance, makes it to the 3rd phase line, while the IX Corps advances only slightly beyond the 2nd phase line. General Ridgway prepares to add more punch to the offensive and simultaneously, he expands the front. The ROK III Corps and the 1st Marine Division will also be thrown against the enemy.

The fifth phase line still stands some distance away at Inchon and from there eastward to Yangp'yong. At this time, General Ridgway's intent remains unchanged, to eliminate as many enemy forces as possible and to gain and retain ground, but without concentrating on fixed lines and positions. His blueprint does not include the recapture of Seoul, unless it falls in line with the advance. Ridgway requests and receives support from Fifth Air Force to prevent the enemy from driving north or south from the Han River.

In the X Corps sector, the 3rd Battalion, 23rd Infantry Regiment (2nd Division), supported by the French Battalion and bolstered by tanks and artillery, moves against the enemy at the tunnels where a patrol had been ambushed on 30 January. The advance over and across snow-filled icy terrain is long and treacherous. The tunnels are reached during the afternoon, but no Chinese are discovered there. The battalion establishes positions at Sinchon, near the Twin Tunnels; however, corps commander General Almond had intended the force to advance farther. Nevertheless, it is about dusk and further progress could prove dangerous. Almond orders a bombardment of a nearby village, thought to be held by the enemy. The order is reluctantly carried out, as a probe determines no enemy there. The barrage is fired, but not directly at the village. Colonel Freeman, the commander of the 23rd Regiment, becomes concerned that the barrage had only informed the enemy of the presence of his force and had invited an attack. His intuition proves correct. Prior to dawn on the following morning, the Chinese attack.

In the 1st Marine Division zone, the search for the enemy continues, but with little success, as the North Korean guerrillas are less than anxious to engage the Marines. Meanwhile, the locals still provide no assistance to the Communists, which makes their task more difficult and they are unable to easily acquire food.

In Air Force activity, the 21st TCS (Troop Carrier Squadron) executes a clandestine mission. A specialized unit of the squadron deposits a UN agent into enemy-controlled territory below the 38th Parallel, at a point in the vicinity of Yonan located on the west coast of Korea. This mission is the first of this type to be recorded during the war.

February 1–6 1951 *In the 1st Marine Division sector,* information from the 7th Marines begins to circulate that the 5th Marines are to expect elements of the NK 25th and 27th Regiments, which are in flight in front of the 7th Marines. The 5th Marines prepare a welcome and deploy, while anticipating a decisive engagement to eliminate the foe during the early days of February; however, the North Koreans disappoint the 5th Marines. The guerrillas approach Topyong-dong and swing north-

ward to evade the 5th Marines. The guerrillas move right into the waiting arms of the 1st Marines, specifically, the 2nd and 3rd Battalions. The Marines close the clamps tightly with the added support of the Korean Marines as the latter (2nd and 3rd Battalions) establishes blocking positions on the escape routes near Sango-ri and Paekcha-dong. The remnant enemy forces scatter and move only in small groups to avoid total destruction.

On 5 February, the North Korean guerrillas encounter the Korean Marines southwest of Yongdok. The Korean Marines, commanded by Colonel Kim Sung Eun, at the request of the 7th Marines, establish blocking positions. One platoon of the 2nd Battalion, Korean Marine Regiment, encounters the Communists at their entrenched positions. The Koreans, after encountering enemy mortar fire and machine gun fire, begin an undisciplined retreat after abandoning their equipment and weapons. The Koreans lose 1 killed, 8 wounded and 24 missing in action. The missing troops later show up minus their weapons.

No U.S. Marines participate in the action, which becomes the sole engagement that ends in a success for the guerrillas. On the following day, the Korean Marines attack in battalion strength with the support of four planes of Marine Squadron VMF(N)-513; however, again the guerrillas escape after raising some minor initial resistance.

February 1 *In the X Corps sector, Second Division zone,* the 23rd Regiment comes under fierce attack at the Twin Tunnels north of the Han River. The attack initiated by the Chinese 125th Division prior to dawn is relentless, but the enemy receives incessant return fire, including the guns of the artillery, accompanying tanks and mortars. The Chinese, after encountering an insurmountable wall of fire, pull back to regroup for a second attack. It occurs at about dawn, when the French contingent holding at Hill 453 is struck by a string of waves, each as ferocious as the one that preceded it. Nonetheless, the French troops, drawn from French forces in Africa, Madagascar and other French garrisons in Asia, hold the ground. Chinese thrusts against the 23rd Regiment continue throughout the day.

The U.S. infantry is bolstered by the 37th Field Artillery Battalion, which had been with them since they established positions there on the previous day. For a while, the situation remains desperate. The French by mid-afternoon lose their high ground and they along with the remainder of the 23rd Regiment have diminished most of their ammunition. However, the remainder of the 23rd Regiment continues to hurl sheets of fire towards the attackers, who seem to continually multiply.

Meanwhile, reinforcements are sped to relieve the beleaguered force. While the fresh elements of the 23rd Regiment drive forward, the 9th Regiment sets itself up to replace the contingent if necessary. One platoon of Company I is pushed from its positions and its leader becomes wounded. Another man, Sergeant Hubert L. Lee, assumes command and leads a charge, but he, too, becomes wounded. Lee disregards his leg wound and drives forward. The enemy drives his contingent back five times, but still Lee adamantly refuses to quit and by this time, he is literally crawling ahead, having sustained two wounds. Lee encroaches the enemy obstacle, forces himself to get up and from a kneeling position, and pours more fire into the enemy until he is yet again wounded. Lee still maintains command and directs the final charge. Lee's actions lead to the attack team eliminating 83 of the enemy and pushing the remainder from the hill. Sergeant Lee becomes a recipient of the Medal of Honor for his extraordinary heroism and leadership under fire.

In the meantime, the Chinese continue to press forward to complete the attack and claim a victory, but the skies clear and planes that had been unable to operate earlier arrive to save the day. A contingent of Marine planes arrives and saturates the enemy formation with bombs. More planes follow as the Marines continue to paper the slopes in front of the French with fire. The Chinese hopes of gaining the hill go up in smoke as they receive riveting fire from the ground troops while they are pummeled from the skies. The slopes remain full of Chinese, but most are deceased. The survivors retreat hurriedly with Colonel Freeman's 27th Regiment in pursuit. The U.S. sustains 45 killed, 207 wounded and 4 missing. The majority of the casualties occur within the French Battalion and the 3rd Battalion, 23rd Regiment. The Chinese suffer about 3,600 casualties. More than 1,200 Chinese dead are counted.

The operation at Twin Tunnels had been launched as a precautionary measure; however, in the process, it had turned into a major victory against the Chinese, who lose the 125th Division as an effective force.

In related activity, while Operation THUNDERBOLT is ongoing, General Almond is authorized by General Ridgway to initiate an offensive (Operation ROUNDUP) to seize Chipyong-ni, which he has concluded is a key defensive position of the Chinese, which provides them with domination on Highway 2, Highway 24 and Highway 24A. U.S. possession, in addition to eliminating a strong point, would also position the Americans so they can trap the enemy forces below the Han. The operation commences on 5 February.

February 2 *In the I Corps sector,* the 35th Infantry Regiment, 25th Division, and the Turkish Brigade launch an attack to reduce Hill 431, which has been raising tough resistance to the I Corps advance (Operation THUNDERBOLT), which had begun on 25 January. The battle continues for several days. The Turks and the 35th Regiment units gain ground on the lower slopes of the hill, but stiff counterattacks push the UN troops back.

In the X Corps sector, during diversionary probes, the village of Hoengsong is seized after some minor resistance is eliminated.

In the 1st Marine Division sector, the Marines continue to search for enemy forces while maintaining control of the MSR, with most of their focus on the stretch between Andong and Yongchon. Meanwhile, between shortages of food and supplies, combined with the relentless pressure of the Marines, the North Koreans continue to evade the Americans. Large groups of Communist forces are not encountered in the sector, but the patrols continue.

In Naval activity, during patrol activities, the USS *Partridge* sustains severe damage and sinks after striking a mine. Eight crewmen are killed and six others are wounded.

February 3 *In the I Corps sector, 25th Division zone,* the violent struggle continues for control of enemy-held Hill 431, but the dogged attempts of the 35th Regiment and the Turkish Brigade are unable to penetrate the defenses. General Ridgway changes strategy by directing General Kean to abort the futile frontal assaults and revert to a flank attack, which commences on the following day.

In the 3rd Division sector, the 3rd Battalion, 15th Regiment, encounters heavy resistance from entrenched enemy positions on a hill in the path of their advance. The battalion plunges forward and engages in a horrific battle for the elevation. The hill is seized due to the doggedness of the assault; but the cost is heavy. Fifteen enlisted men are killed and the wounded list soars.

Following the victory, Colonel Ed Farrell, the 3rd Battalion commander, is evacuated due to his wound. He is replaced by Colonel Clyde H. Baden.

In the 1st Marine sector, a patrol of RCT-7 unexpectedly encounters a North Korean 2nd lieutenant who surrenders, along with three of his men. The lieutenant offers information that exposes exactly how bad things have been going for the guerrillas and how the various units are seeking to survive rather than to engage the Americans. In addition, the officer explains that the North Korean commander of the guerrillas, Major General Lee Ban Nam, has been essentially a recluse, spending his time by himself in foxholes in the heights. On 23 January, another Communist had been captured and papers he was carrying instructed the North Koreans to attempt to break out of the encirclement and make it back to positions in the north. Meanwhile, conditions remain poor for those units unable to escape, particularly knowing they were on their own with no chance of resupply or reinforcements.

February 4 Air attacks ordered by General Ridgway after four days achieve only nominal results against the enemy. In fact, by 5 February, a new Chinese division (114th) arrives in the IX Corps sector.

In the I Corps sector, 25th Division zone, the 35th Infantry Regiment and the Turkish Brigade, bolstered by a heavy artillery bombardment, launch yet another assault to clear the obstinate defenders on Hill 431. The fight carries into the following day, as the troops tangle with the enemy and bone-chilling cold.

In the IX Corps area, 2nd Division sector, the enemy

launches an attack at 0100 against an outpost of the 19th Regiment outside Sesim-ni manned by a platoon of Company A. The platoon, led by Master Sergeant Stanley T. Adams, reacts quickly after Adams spots the force of about 250 troops closing on his positions under a bright moon. Adams leads twelve of his men in an impetuous charge with bayonets fixed. When his contingent reaches a point about fifty yards from the enemy, Adams is struck in one leg by a bullet. He falls, but only momentarily. Once back on his feet, the charge continues. He is knocked down four additional times by the concussion of grenades that detonate and still he is able to lead the attack against a superior force. At close range, the battle rages and the struggle turns to the bayonets and rifle butts.

Despite the overwhelming numbers, the enemy is vanquished. More than fifty of the enemy are killed and the remainder of the force chooses to retire. Adams continues to hold the rear while his detachment heads back to the outpost. Sergeant Adams receives the Medal of Honor for his extraordinary leadership and heroism in the face of the enemy. In conjunction, Adams receives word that his battalion is pulling back. He leads the platoon back to the battalion lines, aware that the battalion is no longer threatened by a surprise attack.

In the 1st Marine Division sector, the 7th Marines receive some unusual assistance in their quest to catch and destroy or capture the North Korean guerrillas in their zone. An R4D aircraft, with an interpreter aboard, spots a large group of Koreans and through the use of a loud speaker aboard the plane, the interpreter, speaking in Korean, urges them to surrender immediately or expect an attack. About 150 begin to surrender by walking with their hands in the air. Those who choose not to surrender are attacked. Marine squadron VMF-323 is called upon and soon after, the group is hit hard with bombs, rockets and napalm; however, it is soon determined that the Koreans had not been soldiers; rather, civilians, as they explain, who were swept up and used as forced laborers by the guerrillas. The plane had actually spotted them as they were in the process of escaping from the Communists.

In Air Force activity, Fifth Air Force, after concluding that the C-47s are unable to maintain sufficient speed to keep up with the B-26s while dropping flares, makes some changes. The Air Force suspends the C-47s and replaces them with modified B-26s.

February 5   The I and IX Corps are up against seven enemy divisions. The Chinese 38th Army has deployed three divisions on the east, while another three divisions from the 50th Army stand at the center, bolstered by the North Korean 8th Division to the west. Other North Korean forces are at Seoul and Inchon.

In the I and IX Corps sectors, Operation THUNDERBOLT is reinitiated. General Ridgway senses that the recent attacks have shaken the confidence of the Chinese. He orders General Milburn (I Corps) to initiate full-scale offensive operations with his armor-infantry task forces (TF Dolvin and TF Bartlett).

Two I Corps divisions (3rd and 25th), bolstered by tanks, advance. The Turkish Brigade and elements of the 35th Regiment maintain attacks against the flanks of Hill 431 and force the enemy to give ground and withdraw to regroup in the terrain, known as the open end of the horseshoe-shaped ridge. Meanwhile, other hills in the area are cleared. TF Dolvin seizes Hills 300 and 178, following the reduction of stiff opposition. Afterwards, TF Dolvin is ordered to move to the rear of the 35th Infantry, which had been in the lead during the advance.

In the meantime, TF Bartlett has a mix-up during the day. It awaits orders to advance from its commanding officer, but Colonel William Bartlett falls on ice and never issues the order. Consequently, the 64th Tank Battalion does not move out on time. Later, under Joseph G. Fowler (executive officer), the tanks roll. Progress remains slow during the advance, but by 8 February, the 25th Division reaches a point within about five miles from the Inchon–Yongdungp'o Road. Meanwhile, the 3rd Division plows forward against opposition and by the 9th, reaches the Han River.

In the 3rd Division sector, its three regiments advance as task forces, each named after the commander of the respective organic tank companies. (TF Tony, TF Myers and TF Fisher). The vanguard of the attack is led by the 65th and 15th Infantry Regiments on the left and right respectively, with TF Myers and TF Fisher in support. Meanwhile, the 7th Regiment supported by TF Tony remains in reserve.

In the IX Corps sector, the advance encounters resistance and progress is tedious, but the land becomes much more of an obstacle than the enemy as the units move towards the Han River. Both the 24th Division and the 1st Cavalry Division face tough resistance from the Chinese 39th Army.

In the 1st Cavalry sector, the 5th Cavalry still acts as vanguard, along with the 7th Cavalry. However, only the 7th Cavalry encounters heavy resistance as it drives towards the Han. In the 5th Cavalry advance, the Chinese resistance diminishes somewhat, which permits the northward advance to continue. However, all across the front, the elements cause obstacles and present natural dangers, due to both ice and mud. Later, during the night of the 5th-6th, the Chinese launch a counterattack against the 3rd Battalion and greatly threaten one unit, Company L. The company resists with ferocity and is able to avoid disaster by mounting a counterattack that routs the Chinese.

In the X Corps sector, Operation ROUNDUP begins. The X Corps offensive is launched in coordination with the attacks of the I and IX Corps advances. The ROK 8th and 5th Divisions on the left and right respectively initiate the advance. The U.S. 2nd Division (General Nick Ruffner) supports the ROK 8th Division. Its support includes elements of the 38th Infantry (1st Battalion), 15th FABn and the 503rd FABn. The U.S. 7th Division bolsters the ROK 5th Division and its support includes elements of the 17th Infantry (2nd Battalion), 49th FABn, 31st FABn and the divisional Recon Company. In conjunction, the 23rd Infantry Regiment at Chipyong and other units, including the 37th FABn and the 1st Ranger Company, are in position to support the northwestward attack of the ROK 8th Division, which is thought to be the most vulnerable to a Chinese counterattack.

Enemy resistance remains light on the first day, but afterwards, it builds. Nevertheless, the advance is hindered more by the terrain than the enemy. The Corps commander, General Milburn, retains his 2nd and 7th Divisions along the line of departure and the reserve division, the ROK 2nd Division, remains weakened from its earlier contest during the Chinese New Year.

In addition, the 187th Airborne Regimental Combat Team is being pulled from the line. The ROKs are en route to Hongchon. All the while, concerns have arisen at Eighth Army regarding a massive Chinese offensive that intelligence has discerned will be launched against Wonju, in the X Corps sector, by 15 February.

In the 1st Marine Division sector, General O.P. Smith has concluded that his Marines have completed the mission in the Pohang region. He responds to a request from General Ridgway as to the time in which the mission will be complete. General Smith informs General Ridgway that the 10th NK Division units in the Marine sector have been sliced down to a strength of about forty percent. He also states that the force is no longer capable of mounting a major attack and that the Marines' mission is essentially complete and awaiting a new assignment.

In Air Force activity, an F-51 Mustang, piloted by Major Arnold Mullins (67th FBS), engages and downs a Yak-9 in the skies about seven miles north of Pyongyang. The kill by Mullins is the sole victory in the sky by an Air Force pilot during February.

February 6

General Thomas J. Cushman, USMC, assistant commanding general, 1st Marine Air Wing, advises the commanding officer, General Harris, that the K-1 airfield at Pusan is nearly complete and will be able to accommodate one squadron on 8 February and an additional one on each succeeding day. In conjunction, K-3, near Pohang, when completed, is scheduled to be the permanent base for MAG 33, but K-1 is to be used in the interim.

In the I Corps sector, armored units advance against some opposition, but most of the obstacles encountered are mines. The advance had been held up for a short time while TF Dolvin awaits TF Fowler, which had been lagging behind due to a late start on the previous day. Ridgway had insisted all units advance abreast for a more galvanized attack and less chance of the enemy penetrating by counterattack. The advance is slowed by minefields along the road, but the enemy had laid them in such fashion that they are easily spotted.

During the advance, elements of I Corps seize North Korean troops affiliated with the N.K. 47th Division in the vicinity of Anyang. The enemy 47th Division had apparently deployed at Kwanak Mountain, south of Seoul, after being relieved at Inchon by the N.K. 17th

Division. TF Dolvin again secures Hills 300 and 178, then as on the previous day, the armor moves back behind the 35th Regiment.

In the IX Corps sector, 24th Division zone, the advance moves cautiously and sluggishly towards the Han River. The Chinese spring a strong assault at a point between the 19th and 21st Infantry Regiments. Both U.S. units resist fiercely, but the Chinese inflict high casualties before the assault is halted.

In Air Force activity, a group of C-54s evacuate 343 sick and wounded troops from Chungju. The planes, attached to the 315th Air Division, transport the troops to Pusan.

In other activity, eight C-54s arrive at Taegu from Japan, each transporting sections of a 310-foot treadway bridge from Japan to Taegu. The bridge is composed of 279 separate sections.

Also, a contingent of six C-119s pass over enemy territory and in an attempt to torment the troops there, the crews drop thirty-two boxes, each one individually booby-trapped to explode once opened. The surprise packages are dropped while the planes are over Kwangdong-ni.

In yet other activity, the 91st Strategic Reconnaissance Squadron executes its initial night photographic mission.

February 7

The I and IX Corps continue to advance (Operation THUNDERBOLT). The enemy raises opposition and it grows more intense as the offensive continues.

In the I Corps sector, as on the previous two days, TF Dolvin again moves to clear Hills 300 and 178. The Chinese, in the meantime, greatly reinforce Hill 300 and with the fresh troops, they are able to prevent TF Dolvin from re-seizing the entire hill. As dusk settles in over the area, TF Dolvin is directed to disengage and return to positions to the rear of the 35th Infantry Regiment at Anyang.

By this time all units of the I Corps attack force are on line, in conjunction with the original directive of General Ridgway. Nevertheless, TF Fowler had not experienced an easy day. During the advance, enemy resistance at one of the targeted hills had been especially ferocious. The 1st Platoon, Company E, 27th Infantry, 25th Division, hits stiff resistance and gets stalled. Two other platoons of the company, led by Lieutenant Lewis W. Millet, execute a bayonet charge against a dug-in force of about 200 troops. The powerful thrust cracks the defenses and the cold steel evicts the defenders on the crest. The platoons follow his lead and the ascent bludgeons the enemy as it moves. Millet, who gets wounded by grenade fragments, takes out two of the enemy during the ascent with his bayonet and a few others with grenades. Captain Millet becomes a recipient of the Medal of Honor for his extraordinary valor and leadership during the assault.

In the IX Corps sector, 24th Division zone, the 19th Regiment, which had come under heavy attack on the previous day, is again hit with a furious assault when it attempts to continue its northward advance. The Chinese pressure forces the regiment to give ground, a hill that the leading 3rd Battalion had passed. The 1st Battalion is pushed back while the 3rd Battalion gets cut off and is forced to fight its way back to the main body.

Recently appointed commander of the 19th Regiment, Colonel Ollie Kinney, is shortly thereafter relieved and transferred to the position of division G-2. He is succeeded by Colonel Peter W. Garland.

In the X Corps sector, during Operation ROUNDUP the ROK 5th Division discovers an enemy force of about 4,000 troops. Plans are laid to attack and eliminate them on the following day.

February 8   General Ridgway directs General Milburn to drive his I Corps against Kwanak Mountain. In conjunction, he requests help from the U.S. Navy and asks for it to send a diversionary force against Inchon

U.S. B-26s of Fifth Air Force (452nd Light Bomber Wing) strike a marshaling yard south of Wonsan. The target is hit with napalm.

on 10 February. Preliminary activity is carried out by the USS *Missouri* (BB 63) and a group of amphibious vessels.

In other activity, Marine Squadron VMF-323 arrives at K-1 from Japan. It will be followed by VMF-214 on the 9th and VMF-312 on 10th. The squadrons are scheduled to move again to K-3, near Pohang, once it is finished.

In the I Corps sector, the advance continues against light resistance. The North Korean opposition that had appeared seems to have moved south to cover the withdrawal of the Chinese 50th Army, but by this day, the North Koreans also are heading north rather than holding positions to resist the advance.

In the IX Corps sector, the Chinese raise stiff resistance. At some points along the advance, enemy counterattacks force withdrawals. In the IX Corps sector, the advance pushes against a point below the Han River, where the Chinese have poured reinforcements in order to hold a bridgehead.

In the X Corps sector, Operation ROUNDUP continues. The Corps' main thrust is handled by the ROK III Corps, which is advancing along Route 29. The South Koreans gain ground beyond Hongsong to the north, northeast and northwest. The ROK 7th Division pushes elements to within several miles of Ch'angdong-ni and the ROK 9th Division stands above Chong-son; however, enemy resistance has slowed progress of the ROKs. The slow-down provides the enemy with an opportunity to bang against the right flank of X Corps. In conjunction, the U.S. 7th Division advances to the rear of the ROK 7th Division.

Also, General Ridgway transfers the ROK 3rd Division to General Almond for the remainder of Operation ROUNDUP. The ROK 3rd Division is assigned the task of continuing the maneuver to come in from the east to encircle Hongch'on, while the ROK 5th Division establishes blocking positions on the exposed right flank. In the ROK 5th Division sector, the enemy launches an attack against the ROK 27th Regiment before the South Koreans are able to launch their offensive. The South Koreans are struck hard, east of Route 29, forcing one battalion to collapse. Afterward, the regiment retires. Fighting continues to rage between the 27th Regiment and the North Koreans into the following day.

In Air Force activity, enemy rail lines in North Korea are attacked by a large force composed of B-26s, B-29s, and fighters. The strikes hit the area that stretches from Hoeryong to Wonsan.

In other activity, Brigadier General John P. Henebry becomes commanding officer of the 315th AD. He succeeds General Willliam H. Tunner. During post–World War II General Tunner handled the Berlin Airlift, but he had been assigned this task on a temporary basis.

February 9 *In the I Corps sector,* Kwanak Mountain is seized by the 25th Division without the support of air cover. Bad weather had cancelled all flights. Patrols from the division drive ahead in the snow to reach positions near Inchon and Yongdungp'o. TF Dolvin, part of the 25th Division, advances to positions from which the city of Seoul can be seen, but no move into the city is attempted. The task force again receives orders to withdraw and take positions to the rear of the infantry. Meanwhile, the 3rd Division pushes against no resistance and TF Myers advances to the Han.

In the X Corps sector, the ROK 5th Division's 27th Regiment finally concludes its hard fighting that had begun on the previous day. During the early morning hours, the North Koreans disengage. Steps are quickly taken by General Almond to restore his right flank. On the following day, Almond orders the ROK 5th Division to establish positions slightly less than fifteen miles northeast of Hoengsong, at about the same place where the North Koreans struck the 27th Regiment.

Also, the U.S. 27th Regiment, 2nd Division, had earlier established positions in Chipyong-ni and afterwards initiated patrols. On this day, a patrol spots a heavy concentration of enemy troops on an elevation, Hill 444, almost five miles east of Chipyong-ni. One battalion, the 1st (9th Regiment), is dispatched north from Yonju, while another battalion moves from the east to reduce the resistance on Hill 444.

February 10 During Operation THUNDERBOLT, progress continues.

In the I Corps sector, the 25th Division seizes the Inchon-Yongdungp'o Road by 1100. In the meantime, no enemy activity is discovered in Inchon; however, the port, earlier destroyed by U.S. forces upon abandonment, is still a massive scene of destruction. Consequently, the planned amphibious diversionary landing is cancelled.

In the meantime, General Ridgway, convinced that the enemy is in retreat, loosens the leash on the advance to accelerate pursuit. In addition, TF Dolvin and TF Fowler are combined as one task force. It races to the Kimpo peninsula, where Task Force Allen moves forward in two columns. The east force effortlessly takes Kimpo Airfield. The troops continue their progress throughout the day and by dusk, the advance of about 11,000 yards gains positions nearly ten miles above the Han River. Other units trailing the task force include the 24th and 35th Regiments. The two regiments and the attached ROK 15th Regiment hold positions along the Han, between the airfield and Yongdungp'o.

Meanwhile, the Eighth Army Ranger Company and the 25th Division's Reconnaissance Company close on Inchon. At about 1700, the reconnaissance force enters Inchon and no enemy troops are discovered; however, at about the same time, the small force of ROK Marines that had been with the amphibious force that aborted the landing arrives at Inchon aboard small boats.

In the 3rd Division zone, operating on the Corps' right, the 65th Infantry Regiment and the 15th Regiment advance to the Han and join with Task Force Myers. The regiments encounter only one sighting of enemy forces near the river. The 15th relieves the 65th

Regiment at the river, which permits the 65th to revert to reserve.

The successful advance to the Han River boosts the morale of Eighth Army. It had driven the Chinese back across the river and forced the Communists to surrender strategic ground, including Kimpo Airfield, Inchon and Suwon, all of which had been required for the U.S. to regain air superiority in the northern reaches of North Korea, particularly MiG Alley.

In the X Corps sector, Operation ROUNDUP begins on the eastern flank. The U.S. 7th Division dispatches one battalion from its positions near P'yongchang to a point about fifteen or sixteen miles east of Hoengsong, in an effort to flush out the North Koreans there and pinch them between the U.S. troops and the ROK 5th Division, which had been ordered to a point northeast of Hoengsong. General Almond also dispatches a contingent of the 187th Airborne Regimental Combat Team to bolster the east flank to the rear of the ROK 5th Division at a point about slightly less than ten miles east of Hoengsong. In conjunction, the ROK 3rd Division, deployed on the fringes of Hoengsong, prepares to jump off on the following day to coordinate with the attack of the ROK 5th Division.

February 11   General O.P. Smith, USMC, arrives in Taegu to confer with General Ridgway with regard to the next mission to be assigned to the Marines. Several possibilities are discussed and Ridgway proposes relieving the 24th Division at the Han River, at the Yoju corridor in the IX Corps sector, and redeploying on the east coast in the event an amphibious landing is required. No decision is reached. However, Ridgway makes it clear that he has confidence in the Marines' ability.

By day's end, the Chinese launch their offensive (fourth phase) in the 2nd Division sector, and by the following morning, as Ridgway had mentioned, the Marines find themselves being ordered to the center of the hornets' nest at the rear of IX Corps, where the brunt of the attack is being felt.

The ongoing offensive, which has carried Eighth Army to the Han River and put the Chinese to flight, causes more complications in Washington. There are differences of opinion on whether to push beyond the 38th Parallel; however, the powers to be, including the Pentagon and the State Department, are in agreement with the British and French that the strategy should be to halt at the 38th Parallel and negotiate with the Communists to terminate the war. In contrast, General MacArthur believes it necessary to continue the attack and he is adamantly opposed to the UN policy of giving the Communists a free, untouchable sanctuary in Manchuria.

In the X Corps sector, the ROK III Corps maintains its progress. The ROK 7th Division deploys in the vicinity of Ch'angdong-ni after first driving through it. The ROK 3rd Division advances along Route 29 to a point about five miles above Hoengsong. Farther east, the ROK 5th Division moves toward its blocking positions on the east flank. Also, the ROK 8th Division reaches a point along Route 29, slightly less than ten miles north of Hoengsong. In the meantime, the ROK 9th Division plows through the Han valley and establishes contact with the ROK I Corps.

In the South Korean I Corps sector, by this date, elements of the Capital Division, which had been joined by the ROK 9th Division, stand in the Taebaek mountains. Kangnung and Chumunjin are both occupied.

In other activity, the 1st Battalion, 9th Infantry Regiment, seizes Hill 444 east of Chipyong-ni, eliminating a threat against the 2nd Division positions. After dusk, the Chinese launch an attack that drives from Hongch'on to the right of the U.S. 2nd Division that strikes the ROK 8th Division. The Chinese also evade the Americans (Support Force 21) at Ch'angbong-ni.

Meanwhile, the Chinese force the regimental headquarters to order the ROK 21st Regiment to withdraw and hook up with the American Support Force 21. The Chinese also pound the ROK 10th and 16th Regiments. Chinese troops flood both sides of Route 29 as they drive forward. By about midnight on the 11th-12th, the command posts of the 10th and 16th Regiments are both overrun. The swift movement also isolates the ROK 20th and 50th Field Artillery Battalions and Support Team A. Shortly thereafter, the ROK units lose all communications between regiments.

February 12   The Chinese offensive that unfolded northeast of Wonju at about midnight continues to gather steam.

In the IX Corps sector, 1st Cavalry Division zone, the 5th Cavalry gathers at IX Corps headquarters in Changhowon-ni, slightly more than ten miles below Yoju. Also, the 7th Cavalry, which had been making remarkable progress, stalls slightly more than ten miles from its objective, the Han River. The enemy is deeply entrenched in the vicinity of Mugam on Hill 578. General Ridgway decides that the hill must be taken before the 7th Cavalry is relieved by the 27th Regiment (25th Division). A full-throttle attack to reduce the obstacle is scheduled for 14 February.

In the X Corps sector, within about one hour after midnight, it becomes apparent that the Chinese had overrun the ROK 8th Division. The supporting American units get caught in the confusion. By about 0100, 2nd Division artillery units request permission to pull back to more tenable positions. The U.S. support team withdraws toward the positions of the 38th Regiment and encounters fierce opposition as it drives eastward. The unit finally arrives at friendly lines by about dawn; however, the cost of the drive is high. Only six men are immediately known to be wounded, but the missing number nearly 150 troops. In addition, two tanks are lost. More than 7,000 South Korean troops are either killed or captured.

The ROK 3rd Division also comes under heavy attack. The ROK 22nd and 23rd Regiments withdraw to the vicinity of Ch'angbong-ni before the Chinese envelop them. By 0245, the Americans (Support Force

21) receive authorization to withdraw. The Chinese, however, had gained positions along Route 29 and pound the troops as they move. En route, Support Force 21 passes abandoned artillery of the 503rd Field Artillery Battalion. The commanding officer of SF 21, Colonel Keith, has no troops in his command who can drive tractors and no explosives. The artillery is left for the enemy. Keith's column, following a tedious flight, joins with the 3rd Battalion.

Finally, at about 1000, the column arrives at the lines of the 3rd Battalion, 38th Regiment (2nd Division). It discovers that the Chinese are also attacking the 38th Regiment. The 38th had been designated as the unit to hold the line at the Route 29 mountain road junction. Keith's artillery is deployed to bolster the positions. The defenders at Hill 300, in the 38th Regiment's zone, are hit especially hard by a large force.

By about 0300, the units are ordered to pull back. One of the troops, Sergeant Charles R. Long, Company M, a forward observer for the mortar section, holds his ground to assist in the withdrawal by directing fire. In addition, as the enemy closes on him, he reverts to resisting with his carbine and grenades. However, the overwhelming enemy force is able to encircle him. Sergeant Long is killed, but his company safely pulls back and afterwards, returns to retake the positions. Long becomes a recipient of the Medal of Honor for his extraordinary valor and selfless sacrifice in the face of the enemy. The ROK 8th Division had nearly been annihilated.

By 1100, the 2nd Division receives orders to designate the 38th Regiment a Regimental Combat Team. Support Force 21 is ordered to withdraw to Hoengsong. Support Force 7, deployed several miles north of Hoengsong near the ROK 3rd Division, also receives orders to withdraw to Hoengsong. In the meantime, the Chinese continue to encircle various units, including one regiment of the ROK 3rd Division. The ROK 5th Division is also being compelled to fight its way towards Hoengsong. The situation continues to deteriorate and by noon, General Almond informs General Ridgway that Hoengsong will be abandoned in order to defend Wonju. The fighting withdrawal continues into the morning of the 13th and casualties become high.

Nevertheless, the Dutch Battalion becomes key to a successful withdrawal. The final units to abandon Hoengsong for Wonju are the Dutch Battalion and the 2nd Battalion, 17th Infantry Regiment (7th Division). The casualty list for X Corps, including the ROK troops, at best estimate (11 February through early 13 February) stands at about 9,800 South Koreans, 1,900 Americans and 100 Dutch. Equipment losses are also heavy. The South Koreans (3rd, 5th and 8th Divisions) lose more than 1,000 weapons, including 14 howitzers and they also lose nearly 90 vehicles. The Americans and Dutch lose more than 300 weapons, including twenty howitzers. The 15th Field Artillery Battalion abandons fourteen howitzers and the 503rd Field Artillery Battalion loses 5 artillery pieces. In addition, the U.S. loses two tanks and just under 300 vehicles.

In conjunction, Far East Air Forces' planes arrive overhead and drop supplies at the airstrip near the X Corps command post at Wonju.

In the 1st Marine Division sector, orders arrive from Eighth Army headquarters that instruct General O.P. Smith to prepare to move out of the Pohang–Andong region and redeploy in the rear sector of the IX Corps to galvanize the lines there where the Chinese are making their strongest thrust. General Smith is also directed to dispatch reconnaissance units to the Chungju region. In conjunction, the 1st Korean Marine Regiment is detached from the 1st Marine Division and attached to the ROK Capital Division, which is deployed on the east coast at Samch'ok.

In Air Force activity, Far East Air Forces makes emergency passes over the X Corps command post and drops supplies. Also, a C-47 plane is struck by enemy antiaircraft fire while it is dropping leaflets during daylight hours. The plane makes a crash landing at Suwon. The incident prompts Fifth Air Force to discontinue the daylight leaflet flights.

In other activity, a contingent of B-26s using guidance of flares strikes enemy positions along the front lines; however, on this mission, two enemy planes in the area use the illumination to attack UN positions.

February 13–16 1952   *In Air Force activity,* H-5 helicopters deliver medical supplies to the besieged elements of the 2nd Division and evacuate more than forty wounded troops. Air Force planes also drop supplies. Fifth Air Force focuses on close-air support missions to bolster the positions of the encircled troops.

February 13   General MacArthur arrives in Korea and confers with General Ridgway. It is decided that Chipyong-ni in the X Corps sector will be held. It remains clear that the I and IX Corps are to hold the line at the Han River.

In other activity, the 1st Marine Air Wing is nearing completion of its consolidation of all units to Korea. At K-1, near Pohang, Lieutenant Colonel Fontana establishes the MAG-33 command post. The squadrons temporarily at K-1 are directed to move to K-3. In the meantime, the support units are en route from Japan. Also, the jets (VMF-311) that had been grounded due to engineering problems during early January are back in operating condition and their arrival from Japan is imminent.

Also, by the end of the month, the all weather Marine Squadron VMF(N)-542 will be based at K-1 near Pusan; however, VMF(N)-513 will operate from K-1. Another group, the Headquarters Squadron (photo pilots), is in the process of transferring from Japan to K-1.

In the I Corps sector, the Communists (North Korean 6th Division, N.K. I Corps) launch a counterattack against the rear near Suwon. Initially, the N.K. 1st Regiment crashes into the 15th Regiment, but fortuitously, the 65th Regiment, composed of Puerto Ricans, deployed in the nearby high ground, is able to intercept

On 13 February, it is decided to hold Chipyong-ni. The 23rd Regiment, 2nd Division, and attached French troops hold the crossroads for several days although surrounded.

the enemy. The 65th at the time is catching a breather from its recent stint at the front. The 65th bolts from its positions and swarms around and upon the invaders and prevents them from penetrating to the divisional command post. The North Koreans are shredded during the night (13th-14th).

On the 14th, the U.S. force scours the area and it is determined that 1,152 enemy troops had been killed (counted). In addition, 353 enemy troops are taken as prisoners. The 65th Regiment is responsible for eliminating nearly 600 of the enemy. Although the enemy attack is repulsed, the fact that they had struck with such force and had gotten behind the lines causes concern. Once the 3rd Division fords the Han on the advance, only the 35th Regiment, the Turkish Brigade and the ROK 1st Division remain on the south side of the Han River across from Seoul. Consequently, a repeat attack could succeed and in so doing, isolate the 3rd Division on the opposite bank of the Han.

In the IX Corps sector, 1st Cavalry Division zone, the

Communists launch a night attack against the 8th Cavalry while it is preparing to participate in a diversionary attack to support the 7th Cavalry, which is held up at Hill 578. The Chinese assault is thwarted, but the lines are penetrated. The 8th Cavalry remains confined to holding the ground and liquidating the intruders. It is unable to jump off on the morning of the 14th in support of the 7th Cavalry.

In the X Corps sector, General Almond attempts to regroup and prepare for the defense of Wonju. The unexpected attack by such a great force, composed of four Chinese divisions and two North Korean divisions, is too strong to halt. However, General Ridgway remains convinced that the resupply ability of the enemy is unable to sustain a prolonged offensive. The enemy swarm into Hoengsong after it is abandoned during the early morning hours of this day, but the Chinese do not initiate pursuit of the U.S. 2nd Division while it moves to Wonju.

By this time, all contingents north of Wonju, including the 38th Infantry (and Dutch Battalion attached),

Top: A contingent of the 15th Regiment, U.S. 3rd Division, engages the enemy as it moves toward the Han River. *Bottom*: A U.S. tank starts its move around a curve as it advances toward the Han River.

187th Airborne RCT, ROK 18th Regiment (ROK 3rd Division) and the 2nd Battalion, 17th Regiment (7th Division) succeed in making it back to positions around Wonju. Meanwhile, the withdrawal by X Corps jeopardizes the forces at Chipyong-ni, which is defended by the 23rd Regimental Combat Team, composed of the 23rd Infantry Regiment (Colonel Paul F. Freeman, 2nd Division), 1st Ranger Company, 37th Field Artillery Battalion, and other units, including Battery B, 503rd Artillery Battalion, Battery B, 82nd Antiaircraft Artillery Automatic Weapons Battalion, Company B, 2nd Engineer Combat Battalion, and the French Battalion.

The Chinese launch a full-scale attack against the defenses of Chipyong-ni at about 2200. The contest lasts throughout the night into the morning of the 14th. Colonel Freeman, after learning of the withdrawal to Wonju, requests permission to abandon Chipyong, but it is denied. He is told to hold and that reinforcements (5th Cavalry and a British Brigade) will be dispatched to ensure the ground is held.

In other activity, the 2nd Division Reconnaissance Company and Company L, 9th Infantry, at Chuam-ni come under assault by elements of the Chinese 116th Division throughout the day. The Chinese attempt to encircle the force after dark and on the following day, a stronger assault is launched.

In the 1st Marine Division sector, departure orders arrive from Eighth Army that instruct the Marines to depart for Chunju, in the rear of the IX Corps on 15 February.

In Air Force activity, priority airlifts develop for the 315th AD. The planes evacuate 800 sick and wounded troops from airstrips in the forward areas, including Wonju. The men are transported to Taegu and Pusan. The operation requires a large number of C-47s and drains the supply. Requests for airlifts from other locations cannot be answered.

— *In Japan:* The Photographic Unit, 1st Marine Division, transfers from Itami Air Force Base to Bradshaw Air Force Base at Pusan. The photographic unit will work in conjunction with the 15th Troop Carrier Squadron.

February 14   The enemy continues its attacks, but the Korean winter is taking a toll on their ranks and enthusiasm. In addition to being pounded by ground forces, aircraft and artillery, the Communists find it difficult to find protection from the frigid cold. Most towns have been decimated, leaving few houses and huts and when they find temporary sanctuary, planes usually attack and destroy the structures. In addition, many of the Chinese are now poorly dressed for the season. It is difficult to acquire medical attention. Nevertheless, those still able continue to maintain the attack.

During the previous November, when the Chinese entered the conflict openly on the side of the North Korean Communists, they were in close proximity to Manchuria and they had bases to their rear, but now,

they are more than 250 miles from the Manchurian border.

In the IX Corps sector, the 5th Cavalry Regiment at Changhowon moves out to open Route 24A and drives to the isolated RCT 23 at Chipyong-ni. The cavalry is bolstered by a contingent of engineers, two tank companies and two artillery battalions. The column is trailed by vehicles carrying supplies and a contingent of ambulances. The advance makes progress until it hits a destroyed bridge, which forces the advance to suspend at Hup'o-ri until the engineers improvise and construct a modified bypass around the obstacle.

Meanwhile, RCT 23, which had earlier been supplied by air, remains isolated until the following day. During the night, the Chinese launch yet another assault against Chipyong-ni. U.S. positions on the north and east are hit hard, but by dawn of the following day, the Communists Chinese fail to make gains. The successful defense of Chipyong-ni eliminates some heavy problems for General Ridgway. If it had fallen, although only a diminutive village of a few huts, the Communists would have gained the road junction there and imperiled the entire Eighth Army front. However, the eastern perimeter is also struck with a severe attack and gains are made by the Chinese. Company G, 5th Cavalry is compelled to abandon its positions by about 0300 on the 15th.

Nearby artillery positions, held by the 503rd Field Artillery Battalion, are deployed from where the battalion continues to pound the enemy. The effective fire keeps the Chinese at bay. The U.S. launches a counterattack at 0400. The force (TF Crombez) is composed of Company G, 5th Cavalry, reinforced by Company F, and a contingent of rangers. The attack gains some of the lost positions of Company G; however, the Chinese push the attackers back and inflict high casualties. A contingent of French troops support the attack and they, too, pull back.

In the 7th Cavalry zone, a scheduled attack to clear the enemy from Hill 578 commences; however, circumstances surrounding the assault cause complications. Scheduled air support had been diverted to Wonju and a supporting attack by the 8th Cavalry is aborted due to an enemy counterattack against the 8th Cavalry on the previous night. Nonetheless, at 0700, following a prolonged artillery bombardment, the 7th Cavalry, supported by a contingent of tanks (70th Tank Battalion) drives against Hill 578. The attack continues against steadfast resistance throughout the day and into the following morning. The Communists continue to come under heavy fire, but still they give no ground. Finally, after about twenty-four continuous hours of gruesome fighting, the 7th Cavalry prevails. Hill 578, through the efforts of the entire regiment, including the attached Greek Battalion, falls on the morning of the 15th.

In the X Corps sector, 2nd Division zone, the 23rd Regiment and its support units at Chipyong continue to come under assault from the attack launched during the previous night. The defenses had been under heavy bombardment and the usual infantry assaults, but the Chinese receive equal punishment from the encircled perimeter. Although the attacks are repulsed, the town remains surrounded and the anticipated reinforcements do not arrive. The 3rd Battalion is struck again at about 0630, but the Chinese fail to break through. At about 0730, the sector defended by the French also repels an attack. The Chinese disengage and withdraw into the heights around the town. Colonel Freeman had become wounded during the night long fight by a shell fragment, but he declines evacuation and remains in command. Planes arrive during the afternoon to drop supplies, but the reinforcements will not make it to Chipyong.

The 27th British Brigade is stalled by heavy resistance and the 5th Cavalry with a contingent of tanks is still at the Han River at Wonju. The Fifth Air Force arrives overhead and drops supplies and ammunition, but the delivery lacks heavy mortar shells and illumination shells. Other airdrops follow for the next three days. The supplies get dropped during night hours at designated spots illuminated by burning rags that had been soaked in gasoline. During the resupply flights, ninety-three transport planes deliver more than 400 tons of supplies and ammunition. After dark, the Communists attack, initially by propelling streams of mortar and artillery shells into the beleaguered perimeter and afterwards with the ground troops that as usual remain oblivious to the artillery barrages. The 2nd Battalion is hit especially hard on the southern sector of the perimeter, where the pressure continues to build.

Although the defenders lack illuminating shells, a Fifth Air Force Firefly (C-47) supports the defense and lightens the skies with flares attached to parachutes that linger overhead for about fifteen minutes to provide a grand view of the charging enemy. The Chinese close and the battle quickly changes to a fierce hand-to-hand contest. Never-ending waves pound against the lines and by 0315, Company G is compelled to give way. It withdraws. In the process, the battery of the 503rd FABn is lost. Meanwhile, the 3rd Battalion is also under heavy assault.

A counterattack is mounted by the 1st Ranger Company and Company F in an attempt to regain the lost ground, but the Chinese refuse passage. The slug-fest continues straight through the night into dawn. Still, no reinforcements arrive, but Colonel Freeman's troops hang on and refuse to capitulate.

Also, during one attack against Company I, an enemy grenade is tossed into a machine gun position and knocks it out. Another machine gun replaces it. Sergeant William S. Sitman, attached to Company I, and his detachment provide protection for the new crew. Meanwhile, another grenade is thrown into the position. Sitman blankets the grenade to save the lives of the others. He is fatally wounded, but the others remain unscathed, able to continue the fight. Sitman becomes a recipient of the Medal of Honor posthumously

for his tremendous heroism during the attack. His actions also save five other men at the machine gun emplacement.

Colonel Freeman had been ordered to evacuate because of his wounds and a replacement arrived during the afternoon of the 13th, but the plane left without waiting to evacuate Freeman. Nonetheless, he had earlier refused evacuation and he continues to hold command, even though Colonel John H. Chiles arrives to assume command.

In other activity, the 2nd Division Reconnaissance Company and Company L, 9th Infantry, at Chuam-ni, again come under heavy assault. The U.S. defenders attempt to withdraw, but the Chinese had established blockages and destroyed a bridge, impeding the pullback. More than 200 casualties are sustained and of those, about 114 are killed.

In the meantime, the Chinese also move against Wonju. Some ground is surrendered by the French and some penetration is made against the 3rd Battalion, 38th Regiment, during the morning. However, by afternoon, all lost ground is retaken. Air support and artillery pound the Chinese columns, but despite heavy losses, the unbroken link in the column continues to advance. Once again, there seems to be more Chinese than artillery shells. The overtaxed artillery units request permission to suspend the bombardment, but they are ordered to continue firing until the final shell is expended. Shortly thereafter, word is passed again that the guns are near collapse from overuse, but the order comes back to maintain fire until the guns explode. The number of Chinese dead continues to climb, yet more walk into the whirlwind of fire. Finally, by about 1500, Chinese losses grow too high and the attack against Wonju is aborted.

As the enemy ranks collapse and the retreat begins, the overworked guns continue to fire into the enemy troops that head north. Just under 650 Chinese dead are counted between midnight on the 13th-14th until dusk on the 14th, but overall Chinese casualties are estimated at 3,200 killed and 2,500 wounded. The devastation inflicted upon the enemy eradicates four Chinese divisions from the field.

In related activity, the British 27th Brigade moves from IX Corps to X Corps during the morning hours. It is attached to the U.S. 2nd Division. Afterwards, the British advance up Route 24 against opposition. Also, the ROK 6th Division arrives later, at about 1100 and it, too, is attached to the 2nd Division. The South Koreans deploy at a place near the convergence of the Han and Som Rivers.

In the ROK III Corps sector, the ROK 3rd and 5th Divisions had pulled back from their respective positions and are in the process of redeploying between P'yongch'ang and Wonju. During the afternoon, both divisions are engaged by North Korean units. The ROK 3rd Division is able to withstand the assaults; however, the 5th Division, farther east, is unable to hold firmly. The division is tossed into more chaos. The ROK sector becomes more disorganized and two divisions, the

ROK 7th and 9th, receive orders from General Yu to withdraw from their respective sectors. The order to withdraw threatens the left of the X Corps lines. In conjunction, North Korean forces at this time are moving against P'yongch'ang.

February 15 The Chinese continue their counterattack against the central front. They drive southeast in force from the IX Corps sector to the X Corps front and isolate the 23rd Infantry Regiment, 2nd Division.

In the IX Corps sector, General Ridgway designates IX Corps with Operation KILLER, designed to eliminate the Chinese and terminate the counterattack.

In the X Corps sector, the 5th Cavalry continues to move to rescue the isolated 23rd Regiment, 25th Division, at Chipyong. Meanwhile, the defenders receive some unexpected help Planes that could not come on the previous day had concluded their mission at Wonju and now arrive to support Colonel Freeman's exhausted troops. Marine and Navy planes plaster the enemy positions by executing more than 130 close-support sorties. Colonel Freeman, the commander of RCT 23, convinced that the threat is now under control, agrees to be airlifted out of the area. Colonel Chiles assumes command.

More supplies arrive when transport planes from Japan drop the desperately needed ammunition. However, some of the parachutes drift into enemy territory. Subsequent attempts to extricate the supplies take a toll as enemy fire inflicts casualties. All the while, the Chinese hold strong positions in front of the advancing 5th Cavalry.

Colonel Crombez concludes that his force will fail to reach Chipyong before dusk. He decides to send armor with infantry atop, a controversial decision. At Chipyong, Colonel Chiles urges Crombez to continue to advance even if it is impossible to bring the vehicles. The column moves out at 1545 and soon after, at Koksu, enemy fire halts the advance. The infantry (Company L, 3rd Battalion) bolts from the tanks to find safer positions, while the tanks work to silence the enemy.

Meanwhile, the tanks are ordered by Crombez to plow forward, but without informing the attached infantry. Chaos follows as the bewildered infantry troops watch tanks leave. Most are able to jump aboard, but others are left stranded. Later, about one mile up the road, the enemy again commences heavy fire and halts the column. The infantry repeats itself and jumps from the tanks to get out harm's way. Soon after, the infantry seeks cover, and the tanks again dash forward, leaving the infantry on its own. Those who are able jump aboard the armor, but a large number — including the 3rd Battalion commander, Colonel Edgar J. Treacy — misses the ride.

Those who catch the train soon find themselves prime targets, as the Chinese continue to bring the armor under attack. The infantry, having only their uniforms as armor, cling haphazardly to the tanks as they charge through the fire. Finally, at about 1700, the battered armor and weary survivors of the infantry arrive at the perimeter, just about the time the 2nd Battalion, 23rd Infantry, 2nd Division, is launching a counterattack. The siege is lifted, but the cost is high. Company L, which had been with the armor, stands at 23 men out of 160 that began the advance. Of the 23, 13 are wounded. One tank had been destroyed and only its driver survived (with serious burns). The stranded infantry had been told that the tanks would return for them, but no relief force is sent.

Later, many of the troops make it back to friendly lines; however, the cost remains high with 12 killed, 40 wounded and 19, including Colonel Treacy, missing. Colonel Crombez had refused Treacy permission to join the relief column, but Treacy jumped aboard anyway, refusing to let his troops undertake such a dangerous mission without him. It is later learned that Treacy had been captured and died from his wounds in captivity.

At Chipyong, the 23rd Regiment sustains 52 killed, 259 wounded and 42 missing. Charles Parziale replaces Treacy as commander, 3rd Battalion.

In the X Corps sector, the U.S. 7th Division is ordered to speed a contingent (31st Infantry Regiment) from the vicinity of P'yongch'ang to the rear of the ROK 5th Division to bolster Chech'on, held by the 32nd Infantry Regiment. To further strengthen the line there, the 17th Infantry Regiment suspends its advance along Route 29 toward Wonju and deploys to the rear of the ROK 3rd Division.

In other activity, the British 27th Brigade continues to advance along Route 24 against nominal resistance, as it attempts to reach Chipyong. At Chipyong, RCT 23 continues to hold, but the Chinese maintain extraordinary pressure against the entire perimeter. The defenders had received supplies by air on the previous day, but again, the ammunition is nearly expended. The Chinese, however, are unable to overwhelm the steadfast combat team.

The most desperate sector is held by the 2nd Battalion, 23rd Regiment. A new counterattack is launched to restore the lost ground, but the strength of Company B, Freeman's last reserve, is insufficient. The attack fails to regain the ground. At about 1200, Air Force and Marine planes arrive to strike the Chinese positions. Later, the Chinese are compelled to disengage. At about 1630, while the planes and artillery maintain a constant attack, tanks are spotted by RCT 23's tanks and to their jubilation, it is a relief column under Colonel Crombez. As the tanks begin to converge, the enemy retires and the flight provides a large amount of targets for the U.S.

Crombez's contingent sustains 3 killed and 4 wounded (armor) and Company L sustains 12 killed, 40 wounded and 19 missing. Chinese casualties, estimated by RCT 23, amount to more than 4,900. TF Crombez estimates about 500 casualties inflicted upon the Chinese during the trek to reach Chipyong-ni. The Chinese had committed elements from about six regiments to the unsuccessful assault to reduce Chipyong-ni. RCT 23 reports 52 killed, 259 wounded and 42 missing.

In the 1st Marine sector, the operation in the Pohang–Andong region known as the guerrilla hunt officially terminates this day. The division begins to move to Chungju in the IX Corps sector; however, the 1st Marine Division remains under Eighth Army rather than IX Corps control. During the period covering the operation (18 January to 15 February) the Marines successfully complete all objectives, including keeping the MSR clear. For the same period, Marines sustain 19 killed in action, 149 wounded in action, 7 who later die of wounds, and 10 missing. In addition, the Marines sustain 1,751 other non-battle casualties, primarily frostbite.

The Marines had essentially knocked the 10th N.K. Division out of action and prevented it from achieving any success. The Marines count 120 enemy dead and another 184 are seized as prisoners, but no estimates are available for enemy wounded.

In the ROK I Corps sector, at 1400, the ROK I Corps assumes control of the SK 3rd, 5th and 8th Divisions.

In other activity, elements of the N.K. V Corps drive against the ROK 3rd Division and for a while, the 22nd ROK Regiment is threatened; however, artillery support is provided by the U.S. 7th Division and the assault is repelled. The ROK 5th Division on the left does not fare well. By day's end, the 5th Division retreats about five miles and it is considered ineffective for the field.

In Naval activity, at Masan, the USS *Wiseman* (DE 667) initiates a program that trains Korean midshipmen of the ROK Naval Academy and other naval personnel from the Service School at the Chinhae Naval Base.

February 16
In the I Corps sector, an enemy force on Hill 185 takes a platoon of the 7th Regiment, 3rd Division, under heavy fire and stalls the attack. Lieutenant Darwin K. Kyle jumps up to defy the intense fire and inspires his men to follow him. Shortly thereafter, an enemy machine gun again stalls the assault. Kyle singlehandedly charges the nest, engages its three occupants in hand-to-hand combat and eliminates all of them. Six men are already wounded when yet another nest opens fire. Kyle again leads an assault and in the process, he takes out four more of the enemy before enemy submachine gun fire kills him. Lieutenant Kyle becomes a recipient of the Medal of Honor posthumously for his extraordinary valor and heroism while leading his troops under fire.

In the IX Corps sector, a pending plan to commit IX Corps to an attack against the flanks of the Chinese salient is postponed due to several reasons, including the inability of the 1st Cavalry Division to field two of its regiments (7th and 8th). The 25th Division, which had relieved the 1st Cavalry Division, initiates an advance to Line Boston at the Han River. Four regiments move out with the British Brigade on the left, the 24th Infantry (center), 27th Infantry (right) and to the far right, the 5th Infantry (24th Division, I Corps). The advance is bolstered by powerful artillery bombardments that eliminate many of the Chinese who otherwise would have increased the resistance.

In other activity, the 1st and 2nd Battalions, 5th Cavalry, depart the vicinity of Hills 143 and 152 respectively and advance to Chipyong-ni. Also, Colonel Crombez, who arrived on the previous night to lift the siege at Chipyong, departs for Koksu'ri. Afterward, supply vehicles and ambulances depart Koksu'ri for Chipyong-ni and en route, the troops gather some U.S. troops, including wounded, along the road. The troops had been stranded during the advance of TF Crombez. The defenders at Chipyong-ni serve as an example of Ridgway's conviction that the Eighth Army could withstand the Chinese with its rejuvenated fighting spirit.

Also, the 7th and 8th Cavalry, relieved at Mugam by elements of the 25th Division, prepare to move to Yonju. The 5th Cavalry participates in the offensive that is being launched. In related activity, Colonel Robert Blanchard replaces Colonel Michaelis as commander of the 8th Cavalry. Michaelis, in command of the regiment for less than one month, is reassigned to other duties in Pusan. The 7th Cavalry, having engaged in vicious combat for a few weeks, including the hard-fought battle at Hill 578, is battle-weary, but in addition, the regiment is hit with an outbreak of typhus, making it incapable of resuming the attack. It is placed in reserve with the 8th Cavalry at Changhowon. Also, the 24th Division remains in its positions outside Yoju, near at the Han River.

In the X Corps sector, some attacks occur along the Wonju Line, but none are substantial, as the enemy offensive begins to subside. The ROK 3rd and 5th Divisions again come under pressure, but neither is forced to give ground.

February 17
Following the end of heavy fighting at Chipyong-ni, the S.K. 6th Division and the British 27th Brigade revert back to IX Corps. The Chinese had used five divisions against the 2nd Division's lines, but the 23rd RCT and the attached French Battalion had held. The Chinese disengage.

In related activity, General Ridgway arrives at Chipyong to confer with Colonels Crombez (5th Cavalry) and Chiles (23rd Regiment).

In the X Corps sector, enemy pressure against the Wonju Line diminishes further and by the following day, it is apparent that the North Korean V Corps has withdrawn from its sector. Although the U.S. had anticipated a heavy assault against Wonju, no efforts have been made by the Chinese since 14 February.

In Air Force activity, during the night (17th–18th), B-26s execute the initial mission that uses a new short-range navigational system for precision bombing missions. The system, known as Shoran, operates with an

Elements of the 27th Regiment, 25th Division, move along a snow covered mountain in the vicinity of Kyongan-ni on February 17. At about this time, the 3rd Division is to hold a sector of the Lincoln Line.

airborne radar device coordinated with two ground beacon stations.

In Naval activity, enemy positions at Wonsan are bombarded by Task Element of UN Blockade and Escort Task Group (TG 95.2).

February 18   *In the Eighth Army area,* General Ridgway during the latter part of this day declines a recommendation by his staff to hold in place and establish a defensive perimeter. Ridgway is unwilling to even consider canceling the offensive and affording the enemy an opportunity to retire in leisurely fashion. Eighth Army is ordered to remain on the offensive. During the meeting with his staff, Ridgway informs them that the 1st Marine Division will anchor the attack as part of IX Corps.

In the I Corps sector, there is no contact with either the North Koreans or the Chinese. The 25th Division sees some action in support of the IX Corps drive. By day's end, it becomes apparent that the Chinese and the North Koreans are abandoning South Korea. It is a significant accomplishment for Ridgway, who, since he assumed command of Eighth Army, has believed his troops could prevail. The victory also proves the theory of Ridgway and others that the Communists could not drive Eighth Army from Korea.

It is estimated that since the previous October, Eighth Army, including the 1st Marine Division and the supporting air and naval units, had decimated about fourteen Chinese divisions. And Ridgway had accomplished the tremendous turnabout in less than sixty days.

In the IX Corps sector, at 0745, the I Corps commander, Major General Bryant E. Moore, informs General Ridgway that one of his regiments (5th Infantry, 24th Division) has reported its front, east of Mugam, to be wide open with no enemy in the way. All fortifications encountered had been abandoned; however, the enemy had apparently departed hurriedly, as many weapons remained, and they had also abandoned large amounts of cooking equipment. The reports are passed on to other units and warnings of a ruse are sent out, but similar encounters occur all across the line, indicating the enemy is in the process of a general withdrawal.

Meanwhile, the 1st Cavalry Division, supported by the British 27th Brigade, and the ROK 6th Division advance towards the heights overlooking the Wonju–Seoul railroad line at a point several miles northwest of Chipyong-ni. The troops are ordered to form a line to prevent the enemy from entering the Han River Valley.

Reconnaissance probes on the previous night discovered that enemy resistance had begun to vanish except for an obstacle west of the river. The Chinese had evacuated their positions in the hills and apparently too fast to consider taking their dead along. The U.S. advance is effortless at the abandoned positions. About 600 dead remain on the field. Large amounts of ammunition and supplies had also been left behind.

The U.S. 24th Division expands the offensive and drives towards Hajin by pushing through the bridgehead, but the entire IX Corps had been ordered to attack by General Moore. The corps is also supported by elements of the I Corps. Its 25th Division advances through the western portion of the bridgehead. Great progress is made throughout the day. The Chinese raise only some sporadic resistance. Opposition throughout the central region dissipates. By 1800, the Han River, near Yongp'yong, is reached by elements of the 24th Division, while the 1st Cavalry arrives to deploy in the Hajin–Chipyong area.

Also, after being directed by General Ridgway to move from Pohang-dong, the 1st Marine Division (minus 7th Marines) arrives at Ch'ungju and prepares to spearhead the IX Corps drive when Operation KILLER commences. In conjunction, the Marines replace the 2nd Division and the 187th Airborne RCT in the vicinity of Wonju. The relief permits the U.S. Army units to rejoin X Corps on the 21st, when the boundary is modified to bring Wonju into the IX Corps jurisdiction.

In the X Corps sector, there is no contact with the Chinese or North Koreans.

February 19 *In the Eighth Army area,* General Ridgway arrives at IX Corps headquarters at Yoju to meet with General Bryant Moore and other staff officers, including Generals O.P. Smith and Lewis B. (Chesty) Puller, both of the 1st Marine Division. General Ridgway continues to work on Operation KILLER, scheduled to commence on the 21st. Ridgway is not totally sure of the combined strength of the Chinese and North Koreans, but best estimates from Intelligence place the opposition at about 6 to 7 new Chinese armies and four North Korean corps (plus, three armies and one corps in reserve).

Also, during the conference in which X Corps attended, the 1st Marine Division learns it is being detached from X Corps and placed under IX Corps control. General O.P. Smith (1st Marine Division) had not been receptive to again serve under General Almond (X Corps), since his experience with him in the previous year during the Inchon–Chosin Reservoir campaign. The Marines also learn that two army units, the 74th Truck Company and the 92nd FABn, are being assigned to the 1st Marine Division for added support. The Marines need no introduction to the 92nd FABn. Under the leadership of Lt. Colonel Leon F. Lavoie, its guns had provided welcome support during the Chosin Reservoir operations.

Although the Marines will spearhead the attack, they will be supported by the entire IX Corps and X Corps, except for the 187th Airborne RCT. The Marines are directed to drive northeastwardly from Wonju and liquidate as many of the enemy as possible during Operation KILLER.

In Naval activity, Task Group 95.9, commanded by Rear Admiral A.E. Smith, is established. Admiral Smith is relieved this day of command of United Nations Blockading and Escort Force (CTF 95) by Vice Admiral William Andrewes. Also, enemy shore batteries in the vicinity of Wonsan initiate fire against the USS *Ozbourn* (DD 846).

February 20 General MacArthur arrives in Korea from Japan. He confers with General Ridgway in the X Corps sector at a forward command post near Wonju. Ridgway doesn't particularly appreciate the conference, as MacArthur's appearance acts as an automatic signal to the enemy that an offensive is underway. MacArthur announces that the offensive had been ordered by him, yet he had no part in it.

A contingent of the U.S. 7th Division climbs Hill 675 on 20 February.

In the 1st Marines sector, the focus is on last minute preparations for the advance by the 1st and 5th Marines scheduled for the following morning at 0800.

In Air Force activity, Far East Air Forces establishes "Special Air Mission." The specialized unit, attached to the 315th Air Division, is assigned the responsibility for handling the flights for high ranking officials, but another task is to execute missions that drop leaflets over enemy terrain and, when needed, to broadcast messages from speakers installed on the aircraft.

February 21   By this date, the Communist salient at Chech'on is eliminated, which foils their attempt to turn the Allied flank.

Operation KILLER commences. The offensive (IX and X Corps) moves against the enemy east of the Han River and south of Line Arizona, which runs from the vicinity of Yangp'yong stretching across Route 29 at a point several miles above Hoengsong and across Route 60, at a point about six miles above P'yongchang.

In the I Corps sector, the units of the I Corps and the 24th Division (IX Corps) deployed along the lower bank of the Han River protect the west flank of the attacking forces.

In the IX Corps sector, the units advance up Route 29.

In the 1st Marine Division zone, General Puller, the assistant division commander, concerned about the 5th Marines' possible delay in reaching the line of departure

in time for the attack, contacts General O.P. Smith to inform him of the snarled traffic on the highway. Smith and General Bryant Moore (IX Corps) at the Marine command post at Wonju deliberate and conclude that the attack will commence on time, with whatever troops are on line. However, the delay causes the jump-off time to be changed to 1000.

The advance to seize the ridgeline several miles south of the heights that dominate Hoengsong is led by the 1st Battalion, 5th Marines. The elements provide most of the resistance as the Marines move under pesky rain, unending mud and slush, but no close range resistance. During the latter part of the afternoon, the enemy engages the Marines, but from great distance. After two fire fights, the enemy retires. The Marines sustain three men wounded. They establish night positions and spend a most uncomfortable night in water-drenched foxholes.

During the early morning hours, the ground remains frozen; however, by afternoon it begins to thaw, causing havoc. In addition to the normal problems associated with nature, the thawed ground exposes land mines that become active and deadly once the ice thaws.

In the X Corps sector, the assault drives up Route 60. As the offensive jumps off, nature delivers unexpected obstacles. The weather had suddenly turned relatively warmer, following about three weeks of continual cold that ranged from about 15 degrees below zero to about 33 to 34 degrees above zero. On this day, the temperature rises to nearly 50 degrees. Subsequently, the region is struck by rainfall and during the next several days, some roads became impassable and many bridges are either damaged or washed out.

In the meantime, the Chinese and the North Koreans had used the time to continue their retreat. The 2nd Division, attacking on the right of the Marines, commences its assault on the 22nd.

February 22   *In the Eighth Army area,* Operation KILLER continues against sporadic resistance. The offensive continues to be impeded by the elements.

In the IX Corps zone, the 1st Marine Division continues its advance with the 1st Battalion, 1st Marines, acting as vanguard. Similarly to the previous day, again the elements become the primary problem impeding the attack. The enemy continues to retreat and raises opposition only from long range.

In the X Corps sector, the 2nd and 7th Divisions initiate their attacks, but the elements create major problems which make the crossing of the Chech'on River hazardous. The river, usually more like a shallow stream, flows wildly at a depth of more than three feet. The lighter vehicles are unable to cross due to the strong currents. The tanks, however, make it across, but it is nearly 48 hours later when the two divisions finally get all units across the river. The 23rd Regiment, 2nd Division, hops aboard the tanks and gets a lead on the other infantry units.

February 23   Operation KILLER continues, but progress remains slow. The condition of the roads interrupts the supply system; however, planes bolster the drive and drop supplies to maintain the efficiency of the offensive. While the ground troops continue to advance in search of the enemy, engineers work tirelessly to repair the roads and the bridges that had been affected by the elements. About 800 sorties (Fifth Air Force) are flown in support of the advance.

In the IX Corps sector, 1st Marine Division zone, the Marines finally encounter opposition. The 1st and 2nd Battalions, 1st Marines, advance together to seize two elevations along a ridge in front of the objective. Marine air support requested on the previous day to bolster the attack does not materialize; however, the artillery provides sufficient punch. The Marines eliminate the resistance and gain the first hill. During the afternoon, they move to evict a contingent of about battalion-strength from deeply entrenched positions on the remaining hill. The assault is augmented by two air strikes. The hill is seized and 61 enemy dead are counted. The Marines lose 1 killed and 21 wounded.

In the X Corps sector, the 2nd and 7th Divisions encounter stiff resistance en route to Chipyong-ni. Urgent calls for air support go out and soon after, the call receives a response. Planes, including Marine Squadron VMF-312, arrive and the Chinese positions are pounded during the afternoon raids.

In Air Force activity, Far East Air Forces Bomber Command executes its initial B-29 bombing mission that uses the more efficient MPQ-2 radar. The planes

strike a bridge located less than ten miles northeast of Seoul.

February 24   *In the IX Corps sector,* the helicopter transporting Major General Bryant E. Moore during Operation KILLER crashes in the Han River. General Moore and his pilot sustain no major injuries. However, less than one hour after the crash, General Moore suffers a heart attack and succumbs. General Moore had only recently assumed command of IX Corps. He is temporarily replaced by General Oliver P. Smith, USMC.

Also, during the crossing of the Chech'on River, one of the tanks strikes a mine and a steel fragment strikes Colonel Cesidio Barberis, the commander of the 2nd Battalion, 9th Infantry Regiment. Although he isn't killed, Barberis is critically wounded and evacuated. He is replaced by Colonel Peter F. Bermingham.

In the 1st Marine Division zone, the 1st and 3rd Battalion, 5th Marines, drive forward and seize the intended Phase 1 objectives. Following an artillery barrage and an air strike, an infantry patrol (1st Marines), supported by one tank, moves into Hoengsong. Afterwards, a platoon of tanks and Company C, 1st Battalion, 1st Marines, enters the village, but the Chinese in the nearby heights to the west initiate mortar and machine gun fire. Two tanks sustain slight yet damaging hits, as their antennae are severed. Nevertheless, the Marines modify their strategy and by the use of a runner, Captain Wray is able to coordinate the enemy's positions. They are soon eliminated by the tanks.

In the meantime, Chinese are spotted by an aerial observer who informs the battalion commander, Lt. Colonel Schmuck, that the Chinese are maneuvering to ambush the patrol as it begins to move deeper into the town. The patrol is ordered to withdraw. Planes are called upon to blast the Chinese as they attempt to set up the ambush.

Captain Wray's contingent moves northwest of the village to a spot known as "Massacre Valley," the scene of a recent ambush of a U.S. Army truck convoy. The survivors are retrieved.

Later this day, enemy fire originating in the high ground northwest of Hoengsong causes problems and kills one Marine and wounds four others. The 2nd Battalion, 11th Marines, returns fire and terminates the enemy fire. By dusk, all divisional preliminary objectives are achieved.

In other activity, General Lewis B. Puller assumes command of the 1st Marine Division in place of General O.P. Smith, who receives temporary control of IX Corps.

In the X Corps sector, the 2nd and 7th Divisions encounter fierce resistance in front of Chipyong-ni. Air strikes are called upon to break up the resistance. Planes from VMF-312 arrive and strike the positions marked with white phosphorous. The enemy is struck repeatedly by napalm and rockets in addition to strafing, which compels the Chinese to abandon their positions. However, Major Daniel H. Davis, executive officer of the squadron, is killed after his plane loses a wing and crashes on his eighth run.

Elements of the 23rd Regiment, 2nd Division, advance to the Hoengsong–Pangnim Road. Conditions remain terrible and there is concern of stretching too far without a proper path for resupply, but orders arrive from X Corps to continue the attack.

Meanwhile, elements of the 7th Division advance to Pangnim.

In Naval activity, two destroyers and other vessels protect the landing of ROK Marines at Sindo–ri Island in Wonsan Harbor without incident.

In Air Force activity, a huge contingent of planes composed of sixty-seven C-119s and two C-47s, attached to the 315th Air Division, distribute by air drop 333 tons of supplies and equipment to the units along the front lines.

February 25 Operation KILLER continues; however, the main advance is suspended temporarily by General Ridgway to await resupply of ammunition and fuel as well as supplies. The entire operation is not halted, thanks to air drops of supplies. Once the supplies are at the front, the attack to the main objective, Phase Line Arizona, resumes. The IX and X Corps maintain the offensive, but the elements remain nasty.

In other activity, General Ridgway issues orders for the second phase of Operation KILLER, to begin on 1 March.

In the IX Corps sector, the ground Marines are disgruntled because they are receiving mostly Air Force support instead of their usual close-air support by Marine squadrons. The 1st Marine Air Wing is under Fifth Air Force jurisdiction and as the advance continues, the U.S. Army and the British units request Marine fighter squadrons. On Feb. 23, the third day of Operation KILLER, the Marine squadrons flew 101 of the 800 sorties. Marine pilots are known for flying support missions just above the helmets of the ground troops if necessary.

Also, the weather impedes the advances of the 1st Cavalry Division and the 24th Division, each advancing on the Marines' left. The Commonwealth Brigade, which replaced the 7th Cavalry, hits severe resistance east of Chipyong. Elements of the Australian and Canadian Battalions attempt to eliminate the obstacles, but the Chinese repel the attempt.

February 26 General Ridgway

unfolds his plan known as Operation RIPPER during a meeting with the commanders of the I, IX and X Corps at Changhowon. The operation is to commence on 10 March; however, the date is later changed to 7 March. Although there had been much discussion in Washington on why Eighth Army should not attempt to cross the 38th Parallel, Ridgway's plan had been accepted by the Joint Chiefs of Staff. The operation is intended to liquidate as many Communists as possible to disrupt their plans, if any, about launching an offensive. Another part of the operation is to regain Seoul.

Also, the Combat Cargo Command continues to overwork its crews and planes to deliver more than 600 tons of supplies and 1,193 passengers to keep the offensive moving. On the previous day, the planes had delivered nearly 500 tons of supplies and just over 1,000 passengers.

In the IX Corps sector, the 1st Marine Division prepares

A view of some Korean mountains from the top of a pole. A lineman repairs a communications wire, a task that apparently does not get too many volunteers.

for the next phase of the operation. While it holds its positions at Hoengsong, the next objective is within sight of the troops that observe the hills to the north of the village. The Marines face a river crossing, without the benefit of a bridge nor engineers to construct a bridge. They also must push their way forward to relieve the ROK 6th Division at the point prior to fording the river.

Nevertheless, they improvise. Major (later General) Edwin H. Simmons (Weapons Company) pulls out a manual on how to construct a "Swiss bent bridge." Simmons hands the book to Sergeant Carmelo J. Randazzo. Randazzo becomes the engineering expert and by dark of the 28th, the bridge is complete in two parts. One length stretches 120 feet to a sandbar and from the sandbar to the opposite bank, the span stretches 60 feet.

In the X Corps sector, as part of Operation KILLER, Company E, 17th Regiment, 7th Division, gets stalled as it attacks a ridge in the vicinity of Maltari. The two squads at the point are prevented from an advance by ferocious fire. Corporal Einar H. Ingman, Jr., assumes command of the point after several men and the two respective squad leaders become wounded. Ingman, without waiting for his command to follow, bolts from his position to silence an enemy machine gun that rivets his men's positions. He eliminates the entire detachment and its gun, but then he is brought under fire by yet another gun. Ingman darts toward the menace, but he is hit by fire and grenades that knock him to the ground. Despite wounds to his neck and face, Ingman rises and continues to charge, using only his rifle. His stamina exceeds normal human expectations and he is able to eliminate the entire second gun crew. But, just after clearing the nest, he collapses into unconsciousness.

By this time, his squads are back on the attack and they finish the task. The enemy force of about 100 troops is vanquished. They abandon the hill and retire. Ingman is rushed to the rear for medical aid. He survives and becomes a recipient of the Medal of Honor for his extraordinary courage and leadership in the face of an overwhelming enemy force.

February 27 Operation KILLER continues. The IX and X Corps continue to advance slowly. By the following day, the IX Corps, operating in the east, is at the heights above Hoengsong and the X Corps reaches positions in the heights just under five miles north of the junction of Routes 20 and 60.

February 28 By this day, the Communist threat in the area south of the Han River folds, terminating weeks of heavy fighting. By the end of this day, the entire line of Eighth Army is restored with no gaps and no enemy forces threatening the lines. The IX and X Corps have each reached Arizona line on the west and east respectively. Operation KILLER continues.

In addition to the recent loss of Major General Moore, some other command changes had occurred during February. Brigadier General Charles D. Palmer replaced General Gay as commander, 1st Cavalry Division (IX Corps), and Brigadier General J. Sladen Bradley assumes command of the 25th Infantry Division. He succeeds General Kean.

March 1 General Ridgway again holds a meeting with his corps commanders at Changhowon to update the plans for Operation RIPPER. The date is changed from 10 March to 6 March; however, the offensive actually commences on 7 March. Later this same day, the operation orders are officially issued. The designated lines are Albany, Buffalo, Cairo and Idaho.

In the IX Corps sector, some units continue to advance to reach the Arizona Line, but they face no heavy resistance. The Chinese 39th Army is deployed to the front of IX Corps.

In the 1st Marine Division zone, the 3rd Battalion, 7th Marines, moves across the new bridge built by regular Marines under the supervision of Sergeant Randazzo. The attack force vanguard advances to the heights north of Hoengsong, with the 3rd Battalion, 1st Marines, trailing. The Marines' arrival on the west bank of the river had been announced by a tumultuous artillery bombardment. In addition, planes arrive, but behind schedule, to deliver air strikes.

The 2nd and 3rd Battalions, 7th Marines, hit resistance. Initially the 2nd Battalion encounters small arms fire and afterward, both Battalions enter an area that is booby-trapped, which stalls the attack. The Chinese remain deeply entrenched and the artillery is unable to evict them. By the middle of the afternoon, it is decided to halt the drive until the following day.

In related activity, the 2nd Battalion, 1st Marines, east of the river seizes Hill 208 and afterwards, joins with the 3rd Battalion, 1st Marines.

In other activity, General Puller informs General Shepherd, commander, Fleet Marine Force Pacific, that Marine close-air support is non-existent and repeated requests go unanswered. He further explains that Navy and Air Force planes arrive and do a good job, but not the same as would be accomplished with Marine pilots. The message is sent in hope of getting back to direct Marine support rather than Joint Operations Center for Fifth Air Force.

In the X Corps sector, the enemy raises opposition in the heights above Route 20. The resistance continues, particularly against the 2nd Division, until the 5th. The X Corps is facing the North Korean III Corps (minus NK 3rd Division).

In Air Force activity, Bomber Command (FEAF) initiates the initial mission of a new interdiction campaign. The B-29s executing the mission are to be escorted by twenty-two F-80s, but headwinds cause problems and the rendezvous does not occur. Nonetheless, the jets arrive over the target area, Kogunyong, prior to the arrival of the B-29s. Consequently, the F-80s run low on fuel and return to base, leaving the B-29s unprotected in the North Korean skies. A band of MiGs attacks the Superfortresses. The B-29s attempt to fight off the MiGs, and succeed in downing one.

However, ten of the B-29s sustain damage and of these, three are unable to return to Japan and make emergency landings in South Korea.

March 2
Although most of the IX and X Corps had reached the objectives along the Arizona Line, other units are continuing to advance towards it.

In the IX Corps sector, 1st Marine Division zone, the advance continues, but while the Communists remain well entrenched in the heights, the Marines trek across rocky ground. The 11th Marines' artillery catapults streams of shells into the enemy positions, but they are not dislodged.

In the 1st Cavalry Division zone, enemy mortars strike the perimeter. The commander of the 2nd Battalion, 5th Cavalry, is killed during the attack. He is replaced by Lt. Colonel Richard L. Irby. The 5th Cavalry has been undergoing other unexpected changes of command. The 3rd Battalion commander, Colonel Treacy had been taken prisoner of war in early February. Charles T. Heinrich replaced Morgan Heasley as commander of the 3rd Battalion.

March 3
In the ROK III Corps area, the corps, which had initiated an offensive along Route 20 during the latter part of February, encounters fierce resistance. It had departed from the sector around Kangnung to establish a defensive line in front of the IX and X Corps. The advancing force, composed of two regiments of the ROK Capital Division, is unexpectedly attacked by elements of the NK 2nd Division at a point about twenty-five miles west of its departure point, at a village known as Soksa-ri. The ambush takes a devastating toll on the regiments and knocks them out of action. The casualties amount to 59 killed, 119 wounded and 802 troops missing.

In the IX Corps sector, the Marines close upon the Arizona Line. At dawn, the final objectives come into sight as the Marines gaze north towards the five enemy-held hills along Phase Line Arizona from west to east, Hills 536 and 533 in the path of the 7th Marines, and Hills 321, 335 and 201 in that of the 1st Marines. The 7th Marines attack is met with fierce resistance at Hills 536 and 333. The 1st Battalion is called upon to cover the left flank of the regiment and simultaneously support the assault against Hill 536. At Hill 333, the enemy holds steadfastly against the 3rd Battalion. At dusk, the summits of both hills remain in enemy hands.

In the 1st Marines zone, at Hill 321, the Chinese are abandoning their positions as the 3rd Battalion, 1st Marines, approach. The Marines overcome the resistance without much effort, but the unit still sustains casualties due to the trek across the nasty terrain. In the meantime, Hills 335 and 201 are secured. By the following day, the 1st Marines executes mop-up operations, while the 7th Marines prepares to mount another assault to take the summits of Hills 536 and 333.

In Air Force activity, Far East Air Forces resumes bombing missions that use radar guided Tazon bombs. These missions had been suspended on 17 January due to a shortage of the bombs.

March 4
In the IX Corps sector, General William M. Hoge, USA, arrives at Yoju to assume command of IX Corps. On the following day, he replaces General O.P. Smith, USMC, the temporary commander. Smith returns to resume command of the 1st Marine Division. In turn, the temporary commander, General Puller, resumes his duties as assistant division commander.

In the 1st Marine Division zone, subsequent to an artillery bombardment, the 7th Marines, at 0800, launches an attack to gain the crests of Hills 536 and 333. The only resistance encountered is the rear guard. The main body had evacuated the area during the night. The 1st Marine Division, having eliminated the five hills along the Phase Line Arizona, achieves its objectives to terminate its part of Operation KILLER by dusk. However, mop-up operations continue on the following day. The 1st Marine Division during the eight days of the operation sustains 48 killed, 345 wounded and 2 missing. The Marines are unable to count all of the enemy dead, because often, when time allows, the Chinese bury their dead before abandoning the area. The Marines however, count 274 dead and they have seized 48 prisoners.

March 5
The date for the commencement of Operation RIPPER is 6 March; however, there is concern that the ammunition supplies are not yet sufficient to ensure all units have ample amounts. The operation is postponed for one day in order to acquire more supplies.

In the IX Corps sector, Major General William J. Hoge assumes command of the IX Corps succeeding the temporary commander, General Oliver P. Smith, USMC. General Joseph Swing, the initial selection by Ridgway, is unavailable. The U.S. Army refuses to release him from his post at the Army War College. General Ridgway had received heat from various sources for selecting General Smith to command an army corps, but he did not acquiesce. Nevertheless, General Smith did find some humor in the way the army rushed to find a permanent commander.

In the X Corps sector, following five days of heavy resistance, the 2nd Division finally scatters the N.K. troops that had been holding formidable positions in the heights. After dark, the North Koreans abandon their positions.

March 6
In the IX Corps sector, all units by this time reach the Arizona Line or have advanced to positions close to it.

In Air Force activity, F-86 Sabres attached to the 334th Fighter Interceptor Squadron, after an absence of several months, again initiate raids from Suwon against targets in the Yalu River area. The 334th Fighter Interceptor Squadron, 4th Fighter Interceptor Group, has no breathing room at Suwon, with its one runway and no taxiway. The pilots must back up the runway after landing to park their planes. The 336th Fighter Interceptor Squadron, another recalled unit, moves to Taegu and stages its jets through Suwon.

March 7   By this day, Operation KILLER achieves only some of its objectives and falls short of liquidating all of the enemy forces below the Arizona line. Nevertheless, IX Corps reports 7,819 enemy killed, 1,469 wounded and 208 captured. In the meantime, the enemy continues to withdraw from its positions.

Operation RIPPER commences at 0545 with a massive artillery barrage that rings enemy positions north of the Han River until about 0615, when the guns switch to targets deeper in the enemy's territory. The offensive is designed to continue to eliminate as many enemy forces as possible. The seizure of territory is not a primary part of the operation.

Naval task forces have been bombarding enemy positions since the previous month and they continue to operate. In addition, the U.S. Navy has commenced several diversionary operations to feign an amphibious attack. The ultimate objective of the offensive is the Idaho Line to the east is along the Han River, less than ten miles from Seoul. From there, it stretches across a portion of the eastern sector of the I Corps sector until it reaches a point near the 38th Parallel.

The attack, which is also supported by Fifth Air Force, is planned to advance in phases to a group of lines, Albany, in the vicinity of Hongch'on, slightly more than ten miles in front of the I, IX and X Corps; Buffalo Line, in front of the I and IX Corps and the Cairo Line, which concerns only IX Corps and signified the gateway to Ch'unch'on.

As usual, General MacArthur arrives in Korea, but in line with the request of General Ridgway, his arrival occurs later in the morning, which permits the offensive to jump off without the enemy getting a premature signal from MacArthur's presence. While at Suwon,

MacArthur, at a press conference, mentions the possibility of a stalemate in Korea. His remarks reflect his displeasure with Washington, which does not agree with his plans, including permitting the Nationalist Chinese to invade the China mainland and a huge number of U.S. reinforcements.

In the I Corps sector, the U.S. 3rd Division and the ROK 1st Division, in the eastern and western areas respectively, are directed to protect the flank and defend Inchon, where the Navy is tirelessly unloading supplies to support the offensive. The 3rd Division maneuvers along the Han south of Seoul to draw attention away from the 25th Division, while the ROK 1st Division advances northwest of Kimpo Airfield.

Meanwhile, the 25th Division, which holds ground east of Seoul, is to drive across the Han River where it converges with the Pukham River and from there, it is to clear the heights above the Pukham River. From there the 3rd Division is to deploy from where it can drive against enemy-held Seoul and to simultaneously defend the IX Corps' left flank.

Prior to dawn, elements of three regiments of the 25th Division cross the river in boats, followed by tanks. The assault regiments are the 27th and 35th, but the 24th Regiment (including Turkish Brigade) also has a key role during the offensive. Shortly thereafter, at sunrise, planes arrive to bolster the advance. The enemy throws up resistance, including road obstacles, but after short bursts of heavy fire, the Communists retire. By dusk, the advance gains less than three miles, but the division pushes elements across the Han River in the vicinity of the Pukham River and establishes a bridgehead on the north bank.

During the night, the Chinese attack the positions of

A Sherman tank (M4) attached to the 89th Tank Battalion in the foreground crosses the Han River near its convergence with the Pukham River on 7 March.

the 2nd Battalion, 24th Regiment, pounding against Companies E and F. The companies are driven from their positions in the heights, but on the following day, a counterattack is mounted and the ground is regained. The Chinese resistance remains heavy for several days and the average ground gained remains about the same.

The 25th Division unexpectedly seizes more than 300 Chinese prisoners during the first day of the operation. After interrogation, it seems apparent that the Chinese have lost much of their fighting spirit, a piece of intelligence that adds to the morale of Eighth Army. Circumstances have changed greatly since the Chinese have ventured so far south from Manchuria and their main bases.

In the IX Corps sector, the primary thrust of the offensive begins. The advance drives towards Chunchon and Hongch'on. The 187th Airborne RCT remains at Taegu, prepared if necessary to support the advance. Four divisions jump off. In the eastern half of the sector, the 1st Cavalry, 1st Marine Division, and the ROK 6th Division plow towards Hoengsong. The 24th Division, operating on the Corps' left, drives forward across the Yongmun Mountains.

In the 24th Division zone, the 19th Regiment encounters stiff resistance in the vicinity of Yonggong-ni. A squad attached to Company I attempts to ascend a hill, but heavy fire halts progress. The squad leader, Sergeant Nelson V. Brittin, under the support fire of the detachment, plows ahead and throws a grenade at the first entrenchment he encounters, but while returning to his detachment an enemy grenade explodes and wounds him. He disregards his injury, grabs more grenades and heads back to eliminate more of the enemy and clear the path for his troops. Brittin expeditiously moves, eliminating obstacles in his way and then, his weapon jams.

He jumps into the next foxhole and with the butt of his rifle and bayonet, he eliminates those in it. But still, the platoon is unable to advance, due mostly to another machine gun nest. Brittin maneuvers to its rear, deposits a grenade and then speeds to the front to finish off the several occupants in the nest. Afterward, the platoon is able to advance, but shortly thereafter, yet another enemy machine gun halts progress.

Once again, Brittin singlehandedly drives toward the nest. Brittin is stopped short of the nest by automatic weapons fire that kills him instantly. His actions, however, inspire the remainder of his command and the objective is seized. Prior to his demise, Brittin had eliminated twenty of the enemy and destroyed four machine gun nests. Sergeant Brittin is awarded the Medal of Honor posthumously for his extraordinary valor under fire.

In the 1st Marines zone, the initial objective is slightly more than five miles distant, just beyond Oum Mountain, but no map is required, as its towering peak is visible from the line of departure. During this offensive, the Marines are en route to reintroduce themselves to the Chinese 66th Army, commanded by General Show Shiu Kwai. The 7th Marines and the 1st Marines on the left and right respectively advance abreast against light resistance.

Meanwhile, the 5th Marines remains in reserve, confined to patrols in the vicinity of Hoengsong. The Hoengsong–Hongchon Road that curves through Kunsama Pass actually parallels the boundary separating the 7th and 5th Marines. During the advance, the Marines are jubilant; the sky is full of MAG-33 squadrons, which more than makes up for an unusual decrease in artillery support due to a shortage of shells. By day's end, all objectives are achieved. The Marines sustain 7 men wounded in action during the advance. Elements of the 2nd Division (X Corps) accompany the Marines and search for troops that had been killed during February (Operation ROUNDUP).

In the X Corps sector, the drive focuses on clearing enemy forces along two separate north-south routes. Also, the ROK 5th Division is reattached to X Corps. Enemy resistance raised by the North Koreans against the 2nd and 7th U.S. Divisions and the ROK 5th Division remains heavy for several days. The 7th Division drills along Route 20, holding the right, while the 2nd Division advances through the Pungam'ni corridor on the left. In conjunction, the ROK troops work the ridges in between the two U.S. divisions.

In the ROK sectors, the ROK I and III Corps move to clear the other part of the sector to the east. The ROK 3rd Division and Headquarters, ROK I Corps (ROK 9th and Capital Divisions), are detached from X Corps and reattached to the ROK III Corps. During Operation RIPPER, the ROK Corps are designated responsibility for clearing Route 30. The I Corps is deployed near the coast, at or near the Idaho line; however, the ROK III Corps is fixed farther inland and it is to drive north through the Taeback ridges to reach the line at a point about five miles above Route 20.

March 8 *In the I Corps sector,* 25th Division zone, the 24th Regiment, which had lost some ground on the previous night, launches a counterattack and drives the Chinese back, then regains the ground. Progress also continues for the 27th and 35th Regiments as the advance moves into the heights of the Pukham valley.

In the IX Corps sector, 1st Marine Division zone, the 7th and 1st Marine Regiments resume the attack and again become jubilant when MAG-12 Marine squadrons are spotted overhead during the trek. The 3rd Battalion, 1st Marines, accompanied by Company A, 1st Tank Battalion, encounters some stiff resistance, but it does not last too long. The 11th Marines pinpoint the area and initiate an artillery barrage that terminates the resistance, again raised by rear-guard troops entrenched mostly in log bunkers.

As the 7th Marines advance, Company A encounters fierce resistance originating on a hill mass to the left of Oum San, several hundred yards distant. Two men of the 2nd Platoon are killed and several others, including Lieutenant Clayton Bush, the platoon leader, are wounded when their positions sustain a direct hit from a high explosive shell. The 1st Platoon takes over and with the support of tanks, the enemy is evicted from the hill. The Marines' system to root them out seems to work well. Initially, the resistance is struck by napalm and then fire from the tanks' 90-mm shells, just prior to the close-quartered assault, when the Marines close and toss hand grenades into the bunkers. By dusk, the Marines reach their assigned zones.

In Naval activity, U.S. and British warships USS *Manchester* (CL 83), USS *Evans* (DD 754), USS *Sperry* (DD 697) and HMNS *Evertsen* (DD), initiate a siege bombardment of enemy-held Songjin.

March 9

In the I Corps sector, 25th Division zone, progress continues as the Division maneuvers to outflank Seoul.

In the IX Corps sector, 1st Marine Division zone, the Marines suspend the advance to await the Army units on the right to move up and come abreast. The 2nd Battalion, 1st Marines, establishes blocking positions, while the 1st and 7th Marines dispatch patrols on the flanks in search of the enemy.

In the X Corps sector, 7th Division zone, Company C, 17th Regiment, encounters heavy resistance near Taemi-dong. Tenacious impenetrable fire from automatic weapons stalls the advance. Captain Raymond Harvey's 1st Platoon is at the point. Harvey takes the initiative to unclog the path. He drives singlehandedly to the first machine gun nest and eliminates it and the crew, then bolts to the next nest and destroys it. The platoon is then able to advance, but only until the next machine gun halts its progress. Harvey, with an apparent propensity for defying the odds, again singlehandedly moves against the third nest and somehow gets through a riveting blanket of fire from where he is able to destroy it, too.

With the destruction of the third nest, Harvey again leads the platoon forward, but he pauses after spotting yet another nest. Captain Harvey springs toward the obstacle and plugs a hole with grenades to destroy the gun and the five members of its crew. By this time, Harvey is wounded. Nonetheless, he refuses evacuation and maintains command. The platoon presses forward, with the remainder of the company trailing. The obstacles are liquidated and the advance continues. Captain Harvey becomes a recipient of the Medal of Honor for his extraordinary actions under fire and his steadfast leadership in the face of the enemy.

March 10

Operation RIPPER continues to push ahead against some enemy resistance, but it is compelled to frequently give ground. Large numbers of Chinese and North Koreans are converging on the area above the 38th Parallel. General Ridgway establishes a command post at Yoju. In addition, he directs Eighth Army headquarters to move from Taegu to Chongju, to conspicuously show the advance is permanent.

In the I Corps sector, resistance against the advance subsides. By this day, the enemy forces have rebuilt their numbers with fresh troops from Manchuria.

In the IX Corps sector, 1st Marine Division zone, the Marines maintain patrols, but the advance remains on hold. In conjunction, to the rear, the Marine service moves up to the vicinity of Hoengsong.

March 11

Enemy resistance, which has often been heavy since the opening of Operation RIPPER, diminishes. This permits huge gains all across the front.

In the IX Corps sector, elements of the corps begin to arrive at the Albany Line. Other units follow during the next two days. The attack to reach the second line begins on 14 March.

In the 1st Marine Division zone, the advance is resumed after the Reconnaissance Company, reinforced with a platoon of tanks, relieves the 2nd Battalion, 1st Marines. The Communists continue to withdraw as the Marines move forward. Resistance in front of the advance remains light, but at Hill 549, a patrol from the 3rd Battalion, 1st Marines, unexpectedly comes under heavy fire. Tanks accompanying the patrol return fire from a distance of about fifty yards, while Marines gnaw forward and from close range, five enemy bunkers are blasted with hand grenades. The patrol, which initially loses one man killed and nine wounded, withdraws. The 11th Marines then plaster the hill to finish destroying any remaining bunkers.

March 12

In the Eighth Army area, General Ridgway holds a press conference at his recently established command post at Yoju. Ridgway proclaims that an Eighth Army offensive to regain the 38th Parallel would be a momentous victory and would ensure that the Communists' thrust had been halted, essentially accomplishing the goal of the U.N.

Also, U.S. planes on reconnaissance missions observe large numbers of enemy troops as they move away from Seoul. Although it isn't a definite sign, it is thought by the Americans that the Communists are preparing to abandon the South Korean capital without a fight.

After dark, patrols from I Corps move across the Han River and discover some enemy positions along the river that have been abandoned. By dusk, the 1st Marine Division, the 1st Cavalry Division and the 24th Division are in positions along the Albany Line.

In the IX Corps sector, the 1st Marine Division advances and in most instances merely occupies ground, as the enemy has retreated. Also, the recovery unit of the 2nd Division, which has been moving with the Marines since the 7th, has retrieved the remains of more than two hundred and fifty troops, primarily from Support Force 21. In addition, the troops recover five operable 155-mm howitzers, thought to have been destroyed by planes when the unit retired. The operation also recovers four of six tanks that had been lost and six M-5 tractors.

General Ridgway had arrived in the Marines' sector during the morning and after departing, he had his pilot fly him over the recaptured area in Massacre Valley near Hoengsong where elements of the 2nd Division (Support Force 21) had been devastated the previous February.

In Air Force activity, a contingent of four RF-80 Shooting Stars, attached to the 36th Fighter Bomber Squadron, are intercepted by a band of 12 MiGs while on a reconnaissance mission in the vicinity of Nansi.

The F-80 pilots engage the enemy, but no MiGs are downed, although several are damaged. During the air duels, two of the MiGs collide and both crash.

March 13   *In the I Corps sector,* the 25th Division's three attacking regiments by this time are fully deployed at the Pukham River (Albany Line). The 35th Regiment, which arrived on the 11th, established its lines on the east side of the river. The west side of the river is occupied by the 24th Regiment. In the nearby high ground (Yebong Mountain mass), the 27th Regiment establishes positions from where it can advance several miles to the Seoul–Chunchon Road in the vicinity of the outskirts of Seoul.

After dark, patrols from the 3rd Division and the ROK 1st Division venture about one-half mile above the Han River without incident. The lack of enemy contact prompts a crossing of the river the following day.

In the IX Corps sector, the 1st Marine Division continues to occupy positions against no resistance along the Albany Line. The IX Corps advance (First Phase, Operation RIPPER, March 7–March 13) reports enemy casualties as 6,413 killed in action and 216 captured. The IX Corps' casualties are reported as 158 killed, 965 wounded and 35 missing in action.

In the X Corps sector, elements of the 2nd and 7th Divisions arrive at the Albany Line.

In the ROK I Corps sector, elements of the ROK 9th Division and the Capital Division hold a line that stretches from the vicinity of the Huangbyong Mountains to the coast, in close proximity to Chumunjin.

A large force of North Koreans, survivors of an earlier operation initiated by the Marines and the ROK 2nd Division, avoided liquidation and on this day approach the ROK line. The division had been trapped in the Pohang-dong–Andong–Yongdok region since February, but it managed to move through the Taebaek Mountains and reach the Chungbong Mountains. The ROK troops, aware of the threat to their rear, funnel two regiments of the ROK 9th Division and a contingent of troops from the Capital Division to engage and destroy the remnant force of about two thousand men. The opposing sides skirmish this day.

In the ROK III Corps sector, the Albany line is reached and some of the units are able to move beyond it.

March 14   Operation RIPPER initiates Phase Two. Eighth Army drives towards the second line, Buffalo.

In the I Corps sector, on the west side of the Pukham River, the 25th Division advances towards a point slightly less than five miles above the Seoul–Chunchon Road. During midday, small contingents of the U.S. 3rd Division and the ROK 1st Division bolt across the Han River, anticipating resistance at a prominent obstacle, Hill 348 several miles south of the capital; however, the positions had been abandoned by the enemy. Other patrols also advance. One unit moves to the Seoul–Chunchon Road without incident, while another advanced to the city's southeastern fringes expecting resistance from Hill 175, a heavily defended part of South Mountain, but it, too, had been abandoned.

General Ridgway's intuition had been correct. The Communists abandoned Seoul without a fight. Elements of the ROK 1st Division move into the capital against no opposition and unfurl the ROK colors on the capitol building. This seizure is the fourth time Seoul has changed hands since the conflict began.

In the IX Corps sector, Hongchon becomes the objective of the 1st Cavalry Division and the 1st Marine Division. The town is secured on the following day and afterwards, the respective forces deploy along the Buffalo line outside the village in position to hold Route 29, which moves northwestwardly towards Chunchon and Route 24 through the Hongch'on River valley.

Also, the 1st Cavalry, operating on the west, moves against Hongchon, while the 1st Marine Division drives against it from the east through the treacherous Oum Mountains. The Marines reach a point several miles outside Hongchon, but after the exhausting trek, they establish night positions rather than continue the drive. Meanwhile, the 1st Cavalry had arrived at the river just west of the village by mid-afternoon. The enemy raises fierce resistance that continues into the 16th and beyond.

In conjunction, the 24th Division, supported by the ROK 6th Division, clears the western sector of the corps' zone effortlessly, due to the total lack of resistance. The advance continues to the lower bank of the Hongchon River and the Chongp'yong Reservoir, still without opposition. The attack to seize Hongchon commences on the following morning.

In Air Force activity, Bomber Command initiates a new tactic. Its B-26s drop a new type of spike on the highways frequented by enemy convoys. Tetrahedral tacks are designed especially for this type of mission and they perform much better that what had previously been used, roofing nails.

In Naval activity, enemy positions and other targets, Chaho, Kyojo Wan, Songjin and Wonsan, are bombarded by Fast Carrier Task Forces (TF 77) from this day until 8 March. The USS *Missouri* (BB 63) participates and receives credit for the destruction of fifteen rail and highway bridges.

March 15   By this date, the offensive has accounted for more than 7,100 enemy dead; however, the Chinese and North Koreans continue to withdraw, making it difficult to greatly increase the numbers and thoroughly liquidate the Communists forces.

In other activity, the 1st Marine Air Wing by this time is authorized to fly forty sorties per day in close-support missions for the 1st Marine Division. Also, Marine Squadron VMF(N)-542 is at about this time heading back to the Marine base, El Toro, California, to be transformed into an all-weather jet (F3D) squadron. Other changes include VMF(N)-312 relieving VMF-212 on the USS *Bataan*. Meanwhile, VMF-212 moves to K-3 at Pohang.

General Ridgway, having Seoul back in the hands of the UN, decides to exploit the Communist retreat by expanding the offensive and moving farther north to the Imjin River. The I Corps plays a larger part in this operation, which becomes known as Operation COURAGEOUS in place of Operations KILLER and RIPPER.

In the I Corps sector, Seoul is searched for enemy remnants, but only some North Koreans who apparently deserted were discovered. Outside the city, patrols scour the area north of the capital and encounter no opposi-

tion until reaching a point about five miles out. North of the capital, it is discovered by aerial observance that the enemy had established defensive positions. Troop concentrations are observed along the route between Seoul and Uijongbu. The Belgian Battalion, attached to the U.S. 3rd Division after its arrival during the latter part of January, is also unsuccessful during its search for the enemy troops in its sector, along the eastern fringes of the capital.

A patrol advances through Hongch'on, seized without opposition by the 1st Battalion, 7th Marines, on 15 March.

Ridgway orders the 3rd Division to move from the south bank of the Han River to positions north of Seoul, along the Seoul–Uijongbu Road, along the Lincoln Line (east sector) next to the 25th Division's positions. The ROK 3rd Division is also ordered to move across the Han River and deploy along the Seoul–Munsan Road along the Lincoln Line (west sector) next to the 3rd Division. The British Brigade is to move from reserve to Yongdungp'o and be prepared to bolster the Lincoln Line. The movement is initiated on 16 March.

In the IX Corps sector, the 24th Division, operating in the extreme left section of the sector and still bolstered by the ROK 6th Division, reaches the lower bank of the Chongp'yong Reservoir. Nearby, the ROK troops deploy in the high ground above the Hongchon River. As the advance continues, the 15th, 24th and 27th Regiments of the 25th Division, operating on the corps' right, reach the Seoul–Chunchon Road by about dusk. Its attached Turkish Brigade advances to a point on the extreme right of the zone to positions slightly less than three miles above the road. Meanwhile, the Turks deploy there near the 24th Division.

In other activity, the Marines hit stiff resistance at a ridge slightly east of Hongchon. While the Marines eradicate the opposition, a contingent, the 1st Battalion, 7th Marines, seizes the town at about 1200 without incident. The 1st Battalion commander, Major Webb D. Sawyer, dispatches a patrol through the demolished village in search of remnant Chinese forces, but none are found. The town was unoccupied, however. Bombs dropped earlier by planes of the Far East Air Force were set to detonate when touched. As the patrol moves back, one jeep is damaged when it detonates a "Butterfly" bomb. Later, while specialists (Company D, 1st Engineer Battalion) work to eliminate the bombs, the battalion moves through and deploys in the heights just northeast of the village. The bomb-clearing operation lasts for three days.

The 1st Cavalry Division remains at the Hongchon River until the remainder of the Marine force moves beyond the opposition on the ridge to join it and reinitiate the advance. Later, General Milburn (I Corps) is directed by General Ridgway to deploy in the high ground just outside the city. Milburn chooses the heights about two miles west of the capital that stretch across the ridge containing Hill 348. Lincoln Line, links with the Buffalo Line in the sector held by the 25th Division. A section of the line is to be held by the 3rd Division; however, the larger part is held by the ROK 1st Division, with the South Koreans receiving responsibility for Seoul and the U.S. holding the lesser portion east of Seoul.

General Ridgway also instructs Milburn to not fortify with full strength; rather, to deploy one battalion, bolstered by some tanks. The South Koreans are instructed to deploy one regiment. Instructions are also delivered that insist that no attack be initiated. Ridgway explains that the present task is to shadow the enemy retreat.

In other activity, the enemy raises fierce resistance east of Hongchon against the Marines. Following day-long fighting, the enemy abandons its positions after dark.

In the X Corps sector, the advance towards the Idaho Line continues. This day, the North Koreans raise resistance, but it is the sole incident during the advance. By the following day, all corps units reach the objective. The 38th Regiment, 2nd Division, had been opposed by North Koreans who held a pass (14th–15th), but the resistance is overrun. The Communists lose 345 killed (counted) and an estimated 800 additional casualties had been inflicted (killed and wounded). The 38th Regiment sustains 12 killed and 156 wounded.

In Air Force activity, a contingent of planes executes an armed reconnaissance mission in North Korea. During the operation, which had been initiated in support of ground forces, one element of the force, led by Lieutenant Clarence V. Slack, Jr., moves against gun positions in the Sunan rail yards. Slack's low level drive draws fire and the remaining planes are able to carry out the raid. However, Slack's plane is hit and it crashes.

In Naval activity, Task Element of TG 95.2 commences a bombardment of enemy positions in the vicinity of Wonsan and inflicts heavy casualties, estimated at 6,000 to 7,000 troops.

In other naval activity, the destroyer USS *Lind* (DD 703) pounds enemy positions at Singi, delivering devastating effects there also. Casualties at Singi are estimated at about 2,000.

March 16   *In the I Corps sector,* elements of the U.S. 3rd Division and the ROK 1st Division, supported by the artillery, cross the Han River against no opposition. The vanguard (2nd Battalion, 65th Regiment) is transported across in boats and DUKWs. As the troops proceed to their positions on the Lincoln Line, they encounter mines and booby traps, but no enemy troops impede their movement. Most of the civilian population in Seoul had departed back in January, when the city was evacuated, but about 200,000 still remained under the Communists domination. Unlike the celebrated takeover during the previous September, following the invasion at Inchon, the city is retaken with no celebration.

In the IX Corps sector, the Marines prepare to eliminate the obstacles east of Hongchon that have impeded their progress. The enemy raises stiff resistance that lasts for the next two days. In the meantime, the 1st Marines encounter heavy resistance north of Hongchon. At 1230, the 2nd Battalion, 1st Marines, drive against Hill 428, but at dusk, despite air strikes by VMF-214, the Chinese still control the hill and continue to fire from concealed mortar positions. After dark, the Chinese abandon the hill.

Meanwhile, the 7th Marines attack toward Hill 399. The 1st Battalion methodically moves from bunker to bunker eliminating the defenders by lobbing hand grenades into the entrenchments. Also, in the corps' western sector, the ROK 6th Division and the U.S.

24th Division encounter nominal resistance near the Hongchon River and the Chongp'yong Reservoir.

In the 1st Cavalry area west of Hongchon, the enemy continues to hold and offer furious resistance. Nevertheless, the corps receives orders to advance. The ROK 6th Division is ordered to move to positions close to the 1st Cavalry to positions, which causes the Chinese to become concerned about their flank. The 1st Cavalry is directed to drive from the river to the Buster Line to place it near the 24th Division along the Buffalo Line. The new position stands about five miles distant. At the conclusion of the advance, the cavalry is aligned to the Marines who hold on the Buffalo Line, the right side of the corps' sector. The 24th Division is ordered to advance and cross the Pukham River on the left side.

In Naval activity, Far East Air Forces launches a record setting number of sorties. The planes fly 1,123 sorties in support of Operation RIPPER, a new high for a single day.

In Naval activity, the East Coast Blockading and Patrol Task Group (TG 94.2) comes under fire by enemy shore batteries at Wonsan.

March 17   During the offensive (Operation RIPPER), General MacArthur arrives in Korea from Japan. He is met by General Ridgway at Suwon and from there they both fly to Wonju in the 1st Marine Division sector. MacArthur and Generals Ridgway and O.P. Smith, riding in a jeep, visit various units on the front.

In the IX Corps sector, enemy resistance still impedes the 1st Cavalry Division in the region near the Hongchon River. The enemy defends strongly, but the Chinese also mount counterattacks. All units advance, but only the cavalry encounters heavy resistance. The ROK forces and the Marines driving on the left hit only sporadic opposition.

In the 1st Marine Division sector, the 1st Battalion, 7th Marines, continues to mop up at Hill 399, which had fallen after a tough fight on the previous day.

In other activity, MacArthur, while in Korea this day, arrives at the command post of the 7th Marines. Also, the 1st Marine Division receives orders to mount an attack toward Line Buffalo. The attack force is to be composed of the 5th Marines after the unit passes through the positions of the 7th Marines and the 1st Marines.

The citizens of Seoul fill the streets on 17 March, two days after the capital is regained from the Communists.

Elements of the 187th Airborne Regiment are in the air aboard C-119 Flying Boxcars, while other planes continue to load paratroopers.

In the X Corps sector, by this day, all Corps units have advanced to the Idaho line.

In the ROK III Corps sector, like the X Corps, all units have advanced to the Idaho line.

In Air Force activity, a contingent of planes from the 36th Fighter Bomber Squadron is intercepted by MiGs while on patrol in the vicinity of Sunchon. No planes are shot down by either side; however, a MiG collides with an F-80 piloted by 1st Lieutenant Howard J. Landry. Lieutenant Landry is killed and the pilot of

The 187th Airborne, accustomed to rugged duty, jumps out of C-119s over nasty terrain.

the MiG also dies. Landry receives credit for the downed Communist MiG, posthumously.

No other planes of Fifth Air Force are lost during the month of March. It is thought the Russians are changing units, which could account for the bad marksmanship of the pilots. The Russians do not change pilots individually; rather they exchange entire units. The new more inexperienced contingents are the No. 303 and the No. 324 Fighter Air Divisions.

March 18   General Ridgway maintains a close eye on the field operations during Operation RIPPER. After analyzing the accumulation of facts collected by intelligence, air observation and information from captives, Ridgway directs the I, IX and X Corps to dispatch reconnaissance patrols into the region between the Hwach'on Reservoir and the east coast.

In the IX Corps sector, the entire corps advances. The 24th Division, which had crossed the Han, joins with the ROK 6th Division, the 1st Cavalry Division and the 1st Marine Division. The momentum swells, but the Chinese withdraw further. After assessing the situation, General Ridgway orders the IX Corps to maintain the attack and seize Chunchon.

In the 1st Marine Division zone, the 5th and 1st Marines advance against only sporadic resistance and make good progress during the trek to the Buffalo Line.

March 19   *In the IX Corps sector,* the ongoing advance continues to make excellent progress and by overwhelming scant rear-guard actions, the units reach the Buster-Buffalo Line towards the latter part of the day.

Meanwhile, the Chinese continue to pull back rather than raise concentrated resistance. The largest prize of the day falls to the ROK 6th Division. A contingent of the 2nd Battalion, 2nd Regiment, acting as the spearhead, surprises a battalion-sized unit just above the Hongchon River. The Chinese battalion sustains 232 killed after the ROKs launch a three-pronged attack. The Chinese also lose much equipment; however, only two of the enemy force are captured.

In conjunction with General Ridgway's orders of the previous day, General Hoge directs his corps to advance to the next line, the Cairo Line. The drive will place the 1st Cavalry Division within striking distance of the objective, Chunchon.

In the 1st Marine Division zone, the attack continues against minimum resistance, mostly some sniper fire and mortars, except in the path of the 2nd Battalion, 1st Marines. As the 2nd Battalion advances, enemy fire originating on ridges west of Hill 330 compels Fox Company to halt. While the battalion pauses to prepare strategy to eliminate the fire, a tank platoon (Baker Company, 1st Tank Battalion) moves forward and directs their fire effectively. The Marines, using the tanks'

The 5th Regiment, 24th Division, after fording the Honogch'on River on 19 March, climbs another enemy-held hill.

90-mm shells as a diversion, scurry along the ridgeline and take out the bunkers with grenades so quickly that the Communists had not yet recovered from the tank fire. The Marines sustain no casualties. Afterward, they establish night positions on Hill 330.

In the 1st Cavalry zone, General Ridgway inserts the 187th Airborne RCT into the attack. The paratroopers are directed to prepare to drop north of Chunchon on 22 March to ambush the Communists as they attempt to escape the advancing 5th and 8th Cavalry Regiments.

However, when the ground troops arrive at Chunchon, they find it abandoned. Ridgway cancels the airdrop, but the paratroopers are committed to bolster the I Corps on 23 March.

In Air Force activity, a flight of B-29s, attached to the 343rd Bombardment Squadron, 98th Bombardment Wing (M), is intercepted by MiGs in the vicinity of Sonchin. One of the attacking MiG-15s is downed by a tailgunner, Sergeant William H. Finnegan.

In Naval activity, the carriers of Fast Carrier Task Force (CTF 77) are informed that the mission of rail interdiction has successfully been completed. Intelligence concludes that the enemy trains were severely hampered by the operation and capable of only using small sections of the rails. By 14 March, traffic along the rails on the northeast coast of Korea is essentially terminated, due to the massive destruction inflicted upon the bridges.

March 20   Eighth Army commences its advance from the Buffalo Line to the Cairo Line.

In the IX Corps sector, the advance continues. General Ridgway prepares to intensify the offensive and attempt to isolate and destroy the NK I Corps, known to be in the vicinity of Uijingbu in front of the Imjin River. Ridgway determines that if he uses the ground forces and bolsters an advance with paratroopers, the enemy could be trapped at Munsan-ni when it retires along Route 1 to cross the Imjin. The operation in conjunction with the paratroopers is set to commence on the 22nd.

In the 1st Marine Division zone, the 1st Korean Marine Regiment is reattached to the 1st Marine Division.

In Air Force activity, Far East Air Forces receives fifteen new jet planes, F-94Bs. The aircraft are all-weather jet fighters. The planes will be added as escorts for the B-29 Superfortress night raids.

March 21   *In the I Corps sector,* the Corps prepares to move toward the Cairo Line, which General Ridgway stretched to the Han River at Haengju. Line Cairo had been drawn above the Lincoln Line at points varying between five to ten miles distant. The I Corps is scheduled to be at the line by the following day to coincide with a planned airdrop of the 187th Airborne RCT on the 22nd at Munsan-ni. En route, the corps encounters some resistance from the Chinese east of Uijongbu and to the west of the village, some North Korean resistance is raised.

The operation is designed to reach two other lines, Aspen and Benton, but the advance is contingent upon the orders of Ridgway, which include a full-scale move by the entire corps to the Benton Line at the 38th Parallel.

In the IX Corps sector, the 1st Cavalry Division arrives at the Cairo Line without having encountered opposition. The progress and lack of enemy forces prompts General Ridgway to cancel a planned airdrop by the 187th Airborne RCT and its attached 2nd and 4th Ranger Companies, which was scheduled for the 22nd. A reconnaissance task force slides into Chun-

chon at 1330 and finds itself in control of the abandoned town. The first encounter with the enemy occurs later at a point about ten miles southeast of the town. The small enemy contingents discovered there raise no opposition; rather the troops scatter from the area at Route 29 and vanish in the Soyang River valley. The town remains under U.S. control. With this seizure, Operation RIPPER has achieved its objectives with regard to real estate, but the purpose is also to destroy as much of the enemy as possible. By this time, it becomes evident that the Chinese are continuing to withdraw, but in addition, they are regrouping for what is an expected attack.

In the 1st Marine Division zone, the 1st Marines and the 5th Marines press forward on the right and left respectively, with the Korean Marines moving up the center. The enemy raises fierce resistance against the Korean Marines as they advance in an area that lacks roads. Airdrops keep the force supplied, and it receives outstanding artillery support, but still, it is a hard-fought advance that continues until the morning of the 24th.

March 22   At Taegu, during the middle of the day, General Ridgway authorizes the airdrop of the 187th Airborne RCT at Munsan-ni. It is scheduled for 0900 on the 23rd, to be coordinated with an armored task force from Seoul that is to hook up with the paratroopers near Munsan-ni. The task force includes 6th Medium Tank Battalion (24th Division, IX Corps), the 2nd Battalion, 7th Infantry (3rd Division, I Corps), elements of the 58th Armored Field Artillery Battalion (3rd Division) and one battery of the 999th Armored Field Artillery Battalion. In addition, the task force includes a pair of British Churchill tanks, both capable of laying down a bridge.

In the I Corps sector, the corps' advance to the Cairo Line begins at 0800. By day's end, despite only nominal opposition along the march, only the ROK 1st Division moving along Route 1 reaches the line. It arrives there about noon, while the 3rd Division, moving along Route 3, and the 25th Division, to its right, establish night positions short of the objective.

In the 1st Marine Division zone, the 1st and 5th Marines encounter only light resistance, primarily by North Koreans who apparently are acting as rear guard for the Chinese 39th and 66th Armies, which continue to retreat ahead of the Marine attacks.

In related activity, the 1st Korean Marine Regiment presses ahead against tenacious resistance at Hill 975.

March 23   Eighth Army initiates a major offensive designed to advance to positions at the Imjin River. Washington had been sending mixed signals regarding a re-crossing of the 38th Parallel, including private reports not to cross due to diplomatic talks and public statements that the choice is up to MacArthur. MacArthur had confined movements, but on this day, he informs Ridgway to disregard his recent orders and to attack in force beyond the 38th Parallel.

Also, Task Force Growdon, an armored contingent, departs Seoul en route to bolster the 187th Airborne

RCT (Colonel Frank S. Bowen), which is flown from Taegu aboard 135 planes at 0730 and dropped over Munsan-ni as part of Operation COURAGEOUS, designed to eliminate the NK I Corps and reach the 38th Parallel. The massive formation is supported by Fifth Air Force aircraft, which attack enemy positions while the planes transporting the paratroopers, protected by Mustangs (P-51s), move above the Yellow Sea to arrive from the west at Munsan.

In other activity, General Ridgway modifies the Benton Line, stretching it to reach Chunchon, where the 1st Cavalry occupies a patrol base, and from there to the IX Corps' right, where the ground is held by the 1st Marine Division. The extension links the Benton Line with the Cairo Line. Ridgway has blueprinted the advance to include bringing I Corps from the Lincoln Line at Seoul to the Imjin River, which would stretch Eighth Army's line slightly less than ten miles from the 38th Parallel, from Munsan to Chunchon (west to east).

In the I Corps sector, TF Growdon, commanded by Lt. Colonel John S. Growdon, passes through the ROK 1st Division along Route 1 as it moves to Munsan-ni. The armor is followed by the ROK force that is to relieve the paratroopers. After passing through and driving up the highway, the armor is barred from crossing a damaged bridge at the Changnung River. While seeking a nearby crossing of the shallow river, a tank in the column strikes a mine. No enemy resistance arises, but more mines there and farther along the route slow the column to a crawl.

Meanwhile, at 0900, on schedule, the paratroopers of Operation TOMAHAWK drop at Munsan-ni, while the armor support remains about fifteen miles away. Other unexpected problems also develop; one of the planes transporting the paratroopers is compelled to return to base due to engine failure. The plane that returned to Taegu is carrying Colonel Arthur (Harry) Wilson, the commanding officer of the 1st Battalion. Nevertheless, the bulk of the force, transported by more than 100 twin-tailed Flying Boxcars, drops as planned slightly northeast of the town, but in the confusion, the elements of the 1st Battalion are inadvertently dropped in the identical zone used by the 3rd Battalion (Delbert E. Munson) and the 4th Ranger Company, instead of a point southeast of the town. The miscalculation causes some problems, as no troops are at the south drop zone. Later, when the remainder of the force (1st Battalion) arrives, it drops in its proper zone, but lacks full strength and the small force for a while remains isolated.

The Communists bring Wilson's contingent under fire from their positions in the heights; however, Wilson directs his troops to safer positions. The Communists remain in the high ground and make no move against the Wilson's troops. Company B, 1st Battalion,

A vanguard of the 24th Division advances across an enemy-built footbridge northwest of Ch'ongp'yong on 23 March.

Elements of the 187th Airborne Regimental Combat Team in the high ground east of Munsan-ni are en route to intercept the enemy forces to the front of the 3rd Division.

moves from the north drop zone to the south zone to bolster the force under Wilson and deter the North Koreans from launching an attack. In the meantime, resistance against the paratroopers remains nominal and Munsan-ni is seized. Afterward, a contingent leaves for the southeast drop zone to rescue troops from heavy enemy fire originating on Hill 216.

By 1700, the rescue has succeeded and the entire force is at Munsan-ni. The operation cost the force nineteen casualties from battle and another eighty-four from accidental injuries during the jump. The enemy sustains 136 killed and 149 captured. The bulk of the NK I Corps at Munsan-ni had retired prior to the arrival of the airborne troops. It was determined that the enemy force encountered was the NK 36th Regiment, 19th Division, composed of about three hundred to

five hundred troops. The armored task force vanguard arrives to join the paratroopers at 1830.

In other activity, the U.S. 3rd and 25th Divisions continue to advance. The 3rd Division, under General Robert H. Soule, encounters resistance; however, it arrives at Uijongbu and takes it effortlessly at 0900. The initial unit to enter is TF Hawkins, composed of elements of the 64th Tank Battalion and contingents of the 15th and 65th Infantry Regiments.

In the 1st Marine Division zone, the units continue to come up on the Cairo Line, but the center of the advance handled by the Korean Marines' 2nd and 3rd Battalions continue to be blocked at Hill 975.

In Air Force activity, in addition to the incidents listed earlier on this same date, helicopters evacuate sixty-eight paratroopers who were injured during the jump.

A Marine Pershing Tank (M26) at a tight spot on a mountain road as the 1st Marine Division advances north and east of Ch'unch'on.

Also, one of the C-119s that transported the paratroopers catches fire en route back to its base and crashes. It is thought the plane might have been hit by bullets.

In other activity, forty-five F-86 jets escort a contingent of twenty-two B-29s on a bombing mission to destroy two bridges in North Korea. The B-29s, attached to the 19th and 307th Bomber Groups, sustain no losses.

March 24 General MacArthur arrives in Korea from Japan to confer with General Ridgway. Before de-

parting for the meeting, MacArthur issues a statement indicating that he is willing to hold a conference with the Communists to initiate a cease-fire. The statement includes MacArthur's opinion that the Chinese were not going to prevail in Korea. His statement causes consternation in Washington. President Truman, awaiting information on the ongoing operation, had prepared a speech, timed to the U.S. drive to the 38th Parallel. The Communists accept MacArthur's statement with disdain. MacArthur's position pushes him farther

Elements of the 5th Regiment, 24th Division, operating on the right of the 25th Division during an Eighth Army offensive, captures enemy troops on 24 March.

from President Truman. Word arrives from the Joint Chiefs of Staff for MacArthur to report to them if he receives a response from the Chinese, but none is actually anticipated. In the meantime, Truman moves toward replacing MacArthur.

General Ridgway extends the Cairo Line from its end in the right of the IX Corps sector, held by the 1st Marine Division, to the east coast at Chosan-ni.

In the I Corps sector, the bulk of the armored task force under Lt. Colonel Growdon arrives at the positions of the paratroopers (187th Airborne RCT) near Munsan-ni by 0700 on the following day. The column had been impeded by mines along the route. Four tanks sustain damage from the mines and another two are damaged by enemy artillery fire on the last leg of the journey. Also, the ROK 1st Division arrives at Munsan-ni to relieve the airborne troops.

At Munsan-ni, General Frank S. Bowen, Jr., commanding officer, 187th Airborne, takes command of TF Growdon. The armor is directed to run patrols along the Imjin River to reconnoiter ferry crossings and to search along Route 2Y, a road that leads to Sinch'on. The mission succeeds in seizing twenty-two enemy troops. Another six are reported killed. The U.S. sustains no casualties; however, one tank is scuttled after it snags in a stream, unable to cross.

In related activity, another contingent, TF Boone, ROK 1st Division, begins to arrive at Munsan-ni prior to noon. Company C, 64th Tank Battalion (on loan to the ROK 1st Division from the U.S. 3rd Division), is the first unit to arrive. Subsequently, the ROK Division under General Paik relieves the paratroopers. The South Koreans assume command from General Bowen at 1700 and deploy around the town. TF Boone establishes positions slightly above the town, while the remainder of the division deploys below Munsan-ni, near Route 1, leading northeastwardly to nearby Pobwon-ni, slightly more than five miles from Munsan-ni.

Despite the success of taking the objective, the NK I Corps still evades confrontation and retires further. In addition, the Chinese 26th Army remains entrenched, prepared to raise strong resistance to the I Corps' 3rd and 25th Divisions. The 25th Division, operating on the corps' right since the previous day, has also encountered large numbers of land mines that have impeded progress. Nonetheless, by dusk, the 25th Division advances to the vicinity of Uijongbu, held by the 3rd Division, which is encountering fierce resistance.

In the 3rd Division sector, the Chinese had fortified their positions at two separate hills. The division jumps off unaware of the firepower on Hill 337 northeast of the village and Hill 468 just northwest of it. The resistance remains tenacious throughout the day; however, Hill 337 is secured by the 15th Infantry Regiment. The enemy maintains control of Hill 468, despite repeated efforts by the 65th Infantry to evict them.

Efforts are undertaken by General Bowen to commit the 187th Airborne in an eastward attack to strike the Chinese that threaten the 3rd Division and catch them between his attacking force and the advancing 3rd Division. The column encounters natural obstacles. At 1800, only a small unit of tanks is able to move out. The remainder of the column's vehicles hold up for fuel. Later, en route, the weather interferes. Some tanks are held up by landslides and then rain further impedes the mission. The tanks return to Munsan-ni; however the remainder of the force, excluding the 2nd Battalion, 7th

Infantry, which had earlier returned to the 3rd Division. The task force under General Bowen arrives at Sinch'on on the following morning.

In the IX Corps sector, the 1st Korean Marine Regiment overcomes the resistance at Hill 975 and afterwards forms along the Cairo Line. Also, the 24th Division continues to advance to the right of the 25th Division (I Corps) en route to the 38th Parallel.

In Air Force activity, a new and larger helicopter, the H-19, is introduced to the Korean War. The H-19 is much more powerful than the H-5 now used to transport the wounded, and it has a greater range of operations.

In other activity, C-46s and C-119s pass over Munsanni and drop large quantities of supplies and ammunition. The planes return on the 26th and 27th to drop more supplies to the troops on the ground. The amount dropped during the three deliveries totals 264 tons.

March 25 General of the Army Douglas MacArthur authorizes the U.N. forces in Korea to cross the 38th Parallel, if it becomes necessary for tactical purposes.

In the I Corps sector, the 187th Airborne RCT arrives at Sinch'on at 0600 and soon the attack is reinitiated. The objective, Hill 228 along the west side of Route 33, is heavily defended by the Chinese. In the meantime, the 3rd Division and the 25th Division reinitiate the advance, but the enemy raises only nominal resistance against both. During the afternoon, armor from the 3rd Division arrives to bolster the attack of the airborne, but still, the resistance repels the assaults.

March 26 *In the I Corps sector,* the Chinese continue to hold Hill 228 against attempts by the 187th Airborne RCT. Later in the day, tanks from the 3rd Division arrive to bolster the assault, but still the Communists do not yield. In conjunction, during the attack to gain the hill, the U.S. armor is able to destroy an enemy T34 tank. It is the first T34 destroyed since General Ridgway assumed command of Eighth Army.

In other activity, the 3rd and 25th Divisions continue to advance against sporadic light resistance.

In the IX Corps sector, late in the day orders arrive instructing the corps to continue to advance to the Benton Line.

In the 1st Marine Division zone, orders arrive to move to a new Cairo Line, but it actually an extension of the present line to the boundary between the IX and X Corps.

In the X Corps sector, the identical order arrives and the X Corps also moves to the Benton Line. The moves of the IX and X Corps remain unopposed; the Chinese have pulled back without contesting the advances.

March 27 While Operation RIPPER continues, General Ridgway convenes a meeting at Yoju with I, IX and X Corps commanders and the commanding officers of the respective divisions. The conference is to map out further strategy with regard to the options facing Eighth Army.

Word is circling that in addition to the Chinese and North Koreans posted above the 38th Parallel, the Russians are also close to entering the conflict against the U.N. force, primarily composed of U.S. fighting troops.

In the I Corps sector, following fierce fighting that began on the 25th, the 187th Airborne RCT seizes control of Hill 228 along Route 33. For the second day in a row, the 3rd and 25th Divisions encounter only slight resistance. Following the capture of Hill 228 at 0900, the paratroopers prepare to attack to clear the high ground along Route 33. Also, later in the day, elements of the 3rd Division arrive to join the 187th Airborne RCT at its position along Route 33. The plan to trap the enemy between the two forces fails to materialize. Two regiments, the 15th and 65th, arrive, but en route, no enemy forces are detected.

In related activity, the 25th Division continues to advance and it, too, encounters only slight sporadic resistance.

In the IX Corps sector, 24th Division zone, the Commonwealth Brigade (Brigadier B.A. Burke) is brought out of reserve to relieve the 19th Regiment (Colonel Peter Garland) and assume responsibility for the center of the line. Burke had recently replaced Basil Coad as commander of the British Brigade.

In Naval activity, the USS *Boxer* (CV 21) relieves the USS *Valley Forge* (CV 45). Two vessels, the *Glendale* (PF 36) and the *Carmick* (DMS 33) collide near Songjin during a fog.

March 28 *In the I Corps sector,* the 187th Airborne RCT reinitiates the attack along Route 33 and again bumps into stiff resistance from strongpoints in the heights along the east side of the highway. Nonetheless, by dusk, the paratroopers secure the ground. In the meantime, the 3rd and 25th Divisions advance against nominal resistance and by the latter part of the day, both divisions arrive at the Aspen line.

While elements of the 3rd Division and the 187th Airborne RCT maneuver to entrap the Communists, the bulk of the enemy in the area is able to slip away and safely cross the Imjin River to continue the northward trek. The 24th and 35th Regiments (25th Division) continue the drive, but the former encounters heavy resistance that halts its progress. By the following day, the 27th Regiment bolsters the 24th Regiment. The combined strength plows through the Communist resistance.

In related activity, the 187th Airborne Regiment reverts to reserve. It moves to Taegu.

In Naval activity, Vice Admiral H.M. Martin succeeds Vice Admiral A.D. Struble as commanding officer, Seventh Fleet. Also, activity gets underway to reopen the port of Inchon.

March 29 I, IX and X Corps continue to advance to their final respective positions to bring Operation RIPPER to a conclusion. No major enemy resistance is encountered. The NK I Corps remains elusive while it withdraws to positions beyond the Yesong River. In related activity, the 187th Airborne RCT departs from the line and returns to Taegu. Also, General Ridgway issues a plan for the next phase, Operation RUGGED.

In the X Corps area, elements of the corps relieve the 1st Marines. In conjunction, the 7th Marines are to revert to reserve in the vicinity of Hongchon and become attached to the 1st Cavalry Division, which is preparing to attack beyond Ch'ongch'on.

In Air Force activity, Far East Air Forces launches B-29s, escorted by fighter planes, on another mission to destroy bridges at the Yalu River. The fading of winter and the thawing of the river once again make the bridges a threat to the UN forces. During the winter months, fighters and light bombers of Fifth Air Force concentrated on destroying the bridges at the Yalu, but their efforts failed to knock out the spans.

March 30   Eighth Army components close on the final phase line, which has become the Benton-Cairo Line. Eighth Army by the following day completes the operation and achieves its goals with regard to territory. The line extends to the 38th Parallel.

In the I Corps sector, 25th Division zone, the 27th Regiment relieves the 24th Regiment and assumes responsibility for the left part of the sector. Also, the 35th Regiment encounters fierce resistance at Chongsong and the supporting artillery is unable to destroy the deep bunkers. Nevertheless, the infantry plods forward and methodically eliminates the obstacles one by one.

In Air Force activity, a band of MiGs intercepts a bombing mission over Sinuiju. During the attack, Technical Sergeant Charles W. Summers, a tailgunner aboard one of the B-29s (28th Bombardment Squadron, 19th Bombardment Group [M]), places a diving MiG in his sights and fires more than 300 shells at it. The MiG takes hits, including some into its air intake, causing it to explode in mid-air. Also, Sergeant Norman S. Greene, aboard another of the B-29s, points his sights to an attacking plane just prior to the actual release of the bomb load on the target. Greene, manning the plane's gun on the left, begins to fire as the MiG attacks from at 8 o'clock. Greene fires about fifty shots at the MiG before it explodes in mid-air.

March 31   The U.S. crosses the 38th Parallel for the second time. Operation RIPPER is complete. The UN forces are on the Idaho Line and all geographical objectives have been gained. The offensive does not eliminate as many enemy troops as expected, because the Communists continue to withdraw rather than engage in a major confrontation. Nonetheless, the advance, which gained a minimum of twenty-five miles, has brought the U.S. forces back to the 38th Parallel. The operation also regained the South Korean capital.

From 7 March until this day, Eighth Army reports that 4,800 Chinese and North Koreans had been captured. In addition, it is reported that enemy casualties had been extremely high. Elements of the 5th Regiment (24th Division), formed as an infantry-armor contingent, encounter opposition and a brisk firefight ensues. The Communists sustain more than 30 killed during the confrontation. Soon after, Colonel Throck-

morton becomes an aide to General Collins. Colonel Arthur (Harry) Wilson of the 187th Airborne RCT replaces him as commander of the 5th Infantry Regiment.

In Air Force activity, during a mission of the 334th Fighter Interceptor Squadron, a Canadian pilot, Flight Lt. J.A.O. Levesque, Royal Canadian Air Force, in an F-86, downs a MiG-15. It is the first kill of a MiG by an F-86 since the previous year. The MiG-15s are lighter, able to climb higher and carry heavier ammunition. The Sabres hold 50-caliber machine guns, while the MiGs have two 23-mm cannon and one 37-mm cannon. The Sabre's guns fire much more quickly, as opposed to the slower weapons on the MiGs. The difference is usually the skill of the pilot that gives the U.S. the advantage. One flaw of the MiG is that at high speeds, the pilots are prone to lose control of the aircraft and another is that at high altitudes, a MiG is susceptible to uncontrollable spins. The Sabres, however, with their adjustable stabilizers, are much more steady. Yet the Sabres are weighed down by a slow climb rate and insufficient acceleration in speed during level flights.

In other activity, the a contingent of the 3rd ARS (Air Rescue Squadron) flying an H-19 helicopter, penetrates enemy lines and picks up about eighteen U.N. troops. This is the initial time the H-19 is committed to a special operations mission.

In yet other activity, the 3rd Air Division grounds its C-119s for repairs and maintenance. While the C-119s are grounded, the workload will be carried by C-47s. By the end of April, the C-119s are back in action.

— In Japan: General MacArthur informs the Joints Chiefs of Staff that about 475,000 enemy troops are Korea, including about 274,000 Chinese; however, it is also estimated that about 478,000 enemy troops are stationed in Manchuria in reserve. The figures raise extra alarms in Washington, particularly because intelligence has deduced that the Communist air forces have also greatly increased. Another concern is that the Soviet Union, already clandestinely involved, may be considering entering the war openly. In Washington, tentative plans are laid for a withdrawal from Korea to Japan if the Russians enter the war.

April 1-21 1950   During this period, while the Chinese continue to mount their forces for an offensive, they string out troops along mountain tops to maintain a vigil for approaching planes. As part of the strategy, the Communist sentinels fire shots to signal the arrival of the aircraft. In addition, the Chinese plant dummy trucks and tanks near antiaircraft guns. As the planes close to attack, they come under heavy fire. During this period, the Marine squadrons lose sixteen planes. Two of the pilots are able to survive by either crash landing or parachuting into friendly lines, but nine are killed and one other is captured. Three other Marine pilots are rescued behind enemy lines and one other crashes in enemy territory, but makes it back to friendly lines.

April 1 Operations RUGGED and DAUNTLESS are initiated. The mission continues until 22 April. The offensive is designed to drive beyond the 38th Parallel and make inroads, while several possibilities about the next phases of the conflict linger. The U.S. and U.N. remain concerned that Russia will enter the conflict with supposed volunteers from Mongolia. Ridgway and MacArthur both conclude that the conflict will not terminate in total victory, rather, by stalemate. Consequently, the offensive is to push north to gain ground prior to a cease fire.

As Eighth Army prepares to launch the offensive, it is known that the Communists also are preparing to initiate an offensive, but intelligence is unable to determine exactly when. Precautions are taken to repel an offensive by redeploying various units to protect Seoul and other strategic targets. The primary objectives of the Eighth Army offensive are the towns of Ch'orwon and Kumhwa, located in the south, and the town of Pyonggang in the north. The layout of the three targets above the 38th Parallel forms a triangle and the area is soon dubbed the "Iron Triangle."

Ridgway designates the first phase line, Kansas. It is drawn in the west from the lower bank of the Imjin River and it stretches eastward passing over the routes to the objectives and continues beyond to the Hwach'on Reservoir. From the reservoir, the line is adjusted to shift northward to a point about ten miles from the 38th Parallel, before tailing off in a southeastwardly direction to terminate at the coast in the vicinity of Hwach'on. The advance is supported by large numbers of Korean reserves who transport supplies on their backs. About 15,000 reserves acting as porters are attached to the advance.

In the I and IX Corps sector, I Corps is directed to work with IX Corps to gain and clear the area that stretches between the Imjin River to the western tip of the Hwach'on Reservoir.

In the 1st Marine Division zone (IX Corps), the orders change. Rather than reverting to reserve, the Marines are directed to continue the attack with two regiments, the 1st and 5th, and to relieve the 1st Cavalry Division (7th Marines attached).

In the X Corps sector, the corps, operating on the east, is directed to secure and hold the ground that runs from the reservoir to Route 24, located in the Soyang River Valley. In conjunction, the ROK I and III Corps are to cover the territory extending from Route 24 to the town of Yangyang.

April 2 Eighth Army continues to prepare for the initiation of Operation RUGGED, designed to advance beyond the 38th Parallel to the Kansas Line, en route to what becomes known as the "Iron Triangle." After Eighth Army reaches the Kansas Line, General Ridgway has a blueprint in place to redeploy particular units to prepare against an enemy counterattack, while IX and X Corps (Operation DAUNTLESS) continue the advance to the primary objective, for the purpose of disrupting the enemy rather than conquering the territory.

The phase lines drawn for the operation are known as the Utah Line and the Wyoming Line. A secondary plan includes a pull-back by the two corps to the Kansas Line if the Communists launch a counterattack. The offensive commences this day; however, it doesn't actually accumulate full steam until 5 April.

In the IX Corps sector, the 1st Marine Division is ordered to go into reserve in the vicinity of Hongchon; however, the 5th Marines and the 1st Korean Marine Regiment are directed to continue the attack. *In the X Corps sector,* General Ruffner assumes temporary command of the X Corps, while General Almond departs for Japan. While Almond is in Japan on April 2-9, General George Stewart temporarily replaces Ruffner as 2nd Division commander.

April 3 General MacArthur again arrives in Korea from Japan as Operation RUGGED (the advance to the Kansas Line) unfolds. The date for commencement had been moved up from 5 April to this day. MacArthur arrives on the east coast within the ROK I Corps zone. General Ridgway and MacArthur confer and concur that the Kansas Line should be held. On this visit, MacArthur moves north by jeep from Kangnung and crosses the 38th Parallel in the ROK 9th Division zone. It is MacArthur's strong opinion that at the conclusion of the operation, the conflict will be at a stalemate.

The enemy forces that stand in opposition to the I and IX Corps are the Chinese 26th, 39th and 40th Armies. Also, the N.K. III Corps, which had evaded the advancing forces during Operation RIPPER, stand in front of X Corps and the ROK I and III Corps. The N.K. III Corps is composed of elements of the 1st, 15th and 45th Divisions, supported also by the 69th Brigade.

In the I Corps zone, the troops near the Imjin River (west) hold in place, but in the eastern sector of the zone, the 24th (IX Corps on loan to I Corps) and 25th Divisions drive north along Route 3 toward the Iron Triangle. The offensive is supported by the 6th, 64th and 89th Tank Battalions, air support and artillery support.

In the IX Corps sector, the advance commences with the Commonwealth Brigade, ROK 6th Division and the 1st Cavalry Division. The 7th and 8th Cavalry Regiments ford the Soyang River and drive toward the Hwach'on Reservoir, slightly north of the 38th Parallel. The Greek and Thai contingents are attached to the 7th and 8th Cavalries respectively. The advance also includes the 7th Marines, which is temporarily attached to the 1st Cavalry Division. The Marines under Colonel Litzenberg advance to the rear of the cavalry.

In other activity, in the 1st Marine Division sector, the 5th Marines and the 1st Korean Marine Regiment maintain the advance.

In Air Force activity, an attempt to rescue a downed F-51 pilot by a helicopter crew of the 3rd Air Rescue Squadron succeeds. The pilot is retrieved in enemy territory southeast of Pyongyang by an H-19 service test helicopter.

In other activity, a contingent of Sabre jets encounters and engages a band of MiGs. The MiGs lose three planes and of these, one is downed by Captain Jabara (334th Fighter Interceptor Squadron), his first. The Sabre jets sustain no losses. In a repeat performance on the following day, the MiGs lose one plane. No losses are sustained by the Sabre jets.

In Naval activity, Logistic Support Force (TF 92) composed of Service Squadron Three and Service Division Thirty-one and United Nations Blockading and Escort Force (TF 95) come under the operational control of the Seventh Fleet. Also, Rear Admiral A.E. Smith is reassigned as commanding officer of the U.N. Blockading and Escort Force (TF 95).

April 4   *In the I Corps sector,* the 25th Division closes on the high ground above the Hant'an River and secures it by the following day. The 24th Division advance encounters nominal resistance except at the right where the enemy stalls the 2nd Battalion, 21st Infantry Regiment, at the western slopes of Kungmang Mountain. The Chinese stand prepared for a tough contest and have permeated the approaches with land mines and barbed wire.

In the IX Corps sector, the British contingent operating on the corps' left had also been stalled by the heavy fire from the heights on Kungmang Mountain.

In the X Corps sector, the 1st Cavalry continues to advance. The 7th Marines, attached to the 1st Cavalry, moves north with the 7th and 8th Cavalry Regiments against nominal resistance, which permits them to be among the first Eighth Army troops to recross the 38th Parallel.

April 5   *In the I Corps sector,* the 24th Division's 2nd Battalion, 21st Infantry, supported by planes and artillery, clears the enemy from the western slopes of Kungmang Mountain early in the day. After the high ground is secured, it is occupied by the 5th Infantry Regiment. The 21st Regiment arrives at the Kansas Line on 6 April. The 24th Division is temporarily attached to I Corps.

In the IX Corps sector, subsequent to the eviction of the enemy on Kungmang Mountain, the British 27th Brigade, operating on the corps' left and stalled by fierce enemy fire, is able to reinitiate its advance. On the following day, the British move to the Kansas Line without incident.

In the 1st Marine Division zone (IX Corps), a heated firefight erupts and some Marines are wounded. An accompanying Navy corpsman, Richard D. Dewert, assists the wounded and himself becomes wounded, but he refuses treatment and continues to brave the heavy fire. On his third run he discovers one Marine had already died and he is wounded again; still, he refuses personal treatment. While attending to another wounded Marine, Corpsman Dewert is struck again, this time with a fatal wound. Hospital Corpsman Dewert is awarded the Medal of Honor posthumously for his extraordinary heroism and selfless sacrifice.

In the X Corps sector, the 23rd Infantry Regiment, which had relieved the 5th Marines, prepares to launch an attack the following day against the Hwach'on Reservoir.

— In Japan: General MacArthur, aware that all assigned forces had crossed the 38th Parallel, informs the Joint Chiefs of Staff that the advance would continue to the Kansas Line. MacArthur's message also mentions that I Corps will commence Operation DAUNT-LESS, designed to move the line forward to Lines Utah and Wyoming.

April 6   Operation RUGGED continues to make progress.

In the I Corps sector, elements of the 24th Division (temporarily attached to I Corps) reach the Kansas Line, which stretches along the south bank of the Hant'an

A contingent of the 32nd Regiment, 7th Division, climbs yet another Korean hill.

River. In the 25th Division zone, General Joseph S. Bradley prepares for Operation DAUNTLESS. He selects the Greek detachment and the 24th Regiment to act as vanguard when the Division crosses the Hant'an River. As part of the ongoing preparations, the 27th Regiment, deployed on the left, is relieved by the Greek contingent, while the 24th Regiment deploys on the right, after relieving the 35th Regiment. The 27th and 35th Regiments, subsequent to being relieved, revert to reserve.

In the 24th Division zone at the Kansas Line, the 19th Regiment relieves the 5th Regiment and the latter prepares to join with the 21st Regiment to be the vanguard of the Division's advance in Operation DAUNTLESS.

In the IX Corps sector, the ROK 6th Division encounters resistance as it moves up the center, but it pushes through and reaches the Kansas Line.

In other activity, the 1st Cavalry Division drives on the right. Its 7th and 8th Regiments advance on the left (east) side of the Pukham River and encounter primitive routes and enemy resistance, raised by elements of the Chinese 39th Army. However, the 7th Marines (attached to the 1st Cavalry) encounters no strong resistance as it pushes forward on the west side of the river. At day's end, the cavalry remains several miles short of its intended positions at the Hwach'on Reservoir.

In the X Corps sector, 2nd Division zone, the 23rd Infantry Regiment (French Battalion attached) initiates its northward attack towards the eastern edge of the Hwach'on Reservoir (Kansas Line). In conjunction, the 23rd is the only regiment on the offensive. The 9th and 38th Infantry Regiments remain in reserve. The French contingent advances to the Kansas Line by 8 April.

In the 7th Division zone, the 17th and 32nd Regiments will attack towards the Kansas Line, subsequent to relieving the ROK 5th Division.

April 7 On this date, the total air defense of the Pusan–Pohang area becomes the responsibility of the 1st Marine Air Wing. In conjunction, the Air Defense Section of the Marine Tactical Air Control Squadron 2 initiates the implementation of the defense system. Also, General Ridgway remains concerned about the possibility of the Chinese opening the gates of the dam at the Hwach'on Reservoir. Ridgway had modified the Kansas Line to place it into the IX Corps zone. Earlier, it had been determined that the dam could not be destroyed by the available bombs. With the modification of the line, the 1st Marine Division is to secure the dam, subsequent to its relief of the 1st Cavalry Division at the Kansas Line.

Also, on this day, the 4th Ranger Company is released from the 187th Airborne RCT and attached to IX Corps. The corps commander, General Hoge, decides to use the rangers to knock the dam's gates out of commission. General Palmer is not aware that the plan is to strike quickly with only the rangers. On the following day, instead of using only the rangers, General Palmer directs the 2nd Battalion, 7th Cavalry, and the attached rangers the task of taking the dam.

In the I Corps sector, 3rd Division zone, an infantry-armor patrol, composed of the 64th Tank Battalion and Company F, 2nd Battalion, 7th Regiment, moves north of the 38th Parallel above the Hant'an River and encounters opposition, which it scatters. During the exchange of fire, the Communists hold positions in bunkers; however, they do not deter the patrol. The Chinese sustain high casualties, including nearly forty troops captured. The patrol, led by Lt. Colonel Wilson Hawkins (64th Tank Battalion), sustains only a few casualties, each of a non-serious nature.

In Air Force activity, a contingent of 48 F-84Es depart Japan to rendezvous with B-29 bombers while they venture into MiG Alley. The bombers pound targets at Sinuiju and Uiju under the protection of the 27th Fighter Escort Wing. MiGs arrive to intercept and of 30 planes on the attack, one is able to break through the jets to reach the bombers. One B-29 is shot down.

In Naval activity, Special Task Force (TF-74) — composed of the USS *St. Paul* (CA 73), USS *Lind* (DD 703), USS *Massey* (DD 778), USS *Fort Marion* (LSD 22), and the USS *Begor* (APD 127) — carries out a demolition mission at Sorye-dong. A landing force, composed of British Marines of the 41st Independent Royal Marine Commandos, executes the landing against no resistance and destroys rails in the area.

April 8 Navy Task Force 77 initiates maneuvers off Taiwan and near the coast of mainland China to show force and discourage the Communists from launching an invasion of Taiwan. Intelligence gathering had picked up the possibility of such an assault during spring. The exercise apparently succeeds. No invasion occurs; however, in the absence of the U.S. Navy off Korea, the Communists had been able to make huge repairs to the rail and bridge system that the carrier planes had destroyed the previous March. The task force and its planes depart the Formosa Strait and resume attacks over Korea on 16 April.

In the IX Corps sector, fierce resistance continues from the previous day above Chunchon, as the 1st Cavalry drives toward the Kansas Line. During the latter part of this day, General Palmer issues orders to the two attacking regiments (7th and 8th) to form in tighter and greater strength on the following day. Both units are stalled, but the pressure against the 8th Cavalry forces it to pull back. To bolster the attack, the 5th Cavalry is plucked from reserve.

In addition, General Palmer prepares the 2nd Battalion, 7th Cavalry, for the task of taking the Hwach'on dam. The attack is scheduled for 10 April. However, in the meantime, at about midnight (8th-9th), the enemy opens the floodgates to catch the cavalry by surprise and impede any progress. The attacking units had been forewarned of the possibility of the attempt to flood the route and the troops are prepared. The waters of the Pukham River rise high, but cause no casualties. The sweeping waters damage some bridges and force the Americans to remove some floating bridges.

In related activity, the enemy forces that had

impeded the cavalry advance withdraw to avoid being trapped by the flood waters, but some forces remain to hold the dam.

The 3rd Battalion, 7th Marines, attached to the 1st Cavalry Division, encounters fierce resistance that originates on a ridge near the western end of the Hwach'on Reservoir. Unable to overcome the mortar and machine gun fire, the patrols also become jeopardized by hand grenades. An urgent call for air support is placed; however, all air traffic for the Marines remains under the control of the Joint Operations Center. The Marines are told help is on the way, but at one point, orders come down that state the 1st Marine Division is not eligible for air strikes until it comes out of reserve. And yet more bureaucracy emerges, but finally after six hours, U.S. Air Force planes arrive. In the meantime, Marine squadrons had been in operation supporting the ROKs and the 7th and 8th Cavalry.

In the 1st Marine Division zone, orders arrive from Eighth Army to relieve the 1st Cavalry Division at Line Kansas and commence an attack toward Line Quantico above Hwach'on and about ten miles below the Iron Triangle.

In the X Corps sector, 2nd Division zone, the French Battalion attached to the 23rd Regiment reaches the Kansas Line; however, it encounters fierce opposition from entrenched positions on Hill 796, in the vicinity of the southern part of the reservoir.

April 9 Operation DAUNTLESS, ordered by General Ridgway in coordination with Operation RUGGED, is set with a commencement date of 11 April.

In the IX Corps sector, the 7th and 8th Cavalry Regiments advance without resistance following two days of hitting tenacious opposition. The regiments arrive at the Kansas Line prior to noon. In related activity, the operation to seize the dam is initiated and General Palmer anticipates its seizure on this day to finalize the mission, prior to being relieved by the Marines on the following day. The 2nd Battalion, 7th Cavalry Regiment, jumps off slightly after noon, but the task becomes more difficult than anticipated. The approaches forbid the passage of tanks. The primitive path is too slim even for artillery, so much so that at points, even a jeep is hardly able to maneuver.

Company F, 2nd Battalion, spearheads the assault to gain Hill 454, located above the dam and afterwards, the rangers that trail are to bolt to the dam and disable the gates. Enemy mortars pound the force and then, more fire pounds the company. Machine guns and small arms stall the advance and prevent Company E from gaining access to Hill 364 along the southern tip of the ridge. Meanwhile, the enemy holding Hill 364 pours fire upon the cavalrymen to bring the attack to a halt. Division artillery to the north is too far from the target to provide accurate fire. An air strike is called upon to crack the resistance, but it fails to dislodge the enemy. The Chinese hold the dam.

General Hoge, the corps commander, and General Palmer, 1st Cavalry commander, agree to commence

another assault on the following day. Lt. Colonel John W. Callaway's 2nd Battalion again gets the task.

April 10 *In the IX Corps sector,* the bulk of the 1st Cavalry Regiment initiates its movement from the Kansas Line; however, the 7th Cavalry remains in place to launch a second attack to seize the dam at the Hwach'on Reservoir. Company G (2nd Battalion, 7th Cavalry), jumps off and as on the previous day, enemy fire prevents progress. The troops have no room to maneuver and they come under fire from the north and the northwest while they are stalled at the base of the diminutive road. The U.S. artillery remains too distant to support the assault and in the meantime, the weather deteriorates, which prevents the possibility of air strikes.

General Hoge concludes that Calloway's 2nd Battalion had not attacked strongly and he decides to attempt yet another assault. General Hoge remains focused on securing the dam prior to withdrawing the 7th Cavalry; however, the 3rd Battalion is already withdrawing from the Kansas Line. Nevertheless, a third assault is planned for the following day.

In related activity, the ROK 1st Division patrols, which had been encountering elements of the N.K. 8th Division near the far bank of the Imjin River, on this day find the enemy positions abandoned. Subsequent patrols advance to the old capital of Korea, Kaesong, more than ten miles above the Imjin River, without detecting enemy presence.

In the 1st Marine Division zone, as the Division prepares to advance from Line Kansas to the Quantico Line, it is directed to postpone its attack. The Marines are directed to confine their activity to patrols.

In the X Corps sector, elements of the 23rd Regiment, 2nd Division, operating on the corps' left (Operation SWING), move along the lower shore of the reservoir in an attempt to eliminate the remaining opposition on Hill 796 and catch the withdrawing N.K. 1st Division. The enemy evades an engagement. Some escape across the reservoir in boats and others pass through Yanggu and speed north. The 23rd Regiment arrives in Yanggu and deploys on the Kansas Line on 15 April. The enemy contingents had been part of the N.K. 1st Regiment (also known as 14th N.K. Regiment).

In the 7th Division zone, the 17th and 32nd Regiments on the left and right respectively drive toward the Soyang River, which stands at the 38th Parallel. The advance is impeded by the elements and the enemy as it crawls towards its objective, Inje, along the Kansas Line, a few miles north of the 38th Parallel. The 7th Division is the sole Eighth Army unit that remains short of the Kansas Line.

— In the United States: The Defense Department issues an order (effective 1 May) that lowers the intelligence standards for the Air Force, Navy, and Marine Corps. The adjustment brings the level equal to that of the Army. For the first time since World War II, the Marine Corps as well as the Air Force and the Navy will be accepting draftees.

April 11 *In the I Corps sector,* Operation DAUNT-LESS commences. It consists of two phases, the first, a drive to the Utah Line, followed by a drive to the Wyoming Line. The 65th Infantry Regiment, 3rd Division, supported by the Philippine 10th Battalion Combat Team and two companies of the 64th Tank Battalion, drives toward the objective. The force pushes up the corps' center. On the corps' right, the 25th Division and the 24th Division (X Corps) drive toward Ch'orwon and Kumhwa against resistance raised by the Chinese 26th and 40th Armies.

In conjunction, the 25th Division encounters heavy resistance as it moves, holding up progress. The 25th Division gets across the Hant'an River after four dogged days to gain positions in the high ground between Route 33 and Route 3, known as the Pogae-san heights. After two additional days, the division arrives at a point about five miles from the Utah Line.

Meanwhile, the 24th Division, on loan from X Corps, drives against resistance originating on the ridges (Kwangdok-san) along the Yongp'yong River.

In the IX Corps sector, the 7th Cavalry again initiates

A U.S. convoy crosses the Soyang River at the 38th Parallel.

an attack to clear the Chinese from the dam at the Hwach'on Reservoir. The regiment, commanded by Colonel William A. Harris, has already expended much of its ammunition and its supplies have dwindled. Although Harris is authorized to commit the entire 7th Cavalry Regiment, he is convinced there is insufficient time to resupply the regiment in time to sustain a full-scale assault.

Since the attack of the previous day, some artillery, two 8-inch batteries of the 17th FABn, and one 155-mm battery of the 4th FABn (1st Marine Division) has arrived to points close enough to support the assault. However, the weather again is inclement and air support is unavailable. The assault is further hampered because much of the cavalry's amphibious equipment had already been moved to Taegu or transferred to the 1st Marine Division as it moved up on the 10th to relieve the 1st Cavalry. Colonel Harris conducts a scavenger hunt and the search comes up with fewer than ten boats to use to carry rangers, but not all are equipped with motors. In addition, boat operators are lacking, which compels Colonel Harris to improvise and use men from his own regiment.

Nonetheless, prior to dawn, two platoons of the 4th Ranger Company push off to take the dam. The rangers safely debark on the eastern peninsula, but the trailing rangers cross in daylight and the Chinese pour fire upon them. In the meantime, the first unit encounters heavy fire as the rangers move to seize the heights. The attack stalls and back on the water, some of the trailing rangers are forced to return to their starting point. All the while, Chinese on the western peninsula rush to bolster the defenses against the attacking force. The rangers under Captain Dorsey B. Anderson remain stalled, prompting Colonel Harris to call up the 3rd Battalion, Company I, which crosses the reservoir at about 1100. Due to the difficulties caused by the lack of boats and motors, the unit is unable to quickly reach the eastern peninsula. By midday, only one platoon reaches the rangers.

In coordination with the attack to seize the dam, a diversionary attack gets stalled before it can advance. A patrol initiated by Company A is unable to evict gunners in the northwest. To further derail the mission, Company E, 2nd Battalion, is still held up at the western ridge, unable to advance from its base. The enemy's fortifications withstand U.S. artillery fire and maintain heavy fire that forbids progress.

Before nightfall, the attack is cancelled. The rangers and Company I are ordered to withdraw rather than risk being overwhelmed during the darkened hours by a Chinese assault. The elements of Company I at the front and the rangers pull back without being harassed by the Chinese. At about dusk, the troops move to the south shore of the reservoir. Just after midnight the rangers and Company I reach the positions of the regiment at the Kansas Line. The mission had been costly, as both units sustain high casualties. The 7th Cavalry is afterwards placed into reserve. Its commander, Colonel William Harris, is transferred to the United States. He is replaced by Colonel Dan Gilmer.

In Naval activity, Fast Carrier Task Force (TF 77) initiates operations in the Straits of Formosa just outside the three-mile limit of mainland China. Carrier planes carry out an air parade that lasts for three days. During the operation, photos of particular potential targets in China are acquired.

— In the United States: General Douglas MacArthur is fired by President Truman. He is succeeded by General Matthew B. Ridgway, who at this time is commander, Eighth Army. With his promotion, Ridgway also receives the other posts held by MacArthur: supreme commander, Allied Powers in Japan; commander-in-chief, U.N. Command in Korea; U.S. commander-in-chief, Far East; and commanding general, U.S. Army, Far East.

Lieutenant General James A. Van Fleet succeeds General Ridgway as Eighth Army commander in Korea beginning 14 April. General Ridgway arrives in Japan from Korea and he makes it clear to the Japanese that all polices will remain in place, with no changes to come.

April 12 *In the IX Corps sector,* the ROK 1st Marine Corps Regiment relieves the 7th Cavalry, 1st Cavalry Division, at the Kansas Line.

In Air Force activity, since the arrival of spring and the thawing of the rivers, the Yalu River bridges remain a high priority of the U.S. Air Force. On this day, forty-six B-29s, escorted by a force of 100 fighters (F-84s), move against the targeted bridges. However, the B-29s fail to maintain a close formation and compel the escort fighters to spread out too far. The planes are met by a large force of about 50 or more MiGs that arrive from across the Yalu. At the approach of the enemy, the escort fighters try to close their ranks, but the MiGs are able by that time to break through and down two of the B-29s while inflicting severe damage to a third that forces it to make an emergency landing at Suwon. In addition, four to seven others are damaged in the skies. The B-29 gunners score seven kills.

One of the tailgunners credited with a victory this day is Sergeant Ercel S. Dye, attached to the 371st Bombardment Squadron, 307th Bombardment Wing (M). Sergeant Dye begins firing at a charging MiG from a distance of 2,000 yards and his finger remains on the trigger when the MiG stands at 50 feet away, veers off, goes into a vertical dive and explodes upon impact. The escort force of F-84s destroys four others in aerial duels.

Another tailgunner, Sergeant Robert A. Winslow, attached to the 30th Bombardment Squadron, 19th Bombardment Group (M), gets a kill when a MiG closes on the rear. Winslow keeps the plane under fire and just as it pulls even closer to pass and reaches a point just above Winslow's plane at a distance of about 50 feet, he lets go with another series of shots that strike paydirt. The MiG sustains successive explosions and crashes. No F-84s are lost.

Although the spans sustain some direct hits, the raids do not succeed in destroying the bridges. The B-29 gunners initially claim ten kills, but the Air Force awards credit for only seven. Of these, Sergeant Billy G. Beach gets credit for two of the downed MiGs. Colonel Meyer and Lt. Colonel Hinton each get one kill (the final one for both men). Other gunners aboard B-29s, including Sergeant Lyle R. Patterson (30th Bombardment Squadron, 19th Bombardment Group, M), Sergeant David R. Stime (371st Bombardment Squadron, 307th Bombardment Wing, M), and Sergeant Royal A. Veatch (30th Bombardment Squadron, 19th Bombardment Group, M), also receive credit for a victory after each gunner downs one of the MiG-15s. In addition, two Sabre jet pilots, Captain Jabara and Captain Howard M. Lane, each down one of the MiGs.

The climbing total of B-29 losses compels General Stratemeyer to suspend B-29 Superfortress attacks in the Sinuiju region. The F-84 Thunderjets are not capable of neutralizing the MiGs. General Partridge reports to Far East Air Forces that it would take the F-86 Sabre jets to handle the MiG threat against the bombers.

— *In Japan:* General Ridgway and General MacArthur meet at the Embassy library in Tokyo. During the meeting, General Ridgway decides to wait until General Van Fleet arrives on April 14 before officially replacing MacArthur. Ridgway returns to Korea to continue to control Operations RUGGED and DAUNTLESS.

April 13 General Ridgway is completing some final issues prior to moving to Japan. However, he will retain much control over Eighth Army after General Van Fleet becomes its commander on the following day. Strategy sessions this day determine that at present, the Chinese are not yet prepared to launch an offensive. Nevertheless, new lines are established by Ridgway's staff in the event that withdrawals are forced by a later Communist attack. Line Delta, the initial line to the south, stretches east to west from coast to coast, originating at Chonchon. Secondly, the Nevada Line, also extending from coast to coast, runs from the west at the lower bank of the Han River and afterward, it pivots northeastwardly toward Yangyang. Line Golden is drawn from the Han River, slightly more than five miles west of the capital, to a point that intersects with the Nevada Line in the vicinity of Yongp'yong.

In other activity, the I Corps continues to advance to the Utah Line. Also, the X Corps and the ROK III Corps maintain the advance to the Kansas Line.

In the X Corps sector, enemy resistance against the 7th Cavalry Regiment in the center and the ROK 5th Division on the right begins to lessen considerably.

In Air Force activity, Fifth Air Force reconnaissance planes discover as many as 400 to 500 MiGs parked on one field in Manchuria. The intelligence brings the dilemma of the U.S. aviators, once again, to the forefront. Even now, at this stage in the war, Congress has not provided sufficient funding for the number of Sabre jets required to neutralize the overwhelming enemy planes and pilots. Nonetheless, the Sabre jet pilots ignore the odds and continue to prevail in the skies.

The U.S. planes are forbidden from chasing MiGs

across the Yalu, but on occasion, some planes stray. And in some instances, pilots intentionally cross the river, apparently accidentally on purpose. The number of kills by Sabre jets sometimes varies from official records. There is combat footage of MiGs with their wheels down as they approach a landing strip and other footage shows parked MiGs on a field in Manchuria.

In Naval activity, Commander Fleet Air, Japan, is designated CTG 96.4. Also, Commander Fleet Air Wing Six is designated CTG 96.2. The designations cause the detachment of Fleet Air Wing Six from the operational control of Commander Fleet Air, Japan.

April 14 General Van Fleet arrives in Korea to assume command of Eighth Army. He is met by General Ridgway upon his arrival. The transfer-of-command ceremony commences at 1700 hours. Ridgway directs Van Fleet not to advance beyond the Wyoming Line in strength and to inform him if it is necessary to move beyond the Utah Line. General Ridgway departs for Japan later in the day, but avoids going to headquarters as a courtesy to General MacArthur, who had not yet departed for the United States. He remains quartered at a hotel in Tokyo.

In the ROK III Corps sector, the ROK 5th Division, after overcoming resistance in the Taebaek Mountains, arrives at the Kansas Line. The advance had been extremely difficult for the troops, who had no roads to ease the march. In addition to the weather and the enemy obstacles, the force had to be supplied by air drops.

In the I Corps sector, the 65th Infantry Regiment, 3rd Division, arrives at the Utah Line. The regiment, bolstered by elements of the 64th Tank Battalion and the Philippine 10th Battalion Combat Team, had encountered contingents of the Chinese 26th Army en route to the line, at points between the Imjin River and Route 33, but the opposition was eliminated. The rapid progress of the 65th Regiment greatly extends the I Corps line, but at this time, there is no indication of an enemy offensive in the works.

Since about 9 April, Eighth Army units have spotted large plumes of smoke. Planes also spot the fires and the origins. The enemy is intentionally starting fires to camouflage daytime troop movements. The nasty weather, combined with the smoke, causes difficulty for the U.S. air operations and for the artillery.

April 15 Eighth Army operations continue, but the enemy, with regard to major combat, remains elusive.

In the X Corps sector, the ROK 5th Division advances in the vicinity of Inje. It encounters and evicts elements of the N.K. 45th Division from their positions. Subsequent to clearing the village, the advance is bolstered during the night by artillery that hammers the ridges above Inje, to further clear the path to the Kansas Line.

In the U.S. 7th Division zone, the 17th Regiment encounters mines and other obstacles along Route 29 as it moves toward the Kansas Line; however, opposition from the N.K. 15th Division had subsided over the past few days. The 17th Regiment establishes contact with the 2nd Division this day. In the meantime, the 32nd Regiment is also pushing towards the Kansas Line against heavy resistance.

In Naval activity, Marine Force Far East (TF-91) is re-designated Marine Air Force Far East (TF-91). Also, Escort Carrier Group (TG-96.8) is dissolved.

April 16

General Van Fleet arrives in the ROK Army zone to confer with the commanders and the South Korean defense minister. Also, the Communists continue to retreat, leaving most of the Eighth Army front much more quiet than usual.

In the IX Corps sector, the British 27th Brigade arrives at the Utah Line. The British had moved across and cleared elements of the Chinese 40th Army from Paegun Mountain while it was en route to the line. The British Brigade is relieved by the ROK 6th Division's 19th Regiment. One contingent of New Zealand artillery remains with the South Koreans, while the brigade moves to Kap'yong as corps reserve.

In the X Corps sector, the ROK 5th Division advances to the Kansas Line against no organized resistance. The division had secured Inje on the previous day and the remaining enemy forces on nearby ridges had apparently been cleared by nightlong artillery bombardments. Also, more contingents of the 17th Regiment, 7th Division, enter Yanggu this day to form with the 7th Division along the Kansas Line. The 32nd Regiment, 7th Division, continues to advance against resistance towards the Kansas Line.

In Air Force activity, Far East Air Forces initiates a short series of missions against Pongyang, Kangdong and Yonpo and various airfields in the vicinity. Between this date and 20 April, B-29s fly about ten sorties each day against the targets.

— In Japan: General MacArthur departs Japan. General Ridgway confers with the headquarters staff subsequent to a farewell ceremony for MacArthur. While MacArthur is being driven to the airport, he witnesses huge crowds of Japanese who had lined the route from Tokyo to Haneda Airport to say farewell. The entourage arrives at the airport at 0700, and an Army band is in place to accompany the flyover by U.S. planes and a nineteen gun salute by an artillery unit. The plane that transports MacArthur and his family arrives in Hawaii before continuing on to the States.

General Ridgway makes some immediate changes. Major General Doyle O. Hickey, acting chief of staff (Far East Command and U.N. Command) is officially appointed to the post. He had been acting chief of staff since the previous September in place of General Almond, who departed as commander of X Corps.

During their final conversation, MacArthur informs Ridgway that if he had the choice of selecting his own successor, "I would have chosen you." Thirteen years later, according to Ridgway, a report surfaces from an interview MacArthur gave to a reporter in 1954 that places Ridgway at the bottom of MacArthur's list of field commanders.

April 17

General Van Fleet moves across the entire front, covering it from coast to coast. Up to this point, the initial phase of Operation DAUNTLESS succeeds. Nevertheless, there is still great concern that the Communists are preparing to strike. Also, The U.S., aware of a massive operation to rebuild the airfields for the People's Air Force since February, launches attacks to destroy the airfields to prevent the Chinese from providing air support to their ground troops. It was earlier decided that premature strikes could not have succeeded in total destruction. This day, B-29s pound the bases and the air attacks continue until the 23rd. The massive air strikes take out the fields and prevent the Communists from providing air support for their spring offensive.

In the I Corps sector, enemy resistance against the 25th and 24th Divisions begins to subside. One patrol, attached to the 5th Tank Battalion, 24th Division, plows along Route 3 and reaches a point about six or seven miles from Kumhwa without incident. Meanwhile, the 25th Division maintains its slow-paced advance.

In the IX Corps sector, on the opposite side of the Hwach'on Reservoir from the X Corps positions, ongoing patrols of the 1st Marine Division and ROK 6th Division search for the enemy. All reports indicate that the Chinese continue to retire. Nevertheless, Eighth Army still anticipates an enemy offensive in the making.

Also, the 1st Korean Marine Corps Regiment deploys elements in the high ground above the Pukham River, west of the dam at the Hwach'on Reservoir and on the ridge inside the Pukham loop, to prepare to evict the Chinese still holding the dam. The 7th Cavalry fails to seize it prior to being relieved by the Korean Marines.

In the X Corps sector, General Almond orders patrols to probe for enemy hot spots above his positions along the Kansas line. The 32nd Regiment, 7th Division, arrives at the Kansas Line.

In Air Force activity, a specialized U.S. and South Korean contingent executes a mission known as Operation MiG. The party gets behind enemy lines in an H-19 helicopter to the scene of a crashed MiG-15 in the vicinity of Sinanju. The detachment succeeds in retrieving particular components of the plane and gets them back to friendly lines where they can be transferred to gather intelligence. En route, the helicopter is hit once by enemy fire, but it returns safely.

In other activity, B-29s, escorted by F-86 Sabre jets of the 4th Interceptor Fighter Wing, attack enemy bridges.

— In the United States: General Douglas MacArthur arrives in San Francisco from Hawaii, where he had been received by large, enthusiastic crowds. Upon his arrival back in the States during the evening, again, huge crowds gather along the route from the airport to the city, causing the motorcade a long delay in

reaching the hotel. On the following day, the people of San Francisco gather again and the city celebrates MacArthur's return with a tickertape parade.

President Truman, by executive order, extends the enlistments of U.S. military personnel, which freezes all discharges.

April 18 *In the I Corps sector,* elements of the 25th Division, including the 35th Infantry Regiment, the 89th Tank Battalion and a contingent of artillery, advance through the Hant'an River valley without incident, until the force reaches a point about five miles from Ch'orwon.

In the IX Corps sector, a small patrol of Korean Marines fords the Pukham River slightly less than five miles west of the dam at the Hwachon Reservoir and afterward discovers the town of Hwach'on undefended, except for eleven Chinese troops, who are quickly seized.

In the X Corps sector, patrols again venture north of the Kansas Line in search of enemy positions, but no major concentrations are located.

In Air Force activity, rescue helicopters come under fire during evacuation sorties. Ten H-5 helicopters (3rd ARS) arrive at the front line to pick up seriously wounded troops to get them to medical facilities. Five of them come under fire; however, all complete their missions and twenty troops are evacuated safely.

April 19 Elements of the attacking units of I and IX Corps are on the Utah Line.

In the I Corps sector, the 25th and 24th Divisions plow forward against the enemy and the elements toward the Utah Line. Enemy fire, combined with heavy rains and primitive roads, slow progress, but the bulk of the 25th Division arrives at the line on the following day. The 24th Division also arrives on the line on the 20th. Eighth Army pauses to catch a slight breather and get the units re-supplied before it reinitiates the

attack. The offensive to reach the Wyoming Line resumes on 21 April.

In the X Corps sector, for the third straight day, General Almond's patrols encounter no enemy strong points north of the Kansas Line. Only sporadic resistance is encountered.

In Air Force activity, the C-119s ground on 31 May begin to come back into service. The first plane to receive some modifications and be reconditioned is placed back in operation.

— *In the United States:* General MacArthur arrives in Washington, D.C., and delivers an address to a joint session of Congress. MacArthur gives his outlook on the conflict in Korea, his thoughts on the Communist threats to the U.S. and the necessity of bringing about victory. The speech, which lasts slightly longer than thirty-five minutes, is interrupted about fifty times with loud, sustained applause.

MacArthur closes by saying:

"I am closing my fifty-two years of military service. When I joined the Army, even before the turn of the century, it was with the fulfillment of all my boyish hopes and dreams. The world has turned over many times since I took the oath on the Plain at West Point, and the hopes and dreams have long since vanished, but I still remember the refrain of one of the most popular barrack ballads of that day which proclaimed most proudly that old soldiers never die; they just fade away. And like the old soldier of that ballad, I now close my military career and just fade away, an old soldier who tried to do his duty as God gave him the light to see that duty. Goodbye."

April 20 Intelligence is unable to provide a specific date for the anticipated enemy counterattack, but it is thought to be between this day and 1 May. Nonetheless, no outward signs of an offensive are spotted in any sector of Eighth Army. Intelligence had determined

The British 29th Brigade takes a pause during its pullback under pressure by enemy offensive.

that the Chinese had succeeded in getting two new Army groups (III and IX) into the region near the Kumch'on–Koksan–Ich'on area. The information leads the U.S. to speculate that the attack, when launched, will pour across the Imjin River from the north and northwest.

General Van Fleet informs General Ridgway that all units are either at or close to their respective Lines (Kansas and Utah) and that Eighth Army will initiate the next phase of Operation DAUNTLESS on the following day. General Van Fleet, in addition to directing the I and IX Corps to advance to the Wyoming Line, requests of Ridgway authorization to have the X Corps and the ROK I and III Corps push to Kansong, a town situated along the coast near the junction of Route 24 and the coastal road. The X Corps objective stands slightly more than twenty miles above Yangyang. Ridgway authorizes the plan, but he modifies the route of attack by shortening the arc of the eastern sweep. The operation is to commence on 24 April.

In other activity, two planes attached to Marine Squadron VMF-312 aboard the light carrier *Bataan* encounter and engage four enemy Yak fighters in the Pyongyang–Chinnamp'o area. Three of the enemy planes are destroyed; one escapes.

In the I Corps sector, the 3rd Division under General Robert H. Soule, unlike the 24th and 25th Divisions, had made long gains during the advance. The Corps' line, due to the progress of the 3rd Division, extends from the mouth of the Imjin River to a point about ten miles from Ch'orwon, which gives the I Corps about thirty miles to defend if the Communists launch an attack. The ROK 1st Division, on the 3rd Division's left, holds ground at Route 1 that extends from the mouth of the Imjin to a point about fifteen miles distant, known as the Korangp'o-ri bend. The 3rd Division stands at the Korangp'o-ri Route 33 sector. It is augmented by the British 29th Brigade.

In the X Corps sector, patrols advance to a point about two miles above the Kansas Line, but still, the enemy remains elusive.

April 21   Marine planes attached to a carrier encounter enemy aircraft for the first time over Korea. Two Yaks are downed by Captain Philip C. DeLong, while another Marine pilot, 1st Lieutenant Harold U. Daigh, downs one plane and inflicts damage upon one other.

Also, The U.N. forces, composed primarily of U.S. troops, advance beyond the 38th Parallel as the final phase of Operation DAUNTLESS commences. The 1st Marine Division launches an attack in its zone in coordination with the operation. The Marines drive toward the area above the Hwach'on Dam. At the same time, the elusive enemy that has been difficult to engage since about the 11 April initiates an offensive on this day.

In the I Corps sector, 3rd and the 25th Divisions push off for their respective objectives. The 25th advances towards Ch'orwon while the 24th drives towards

Kumhwa, the latter at the point of the Iron Triangle. Both divisions move beyond the Kansas Line and gain, at some points, about five miles, against minor sporadic resistance. Meanwhile, the 25th Division moves across the Pogae-san heights en route to Ch'orwon, but the task is much more difficult, as the troops are hit by heavy artillery fire. After dark, the Chinese attack the Utah Line particularly hard in the zone of the Turkish Brigade at Route 33. During the night (21st-22nd), patrols discover that the Chinese have fortified positions at the Imjin River.

In the IX Corps sector, no enemy opposition is encountered. The ROK 6th Division moves in the Kwangdok-san ridges, alongside of the 24th Division (on loan to I Corps).

In the 1st Marine Division zone, after a three-week delay, the Division is directed to initiate its attack from the Kansas Line to Line Quantico. The attack is to begin the following day.

In the X Corps sector, patrols of the 2nd and 7th Divisions encounter large concentrations of North Korean troops in the area east of the Hwach'on Reservoir. The discovery of various concentrations of enemy units, some of which contain up to 1,000 troops, is a signal to Eighth Army that they are relieving and reinforcing units, but still, there is no absolute evidence to prove a counterattack is imminent. Also, Marine Air Group 12 (Forward Echelon) begins to operate from the airport in Seoul.

In Air Force activity, a plane (SA-16) attached to the 3rd Air Rescue Squad takes off for the scene of a downed enemy Yak pilot in the vicinity of Chinnamp'o to try to retrieve him for the purpose of gathering intelligence; however, after the plane lands and puts out a raft, enemy fire becomes too heavy. The mission is aborted and the plane takes off without harm and without the enemy pilot.

Also, Major Blake, on a mission as part of the 13th Bombardment Squadron, comes under heavy fire from antiaircraft guns as his bomber approaches the target. Despite the lack of gun turrets on his B-26, Blake passes at low levels and bombs and strafes the marshaling yard at Songchon. His plane sustains some damage to the radio antennae, but Blake destroys one locomotive, damages another and damages about 15 boxcars. After expending all of his ammunition, including machine gun shells, Blake chooses to remain overhead until daylight to try to detect moving trains. After dawn he calls for fighters and guides them to the marshaling yards.

April 22–July 8 1951. FIFTH DESIGNATED CAMPAIGN: CCF SPRING OFFENSIVE.

April 22   The Communists launch a spring offensive (fifth phase). Aerial observation spots large concentrations of enemy forces to the north of I and IX Corps and more are detected northwest of I Corps. More enemy units are spotted east of the Hwach'on Reservoir above Yanggu and Inje. The combined Communist

U.S. troops (25th Division) assist a wounded soldier on 22 April to get him down a hill to medical aid.

force moving against Seoul numbers about 270,000 troops and includes the III, IX and XIX Army Groups. The Chinese, following a four-hour bombardment, unleash three armies in a two-pronged assault. Under a full moon amid endless sounds of whistles, flares and blaring bugles, the Chinese launch the first phase of the attack against Eighth Army troops in central Korea, as a diversion. The primary assult is thrown against I and IX Corps to encircle and destroy Eighth Army defenders and seize Seoul. About 50 percent of the available enemy forces in Korea participate in the attack; however, it is not heavily supported by artillery, nor does it receive close-air support. Nonetheless, by the following day, the Communist offensive is in full swing across the entire Korean peninsula.

In the I Corps sector, the advance to the Wyoming Line is reinitiated. Enemy resistance is encountered, but on the left flank, the coveted dam at the Hwach'on Reservoir is seized effortlessly by the 1st Korean Marine Corps Regiment. It becomes apparent on the ground that the enemy offensive is underway, as civilians approach from the northwest. More evidence is discovered in the 3rd Division zone, when a patrol captures a soldier attached to the Chinese 34th Division, 12th Army.

At about 1700, air observers in the 25th Division zone spot a huge column with vehicles and artillery as it moves down Route 33, on a collision course with the Turkish Brigade. Meanwhile, in the 24th Division sector, other enemy ground troops are spotted on Route

33. The U.S. initiates an artillery attack to impede progress. As General Bryan directs the 24th Division in preparation for an imminent attack, the ROK 6th Division, positioned beside the 24th, seems to be in line for a direct assault. Elements of the 24th Division had seized prisoners attached to the Chinese 59th Division.

In the 25th Division zone, as anticipated, the brunt of the enemy assault strikes the Turkish Brigade. Following a heavy artillery bombardment, which lasts several hours, the Chinese strike the Turks' perimeter along Route 33. At about midnight, elements of the Chinese 179th Division (III Army Group) plow into the Turkish lines and the positions of the 24th Regiment. The Turks are split into several isolated contingents as the Chinese push through between the Turks and the left flank of the 24th Regiment. Artillery support is cancelled due to the close-quartered fighting. The Chinese pound against the lines throughout the night and by dawn, they are threatening also the 27th Infantry Regiment. Some enemy forces penetrate about two miles beyond the front lines.

At dawn the Chinese strike the Division's right, defended by the 27th Regiment. However, the 27th Infantry throws up a wall of fire that the Chinese are unable to penetrate. After less than one hour of failed attempts and high casualties, the Chinese disengage. General Sladen Bradley, the division commander, directs the 24th and 27th Regiments to pull back about two miles. The Turkish brigade is directed to leave the line to regroup. Despite the harrowing night, the Turks emerge with much less damage than expected. Nevertheless, one of the isolated Turkish contingents, a full company, is annihilated. The reserve 35th Infantry Regiment assumes responsibility for the Turkish zone.

In the 3rd Division zone, the Chinese also strike at about midnight of the 22nd-23rd. The initial thrust against the 65th Infantry Regiment hits the Philippine 10th Battalion Combat Team and knocks it out of its positions, but otherwise, no gains are accomplished. Throughout the night, the two enemy divisions (34th Division, 12th Army and 29th Division, 15th Army) expend many troops. During the morning of the 23rd, the Filipinos mount a counterattack and regain the ground they had lost at the beginning of the fight.

In the meantime, the attacks subside, but the withdrawal of the Turks has left the right flank of the 65th Regiment exposed. Also, the regiment's perimeter remains under threat by the Chinese XIX Army Group, which is pressing against the British 29th Brigade deployed in the southwest. The British also come under severe attack at about midnight. The enemy crashes through a hole that exists between the Northumberland Fusiliers and the Belgians along the Imjin River near Hill 194.

Word is passed from the Belgians that the enemy is moving to unguarded crossings. Reinforcements attached to the Ulster battalion speed toward the two suspected bridges, but Chinese forces ambush the column. The unit is nearly annihilated. The Chinese, meanwhile, continue to pour into the region with some moving to assault the Belgians at Hill 194, and others heading straight to the two unguarded bridges. Soon after, Company Z (Northumberland Fusileers), deployed on Hill 257 on the opposite bank, is attacked. Another objective that comes under attack by the forces that cross the bridges is Company X, also of the Fusiliers, deployed on Hill 162 along the Imjin, but downstream from Hill 257.

Company Y, deployed in the right tip of the zone, evades attack, but the enemy advances on both sides of their lines. The Chinese dominate the bridges from positions at Hill 257 and at dawn, their artillery fire prevents U.S. reinforcements from accessing the Hant'an crossing along Route 11. In addition, Chinese reinforcements continue to arrive to bolster the assault against Hill 294, held by the Belgians. At about dawn, the British commander concludes that a pullback is necessary.

In the IX Corps sector, the advance continues without encountering any heavy resistance. Later in the day, the ROK 6th Division captures members of the Chinese 60th Division. Other Chinese are captured by the Turkish Brigade. Information gathered from the POWs indicates that an attack by the enemy would be launched subsequent to dusk. In the ROK 6th Division zone, the advance towards the Wyoming Line is halted by about 1600. The commanding officer, General Chang, disregards the advice of his KMAG advisor regarding the deployment of the division and deploys his reserve (7th Regiment) too close to the front, immediately behind his 2nd Regiment. The 2nd Regiment and the 19th Regiment fail to establish defensive positions as ordered. Within about four hours, the Chinese strike the ROK 6th Division, which collapses. The ROK 2nd and 19th Regiments retreat haphazardly, leaving great quantities of weapons and equipment for the Communists. The reserve 7th Regiment, after seeing the stampede, also retires aimlessly.

The failure to stand and fight jeopardizes many other units. The New Zealand artillery contingents in support of the 6th Division are compelled to withdraw. Nearby, the South Korean artillery battalion, unprotected after the abandonment of positions by the 6th Division, is caught by the Chinese before it can retreat. The Korean artillerymen, like the infantry, abandon their weapons. U.S. units in support of the South Koreans are also compelled to pull back; however, the Americans carry out all their equipment and weapons. They head eastward to link with the 92nd Armored FABn, but the route is clogged by retreating Koreans and abandoned vehicles.

When the elements of Company C, 2nd Chemical Mortar Battalion, and the 2nd Rocket Field Artillery Battery arrive at the lines of the 92nd Armored FABN positions, much of their weapons have been left behind along the unpassable road. While the U.S. toils to fill in gaps and hold against the attacks, the ROK 6th Division continues to run. General Chang is unable to regroup any of his command until about dawn on the following day at positions about ten miles from where they were supposed to be. The 24th Division and the 1st Marine Division are both severely jeopardized.

In the 1st Marine Division zone, the 7th and 5th Marines advance on the left and center, with the 1st Korean Marine Regiment moving on the right. In conjunction, the 1st Marines are kept in reserve. During the day, the advance meets with little opposition. All the while, the enemy pours troops into the vacated positions of the ROK 6th Division. At 2130, word arrives that west of the division positions, the ROK 6th Division is under strong pressure. Just after 2200, orders arrive instructing the Marines to cancel the scheduled resumption of the advance (at 0800 on the 23rd) and instead, consolidate their positions. At about the same time, the ROKs collapse, which creates a huge hole.

The Chinese plow through the gap and punch against the 7th Marines with the brunt of the assault, but the 5th Marines also come under attack. The 1st Battalion, 1st Marines, is called from reserve to move up and fill the gap on the division's left flank. Meanwhile, the retreat of the ROKs jams the roads and hinders the advance of the 1st Marines. Just before midnight, the Chinese strike the Korean Marines (2nd Battalion) at Hill 509 on the right and maneuver to partially surround the 1st Battalion.

At the same time, the center of the perimeter, held by the 5th Marines, sustains a tenacious assault. At the 1st Battalion, 5th Marines' command post at Hwach'on, a contingent is immediately dispatched to gain Hill 313, the dominating point that controls the town. A bitter contest ensues as, the Marine platoon and the Chinese each covet the hill. The Marines lose 7 killed and 17 wounded. Reinforcements from the 2nd Battalion, 5th Marines, move to reinforce 1st Battalion, but by dawn, the situation eases. The Marine platoon holds Hill 313; the Chinese had abandoned it during the night.

In the 7th Marines area along the Division left, the 1st Battalion braces against the onslaught of about 2,000 troops of the 358th Regiment, 120th Division, Chinese 40th Army. Despite the overwhelming odds, the Marine 1st Battalion holds steadfastly, thanks in great part to the support of artillery.

During the battle, PFC Herbert A. Littleton, Company A, 1st Battalion, is on guard when the attack is sprung. He alerts the forward observers and remains at his post to help guide the artillery, but just after more Marines rush to join him, the enemy tosses a grenade in their positions. Littleton spots the live grenade and blankets it with his body to save the others. His sacrifice spares the others and permits them to support the artillery. PFC Littleton is awarded the4 Medal of Honor posthumously for his selfless sacrifice.

The 1st Battalion, 1st Marines, move up in time to help hold the line west of Hwach'on. By dawn on the 23rd, the American and South Korean Marines had thrown back the attacks. The town of Hwach'on and the dam are preserved. No further attempts to gain it are made.

With the arrival of dawn on the 23rd, it is apparent that the Chinese fail to exploit the gap on the flanks, opened with the retreat of the ROK 6th Division. Only frontal attacks had been thrown against the Marines.

In the X Corps sector, elements of the N.K. 45th Division launch attacks against the 32nd Infantry Regiment on the 7th Division's right flank, but no progress is made. However, the ROK 3rd Division, holding the east flank, is hit hard. Before noon on the following day, the Communists drive the ROKs back and create a gap with which to reach Inje.

In the ROK III Corps sector, contact is made with elements of the N.K. 12th Division (V Corps) by the ROK 5th Division at a spot above Inje. Prior to this day, the ROKs had been encountering elements of the N.K. 45th Division.

In the 25th Division zone, pressure by the Chinese and North Koreans prompts the Marines to order the air support section of MCTACS-2 to pull back about six miles and reestablish positions about one mile north of Chunchon. On the 24th, the unit again withdraws to a point about four miles south of the town.

In Air Force activity, by this date, the airfield at Suwon has been improved above its primitive condition and additional Sabre jets of the 334th and 336th Fighter Interceptor Squadrons of the 4th Fighter Interceptor Wing are now there, which permits the U.S. to dispatch more planes into MiG Alley. The planes on this afternoon get an opportunity to unfold their recently developed tactic, which has been made possible by adding two planes to each flight, bringing the total from four to six planes. With the added power, the Sabres expect to neutraize the MiGs that attack and separate the formation into two pairs. A patrol of 12 Sabres is intercepted by a band of 36 MiGs while on patrol by the Yalu River. When the MiGs use their tactic of one diving and one climbing, they discover that four Sabres pursue the one that climbs and two chase the one that dives. In addition, the Communists discover that their timing is bad, as another twelve Sabres arrive to relieve the one already engaged. The tactic works well. Four of the MiGs are destroyed and another four sustain damage. One of the downed planes is credited to Lt. Colonel Eagleston. It is Eagleston's second and final kill of the war. Captain Jabara also gets one kill, his fourth.

April 23–27 1951 The U.S. Marines engage and halt the Chinese Communist offensive and prevent them from turning the IX Corps' flank.

April 23 Far East Air Forces concludes a series of devastating raids against enemy-held airfields. B29s have been saturating the airfields, particularly those in the forward areas in the vicinity of Pyongyang, since the 17th. On this day, the planes also execute about 340 sorties in close-air support missions. The bombers succeed in eliminating air support for the enemy offensive launched the previous day.

In other activity, prior to noon, General Van Fleet determines that the positions of the I Corps and the IX Corps have become undefendable, subsequent to the hasty retreat of the ROK 6th Division on the previous day. General Van Fleet aborts the advance to the Alabama Line (scheduled for 24 April) and he directs I and IX Corps to establish entrenched positions along the Kansas Line. Nonetheless, by day's end, the corps perimeter remains in peril due to enemy pressure. During the latter part of the day, it is suggested to abandon the Kansas Line for the Golden Line, just to the front of Seoul, but General Van Fleet prefers not to grant the enemy more territory without having them pay a stiff price.

In other activity, Naval Task Force 77, operating in the Sea of Japan, changes its fast carrier mission from interdiction to close support. Other air support includes USMC fighter squadrons, five of which are landbased in southeastern Korea and a sixth aboard the escort carrier *Bataan.* The ground troops are also supported by the Fifth Air Force, which on this day carries out 340 sorties. The 1st Marine Air Wing flies 205 sorties and of these, 153 are in support of the front, including the I Corps as the 24th and 25th Divisions and elements of the 3rd Infantry Division withdraw to the Kansas Line.

In the I Corps sector, at Hill 194, defended by the Belgians in the British 29th Brigade zone, a heavy enemy assault is launched. Reinforcements from the U.S. 2nd Battalion, 7th Infantry Regiment, bolstered by tanks, move against the two bridges that had been unprotected but now remain under the guns of the Chinese. Heavy fire from the heights at Hill 257 prevents the Americans from attempting to force the Hant'an crossing.

A contingent of the 25th Division is deployed in the hills south of Ch'orwon, April 23.

British Brigadier Thomas Brodie pulls back his force and draws a line about two miles below Hill 257 and deploys on both sides of Route 11.

Meanwhile, Brodie requests help from General Soule, who dispatches the 1st Battalion, 7th Infantry Regiment, to bolster the British positions. The Gloster Battalion, holding near Route 5Y, had engaged the Chinese since the previous night on Hill 148 west of the road and Hills 144 and 182 on the opposite side of the road. Company A, on Hill 144, remains unscathed, but Company D, at Hill 182, sustains high casualties, but surrenders no ground. At Hill 148, Company A repels the enemy throughout the night, but by dawn, the remaining able-bodied troops are unable to continue to hold. The positions at an ancient castle near the summit of the hill are abandoned. Company A establishes an ambush at the Imjin and after successfully eliminating many Chinese, the unit retires without sustaining any casualties. After dawn (23rd), the battalion redeploys in the vicinity of Solma-ri. Company A occupies Hill 235 and the remainder deploys nearby on either side of the road.

During the early part of the day, the Chinese attempt to ford the Imjin in force at several locations, but artillery fire and air strikes halt the penetrations prior to noon.

In related activity, the ROK 1st Division, bolstered by tanks, repels several intrusions. The 12th ROK Regiment eliminates the probing attacks by about noon. Other elements push out in front of the perimeter and

engage enemy forces until dusk. The regiment inflicts high casualties on the enemy. About midnight (23rd-24th), the Communists again strike the ROK 1st Division. Later, after the ROK 6th Division again abandons its positions, the British Brigade is in the line of the Chinese advance. The South Koreans halt their flight after getting to the rear of the Australians.

At about 2200, a platoon of U.S. tanks (4th Platoon, Company A, 72nd Tank Battalion), under orders to withdraw as the Chinese approach, had been one of the units on guard at an outpost by the Kap'yong River while the South Koreans retreated. Suddenly, the unit comes under fire as the approaching troops, thought to be ROKs, actually are Chinese. The tankers resist the hordes tenaciously and with the hatches open. The engagement costs the platoon two of its tank commanders and its commanding officer before it is able to turn and retire and hook up with the 2nd platoon at the Kap'yong ford. En route, another tank platoon (1st Platoon) intercepts the 4th Platoon at the blocking position.

Chinese troops compel the 4th Platoon leader to return to the island ridge, while the remainder of the platoon continues toward the ford. In the meantime, the Chinese continue to flood through the gaps. The Australians on Hill 504 maintain a steadfast defense, despite the lack of artillery support. Repeatedly, the Australians repel assaults. The Chinese gain two positions held by platoons, but one is later regained. During the night-long contest, the U.S. tanks on the island hold the

U.S. troops in search of enemy near the Hant'an River.

ground, but Company B, 2nd Chemical Mortar Company, deployed behind the Australians, had pulled out and abandoned its vehicles and weapons. The 213th FABn and the New Zealanders, also deployed to the rear of Hill 504, had been ordered to pull back by Brigadier Burke when Chinese pressure became too great. Nevertheless, the Australians hold.

By about dawn on the following day, the Chinese again sustained heavy casualties. Their attacks subside. However, at about midnight (23rd-24th), the Communists reinitiate contact and engage some units of the 24th and 25th Divisions. The ROK 1st Division and the British 29th Brigade, each deployed along the Imjin

River, also come under attack. Company B, holding the battalion's right flank, becomes surrounded.

Meanwhile, within the British zone, Company C, along Route 5Y, is directed to withdraw to positions between Companies A and D near Hill 235, but Brigadier Brodie is convinced that the troops on the right flank would not be able to penetrate the Chinese to reach safety. The isolated unit, Company B, spends the night repelling all attempts to destroy it.

In the 3rd Division zone, General Soule orders a pull-back from the western part of the zone along the Utah Line. At about noon, the 65th Infantry Regiment begins to drop back by passing through the 7th Infantry

Regiment. As the leap-frog move unfolds, the 3rd Battalion, 65th Infantry, bolstered by tanks (64th Tank Battalion) and the 3rd Reconnaissance Company deploy slightly above the Hant'an River along Route 33 to defend there until the Belgian contingent on Hill 194 is able to extricate itself. The 1st Battalion, 7th Infantry Regiment, supported by tanks, moves up Route 11 to attack Hill 675 on the summit of Kamak Mountain.

Later at about 1800, the 1st Battalion pivots and moves north against Hill 257, but only minimal progress is made by 2000. In the meantime, the Belgians are able to abandon their positions and reach relative safety on Route 33, which leads them to an assembly zone at the junction with Route 11. In conjunction, the 1st Battalion, led by Colonel Weyand, breaks off its attack and rejoins the 7th Regiment along the Kansas Line. Also, once the Belgians form with their vehicles and head to the line, the 65th Infantry's 3rd Battalion and its supporting armor and reconnaissance units abandon the blocking positions at the Hant'an River and head for the Kansas Line.

Meanwhile, the Philippine 10th Battalion Combat Team, expected to plug the hole in the British Brigade's line, arrives at the brigade's headquarters at about 2000, but too late to attempt to deploy between the Gloster Battalion and the fusiliers.

At about midnight, the Communists press against the entire 3rd Division line. Meanwhile, the beleaguered ROK 6th Division (IX Corps) remains scattered, but more than 2,000 troops had been regrouped by General Chang. He is directed to move his force several miles north to the Kansas Line. The Chinese, however, rip into the positions of the 24th Division (on loan to I Corps) at the center of the line to open a hole between the 19th and 5th Infantry Regiments. The struggle continues through the early morning hours and some units are compelled to give ground. General Bryan orders his reserve 21st Regiment to seize the high ground, where the penetration first occurred, but the Chinese arrive before the regiment could take it. The Chinese are able to drive a wedge that penetrates about three miles, but General Bryan readjusts his regiments, drawing them back and forming a galvanized line. Chinese pressure remains constant, but the line holds.

After General Bryan learns of his unprotected flank because of the ROK 5th Division's retreat, he directs the 21st Regiment to plug the gap. The Chinese again fail to take advantage of the hole, instead launching frontal attacks. Patrols of the Eighth Army's Ranger Company (attached to the 21st Regiment) move out in an eastward direction, but no Chinese forces are discovered on the flank. The division manages to withdraw to the Kansas Line by 1800.

After dark, the Communists again strike the ROK 6th Division and as on the previous night, it immediately collapses and runs. The retreat causes pandemonium as the roads clog. The New Zealanders had sped to support the ROK 6th Division, but before the contingent could prepare its defense, it, too, becomes jeopardized. In addition, the 27th British Brigade's positions become threatened.

In the 25th Division zone, in the eastern section, by dawn, enemy pressure lessens. The Division is able to reach the Kansas Line during the afternoon. After arriving, the 24th and 35th Regiments redeploy on the ridges that the division previously held between the Yongp'yong and Hant'an Rivers. In conjunction, the 27th Regiment and the Turkish Brigade set up positions at the Yongp'yong River.

In the IX Corps sector, 1st Marine Division zone, preparations are being completed for the advance to the Alabama Line, but by about 1100 on the following day, the operation is cancelled. The 1st Marine Division is ordered to form a line that extends from the dam at the Hwach'on Reservoir in a southwestwardly direction that traces the Pukham River. The line is designated Pendleton. The 3rd Battalion, 1st Marines, are taken by truck from the village of Todun-ni along the west bank of the Pukham River to Hill 902, but the Chinese also are en route to gain the hill, aware that it controls the river where the 1st Marine Division would have to cross.

The Chinese are unable to arrive first. Companies G, H and I, 3rd Battalion, 1st Marines, occupy three separate ridge lines that straddle the path to the hill mass, with mortar and machine gun support to their respective immediate rears. By mid-day, the three Marine regiments complete the establishment of a line formed in what might be described as a fish hook, but some separations exist between the regiments. Nonetheless, the Marines are prepared for an expected Chinese night assault.

By day's end, it becomes evident that the ROK 6th Division remains unstable and disorganized, which places the Marines in further jeopardy. In conjunction, the 11th Marines (Marine Artillery) is deployed at Chich'on-ni. The 92nd FABn and the other units, including the 987th FABn, that were driven back subsequent to the retreat of the ROK 6th Division are directed to form in the vicinity of the 11th Marines. During the operation to move to the Kansas Line, observation planes detect large numbers of Chinese moving through the vacated positions of the ROK 6th Division. The Marines conclude that these forward forces are en route to sever the supply line.

At Horseshoe Ridge, defended by the 1st Battalion, 1st Marines, elements of the Chinese 120th Division launch an attack at about 2000. Several hundred Chinese rush in successive waves and compel a forward position of Company C to pull back under the relentless thrust, which includes machine gun and mortar fire and, from close-range, hundreds of grenades. The Marines, however, hold the ridge, despite about four hours of non-stop combat and a simultaneous eerie serenade of Chinese chants and yells. At about midnight, the 3rd Battalion, 1st Marines, is attacked, but Companies G, H and I receive the brunt of it. At Company G's outpost, the Communists overrun the small contingent and force it back.

A nearby contingent led by Tech Sergeant Harold E. Wilson attempts to return fire and cover the retirement. Wilson becomes wounded twice as he assists the survivors from the outpost. The heavy fire continues to pour down from the heights. Despite his wounds, Wilson refuses evacuation and maintains control over his contingent. Meanwhile, he is wounded twice more and incapacitated, unable to use his arms to fire. Undaunted, Wilson continues to hand ammunition and weapons to his fellow troops and in addition, he finds time to call for reinforcements. When they arrive, he also directs them against the enemy. Wilson continues in extreme pain, but he refuses to quit and his men follow suit. At dawn, the enemy has been repulsed and the ground remains under the control of C Company. Wilson becomes the recipient of the Medal of Honor for his outstanding leadership and courage in the face of the enemy.

Other units that come under attack include the 3rd Battalion, 1st Marines, and the 3rd Battalion, 7th Marines. Nonetheless, by dawn, the Marines remain in place and the Chinese sustain a huge number of casualties.

In other activity, the ROK 6th Division is expected to arrive at the Kansas Line; however, by the latter part of the afternoon, it remains in place, still unprepared to move. General Hoge, concerned about the absence of the ROKs on the Kansas Line, directs the British 27th Brigade to deploy and defend the Kap'yong River Valley to the rear of the South Koreans. Hoge wants to assure that the Chinese cannot sever Route 17 and take the village of Kap'yong. The blocking positions guard against intrusions along both valley approaches.

Elements of the Royal Australian Regiment deploy at Hill 504 and a contingent of the Princess Patricia's Canadian Light Infantry spreads out on Hill 677. The British positions are supported by U.S. contingents, including elements of the 72nd Tank Battalion, 2nd Chemical Mortar Battalion and the 74th Engineer Combat Battalion.

In the ROK III Corps sector, at about midnight (22nd-23rd), while the corps prepares for an advance on the following day to the Alabama Line, the Communists strike the positions of the ROK 35th Regiment, ROK 5th Division, at midnight. The Communists continue to pound the regiment and by dawn, the South Koreans take flight. In the meantime, the North Korean 12th Division funnels into the zone. The enemy advances into a large gap between the 35th and the 5th Regiments (7th ROK Division). Although 35th deserts its positions, the ROK 5th Regiment attempts to hold, but it too is compelled to retreat or risk entrapment. The 5th Regiment makes a disciplined fighting withdrawal. Afterwards, all ROK forces in the vicinity of Inje come under the control of Colonel Min Ki Shik, the commander of the 5th Regiment.

In Air Force activity, F-86s attached to the 336th Fighter Interceptor Squadron begin to operate from the airfield at Suwon. From this location, the F-86s are able to stay in the air on target for longer periods when operating in the area near the Yalu River, known as MiG Alley.

Also, in an effort to bolster the offensive, Far East Air Forces presses its capacity in the air by initiating more than 1,000 sorties on this day. The performances of the pilots remain identical for the next three days, with an average of 1,000 combat sorties each day. The planes achieve great success and inflict heavy casualties upon enemy forces and in the process huge amounts of supplies are also destroyed.

April 24 *In the I Corps sector,* the 24th and 25th Divisions and elements of the 3rd Division are now on the Kansas Line. The Communists, at about midnight (23rd-24th), launched attacks against some units, but heavier assaults had been thrown against the ROK 6th Division and the British 29th Brigade at the same time. On this day, the attacks intensify. Despite heavy support for the 1st Marine Division, Marine squadrons also support I Corps with 57 sorties.

In the 24th Division zone, Hill 664 is gained by the Chinese 179th Regiment, giving it dominating high ground; however, throughout the day, the Chinese fail to push the 24th Division from its positions. The line is augmented by two battalions of the 27th Infantry Regiment (25th Division) that deploy at the base of Hill 664. Repeated assaults are repelled. Some minor gains are made against the 17th Regiment, but U.S. counterattacks regain the lost ground. Although the 24th Division holds the line, it discovers that large numbers of Chinese forces are gathering in positions to strike the right flank, held by the 21st Regiment, and other attacks against the front.

In the British 29th Brigade zone near Solma-ri, along Route 5 at Hill 235, as dawn emerges, Company B, Gloster Battalion, still holds its ground but the situation deteriorates. The Chinese prepare to liquidate the isolated command. Under cover fire, the beleaguered troops try to break out by descending the south slopes, but the trek turns into tragedy. Only twenty men escape the Chinese fire to reach the main body at Hill 235.

At Hill 235, the Chinese mount a furious attack and temporarily gain the summit, but the casualty rate had been so high that a counterattack regains the ground. The Gloster Battalion receives word that reinforcements are en route, but in the meantime, the Chinese are massing for a full-scale attack. Complications develop as the reinforcements encounter problems.

In the 3rd Division zone, events of the previous night cause General Soule to modify his lines. The Chinese had on the previous night shadowed the 1st Battalion, 7th Regiment (3rd Division), as it withdrew from the vicinity of Hill 257 and afterwards, attacked elements of the Northumberland Fusiliers and the Royal Ulster Rifles at their positions near Route 11, about two miles south. On this day heavy fighting breaks out between the enemy and Company B, 1st Battalion, 7th Regiment, in the vicinity of Popsu-dong. The attack is too strong to thwart. Orders to retire arrive, but Corporal

Clair Goodblood, a machine gunner from Company H attached, volunteers to cover the withdrawal.

Meanwhile the assault continues and waves of enemy troops storm the area. Another man assists Goodblood with the Herculean task of keeping the enemy at bay, but a grenade is tossed into their position. Goodblood slams himself over the other man to protect him, but to no avail, the grenade wounds both. Goodblood resists evacuation, instead insisting on getting the other trooper out. The badly wounded Goodblood remains at his machine gun to ensure the withdrawal succeeds. Eventually the enemy overruns his position, but when the command returns and retakes the ground, Goodblood is not alone. About 100 enemy dead are still in the field to the front of his silent gun. Corporal Goodblood is awarded the Medal of Honor for his extraordinary heroism and his selfless sacrifice.

In another fierce contest, Company H, 3rd Battalion, comes under a heavy assault during darkness. The enemy is introduced to Corporal Hiroshi Miyamura, a New Mexican who leads a squad of the machine gun section. Miyamura first bolts from his position with a rifle and fixed bayonet to protect his squad. In the brief contest, about ten of the enemy fall to the steel, but afterwards, the machine gun takes over, until the position becomes untenable due to the exhaustion of his ammunition.

Still Miyamura pauses at the gun after he directs the remainder of his detachment to withdraw. The fighting corporal disables the gun and then, with his bayonet, fights his way back to another machine gun and continues to fire against the hordes of enemy troops. When last spotted by the survivors of his squad, he was heavily engaged against a large number of enemy troops. Corporal Hiroshi H. Miyamura, known as "Hershey," is awarded the Medal of Honor for his extraordinary heroism against insurmountable odds. At this time, there is no knowledge of the corporal's fate; however, he is not killed; rather captured. He survives brutal treatment and loses about fifty pounds in captivity.

In the meantime, the Gloster Battalion's withdrawal to Hill 235, linked with the pull-back of the 7th Regiment, creates a large gap of about four miles. General Soule orders British Brigadier Brodie to dispatch a battalion to block the hole. In addition, Brodie is directed to dispatch a contingent of tanks, supported by infantry, to advance and clear Route 5Y, to permit reinforcement of the Gloster Battalion.

Six Centurians attached to C Squadron, 8th Hussars, and four tanks of the 10th Philippine Combat Battalion shepherd three rifle companies; however, the Centurians are too large to pass some points on the road, leaving only the light tanks of the Filipinos to complete the trip.

The Glosters remain under the impression that the full complement is en route and Colonel Carne has determined that his force is not sufficiently strong to fight its way out of the trap.

In the 65th Regimental zone, the Chinese strike the area with mortars and small arms, while the Northumberland Fusilier and Royal Ulster Rifle Battalions fight off strong frontal assaults by the Chinese 188th Division. Some elements of the enemy division manage to penetrate to the rear of the two battalions.

Also, by about dusk, the situation along the entire 7th Infantry Regiment perimeter becomes calm. During the afternoon, the lull in the battle permitted the 1st Battalion, 7th Regiment, to relieve the 3rd Battalion, 65th Infantry Regiment, at the center of the regimental line. Once relieved, the 3rd Battalion moves to rejoin its main body to prepare to extricate the isolated Gloster Battalion. A few hours before midnight, the tranquility along the 7th's line is shattered.

The Chinese press the entire line and by about 0230, the 2nd Battalion becomes encircled. Nevertheless, through some complicated maneuvers, the isolated battalion is able to splinter into small contingents and break through the Chinese lines to reach friendly forces by about dawn (25th). The 1st and 3rd Battalions, still under the regimental commander Colonel Boswell, thwart the repeated assaults and hold the line. A group of Gloster troops, captured on the previous night, escape harm when U.S. planes strike the Chinese positions near Hill 675. They also literally escape and reach friendly lines during the morning. It is learned from the escapees that at least 1,000 Chinese are deployed at Hill 675.

The decision to continue the relief effort is suspended until the following day. Nevertheless, during the afternoon, it is learned that the Philippine 10th Combat Battalion Team had broken through with the Centurians trailing, so again the strategy is changed and the attack to rescue the Glosters is reinitiated. Soon after, the tank on the point loses a track from either a mine or mortar fire and it blocks the route. The Chinese pour fire upon the stalled tank and ground troops descend the heights to reach it. In the meantime, two of the heavier Centurians advance and move cautiously past the stalled Filipino column. The tanks move only a short distance farther due to the thinning of the path, but they do manage to rescue the jeopardized crew in the disabled tank.

The attack is cancelled and the relief force is ordered to withdraw. In the confusion of the order, the 10th Battalion Combat Team inadvertently is directed to retire, rather than hold a blocking position as earlier ordered. The Gloster Battalion remains stranded. The failure of the ROK 6th Division to hold its positions, combined with the deteriorating situation of the beleaguered British contingent, the I Corps is unable to execute a withdrawal on schedule as planned by Eighth Army. While efforts are undertaken to extricate the British, the Chinese maintain enormous pressure against I Corps.

In the ROK 1st Division zone, the Communists had suspended their attacks at about noon on the previous day, but later, at midnight (23rd-24th), again an attack is launched. The ROK 12th Regiment is compelled to surrender ground where it stood on the right flank along the Imjin. By dawn, elements of the Chinese 190th Division shoot across the Imjin at several places in the vicinity of Korangp'o-ri, where earlier contingents of the 189th Chinese Division had crossed. The enemy forces break into various columns and some penetrate between the 11th and 12th ROK Regiments, while others drive south between the 12th Regiment and the isolated Gloster battalion.

Following a day-long counter-attack, the ROKs, supported by Company A, 72nd Tank Battalion, regain the gap and establish entrenched positions there between the two ROK regiments. The penetration causes great concern at corps headquarters. General Milburn moves to bolster the line to protect Seoul. The only available reserve, the 15th Regiment, 3rd Division, speeds to establish a line slightly more than five miles behind the ROKs where Route 1B can be blocked. General Milburn dispatches the 2nd Battalion, 15th Regiment, to secure another secondary road, Route 2X. By about 1800, the 1st Battalion encounters an enemy roadblock near Uijongbu and immediately eradicates it. The enemy loses twenty defenders and the rest abandon the obstacle. Afterwards, the 15th Regiment, rather than risk unnecessary casualties, suspends its clearing operation until dawn on the following day.

Also, about dusk, the 25th Division in the eastern corps sector comes under a tenacious assault that continues relentlessly until about midnight (24th-25th). The Americans fight off elements of three divisions (Chinese 29th, 81st and 179th). During the attacks, the 24th and 27th Regiments give ground and withdraw southward about one mile, but the Chinese pursue. While the 25th Division attempts to halt the Chinese progress, the 24th Division holding the corps' right sector also is struck. The pressure becomes too high, which compels General Milburn at 0500 (25th) to order a pullback to the Delta Line.

In the IX Corps sector, 1st Marine Division zone, the 1st Marine Division withstands a night-long attack against its line and inflicts large numbers of casualties against elements of the Chinese 40th Army (359th and 360th Regiments, 120th Division) and the Chinese 39th Army (115th and 116th Divisions). After daybreak, the division withdraws from its Pendleton Line to the Kansas Line. During the final phase of the attack, the Chinese manage to get behind the Marines to strike against the 92nd Armored Field Artillery Battalion as it is beginning to move out. The troops redeploy to defend and soon after, they are bolstered by Marine tanks. The enemy pays another steep price and fails to interrupt the withdrawal. The attacking force of between 200 and 300 troops is decimated. The 92nd sustains four killed and eleven wounded.

The largest problem during the attacks seemed to have been maintaining an ammunition supply. Marines in some instances became runners to hand carry ammo to the front, after transporting wounded Marines to safety.

One VMO-6 helicopter, piloted by Lt. Robert E. Matthewson, is downed during the morning while attempting to evacuate wounded. Although the helicopter is destroyed, he survives. Another helicopter arrives to lift him to safety, but he declines the offer and instead picks up an M-1 rifle to join the infantry as they withdraw.

In related activity, some enemy forces attempt to shadow the Marines as they move toward the Kansas Line, but the fighting withdrawal of the rear-guard receives support from planes and artillery. Forty-nine Marine Corsairs and forty Navy and Air Force Ads shepherd the Marine pullback. Three Corsairs and one observation plane are downed by the Chinese during the operation. However, the pull-back is successful, so much so that by dawn on the 25th, the Marines' perimeter is free of major opposition. The 120th Division (40th Army) and the 39th Army's divisions fail to mount any future major attacks during the offensive. The move to the Kansas Line is necessitated primarily because the ROK 6th Division is still unable to move into position.

On this day, General Chang informs General Hoge that he is in the process of regrouping about four thousand to five thousand men in his command that converged on positions behind the Australians on Hill 504. At Hill 504, the Australians continue to hold against ferocious attacks. They have no artillery support, but still, they hold.

The commanding officers request reinforcements from British Brigadier Burke. The Australians lose a little ground, but from the new command post, some good fortune arrives. The New Zealanders have by this time regrouped and redeployed to provide artillery. The defenders on Hill 504 also are greeted by the sound of Marine Corsairs. The combined fire of the Australians, the artillery and the Corsairs shreds the attacking columns. Repeated assaults are repelled; however, during one of the air strikes, an Australian unit is inadvertently hit with napalm. The accident costs the lives of two men and it wounds several others. Despite the apparent success, the Australians on Hill 504 remain in peril due to a large hole between them and the Middlesex positions.

Prior to noon, Brigadier Burke orders the hill abandoned. The U.S. tanks (72nd Tank Battalion) on the island ridge transport Colonel Ferguson from his command post to Hill 504 to execute the withdrawal. The tanks bring out wounded and then they return across the field of fire to transport ammunition and supplies to the troops on the hill. Defying the odds, the tanks also pick up volunteers from Company B, 74th Engineer Battalion, and transport them to the abandoned positions of the mortar company that fled the previous night. The engineers, afterwards, are protected by the tanks as they gather some of the equipment that they had earlier abandoned.

In the meantime, the Australians move off Hill 504, while the tanks push to the north to block the ford and prevent the Chinese from moving through the Kap'yong Valley to overwhelm the Australians as they withdraw.

As the Australians descend from Hill 504, the Chinese begin to ascend, but unexpectedly, they are greeted by smoke signals. The New Zealanders pound the slopes with artillery shells that deliver the smoke screen. The New Zealanders also present the Chinese with a large dose of high explosive rounds as they descend one company at a time while covering the rear. Both the Australians and the New Zealanders move through the Middlesex lines slightly after dusk.

In related activity, after the Australians evade the Chinese, the Canadians on Hill 677 become the prey. The Chinese launch the attack against Hill 677 at about 2200 and the battle continues through the night.

In the X Corps sector, at about dawn, the ROK 5th Division is struck by the N.K. 12th Division. The defenders collapse and the Communists drive easily to Inje. At the lines of the U.S. 7th Division, the N.K. 45th Division plows against the 32nd Regiment, positioned left of the ROK 5th Division, but here the Communists do not fare well. And nearby, at the west flank of X Corps perimeter, the 23rd Regiment, 2nd Division, also holds firmly.

During the enemy assault, the North Koreans converge upon a draw near Tokko-ri, but while there, unexpectedly, an iron storm overwhelms them. A U.S. forward observer for artillery spots the enticing target and alerts the artillery. Shortly thereafter, the relentless bombardment commences and scores a massive series of direct hits on the troops numbering about 400. The artillery observer who detected the formations informs headquarters that only two North Koreans came out of the gully. The ill-fated advance of the N.K. 45th Division is unable to gain territory, but once the 32nd Infantry Regiment abandons its positions to deploy on a ridge and link with the ROK 5th Division that had been shoved below Inje, the North Koreans occupy the 32nd's positions.

In the ROK III Corps sector, the NK 6th Division drives against the III Corps positions and penetrates to a point several miles below Inje, but the ROKs are able at that time to halt the momentum.

In Air Force activity, a B-26 light bomber gets shot down by enemy fire in the vicinity of Ch'orwon. The 3rd Air Rescue Squadron dispatches an H-19 helicopter to rescue the pilot and the navigator. The rescue attempt is not an easy task. The helicopter first rescues the pilot and the navigator is then rescued, but under special circumstances. The navigator had broken his leg and is captured by two enemy troops. Nonetheless, he is able to seize one of his captors' guns and the enemy then flees. Both men are safely retrieved and brought back to friendly lines. During the retrieval, the rescuers work while fighter planes circle and keep the enemy pinned down.

April 25 General Van Fleet remains concerned about the security of Seoul, particularly since the I Corps had withdrawn from the Imjin River, which provided an opportunity for the Communists to slip across the Han River estuary without being detected. If accomplished, they enemy could effortlessly drive down the Kimpo peninsula to the rear of the capital and capture Inchon along with Kimpo airfield and the airport at Seoul. To thwart such enemy progress, Van Fleet requests support from the U.S. Navy. He gets it from Task Force 95. By the following day, planes from the western section of the task force maintain vigil over the area where it is thought a crossing might be attempted. The USS *Toledo* embarks from the Sea of Japan to the area near Inchon, from where it can provide its guns to the operation.

In the I Corps sector, prior to dawn General Milburn concludes that the I Corps must abandon the Kansas Line due to Chinese pressure. At 0500, the order for the corps to withdraw is issued. General Milburn remains concerned about the isolated Gloster Battalion. To maintain cohesion during the withdrawal, the 24th and 25th Divisions are to commence the move at 0800; however, the 3rd Division and the ROK 1st Division are to hold in place until the beleaguered Gloster unit is retrieved. As it turns out, the relief efforts fail and the cost is high, due in part to bad communications. The Gloster Battalion on Hill 235 apparently believes that help is en route and that the troops can hold. The general withdrawal causes one attempt by the 65th Regiment, 3rd Division, to be cancelled, but another contingent from the only available reserve, the 64th Tank Battalion and the 65th Infantry tank company, is available.

British Major Huth suggests that tanks alone would be unable to break through to the trapped command, and his opinion is based on his experience of the previous day's rescue attempt. Nevertheless, no strong infantry is included. The commander of the 65th Infantry tank company is informed also that he is not to commit his full company. The one tank platoon that departs is short one of its tanks. During the planning, the 3rd Division commander, General Soule, is unaware of just how bad the situation is for the Gloster Battalion.

All the while, the ROK 1st Division is attempting to advance to secure ground lost by the ROK 12th Regiment of the previous day. The ROKs are supported by elements of the 73rd Heavy Tank Battalion. General Kanh intends to have his force clear the area and break through to the Gloster Battalion. While the Gloster Battalion attempts to hold, the initial rescue team hits opposition short of its target and is halted. The fire fight costs the tanks most of their ammunition and they cancel the advance.

By about noon, the ROKs become stalled. In the meantime, at about 0900, the Glosters are directed by Brigadier Brodie to fight their way out of the trap. At about the same time Brigadier Brodie instructs the Northumberland Fusiliers and the Royal Ulster Rifles to retire southward along Route 11, through the lines of the Belgians. The retreat of the British is hotly pursued by the Chinese, costing the British dearly. Many wounded are left unprotected on the tanks as heavy Chinese fire rips the tanks as they race for safety.

Artillerymen of the 204th FABn, deployed north of Seoul, initiate a barrage with their "Long Toms."

Chinese fire disables some of the tanks and the occupants are apparently all killed. Later, Brodie is able to get the mangled forces back to the Delta line.

Meanwhile at about 0900, the Gloster Battalion under Colonel Carne attempts to break out, but not in the direction of the advancing 65th Infantry tank company; rather, Carne intends to head southwest from Hill 235. Colonel Carne directs the troops to withdraw, but he informs them he is staying with the wounded, about fifty troops. Suddenly others — including the chaplain, the battalion surgeon and some medics — also decide to stay. About 100 men with Captain M.G. Harvey take a separate route than the main body. Soon Harvey's group encounters two Chinese as they enter the valley, but both are eliminated. Later they are spotted by an observation plane, but the Chinese also detect the men

and more troops are hit. Eventually, they encounter American tanks, but initially the tankers mistake them for enemy and six more troops are wounded.

The Gloster survivors reach safety with the tanks and the ROKs at about 1400. Most of the remainder of the battalion that attempted to break out had been captured en route.

Meanwhile, in the 7th Regiment zone, heavy fighting continues from the previous day. Company A, 1st Battalion, near Popsu-dong continues fighting a delaying action, while the 3rd Battalion pulls back. Two squads have already repelled repetitive assaults, but more of the enemy continues to press against their diminutive positions on the right flank and threaten to isolate the contingents.

Corporal John Essebagger, Jr., with one of the

The 65th Infantry, 3rd Division, traverses a valley road during late April. The regiment reverts to reserve on 27 April.

squads, senses the danger as the noose closes. He volunteers to hold the line to provide cover fire for a withdrawal. The squad, under cover fire from Essebagger, safely evacuates. Essebagger manages to eliminate a high number of the enemy but is finally overrun. Corporal Essebagger is posthumously awarded the Medal of Honor for his tremendous heroism under fire and his selfless sacrifice to save others.

In the 3rd Battalion area, the enemy launches a ferocious attack against Company I. Two troops try to stem the tide, but the enemy fire kills one of the troops, leaving Corporal Charles L. Gilliland to stand alone with his automatic rifle. Rather than retreat, Gilliland holds his ground and pours fire into the attackers, but the odds are too great. He bolts from his foxhole in pursuit of two of the enemy who had penetrated his sector. He eliminates both with his pistol. In the process, Gilliland is wounded in the head. He refuses treatment and when orders arrive to pull back, he volunteers to hold the line to provide cover fire. The company safely retires. Corporal Gilliland is killed. He is awarded the Medal of Honor posthumously for his extraordinary courage and selfless sacrifice.

Also, the Chinese 354th Regiment, bloodied by the Australians at Hill 504 on the previous night, also moved against the Canadians holding Hill 677. The Chinese had been reinforced by elements of the 118th Regiment. Aware of the impending threat, the Canadians under Lt. Colonel J.R. Stone switched a contingent from positions on the northern slopes to a southern slope on Stone's intuition that the Chinese might move against the rear. The attack, beginning with machine gun fire and mortars, had struck at 2200 on the 24th, but the Canadians had not been caught off-guard. While Company B defended the southern slope, the remainder fought off frontal assaults. The Canadians received some additional support from a bright moon, which fortuitously illuminated the targets. A large contingent of Chinese is whacked decisively by artillery as they move across the Kap'yong River heading east.

While the New Zealanders hammer the enemy at the river, the Canadians mow down the Chinese that

emerge from a gully during the frontal attack. In the meantime, the rear approach comes under attack, but here, too, the troops of Company B repulse the initial charge. Afterward, some ground is lost to a second attack, but subsequent assaults throughout the night into dawn (25th) are repelled at the rear.

At about 0200 on this day, the Chinese mount a tenacious assault against the front of the perimeter. Company D, holding the left flank, is nearly overwhelmed by an enormous force, but the commander calls in artillery upon his own positions. The artillery succeeds in bolstering the positions and the Canadians push the Chinese from the crest. By dawn, with the added support of tanks attached to the U.S. 72nd Tank Battalion, the Chinese abort the attacks against the flanks. The hill remains under Canadian control. However, the Chinese hold ground along the Kap'yong Road, which prevents the British from getting supplies to the beleaguered force.

Meanwhile, Lt. Colonel Stone defies the odds and requests an air drop. About six hours later, planes from Japan fly over and deposit ammunition and supplies. The Canadians (Patricia's Canadian Light Infantry) compel the Chinese to abandon the attack during the latter part of the afternoon. The Chinese sustain high casualties for their failed attempt to seize the hill. The Canadians lose ten killed and twenty-three wounded.

Also, during the operation to withdraw, the 25th Division's route includes two bridges, one at Route 3 and another at Yongp'yong. The Chinese earlier gained Hill 664, several miles north of the Route 3 crossing, prompting General Bradley to deploy the 3rd Battalion, 27th Infantry, in front of the bridge to block any Chinese advance. The entire 27th Regiment receives responsibility to keep both bridges secure for the withdrawal.

By the evening, the 27th Regiment arrives at the Delta line. In the meantime, the 5th Infantry Regiment (on loan from IX Corps, 24th Division), is deployed along Route 3A a few miles to the rear of the Kansas Line. It is directed to cover the pull-back of the 19th and 21st Infantry Regiments and its support units, including the 555th FABn and Company D, 6th Medium Tank Battalion.

The 5th Infantry anticipates the arrival of the 8th Ranger Company, but before it can arrive, the Chinese encircle it. The Rangers attempt to hold at Hill 1010 just off the right flank of the 21st Regiment. The 5th Regiment moves out to rescue the rangers.

In the meantime, the 19th and 21st Regiments reach the Delta Line. The 21st Regiment is attacked by the Chinese after its arrival, but the enemy thrust from the east is repulsed. Subsequently, the ROK 6th Division in the IX Corps and the 21st Regiment make contact on the line. While the regiments establish their new positions, the rangers attempt to break through the Chinese lines. A contingent of tanks moving toward the embattled hill spots some rangers who broke out. Sixty-five exhausted rangers are picked up. They are the survivors of the 8th Ranger Company.

After the surviving rangers are brought to safety, the 5th Regiment and its support units initiate the move to the Delta Line. En route, Chinese holding high ground on opposite side of the escape road pound the column and hit the 555th FABn especially hard. The column stands less than one mile from the Delta Line when it comes under the heavy assault.

Colonel Wilson's forces return fire and succeed in eliminating the threat on the east side of Route 3A, but even more fire continues to pour down from the west side. Successive attacks fail to eliminate the enemy. The 1st Battalion is repulsed three times and the 2nd Battalion also is stymied. In addition, a contingent of tanks attempt to quell the fire, but it costs Company A, 6th Medium Tank Battalion, two of its tanks and the infantry atop them. No reinforcements arrive from the Delta Line, but a separate road is discovered and the column takes the circuitous route unhindered by the Chinese, and arrives at the lines of the 19th Regiment slightly after dusk.

In the IX Corps sector, the 1st Marine Division galvanizes its positions at the Kansas Line. On the previous day, subsequent to moving from the Pendleton Line, the Chinese entered Hwach'on and covered the area, including where the dam is located, but the Marines retired unhindered by pursuers. On this day, the Marines' zone remains relatively tranquil.

The casualties incurred by the 1st Marine Division on 24–25 April amount to 18 killed and 82 wounded, which brings the total casualties since 1 April to just under 300. The IX Corps instructs the 1st Marine Division to be prepared to move back to Chunchon on the 26th to deploy on the south bank of the Soyang River to guard the service units as they withdraw their respective supply depots. The Chinese assaults in the IX Corps zone had failed, but they change strategy and try to penetrate the I Corps to seize Seoul.

In the X Corps sector, the U.S. 2nd Division modifies its positions to adjust to the absence of the 1st Marine Division. The 23rd Regiment pulls back to positions near the eastern fringes of the Hwach'on Reservoir. The redeployment places the regiment about online with the Marines who are deployed along the Kansas Line at the western end of the reservoir in the vicinity of Yuch'on-ni.

The X Corps commander, General Almond, initiates several directives to blunt the enemy offensive. The ROK 5th Division is ordered to mount a counterattack to regain Inje, which the division had surrendered on the previous day. The town is seized, but the Communists afterward force the South Koreans to retire. The ROK III Corps, expected to join in the attack, never advances. Almond also directs the 2nd Division to initiate contact with the 1st Marine Division on a daily basis to ensure a coordinated effort against any potential threat.

General Ruffner establishes TF Zebra, composed of elements of the 72nd Tank Battalion and the 2nd Reconnaissance Company, bolstered further by a French Battalion and a Netherlands battalion. The 1st Ranger Company joins TF Zebra, which is commanded by Colonel Elbridge L. Brubaker. In related activity, after General Almond is informed of the failure to retain Inje, he orders yet another assault to commence on the following day.

April 26 Although the enemy continues to attack toward Seoul, the ferocity of the assaults is lessening largely because the Communists have sustained devastating numbers of casualties, estimated to be nearly 50,000 along the I Corps lines. The Communists sever

A U.S. M46 Patton tank tows a disabled tank through Uijongbu.

U.S. troops near Uijongbu. A battalion commander on a field phone reports his positions.

the highway that links Seoul with Chonchon (Central Korea) and Kansong (East Coast).

General Van Fleet, Eighth Army commander, establishes another defensive line that runs from coast to coast. The line begins just above Seoul and uses the existing Golden Line and stretches across Korea to the vicinity of Yangyang on the east coast. Van Fleet's new line receives no name and is soon dubbed the "No Name Line." The section covering the Pukham and Han corridors falls into the area where the 24th Division is deployed. Consequently, responsibility for that region falls to the IX Corps. The 24th Division, on loan to the I Corps, is posted in position to guard the corridors; therefore on the following day, the 24th Division reverts back to IX Corps.

The carrier USS *Toledo* (CA 133) arrives off Inchon to provide air support in the event the Communists at-tempt to penetrate Seoul. Also, the 1st Marine Division commander, Major General O.P. Smith, is relieved by Major General Gerald C. Thomas.

In the I Corps sector, the enemy continues to press against the recent line of defense, the Delta Line. The line is meant to stand only temporarily as the corps withdraws towards the Golden Line. Prior to noon, General Milburn issues orders to withdraw to positions in the vicinity of Uijongbu.

Nightlong enemy attacks make inroads against the ROK 1st Division. After dusk, the Communists strike against the entire corps front, except for the lines of the 24th Division, which holds the right section. However, there is action in the sector. A unit of Company C, 21st Regiment, becomes isolated during the day when the platoon is ordered to pull back.

Sergeant Ray E. Duke, once aware of the predicament,

An F80 Shooting Star (top left) leaves the area after striking enemy positions on hill near Ch'orwon.

leads a charge to extricate the isolated troops. The attack succeeds but afterward another one is launched. Duke, wounded by this time, continues to rally his men and soon after, he is wounded yet again. The platoon is ordered to withdraw, but Duke's wounds in both legs forbid any walking. Two others carry him out, but Duke becomes concerned for their safety and orders them to leave him. Sergeant Duke holds his positions and continues firing at the attacking troops until he is killed. Sergeant Duke is awarded the Medal of Honor posthumously for his extraordinary actions under fire.

The assaults against the 25th Division focus upon the 27th Infantry Regiment. Some ground is gained by the attacks, but with the support of radar-controlled bombs and flares bursting overhead as the Chinese push forward, they are halted with devastating results. Other heavy attacks strike the 65th Regiment (3rd Division) and the ROK 1st Division west of Uijongbu. The Chinese meet a wall of artillery fire and air strikes also descend upon them as they are repelled by the 65th and the ROKs along the left sector of the 3rd Division's lines.

In the meantime, the 15th Regiment to the right of the ROKs is compelled to surrender some ground. Nearby in the area defended by the 11th Regiment and a tank destroyer battalion, a North Korean force smashes through and inflicts high casualties on the troops of the tank destroyer battalion. The enemy thrust is capped by counterattacks of the South Koreans, bolstered by U.S. tanks.

In the IX Corps sector, a planned attack by the ROK 5th Division (X Corps) to regain Inje is aborted due to yet another debacle caused by the ROK 6th Division on the left part of the IX Corps sector on the previous day. The IX Corps, due to the I Corps' changes, modifies its lines to conform with the adjusted positions of the I Corps. In conjunction, the 1st Marine Division pulls away from the Kansas Line and redeploys along the Pukham River in the vicinity of the northern fringes of Chunchon and then the line curves along the lower bank of the Soyang River.

The Marine zone remains quiet during the night of the 25th-26th except for several small probing assaults and some mortar fire. Other adjustments in IX Corps include the redeployment of the ROK 6th Division, which is directed to pull back and form the line that links with the right flank of the I Corps. In addition, the British 28th Brigade redeploys in the evacuated positions previously held by the Australians and Canadians in the high ground above Kap'yong.

In the X Corps sector, adjustments are ordered by General Almond to maintain alignment with the IX Corps. The new positions link with the Marines at the Soyang River and extend toward the vicinity of Yanggu, from where it stretches southeast to the ROK 5th Division positions.

In Air Force activity, Far East Air Forces initiates an attack by B-29s during the night (26th-27th) against enemy forces that are converging to launch an attack against IX Corps. The Superfortresses pound the enemy positions and succeed in causing the Communists to abort the attack.

April 27   *In the I Corps sector,* at 0600, the 24th Division reverts to the IX Corps. In conjunction with the jurisdiction transfer, the boundary between the two corps is similarly adjusted.

In other activity, General Milburn issues orders to with draw to the next line, just above the Golden Line in front of Seoul.

In the 25th Division zone, the Chinese strike against

On 27 April, the 24th Division reverts to IX Corps. In this picture the 24th is pulling back to new defensive lines.

An infantryman of the 24th Regiment, 25th Division, is deployed in the hills along the Wyoming Line.

the 27th Infantry Regiment as it prepares to move from the first phase line. The 35th Regiment also comes under attack while it tries to establish positions to cover the besieged 27th Regiment. The fighting continues throughout the morning and into the afternoon. Later the regiment makes it to the second phase line.

In the meantime, the Chinese strike also at the 3rd Division and hit the 7th Cavalry, which had on the previous day reinforced the 3rd Division. The flank of the 3rd Division might have been very vulnerable had it not been covered by the cavalry. The cavalry, by the afternoon, eliminates the attacks, which originated from the northeast. The cavalry had come under assault as part of the thrust against the ROK 1st Division's 15th Regiment.

Following the confrontations, the 7th and 15th Regiments form along the second phase line, while the 65th Regiment is placed in reserve. The 7th Cavalry, which remains to bolster the 3rd Division, deploys on the left alongside the 7th Regiment in the center of the line.

The ROK 1st Division area calms during the afternoon and the division reaches the second phase line. The divisional perimeter remains tranquil throughout the night.

In the IX Corps sector, the front remains relatively tranquil during the night, again exhibiting the enemy's inability to launch strong attacks there. A withdrawal to the No Name Line continues.

April 28

Eighth Army receives word from General Van Fleet that he intendts to hold firmly at the No Name Line and in so doing retain Seoul. Van Fleet's directives unambiguously dictate no retreat from the line, unless it is his order. Van Fleet further stipulates that if a withdrawal becomes necessary due to pressure against Eighth Amy, the forces are to move back to the Waco Line, which will still keep the Eighth Army positions above the Nevada Line.

In the I Corps sector, General Milburn again issues orders to withdraw. This move places the corps at Line Golden. The withdrawal causes the other forces to move back to No Name Line. Concentrated efforts over the past several days had continued to focus on discipline and determination to preserve the capital, Seoul. During the morning the various corps units initiate the withdrawal. No heavy assaults are launched by the enemy, but some North Korean contingents are spotted above the Han River in the vicinity of the village of Haengju. Artillery units and the big guns of the USS *Toledo* pound their positions to prevent a crossing of the Han. The bombardment succeeds and the troops that survive the fire storm retire. Earlier in the day, the 7th Cavalry, temporarily attached as support for the 3rd Division, engages a Chinese contingent, and the cavalry is unscathed. Later the 7th Cavalry reverts back to the 1st Cavalry Division.

In related activity, the ROKs are able to withdraw without incident to reach the Golden Line earlier than expected. While the enemy intrusions have subsided, Eighth Army prepares to launch a counterattack. The 3rd Division (minus the 65th Regiment in reserve) receives the order to launch the attack. Also, the remainder of I Corps establishes defensive positions to protect the capital.

The ROK 1st Division comes under attack toward the latter part of the day. Once again, the guns of the USS *Toledo* stationed off Inchon lend their support and combined with the artillery and supporting tanks, the South Koreans force the Communists to abort the assault. At about dawn on the 29th, armored patrols are dispatched.

April 29

It is sometimes reported that on this day, a massive force of about 6,000 enemy soldiers attempt to cross the Han River to use the Kimpo peninsula to get behind Eighth Army and seize Seoul, but no official government records document the attempt. However, on the previous day, a large enemy assault at the Han was aborted due to heavy naval and artillery fire.

In the I Corps sector, Fifth Air Force planes attack enemy forces west of Seoul and inflict heavy casualties.

In the 25th Division sector, some enemy troops form for an attack, but it is not launched. After dusk, artillery fire and air attacks break up the force. Meanwhile, the 3rd Division holds steadfastly in its zone slightly outside Seoul.

Also, the ROK 1st Division dispatches patrols in search and pursuit of the N.K. 8th Division, which had unsuccessfully attacked the previous night. In less than three miles, the patrol finds more than nine hundred enemy dead in the field.

In the IX Corps sector, withdrawal to the No Name Line continues.

In Naval activity, the U.S. Navy initiates a diversion mission to relieve pressure against Eighth Army. The warships USS *Helena* (CA 75), USS *Manchester* (CL 83), USS *Bausell* (DD 845), USS *Rogers* (DDR 876), USS *Agerholm* (DD 826) and the USS *Anderson* (DD 786) plaster various targets on the east coast of Korea in the vicinity of Kojo-Tongchon. The USS *Okonogan* (APA 22), USS *Telfair* (APA 210), and USS *Winston* (AKA 94) execute an amphibious landing. The operation continues into the following day.

April 30

The Chinese offensive is halted north of Seoul and north of the Han River. General Van Fleet orders Eighth Army to fortify the line designated No Name, to bring it up to the level of the Golden Line, which provides Seoul with a staunch umbrella of protection. General Van Fleet makes it clear to the various commanders that despite the casualties inflicted upon the enemy, he expects yet more attacks. The fortifications are to bolster as much as possible the entire line, with expectations that the attack would come from the east or against the front at Seoul. Van Fleet is also concerned with the dam at the Hwach'on Reservoir, which still stands. Rather than risk the Chinese flooding the area, he requests and receives air support to partially knock out the flood gates. Naval Task Force 77 sends a contingent of AD Skyraiders on this day. The dive bombers knock out one gate and on the following day, they return to finish the task.

During the Chinese spring offensive (22 April to 30 April), the number of U.S. Army casualties up to 29 April amounts to 314 killed and 1,600 wounded. Estimates of enemy casualties for the period 22 April through 30 April vary. Eighth Army reports 13,349 known killed and 23,820 estimated killed. The reports also account for 246 POWs. The United Nations Command reports estimate enemy casualties for the same period as 75,000 to 80,000 killed and wounded. Of those, 50,000 casualties occurred in the Seoul region. There is no exact official count, but it is known that the enemy casualties were extremely high.

In the I Corps sector, the units will deploy to protect the approaches from Uijongbu. The units include the 25th Division, 1st Cavalry Division and the ROK 1st Division along the line. The 3rd Division and the 29th British Brigade stand in reserve. Also, in the I Corps sector, the line is defended by the ROK Capital Division and the ROK 11th Division.

In the IX Corps sector, the British 28th Brigade, 24th Division, ROK 6th Division and 7th Division (X Corps) stand along the No Name Line. The reserve is composed of the 187th Airborne RCT and it is deployed along the south bank of the Han River to the rear of the 24th Division to thwart an attack if one is launched through the Pukham Valley. The 7th Division had been directed to move from Eighth Army's east flank in X Corps to stiffen the center of I Corps by deploying at positions from which it can bolster the ROK 2nd and 6th Divisions.

Also, by this date, the 1st Marines become reserve, while the 5th Marines, 1st Korean Marine Regiment, and 7th Marines deploy along the No Name Line.

In other activity, the 1st Marine Division is for the third time in eight months transferred to the operational control of X Corps. The Division is to deploy in the western corps sector subsequent to its boundary with IX Corps being shifted slightly more than ten miles to the west.

In the X Corps sector, 1st Marine Division comes under the operational control of X Corps, having passed from IX Corps. The 1st Marine Division and the 2nd Division (minus the reserve 65th Infantry Regiment) hold the corps' left to defend the Chunchon–Hongch'on region. The corps' right is held by the ROK 5th and 7th Divisions.

In the ROK III Corps sector, the zone is held by the ROK 9th and 3rd Divisions.

In Air Force activity, Fifth Air Force continues to press the enemy by pounding their positions. On this day, 960 sorties are executed. During the day's action, two downed pilots are retrieved behind enemy lines in separate missions by two H-5 helicopters, one of which is hit by enemy fire. Nonetheless, both pilots and both helicopters return to friendly lines safely.

In other activity, enemy fire brings down three out of four F-51s that attack enemy targets at Sinmak. The high loss indicates to Far East Air Forces that the enemy has initiated the use of radar controlled anti-aircraft guns.

May 1951 *In Air Force activity,* Fifth Air Force establishes a radar station on Chodo, located in the Yellow Sea. From there, the radar direction center remains effective as far away as the Yalu River on the border with Manchuria. With the addition of the facility, the Sabre jets receive support that aids their efforts. During the month of May, the center is responsible for the downing of 6 of the 27 MiGs that are shot down by pilots of Sabre jets. The Sabres also shoot down an additional 6 planes. However, during May, the Communists, also supported with more modern radar, down five F-86s, three F-84s and one F-51 Mustang. Also, the 4th Fighter Interceptor Wing begins an experiment by carrying 1,000-pound bombs for use in air-to-ground operations, but the aircraft is unsuitable for the task. Subsequently, with the arrival of the F-86F, the plan becomes feasible.

May 1 Although the Communists sustained high casualties during the offensive, intelligence estimates place more than 500,000 Chinese troops in Korea, bolstered by just under 200,000 North Koreans. Intelli-

gence also estimates that about 300,000 troops are within striking distance of Eighth Army. The enemy, however, continues to have supply problems. All corps initiate patrols that stretch out as far as five miles from the line in search of enemy forces. The patrols continue into the following day, but only near the I Corps sector are any Communist elements detected in strength. An ROK 1st Division patrol discovers elements of the N.K. 8th Division along Route 1.

In the meantime, all units continue to strengthen the line in their respective sectors. The land in front of the lines is augmented by barbed wire, mines and drums that contain a mixture of napalm and gasoline. Patrols in the X Corps sector stretch westward and General Van Fleet also orders forward patrol bases to be established about five miles out along a line leading east to Route 24. In line with General Van Fleet's corps adjustments for the next enemy attack, Eighth Army as of this date, is deployed from left to right: I Corps — ROK 1st Division, 1st Cavalry Division and the 25th Infantry Division; with the 3rd Infantry Division and the British 29th Brigade in reserve; IX Corps — the British 27th Brigade, 24th Infantry Division, 5th and 6th ROK Divisions and the 7th Infantry Divisions, with the 187th Airborne RCT in reserve; X Corps—the 1st Marine Division, 2nd Infantry Division, and 5th and 7th ROK Divisions; ROK III Corps–ROK 9th and 3rd Divisions; ROK I Corps — Capital Division and ROK 11th Division.

In Naval activity, the USS *Helena* (CA-75) comes under extremely heavy fire from enemy shore batteries deployed in the vicinity of Wonsan.

May 2 Eighth Army continues to strengthen the No Name Line and the corps continues to form a regimental combat team to respond quickly to any Communist intrusion.

In the I Corps sector, patrols continue to scout the front in search of the enemy. In addition, preparations are underway to advance the front east of Route 24 to the Missouri Line.

May 3 By about this time, Eighth Army is focusing on patrol bases to maintain contact with the enemy. Also, by this time, the artillery units' acute ammunition shortages have ended. The artillery units are under orders to execute fire each day, but the 11th Marines react with a protest, proclaiming that the troops are seldom in contact with the enemy. The artillery shells are, as some would contend, wasted, until later in the month when the Chinese again attack. The shortage of ammunition again occurs.

In the X Corps sector, the Marines continue to bolster their positions along the No Name Line; however, there is a lull in the combat as the enemy apparently prepares to launch the next phase of its spring offensive. The attack is anticipated along the eastern sector of the Eighth Army perimeter.

In Naval activity, carrier planes attached to the USS *Princeton* (CV 37) attack and damage the Hwach'on Dam.

A squadron of F-9F Panther jets prepares to land on the USS *Princeton* (left center). The USS *Philippine Sea* is nearby (upper right).

May 4 *In the I Corps sector,* a contingent of the 12th Regiment, ROK 1st Division, moves up Route 1 to establish a patrol base. In the 25th Division zone, the establishment of a patrol base is complicated by a shortage of reserve troops. To solve the problem, the 7th Infantry (3rd Division) is pulled from reserve.

In the IX Corps sector, 1st Cavalry Division zone, the 7th Cavalry is designated as the unit to establish an advance patrol base in the vicinity of Uijongbu.

— *In the United States:* A bill that authorizes the Marine Corps to double its size to 400,000 is passed unanimously by the U.S. Senate. In addition, the commandant of the Marine Corps is to become a consultant to the Joint Chiefs of Staff.

Top: An AD Skyraider on the deck of the USS *Princeton* prepares to take off on a mission. *Bottom*: U.S. Navy carrier planes (AD Skyraiders) strike the Hwach'on Dam.

May 5 The Canadian 25th Infantry Brigade arrives in Korea.

In Air Force activity, enemy fire shoots down an F-51 in the skies north of Seoul. A crew attached to the 3rd Air Rescue Squadron is alerted and dispatched to attempt to rescue the pilot. They take off in an H-5 helicopter, locate the pilot, and successfully retrieve him. Enemy ground troops open fire, but no harm comes to the crew or the pilot.

May 6 The Imperial Ethiopian Expeditionary force (known also as the Kagnew Battalion) arrives in Korea.

The Ethiopian force is not a heavily trained combat outfit and it has arrived with no equipment or weapons.

In Naval activity, Rear Admiral G.R. Henderson relieves Rear Admiral R.A. Ofstie as commander, Carrier Division 5 and Task Force 77.

In other activity, the vessels USS *Helena* (CL 75), *Orleck* (DD 886), *Fiske* (DD 842), *Buck* (DD 761) and HMS *Cockade* (DD), initiate a bombardment of enemy targets in the vicinity of Kansong and Kosong to soften enemy resistance for the ROK troops in the area. The operation continues into the following day as the ROKs advance to the Missouri Line. A patrol of the 1st Korean Marine Regiment reports that the naval fire had inflicted devastating damage to enemy targets and spared the ROK troops from possible annihilation.

May 7   The six ROK divisions in the eastern sector of the line initiate a move to the Missouri Line.

In the I Corps sector, the advance encounters only minimal sporadic opposition.

In Air Force activity, the 39th Fighter Bomber Squadron, 35th Fighter-Bomber Group, is transferred into the 18th Fighter Bomber Group, commanded by a new CO, Colonel William P. McBride. This is a component of the plan to combine all F-51 Mustang squadrons into one contingent. It occurs while the 35th Group is converting their aircraft.

In Naval activity, the USS *Hoquiam* (PF 5), operating off Songjin, comes under fire by enemy shore guns. One seaman is injured.

May 8   The advance to the Missouri Line by the ROKs continues.

In the I Corps sector, the ROK 1st Division advances up Route 1, and on this day, some N.K. resistance is encountered. Skirmishing continues during the advance, but by the following day, the South Koreans compel the enemy to retire.

In the X Corps sector, the ROK 5th and 7th Divisions advance on the Corps' right.

In the ROK III Corps sector, the 3rd and 9th Divisions move forward.

In the ROK I Corps sector, the 11th and Capital Divisions advance.

In Air Force activity, two U.S. ground troops caught in enemy territory north of Seoul are located and extricated by an H-5 helicopter attached to the 3rd Air Rescue Squadron.

May 9   General Ridgway and Ambassador Muccio meet with South Korean President Syngman Rhee. Ridgway informs Rhee that leadership within the ROK forces is poor and must be improved.

Also, the Fifth Air Force strikes enemy positions in the vicinity of Sinuiju, near the Yalu River. The 1st Marine Air Wing participates in the attack, which is executed by several hundred planes, including Marine Corps Corsair fighters and Panther jets. The massive strike against the enemy airfield and vicinity is executed by 312 planes and the attack results in the destruction of 15 enemy jets and 100 buildings.

In the I Corps sector, enemy resistance against the ROK 1st Division is terminated. The division establishes a patrol base along Route 1 and then returns to the No Name Line.

In the ROK I Corps sector, a contingent of the ROK 11th Division, a tank destroyer battalion, moves well beyond the Missouri Line and enters Kansong, slightly more than fifteen miles above the line. Kansong is strategically located where Route 24 terminates at the coastal highway.

In the X Corps sector, the ROK 5th Division arrives at the Missouri Line.

In Air Force activity, the airfield at Sinuiju is pounded heavily by a combination of Air Force F-51s, F-80s and Marine Corps F4-Us. The strike force is protected by U.S. Navy F9Fs and Air Force F-84s and F-86s. During the attack, a contingent of about 50 MiGs arrive from Antung on the opposite side of the Yalu River in Manchuria, but their attack is mild at best and in one instance, a group of eight MiGs passes within one hundred yards of a formation of Sabre jets, but it makes no move to attack; rather it keeps moving. The attack damages the airfield sufficiently to knock it out of action.

May 10   Preparations continue for a move by Eighth Army to the Kansas Line; however, intelligence reports continue to point to an imminent Chinese offensive. By this time Communist resistance is becoming more tenacious. In addition, it has been determined that the enemy now has about 1,000 planes available and that about fifty new enemy airfields are nearly completed. Large concentrations of enemy troops are detected in the area north of the I Corps.

In Naval activity, a contingent of U.S. Air Force personnel, transported by a contingent of Amphibious Task Force (TF 90), arrives at Inchon from Okinawa.

May 11   General Van Fleet cancels a plan to advance to the Kansas Line, scheduled to begin on 12 May with an attack toward the Topeka Line. The attack had been scheduled on 9 May, but the situation has changed. Intelligence informs Van Fleet that the enemy offensive is about to be reinitiated imminently. Initially Eighth Army knows about eight separate Chinese armies. Four (12th, 20th, 60th and 64th) are not in the immediate area. Of the four (15th, 27th, 63rd and 65th) that are in nearby sectors, intelligence can find only one division out front.

Later Van Fleet is informed that five of the armies are staging in the region west of the Pukham River from where they are positioned to launch an attack against the west central sector. Although the primary attack is cancelled, the ROK III and I Corps remain under orders to continue their attack toward the Missouri Line. Later the orders will be modified, instructing the ROKs to stay ahead of the No Name Line, but to postpone the advance to the Missouri Line.

In the I Corps sector, the 3rd Division is still scheduled to move into corps reserve, but this day, combat teams form to prepare to support any corps sector. The

7th RCT assembles in Seoul, from where it is positioned to speed to support the I Corps. The 65th RCT deploys about twenty miles southeast of Seoul near Kyongan-ni, from where it can bolster the IX Corps. The 15th RCT forms in the vicinity of Ichon, near the junction of Route 13 and 20, about thirty-five miles southeast of Seoul, from where it can augment the X Corps.

In the IX Corps sector, a contingent of the ROK 9th Division moves into Inje during the afternoon without incident.

In Naval activity, the USS *Orleck* (DD 886), guided by a shore fire control party (ten Marines in group acting as eyes of naval ship) pound enemy positions along the east coast of Korea and inflict about 300 casualties. Also, pursuant to requests by the U.S. Air Force at the end of April, planes attached to Fast Carrier Task Force (TF-77) are launched against four specific enemy targets — rail bridges. Three of the bridges are demolished.

May 12 While Eighth Army continues to reinforce its defenses, the ROK III and I Corps press forward toward Inje and Yongdae-ri with a full scale attack. The ROK 3rd, 9th, 11th and Capital Divisions all participate. A reconnaissance contingent of the ROK 9th Division that had entered Inje on the previous day encounters an enemy force slightly beyond the town and drives it off before returning to the main body; however, the main attack is unable to reach its objectives due to a combination of the distance involved (Yongdae–ri is nearly fifteen miles northeast of Inje) and the amount of resistance encountered. Meanwhile, Eighth Army still has no complete picture of where the enemy is deployed.

— *In the United States:* General O.P. Smith, recently transferred commander, 1st Marine Division, assumes command of Fleet Marine Force Pacific Troops and Marine Barracks, Camp Pendleton.

May 13 By this date, more intelligence is collected and it becomes evident that large enemy forces are shifting from positions in the west and west central regions to the east, but there is no precise information on when and from where the attack will be launched. Intelligence determines that the Chinese have advanced five armies into the region to the front of Chunchon–Inje area, a huge threat against the X Corps and the ROK III Corps. In the meantime, the elements begin to work against Eighth Army, which will impede air observation missions.

In Air Force activity, a contingent of the 4th Fighter Interceptor Wing, while on a mission (experimental) as a ground attack force, encounters enemy fire. The planes are carrying 1,000-pound bombs. One of the pilots, Bud Mahurin, a World War II ace, is shot down and captured.

May 14 The No Name Line is heavily fortified in preparation for a Communist offensive. The line is bolstered by interlocking machine gun positions, an unending series of miles, and strategically placed drums of

napalm and gasoline, each set to detonate by electrical devices. The line is also augmented by barbed wire.

Also, the Canadian 15th Infantry Brigade, in reserve, is ordered to move from Pusan to Kumnyangyang-ni, slightly less than twenty-five miles southeast of Seoul. The Canadians are to deploy and defend against an enemy attack, if it emerges from the Pukham or Seoul–Suwon corridors.

In the IX Corps sector, the 187th Airborne RCT prepares to launch an attack toward Kap'yong on the following day. On this day, weather prevents observation planes from initiating any missions and as the day progresses, the heavy rains also hinder ground reconnaissance patrols.

In other activity, General Van Fleet visits the 24th Division perimeter and after observing the defenses, concludes that the division has not properly bolstered the lines.

May 15 The Chinese reinitiate the offensive with a force estimated at 21 divisions, supported by 9 North Korean divisions on the flank. The main attack strikes X Corps and the ROK III Corps.

In the IX Corps sector, the 187th Airborne RCT aborts its planned attack against an enemy force, thought to be in an assembly area near Kap'yong, due to inclement weather, which has caused the roads to become too poor for travel.

In the X Corps sector, the ROK 5th and 7th Divisions are struck hard by the Chinese. By the following day, the ROKs are driven from the high ground to the right of Chonchon.

In Air Force activity, Far East Air Forces launches daylight strikes against enemy positions to impede their progress.

May 16–20 1951 The Communists maintain pressure against the UN forces in Korea. In an effort to sustain the ground troops, Far East Air Forces maintains an aggressive campaign to keep the troops supplied with rations, equipment and ammunition. During this five-day period, the aircraft attached to the 315th AD deliver an average of 1,000 tons of supplies each day.

May 16–23 1951 The Chinese launch the second and final phase of the Spring Offensive. The attacks are halted by the 23rd. By 30 May, Eighth Army is again positioned at the Kansas Line.

May 16 Eighth Army continues to bolster its defenses. The most solid information on the enemy intentions had come from captives picked up during the past week. According to one captive caught above Seoul, the 2nd Division, X Corps, and the ROKs along the eastern part of the line are the primary objectives. The information proves true during the latter part of this day, when the Chinese offensive (fifth phase, second and final effort) is re-ignited.

The Chinese 60th, 15th and 12th Armies strike from positions above the Soyang River from the vicinity of Chunchon to Naep'yong-ni (Battle of Soyang-gang). This is the start of the Second Chinese Communist

Spring Offensive. The 27th Army launches its attack against the ROK 5th and 7th Divisions. In addition, the N.K. V Corps and II Corps strike the eastern sector of the line. The strength of the attacking force is estimated at 21 Chinese divisions, supported by 3 North Korean divisions.

In the IX Corps sector, a contingent of the 7th Marines holding along Route 29 is attacked during the night in a contest that lasts about four hours. Captives seized by the Marines provide evidence that the Chinese III Army Group is in the area and in position to threaten the X Corps.

In the X Corps sector, the ROK 5th and 7th Divisions are hit with heavy attacks with the main thrust penetrating between the two divisions. The Chinese 87th Division, 27th Army, drives toward Sangam-ni as the ROKs again collapse quickly. By midnight (16th–17th), both divisions are authorized by General Almond to withdraw to the No Name Line. The infantry units scatter haphazardly, but the artillery units of both divisions make it safely down Route 24 to reach the lines of the U.S. 2nd Division. By noon on the following day, the ROK 7th Division is still disorganized. The only available ROK 7th Division forces on the field are two battalions of the reserve 3rd Regiment.

In the meantime, the ROK 5th Division is able to get forces to the right flank of the 2nd Division. The 2nd Division becomes jeopardized due to the collapse of the ROK 7th Division. The division is defending a fifteen mile front with the 9th and 38th Regiments holding the left and bolstered further by Task Force Zebra, which holds the right side of the perimeter. The French Battalion stands about five miles behind the lines of TF Zebra, and remains the only reserve in the division zone.

In the 38th Regiment's zone, the attached Netherlands Battalion is posted on Hill 710 and Hill 975 to augment the 1st Battalion, 38th Regiment. Daylight attacks against the 2nd Division's lines indicate that stronger attacks are imminent. Meanwhile, the French and Dutch Battalions, along with the U.S. 23rd and 38th Regiments, drive southward to secure the MSR. At about dusk, the Communists pound against the lines of TF Zebra and the 38th Regiment in an attempt to penetrate between the two units. The attacks continue until about dawn on the following day. In conjunction, during 16th–17th, the 38th FABn fires more than 10,000 rounds.

In the 1st Marine Division zone, the perimeter is not tested by the Chinese. However, during the early morning hours of the following day, the Chinese make contact.

May 17–22 1951   Far East Air Forces continues to support the ground troops as they attempt to quell the enemy offensive. B-29s attached to Bomber Command execute ninety-four sorties against the enemy ground troops and of these, most are after dusk and designed to deter enemy night attacks. Superfortresses undertake other missions during this time.

May 17   The U.S. Air Force intensifies its support to bolster X Corps. Orders from General Stratemeyer stipulate that a minimum of twelve medium bombers be committed for night runs to pulverize suspected enemy positions in front of the Eight Army lines, within the X Corps sector. Enemy targets selected by X Corps become the recipients of the bomb loads, composed of about three hundred and fifty 500-pound bombs.

In the face of the enemy's re-initiation of the offensive, the ROK Army Headquarters, ROK III Corps and I Corps pull back to the No Name Line. During the early morning hours, the 30th FABn, ROK 9th Division, gets snagged by an enemy roadblock as it moves back. The 11th Regiment, ROK 3rd Division, trailing the 30th FABn, also gets tangled in the roadblock. By the latter part of the day, the artillery that survives and the 11th Regiment moves back toward Hyon-ni to the north to establish positions there.

Also, the scattered ROK 5th Division is later able to regroup and make it to the right flank of the 2nd Division. The No Name Line, by about 0100, is stabilized and secure, but in the X Corps sector, the attacks continue relentlessly.

In the IX Corps sector, the boundary is shifted about four miles to the east to modify positions prior to an expected heavy attack against the X Corps. The 1st Marine Division is directed to relieve the 9th and 38th Regiments, 2nd Division (X Corps), which permits the two X Corps regiments to extend farther eastward. In addition, the ROK III Corps and I Corps are ordered to withdraw to the Waco Line, more than fifteen miles below the No Name Line. General Almond is directed by General Van Fleet to realign his forces to the southeast, where a link is to be made with the ROK III Corps at the Waco Line.

In the X Corps sector, two battalions of the 3rd Regiment, 7th ROK Division, stand their ground and engage elements of the Chinese 81st Division in the vicinity of Sangam-ni. In the 2nd Division sector, by about dawn, concentrated attacks against the 38th Regiment and TF Zebra terminate, but the fighting does not end at other spots that remain contested in the sector. At about the stroke of midnight (16th–17th), elements of the Chinese 45th Division, 15th Army, drive against the positions of the 2nd Battalion, 38th Regiment at Hill 755, defended by Company E. In less than three hours, Company F comes under siege at Hill 755. It withdraws to positions to the rear of the 3rd Battalion.

In the meantime, in the 1st Battalion zone, Hill 1051, held by Company A, and Company C, on Hill 914, remain under attack since the previous night. Assaults that had begun at about dusk on the previous day continue to fail, but the pressure to hold becomes too great. As the Chinese ascend the slopes, their numbers quickly lessen due to the defenders and an avalanche of artillery fire, combined with deadly mines and illumination flares. The U.S. forces at most points remain steadfast after having inflicted huge numbers of casualties against the attack force.

Company A, at Hill 1051, is struck with a severe blow at about 0200, but it holds. A contingent of Netherlands troops is rushed to support the beleaguered platoon at dawn, but Chinese opposition is too stiff to break through. Subsequently, the full battalion prepares to advance to rescue the defenders at Hill 1051, but too late.

In the meantime, Company C is compelled to abandon Hill 914. The Chinese begin to flow into the gap about one hour prior to noon, due in part to the inability of the Dutch and French contingents to plug the gap. At 1300, the Netherlands force is directed to advance, but the force stays in place. Finally, after more prodding, the Netherlands Battalion advances at 1500, but it makes no progress against the Chinese forces in front of it. Colonel Chiles, X Corps G-3, at about 1430 takes charge of the X Corps front, including TF Zebra, the French Battalion and the reserve 23rd Regiment. Reinforcements are en route to bolster the positions. They include the ROK 8th Division and the 3rd Division (minus the 7th and 65th Combat Teams). The 3rd Division reinforcements arrive first just before noon, when the vanguard of the 15th RCT moves into the area. The remainder of the division will be in place by the following day. The X Corps also receives an influx of artillery units, borrowed also from IX Corps.

General Van Fleet intends to halt the attack and deliver a punishing blow to the enemy. Earlier, Van Fleet had stated: "I welcome his [Chinese] attack and want to be strong enough in position and fire power to defeat him." Preparations had been made to increase the artillery against the Chinese during this offensive by about 500 percent and according to the situation, the pace could be maintained for seven days without resupply. While the ammunition is a priority, it is accepted that other supplies would not be delivered on a regular basis for the duration of the offensive.

The order to execute the monstrous bombardments upon suspected enemy positions is issued late on this day. On the following day, more than 41,000 rounds are expended and the total increases on successive days. Also, the artillery attacks are augmented by radar-guided air strikes. Planes deliver 500-pound bombs against targets of Chinese troop concentrations, some of which are less than 500 yards from the perimeter.

The afternoon remains relatively quiet, but the Chinese, despite sustaining heavy losses, continue to mount more forces against the X Corps lines. The X Corps boundary is realigned to move southeast and connect with the ROK III Corps at the Waco Line, below the No Name Line. Late in the day before dusk, large concentrations of enemy troops are detected as they filter through the gap to strike the front of the 38th Regiment, 2nd Division, and near the front of the 23rd Regiment. The attack force is composed of elements of the Chinese 45th Division.

Air strikes are called upon and the artillery commences a tumultuous bombardment that causes high enemy casualties, but the Chinese ignore casualties and continue to press. The 3rd Battalion, 38th Infantry

Regiment, is struck with a strong blow and some penetration occurs. Nevertheless, the toll extracted by the 3rd Battalion, coupled with the air and artillery, thins out the force and the Chinese fail to sustain their thrust. The 3rd Battalion regains the lost terrain and ousts the enemy from the lines by the early hours of the 18th.

Along the eastern sector of the 2nd Division zone, the Chinese also sustain horrific casualties, but again, they are not dissuaded as they funnel through the area between Hill 1051 and Hill 914. Undaunted by the relentless bombardment, the Chinese (181st Division, 60th Army, attached to 12th Army) walk through the enfilade of fire, oblivious to the shells, bombs and the massive amount of dead Chinese that they pass over as if stepping on a leaf or tree branch.

Before dusk, the Chinese reach the positions of the French Battalion at Hill 975. The French hold their ground, but only for about two hours before they are compelled to withdraw, giving the Chinese an opportunity to hammer the left flank of the 23rd Regiment during the early morning hours of the 18th.

In the meantime, to the front of the left flank of the regiment, Company F comes under attack, but it completely suppresses it by about midnight (17th-18th). After failing to make progress the Chinese disengage and head east.

At the same time the 23rd Regiment is repulsing the enemy, the ROK 5th Division elements, deployed on the right flank, come under attack, but General Almond authorizes a withdrawal to positions east of Chaun-ni. By morning of the 18th, the entire 38th Regiment becomes imperiled.

The same circumstances face the 1st and 2nd Battalions, 38th Infantry, which became jeopardized after the Netherlands Battalion, without a fight, abandoned its positions on Hill 975. Much pressure is placed upon the 1st and 2nd Battalions (38th Regiment) until daylight on the 18th, but by then the forward companies eliminate the threat. However, Companies A and F are isolated and unable to breakthrough from their positions to the rear of Company B, which remains encircled. In the meantime, the 3rd Battalion at Hill 800 and beyond to the southeast through Han'gye to Hill 693 remains intact and under no immediate threat.

In the 1st Marine Division zone, a contingent of Chinese, about regimental strength, manage to get through to the rear of a Korean Marine patrol base in an attempt to strike the 2nd Division; however, a recent move by elements of the 3rd Battalion, 7th Marines, puts them in position to greet the Chinese. At about dusk, the battalion completes a roadblock at the Morae–Kogae pass along the Chonchon road, and by midnight (17th-18th), it is reinforced by Company G, to place the entire regiment there.

Although the Marines had not expected the Chinese, it becomes apparent that the Chinese's thoughts of a free run to the 2nd Division are shattered by the fortuitous move of the 3rd Battalion. At the northern tip of the Marines' perimeter, the Chinese are welcomed by a surprised Company I, a platoon of

Company D, tanks, and a weapons company platoon. The Chinese are caught completely off guard, but they return furious fire. The exchange transforms the area into a cauldron of fire. Two tanks are lost, and the Chinese attempt unsuccessfully to destroy another. The fight continues into the following day.

In Naval Activity, Rear Admiral R.A. Ofstie, having recently been relieved of his command of Task Force 77 by Admiral Henderson, becomes Chief of Staff, Naval Forces Far East. He succeeds Rear Admiral A.K. Morehouse.

May 18   General Van Fleet, after assessing the situation, makes a decision at about midnight (17th-18th) to bolster the eastern sector of the X Corps, due in great part to the inability of the South Koreans to hold their positions. The remaining 3rd Division contingents are directed to move eastward from Seoul and other units will follow, including the 7th RCT and the 65th RCT, which will redeploy on the 19th and 20th respectively. In conjunction, the 15th RCT is unaffected; it is to remain attached to the 2nd Division. Van Fleet also directs the I Corps, IX Corps and the 1st Marine Division to dispatch patrols and prepare to attack a phase line (Topeka).

In the IX Corps sector, the 7th Marines are ordered to withdraw from blocking positions along Route 29 and relieve the 1st Marines at its positions on the right sector of the zone, along the No Name Line, to permit the 1st Marines to relieve the 9th Infantry Regiment (X Corps). On the division's left flank, the 5th Marines relieve the 38th Infantry Regiment (X Corps) after elements of the 7th Division (X Corps) redeploy in the 5th Marines sector.

In the X Corps sector, subsequent to the pull back on the previous night by the French Battalion on Hill 975, elements of the Chinese 181st Division effortlessly gain access to Route 24, which enables the enemy to strike at the left flank of the 23rd Infantry Regiment at Chaun-ni by about 0330. Other enemy contingents advance to positions in the heights west of Chaun-ni to place the Chinese between the village and the French Battalion, which had withdrawn to some high ground on the fringes of Putchaetful.

In the X Corps sector, General Almond orders a boundary shift. The boundary is extended slightly less than fifteen miles to connect corps with the Waco Line and the ROK III Corps at Habae-jae. During the three-day battle (16th-18th), General Ruffner, 2nd Division

Marines on patrol. The silhouette of one Marine can be seen in the rear doorway, while other Marines move toward the front of a hut. One enemy casualty can be seen. His boots are visible in the doorway.

The smoking lamp is lit. A trio attached to the U.S. 7th Division pauses to smoke cigarettes along a road in the vicinity of Chungbangdac south of the Hongch'on River on 22 May.

commander, reports 900 killed, wounded and missing. He reports Chinese and North Korean losses at 39,000.

In the 2nd Division zone, the 1st Marines (IX Corps) completes relief of the 9th Regiment, which permits the 9th Regiment to complete its redeployment to bol-

ster the 38th Regiment. By noon, the 1st Battalion, 9th Infantry, begins to establish positions between the 2nd and 3rd Battalions. During the realignment of the 2nd Division line, the 2nd and 3rd Battalions are directed to punch forward to attempt to rescue Company B,

38th Regiment, which has not been able to break out of its encirclement at Hill 724 because of the Chinese that had massed on Hill 710 to the rear of Companies A and F.

Another attempt to rescue the beleaguered unit is scheduled to commence at about 1800. Planes expected to support the advance are compelled to return to base due to a sudden unexpected storm. Cancellation of the air power is followed by the suspension of a massive artillery barrage. Meanwhile, the 9th Regiment — bolstered by Company G (38th Regiment) and the Dutch battalion — is en route to extricate the trapped units.

By the following morning, when stragglers that reach the positions of the 9th Regiment are counted, the casualties are extremely high. Company A stands at eighty-nine men and two officers. Company B accounts for seventy-four enlisted men, but no officers. Company F accounts for no officers and eighty-one enlisted men. The other units in the 1st and 2nd Battalions of the 38th Regiment also sustain high casualty rates.

Meanwhile, the 3rd Battalion, 38th Regiment, holds Hill 800 and awaits the arrival of the 5th Marines, which on the following day is to fill the gap there between the 3rd Battalion and two battalions of the 9th Infantry Regiment. The Chinese, however, advance after dark to seize Hill 800. Company K, defending the summit, receives an enormous amount of support. With each successive assault, artillery strikes are called upon and the Chinese continue to get raked with relentless fire. All the while, the troops of Company K wait in the security of the defenses. The attacks continue until dawn on the following day, but the crest remains unscathed and the Chinese lose about 800 troops to the artillery bombardments.

In the 23rd Regiment zone, orders direct the regiment to redeploy along the new line in positions east of Route 24; however, the Chinese block the only route capable of carrying vehicles. To add to the crisis, a mix-up in communications causes more problems. The French inform the 72nd Tank Battalion that the road from Chaun-ni is mined. The information is passed on to Chaun-ni, but it does not reach the officers. Consequently, the supply trains of the 2nd and 3rd Battalions, some tanks of the 72nd Tank Battalion, along with a contingent of a mortar company face mines and a wall of fire, unless the Chinese can quickly be evicted.

Elements of the 2nd and 3rd Battalions, bolstered by a platoon of tanks, attempts to clear the way, but the Chinese force is insurmountable. The 3rd Battalion advances to positions near the roadblock by early afternoon, while the 2nd Battalion works to clear other enemy forces along the road, but to no avail. Orders arrive instructing the supply trains and accompanying units to plow through the blockade, while the 2nd Battalion moves to join with the 3rd Battalion for a combined withdrawal. Still unaware of mines along the route, the convoy, led by tanks, rolls out of Chaun-ni, but after traveling only a short distance, the lead tank hits a mine and stalls the entire convoy.

The Chinese, meanwhile, remain perched in the high ground on opposite sides of the road and immediately open fire. Pandemonium breaks out as the drivers, including tankers, attempt to escape the fire by abandoning the vehicles. The second tank in the column rams its way through the iron debris and gets ahead of the disabled tank, but to no avail. Soon after, it also loses a track to a mine. Attempts are made to get the convoy off the road and onto a stream bed leading southward. There, too, the enemy totally disrupts the withdrawal. Drivers again abandon vehicles, some of which are halted by collisions and others afire by burning ammunition.

The troops flee toward the 2nd and 3rd Battalions and accompany them on yet another tedious and dangerous phase of the withdrawal. The rear guard of the force is Company C, 72nd Tank Battalion. At about 1830, even the weather turns against the retreat. Heavy rain begins to saturate the area. Nonetheless, by about midnight, the 2nd and 3rd Battalions reach positions behind the 1st Battalion. In the meantime, the Chinese enjoy a scavenger hunt among the abandoned vehicles.

The ROK 5th Division, positioned east of Chaunni, is forced to retire in disorderly fashion. The ROKs halt the retreat at positions slightly south of Hill 683, but only some are there. Many more South Koreans are scattered all about. Also, elements of the ROK 7th Division holds the X Corps' east flank at positions southeast of Hasolch'i, slightly below P'ungam-ni. The bulk of the division is like the ROK 5th Division, scattered as far away as the ROK III Corps sector.

In the X Corps zone, a night-long battle at the Morae–Kongae pass ends successfully for the 3rd Battalion, 7th Marines. The Chinese had mounted a tenacious assault, but a counterattack by Company I regains the ground and suppresses the assault, while other Marines and tanks bolstered by artillery maneuver to seal off the enemy's rear. By dawn (18th), the Chinese sustain a devastating defeat. Air support again arrives late at about 1030, but still there are plenty of enemy targets in the area. The Chinese lose 112 killed (counted) and 82 POWs. The U.S. loses 7 killed and 19 wounded.

In other activity, the 1st Marine Division, acting on Eighth Army orders, shrinks its perimeter to support the 2nd Division on the east. While the 1st Marines speed to relieve the 9th Infantry, 2nd Division, the 7th Marines pull back to the No Name Line to relieve the 1st Marines. In conjunction, the 5th Marines pull out of the division's left flank to relieve the 38th Infantry Regiment on the far right. In turn, the relief by the Marines allows the 2nd Division the flexibility to deploy from where the Chinese moving from the east can be engaged and halted.

In the ROK III Corps sector, the 5th and 9th ROK Divisions each receive orders to withdraw to the Waco Line. Both divisions are attacked and each collapses. The South Koreans lose several hundred vehicles and all of their artillery.

In Naval activity, Fast Carrier Task Force (TF 77) launches planes in support of Eighth Army. The day is costly, as 6 aircraft (5 F4U, 1AD) are lost, the highest casualty rate to this point in the conflict. Two of the pilots are rescued, but three others are killed and one is missing.

Also, the vessels USS *Duncan* (DDR 874), *Brinkley Bass* (DD 887), and the *Leonard F. Mason* (DD 852) combine their fire power and propel more than 1,000 rounds of 5-inch shells against enemy positions at Wonsan. Enemy shore batteries on Kalma Gak return heavy fire, but no damage or casualties are sustained by the naval warships.

May 19   The Communists continue to mount high casualties as they maintain the offensive. Meanwhile, Eighth Army continues to modify its lines and strategy to terminate the attacks. By this day, the fighting tilts to the eastern part of the lines. By darkness, the entire eastern front is threatened by the total strength of the Chinese IX Army Group, positioned primarily between Han'gye and Soksa-ri. At Soksa-ri, only one platoon of the Reconnaissance Company (3rd Division) is positioned. However, General Van Fleet is convinced that the Chinese are stretched too far. After checking along the entire front, Van fleet concludes that a massive counterattack will crack the Chinese offensive. He schedules the offensive by the I and IX Corps, against enemy supply areas and communications centers in the vicinity of Mansedari, Hwach'on and Inje, to begin on the following day. General Ridgway arrives at X Corps from Japan and confers with Generals Van Fleet, Almond (X Corps) and Hoge (IX Corps) at Hoengsong. Eighth Army urgently requests full-scale air support to stem the tide.

In the X Corps sector, another difficult day emerges as the Chinese relentlessly move to overwhelm the X Corps.

In the 2nd Division zone, stragglers from the 23rd Regiment continue to arrive at the 9th Regimental positions, following the failed attempts to extricate the isolated units. The 23rd Infantry Regiment and accompanying units sustain 72 killed, 158 wounded and 190 missing. More than 150 vehicles, including some tanks, are lost. The regiment inflicts upon the enemy more than 2,200 killed and 1,400 wounded. The 23rd Regiment captures 22 Chinese soldiers attached to several divisions, the 31st, 35th and 181st.

Also, elements of the 3rd Division arrive from Seoul. The 3rd Battalion, 7th Infantry Regiment, deploys to hold Route 20 and to protect against intrusions from the mountain paths northwest of their line. The remainder of the 7th Infantry arrives later and deploys in the vicinity of Ami-dong.

At the divisional right, the 15th RCT (on loan from 3rd Division) passes through the ROK 3rd Regiment and gains P'ungam-ni prior to noon. Afterward, the 15th RCT gains the high ground to the northwest of the village. The ROK 3rd Regiment and several contingents of the ROK 7th Regiment shadow the 15th RCT to positions north and northeast of P'ungam-ni.

In the 23rd Regiment zone, prior to dawn, again, the Chinese launch an attack. The regiment calls for assistance from artillery and by air strikes to inflict more casualties upon the 181st Regiment. Meanwhile, the 1st and 3rd Battalion remain under great pressure until about noon, when the skies clear and planes arrive to support counterattacks. After eliminating the threat, the battalion advances to positions near Route 24, below Hasolch'i.

In the meantime, the 9th Regiment continues moving to its positions above Hasolch'i after dusk. The 1st Battalion deploys to the right of the ROK 35th Regiment. The 2nd Battalion moves to positions to the rear of the ROK 36th Regiment. Also, the French Battalion is prevented from linking with the ROK 36th Regiment, positioned northwest of Hasolch'i.

Also, the 2nd Division receives a huge amount of support from the U.S. Air Force, which delivers about 700 radar controlled bombs after dark to help smash the enemy troop formations in front of the 2nd Division. In the 3rd Division zone, elements of the Chinese 93rd Regiment, 31st Division, arrive after dusk and compel a small reconnaissance contingent of the 3rd Division to evacuate the their positions in Soksa-ri.

In the ROK III Corps sector, disorder remains rampant as troops from various units are still scattered about. None of the units reach the Waco Line.

In the ROK I Corps sector, the Capital Division and the 11th Division remain disciplined and the units are able to arrive at the Waco Line.

In Air Force activity, enemy fire shoots down an F-51 in the area southwest of Ch'orwon. An H-5 helicopter from the 3rd Air Rescue Squadron is dispatched to attempt to rescue the pilot. The mission is successful and the pilot is retrieved and brought back to friendly positions; however, enemy fire is encountered while the crew is bringing the man aboard.

May 20   Operation STRANGLE commences. The operation is designed to destroy the enemy's rail and vehicle traffic where it can be caught in North Korea. The operation is unfolded primarily with air power, but the planes are not able to provide sufficient air power to the ground troops. Eighth Army for some time receives fewer than 100 sorties a day. Operation STRANGLE continues into September.

Also, the I Corps and IX Corps initiate counterattacks (Operation DETONATE), while the X Corps continues to fend off the remaining attacks in its area. The Communists against X Corps continue to sustain extremely high casualties without making progress.

Also, by this date, the Communist offensive is halted, unable to gather any momentum against the galvanized Eighth Army.

In the I Corps sector, the advance moves toward the major road center in the Yongp'yong River valley; however, the orders will be modified and on 23 May, subsequent to rearranging the IX Corps–X Corps boundary in an eastward direction, the IX Corps will assume responsibility for the road hub west of the Hwach'on Reservoir and the security of the Hongch'on–Chunchon–Hwach'on Road. In conjunction, the modified orders give X Corps responsibility for the road centers east of the Hwach'on Reservoir.

On this day, General Milburn directs a three-division advance. The 1st Cavalry Division advances up Route 33, while the 25th Division drives north along Route 3, toward the Yongp'yong River valley. In addition, the ROK 1st Division advances toward Munsan-ni.

In the 25th Division zone, Company E, 35th Regiment, engages an enemy contingent in the vicinity of Seoul. During the struggle, just as the vanguard approaches the positions of the enemy, a grenade is tossed into the ranks. Sergeant Donald R. Moyer spots the live grenade and to save the lives of the others with him, he dives on it and takes the full blast. Sergeant Moyer receives the Medal of Honor posthumously for his selfless actions on behalf of his fellow soldiers. The hill is later taken.

In the IX Corps sector, the counterattack is executed by the 24th Division and the ROK 2nd, 6th and 7th divisions. The IX Corps objective is to pursue and engage the enemy reserves; however, the progress of the attacks rates poor at best, despite only minimum opposition.

In the X Corps sector, 2nd Division zone, elements of the Chinese 34th Division strike the positions of the 9th Infantry Regiment northeast of Hasolch'i. Following the massive air bombardment of the previous night, this is the only heavy attack to commence by dawn. Nevertheless, the defenders, Company C, receive massive support, including air attacks and artillery, bolstered further by a counterattack launched by Company A. The attacking force of about five hundred troops is liquidated.

In other activity, elements of the 7th Regiment, 3rd Division, in battalion strength, advances to evict the Chinese that occupied Soksa-ni on the previous night, but the Chinese repulse the attempt. Nearby, above Soksa-ri, the Chinese strike against the 23rd ROK Regiment (3rd Division).

In the 23rd Infantry Regiment zone, the left flank is hit by the 181st Regiment, which emerges from the Naech'on River valley. The Communists move through a wall of withering fire while planes deliver yet more killing power. The fire is so overwhelming that the Chinese halt and retire before crashing into the regimental line. To the rear of the devastated 181st, more Communists gather to again brave the deadly fire; however, Eighth Army relentlessly maintains its artillery fire and B-29s saturate the various gathering places of the enemy formations. The powerful display riddles the Chinese and prevents any attacks against the 2nd Division throughout the night of 20–21 May.

General Ridgway (far right) discusses strategy with (from left to right) Major General William M. Hoge (IX Corps commander), Blackshear M. Bryan (24th Division commander) and Lt. General James A. Van Fleet (Eighth Army commander).

The convincing efforts against the 12th Army galvanizes the division. General Almond had withdrawal plans in effect, but prior to execution, he concludes that the line will hold steadfastly and he aborts the withdrawal. Instead, he directs his attention to modifying the lines to prevent the possibility of an attack from the east.

While the 2nd Division remains in place like a steel picket fence, Almond prepares to take Soksa-ri back on the following day. The lines are further strengthened by the arrival of the 65th RCT (3rd Division). Another contingent, the ROK 8th Division, arrives in the vicinity of Chech'on, giving General Almond the option of dispatching the South Koreans from there to augment the eastern flank of X Corps. The ROK 8th Division had been operating in South Korea engaged in eliminating guerrillas behind Eighth Army lines. General Almond also has elements of the ROK 7th Division at P'ungam-ni, as well as elements of the battered 38th Regiment.

In the 1st Marine Division zone, the 1st Korean Marine Regiment attacks with the IX Corps; however, the three U.S. regiments remain in place. During the early morning hours, again the Chinese are surprised when they unexpectedly encounter Marine forces. At about 0445, a large contingent of about regimental strength encroaches the lines of the 3rd Battalion, 5th Marines, expecting to occupy the positions, but not anticipating that the Marines already hold it. The surprise is deadly and one-sided. By 0930, the Chinese are introduced to every available weapon of the 7th Marines. The Marines count 152 dead and collect fifteen prisoners. The Chinese survivors flee into the hills.

In Air Force activity, a contingent of Sabre jets on a mission get intercepted by about 50 MiGs. The Sabre pilots call for support, but in the meantime, they engage the MiGs in a wild shoot-out in the skies. One of the pilots, Captain Jabara, has problems with his plane; he cannot drop one of his wing tanks. Nonetheless, he maintains a stable flight. The Communists lose three MiGs, two of which are downed by Captain Jabara for his fifth and sixth kills. The Sabre pilots note a possible fourth kill and they report five MiGs damaged. Subsequent to the less than sterling performance, the Russians who had piloted the MiGs fail to show up for awhile, but they return to the skies on 31 May. Captain Jabara becomes the first jet-to-jet ace.

In Naval activity, U.S. warships continue to operate off Wonsan. Enemy shore batteries inflict slight damage to the USS *Brinkley Bass* (DD 887) and inflict casualties. One seaman is killed and nine others are injured before the ship pulls back out of the range of the guns.

Also, the USS *New Jersey* (BB 62) initiates its activity in the conflict by pounding enemy positions in the vicinity of Kansong and afterward at Kosang and Wonsan. On the following day, the USS *New Jersey* sustains minor damage to gun turret No. 121 after being fired upon by an enemy shore gun. One seaman is killed and three others are wounded.

In other activity, with air support provided by the USS *Bataan* (CVL-29) and naval surface support fire, British commandos land on the west coast of Korea across from Cho-do Island. The operation continues into the following day, with warships, including the USS *Toledo* (CA-133), providing continued naval surface support fire.

— In Japan: General George E. Stratemeyer, the commanding officer of Far East Air Forces, suffers a severe heart attack. On the following day, he is replaced by General Partridge. Partridge's position as commander Fifth Air Force is temporarily filled by Major General Edward J. Timberlake, Jr., USAF.

May 21 The Chinese offensive begins to slacken along Eighth Army's front, except in the ROK III and I Corps sectors. However, the Eighth Army offensive of the I and IX Corps accelerates in an effort to drive the Chinese back and inflict punishing casualties. Toward the latter part of the day, the ROK III Corps receives orders to hold and make no additional withdrawals. The order stipulates that the corps re-establish its defensive positions along Route 20. Also, at about the same time, the ROK I Corps is directed to withdraw from its positions along the Waco Line and establish new defensive positions that protect Route 20, the section that stretches between Yuch'on-ni and the coast at Kangnung.

In the I Corps sector, the progress continues and the entire force closes on the Topeka Line. Elements of the ROK 1st Division enter Munsan-ni prior to noon.

In the IX Corps sector, the counterattack continues to make slow progress.

In the X Corps sector, General Almond orders an attack to regain Soksa-ri.

In other activity, the 187th Airborne RCT is released from IX Corps reserve. It moves to positions to the right of the 1st Marine Division, which places it to the left of the 2nd Division. Also, in the 7th Division zone, a platoon of Company F, 17th Regiment, attacks an enemy position in the heights in the vicinity of Monyeri. Enemy fire stalls the advance and grenades that plop down the slope cause the troops to scatter for safety. Sergeant Joseph C. Rodriguez, 2nd Platoon, jumps from his protected position and pushes toward the enemy. He sprints through the raging enemy fire for about sixty yards, then deposits a few of his grenades directly into the first foxhole he spots. Immediately he bolts forward and eliminates an automatic weapon with another delivery of grenades. Following his impetuous climb, Rodriguez reaches the summit and immediately liquidates the occupants of two additional foxholes. Still on the hunt, Rodriguez locates the remaining gun emplacement and takes it out to ease the path to the summit for the rest of his command. Rodriguez receives credit for the elimination of fifteen of the enemy. The enemy is routed. Rodriguez becomes the recipient of the Medal of Honor for his extraordinary heroism under fire.

In Air Force activity, a contingent of four F-86 Sabre

jets led by Lieutenant Baldwin encounters and engages a band of MiGs in the skies over Kyebang-san. The patrol, which had arrived from Japan, is hitting bad weather and its target is in a mountainous area. However, the Sabres contact a tactical controller who guides them through the foggy weather to spot the target, a force the size of about two battalions, placed to threaten friendly troops.

The planes arrive over the target just as the enemy is ascending a steep draw. But the Americans, in addition to the rain and overcast skies, are greeted by heavy antiaircraft fire. The combination of poor weather and low fuel compels the tactical control plane to depart the region. Nevertheless, the Sabre jets execute an attack. The strafing runs are so effective that the friendly ground troops get the needed relief and take the ground, where they discover and count about 700 enemy killed by the air attacks. They find huge stacks of equipment and supplies — no longer of any use. The planes had also destroyed the supplies.

— *In Japan:* Major General Partridge, commander Fifth Air Force, succeeds General George E. Stratemeyer as commander Far East Air Forces. General Stratemeyer had suffered a heart attack. Major General Frank E. Everest succeeds General Partridge as commander Fifth Air Force; however until Everest can arrives to assume command, Major General Edward J. Timberlake becomes temporary commander.

May 22 The Communist focus, according to Eighth Army intelligence, seems to be against objectives along Route 20, Py'ongch-ang and Yongwol, and from there to Kangnung, but General Van Fleet remains convinced that the Communists' attacks are fizzling out. Van Fleet directs the ROK I Corps to bolster the positions along Route 20 by establishing defenses to thwart an assault from the east. The orders stipulate that if enemy pressure prevents the I Corps from holding there, it is to form to protect the road hub at Kangnung.

Meanwhile, the enemy forces in the X Corps zone initiate a withdrawal subsequent to dusk. Although enemy intentions remain uncertain to Eighth Army, the Chinese apparently have concluded that the casualty rates sustained during the offensive have been too great to continue the advance. Nevertheless, the Communists still have enormous reserves in the region. All the while, the Eighth Army counterattack continues in the I and IX Corps sectors.

In the IX Corps sector, still only slight progress is accomplished. The full corps attacks reach no farther than the Georgia Line. The corps' poor progress prompts General Van Fleet to commit the X Corps to join in on the following day to strengthen the assault.

In the X Corps sector, recently formed Task Force Yoke, led by Colonel Lawrence K. Ladue, moves to take control of Habae-jae to prevent the Chinese from using it as a path to strike the line. TF Yoke is composed of the 2nd Battalion, 38th Regiment, a large contingent of the 72nd Tank Battalion, one platoon of the 15th Infantry's tank company and the greater part of the ROK 3rd Regiment. In addition, TF Yoke includes one battery of the 300th FABn and a tactical air control party.

The task force advances through the lines of the ROK 7th Division near P'ungam-ni en route to the Habae-jae road junction; however, the objective is not achieved. The advance, due in great part to the tardiness of the ROKs, misses the mark by less than five miles. Later, Task Force Able is formed to resume the task of seizing Habae-jae.

The task force is initially composed of the 15th RCT and two units from TF Yoke, the ROK 3rd Regiment and the 300th FABn; however, the force is altered. Almond returns the ROKs to the 7th Division and replaces them with the 3rd Battalion, 15th Infantry Regiment. One company of the 72nd Tank Battalion is added. The advance is set for the following day. Colonel Ladue, commander of TF Yoke, succumbs two days later due to a heart attack.

Also, the 187th Airborne RCT initiates an advance up Route 24 to seize the high ground near Han'gye. The afternoon advance encounters only light resistance and effortlessly gains the objective. In related activity, regarding the primary attack, the 2nd Division, reinforced with the 187th Airborne RCT, moves against Inje, while the 1st Marine Division pushes toward Yanggu (Hongch'on–Omyang–Yanggu axis). During the arduous trek to Yangu, the 1st and 5th Marines sustain many injuries due to the nasty terrain. The Marines attack toward Hill 1051, which had been seized by Chinese on 17 April. The 5th Marines while advancing and engaging rear-guard units of the Chinese 15th Army through some fortuitous luck, discover eleven 2nd Division troops that had been wounded and unable to reach friendly lines during the earlier Chinese attack.

In the ROK III Corps sector, the ROK 3rd Division, commanded by General Kim Jong Oh, and 9th Division, led by General Choi Suk, again are unable to complete tasks assigned to them and both divisions are mauled by the Chinese by early afternoon. The lines of both units collapse and their command posts vanish as the Communists overrun positions effortlessly. Some units of the ROK 3rd Division are discovered on the following day at positions fifteen miles below Hajinbu-ri.

Also on the following day, some elements of the ROK 9th Division, through the efforts of a KMAG advisor, begin to regroup about five miles southeast of Hajinbu-ri. By the latter part of the day, General Van Fleet concludes that the ROK III Corps is no longer cohesive. The III Corps is designated inactive. The ROK 3rd Division is transferred to the ROK I Corps, while the ROK 9th Division is placed under the jurisdiction of X Corps. The failure of the South Koreans increases the difficulty for Eighth Army, but Van Fleet remains convinced that the Communists are in the process of a major withdrawal. He removes the ROK Army forward headquarters from the field and Van Fleet himself assumes responsibility for the ROK I Corps.

In the ROK I Corps sector, during the early morning hours, the Communists smash into the ROK 20th Regiment, 11th ROK Division, at Yuch'on-ni. The regiment is driven out by the elements of the N.K. II Corps.

In Air Force activity, Fifth Air Force executes a large number of close-air support sorties and reports that the attacks inflict about 1,700 casualties on the enemy.

May 23 *In the I Corps sector,* Task Force Able, commanded by Lt. Colonel Thomas R. Yancey, resumes the attack toward Habae-jae road center, in place of TF Yoke, which had not been able to seize it on the previous day. Although the task force is only several miles from the target, it, too, is unable to reach the objective due to the rough terrain.

In the 3rd Division zone, the advance continues against North Korean rear-guard units. Elements of the 1st Battalion, 7th Infantry Regiment, reach the pass north of Soksa-ri.

Also, the 65th Infantry Regiment reaches positions west of the 7th Regiment, while the ROK 9th Division holds the rear of the advance in reserve.

In the IX Corps sector, after some modifications are made amidst the forces, the corps finally experiences some progress and gains ground. Nonetheless, the largest advances move only slightly more than five miles against the Chinese 63rd and 64th Armies, which continue a hurried retreat. The task force, composed of tanks and the 1st Battalion, 21st Regiment (24th Division), led by General Bryan, makes the deepest penetration and seizes Kap'yong.

In the X Corps sector, the ROK III Corps sector is assumed by X Corps subsequent to the ROK III Corps being dissolved on the previous night by General Van Fleet. Also, the 1st Marine Division initiates its attack northward toward Yanggu at the eastern tip of the Hwachon Reservoir, to secure the road hub at the eastern tip of the reservoir. The advance is led by the 1st and 5th Marines. Meanwhile, the 7th Marines, after being relieved by a contingent of the 7th Infantry Division (IX Corps), moves to the east to operate on the Division's right flank.

In other activity, a contingent of the 2nd Division, including the 187th Airborne RCT (attached), is directed by General Almond to establish a bridgehead at the Soyang River and from there advance to Inje.

In Air Force activity, Brigadier General Robert H. Terrill assumes command of Far East Air Forces Bomber Command. He succeeds General Elbert Briggs. General Briggs will return to the States in June to assume the position of deputy commander, Fifteenth Air Force, at March Air Force Base in California.

In Naval activity, two LSMRs (Landing Shore Medium Rocket) launch a huge barrage against enemy positions at Wonsan during their initial action at the siege of Wonsan. The two vessels fire more than 4,900 rockets during a 35-minute period as part of Operation FIREBALL, executed by cruisers and destroyers.

May 24 General Van Fleet continues to become impatient with the tardiness of the offensive. He is convinced that if the corps commanders quicken the pace, the Chinese and North Koreans attempting to withdraw can still be caught in a vise and destroyed.

In other activity, the saga of a group of 18 Marines and one U.S. Army interpreter captured during the previous year ends at U.S. lines. The captives had been brought to the Communist lines near Ch'orwon, probably to be used as laborers during April. During an artillery barrage, the Chinese guards seek cover while the POWs flee. On the following day while concealed in the heights, the band fabricates a sign from wallpaper stripped from a nearby destroyed house, reading: "POW 19 RESCUE." A pilot in an observation plane spots the sign. On the 26th, several tanks roar to the area and rescue the men.

In the I Corps sector, the advance pushes up Route 3 toward the Kansas Line. Elements reach the line on the following day.

In the IX Corps sector, the objective is the Topeka Line at a point in the 7th Division's newly assigned area, just above Chunchon. General Ferenbaugh, the 7th Division commander, is directed by General Hoge to dispatch an armored force toward Chunchon to discover crossing sites at the Soyang River. Task Force Hazel is formed for the task, but it is only a light unit, composed only of a platoon of tanks, the 7th Reconnaissance Company and a contingent of engineers. The task force comes under heavy attack by small arms and machine gun fire along Route 29 near Sinjom, about eight miles from Chunchon.

Captain Hazel, immediately after coming under attack, pulls back the vanguard, which consists of jeeps and half-tracs, then pushes eleven tanks to the point. The Chinese continue to pound against the tanks as they drive through the pass; however, the enemy fire strikes only harmless blows against the armor. Despite being intercepted by an enemy force of regimental strength, by the latter part of the afternoon, the armor rolls into Chunchon. Captain Hazel is ordered to remain in Chunchon and await reinforcements, two tank platoons carrying supplies and ammunition.

In the meantime, General Ferenbaugh moves out to catch up with the task force to oversee the operation. After Hazel's armor enters Chunchon, the tank crews scour the town and the river banks. About 100 Chinese are discovered and of those, some are either killed or captured while others escape.

Also, at Hill 302, the tank crews spot a large Chinese contingent attempting to flee. The tanks unleash an avalanche of fire upon the hill. The Chinese continue to flee without returning fire.

Meanwhile, after no communication from General Ferenbaugh, grave concern arises. When Captain Hazel is asked if the general is at Chunchon, Hazel replies that he didn't even realize the general was en route. A special unit moving up the road solves the mystery. The troops come upon the place where General Ferenbaugh's two-jeep convoy had been ambushed at 1630. Two men were killed, but the general, his driver and aide escaped harm and sought concealment off the road.

Top: A contingent of the 31st Regiment, 7th Division, in action near Ch'onchon on 24 May. One of the troops, a casualty, receives aid from a medic. *Bottom*: The 34th Regiment is deployed in the hills near Ch'unchon.

A platoon of tanks led by Lt. Ivan G. Stanaway, while preparing to move out to reinforce Captain Hazel, speeds to the point of ambush and encounters some opposition. Nevertheless, the tankers rescue the wounded man along the road. Soon after, General Ferenbaugh and the others are located. The tanks wait patiently until dark, unaffected by the small arms fire. At that time, the general and the other two men abandon their concealed position, reach the tanks in single file and climb aboard by squeezing through the escape hatch. By about 2100, the tanks and the general's contingent return to the lines of the 38th Infantry.

In related activity, the situation at Chunchon changes. Captain Hazel receives new orders that direct him to abandon the village and return due to concerns that resupply might not be possible. During the pullback from Chunchon, two tanks in Captain Hazel's command are lost; one is destroyed after it runs out of fuel and another drops off the road into a gully. Otherwise, the contingent sustains no damage from the enemy. However, some captives held atop the tanks are struck by small arms fire.

In the X Corps sector, the offensive continues in an effort to push the enemy to positions that might trap it between the IX and X Corps. The 2nd Division initiates a drive to the Soyang River to secure the Umyang-ni bridge with an armored force. The task force is initially commanded by Colonel Brubaker, but while he is en route P'ungam-ni, Colonel William Gerhardt takes command of the force at Han'gye. The operation gets a late start at 1300. The spearhead of the column takes precautions on the road to avoid mines, but this slows the drive. An irritated General Almond orders the tanks to open the throttles and advance. In the meantime, the main body remains at Han'gye, prompting Almond to relieve Colonel Brubaker (commander 187th Airborne).

In the meantime, the vanguard, led by Major Charles A. Newman, races toward the objective. Just below Umyang-ni the armor encounters an enormous force of Chinese that numbers several thousand. The Chinese are startled by the sudden appearance of a line of tanks and raise no resistance. They break for safety while the tanks open fire. Afterward, the tanks roll into the town and scour the area near the river for more enemy troops.

In the meantime, enemy contingents continue to run north as the tanks maintain a stream of fire upon both banks of the Soyang River. Later, about 1830, the main body of Task Force Gerhardt arrives to join the vanguard.

In the 2nd Division zone, the 38th Infantry Regiment advances to a position slightly less than ten miles from Hyon-ni-on, but the progress is hindered by poor road conditions more so than enemy resistance. On the following day, the 24th Regiment is removed from reserve to secure the Soyang bridgehead. In the meantime, the 187th Airborne Task Force (minus the contingent attached to TF Gerhardt) moves up Route 24 on the side of the road opposite the Marines and makes only slight progress against heavy resistance. On the following day,

a contingent punches through the resistance and fords the Soyang River to establish a bridgehead.

In the 1st Marine Division zone, on the corps' right, the advance up Route 24, to the rear of TF Gerhardt, reaches the area around Yanggu, which is secured; however, the 7th Marines jumps off late, due to a vehicle shortage and enemy resistance. Consequently, the Marines end the day short of the objective, the high ground west of Umyang-ni. The 7th Marines maintain the move toward the Soyang River.

In related activity, the 2nd and 3rd Battalions, 5th Marines, encounter heavy resistance as they advance toward their objective, several hills north of Han'gye. Hill 1051 is spotted as the origin of the enemy fire. Artillery fire is requested to clear the hill. Shortly thereafter, the summit and the southeastern slopes are engulfed with fire that promptly evicts the Chinese, who flee northward. By about 1300, Hill 883 is gained by Company D. The Marines continue their advance and by midnight, Colonel Hayward, commanding officer, reports that the objective of the 5th Marines has been secured.

In Naval activity, the USS *Manchester* (CL 83) and the USS *Brinkley Bass* (DD 887), operating in the vicinity of Wonsan and using night radar, commence firing upon an enemy formation and cause the group to disperse. The *Manchester* seizes four enemy sampans that contain eleven enemy dead and one wounded.

In Air Force activity, the 136th Fighter Bomber Wing (Air National Guard), which had previously arrived in Japan from the U.S., initiates its initial combat mission of the war in Korea. The troops are drawn from Texas and Arkansas.

May 25 *In the IX Corps sector,* TF Hazel against sets out for Chunchon, this time supported by one battalion of the 17th Infantry Regiment (7th Division). No ambushes are encountered and the enemy is not found along the route or in Chunchon. Apparently, the Chinese believed that the tank column that entered Chunchon on the previous night had been the spearhead of a large force and rather than engage, they retired. Nevertheless, the air observers spot large enemy formations, one composed of more than ten thousand troops, along and near Route 17 above the village. Afterward, well before noon, artillery and air attacks pummel the retiring enemy forces.

In the meantime, the remainder of the 17th Infantry speeds to Chunchon and initiates pursuit from there at about noon. To add to the dilemma of the Chinese, the 21st Infantry Regiment, 24th Division, is advancing up the Kap'yong–Chiam-ni road en route to link with the 17th Regiment, 7th Division, at Chiam-ni.

Observation planes continue to shadow the advance and while on patrol, a sign (later discovered to be made of wallpaper and shells) is spotted southeast of Chunchon. It reads: "POW 19" and is underscored by shells with the word "rescue." The pilot accepts the message as urgent and drops a note to the tanks in the town. Soon after, eighteen Marines and one soldier are soon greeted by three of Captain Hazel's tanks. The troops had been seized at the Changjin Reservoir during the previous November and abandoned when the town was evacuated this day.

Just before dusk, observation planes on patrol detect a large group of Chinese moving west toward Route 24 (X Corps troops are en route there); however, an escape hatch remains there and the enemy continues to move across the road throughout the night. In conjunction, elements of the Chinese 106th Regiment, 34th Division, take advantage of the absence of U.S. troops and establish defensive positions to protect the retreat. Task Force Gerhardt (X Corps) is within striking distance, but the commander fails to dispatch any units, despite his awareness that a twenty-truck convoy had been ambushed and only one vehicle had survived.

In the X Corps sector, as in the IX Corps sector, aerial observers detect large enemy formations attached to the Chinese 12th and 15th Armies as the units retire from positions below the Hwach'on Reservoir. The X Corps troops react by increasing the pact to reach Hwach'on town, while artillery and planes deliver devastating blows against the columns, formed by more than 10,000 troops and unending rows of vehicles, as they head north.

In the 2nd Division zone, the 23rd Infantry Regiment arrives at the Soyang River and lays a bridge across the river to ease the path of trailing units en route to Inje, another strategy needed to cut off the retreating enemy.

Also, General Ruffner is alerted to an ambush of twenty vehicles attempting to drop back and get supplies. Of twenty trucks, nineteen are destroyed and only two drivers survive. The 23rd Infantry Regiment is ordered to advance to liquidate the roadblock, but not until dawn on the following day.

In the 38th Infantry Regiment zone, the North Koreans raise fierce opposition below Sangam-ni and halt the regiment's progress. In conjunction, the 9th Infantry Regiment advances, but encounters no opposition. The Communists in the 23rd Infantry's zone continue to retire through the gap between the front of the Marines (X Corps) and TF Gerhardt in the vicinity of Umyang-ni.

Meanwhile, the North Koreans being pursued by the 38th Regiment maintain their retreat toward Inje. General Almond forms Task Force Baker, using elements of Task Force Gerhardt and the remaining units of the 187th Airborne RCT. The task force sets out on the following day to secure Kansong along the coast.

Other action following the establishment of the bridgehead at the Soyang River includes placing the 2nd Division (minus the 9th Infantry) into reserve. The ROK 5th Division assumes responsibility for the 2nd Division zone stretched between Route 24 and the P'ungam-ni–Hyon-ni–Inje road. Other corps changes include the 3rd Division assuming responsibility for the area protected by Task Force Able, which is disbanded. The 3rd Division continues to keep the ROK 8th and 9th Divisions attached.

In the 1st Marine Division zone, the 1st Marines reaches its objectives, short of the Soyang River. At that point, the Marines are relieved by the 1st Korean Marine Corps Regiment. The 1st Marines are placed in reserve. Meanwhile, the 7th Marines, advancing to the rear of the 5th Marines, continues advancing toward the Soyang River.

May 26–28 1951   During this period of the ongoing U.S. offensive, the remaining Communist forces below the 38th Parallel either escape north of the parallel or are driven beyond it. However, some scattered forces remain south of the 38th Parallel. During this period, great numbers of enemy forces surrender, many without attempting to resist. In addition, the Chinese have broken one of their traits by risking disaster and moving during daylight hours to escape the wrath of Eighth Army. Chinese retire while the North Koreans are sacrificed in rear actions to permit the Chinese to flee without a fight. The Communists come under attack by planes and artillery that devastate their ranks.

May 26   *In the I Corps sector,* the 3rd Division, reinforced, advances against sporadic resistance. The 7th Infantry Regiment effortlessly reaches its objective, the road junction east of Habae-jae.

In the IX Corps sector, the 17th Infantry Regiment, 7th Division (X Corps) and the 21st Infantry Regiment, 24th Division (IX Corps), both converge upon Chiam-ni. Several miles southwest of the town, the regimental headquarters of the 17th Regiment and the medical detachment establish positions separate from the infantry units. In the meantime, the 19th Regiment, 24th Division, in the center, drives toward positions within several miles of Chiam-ni. The ROK 6th Division is directed to shift from the center to the east and advance with the 7th Division.

During the day's operations, some of the Chinese caught below Chiam-ni escape the trap set by the three closing regiments; however, others remain in the area. One group drives against the non-infantry contingent outside Chiam-ni slightly after midnight (26th-27th); however, despite no infantry units, the headquarters and medical personnel hold steadfastly and pulverize a contingent of about three hundred. More Chinese follow and they, too, fail to break through. The Chinese even attempt close-quartered fighting and still find themselves on the short end, with high casualties. Failing to penetrate and shoot through to safety, the enemy bolts for the high ground and from there attempts to harass the perimeter.

By about dawn (27th), riflemen arrive from the south to take over the fight. The 5th Infantry, 24th Regiment, eliminates the last of the assault troops. The Americans lose two killed and twenty wounded while defending the perimeter. The Chinese sustain about three hundred killed, and about two hundred and fifty wounded. In addition, four hundred and fifty Chinese are captured.

In the X Corps sector, recently formed TF Baker advances toward the coast to seize Kansong. Also, the 23rd Regiment, 2nd Division, advances at dawn to knock out the roadblock along Route 24. The enemy defenders there, attached to the Chinese 12th Army, are eliminated.

The advance moves forward up Route 24 toward Inje after fording the Soyang River in late morning. Later, the enemy again raises resistance and prevents the 23rd Regiment from breaking through to Inje.

In related activity, the 7th Marines advance on the west flank of the 23rd Infantry Regiment. The Chinese had been retiring in a northwesterly direction, but subsequent to the elimination of nearly the entire 106th Division, the retreating forces pivot and move to the northeast toward Yanggu. The 2nd Division is ordered to seize Inje to provide easy passage across the Soyang River and through the town to speed its pace to Kansong.

General Almond, X Corps commander, and General Van Fleet remain convinced that the opportunity to cut off and eliminate many Chinese below Route 24 is still available. In addition to the formation of TF Baker by General Almond, this day he directs the 3rd Division to form Task Force Charlie, composed primarily of 7th Infantry Regiment, and attack northeastward to the coast to capture and secure Yangyang.

The advance of TF Charlie experiences problems. The task force hits mines and an impassable bridge that suspends further progress after a gain of under five miles. The pursuit continues across the entire corps front and during the afternoon, the skies clear, giving the advance the support of air attacks. Air observation planes spot more large enemy formations as they move hurriedly north and west of Inje. The information is forwarded to headquarters. Soon after, artillery in support of the 38th Infantry's advance catapults streams of fire toward designated targets above Inje.

Later, fighter planes arrive overhead and deliver more punishing blows. The Communists attempt to outrun the shells and bombs, but without much success. In addition to the artillery and fighter planes, the Communists also become the recipients of about thirteen tons of bombs delivered on target by B-29s. Despite the overpowering bombardments and strafing runs, the 38th Regiment is unable to break through a blockage established by the N.K. 19th Regiment, 13th Division, in front of Hyon-ni.

In the 1st Marine Division zone, the advance toward Yanggu continues.

In the ROK I Corps sector, the South Koreans enter Kansong. Consequently, TF Charlie is ordered to halt its attack on the village.

In the 7th Marines sector, the 7th Marines close on the Soyang River. The 2nd Battalion crashes into an enemy ammunition dump and seizes the remnant forces there, 27 troops, some of whom are wounded and apparently left behind. The Marines also confiscate a huge amount of ammunition and supplies, including 100,000 rounds of small arms ammunition, 12,000 mortar rounds and 9,000 grenades. By dusk, the 7th Marines arrive at the south bank of the Soyang River.

May 27 The U.S. counterattack continues to make progress as the Chinese and North Koreans maintain

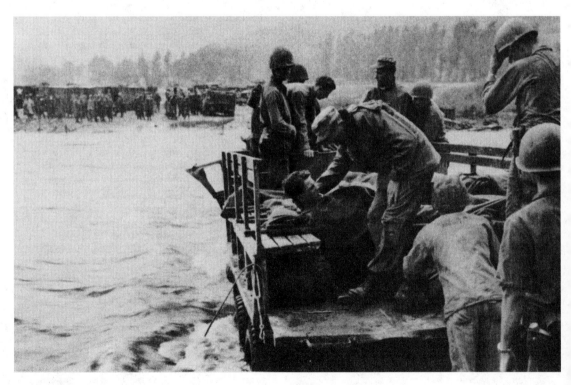

The U.S. 2nd Division sustains casualties during the fight to seize Inje. Some of the wounded are transported across the Soyang River.

Top: U.S. planes pass over positions of the 187th Airborne RCT (vicinity of Umyang) and drop supplies. *Bottom*: Sherman tanks (M4s) attached to the 1st Cavalry Division cross the Imjin River.

their respective retreats. Eighth Army progress remains behind the schedule expected of it, prompting General Van Fleet to plan a new phase, Operation PILE DRIVER. Van Fleet's blueprint calls for the I and IX Corps to sever the enemy communications by securing the Wyoming Line, which will also provide domination of the area at the base of the Iron Triangle. The operation also encompasses the simultaneous establishment of a solid defensive wall to prevent the enemy from exiting the triangle from the northwest, along the primary

roads leading to Chunchon and the Hwach'on Reservoir.

In other activity, Major General Thomas J. Cushman succeeds General Harris as commander 1st Marine Air Wing. In conjunction, Brigadier General William O. Brice, recently arrived from the U.S., succeeds General Cushing as deputy commander.

In the IX Corps sector, at Chiam-ni, some Chinese still search for a route of escape, but the clamps continue to tighten. One group tries unsuccessfully to break out during the early morning hours. Afterward, all escape routes close. The 17th and 21st Infantry Regiments discontinue their respective operations around Chiam-ni and moved to participate in the main advance along Route 17, but the 5th Infantry Regiment, supported by the ROK 19th Regiment, 6th ROK Division, begins a mop-up of the area. About 2,000 Chinese are captured.

In the X Corps sector, despite poor weather, some air observations flights operate, and reports continue to indicate strong enemy forces on the retreat. One group of about seven thousand is detected as it drives north along the Hyon-ni–Inje Road in front of the 38th Infantry Regiment. Meanwhile, TF Baker drives toward Inje at full speed, avoiding some enemy units as it moves, aware that the trailing 23rd Regiment will engage them. The North Koreans raise opposition and impede the advance of the 23rd Regiment. TF Baker plows into Inje at 1430, but the 23rd Regiment encounters stiff opposition. Nonetheless, by about dusk, Hyon-ni is secure. Later, Task Force Baker and elements of the 23rd Regiment secure the town, but by that time it is too late to push to Kanyong.

In the 1st Marine Division zone, the attack advances to a point slightly more than five miles from Inje.

In the X Corps sector, the 1st Marine Division (5th and 7th Marines) continues its advance against a vanishing enemy.

May 28

The elements again are uncooperative, preventing any air activity until the afternoon. Nonetheless, activity across the Eighth Army front continues to focus on destroying as many enemy troops as possible. Also, General Ridgway arrives in Korea from Japan to confer with General Van Fleet in Seoul. The conference regards Van Fleet's intent to attack beyond the Kansas and Wyoming Lines and secure the T'ongch'on area near the coast. Van Fleet seeks permission to penetrate farther to engage the enemy troops that escaped the trap that was expected to nab them at Route 24. Ridgway, however, is adamantly opposed to stretching the lines to the T'ongch'on region, which in his opinion would be too risky. Nevertheless, Van Fleet receives authorization to modify the Kansas Line where it stretches east of the Hwach'on Reservoir.

In the I Corps sector, General Milburn plans a three-division advance to the Wyoming Line. The objective of the 1st Cavalry Division on the corps' right becomes the section of the line southwest of Ch'orwon to the Imjin River. The 25th Division is to advance on the right of Route 33 to seize Kumhwa at the eastern point of the triangle, while the 3rd Division drives forward to seize Ch'orwon. The full-scale advance for the I Corps is set for 3 June, followed two days later by the IX Corps.

In the IX Corps sector, General Hoge, like General Milburn in the X Corps sector, plans for a three-division attack to reach the Wyoming Line. The 7th Division and the ROK 2nd Division are to seize the terrain above Route 17, extending northwest from Hwach'on to the Iron Triangle. In conjunction, the ROK 6th Division is directed to take the territory above the western side of the Hwach'on Reservoir from Route 17 to the Pukham River.

In other activity, at Chiam-ni, the 5th Infantry Regiment and the ROK 19th Regiment continue to mop up. The Chinese, still trapped, surrender in large numbers. The total of captives gained stands at 38,000 troops.

Meanwhile, the 17th Regiment, 7th Division, drives up Route 17 and encounters some tenacious resistance. Nevertheless, the regiment overcomes the Chinese covering forces and pushes to Hwach'on, which it reaches by about 1400.

In related activity, the main body of the ROK 6th Division advances on the right against no opposition, but makes little progress as it reaches the area west of the reservoir. Consequently, the Chinese still have open escape routes near the Hwach'on Reservoir. The air observation flights that resume during the afternoon discover that the area below the reservoir had surely been evacuated.

Meanwhile, the 17th Infantry Regiment pushes beyond the village of Hwach'on. But the 20th Chinese Army, which slipped through the lines, posts elements above the village that halt the advance. In addition to the disciplined troops north and east of Hwach'on, other elements of the Chinese 20th Army raise ferocious opposition farther west against the advance of the 24th Division and the ROK 2nd Division.

May 29

At Seoul, the talks between Generals Ridgway and Van Fleet conclude. General Van Fleet is directed to provide Ridgway with a blueprint that estimates the Eighth Army situation as far out as sixty days. In conjunction, the report is also to include Van Fleet's suggestions for future operations. With regard to the advance to the Wyoming and Kansas Lines, Ridgway anticipates strong opposition in the terrain below the Iron Triangle and along the flanks there. Nonetheless, it is thought that the objectives can be achieved within two weeks.

In the X Corps sector, the 5th and 7th Marines each encounter tenacious enemy resistance. Calls are made to get immediate air support; however, the Marines still are not able to maintain direct support from the Marine squadrons. The Marines request 92 sorties and receive only 55. In addition, only 20 are handled by Marine Corsairs or Panther jets. Thirty-five sorties are executed by Air Force Mustangs and jets. Marines who are accustomed to immediate and direct support are essentially left to clear the resistance from the ground. Most flights arrive between two and four hours late. In one incident within the 5th Marines zone, Company C, 1st Battalion, becomes heavily engaged near Kwagch'i-dong.

A rifleman and scout, PFC Whitt L. Moreland, uses his skills to support the elimination of an obstinate position. Moreland afterward leads a detachment against a heavily fortified bunker. As the unit approaches the obstacle, enemy grenades land in their midst. Moreland shoves a few away, but one remains to endanger him and others nearby. He dives on it to save the lives of the others. PFC Moreland receives the Medal of Honor posthumously for his selfless sacrifice.

In Naval activity, the USS *Stickell* (DD 888) and USS *Burlington* (PF 51) land a raiding party near Songjin. A few small boats are destroyed. The party sustains no casualties.

May 30   By this date, Eighth Army is back on the Kansas Line. Subsequent to the recent discussions with General Ridgway, General Van Fleet makes preparations to carry out Eighth Army objectives, which will also include contingency plans. While plans are being drawn for the advance (Operation PILE DRIVER), the weather again acts against the operation. Heavy rains strike across the area and continue during the following day, causing nasty consequences for the troops and vehicles that must move along the water-clogged ground and roads. While the I and IX Corps prepare to attack, it becomes evident, as predicted by General Ridgway, that the Communists are willing to pay a huge price to hold the Iron Triangle. Patrols from each corps encounter resistance.

May 31   According to reports, the enemy sustains more than 62,000 casualties during the U.S. counterattack, which began on 20 May. When the Chinese offensive is added, enemy casualties rise to more than 73,000 and include 44,705 killed, 19,753 wounded and 8,749 captured. Of the casualties, the 1st Marine Division reports 1,870 killed (counted) and 593 captured. Eighth Army estimates of enemy casualties for the last half of May include 17,000 killed (counted) and 17,000 POWs. Eighth Army reports 33,770 casualties for all of May, with most sustained by the South Koreans. American casualties amount to 745 killed, 4,218 wounded and 572 missing. In addition, Eighth Army sustains 6,758 non-battle casualties, mostly from disease.

In the IX Corps sector, the casualties for May, including the Chinese offensive and the U.S. counterattack, amount to 341 killed, 2,011 wounded and 195 missing.

In the X Corps sector, 1st Marine Division zone, the 7th Marines encounter a treacherous pass that leads into Yanggu. The Marines atop the ridges that overlook the pass begin a slow and methodical descent to clear the enemy. General Van Fleet, who happens to be at the 7th Marines' positions, looks up at the towering ridges and in amazement asks: "How did you ever get the men up those cliffs?" Colonel Nickerson responds with a succinct answer: "They climbed." By dusk, the Marines complete their descent, evict the enemy and gain control of Yanggu and its airfield as well as the surrounding heights. In the meantime, the 5th Marines reaches positions about 6,000 yards northeast of Yanggu. During the month of May, the 1st Marine Division sustains 75 killed, 8 who die of their wounds, and 731 are wounded in action.

In other activity, the enemy launches an attack against Hill 120, defended by a contingent of the 187th Airborne Regiment. The Communists support the

ground troops with artillery, machine guns and mortars. The diminutive force, attached to Company G, is unable to withstand the superior numbers of attackers because of expending their ammunition. The platoon is ordered to withdraw.

Corporal Rodolfo P. Hernandez, although wounded, attempts to hold the line while the others retire. Hernandez fires into the rushing forces until his weapon fails. The sentinel continues to battle with a rifle and bayonet until his wound (a combination of a grenade, bayonet and a bullet) forces him to drop in place, unconscious. However, his actions save the others and they return to retake the ground. Corporal Hernandez is awarded the Medal of Honor for his extraordinary courage in the face of the enemy.

In Air Force activity, Fifth Air Force initiates Operation STRANGLE, designed to destroy the supply lines of the enemy. Also, a contingent of B-29s is intercepted by MiGs in the vicinity of Sinuiju. The Superfortresses and their escort planes engage the attack force and when the air battle subsides, the Russians lose four MiGs, against no U.S. losses. The gunners aboard the B-29s take out one of the MiGs and two others are downed by the Sabre jets.

In Naval activity, Rear Admiral A.A. Burke, recently appointed commanding officer, Cruiser Division 5, aboard the USS *Los Angeles* (CA 135), arrives off the east coast of Korea and assumes command of Bombline Element (TE 9.28).

Summer 1951   During the summer, the Soviets and the Chinese have amassed about 445 MiG-15s across the Yalu River, where they remain safe from U.S. forces. Far East Air Forces, at this time, has only 89 F-86s (Sabre jets) in its force. Only 44 are assigned to the 4th Fighter Interceptor Wing, which greatly curtails its efficiency against the MiGs. To add to the dilemma, at times due to maintenance, about half remain out of service.

Lieutenant General Otto P. Weyland, recently appointed FEAF commander, has constantly requested additional planes but his pleas are met by deaf ears in Washington. The consensus in D.C. continues to focus on the Soviet threat to Europe. The massive cutbacks in the military following the close of World War II continue to hurt the troops in the theater. Nonetheless, the top brass in the Air Force will begin to replace the F-86As with F-86Es, but not on a large scale; rather, one at a time.

It is well that the E-model, featuring a "flying tail" (a horizontal stabilizer moving as one unit) and hydraulically powered flight controls that substantially increased maneuverability, begin to arrive, because the 4th FIW is now faced with an improved MiG, the MiG-15bis. This version has a more powerful engine that gives it a higher maximum speed and a greater operational altitude.

June 1   Eighth Army issues orders to all Corps to bolster the Kansas and Wyoming Lines. In conjunction with General Ridgway's recent instructions to

General Van Fleet to suspend any major attacks toward the T'onch'on region, each corps is directed to initiate only limited attacks and strong reconnaissance missions in addition to their normal patrols.

In an effort to further solidify the defensive line, all civilians are moved from an area five miles behind the Kansas line to a point above the line where forward patrol bases are located. The relocation of the civilians permits the troops to more easily deal with and identify the enemy, while the defenses are being more heavily fortified.

The full-scale attack is scheduled to jump off in the I Corps area on 3 June. In the meantime, on this day the weather clears, but the enemy resistance continues to be aggressive.

In the X Corps sector, 1st Marine Division zone, the 5th and 7th Marines launch an attack toward the Kansas Line. The 2nd Battalion, 5th Marines, encounters fierce resistance at Hill 651, defended by about 200 North Koreans. The attacks by noon are still unable to dislodge the Communists, but air strikes are requested to quicken the eviction. Four Marine planes arrive and plaster the slopes with bombs and strafing runs, which succeed in cracking the defense wide open. The Marines afterward push forward and seize the hill.

Also, 1st Marine Aircraft Wing initiates its plan of deploying one squadron at Hoengeong, which is located to the rear of the 1st Marine Division.

In Air Force activity, a band of 22 MiGs attacks a group of B-29s attached to the 343th Bomber Squadron. One of the B-29s is shot down, but the Superfortresses' gunners down two of the MiGs. The Russians again, after failing to make progress against U.S.

pilots, sink into temporary invisibility and do not return to the skies until 17 June. Also, one other B-29 is damaged.

In other activity, a flight of F-86s, attached to the 336th Fighter Interceptor Squadron, encounters a band of 18 MiGs near Sinanju while it is escorting a B-26 bombing mission. A U.S. Navy exchange pilot, Lieutenant Simpson Evans, Jr., attached to 336th Fighter-Interceptor Squadron, 4th Fighter-Interceptor Group, gets the victory. The plane is set afire and the wing falls off, causing the MiG to crash.

Another pilot attached to the 336th Squadron, Captain Richard O. Ransbottom, also gets one of the MiGs. Ransbottom knocks the MiG out after three bursts of machine gun fire. The pilot is able to eject, but his plane crashes in flames.

In yet other activity, Far East Air Forces Special Air Mission transports a group of fifteen South Koreans that parachute behind enemy line on a mission to gather components of a crashed MiG. The entire contingent is captured.

—*In Japan,* Major General Frank F. Everest, USAF, assumes command of the Fifth Air Force (Major General Edward J. Timberlake had been in temporary command after General Stratemeyer suffered a heart attack and was hospitalized).

— *In the United States:* The 3rd Marine Brigade is activated at Camp Pendleton, California.

June 2   *In the I Corps sector,* final preparations are made for the attack scheduled for the following day.

In the 25th Division zone, a contingent of Company

A U.S. observation plane is on a mission above mountains in search of enemy movements and positions.

C, 24th Regiment, engages an entrenched enemy position in the vicinity of Chipo-ri. The platoon leading the attack gets stalled by intense fire. The platoon leader becomes wounded, but he is evacuated. Meanwhile, Sergeant Cornelius H. Charlton assumes command, then continues the attack by ascending farther up the slope, despite the heavy fire. Charlton takes the point and single-handedly eliminates two gun positions and six defenders. Soon the platoon is again stalled by heavy fire. Undaunted, Charlton leads yet another attack, until he is felled by grenades. Despite a serious chest wound, Charlton refuses medical aid and instead leads yet another charge that seizes the ridge.

Upon gaining the crest, Charlton notices that the reverse slope contains another gun emplacement. Singlehandedly, Charlton drives straight into the position and takes it out with grenades. The company gains control of the hill and the enemy retires. Charlton, however, succumbs from his wounds. He is awarded the Medal of Honor posthumously for his extraordinary leadership in the face of the enemy and for his tremendous individual heroism.

In the IX Corps sector, patrols continue, but the jump-off for the main assault remains three days off.

In the X Corps sector, 1st Marine Division zone, the 1st Battalion, 5th Marines, advances toward the Kansas Line. Intense enemy fire holds up the advance until tanks arrive to add some punch to the drive. The tanks pour fire into the log bunkers, providing time for the Marines to reach the forward slope of Hill 610. Meanwhile, the 2nd Battalion, 5th Marines, continues to drive along a parallel ridge. The enemy positions on Hill 610 are completely eliminated by 1945. Afterward, the 2nd Battalion jumps out and advances another 5,000 yards. Later, the enemy mounts a failed counterattack against Hill 610.

In other activity, the 1st Marines prepares to relieve the 7th Marines as ordered the previous night. The 1st Marines arrives at the assembly area at 0630, but shortly thereafter, an enemy mortar strikes a gathering of officers, killing the artillery liaison officer and wounding four company commanders. More than thirty enlisted men are wounded. Lieutenant Colonel Homer E. Hire is unharmed. Nevertheless, the scheduled operation to pass through the 7th Marines and continue the attack is suspended until the following day.

In Naval activity, the *Begor* (APD 127) and Underwater Demolition Team 3 (UDT 3), operating on the east coast of Korea in the vicinity of Kojo, lands a group of ROK guerrillas on Song-do Island during the night of June 2–3.

June 3   Operation PILE DRIVER commences. The I Corps launches its advance from the Kansas Line to the Wyoming Line. It encounters tenacious resistance as the Chinese anchor themselves to hold the Iron Triangle. Following a couple of clear days, the rains again descend upon Eighth Army sectors to further hamper the advance.

In the X Corps zone, the 1st Marines, which had sus-

pended the attack for one day, moves out to seize the objective, designated X-RAY. The 2nd Battalion, 1st Marines, drives toward Hill 516, while the 3rd Battalion advances along a parallel ridge. Planes attached to VMF-214 and VMF-323 support the advances and the objective is secure by 1900.

Also, the 1st Battalion, 5th Marines, supported by air attacks, drives to seize Hill 680, which falls by about 1400. Then the Marines move against nearby Hill 692. Air support is requested after the attacking force is halted by intense enemy fire. However, fog sets in and delays the planes. At about 1600, the attack is resumed without air cover, but as the Marines approach the summit, the planes arrive to drop napalm. The Marines scatter to avoid becoming casualties of the friendly fire. While they run to seek cover, enemy fire inflicts some casualties. Once the planes complete their passes, Company A reinitiates the attack and gains Hill 692.

The day's fighting terminates the Battle of Soyang-gang, which had begun on 16 May. The Marines continue the offensive in their new zone of responsibility, east of the Hwach'on Reservoir.

In Air Force activity, during a resupply flight, friendly ground artillery fire downs two C-119s as they are in the process of dropping supplies. The tragedy compels the U.S. to change its method of identification to distinguish friend from foe during the Air Force's air-drop flights.

June 4   Bad weather and continuing stiff oppositions impedes the advance of the I Corps as it punches its way toward the Wyoming Line.

In the X Corps sector, the ROK 5th Division advances toward the Kansas Line in coordination with the 1st Marine Division, the latter already on the move toward the line and the Punch Bowl.

In other activity, the 1st Korean Marine Corps Regiment relieves the 5th Marines. The Korean Marines receive the task of seizing Hill 1316 (Taeam-san).

In the ROK I Corps sector, the Corps has advanced against light opposition and by this date, its three divisions reach and deploy along the Kansas Line to protect the area that stretches across a ridge to the front of Route 24.

In Naval activity, Marine Fighter Squadron VMF-312 departs the USS *Bataan* (CVL 29) for Itami Air Force Base, Japan.

June 5   Two F-80s on patrol spot several Communist MiG-15s at 39–52 N, 12–50 E, the deepest southern penetration by enemy jet fighters at this point in the conflict, with the exception of one incident the previous year, when a naval helicopter had come under attack in the same zone during December 1950.

Also, the IX Corps commences its advance to the Wyoming Line. Like the I Corps, it too becomes hindered by inclement weather and tough resistance as it slowly grinds forward.

In the X Corps sector, 1st Marine Division zone, the Korean Marines move to seize Hill 1316, defended by North Koreans who had been directed by the Chinese to "hold until death." The hill is located in extremely nasty terrain and the battle to gain it lasts five day without any success by the Korean Marines. On 10 June, the strategy to take the hill changes.

In the 7th Division zone, a contingent of Company I, 31st Regiment, led by 1st Lieutenant Benjamin F. Wilson, moves against an obstinate enemy position in the vicinity of Hwach'on–Myon. The vanguard gets stalled as it presses ahead, but Wilson speeds to the point and takes his own action. He drills toward the position with his rifle and grenades, takes out the position and its four defenders, then races forward to the next obstacle. Wilson, leading a charge with his troops' bayonets fixed, takes the next obstacle and about 27 defenders are eliminated. The Communists mount a counterattack to regain the ground, but again, Wilson takes action before his command, which is regrouping, can be overwhelmed.

Single-handedly, Lieutenant Wilson bolts forward, takes out seven of the attackers and wounds two others. The enemy, apparently stunned Wilson's action, retreats hurriedly. The contingent then completes its regrouping and moves against its primary objective, but when it reaches a point about fifteen yards from it, the enemy commences fire. The fire becomes impenetrable, which compels the troops to pull back. During the withdrawal, Wilson becomes wounded.

Meanwhile, the enemy mounts yet another counterattack. The company resists, but the company commander and the platoon leader become wounded. Wilson, despite his own wound, leads a counterattack and throws the enemy back, buying enough time for the company to make a disciplined withdrawal. Lieutenant Wilson becomes a recipient of the Medal of Honor for his services above and beyond the call of duty.

In Air Force activity, Colonel Ralph H. 'Salty' Saltzman assumes command of the 18th Fighter Bomber Group. He succeeds Colonel William P. McBride.

June 6–8 1951   The Chinese continue to resist in front of the Iron Triangle, but the I and IX Corps maintain pressure, which finally punctures the enemy lines on 8 June.

In the X Corps sector, 1st Marine Division zone, the 1st Marines continue to advance against building resistance.

June 6   *In the X Corps sector, 1st Marine Division zone,* the advance to the Kansas Line continues. The Marines' objectives are five ridgelines that run northwest to southeast along the Kansas Line. At 1300, the 5th Marines moves out to seize Hill 729. Air support does not arrive until 1400 due to fog. Nevertheless, by 2100, the 2nd and 3rd Battalions, 5th Marines, regroup on the first ridge and for the next ten days, they secure the four remaining ridges.

June 7   In the IX Corps sector, 7th Division zone, the Communists launch an attack against a contingent of Company F, 31st Regiment's perimeter near Pachidong. Elements of the company are deployed on two strategic hills separated by a large saddle. The enemy strikes at 0300 and the fire immediately becomes fierce. Four of the defenders are immediately wounded, but while the contingents defend, the wounded are

Sikorsky helicopter is on a dangerous slope, held down by Marines during high winds.

A Marine casualty receives plasma from a medic after being wounded by a mine. Four other Marines also sustained wounds from the explosion.

evacuated. A machine gun manned by PFC Jack G. Hanson becomes extremely important, situated where it can protect the command post and the weapons platoon. Hanson volunteers to hold his position to permit the platoon to withdraw to more tenable positions. The 1st Platoon is able to retire and regroup for a counterattack.

Soon after, the assault is launched and the ground is regained. PFC Hanson remains at his machine gun, but he had been killed. His machine gun had expended its ammunition but Hanson remained at his post. He is discovered with his pistol in his right hand, a blood-ied machete in is left hand, surrounded by 22 dead enemy troops. PFC Jack Hanson is awarded the Medal of Honor posthumously for his extraordinary courage in the face of a superior numbered enemy.

In Air Force activity, Far East Air Forces initiates a three-day campaign by B-26s and B-29s that saturates enemy positions in the Iron Triangle during the darkened hours. The planes drop radar-directed 500-pound bombs that burst over the heads of the enemy troops and spread fragments over a wide area. The Air Force's campaign is designed to loosen the resistance against imminent attacks by the friendly ground troops.

A Sikorsky helicopter approaches a landing site to evacuate wounded Marines.

In Naval activity, a raiding party debarks from the USS *Rupertus* (DD 851) at Songjin and soon after comes under enemy fire. The contingent returns to the ship without sustaining any casualties. Three prisoners (North Koreans) are seized and carried back to the ship.

June 8 The Communists' resistance cracks and the I and IX Corps increase the pace of their respective advances toward the Wyoming Line.

In the X Corps sector, 1st Marine Division zone, the Marines continue to advance toward the Kansas Line, but Major General Gerard C. Thomas becomes concerned about climbing casualties. He commits the greater part of the reserve 7th Marines to add more strength to the attack. Only the 3rd Battalion, 7th Marines, remains in division reserve.

In other activity, the ROK 7th Division is ordered to drive above the eastern sector of the Hwach'on Reservoir to secure it and gain the Kansas Line. The 1st Marine Division drives against North Korean resistance in front of the lower portion of the Punch Bowl.

June 9–11 1951 Elements of the I and IX Corps reach their objectives at the Wyoming Line. Communist forces have withdrawn farther north.

In the X Corps sector, the advance to the Kansas Line continues.

June 9 *In the X Corps sector, 1st Marine Division zone,* the reserves (7th Marines) join the advance to the Punch Bowl. Heavy resistance continues, but the Marines also face especially nasty terrain and lousy weather. The advance is hindered by many natural obstacles, including landslides that frequently block the routes and at times cause vehicles to veer off the roads. Frequent fog also creates problems by preventing air cover.

In the 1st Marines zone, during the early morning hours as the 2nd Battalion prepares to advance, an enemy mortar barrage strikes the lines just prior to an enemy attack by a company-sized contingent of North Koreans. The attack is easily repelled and the North Koreans sustain heavy casualties. After eliminating the North Korean attackers, the advance jumps off on schedule and as the 1st and 2nd Battalions advance, the resistance continues to be heavy. Nonetheless, prior to noon, the Marines seize the first ridge and by 1600, with the support of elements of the regimental anti-tank company, the second ridge is gained.

In the 7th Marines zone, the 1st Battalion advances along the ridgeline, while the 2nd Battalion punches forward through the valley to secure Hill 420. The North Koreans raise heavy resistance, primarily from mortars and artillery fire; however, the Marines secure the hill prior to dusk. The Marines count 85 N.K. dead and they capture sixteen others.

In Naval activity, in an effort to expedite the exchange of information between TF-77 and forces in the vicinity of Wonsan, the U.S. Navy initiates an air drop and pick-up station on Yo-Do Island.

June 10 *In the I Corps sector,* elements of the 3rd Division, ROK 9th Division and the 10th Philippine Battalion seize high ground south of Ch'orwon. In the meantime, the 25th Division and the Turkish Brigade reach positions within several miles of Kumhwa.

In the X Corps area, the ROK 7th Division arrives at

U.S. Army engineers move in front of a tank along a road south of Ch'orwon on 10 June to clear any mines laid by the enemy.

the Kansas Line, the objective of Operation DETO-NATE. The Marines, meanwhile, trudge across the rugged terrain against heavy resistance and make only slow progress.

In the 1st Marine Division zone, enemy resistance prompts a change in strategy. General Almond confers with Colonel Wilbur S. Brown (Commander, 1st Marines) and afterward, by 1100, the entire 2nd Battalion is committed to bolster the assault. During the ferocious contest, Corporal Charles G. Abrell, Company E, 2nd Battalion, 1st Marines, participates in a charge against a fortified enemy gun position. Abrell, already wounded, closes on the position, but he is hit twice more while he is at the point within striking distance of the obstacle. Despite, or possibly because of, the three wounds, Abrell continues to advance, while he calls for the others to follow. With a grenade in his hand, Abrell pulls the pin and dives into the bunker. The entire enemy gun crew is killed and Corporal Abrell is mortally wounded. Corporal Abrell is awarded the Medal of Honor posthumously for is selfless courage in the face of the enemy.

The Communists raise tenacious resistance throughout the day. By dusk, both battalions are short of their objectives and although many Communists had been liquidated by grenades and bayonets, they still hold steadfastly. The 11th Marines in support of the attack

coordinate their fire and deliver a relentless barrage to soften the resistance. In addition, air strikes bolster the ground troops, but in the end, it is the infantry that finally evicts the defenders from their log bunkers. The Marines secure their final objective including Hill 802 prior to midnight (10th-11th). The Marine casualties for this attack include 14 killed in action and 114 wounded in action. The 1st Battalion, 1st Marines, which seized Hill 802, sustains 9 killed and 97 wounded.

Colonel Brown moves to the front to observe the final assault. Later, he states: "It was a glorious spectacle, that last bayonet assault. In the last analysis, 2/1 had to take its objective with the bayonet and hand grenades, gnawing its way up the side of a mountain to get at the enemy. It was bloody work, the hardest fighting I have ever seen."

Also, the 1st Korean Marine Regiment, following five days of failed attempts to gain Hill 1316, at 2000 prepares to mount a night attack. The defenders are caught completely off guard when they are struck by the weight of three battalions at 0200 on the 11th.

In other activity, the ROK 5th Regiment secures its objectives during the morning hours.

In Air Force activity, the 315th Air Division is able to expand its resupply operations with the opening of the airfield at Chunchon to cargo planes. The airfield, located slightly below the 38th Parallel, about fifty miles northeast of Seoul, expands the ability of the planes to resupply the troops in the field by air drop.

In Naval activity, two PB4Y-2 planes initiate action to assist the night operations. The aircraft drop flares to illuminate the target areas for Marine Squadron VMF-323.

— *In Japan:* Lt. General Otto P. Weyland assumes command in Tokyo of Far East Air Forces, replacing General Partridge. Partridge had been commanding officer of Fifth Air Force until May 21, when he succeeded General Stratemeyer as commander FEAF.

June 11 *In the I Corps sector,* the Communists, facing pressure from the 3rd Division, ROK 9th Division and the Turkish Brigade, abandon Ch'orwon and Kumhwa. The gains of the 3rd and 25th Divisions continue to press the Communists. Two tank-infantry forces drive across the Iron Triangle to P'yonggang and enter it on the 13th.

In the X Corps zone, 1st Marine Division sector, the 1st Marines recuperates for only a short while following the tenacious battle on the previous day. The advance continues with the 3rd Battalion taking the lead; however, by this date, the North Koreans in front of the advancing 1st Marines are no longer able to raise strong resistance. By 14 June, the Marines reach the Brown Line, an extension of the Kansas Line.

In other activity, the 1st Korean Marine Corps Regiment launches a full-scale attack, turning the table on the North Koreans defending Hill 1316 and the adjacent ridges. The defenders, totally surprised, are unable to react quickly enough to resist the three-battalion onslaught. Hill 1122 falls and the enemy withdraws from the shoulder, providing the Korean Marines an easy task to seize Taeam-san (Hill 1316). The Korean Marines sustain about 500 casualties during the operation.

In Air Force activity, an F-51, while on a mission, gets shot down in the vicinity of Kyomipo. The pilot ejects and lands in the Taedong River. A rescue plane attached to the 3rd ARS arrives to pick up the pilot at just about dusk and despite enemy fire originating on either side of the river, the SA-16, with its lights off, safely passes low hanging electrical transmission wires, then lands on the river, which is filled with debris and rocks. Nevertheless, the pilot is successfully extricated.

June 12 The I and IX Corps strengthen their positions along the Wyoming Line.

In Naval activity, the USS *Walke* (DD 723) strikes a floating mine at 38–52 N, 129–25 E. Twenty-six enlisted men are killed and 35 receive minor wounds.

June 13 *In the I Corps zone,* patrols from Ch'orwon and Kumhwa push forward to P'yonggang at the tip of the Iron Triangle and enter the town without incident. Although the town is deserted, the Chinese have not totally abandoned the region. They are redeployed in dominating ground northeast and northwest of P'yonggang. The patrols, detecting the enemy strength, then pull back out of the town.

In the IX Corps sector, Chinese forces are detected northeast of Kumsong.

In the X Corps sector, North Koreans hold positions east of the Hwach'on Reservoir.

June 14 The USS *Thompson* (DMS 38), while operating against the enemy off Songjin on the 99th day of the siege, sustains fourteen hits by shore batteries. The vessel sustains some damage and in addition, three men are killed and another three are wounded. One other seaman receives a superficial wound.

June 15 By this day, all geographical objectives of Operation PILE DRIVER are attained. Also, an infantry battalion from Colombia arrives in Korea. Colombia is the final member country to send ground troops to the United Nations forces. However, some additional British units (headquarters and service contingents) also arrive during June. The British units would later, during the latter part of July, be formed with other United Kingdom contingents as the 1st Commonwealth Brigade.

In Air Force activity, Fifth Air Force headquarters, located at Taegu, relocates again to Seoul.

June 16 By this date, Eighth Army achieves its objectives, as elements of all units have arrived at their respective positions along the Wyoming-Kansas Line.

In the X Corps sector, The 1st Marine Division reaches its objective, a line extending from the Hwach'on Reservoir to the Punch Bowl.

June 17 *In the I Corps sector,* the Communists reoccupy P'yonggang.

In the X Corps sector, the advance continues toward the Kansas Line. The 7th Marines, which had joined in the attack on the 9th, still lacks the 3rd Battalion, but it prepares to come out of reserve on the following day. The 3rd Battalion, 7th Marines, is at this time the sole unit in division reserve.

In Air Force activity, a band of about 25 MiGs attacks a formation of Sabre jets near the Yalu River in the vicinity of Sinuiju. The enemy is especially aggressive, but to no avail. The U.S. sustains no losses; however, the Communists sustain one MiG destroyed and six others damaged. The MiG is downed by Captain Samuel Pesacreta, attached to the 4th Fighter-Interceptor Group. Captain Pesacreta's contingent of four F-86s had been attacked by eight MiGs.

Also, a Polikarpov Po–2 biplane, a type of aircraft from the pre–World War II days dubbed "Bedcheck Charlie," makes a usual bombing run over Seoul. The plane, which rarely scores great damage and can hardly reach 100 miles per hour, scores a big hit on this day. Its bomb strikes the ramp at Suwon and destroys one Sabre jet of the 335th Fighter Interceptor Squadron and inflicts damage on eight others.

— *In Japan:* Fifth Air Force issues a warning, stating that the Communists have increased their number of planes in Korea from about 800 in mid–May to about 1,050 at present. Despite constant air strikes against the Communists' airfields in North Korea, the fields remain operable. At this time there are an estimated 58 Communist divisions in Korea. The U.S.–U.N. air strikes have not halted the flow of supplies and ammunition that continues to arrive to maintain their resources.

June 18 *In the X Corps sector, 1st Marine Division zone,* the advance closes on the east-west hill that identifies the Brown Line. The terrain is too difficult to mount an attack except directly from the front. The enemy-held ridge is defended by the 1st Battalion, 41st Regiment, N.K. 12th Division. The Marines ascend the ridge and just as they approach the crest, the North Koreans, concealed on the opposite slope, launch an attack. Company G, 7th Marines holds solidly and repels five successive charges. Company I participates in the fifth enemy assault and it, too, refuses to budge. At about dusk, the brutal contest ends. The Marines establish night positions and prepare to resume the attack on the following morning.

In Air Force activity, a group of 40 MiGs encounters and intercepts a formation of F-86 Sabre jets during the morning to ignite another wild fight in the skies. The Russians fare poorly and lose a minimum of five of their MiGs, two of which are downed by Lieutenant Ralph D. Gibson. Nevertheless, the Russians do shoot down one Sabre jet, the second Sabre lost during the war. Another pilot, Captain Erwin A. Hesse, 4th Fighter-Interceptor Group, also receives credit for downing one of the MiGs.

In Naval activity, the USS *Evans* (DD 754), operating off Wonsan, comes under fire by enemy shore guns, but no major damage is sustained; however, some sailors receive minor wounds.

June 19 *In the X Corps sector, 1st Marine Division zone,* the Marines prepare to complete the seizure of the ridge along the Brown Line, but the enemy absconded during the night (18th-19th).

In Air Force activity, again a band of MiGs intercepts

and engages a formation of F-86 Sabre jets in MiG Alley. It is the third consecutive day that the Russians have come out to fight. The Sabre jets manage to damage four MiGs, but one Sabre jet is lost.

— *In the United States:* President Truman signs a bill that lowers the age of those eligible to be drafted to eighteen and one-half.

June 20 *In the X Corps sector, 1st Marine Division zone,* the modified Kansas Line is completely secure by noon. Preparations to bolster the line are begun immediately.

In Air Force activity, F-51 Mustangs intercept the contingent of six Il-10s (Ilyushins). Two of the enemy craft are shot from the sky, but neither kill is officially credited to the pilots. Three others are damaged. One of the pilots to get a victory is Lieutenant James B. Harrison. It is the last official kill by an F-51 pilot during the conflict.

While the Mustangs engage the Il-10s, MiGs arrive, but at the same time, Sabre jets arrive to bolster the F-51s. During the air battle, one of the MiGs moves away from the Sabres and hits one of the Mustangs with shells that rip off one of its wings. The pilot is unable to bail out and goes down with his plane.

In Naval activity, Rear Admiral G.C. Dyer relieves Rear Admiral A.E. Smith as Commander United Nations Blockading and Escort Force (CTF 95). Also, carrier planes encounter MiGs while operating against enemy propeller aircraft along the west coast of Korea. It is the first recorded incident of MiGs coming to the support of conventional aircraft under attack.

In other activity, the USS *Brinkley Bass* (DD 887) initiates SCAB (ship control of aircraft bombing) when it controls and guides a B-26 bomber-run in the vicinity of Wonsan.

June 21 *In the X Corps sector, 1st Marine Division zone,* the 1st Marines and the 1st Korean Marine Corps Regiment stretch their right and left flanks respectively,

A squadron of F-86 Sabre jets prepares to take off for MiG Alley.

which pinches out the 7th Marines. The 7th Marines revert to reserve.

June 22   The 1st Marine Division, as of this date, terminates two months of continuous fighting against the Chinese spring offensive. The Marines are directed by Eighth Army to establish patrol bases on the Badger Line, but when General Almond arrives at the 1st Marine Division command post, it is decided that stretching out patrol bases while units are still in contact with the enemy is risky and the idea is shelved. However, on the following day, again orders arrive directing the patrol bases be set up.

June 23   The 1st Marine Division is again instructed to establish patrol bases. The order is reluctantly carried out. The Marines are aware that each of the three battalion patrol bases will become susceptible to enemy incursions and may be encircled and imperiled.

— ***In the United States:*** A hint of a possible cease fire in Korea is spoken by the Soviet representative to the U.N. during a broadcast (U.N. Price of Peace) in which Jacob Malik claims that the warfare in Korea is the fault of the United States. However, toward the end of the program, Malik slips in the proposition that the Soviet Union thinks that the war could be stopped by mutual agreement of both sides pulling back from the 38th Parallel.

The U.S. shows no outward signs of accepting the suggestion as genuine, but steps are taken in the event that a cease fire might be in the works. Diplomatically, the U.S. probes to discern the credibility of Malik's remarks. Militarily, the Joint Chiefs of Staff and Eighth Army assess the situation on the ground in Korea to determine where a dominating line should be drawn prior to any talks with the Communists.

June 24   (Korea) In the I Corps area, 3rd Division zone, the Communists launch a strong assault at about 0200 against the 15th Regiment sector. About two battalions chash against the perimeter. Company B, holds firmly for awhile, but the overwhelming strength threatens the entire line. PFC Emory L. Bennett bolts from his foxhole carrying his automatic rifle to attempt to stem the tide, while his outfit regroups. All the while, the enemy continues to press forward and some penetration occurs. Orders to pull back are given, but Bennett, although wounded, volunteers to maintain his one-man defensive line. In conjunction, the contingent safely pulls back, thanks to the rear guard fire, attributed to Bennet's weapon. Nonetheless, PFC Bennett sacrifices his life to save the others. Bennett is awarded the Medal of Honor posthumously for his extraordinary heroism and his selfless sacrifice to save the remainder of the command.

— ***In the Soviet Union:*** In a move that catches the attention of the U.S., two newspapers in the Soviet Union publish the entire context of the recent statement made by Jacob Malik with regard to a cease fire in Korea. The article signals Soviet approval of a cease

fire. On the following day, influential newspapers in China publish Malik's statement. The U.S. senses that the Communists are ready to initiate talks to bring about a cease fire.

June 25   A staff officer from headquarters in Japan arrives in Korea to discuss strategy with General Van Fleet regarding where the line should be drawn with regard to negotiations with the Communists. The possible location considered by General Ridgway and Van Fleet had been the Kansas Line, but Ridgway is considering a forward line about twenty miles above the Kansas Line and another ten miles out front as an outpost line. General Van Fleet is not in favor of extending beyond the Kansas Line due to the possibility of unnecessary casualties, but only recently, during the counterattack, it had been Van Fleet that had been in favor of a much deeper penetration.

Also, one year has passed since the Communists unleashed their invasion of South Korea on June 25, 1950. Since that fateful day, about 1,250,000 men have been killed, wounded or captured. Of those horrific numbers, about one million of the casualties have been the Communist Chinese and the North Koreans. Other victims include about two million civilians who died from various causes, including warfare and disease. The Communists, one year after the invasion, hold much less territory, having lost about 2,100 square miles. In addition to the massive loss of equipment, including 391 planes, 1,000 artillery pieces and countless small arms, North Korea has been reduced to rubble.

Essentially, by this time, the Chinese Communists under Mao Tse-tung's "volunteers" had sustained a devastating defeat and a loss of face as the great offensive (Fifth Phase) failed to gain any objectives and surely Seoul would not become a present by May Day as promised. Although Eighth Army initially sustained tremendous setbacks due to being unprepared for the conflict, at this time the Eighth Army is at a razor's point and Generals Ridgway and Van Fleet are prepared to finish the job and bring victory to the people of the Republic of South Korea. But diplomacy and the situation in Washington are prodding to turn to the peace table and settle on a stalemate. General Ridgway is informed this day by the Joint Chiefs of Staff that cease-fire negotiations are expected to begin soon.

In Air Force activity, the 8th Fighter Bomber Group moves its operations to Kimpo Air Base in Seoul, subsequent to repairs being completed on the runway to lengthen it. The unit reinitiates its combat sorties from there, while work continues on the runway.

In other activity, a flight of F-86 Sabres, led by Captain Milton E. Nelson (335th Fighter-Interceptor Squadron, 4th Fighter-Interceptor Group), encounters a large force of enemy planes in the vicinity of Sinuiju. The American patrol comes under attack. Captain Nelson maneuvers and gets behind one of the MiG-15s. Nelson knocks the MiG from the sky, leaving the enemy 24-plane contingent short one aircraft. Nelson, who had won a victory in the same area on 20 May, will achieve others here on 9 July and 11 July.

June 26 *In the X Corps sector, 1st Marine Division zone,* a contingent of Marines pushes out ahead of the perimeter and establishes a patrol base on Hill 761; however, the isolated battalion comes under heavy mortar fire and by the following day, it is ordered back to the main lines.

In Air Force activity, the recently arrived 136th Fighter Bomber Wing, which executed its initial combat mission on 24 May, on this day encounters a band of MiGs. The F-84 ThunderJets, while providing an escort to B-29s to the airfield at Yongyu, are intercepted. One of the MiGs is downed and credit is claimed by 1st Lieutenant Arthur E. Olinger and Captain Harry Underwood. The MiG had been able to evade a flight of Sabres before it encountered the ThunderJets. This is the first kill of the war for the Air National Guard.

— *In China:* The Chinese Communists broadcast their approval of cease-fire talks by acknowledging the comments of Jacob Malik, the Soviet representative to the U.N., one day after Chinese newspapers had printed the context of his remarks. However, the Communists stipulate that the U.S. must acquiesce to the often repeated Communist demands that Formosa (Taiwan) is to be returned to Communist (Red) China and all United Nations forces must be withdrawn from Korea. They also demand a seat at the U.N.

June 27 The U.S. notices changes in the Communists' broadcasts. Pyongyang radio continues to encourage the eviction of the U.S.-U.N. forces, but on this day, the statement changes from "drive the enemy to the sea" to "drive the enemy to the 38th Parallel." President Truman authorizes General Ridgway to publicize an offer to negotiate a cease-fire.

In Naval activity, South Korean guerrillas bolstered by U.S. naval surface ships spring a raid on enemy-held Chong Ye-ri, on the west coast of Korea. The guerrillas seize several prisoners and they destroy two ammunition depots.

— *In the Soviet Union:* The U.S. directs its ambassador to the Soviet Union in Moscow to inquire about the Soviet positions with regard to the demands of the Chinese on the previous day. Deputy Foreign Minister Andrei Gromyko informs Ambassador Alan G. Kirk that the position of the Soviet Union does not include any contingencies such as territorial claims; rather the talks from the perspective of the Soviets should be confined to military matters. The Soviets, through Gromyko, inform the U.S. representative that territorial and political matters should be discussed later and separately from the military matters.

June 29 Enemy shore batteries in the vicinity of Wonsan harbor return fire against the USS *Tucker*

(DDE 875). The vessel sustains some minor damage and one man is slightly wounded.

June 30 A Marine Tigercat squadron (VMF 513) known as the Flying Nightmares engages and destroys a PO-2 above Seoul by the Han River. It is the first PO-2 downed by an F7F. The PO-2s are not constructed of metal and while they had been raiding the area around Seoul, the Marine squadrons had difficulty tracking them, as they avoided detection by radar.

The strength of the Marine Corps on this date stands at 192,620 men.

In Naval activity, the siege of Wonsan, which includes a naval bombardment, continues on this, the 134th consecutive day.

— *In Japan:* Following a long period of political maneuvering in the U.S., the U.N. and by the Russians and Chinese, the stage is set by Washington to delegate General Ridgway to publicly offer a cease fire in Korea. The preceding maneuvers had been complicated, as the U.S. does not officially recognize either the Chinese or North Korean authorities. In turn, the Chinese take no responsibility for the Chinese troops claimed to be volunteers, but the Chinese commander is authorized to act on their behalf.

At 0800, as directed by the Joint Chiefs of Staff, General Ridgway broadcasts the statement. The statement suggests that if the Communists agree to talks, a meeting could be convened in Wonsan Harbor aboard a Danish hospital ship. The cease fire offer is addressed to the commander in chief of the Communist forces in Korea. The Communists reply to General Ridgway's proposal on the following day.

July 1 The Communists respond to General Ridgway's cease-fire proposal of the previous day. In China and Korea, Peking radio and Pyongyang radio simultaneously break into their respective programming to broadcast a combined reply from Peng Teh-huai (China) and Kim II Sung (N.K.) which essentially agrees to talks; however, the Chinese prefer to meet at Kaesong rather than at Wonsan harbor. As part of the Communist reply, a proposal to call an immediate cease fire for the duration of the talks is made.

U.S. officials realize by the offer means the Chinese are not prepared to attack and need a cease fire to rebuild their devastated units and bring in yet additional fresh troops. General Ridgway agrees to meet with the Communists at Kaesong, but the cease fire proposal is ignored. As earlier directed by the Joint Chiefs of Staff, Ridgway intends to continue operations, including missions by the Fifth Air force. A preliminary meeting occurs on 8 July.

In the I Corps sector, infantry supported by tanks moves to clear the Sobang Hills of the Chinese who had re-occupied the area subsequent to the Eighth Army's June offensive; however, the Chinese are able to hold the ground.

Also, the commander of the 67th Tactical Reconnaissance (Intelligence) Wing, Colonel Karl L. (Pop)

Polifka, while on a mission in the vicinity of the front lines near Kaesong, is hit by enemy fire. His plane, an RF-51, crashes and Colonel Polifka is killed. He is temporarily succeeded by Colonel Bert N. Smiley until the permanent successor, Colonel Vincent W. Howard, assumes command on 4 July. Colonel Polifca had been the first pilot to spot the Japanese fleet while it moved toward Port Moresby during May 1942, just prior to the eruption of the Battle of the Coral Sea.

July 2   Typhoon Kate strikes and hinders operations, including those of Fast Carrier Task Force 77, which is unable to launch planes.

July 3   In response to news of a downed pilot in North Korea, a Navy helicopter pilot, Lieutenant John Kelvin Koelsch, volunteers to take the rescue mission.

Lacking fighter coverage, he descends to low level below the clouds and locates the downed pilot, despite weather conditions that include a total overcast. Koelsch defies tenacious enemy fire and lands. The pilot, wounded, is raised into the helicopter, but more fire strikes the helicopter and it crashes into the mountain. Koelsch gets his crew and the wounded pilot out of the helicopter and together, they vanish in the woods to evade capture. Nine days later, the group is captured. Lieutenant Koelsch is later awarded the Medal of Honor for his heroism and leadership under fire. Koelsch succumbs while imprisoned by the Communists.

In other activity, the USS *Everett* (PF 8), operating off Wonsan, sustains minor damage from enemy shore batteries. One seaman is killed and seven are wounded.

Troops of the 7th Regiment, 3rd Division, in action atop a hill on 3 July.

Elements of the 7th Division in action in the Iron Triangle on 3 July.

July 4 *In the I Corps area, 3rd Division sector,* Company B, 7th Regiment, seizes Hill 586, but the contest is extremely difficult and drains the victors. While the contingent attempts to catch a breather, the enemy prepares for a counterattack. After dark it is launched and the 1st Platoon is hit heavily and compelled to pull back. Sergeant Leroy A. Mendonca remains in his position to provide cover fire. The enemy comes under a wall of fire form Mendonca, until he exhausts his ammunition and they encounter his rifle butt and bayonet as he attempts in vain to block the rushing wave. The platoon rejoins the main body and the hill is retained after the enemy is routed. Sergeant Mendonca gives the ultimate sacrifice to save the command. He is credited with the elimination of about 37 enemy casualties prior to his demise at his post. Mendonica is awarded the Medal of Honor posthumously for his extraordinary heroism under fire and his selfless sacrifice to save others in his command.

In Naval activity, Bombardment Element (TE 95.21) encounters fierce return fire from enemy shore batteries at Wonsan. On the following day, Wonsan is struck heavily.

July 5 The enemy at Wonsan has recently bolstered its positions and reached a capacity from which U.S. warships become threatened with heavy fire. Carrier planes pummel selected targets in the Wonsan area. The mission includes 247 sorties.

In other naval activity, warships bolster a mission executed by about 600 ROK troops who launch a raid upon the mainland opposite Cho-do Island.

July 6 *In Air Force activity,* a tanker (KB-29M), attached to an air materiel command but flown by a crew of the strategic air command and attached to the 43rd Air Refueling Squadron, refuels four separate RF-80 Shooting Stars. The task is accomplished in enemy territory while the planes are in flight engaged in reconnaissance missions. This is the first in-air refueling that occurs over enemy territory during a combat mission.

In Naval activity, the USS *Evans* (DD 754) lands a shore fire control party (SFCP) on Hwangto-do Island, located in the southern section of Wonsan Harbor, to direct fire. Three destroyers blast the area and level buildings and a torpedo station.

July 7 *In the X Corps sector, 1st Marine Division zone,* the 1st Korean Marine Corps Regiment is notified that it will be receiving orders to move out on the following day to establish a patrol base on Taeu-san.

In Naval activity, a shore fire control party and elements of the 1st Korean Marine Regiment debark the USS *Blue* (DD 744) at Wonsan to establish an observation post from which the fire of warships can be directed against enemy targets.

July 8 A U.S. three-man liaison team meets at Kaesong with Communist representatives to set up the official armistice talks. The date agreed upon is 10 July. After sitting across the negotiating table from the U.S. representatives, the Communists notice the difference in height between the two sides. They saw off part of the legs of the chairs to make the U.S. representatives appear shorter. Another piece of mischief by the Communists occurs when the chairs are arranged so the U.N. representatives are facing north, where the losers are made to sit in Asia during negotiations.

Communist photographers make good use of the shots of the participants at the table and when the pictures are viewed across Asia, they give the illusion of defeated Americans. An even more devious tactic is used when the Communists insist that all vehicles fly white flags for identification purposes, but when the photos are distributed, it gives the impression to the Orientals that the U.N. had capitulated. They also insist that the U.N. representatives remain unarmed; however, when the U.S. representatives and accompanying troops are photographed without arms, the pictures show the Communists well armed.

The Communists also outdo the U.S.-U.N representatives, as they received a confirmation that the peace talks will be held at Kaesong, which is directly in the path of the Eighth Army. The Communists realize that by holding the talks in Kaesong, the Americans will be unable to advance and secure the strategic road center there.

In the X Corps sector, 1st Marine Division zone, elements of the 1st Korean Marine Corps Regiment move out to establish a patrol base at Taeu-san at 1030, but little progress is made. Enemy mortar and machine gun fire halts the advance on the right, while the left section manages to reach Hill 1100, still short of Taeu-san.

In Air Force activity, a four-plane contingent of F-86 Sabre jets led by Lieutenant Richard S. Becker (334th Fighter-Interceptor Squadron, 4th Fighter-Interceptor Group) encounters a pair of MiGs in the skies over Pyongyang. He takes one of the two MiGs by machine gun fire from his F-86. The MiG, after being struck, begins to spin out of control and rolls into a dive that takes it directly into the ground about one mile south of the Pyongyang East Air Field.

July 9–November 27 1951.
SIXTH DESIGNATED CAMPAIGN:
THE U.N. SUMMER-FALL OFFENSIVE.

July 9 General Ridgway appoints Vice Admiral C.T. Joy, USN, as chief of the U.N. delegation that will convene with the Communists for the truce talks at Kaesong. Others in the delegation are Major General

Communist representatives at Kaesong are (left to right): Major General Hsieh Fang (Chinese Army); Lt. General Teng Hua (Chinese Army); Lt. General Nam II, chief delegate; Major General Lee Sang Cho (N.K. Army) and Major General Chang Pyong San (N.K. Army).

UN representatives at Kaesong are (left to right): Major General Lawrence C. Craigie (USAF); Major General Paik Sun Yup (ROK I Corps commander); Vice Admiral C. Turner Joy (Far East naval commander), acting as chief delegate for U.N; Major General Henry I. Hodes (deputy chief of staff, Eighth Army) and Rear Admiral Arleigh A. Burke, USN.

L.C. Craigie, USAF, Major General H.I. Hodes, deputy chief of staff, Eusak, Rear Admiral A.A. Burke, USN, and Major General Paik Syn Yun, ROK Army.

In the X Corps sector, 1st Marine Division zone, the Korean Marines reinitiate the advance to establish a patrol base at Taeu-san. The full weight of the battalion pushes forward on the right, but similarly to the previous day, the enemy halts the advance. In the meantime, the troops that had reached Hill 1100 on the previous day are driven back.

Hill 1001 is seized by the 1st Battalion, but it is apparent that Taeu-san can not be seized by the Korean Marines. During the operation, the Korean Marines sustain 222 casualties. Subsequently, the task is given to the 2nd Division. Taeu-san is designated Hill 1179.

July 10 Armistice negotiations begin at Kaesong on this day in an attempt to bring a conclusion to the conflict that has been ongoing since June of the previous year. Admiral C. Turner Joy (commander Far East Naval Forces) leads the U.N. command negotiations. Admiral Joy informs the Communists that the U.S.-U.N. will not under any circumstances suspend action unless and until the negotiations are completed. The Communists, who recently requested an immediate cease fire, are not in a position to contest. Consequently, they are compelled to agree to a continuation of hostilities.

The U.S. also maintains a naval blockade of Korea's east and west coasts and the U.S. Navy and Air Force maintain consistent bombardment of Communist shore batteries. From the beginning of the war until now, the Communists have sustained horrendous casualties that total almost one million. The recent spring offensive by the Communists helped to dramatically increase the numbers. The huge losses and inability to overwhelm the U.S.-U.N. forces is apparently the primary reason the Communists have agreed to talk about a cease fire.

A signal corps team at work making repairs to a communications line along a mountain pass south of Hwach'on.

The U.S. is inclined to believe the Communists are stalling for time to rebuild their shattered forces.

At this time, the front extends from the Imjin River to Ch'orwon, then parallels the base of the "Iron Trian-gle" before swinging southeast to the lower tip of the Punch Bowl and from there it runs north and east to the Sea of Japan at a point above Kaesong. At Kaesong, the neutrality of the place is not conspicuous. The Chinese carry Tommy guns and attempt to intimidate U.N. envoys. In addition, the Chinese propagandize the "white flags" on the U.N. jeeps, attempting to transform the neutrality into a scene of surrender or capitulation. The film is played throughout Asia.

As the talks begin, the U.S. holds 163,000 POWs, most of whom are North Korean. The U.N. has sustained about 294,000 casualties and of these, the South Koreans account for 212,500. U.S. casualties stand at 77,000, mostly sustained by the U.S. Army, which loses 11,327 killed and 42,900 wounded. Of the wounded or injured in action, 1,075 later succumb from their injuries. In addition, 6,088 soldiers are captured and of these, 2,583 die while held in captivity by the Communists. Another 3,979 soldiers are reported missing in action and among these, 3,323 are subsequently declared dead.

In Air Force activity, a contingent of F-80s, while on a mission, spot an enemy convoy stalled at an impassable bridge. The pilots of the F-80s relay the information and location to Fifth Air Force. Shortly thereafter, every available aircraft is directed to converge on the convoy. The planes deliver a massive amount of bombs, rockets and machine gun fire that shreds the stalled column. It is reported that more than 150 vehicles, including about 50 tanks, are demolished in the attacks.

— *In the United States:* The Marine Corps will accept 7,000 draftees to help bolster its force of 194,000 troops to bring it closer to its authorized strength of 204,000. This is the first time the Marines has drafted men since World War II.

July 11–12 1951 Operation CAVE DWELLER commences. The USS *New Jersey* (BB 62) and USS *Leonard F. Mason* (DD 852) combine their firepower to blast enemy positions, supply depots and troops formations in the vicinity of Kensong. Estimates of enemy casualties are 129 killed.

July 11 General Ridgway prepares for operations to further destroy the enemy and force a quick decision for an armistice at Kaesong. Restrictions upon Eighth Army on operations had been lifted on the previous day by the Joint Chiefs of Staff, giving Ridgway authorization to expand the lines. In addition to the normal air and ground operations, Eighth Army is preparing to execute Plan Overwhelming, set tentatively for commencement on 1 September. The plan, designed by General Van Fleet at the request of Ridgway, calls for an offensive to move the line from Kansas to the P'yongyang–Wonsan Line. However, Van Fleet is convinced he can do much more to damage the enemy when operating from the Kansas Line. Meanwhile, Ridgway considers the possibility of high casualties and the remote possibility of a settlement at Kaesong.

In Naval activity, U.S. warships, including the USS

USS *New Jersey* in action off the east coast of Korea.

The battleship *New Jersey*'s guns in action, in a close-up view of a bombardment of enemy positions along the east coast of Korea.

Blue (DD 744) and the USS *Evans* (DD 754), operating near Yo-do Island, come under fire from enemy shore batteries; however, no damage is sustained.

July 12 *In the X Corps sector, 1st Marine Division zone,* the Marines inform X Corps that the patrol base established by the 1st Korean Marine Regiment near Hill 1001 is to be considered the 1st Marine Division patrol base.

July 13 A plane (VMF[N]-513) piloted by Captain Donald Fenton spots and destroys a PO-2 in the vicinity of Seoul. It is the second elusive non-metal biplane destroyed over Seoul.

July 14 *In the X Corps sector, 1st Marine Division zone,* combat for the past two weeks has not been too heavy. Nonetheless, the casualties, including the Korean Marines (attached), amount to 55 killed, 360 wounded and 22 missing.

In other activity, Marine squadrons (MAG 12) at K-46 near Hoengsong abandon the field and move temporarily to K-1 near Seoul. Subsequently, MAG 12's new field will be K-18, on the east coast at Kangnung, about forty miles to the rear of the 1st Marine Division lines and just slightly below the 38th Parallel.

In Naval activity, elements of the British 41st Independent, aboard an LST, arrive from Wonsan at Yo-do Island.

In Air Force activity, one plane attached to the 452nd Bomber Group launches an attack against two separate enemy convoys it spots during the darkness in the area north of Sinanju. The crew of the B-26 light bomber reports both columns devastated with a combined loss of 68 vehicles either destroyed or damaged.

July 15 *In the X Corps sector, 1st Marine Division zone,* the 2nd Division completes its relief of the 1st Marine Division. The 2nd Division is then designated as the attack force to push the Kansas Line forward to the Punch Bowl. The 2nd Division is flanked by the ROK 5th and 7th Divisions on the east and west respectively.

U.S. planes strike an enemy industrial complex. The target is hit with napalm bombs.

July 16 *In the X Corps sector,* the 1st Marine Division is in the process of moving to the rear of X Corps. The maneuver is completed by the following day.

July 17–31 1951 By this date, nearly all of the 1st Marine Division is in X Corps reserve. The exception is the 5th Marines, which is in the vicinity of Inje as "ready reserve," under the operational control of X Corps. Subsequently, the 3rd Battalion, 11th Marines, is attached to the operational control of the 2nd Division.

In related activity, the 7th Marines and the Division Reconnaissance Company move to the vicinity of Yanggu to participate in training and to support the building up of the fortifications there. Also, by about this time, General Almond is relieved as commander of X Corps by Major General Clovis E. Byers. General Almond returns to the States.

In Naval activity, Communist shore batteries on Kalmagak, Umi-do and Ho-do Pando bombard naval warships (TE 95.21) operating off Wonsan and the U.N. positions on islands. Fire is continuous and well coordinated. The USS *O'Brien* (DD 725) sustains only one minor casualty. The LSMR (rocket ship) 409 and the LSMR 525 sustain only minor damage. Other U.S. warships speed to the area to augment the force already there. Task Element 77.14 (USS *Helena* [CA 75] and accompanying destroyers arrive and Task Element 77.11, USS *New Jersey* (BB 62) moves to bolster the relief force. The *Helena* is on site by evening. Also, the USS *New Jersey* arrives during the early morning hours of the 18th.

July 18 Operation KICKOFF commences at 1500 in Wonsan harbor. The warships initiate what becomes a daily ritual. The vessels maneuver at five knots, moving clockwise and firing effectively at known enemy positions, where the batteries had been used to threaten the U.S. Fleet. The bombardments begin each day at the same time and continue until dusk.

July 21 At Cho-do Island, following a clandestine operation, a contingent of the 6004th Air Intelligence Service Squadron terminates a mission that began one week ago in an effort to disassemble components of a downed MiG-15. The crashed aircraft contains many parts that help the U.S. unlock its secrets. The detachment is provided with protection while the operation is in progress. The mission succeeds in salvaging the parts, the most ever from a captured MiG. The protective force includes planes, attached to a British carrier, that maintain low level flights, while Fifth Air Force executes high level flights. A vessel that contains a crane is provided by the U.S. Army.

Also, a Marine patrol composed of three F4-Us is attacked by 15 MiGs at a point when the Marines' F9Fs are nearly out of fuel. The Marines fend off the MiGs, which show little aggressiveness, then head for cloud cover. One of the planes fails to return to base. The fate of the pilot, Lieutenant Richard Bell, is for a while unknown, but he is captured. Bell returns during the POW exchange in 1953.

U.S. Army engineers make road repairs at a spot near Inje on 21 July. Torrential rains caused large washouts. A deep drop can be seen in the center.

July 22-24 1951   The Communists' demand for the withdrawal of all foreign troops from Kaesong goes unheeded. Consequently, the truce talks are temporarily aborted.

July 24   The 116th Fighter Bomber Wing (Air National Guard), composed of F-84 ThunderJets, arrives at Japan. The wing, the second National Guard air unit to arrive, will be based at Misawa and Chitose Air Bases in Japan. The 116th is the second Air National Guard aviation unit to arrive in the theater. It follows the 136th Fighter Bomber Wing, which came the previous May. The 116th had come in from its base in Georgia. The arrival of both Air National Guard units does not necessarily improve the combat capabilities for Far East Air Forces.

In conjunction with the arrival of the F-84 Thunder-Jets, elements of the 27th Fighter Escort Wing provide training for the crews, but the 27th has been returned to Strategic Air Command due to the efforts of General Curtis LeMay. Once the training period is completed, the 27th departs for the States. The acute shortage of Sabre jets continues to impede operations and raise the danger level for those pilots in the theater. Far East Air Forces is in urgent need of about a fifty percent increase in Sabres, but the Air Force chief of staff, General Hoyt Vandenberg, will inform FEAF to expect no more than a ten percent increase.

July 25   British warships initiate a bombardment of enemy positions near the Han. The HMS *Cardigan Bay* (PF), HMAS *Murschison* (PF), ROKN *Apnok* (PF 62), and several minesweepers participate.

In Air Force activity, Fifth Air Force officially orders the establishment of the air defenses of South Korea. The defensive measures are to be undertaken by the 502nd Tactical Control Group and its attached units.

July 26   The maintenance crews of MAG 12 abandon K-46 at Hoengsong and join the squadrons at K-1. The airfield had been abandoned due to chronic maintenance problems caused by the primitive, rocky runway.

July 27   Major General Christian F. Schilt assumes command of the 1st Marine Aircraft Wing.

July 28   The USS *Los Angeles* (CA 135), subsequent to the recent mine-clearing operation in the Haeju Man channel, arrives and bombards enemy positions in the area. In the meantime, British warships continue to bombard the area along the north bank of the Han River.

July 29   *In Japan:* Regimental Combat Team 160, 40th Infantry Division, undergoing amphibious landing exercises at Chigasaki Beach, completes its training.

In Air Force activity, a contingent of U.N. jet fighter-bombers and some reconnaissance planes operating near Pyongyang spot a group of MiG-15s, but the planes avoid contact with the enemy aircraft.

July 30   A huge contingent of fighter bombers, composed of 354 Air Force and Marine Corps squadrons protected by ninety-one F-80s, strike enemy targets in the vicinity of Pyongyang.

July 31 The USS *Helena* (CA-75), while bombarding enemy positions in the vicinity of Wonsan, is struck by enemy shore battery fire, but no major damage is sustained.

August 1 At this time, the 1st Marine Division reports its strength as 1,386 officers and 24,044 enlisted men. In addition, the division has 165 interpreters and 4,184 civilians, the latter known as cargadores (laborers).

A U.S. carrier en route to Japan. Its deck is covered with F-84 Thunderjets that will join the air war in Korea.

An Eighth Army convoy of trucks moves along a recently repaired road leading into Inje on 1 August. The road is similar to many others, a single lane with a deep drop-off.

August 6 By this date, LSMRs (rocket ships), according to Navy reports, have fired more than 100,000 rockets at enemy positions. Also, the USS *Carmick* (DMS 32), operating in the vicinity of Chongjin, destroys four sampans and seizes 13 fishermen (enemy).

August 10 The carrier USS *Princeton* (CVE 37), after being detached from TF-77, moves to Yokosuka, Japan, and from there it embarks for the United States.

August 11 The truce talks in Kaesong resume after the Communists agree to maintain Kaesong as a neutral site.

In Naval activity, the enemy at several locations fires

upon U.S. Navy warships. Near Ho-do Pando, the USS *Dextrous* (AM-34) comes under attack from shore batteries and sustains two strikes that inflict casualties. One sailor is killed and three others are wounded. The vessel sustains some damage.

Also, the destroyer USS *Hopewell* (DD 681), coordinating with a SFCP party on Hwangto-do Island at Wonsan Harbor, initates a bombardment of enemy positions. Also, warships continue to blast Communist positions in the vicinity of the Han River's north bank.

August 12   *In the X Corps sector,* the 2nd Division is informed that a possible attack is being planned against Hills 983, 940 and 773. Just after midnight (12th-13th), a directive arrives instructing Division to draw up plans to seize the hills in question and submit the plan to X Corps.

August 13   *In the X Corps sector,* orders arrive instructing the 2nd Division to decrease its boundary. The directive is an extension of an earlier order to plan for an attack against Hills 983, 940 and 773. That sector of the boundary, which is reduced, is taken over by the ROK 7th Division.

August 14   Although newspapers in the United States continue to speak of the possibility of a truce in Korea, various directives that spread through Eighth Army discount that possibility. On this day, all divisions in Korea receive word that Eighth Army had been in receipt of requisitions for winter clothing, surely signaling that the troops would be spending a second winter in Korea.

In the X Corps sector, the 2nd Division is informed that the attack to seize Hills 983, 940 and 773 is imminent. In conjunction, the ROK 36th Regiment (7th ROK Division) is attached to the 2nd Division. The ROKs are to spearhead the assault. In conjunction, Company B, 72nd Tank Battalion, is attached to the 7th ROK Division to augment its offensive strength.

In Naval activity, the destroyer USS *William Seiverling* (DE 441), operating off Tanchin, halts Communist fishing sampans and seizes 9 men.

August 15   *In the X Corps sector,* an attack against an ominous ridgeline, which had been included in Eighth Army's planning while negotiations continue at Kaesong, is now in the final planning stages. The assault is scheduled to commence on 18 August. The enemy-held objective, later known as Bloody Ridge, includes three hills, 983, 940 and 773, but the ridges that link the hills must also be secured. On the western end, four separate rugged ridges converge to form Hill 983, which is also the highest peak. Hill 940 lies east of Hill 983, along the center of the ridge on the opposite side of a deep ravine and farther east, about 1,000 yards, the Communists hold Hill 773.

Each of the hills is well defended and the fortifications are camouflaged. The bunkers are often linked and built so well that they are shielded from artillery and air strikes, which essentially leaves the job of clearing to the ground troops. Each of the three enemy-held hills

are a threat to the 2nd Division, as the North Koreans are able to use them as strategic observation posts to maintain a vigil on the western zone along the Kansas Line at Hill 1179 (Taeu-san), a 3,890-foot-high mountain defended by about one regiment (1,700 troops). The 2nd Division had earlier eliminated the enemy east of the hill, but with three obstacles remaining, Eighth Army had directed that they be destroyed.

The 9th, 23rd and 38th Regiments have been dispatching patrols to evaluate the enemy's intent and it is concluded that no offensive action is imminent. However, the enemy artillery posted along the ridgeline makes it mandatory that the hills be seized. During this month of August, while the troops must endure the trials of combat, nature is also working against Eighth Army. Frequent heavy rains sometimes reduce the roads to mud and inflict damage to the bridges. Engineers work tirelessly to keep the roads open and the bridges operable, but fierce enemy artillery bombardments constantly interfere and often the engineers are ordered to suspend their work. In conjunction, to soften resistance, fighter planes strike the enemy area during the night (15th-16th) and deliver napalm while strafing the ridges; the rear slopes are struck by a B-26 that drops 500-pound bombs.

August 16–17 1951   *In the X Corps sector,* the preliminary stages of the offensive to gain the area soon to be known as Bloody Ridge continue. Enemy positions continue to come under bombardment in an effort to soften the resistance against the ROK 7th Division before its attack.

— *In Japan:* The final contingent of the 40th Infantry Division, Regimental Combat Team 224, completes its training (amphibious) at Chigasaki.

August 17   A Chinese security patrol is ambushed near the "neutrality zone." The Chinese at Kaesong protest and insist that the U.N. apologize. After an investigation, it is determined that the ambush had been staged by South Korean partisan irregulars who acted out of the U.N. and South Korean government jurisdictions. No apology is made.

In the X Corps sector, the 2nd Division initiates a preattack bombardment against Hills 983, 940 and 773, in an attempt to soften resistance for the ROK 36th Regiment, ROK 7th Division, which will launch the attack on the following day. The enemy is struck by planes and artillery; however, the North Koreans are not too hard-hit. Their bunkers are deeply entrenched and well camouflaged. Many of the bunkers are linked and some are spacious enough to quarter more than fifty troops.

In Naval activity, Special Bombardment Group TG 95.9 is established. It is composed of the vessels USS *New Jersey* (BB 62), USS *Toledo* (CA 133), the Dutch destroyer *Van Galen* (DD) and USS *Agerholm* (DD 826). Also, the British continue to plaster enemy positions along the north bank of the Han River. The HMAS *Murchison* (PF), HMS *Cardigan Bay* (PF) and the HMS *Morecombe Bay* (PF) participate; however, due to the imminent arrival of a typhoon, the ships abandon the area for safer waters.

August 18–20 1951   Typhoon Marge sweeps into the area. The 1st Marine Air Wing evacuates Korea for Japan. The air units return on 21 August.

August 18–September 5 1951 BATTLE OF BLOODY RIDGE *In the X Corps Sector zone,* following the lifting of a two-day bombardment, the ROK 36th Regiment, ROK 7th Division, advances through a thick and murky fog toward a ridgeline that includes Hills 983, 940 and 773. Hill 983 stands

in the west at the convergence point of four knife-like ridges. Hill 940 lies east of Hill 983 on the opposite side of a huge ravine and farther east is the other major link, Hill 773.

In an attempt to bolster the assault, the 2nd Division uses elements to draw attention from the primary attack. The 23rd Infantry Regiment attacks in the east against fierce resistance and the 38th Regiment attacks northeast of the targeted three hills. The 38th Regiment is able to secure its objectives in the heights there and afterward, its guns bolster the ROK attack. The attack is also bolstered by an im-

A contingent of the 2nd Division ascends Hill 1179 (Taeu-san). Stretcher bearers are among the column.

Wounded troops attached to the U.S. 2nd Division, able to walk, descend Hill 1179 (Taeu-san).

mense amount of artillery support, which includes the four division artillery battalions and three other artillery battalions, composed of two medium and one 105-mm battalion. Other support units include several tank companies and two heavy-mortar companies.

Meanwhile, the ROKs initiate the frontal assault.

Initially, the resistance is nominal, but as the ROKs encroach the slopes of the respective objectives, the resistance intensifies. Small arms fire rings down upon them as they ascend the slopes. Machine gun fire and mortars, as if synchronized, pour down from each of the three respective hills.

The ROKs, however, continue to drive up the

slopes and en route to the summits, often the Communists pop out of their bunkers to ignite close-quartered fighting. The ROK 36th Regiment maintains its discipline and tenaciously drills forward, eliminating bunkers as they ascend. Nevertheless, by the latter part of the afternoon, the enemy fire becomes too fierce to penetrate. The attack is suspended.

The 23rd Regiment, 2nd Division, which had launched a diversionary attack, secures Hill 1059 with Company G; however, the enemy artillery fire against the advance of Company E compels it to halt and retire. After dark, the ROKs re-ignite the attack, still exhibiting great persistence, a trait that often in the past had been lacking with ROK units.

In the meantime, the 2nd Division informs the 9th Infantry Regiment to be ready to jump to relieve the ROKs in the event they succeed in seizing the hills; however, the North Koreans are equally determined to hold the real estate. The 2nd and 3rd Battalions claw forward to within several hundred yards of their objectives, but at that point, the enemy fire forbids further advancement. The ROKs establish night positions and prepare to resume the fight on the following morning.

At dawn on the 19th, it quickly becomes apparent that the Communists had not abandoned their positions. Enemy fire continues to be heavy against all units at the respective hills and the enemy guns also begin to bombard the support guns of the 38th Regiment. All the while, the ROKs slowly but methodically grind forward against the menacing fire. At Hills 940 and 773, the ROKs attain positions slightly more than 200 yards from the respective summits and at Hill 983, on the west and the highest peak on the ridge, they hammer their way to positions slightly more than fifty yards from the summit. Once again, the ROK 36th Regiment establishes night positions, still determined to take the objectives. Meanwhile, the 2nd Division continues to support the assault, but no U.S. units are ordered to relieve the ROKs.

On the 20th, the ROKs finally begin to achieve some success for their tireless efforts. On the slopes of Hills 940 and 983, the stamina of the ROKs greatly outweighs that of the Communists and the ROKs gain the advantage as they begin to punish the defenders on the respective hills, but still the summits continues to be defended by deeply entrenched troops in formidable bunkers that are being eliminated one by one.

At Hill 773, the ROKs battle relentlessly again, outweighing the defenders' determination. The summit is gained and secured by 1800. Immediately, the South Koreans establish defensive positions in expectation of a counterattack. As anticipated, the Communists, determined to oust the ROKs, mount a counterattack to evict them from Hill 773, but it is met with rigid, non-bendable resistance from the ROK 36th Regiment. Although the South Koreans hold the summit, the situation becomes close to a crisis. Ammunition and supplies have been greatly depleted during the heated contest, and still, the remaining hills must be secured.

The North Koreans remaining on Hills 940 and 983 continue to dominate, but the rugged determination of the ROKs carries over from the previous day. After another tenacious day of battle, both hills fall to the 36th Regiment. In addition to securing all of its objectives, the 36th ROK Regiment enjoys a pause in the combat; the North Koreans either choose not to attack or are unable to launch a counterattack during the night (21st–22nd), permitting the regiment to catch a breather.

Nevertheless, the depletion of supplies remains a huge concern. While the ROKs and the 2nd Division are maneuvering to seize the objectives, the negotiations in Kaesong are deteriorating. The Communists have been stalling for time; however, on the 22nd, after apparently concluding that their demands are being ignored, the Communist leader, Nam II, proclaims that the U.N. had, through air attacks, attempted to kill his delegation and abruptly cancels the meetings at Kaesong.

The ROKs have up to this point gained the objectives, but their task is extended to include several other unnamed hills slightly north of their present positions. However, the North Koreans exhibit no signs of withdrawing as they had in the past, which makes it plain that the contest to secure the no-name hills will be yet another grueling advance.

Enemy artillery remains extremely active on the 23rd and based on the amount of fire, there is no lack of ammunition or guns, despite a Herculean effort by the Air Force bombers to halt the flow of Chinese arms. The ROKs move cautiously toward the hills designated A, B and C. Elements of the 2nd Division continue to dispatch reconnaissance patrols. None of the patrols encounter any heavy resistance until 24 August, when the North Koreans try to deliver a killing blow to the ROK 26th Regiment and terminate the advance before the troops reach the objectives.

As the ROKs push ahead on the 24th, the resistance galvanizes. The Communist counterattack succeeds in bringing the advance to a halt. In addition, the North Koreans initiate attacks against elements of the 2nd Division, including patrols of the 38th Regiment and others posted near Hill 1059. By the following day, the 2nd Division takes steps to augment the ROKs. The 9th Infantry Regiment shifts toward the area near Hill 983 to initiate contact with the ROKs positioned on the southwest slope, while the 38th Infantry Regiment moves hurriedly to establish a link with the ROKs at Hill 773.

All the while, the ROKs are instructed to focus their attack against the undesignated hill known as "C," which stands to the front of Hills 940 and 773. Still the North Koreans maintain an iron wall of resistance on the 25th, preventing the ROKs from gaining ground in front of Objective C.

However, in the zones of the U.S. 38th Regiment, again the North Koreans become elusive and avoid major contact with the Americans. Subsequently, as part of an X Corps offensive, the seizure of Objective "C" becomes the responsibility of the U.S. 9th Infantry Regiment.

During the night (25th–26th), the Communists revert back to their tactics of night assaults. At 0245, the North Koreans holding positions to the north of Hill 983 execute a two-pronged assault. While some units surge forward with a frontal assault, other contingents maneuver to gain positions between Hills 940 and 983. The gains threaten Hill 940 and Hill 983, the latter becoming encircled by 1200.

In the meantime, elements of the 38th Regiment, holding positions north of Pia-ri, come under fierce attack. Unable to release the pressure, the troops are compelled to withdraw slightly more than one thousand yards. At Hill 983, the situation has severely deteriorated and the ROK positions become untenable; however, there is no route of escape. By 1430, with no options, the surviving members of the 36th ROK Regiment are compelled to capitulate.

Meanwhile, after news of the fall of Hill 983 and of the retreat of Companies F and G north of Pia-ri, steps are hurriedly taken to plug the line. Company E at the Kansas Line is rushed to reinforce Companies F and G, while at Division headquarters, plans are modified to include the recapture of Hill 983.

The task of evicting the North Koreans is delegated to the 9th Infantry Regiment. The North Koreans, however, do not remain dormant during the day. Later, about one and one-half hours before midnight (25th–26th), elements of the 38th Regiment (2nd Battalion) move to Hill 773 to augment the contingent of the ROK 36th Regiment there, which has been able to throw back repeated attacks that were launched prior to dusk.

As scheduled, during the morning of the 27th, the 9th Regiment advances to seize its objectives, but enemy resistance continues to block all progress of the attacking 2nd Battalion. Consequently, at dusk, Hill 983 remains under Communist control.

In the meantime, X Corps remains determined to conquer the objectives, particularly to prevent the enemy from maintaining positions from which they can continue to observe X Corps' positions and operations, but equally important, because Hills 983 and 773 dominate the Hwach'on Reservoir, the source of the capital's electricity. The depth of the artillery in the fullest sense is brought to bear upon the crafty enemy defenses on Hill 983.

Subsequent to dusk, the 2nd Division catapults thousands upon thousands of rounds that rock the slopes and plant an iron picket fence composed of more than 22,000 shells. While the thunderous artillery bombardment pounds the enemy positions, the 3rd Battalion prepares to pass through the beleaguered 2nd Battalion to continue the assault.

As dawn emerges on the 28th, the 1st Battalion

remains at the Kansas Line while the 3rd Battalion, 9th Infantry Regiment, takes the point to spearhead the assault against the unyielding defenders at Hill 983, but another enemy again enters the contest. The inclement weather, in its predictable manner, has transformed the roads into giant pits of mud. The condition of the roads causes delays in the battalion's jump-off until afternoon.

Meanwhile, the North Koreans sustain the identical torrential rains, but they are unaffected by the poor conditions of the road and wait in their camouflaged bunkers for the advancing infantry. As the 3rd Battalion drives toward the objective, the resistance refuses to falter; however, the 3rd Battalion presses ahead despite the rings of fire. Company I and Company F lunge forward inch-by-inch and yard-by-yard and by darkness, following the dreadful trek, still fall short of the prize. The summit remains a long three hundred yards or so from their grasp. As the sun sets the 3rd Battalion attempts to establish night positions to protect against a counterattack; still the weather refuses to relent. The pesky, irritating rain that has helped to bog down the advance increases in intensity and inundates the area. The slopes of the hill are transformed into a series of unruly streams of water that funnel into the ravines and the mountain streams.

While the 2nd Division continues to implement strategy to end the quest for Hill 983, the raging flood waters wreak havoc on logistics. Bridges, including the primary Bailey bridge (LaDue bridge) at the Soyang River, sustain damage during the night of the 28th when a runaway pontoon bridge gets tossed against one of its anchors, damaging the northern end. Traffic on the double-span is curtailed, but the problem becomes especially complicated because of the great need to maintain the flow of ammunition and supplies. A circuitous route is used to ease the pressure.

Vehicles at Chunchon are ordered to move out with supplies. Toward the latter part of the day, the 2nd and 3rd Battalions, both of which have sustained grueling punishment during the advance, are informed that they will be joined by the 1st Battalion on the 29th. Nonetheless, the North Koreans hold steadfast throughout the day's fighting.

While the North Koreans attempt to cling to their positions, including Hill 983, X Corps moves to add more muscle to the attack. In addition to the continuation of the assault to gain Hill 983, X Corps on 29 August orders a larger attack, scheduled for 31 August. In the meantime, the 9th Infantry continues to slug its way forward against resolute opposition, carrying the prolonged battle into the next day, still without a victor at the ridge that becomes known as Bloody Ridge through an article in *Stars and Stripes*.

Prior to dawn on 30 August, the 9th Infantry Regiment resumes its attack to clear the ridgeline that encompasses Hills 983 and 940, as well as the lingering defenders farther north at Objective "C," the

The 9th Regiment, 2nd Division, ascends Hill 940 during the Battle of Bloody Ridge (18 August–5 September).

unnamed hill that had not been secured by the ROKs. The 1st and 2nd Battalions press ahead against continuing opposition, which has been reinforced by a contingent estimated to be about 1,000 troops. The slug-fest at Hill 940 rages throughout the day without success.

In the zone of Company A, the casualties rise to about fifty percent and the list includes the company commander (wounded). Orders arrive to pull back, but in the meantime, Lieutenant John H. Dunn, who had assumed command, is also killed. Command reverts to an artillery officer, Lieutenant Edwin C. Morrow. During the withdrawal the troops receive cover fire requested by Morrow. Seven battalions of artillery lay smoke to aid evacuation of the wounded that have to be carried down the slopes.

In the meantime, the 3rd Battalion, 38th Infantry Regiment, moves to relieve the ROKs at Hill 773, but they had already absconded and instead, as the battalion moves up the slopes, the troops are met by North Koreans. Following a tenacious fire fight, the battalion is pushed from the hill.

After a while, the battalion regroups and plows up the slope a second time, only to be halted short of the summit. It loses a hill thought to have been controlled by the ROKs. At dusk, after concluding a brutal contest and sustaining high casualties, the U.S. contingents establish night positions and prepare to spend another uncomfortable and restless night prior to the next attack, most probably before the sun rises.

On 31 August, at 0400, the 1st Battalion, 9th Infantry Regiment, forms at the assembly area where it had originally occupied positions prior to the attack. Despite lack of sleep, the troops are ordered to be ready in case of an attack. After a suspension of several hours, the trucks move to the vicinity of Worunni, where again they are stalled until nearly 1200. Then a short ride takes them to a point from which they attack Hill 773 from the east.

Company C, in the lead, reaches the tip of the ridgeline and swings left to attack the first knoll that stands between the column and the objective. The trek is effortless, as the knoll is controlled by elements of the 38th Regiment, who recently established an outpost there. The column advances in

U.S. armor (Quad 50s) is in action to bolster the 9th Regiment's attack against Bloody Ridge.

single file obscured by fog, but a more ominous sight is the haze and low clouds that completely cloak Hills 773 and 940, as if they don't exist. Nevertheless, the vanguard of the column out in front of the first knoll realizes that, at any time, the next step could ignite the fight for the hill.

As the scouts on the point arrive slightly beyond the first knob, sudden but anticipated enemy machine gun fire strikes with effect. A brief fire fight erupts with devastating results. Several troops and the commanding officer of Company C are wounded. Meanwhile, the enemy remains unscathed, as their positions are about two hundred yards away and contained in fortified bunkers. Soon after, the two remaining officers become wounded

and at about the same time, the fire becomes so heavy that the advance is halted.

The battalion commander, Lt. Colonel Gaylord Bishop, is posted at the 38th Regimental positions on a hill east of the road, placing him within sight of the fight. Visibility is poor and Bishop is informed of the situation by radio. He directs Company B to jump to the front and continue the attack. The 1st Platoon, led by Lieutenant Joseph W. Burkett, takes the point and leads the drive toward the first knoll under support fire from the remainder of the company and elements of Company C. The advance has no artillery or air support due to the fog, but four machine guns provide some comfort as Burkett drills forward through the fog.

Resistance against the platoon remains light, giving the platoon leverage to reach the knoll, but as it arrives at the diminutive hill caution rules as they await some deadly grenades to come tumbling upon them. None are tossed. Burkett lunges up the hill and throws a grenade over to the reverse slope, while several of his troops trail the grenade and discover abandoned positions.

Burkett leads his platoon toward the next knoll, but en route, in addition to losing radio contact, the support fire from the machine guns also ceases, causing great concern, particularly because at about the same time, the enemy fire intensifies. Nonetheless, the platoon forges ahead directly into the path of incoming grenades that cause the vanguard of the platoon to scatter. Fortunately, the grenades continue to tumble farther down the hill and detonate without causing any casualties.

After the grenades harmlessly explode, more follow, but Burkett detects the bunker from which they came and moves to liquidate the position. Meanwhile the second grenade toss does inflict casualties, some due to the troops not attempting to get out of harm's way. In the meantime, several BAR teams rush to support the beleaguered platoon. Immediately after their arrival, PFC Domingo Trujillo, standing straight up, fires his BAR directly into the bunker, but unbeknownst to Trujillo, the bunker remains deadly. As he lowers his BAR, another BAR man spots a North Korean in the bunker preparing to fire. In an instant, the 2nd BAR misfires and Trujillo is hit directly in the chest and neck, killing him instantly.

Lieutenant Burkett, although hindered by the fog, orders his troops to provide cover fire while he maneuvers to get atop the bunker. Shortly thereafter, Burkett bolts through the haze to the opposite side of the knoll and squirms along the ridge to a point he believes is just above the bunker. He pulls the pin and deposits it right on top of the bunker and then for good measure drops another. Meanwhile, another soldier tosses several more grenades to Burkett and each is dropped into the bunker.

To Burkett's surprise, the six grenades had apparently only stirred the hornet's nest. The bunker that defended the frontal approach to the crest also had a back door. A North Korean bolts through the door and tosses at least five grenades at Burkett, who hurriedly dives down the ridge, but not quickly enough. The first wave scores no harm, but as he warns a sergeant, another grenade lands farther up the slope and explodes about five or six feet from where they stand. Both Burkett and Sergeant Hartman, the man who initially tossed the grenades to Burkett, are both wounded.

Burkett is still able to direct his platoon. He orders the men to withdraw out of the range of grenades and remain there until he can return with help. Nonetheless, Burkett is overruled by the regimental commander, Colonel Bishop, who concludes that it is too late to reinitiate the assault. He orders Company B to establish a night perimeter and resume the attack on the following day. Meanwhile, other troops from Company B are dispatched to assist with the evacuation of the wounded from Lieutenant Burkett's platoon.

At dawn on 1 September, the weather is cooperating. The daylight is no longer obscured by fog and haze. Still, the crack of dawn signals another day of gruesome combat. After another restless night, the 9th Infantry Regiment moves out to vanquish the remaining defenders on Bloody Ridge, held by the Communists since 18 August. The attack is spearheaded by Company A. Due to the absence of fog, artillery is able to support the advance. Cover fire is applied along the ridgeline between Hills 773 and 940 and the former also becomes the recipient of mortar and heavy machine gun fire, supplied by Company C, which also supports the assault. As the vanguard reaches the point of advance gained on the previous day by Company B, again, the North Koreans pour fire upon the attacking platoon.

A second platoon, led by the company commander Lieutenant Elden Foulk, speeds forward and it, too, incurs casualties, including Lieutenant Foulk. Despite a serious wound, Foulk makes it back to the lines of Company C and just before he collapses, Foulk requests reinforcements for Company A. Once Colonel Bishop is informed, he throws Company B back into the fight. The reinforcements sprint to the lines of Company A and jump ahead, drilling straight toward the obstinate bunker that has halted progress. After the reinforcements close on the obstacle, a few grenades clear the way. The ferocious resistance on the third knoll is terminated by 1000.

Having secured the first three knolls, the 9th Regiment focuses on the next objective, the tallest peak of the ridge that encompasses Hill 773, a ridgeline known as the question mark due to its curvature that seems to form a hook at the tip. It stands less than 300 yards distant, but in the hills of Korea, 300 yards, at times, are measured by inches and underscored with blood and steel. The advance pushes forward at about 1400 and casualties mount on both sides. Company B is operating with only about fifty troops. As the vanguard pushes ahead, suddenly, enemy fire originating on Hill 940 pounds the unit just about the time the troops encounter several more bunkers, each of which are heavily fortified. Occupants of the concealed bunkers begin to lob grenades that wound more troops. Company B is compelled to withdraw, but only for a short time.

Quick thinking on the part of the commanding officer, Captain Edward Krzyzowski, places the company back on the offensive. A runner acquires a bazooka and ammunition to level the field. The first bunker is liquidated and then a second is destroyed by an agile soldier, PFC Edward K. Jenkins, who slivers into position above the obstacle and maneuvers into position from where he drops several grenades upon the defenders to silence the guns there. In a short while, Jenkins destroys the third bunker as he positions himself from where he can attack. After catching three grenades tossed to him, he deposits two of them into the laps of the defenders to terminate the resistance.

Progress is still stalled; yet another one emerges and the fire halts the advance. Attempts are made to inch forward to knock it out, but the twenty-five yards separating them is also covered by several other positions that place the empty space in a menacing cross-fire. After assessing the odds and the fast-approaching darkness, it is concluded that the combined guns on Hill 773, those on the peak of the question mark and the longer-range weapons on Hill 940 make the bunker a task too risky. Companies A and B, now holding a combined strength of only forty some able-bodied men, cancel the advance and establish a night perimeter.

At dawn on 2 September, the quest to secure the objectives continues. No major assaults are launched; however, small probing advances press against Hill 773 and discover the occupants are prepared to fight. The advancing platoons are each greeted with hand grenades tossed from the high ground on the slopes.

Meanwhile, urgently needed replacement troops are assigned to the 1st Battalion. The beleaguered 1st Battalion, 9th Infantry Regiment, receives more than 150 replacements, including 6 officers. Company A and Company B are each bolstered by 65 men and Company C receives 20 men. In addition, each company receives 2 officers. The force is augmented by artillery fire, air strikes and mortars, focused primarily against Hill 940 and the western sector of the ridgeline.

Although no large sized assaults are initiated, Lieutenant Mallard, acting commander of Company C, establishes an outpost on the most recently captured knoll and from there, he is able to communicate by radio with some tanks. The tanks in turn pound various targets selected by Mallard. The clear skies allow heavy mortars to focus upon Hill 773. Enemy-held Hill 940 is pounded by artillery and to further inflict punishment upon the enemy, planes arrive to strike the western portion of the ridgeline.

As daylight arrives on 3 September, the 9th Infantry fine tunes its strategy for the attack. At 0900, the assigned platoon of Company C is directed to move to spearhead the assault; however, before the advance jumps off, orders arrive from Colonel Bishop to hold in place until an imminent air strike is carried out. At about 1030, planes arrive and deliver napalm upon targets selected by the Company A, whose commander, Lieutenant Robert D. Lacaze, had replaced Lieutenant Foulk of the 2nd after he had been wounded. Lieutenant Mallard continues to control the tanks' fire and the mortar units. Hills 773 and 940 are deluged with an avalanche of fire.

In early afternoon, the air strikes are completed and Company C jumps off, but its composition has greatly changed in the past few days. Of the three platoons, the combined strength is about 85 troops and of these, two of the platoons are battle hardened while the other is composed primarily of replacement troops. In a short period of time, the fresh troops will receive their baptism of fire.

The vanguard leads the way around the curve of the question mark and immediately encounters obstacles. The obstinate bunkers present less of a challenge than that which would be encountered if the attack moved directly over the treacherous ridge against heavy machine gun fire from Hill 940; however, the task remains daunting. The advance presses against the first of a trio of bunkers and then the second, but as they move forward, it begins to rain grenades. The grenade launching originates on the opposite side of a steep ravine that separates the North Koreans there by only a few, but deadly, yards.

The troops sustain high casualties, primarily from the grenades, but the first two bunkers are destroyed. The third bunker, however, is able to halt the advance. The platoon is too badly battered to continue. A second platoon, also battle tested, moves out to continue the attack, but it, too, comes under devastating grenade and small arms fire, which inflicts high casualties.

All the while, the third bunker operates under the protection of cover fire from adjacent positions, jeopardizing both platoons. Through the earlier actions of Colonel Bishop, 6 men who had taken a course in flame throwers arrive during the morning to bolster Company C, at about the same time that both platoons stall at the steps of the third bunker. Soon after, Lieutenant Mallard dispatches his third platoon along with the flame throwers. A platoon from Company A covers as reserve while the final Company C platoon advances.

Heavy fire impedes the advance. One of the three accompanying flame thrower teams is victimized by the enemy fire, but only the flame thrower is hit, sparing the men from harm. The two remaining teams make it to positions just under the summit and point the flame throwers toward the sky before pulling the trigger. The flames are propelled on an angle that carries the burning jelly over the top of the knife-like ridge and onto the reverse slope, jolting the Communists into a frenzy as they abandon the bunker.

The flame thrower trainees are now battle tested and their clearance operation opens the way for the remainder of Company C to swerve around the hook of the question mark and into the path leading to two additional bunkers, the final obstacles in front of Hill 773. The advance continues and the bunkers are silenced.

Afterward, there is a final thrust to the summit and Hill 773 is back in the hands of the U.S. The quest on this day drains Company C from its starting complement of about 85 troops to a force about the size of a platoon.

Lieutenant Mallard directs his weakened Company

C to establish night positions and with authorization from Colonel Bishop, he uses the Company A platoon and incorporates it into Company C to strengthen the perimeter and provide him with an opportunity to merge the fresh troops with his veterans. Although much progress had been accomplished, the North Koreans continue to threaten the positions and inflict more casualties.

Shortly after securing Hill 773, Lieutenant Mallard is struck and wounded by friendly fire when an artillery shell inadvertently drops short of its target. While he is moving back to receive medical attention he encounters Captain Krzyzowski, who is directing Company B's deployment in the area vacated by Company C. While they exchange information, fire from an enemy machine gun on Hill 940, 1,000 yards distant, strikes and kills Krzyzowski. The wounding of Mallard and the death of Krzyzowski is a costly blow. Only two officers remain among the three infantry companies of the 1st Battalion, 9th Infantry Regiment.

Circumstances unexpectedly change for the 9th Infantry Regiment on 4 September as the men peer at the death and destruction on the ridge, which by this day has been shattered by a combination of air strikes, artillery bombardments and the direct fire of tanks. The 9th Infantry is ordered to suspend its advance toward Hill 940 due to a planned full-scale attack. The bomb-scarred ridge is pummeled with more bombs and napalm and the attack is underscored with earth-shattering artillery bombardments.

While the 9th Regiment has encroached but not reached the summit of the ridge the 38th Regiment, as part of the ongoing X Corps' offensive, has pierced the enemy's defenses. On this day it secures Hills 660 and 774 north of Pia-ri. Elements of the 38th Regiment, on 26 August, had been pushed from positions north of the village to positions about 1,000 yards below the village. But now they have retaken the ground and are in position to provide its guns to bolster the 9th Regiment at Bloody Ridge. In addition, the 23rd Regiment is directed to move west into another cauldron, designated Objective "N," a stretch of the ridge leaning northward from Hill 983 to Hill 778.

At dawn on 5 September, the target is Hill 940. Yet again, the overtaxed troops of the 9th Regiment ascend the slopes to the summit, but this advance succeeds. The ground troops charge to the summit to deliver a resounding blow that ensures victory. The ground troops of the 1st and 2nd Battalions literally pass hundreds of North Korean corpses as they ascend the slopes, in what becomes the final assault on Bloody Ridge. The troops still on the crest bolt from their positions in an attempt to escape. The 9th Infantry Regiment permanently secures the hill at about 1400. Communist losses in defending the blood-stained ridge amount to more than 4,000 killed and about 7,000 wounded. While the 9th Infantry Regiment is securing its objective, the 23rd

Regiment also scores successes during its supporting role against Objective "N." (*See also,* **September 5, 1951.**)

Despite the horrific losses inflicted upon the North Koreans on Bloody Ridge, the Communists, after retiring from the ridgeline, immediately begin to regroup and form a new line of defense from which to terminate the continuing progress of the 2nd Division. The North Koreans replenish their grievous losses with several new battalions and form a new defensive line in yet another rugged ridgeline that extends north to south and encompasses Hills 851, 931 and 894.

At Hill 894, to the south, the curvature of the slopes swing in a southwestward direction and begins to level out with a group of smaller hills near the village of Tutayon. This defensive line becomes the next battleground for the 2nd Division. Like Bloody Ridge, this new killing field receives a name that overshadows the respective hills, Heartbreak Ridge.

August 18   *In Air Force activity,* Far East Air Forces commences Operation STRANGLE, designed to destroy and damage the enemy rails in North Korea. The Air Force had commenced a similar operation with the identical name on 31 May to destroy enemy supply lines. Also, a 2-plane patrol attached to the 334th Fighter Interceptor Squadron, 4th Fighter Interceptor Group, led by 1st Lieutenant Richard S. Becker, encounters and attacks a solitary MiG-15 in the vicinity of Sinuiju. Becker knocks it out at 1115 following a short hunt and then within a few minutes, at 1121, Becker pumps several bursts of machine gun fire another MiG-15 and damages it severely, but it remains in the air. He closes further and from a distance of about 200 feet, he again pulls the trigger and the MiG catches fire, while the pilot ejects from the aircraft.

August 19   *In the I Corps sector,* following a four-day struggle, elements of the 2nd Division seize the crest of Hill 1179 (Taeu-san), in the vicinity of the southwestern tip of the Punch Bowl. Earlier, ROK troops had failed to seize the objective.

August 20   Enemy shore batteries fire upon the destroyer USS *Uhlmann* (DD 867) while she operates off Ho-do Pando Island at Wonsan. The *Uhlmann* returns fire and knocks out two guns of the seven that had been spotted. The warship aborts further fire due to the activity of a friendly contingent on the ground in the same area. The *Uhlmann* sustains no damage.

August 22   At Kaesong, the Communists, having made good use of the partial lull in battle to refurbish their forces, use another delaying tactic. The Communist representatives at the peace table in Kaesong abruptly walk out of the meeting after claiming falsely that U.N. planes had broken the neutrality of Kaesong by dropping napalm bombs. After dusk, the Communists and a USAF team, using flashlights, inspect the supposed location of the bombing by a U.N. plane. Colonel Andrew J. Kinney and his party discover a hole

A pontoon bridge in the I Corps sector, 3rd Division zone, was overwhelmed by flash flood and washed about 300 yards downstream.

and evidence of exploding grenades. No scorching from napalm was found, but there were some unexplainable metal parts, including the tail-fin of a rocket. Nevertheless, the Chinese demand a "confession" and an "apology." None is given.

In the X Corps sector, 1st Marine Division zone, the division is informed that it is to prepare for a return to offensive action.

In Naval activity, the cruiser USS *Toledo* (CA 133) continues to operate off the east coast of Korea in support of the X Corps and the ROK I Corps. Also, the USS *Essex* (CV 9) joins Fast Carrier Task Force 77 in place of the USS *Princeton* (CV 37), which recently embarked for the U.S. The *Essex* is the first carrier capable of carrying jets to arrive in the war zone. By the following day, the jet fighters (F2H McDonnell Banshees) engage in their first combat missions.

August 23   At Kaesong, the Communists halt the negotiations, claiming erroneously that the United Nations had violated the neutral territory.

In Naval activity, the cruiser USS *Los Angeles* (CA 1351) arrives on the east coast of Korea to relieve the cruiser USS *Toledo* (CA 133).

August 24   Missions carried out this day and the next by light bombers (B-26's) report more than 800 enemy vehicles destroyed during the ongoing night raids against enemy supply lines.

In Air Force activity, Colonel Benjamin S. Preston, Jr.

(336th Fighter-Interceptor Squadron, 4th Fighter Interceptor Group), while leading a patrol encounters a group of four MiG-15s. Preston's four Sabre jets attack. The trailing MiG is picked up by Preston, who from a range of about 500 feet snaps off six bursts of machine gun fire that downs the enemy plane. While the MiG plummets, the pilot is able to bail out at an elevation of about 9,000 feet to free himself of the burning aircraft. Also, Captain Jack A. Robinson (334th Fighter Interceptor Squadron, 4th Fighter Interceptor Group), while on patrol in the vicinity of Taechon, observes a MiG traveling alone. Robinson closes for the attack and releases a string of machine gun fire that strikes and downs the MiG.

August 25   The USS *Essex* (CV-9) launches fighter planes to fly escort for U.S. Air Force bombers on a mission over the enemy rail yards at Rashin. It is the first time during the Korean War that U.S. Navy planes escort an Air Force bomber mission. It also becomes the first mission in which U.S. Navy fighters fly as escort for Air Force bombers on a combat mission. Other naval surface craft involved with the mission include the USS *Helena* (CA 75), USS *Harry E. Hubbard* (DD 748) and the USS *Rogers* (DDR 876).

August 26–28 1951   Transport Division 13 initiates an amphibious demonstration near Changjon to cut the resistance in front of the ongoing advance of the ground troops. Amphibious vessels, the cruiser

USS *Helena* (CA 71), the battleship *New Jersey* (BB-62), a contingent of destroyers and some minesweepers participate during some portions of the operation.

August 26   The 1st Marine Division informs all of its components that offensive actions are imminent. At this time, the Division is deployed as follows: the 1st Marines at Chogutan, the 5th Marines in the vicinity of Inje, the 7th Marines near Yanggu and the 1st Korean Marine Regiment at Hangye. The division command post and the service units are posted along the Hongchon–Hangye Road near Tundong-ni.

In conjunction, the 11th Marines (minus) with the 196th FABn (11th Marine Regiment Group) is at this time an element of X Corps artillery. The 2nd Battalion, 11th Marines, is attached to the 1st Marine Division, while the 3rd Battalion is attached to the 2nd Infantry Division.

August 27   *In the X Corps sector,* Communists seize the recently captured Bloody Ridge from the ROK 5th Division during the night of the 27th-28th. The U.S. 9th Infantry Regiment, 2nd Division, attacks, but fails to regain the hill. Subsequent to the loss, it is decided to commit a five-division attack in the X Corps sector.

In related activity, 1st Lieutenant Lee R. Hartell (Battery A, 15th FABn, 2nd Division), attached to Company B, 9th Regiment, comes under attack near Kobangsan-ni, during the early morning hours. Hartell, as a forward artillery observer, does not withdraw, despite overwhelming numbers of the enemy who encroach his position. Instead, he remains in place to direct the artillery. He is about to be overrun, but still he maintains his hold on the microphone, while calling for flares. Just in time a protective wall of fire arrives that drives the Communists back, but only for a short time. Soon after, yet more of the enemy arrive, but Hartell, by this time mortally wounded, continues to guide the artillery and in his last directives, he urges both artillery batteries without pause. Lieutenant Hartell is awarded the Medal of Honor posthumously for his intrepid courage in the face of the enemy.

In the 1st Marine Division zone, the 5th and 7th Marines are directed to move to the region south and west of the Punch Bowl to relieve U.S. Army and ROK units at Bloody Ridge. The 1st Korean Marine Regiment also moves with the other two regiments, but the 1st Marines is to remain in division reserve. Early on this day, the 7th Marines near Yanggu prepare to move to the Soyang River, but no trucks arrive until 2100. In conjunction, the 5th Marines at Inje are to trail the 7th Marines. Meanwhile, the troops are under a constant rain. The 3rd Battalion finally arrives at the 7th Marines command post at Sohwari at 0300 on the 28th.

August 29   X Corps orders a larger attack, described as a "limited offensive." The attack is to commence on 31 August. The advance is in conjunction with the ongoing battle to control Bloody Ridge in the 2nd Division zone.

In the 1st Marine Division zone, the 3rd Battalion, 7th Marines, arrives at Sohwari at 0300, following a tedious day of waiting at the jump-off point until nearly midnight. After arriving, the Marines discover their bivouac area is flooded, which forces the troops to remain in the trucks to attempt to get a little rest. In

An LST laden with boxcars awaits unloading.

A crane unloads a boxcar at Pusan.

addition, the assembly area is on the opposite bank of the Soyang River. The first contingent to attempt to cross is Company H, but the trek becomes so perilous that the remainder of the battalion must be carried by DUKWs. Nevertheless, both battalions, the 2nd and 3rd, are on the opposite (west) bank by mid afternoon to begin relief of the U.S. Army and ROK units.

Also, two battalions of the 1st Korean Marine Regiment, to the left of the 7th Marines, assume responsibility for the area formerly held by contingents of the

2nd Infantry Division and the ROK 8th Division. The 1st Battalion, 7th Marines, on the west bank of the Soyang, relieve elements of the ROK 8th Division at a hill position about one and one-half miles north of Topyong. During the evening, enemy mortars strike the lines without harm.

August 30 *In the X Corps sector, 1st Marine Division zone,* the 1st and 3rd Battalions, 1st Korean Marine Regiment, are positioned to the rear of the line of departure on Hill 755. The Korean Marines make last minute preparations for the attack, scheduled to commence on the following morning. In conjunction, the 2nd Battalion holds at the regimental positions on the Kansas Line. In the meantime, the 2nd and 3rd Battalions, 7th Marines complete relief of the ROK 8th Division. Back on the opposite bank of the Soyang, the 1st Battalion, 7th Marines, had relieved elements of the ROK 8th Division on a hill position about one and one-half miles north of Topyong.

August 31 *In the X Corps sector,* in conjunction with the ongoing attack by the 9th Infantry to gain Hill 983, X Corps commences an offensive all along the front, which actually is a full-scale drive to the Hays Line. The 2nd Division's objectives, aside from Hill 983, is a hill mass that runs north-south in the eastern sector of the divisional zone. The targeted ridgeline stretches into the 1st Marine Division zone as it swerves into the northern rim of the Punch Bowl and intersects with an east-west ridge there. The Punch Bowl is cut from the 2nd Division zone and left for the Marines and the ROK 5th Division. The section delegated to the 2nd Division extends about 3,000 yards and includes a formidable enemy-held position, Hill 1243. The 38th Infantry is delegated Hill 1243.

In the 23rd Infantry Regimental zone, two battalions remain in reserve for use at any point in the divisional sector and the other battalion holds in place along the Kansas Line. The path to Hill 1243 is notched with a series of other hills that must first be secured prior to the primary target, Hill 1243, known as Kachilbong by the locals. Those initial obstacles include 1059 and 1181 and each of them that lean northeast from Taeu-san is as ominous as the largest of the group. The effort to secure the entire group will not be supported by tanks due to the nasty terrain.

The vanguard of the 23rd Infantry, the 1st Battalion, moves out at dawn. After a few hours, the resistance accelerates and becomes intense. Company C, at the point, plows into a large enemy force, but holds its ground. In the meantime, the other companies move up to reinforce, with one pivoting in an attempt to corral the opposition, but the North Koreans slug it out and give no ground. The intense combat terminates at dusk with no clear victor.

In the 1st Marine Division zone, an attack is launched against the northern section of the Punch Bowl. The 7th Marines and the 1st Korean Marine Corps Regiment commence an attack at 0600 to seize the X Corps' objective, designated Yoke, a ridgeline running west to east from Hill 930 through Hill 1026 and beyond to Hill 924 to the east. In conjunction, the first objective, the hill mass northeast of Topyong, is presently occupied by the 1st Battalion, 7th Marines.

Meanwhile, the sector of Yoke Ridge, east of Hill 924, lies in the path of the 3rd Battalion, 7th Marines. Hills 924 and 1026 are to be secured by the Korean Marines. Also, the 1st Tank Battalion is ordered to prepare to support the attacking regiments.

In related activity, the 5th Marines are to patrol the Kansas Line and the 1st Marines remain in X Corps reserve in the vicinity of Hongchon. The 3rd Battalion, 7th Marines, initially encounters light resistance, but as the advance continues, the opposition becomes heated and the slopes of Hill 702 are inundated with mines. The attack is suspended during the latter part of the afternoon. In conjunction, the Korean Marines also come to a halt.

In other activity, Marine Transport Helicopter Squadron 161 arrives in Korea. The unit will get organized and begin to move to Airfield X-83, near Sowo-ri, where VMO-6 is stationed.

September 1 Planes attached to Far East Air Forces, directed by the destroyer USS *Hopewell* (DD 681), carry out bombing and strafing missions in the vicinity of Wonsan on this day and the next.

In the X Corps sector, 2nd Division zone, the commander, Major General Clark L. Ruffner, having completed his regular tour of duty, departs for the U.S. The assistant commander, General Thomas de Shazo, assumes temporary command, until Ruffner's replacement, Major General Robert N. Young, arrives to assume command on 20 September. At this time, the 2nd Division has the highest rate of deaths in action.

In other activity, the 23rd Regiment resumes its advance toward Kachilbong (Hill 1243). The attack receives a huge assist by a thunderous artillery bombardment that strikes like a jackhammer to loosen the resistance. As the troops advance, the enemy attempts to repel the advance, but to no avail. Cracks in the defense appear and as the momentum builds, the North Koreans pull back, permitting the 1st Battalion to ascend the slope of Hill 1059 and plunge upon the summit by 1100. Afterward, the regiment makes quick progress as it drives along the ridge toward the next objective, Hill 1181, which is seized by about 1900.

Once Hill 1181 is secure, the regiment establishes night positions. In addition to the full complement of the regiment, other troops had been attached to assist in the tedious task of maintaining supplies and ammunition, which can be carried only by people in this terrain. The regiment gets assistance from Korean laborers, headquarters and service company, and some crewmen from the tank units who help transport the ammunition.

In related activity, the Communists strike the positions of the 2nd Reconnaissance Company (2nd Division) with mortars and artillery fire. Sergeant Charles W. Turner takes notice that the assault is pinpointed

The summit of Bloody Ridge, Hill 983, in the hands of the 2nd Division. The battle for Bloody Ridge raged from August 18 through September 5.

toward the tanks. He speeds to the tanks about 100 yards distant, mounts a tank and takes over the machine gun, then while pouring fire into the enemy positions, he directs fire for the tank's 75-mm gun. With Turner atop the tank and exposed, the armor is struck more than fifty times. Seven enemy machine gun nests are destroyed, but during the fierce engagement, Turner is killed. Lieutenant Turner is awarded the Medal of Honor posthumously for his extraordinary heroism under fire.

Also, in the 9th Regimental zone, the Communists launch an attack with contingents of three separate divisions. The positions of Company A, 1st Battalion, near the Naktong in the vicinity of Agok, are bashed, but no penetration occurs; rather, the unit is bypassed, which jeopardizes it and places it in near isolation. Soon another enemy unit encroaches its positions, but it is spotted. PFC Luther H. Story takes over a machine gun from his wounded gunner and then focuses on the approaching hordes as they ford the river. Story eliminates about 100 of the enemy. However, as usual, more take their place.

The intrepid actions of Story forestall disaster, but in a flash, he spots a truck closing on their positions and it contains troops and a trailer laden with ammunition. Story bolts to the road, then flings grenades. After exhausting his supply, he slithers back to his squad to get more and then throws them at the truck. Nonetheless, the enemy continues to press forward. Company A is ordered to withdraw, but Story, although wounded, volunteers to remain to afford cover fire. When the final elements of his unit depart, he is seen fighting off a far-superior force. PFC Luther H. Story is awarded the Medal of Honor posthumously for his extraordinary actions and heroism under fire.

In the 7th Division area, the 17th Regiment is heavily engaged with the enemy in the vicinity of Chup'a-ri. One platoon becomes stalled by vicious enemy fire that kills the platoon leader. Corporal William F. Lyell takes command and leads an attack against the heavily fortified positions, but the platoon again stalls. Lyell moves quickly despite the fire and confiscates a recoilless rifle with which he proceeds to knock out the obstacle to permit the attack to resume. Soon after, two other enemy positions stall his platoon. Lyell remains undaunted. He grabs a supply of grenades and single-handedly charges two bunkers and eliminates both; however, he becomes wounded. Nonetheless, Lyell leads his command to the north slope, from which the troops are positioned to fire into the enemy resistance. In the meantime, reinforcements rush to the slope, but Lyell is mortally wounded while providing cover fire. Corporal Lyell is awarded the Medal of Honor posthumously for his extraordinary actions in the face of hostile fire.

In the 1st Marine Division zone, the 3rd Battalion, 7th Marines, and the 1st Korean Marine Corps Regiment reinitiate the attack to seize objective, Yoke. The 3rd Battalion, Korean Marine Regiment, passes through the 3rd Battalion, 7th Marines, and drives toward a ridge on the flank of the ridgeline objective. After a dogged fight, the Korean Marines encroach the crest of Hill 924 by 1700, yet the Communist North Koreans are able to hold until about 2100 before the objective is secured, only to be lost again by a furious counterattack at midnight (1st–2nd).

In the meantime, the 3rd Battalion, 7th Marines, encounters tenacious North Korean resistance near Hill 702. The Communists launch five counterattacks against the 7th Marines on Hill 602 and some penetrate

the lines of the 3rd Battalion. Patrols of the 1st Battalion, 7th Marines, operating on the opposite bank of the Soyang River, see the distress and call for air strikes to aid the 3rd Battalion. The 11th Marines also saturate the enemy positions with an avalanche of fire. The all-day engagement breaks off at dusk.

In related activity, Air Force planes arrive to drop ammunition and supplies to the Korean Marines; however, of thirty-nine additional air drops in X Corps during the month of September, this is the only one that is delivered to the 1st Marine Division. All other supplies have to be delivered by Korean laborers.

In Air Force activity, a contingent of the 335th Fighter-Interceptor Squadron, 4th Fighter-Interceptor Group, encounters MiGs in the vicinity of Sinanju. Major Winton W. Marshall, the leader of one section of the flight, drives directly into a pack of 30 to 50 enemy planes. No U.S. planes are lost.

In Naval activity, enemy shore guns (anti-tank artillery, mortars and machine guns) strike the HMAS *Murchison* (PF) while the vessel is operating against Communist positions along the north bank of the Han River. The British sustain three wounded, two seriously.

September 2 *In the X Corps sector, 2nd Division zone,* the 38th Regiment bolts from its positions on Hill 1181 en route to Kachilbong (Hill 1243); however, enemy pressure again becomes heavy. The advance, led by the 3rd Battalion, is subjected to artillery fire and mortars, as well as the entrenched enemy. The vanguard force presses forward and eliminates strong points as it moves. Enemy machine guns and burp guns are silenced to ease the pathway. The fire intensifies as the advance encroaches the summit, but the ascent continues, step by step. Darkness settles over the area; however, the illumination of gunfire signals that the battle continues unabated, exhausting both the defenders and the attackers to the point that the side with the most stamina will prevail.

The summit suddenly becomes silent at 2145 when the contest ends. The beleaguered 38th Regiment vanquishes the defenders and holds the hill as the victors. Despite exhaustion, there is no time to relax until a perimeter is established to safeguard the summit. Subsequently, on 7 September, the 38th Regiment is relieved on the ridgeline by the ROK 5th Division.

In the 1st Marine Division zone, the Marines again reinitiate the attack to seize objective Yoke. At Hill 924, the Korean Marines, who participated in a see-saw battle for control of the hill on the previous day, mount a furious assault at dawn. The 11th Marines support the advance and by noon, the objective is secured. Following the capture of Hill 924, the 2nd Battalion, 1st Korean Marine Regiment, moves through the 2nd and 3rd Battalions to lead the way to Hill 1026, to the west.

In the meantime, the 3rd Battalion, 7th Marines, which had turned back at least five counterattacks on the previous day, is again struck before it can jump off to seize its objective. However, the Marines repulse the attack by 0700, and regroup to move against Hill 602. At about 0900, the attack commences. Supported by 11th Marines' artillery, the summit is secure by about 1100. The North Koreans mount several counterattacks to reclaim the hill, but all fail. At about 1500, the North Koreans disengage and retire.

In Air Force activity, a contingent of four F-86 Sabre jets, attached to the 335th Fighter-Interceptor Squadron, 4th Fighter-Interceptor Group, led by Major Winton W. Marshall, encounters a pack of six MiG-15s in the vicinity of Sinanju. Major Marshall moves in close behind the trailing plane and flames it with several bursts of fire. The plane sustains a hit in the fuselage and afterward, Marshall pours another burst of machine gun fire to down the MiG. The enemy pilot is spotted after he bails out. Also, Colonel Francis S. Gabreski, the commanding officer of the 4th Fighter Interceptor Wing (later, 51st Fighter Interceptor Wing) engages and destroys one MiG-15 in the skies northwest of Taechon.

September 3 *In the X Corps sector,* the 2nd Infantry Division and the ROK 5th Division continue to advance west of the Punch Bowl against minimum resistance to make substantial gains.

In related activity, the 9th Infantry, since 31 August, has been engaged in the vicinity of Tondul at Hill 700. Captain Edward C. Krzyzowski had eliminated several obstacles on the first day of the conflict and on the succeeding days, he continues to take a lead in the attacks. Often he singlehandedly eliminates obstinate enemy positions. Krzyzowski, although seriously wounded, ordered his command to pull back while he provided cover fire. On this day, again Krzyzowski leads the way. Initially several positions are overrun, but still, enemy fire is able to stall the advance. Krzyzowski maneuvers into position on a knoll to direct mortar fire, but before he can direct the fire, he is slain by a sniper. Captain Krzyzowski is awarded the Medal of Honor posthumously for his extraordinary heroism under fire.

In the 1st Marine Division zone, the 3rd Battalion, 7th Marines, fortify their positions on Hill 602. The 1st Korean Marine Regiment reinitiates its attack to gain Hill 1026. In conjunction, the 2nd Battalion, 7th Marines, comes out of reserve and fills in a part of a new sector that occurred when the 7th Marines' zone was stretched to cut down the length of the Korean Marines' area.

The North Koreans react tenaciously against the Korean Marines and mount a ferocious counterattack, but following a brutal contest that lasts more than three hours, the 1st Korean Marine Regiment prevails. Later, at 1230, the North Koreans again mount a strong attack to regain the hill, but they fail. By about 1430, the Communists disengage and retire.

By 1800, all X Corps objectives of Ridge Yoke are accomplished and the 1st Marine Division holds the entire Hays Line, which is also the complete northern rim of the Punch Bowl. The North Korean defenders are victimized after four difficult days of combat; how-ever, the cost of victory had been expensive. Casualties, including the Korean Marines, amounts to 109 killed and 494 wounded. The Communists lose 656 killed (counted) and 40 are captured.

In Naval activity, Vice Admiral I.N. Kiland, USN, commander Amphibious Force Far East (CTF 90), is succeeded by Rear Admiral T.B. Hill (commander Amphibious Group 1).

September 4 *In the X Corps sector, 1st Marine Division zone,* the Marines consolidate their positions along the Hays Line. In conjunction, patrols are dispatched northward in search of enemy units, while preparations are made to commence the next phase of the 1st Marine Division's attack. In the course of the operation to seize Ridge Yoke, it became apparent that the Communists had taken advantage of the lull in combat while peace talks were underway in Kaesong. The Communists' fire power during the recent Marine operation was almost equivalent to that of the 11th Marines and U.S. Army units that supported the Marines.

While the Communists managed to build their arsenal in Korea, the 1st Marine Division concludes that the next phase of the attack must be postponed until 9 September, to allow time to replenish artillery and mortar ammunition. The supply depot, Ammunition Supply Point (ASP) 60-B, is located about five miles to the rear of the guns and just under fifty miles from Hongch'on. Due to the extremely poor condition of the road, which for most of the distance is a slim serpentine path, the time required to make one round trip is about twenty-five hours. All the while, about fifty trucks will not be available for other division uses.

In related activity, during the daylight hours, patrols are unable to spot the enemy, but during the night (4th-5th), the North Koreans strike positions of the 5th Marines along the Kansas Line. Similarly, in the 7th Marines area, about five miles in front of the 5th Marines, patrols move out from the Hays Line without encountering the enemy. The Communists continue to strike the Marine perimeter with artillery; however, the locations of the guns are concealed.

In Naval activity, Fast Carrier Task Force (TF 77) sustains the loss of four planes, three by enemy fire and a fourth by mechanical difficulties. Three pilots are killed and the one who survives sustains injuries from burns.

September 5 *In the X Corps sector, 2nd Division zone,* the 2nd Battalion, 23rd Infantry Regiment, in coordination with the 9th Infantry Regiment, attacks and seizes Objective "N" slightly after 1600. The battalion was bolstered by Company B and Company C, 72nd Tank Battalion. While the 2nd Battalion secures its objective, the 1st Battalion encroaches the summit of Hill 618. Shortly after Objective "N" is secured, Hill 618 comes under the control of the Regiment. Control of Hill 618, west of Bloody Ridge, gives the regiment a strategic piece of real estate that is a natural blockage along the MSR, causing the curve in the road running northward to swerve eastward.

Top: A rescue helicopter lands on the USS *Boxer* following the rescue at sea of a downed pilot. *Bottom*: A U.S. Navy tanker refuels a destroyer (left) and a cruiser (right) in the Sea of Japan.

In Naval activity, CTG 95.6 is ordered to initiate a minesweeping operation in the area from Wonsan to the waters near Hungnam, to clear the way for warships to patrol the area from which their guns can safely reach their targets. Hungnam is scheduled to come under bombardment for the first time since X Corps abandoned it, during the period following the Chosin Reservoir campaign of the previous year.

September 6 *In the I Corps sector,* 3rd Division zone, the positions of Company L, 3rd Battalion, near Ch'orwon on Hill 284 come under attack during the night (6th-7th). Small outpost positions are overrun. During the savage exchange, Corporal Jerry K. Crump observes two enemy troops closing on a friendly unmanned machine gun. The two troops are killed, both by bayonet. Afterward, he moves back to his foxhole, now inhabited by four other men of the command and each is wounded. Shortly thereafter, an enemy grenade is tossed into the foxhole. Crump, in an attempt to save the others, blankets the grenade with his body. All survive. Corporal Crump is awarded the Medal of Honor for his extraordinary heroism in the face of the enemy.

In the X Corps sector, 2nd Division zone, the 23rd Infantry Regiment relieves the 9th Infantry Regiment, the latter having just completed a prolonged hardfought series of battles for Bloody Ridge. After completing the relief, the Company E, 23rd Regiment is dispatched to occupy Hill 785, located northwest of Objective "N." Company F deploys on Hill 778 northeast of Objective "N."

In other activity, toward the later part of the night, an enemy contingent operating from Hill 618 launches an unsuccessful attack against Company I.

September 7   *In the I Corps sector,* the Communists launch a strong assault against the positions of Company I, 3rd Battalion, 35th Regiment. One man, Private Billie G. Kanell, defies the mortar and artillery barrage to fire at the approaching ground troops. A grenade lands near Kanell and two nearby troops, but Kanell blankets the grenade to save the others. He survives, but is badly wounded. Shortly thereafter, yet another grenade is thrown at the small group and again, Kanell, unable to move quickly, still gathers the energy to smother the grenade with is body to save the others. Private Kanell is awarded the Medal of Honor posthumously for his extraordinary courage in the face of the enemy and for his selfless sacrifice to save others.

In the X Corps sector, 2nd Division zone, Division command post is moved to a place near the eastern sector of the Hwach'on Reservoir. The 38th Infantry Regiment is relieved at Kachilbong (Hill 1243) by the ROK 5th Division. (*See also,* **September 2**, 1951.)

Also, reconnaissance patrols operating west of Hill 1181 near Kachilbong encounter enemy units on Hill 868. Other enemy contingents are discovered north of Hill 660 at Hill 703.

September 8   Naval ships operating on the west coast of Korea land a contingent of about 200 ROK guerrillas who launch a raid against enemy positions. Estimates of enemy killed are slightly more than 100. Also, the USS *Seiverling* (DE 441), while operating off Wonsan, comes under enemy fire from shore positions. The *Seiverling* is struck several times, but no casualties are sustained.

In the X Corps sector, 2nd Division zone, the Division's artillery units and the 72nd Tank Battalion support ROK attacks this day and the next. The ROK 5th Division at Kachilbong dispatches a contingent north, against an enemy strongpoint at Hill 1211, but the assault fails to make progress. Another attack supported

by elements of the 72nd Tank Battalion is launched by the 7th ROK Division to secure Hill 883, but it, too, fails to gain the objective.

September 9   *In the X Corps sector, 2nd Division zone,* the 1st and 2nd Battalions, 38th Infantry Regiment, move to the ridge that curves west off of Hill 1181 to secure and occupy it, but the move fails; the Communists have gained positions there. The enemy penetration causes complications, as the Communists who had infiltrated the area also plant mines. Two tanks hit mines as they patrol along the Pia-ri–Worun-ni Road.

In the 1st Marine Division zone, orders are issued that instruct the 7th Marines to prepare to commence an attack on 11 September to seize Objectives Able (Hill 673) and Baker (749).

In other activity, the 1st Marines receives orders that detach the unit from X Corps reserve and place it under the 1st Marine Division, with orders to prepare to pass through the 7th Marines once the objectives are secured. Then they are to extend the attack against Objective Charlie, a ridgeline that stretches northeast from Hill 1052. One company of the 5th Marines is to remain on the Kansas Line, while the remainder of the regiment moves into 1st Marine Division reserve.

Also, Marine Transport Helicopter Squadron 161 completes its transfer to Airfield X-83. The large transport helicopters will be used to drastically change combat supply tactics within three days. The squadron now consists of 15 HRS-1 Sikorsky helicopters. The helicopters are able to carry more troops (4 to 6 men in full gear) and can transport three to five casualties in litters.

In Air Force activity, a group of 28 F-86 Sabre jets operating in the area between Sinanju and Pyongyang is intercepted by a massive force of 70 MiGs. A group of 6 Sabres under Captain Richard S. Becker (334th Fighter Interceptor Squadron) on the patrol in the area between Sinanju and Pyongyang spots a force of 30 MiGs flying above the Sabres. Soon after, Becker spots yet another large formation closing on his command. Despite the odds, Becker orders the squadron to attack right into the enemy formation. The impetuous pilots totally disrupt the Communists. The Communists break their formation, but during the ongoing maneuvering, Becker gets separated from his squadron. Meanwhile, as he prepares to withdraw, Becker spots another contingent of about 15 planes. Rather than withdraw, Becker on his own dives toward the enemy and again the enemy becomes unbalanced. The aggressiveness of Captain Becker keeps him safe through the battle and he downs one of the MiGS, bringing his total for kills to five.

Also, during the air battles Captain Ralph D. Gibson, 335th Fighter Interceptor Squadron, also downs a MiG, his fifth kill to date. Both Becker and Gibson become aces. They join Captain James Jabara, who became the first jet-to-jet ace during the previous May. In conjunction, each of the officers, Creighton, Becker and Fisher, receive the Silver Star for their heroism and leadership under fire.

September 10–12 1951 *In the X Corps sector, 2nd Division zone,* the 38th Regiment takes action against enemy elements that had been encountered at Hill 868 on the 7th. The day-long assault by Companies A and G gnaw through the resistance and begin to ascend the slopes; however, ferocious resistance prevents the units from securing the summit. Night positions are established and on the following day, three companies attack. Company E maneuvers to positions from which it ascends from the southwest, while Companies A and G grind forward from the northeast. Again, the enemy pours continuous fire upon the assault troops. The ascents on either side are able to encroach the summit, but the Communists refuse to budge.

The first to grasp a hold near the crest is Company E, which reaches a point slightly more than fifty yards from the crest by about 1830, but the enemy is prepared to react and the force is met by grenades in such numbers that the assault is halted. Meanwhile, the other units maintain the assault and reach positions nearly within arm's reach of the crest, but here too, the Communists compel the force to pull back. While the enemy holds formidable positions, the 38th Regiment refuses to disengage.

The regiment establishes night positions and prepares to reinitiate the attack on the 12th with additional fire power. Following two unsuccessful days of combat, the attack commences with Companies A, E, G and I synchronized. The four companies advance in unison and the combined power eventually wears down the resistance. Nevertheless, the advance again is blood-filled, as the infantry drills to the summit and secures it by mid-afternoon.

In other activity, the 9th Infantry Regiment initiates the relief of the 23rd Regiment and completes the operation by 11 September. Company B, 72nd Tank Battalion, which has been attached to the 23rd Regiment, is attached to the 9th Regiment to provide support.

In the 1st Marine Division zone, the Advanced Echelon HMR 161 (Helicopter Transport Squadron) arrives at Nayhon-Ri, from where it will support ground operations of the Marines.

In Air Force activity, Captain Ward M. Millar, an F-80 pilot, following a harrowing set of circumstances, finds himself in territory south of Pyongyang. Captain Millar, attached to the 7th Fighter Bomber Squadron, had been shot down. He ejected and upon landing broke both of his ankles. The Communists captured him. About two months later, Millar escaped with the aid of a North Korean sergeant. Both then evade the Communists for about three weeks. On this day, an H-5 helicopter locates Millar and the North Korean and retrieves both men, then transports them back to Seoul.

In Naval activity, the USS *Redstart* (AM-378) and the USS *Heron* (AMS-18), while operating in the vicinity of Wonsan, are each struck by enemy shore batteries.

September 11 *In the X Corps sector, 2nd Division zone,* the 23rd Regiment, upon relief by the 9th Infantry Regiment, initiates relief of the 38th Infantry, beginning with the units not engaged against Hill 868. The entire regiment is relieved by 13 September.

In the 1st Marine Division zone, the 7th Marines initiates the assault to gain Hills 673 and 749; however, the ground between the Marines and the objectives include three formidable and dominating enemy-held positions, Hills 812, 980 and 1052, on Kanmubong Ridge, about 4,000 rugged yards from the primary objectives. And yet, one other obstacle had to be taken first, Hill 602, just to the front of the spearhead of the attack, the 3rd Battalion, 7th Marines. At just about dawn, Company H, 3rd Battalion, in the center, prepares to jump off, but inclement weather delays the assault. With the element of surprise lost, the ascent up the hill is easily detected. The Communists halt the advance at about the mid-way point.

Company I moves up the southwest spur of the hill to divert attention and release some pressure from Company H, but while H Company is able to reach a point about fifty yards from the crest, Company I somehow gets off course and ends up on the spur with H Company at about 1245. All the while, the North Koreans from their dug-in bunkers steadily pour machine gun and mortar fire into the Marine positions. Before dark the North Koreans launch two counterattacks that succeeded in pushing the Marines back.

Equally tenacious resistance is raised on Hill 673 (Objective Able), in the 1st Battalion zone, causing the 1st Battalion to also establish night positions short of the objective. During the darkness, the 2nd Battalion moves out and reaches positions behind the North Koreans on Hill 673 and prepares to strike from the rear.

September 12 *In the I Corps area, 25th Division zone,* Company B, 27th Regiment, engages the enemy in a fierce battle in the vicinity of Kumhwa. The intense enemy fire stalls the attack. Lieutenant Jerome A. Sudut attempts to clear the blockage; he drives directly toward the obstacle and ignores the wall of fire directed at him from the bunker. Sudut succeeds in destroying the obstacle and three occupants while the others retire hurriedly. Although the thrust succeeds, Sudut becomes seriously wounded. Nonetheless, he refuses evacuation and instead leads the next assault.

The abandoned bunker had in the meantime been reoccupied by the enemy who had used connecting trenches without being discovered. The platoon is again stalled. Sudut and one rifleman advance, but the rifleman is wounded. Sudut moves forward and eliminates three of four occupants before running out of ammunition. The remaining enemy soldier is greeted by Sudut, armed only with his trench knife, but still he prevails. The actions of Sudut inspire the command and they follow to seize the objective. Lieutenant Sudut had been wounded fatally. He is awarded the Medal of Honor posthumously for his intrepid actions and unwavering leadership in the face of the enemy.

In the X Corps sector, 2nd Division zone, Company B, 23rd Infantry Regiment, secures Hill 702 without a major contest by mid-afternoon.

In the 1st Marine Division zone, the 2nd Battalion, 7th Marines, which had maneuvered behind the North Koreans on Hill 673 without being detected, springs from its positions at the first crack of sunlight. The attack catches the Communists totally off guard. Although the 1st Battalion is slowed tremendously by mines that pepper the slope, the troops complete the ascent by 1415. During the ascent, Company B halts due to a wall of fire. Sergeant Frederick W. Mausert III, an acting platoon leader, bolts form his cover to retrieve two wounded Marines. Mausert receives a head wound but he refuses evacuation. Within minutes, Mausert leads a bayonet charge and en route to the objective, he gets hit again. His helmet absorbs the shot. He is knocked down but otherwise okay.

Meanwhile, as the troops are ready to take the final objective, the crest, enemy fire again stalls the attack. Mausert refuses to halt. He jumps ahead, runs directly toward the enemy machine gun to draw fire away form the remainder of his command, and stops only when the fire cuts him down. Still, Mausert remains adamant about leading his men to the crest. He ignores his multiple wounds, bolts to the summit and destroys a machine gun nest before he is fatally wounded. Sergeant Mausert is awarded the Medal of Honor for his extraordinary courage in the face of the enemy.

In the meantime, the 3rd Battalion, 7th Marines, seize its objective, Hill 602, and all attacking units reach the summit by 1030. During the attack, Second Lieutenant George H. Ramer leads his 3rd Platoon against a heavily fortified position. During the treacherous ascent, the bulk of his command becomes wounded. Lieutenant Ramer, with the able bodied men of the platoon, continue the climb and once at the crest, Ramer singlehandedly destroys an obstinate bunker. Ramer and eight other Marines seize the summit. However, the positions become untenable. Ramer, having sustained two wounds, directs the remainder of his contingent to seek shelter, but he refuses evacuation and holds the crest until the enemy finally overwhelms him. Lieutenant George Ramer is awarded the Medal of Honor posthumously for his extraordinary courage under hostile fire.

Later, at slightly after 1710, the 2nd Battalion reports Hill 749 (Objective Baker) secure; however, the North Koreans retain positions on the slope and threaten the Marines. Later, when the 1st Marines begin to relieve the 7th Marines, the 2nd Battalion is too engaged and some units are isolated, making the change impossible. Subsequently, a two-battalion surge secures the objective.

Fox Company, 2nd Battalion, is not relieved by the 1st Marines until 1100 on the following day. During the two-day contest, the Marines sustain 22 killed and 245 wounded. Enemy killed are calculated only by actual count, which is, for the identical time period, 30 killed and 22 prisoners.

In other activity, during the night (12th-13th), the 1st Marines relieves the 7th Marines and assumes responsibility for the zones of the 1st and 3rd Battalions, which pass into reserve. The helicopters are able to carry only two wounded Marines per trip, prolonging the evacuation mission.

September 13–October 15 1951 THE

BATTLE OF HEARTBREAK RIDGE Having recently cleared Bloody Ridge of the enemy, X Corps now prepares to eliminate the next North Korean line of defense, a ridgeline north of Bloody Ridge and equally treacherous. After being driven from their prior positions, the Communists retired to a series of razor-tipped ridges that include Hill 894, on a straight line about three miles north of Bloody Ridge, Hill 931, north of 894, standing as the tallest peak on the ridge, and beyond, the final major obstacle, Hill 851, sometimes referred to as the needle. The ridges are nestled between the Sat'ae-ri Valley and the Mundung Valley on the east and west respectively.

The North Korean 12th Division (N.K. III Corps) is deployed on the west bank of the Suip-ch'on River in the high ground above it to dominate the Mundung-ni valley. The other primary unit, the 6th N.K. Division, also of the N.K. III Corps, is deployed to defend Heartbreak Ridge and the Sat'ae-ri Valley.

Although Eighth Army is not focused on real estate for the sake of gaining it, the ridgeline that stretches about seven miles, specifically because of its strategic location, poses a tremendous threat to X Corps positions, mandating that the resistance there be leveled to prevent any catastrophic events from occurring to disrupt the U.N. bargaining power with the Communists.

The 2nd Division, which prevailed at Bloody Ridge after a prolonged duel, again receives the task. It is given responsibility for securing the southern portion of the ridgeline to cut off any possibility of the valleys being used as a funnel to threaten the lines west of the Punch Bowl. The key to the domination of the valleys is Hill 931. However, the enemy has tirelessly fortified the ridges and used their excellent skills to camouflage their positions to gain extra advantage during the eight days since they had been driven from their final bastion at Bloody Ridge.

During the final planning session, there is no unanimous consensus on the degree of resistance the Communists are willing to raise to hold the ground. In the recent past, the North Koreans, under orders from the Chinese, have been holding their ground, but at Bloody Ridge, their losses were extremely high, apparently bringing some on staff to conclude that the resistance would not remain rigid for too long. Others, including the commander of the artillery, remain convinced that they will "fight like hell" to hold the terrain.

At this time, General Ruffner has transferred back

Company B, 23rd Regiment, 2nd Division, moves up to relieve Company C during the fighting on Heartbreak Ridge (13 September–15 October).

to the U.S. The 2nd Division is now commanded by the acting division commander, Brigadier General Thomas E. de Shazo. He decides to launch the assault with only one regiment, the 23rd, rather than two, based on his leaning toward the theory that resistance will not be too substantial. Backup plans in place have the 9th Regiment prepared to lunge toward Hill 728 immediately after the fall of Hill 894.

At 0600, following a preliminary artillery attack of one-half hour, the 3rd Battalion, 23rd Regiment, led by Lt. Colonel Virgil E. Craven, advances north from Hill 702 as the spearhead of the assault force. A protective umbrella of artillery fire supports the drive. The 37th FABn assumes responsibility for direct and immediate support, while other units — the 38th FABn, 96th FABn, 503rd FABn and one battery of Company C, 780th FABn — add supplemental support. The 37th and 38th FABns are posted several miles southeast of the objective. The 96th is deployed more than five miles south of the objective

A U.S. soldier attached to the 23rd Regiment, 2nd Division, pauses for a rest near an enemy casualty during the fighting on Heartbreak Ridge.

and the 503rd is positioned nearly ten miles southeast of the ridgeline. Even farther back, Company C, 780th FABn, is deployed slightly more than ten miles south of the ridge.

As the advance progresses there is an ever-increasing anxiety caused by the lack of serious resistance. The veterans and the replacements each realize that the tranquil appearance of the valley is but a ruse to conceal a cauldron of fire on the brink of erupting at any time. The apprehension of the vanguard is not confined; rather, it is evenly spread within the ranks of Lt. Colonel Henry F. Daniels' 2nd Battalion, which is directly behind the 3rd. Initially, there is an ominous silence as the advance ventures through the Sat'ae-ri valley en route to the east-west spur of the ridge upon which the ground troops will traverse to the core of Heartbreak Ridge. From there the regiment splits to take out Hill 851 to the north with one battalion, while the other pivots to the south to seize 931 and 894.

As the troops advance, the resistance becomes severe, much more so than the strategy session had anticipated. Nevertheless, the 3rd Battalion presses ahead and then, the North Koreans open the flood gates. The columns are pounded with ravaging artillery barrages and menacing mortars. Casualties are

incurred. With each yard gained, more casualties are sustained, yet, still the advance continues. The grueling trek to the east-west spur continues to slowly wedge through the walls of fire.

The 3rd Battalion reaches the spur and begins the ascent, but soon after, the North Koreans, holding concealed positions, reveal their presence and unleash deadly streams of fire from machine gun and mortars. That ferocious burst of firepower, added to the incoming artillery fire, forbids passage and compels the 3rd Battalion to essentially hug the ground at the foot of the hill. The heavy resistance also prompts a change in the schedule, as the 9th Infantry had been awaiting word on the seizure of Hill 894 as a signal to move against Hill 728. With the obvious stall in the advance, the 9th Regiment's attack is suspended.

In the meantime, the 2nd and 3rd Battalions establish night positions and prepare to spend another uncomfortable, sleepless night in the Korean wilderness.

On the morning of 14 September, General de Shazo moves to get the attack back on track. He directs the 9th Regiment, at Yao-dong, to abort its plans to seize Hill 728 and focus on relieving the overwhelming pressure on the 23rd Regiment by attacking Hill 894. The 2nd Battalion, 9th Regiment, moves toward the objective, Hill 894. The attack is supported by elements of Company B, 72nd Tank Battalion, and further augmented by the heavy mortar company and a battalion of 155-mm howitzers to help insulate the troops and level the field if strong resistance lies in the path. After the battalion surges forward, it meets only nominal resistance, which permits quicker than expected progress.

By dusk, the battalion holds positions less than 700 yards from the summit of the objective. The attack is suspended for the night. The troops establish a night perimeter and begin preparations to continue the assault on the morning of the 15th. Unlike the most recent struggles to claim ownership of the dreadful real estate in this region of Korea, the 2nd Battalion has sustained extremely light casualties.

On the 15th, the stalled 23rd Regiment resumes its attack to break through the resistance and thread the line between Hill 931 the dominant peak on the ridge and Hill 851. The enemy still commands the approaches with positions at various angles that seal the slope and keep the regiment from ascending beyond the lower portion of the hill.

In the meantime, the 2nd Battalion, 9th Regiment, resumes the ascent on the southwestern slope of Hill 894. After a rough climb on the ragged slope, the vanguard bursts upon the summit during the afternoon to the dismay of the defenders, who are handily evicted. The battalion accomplishes its mission with only 11 casualties. The main mission in the seizure had been to press the enemy sufficiently to reduce the resistance against the 23rd Regiment, but the capture has no effect. The 23rd Regiment is unable to capitalize and ends the day at the lower portion of the ridge.

On the 16th, the circumstances of the 23rd Regiment remain dismal; however, other than the conquest at Hill 894, the entire 2nd Division continues to be impeded by the aggressive defense of the ridge. Even the continuous artillery bombardments and air strikes fail to collapse the iron resistance. The North Koreans burrow down during the massive strikes and when the artillery silences, they return to their guns. While the 23rd Regiment attempts to modify its attack by switching from a column formation to advancing abreast, the commanding officer also alters the tactics. Colonel Adams orders the 2nd Battalion to pivot and move southwest toward Hill 931, while the 3rd Battalion maintains its drive to the west. In another support move, elements of the 1st Battalion, Company C, move against Hill 931 by passing through the positions of the 9th Infantry Regiment at recently captured Hill 894 to launch an assault from the south.

As the separate units push ahead, each is easily observed by the North Koreans who wait patiently in their bunkers for the Americans to come within range of their small arms and grenades. As the day passes, casualties continue to mount, but still the men climb and eventually encroach the summit of Hill 931, only to find themselves on the receiving end of cascading grenades and machine gun fire. The hill and the ridgeline remain under North Korean control.

In the meantime, because the American regiments have not gained control of the hills or the valleys, the Communists continue to effortlessly resupply and bring in fresh troops. On the 16th, the N.K. 13th Regiment, 6th Division, moves onto the ridge and relieves the N.K. 1st Regiment.

By the termination of the fighting on the ridge on the 16th, the U.S. forces begin moving beyond exhaustion. Their relentless pursuit of victory has brought forth no results, yet there are no signs of giving up the struggle. Of course the morale droops, but primarily because of the difficulty of the terrain and the inability to quickly acquire supplies.

Unlike the Communists, the U.S. troops experience terrible logistics problems. Often, the Korean laborers abscond, abandoning the supplies as they flee. The roads are jammed due to the enemy's ability to pour fire at all strategic points that lead to the 23rd Regiments' positions. Another equally disturbing fact is that the task of evacuating the casualties is equivalent to walking through a firestorm. The trek back from the front of the regiment's positions while carrying a wounded soldier in a litter can take as long as eight to ten hours. And there is no indicator of the situation changing for the better. Nevertheless, the struggle to gain superiority continues on the 17th and the 18th. Still the Communists hold.

On the 17th, Company C, 23rd Regiment, comes under a vicious attack. One platoon holding strategic ground is hit by wave after wave. PFC Herbert K. Pililaau volunteers to hold the ground to afford cover fire while his exhausted platoon, upon orders, pulls back. He expends his automatic weapon ammunition, then reverts to grenades and when that supply is expended, Pililaau takes on the enemy that closes upon him with hand-to-hand combat. His final stand is accomplished with his fists and trench knife, but finally the enemy overruns his one-man line. On the following day, when Corporal Pililaau's body is retrieved, the detail counts more than forty enemy dead around him. Corporal Pililaau is awarded the Medal of Honor posthumously.

On the 19th, the contest is again reinitiated, but while the troops slug it out with the North Koreans, Colonel Lynch concludes that changes should be made to turn the tide of the battle to break the stalemate. Colonel Lynch, the commander of the 9th Infantry Regiment, is convinced that the assault must be enlarged and strengthened to punch a hole in the resistance that to this point has remained nearly invincible. His theory is that if he dispatches his 1st Battalion to seize Hills 867 and 1024, both located less than five miles south of Hill 894, which is presently held by the 9th Regiment, it will appear as if a major assault is being launched from the west. If the ruse works, he contends, the North Koreans will take the bait and slim their lines on the ridge to thwart the threat. However, General de Shazo, the acting commander, disagrees. He contends that the priority of X Corps, by a directive of General Byers, remains Hill 931, where the enemy had repulsed an attack by elements of the 9th Infantry Regiment on the 16th.

On the following day, 20 September, General de Shazo reverts back to the position of assistant division commander as General Young arrives and assumes command of the 2nd Division. Colonel Lynch's idea of the previous day is well received by Young. The plan is put into effect and the diversionary attack across the Mundung-ni Valley is scheduled to commence on 23 September, with Hill 1024 as the initial objective.

Meanwhile, there are no changes in the zone of the 23rd Regiment. It continues to grind forward with similar results, unable to permanently crack through the resistance. Throughout the 22nd, Hill 931 is assaulted from two sides, but at day's end, the North Koreans are able to hold the crest. On the following day, the 1st Battalion climbs to the summit, but during the early morning hours of the 23rd, it sustains severe casualties. The battalion, after expending all of its ammunition, relinquishes the crest to the N.K. 3rd Regiment, 12th Division.

During the 22nd, while the 9th Regiment prepares for its upcoming assault, General Van Fleet directs X Corps to expand its west flank to bring it alongside the IX Corps positions. Pursuant to Van Fleet's order, General Byers orders the ROK 7th Division to prepare to advance to seize yet another elevation, Hill 1142, which stands northwest of Hill 1024. The additional objective becomes another component in the attempt to draw forces away from the 23rd Regiment.

The two attacks jump off on the 23rd and unlike the 23rd Regiment, both forces, the 9th Regiment and the ROKs, push forward and gain ground. The attack continues to gain ground on 24 September in both zones. On the 25th, Hill 1024 is gained by the 9th Regiment. Meanwhile, the ROKs maintain their progress against Hill 1142.

The strategy of the X Corps begins to show success. The Communists feel the pressure closing against Heartbreak Ridge. The North Koreans anticipate an attack against another strategic point, Hill 867, farther north in the Mundung-ni valley. To counteract the 2nd Division movements, the Communists dispatch the N.K. 3rd Regiment, 6th Division, from its positions on Heartbreak Ridge, to forge a defensive line at Hill 867.

On the 26th, while the ROKs take Hill 1142, still the pressure against the 23rd Regiment remains rigid. During the day's contest, the French Battalion takes over for the 2nd Battalion and pushes south, but without any progress. In conjunction with the southern push, the 1st Battalion, 23rd Regiment, contin-

ues to grind north against near-impregnable positions of the heavy mortar and machine gun crews at and along the approaches to Hill 931. The 2nd Division had launched the attack on 13 September and as of this date, the casualties have risen to well more than 1,600 men. The 23rd Regiment has been hit the hardest; its casualties soar to more than 950 troops.

Colonel Adams, the regimental commander, on the 26th informs General Young that the ongoing operation is destined to accomplish only more grievous casualties unless the plan of attack is drastically modified. Adams concurs with the strategy of Colonel Lynch, 9th Regimental commander, and requests the attack be greatly expanded to compel the Communists to slim their defenses on Heartbreak Ridge, to defend against a wider assault. General Young and General Byers, X Corps commander, consider Colonel Adams' plan and by the following day, it is authorized.

The 23rd Regiment is ordered to halt its attack while new plans are drawn to execute a full-scale divisional assault, through both the valleys with the support of all available artillery and armor. The operation is later dubbed Operation TOUCHDOWN. The operational order is issued on 2 October in an effort to transform the two valleys of death into places of victory.

The preliminaries prior to the attack depend heavily on logistics to ensure that each participating unit has sufficient ammunition to sustain the attack for the duration. The transport crews become overtaxed to fulfill the requisitions, particularly because of the arduous trek from the rear to the front along pot-holed paths. Having learned from the debacle of the 23rd Regiment on Hill 931, supply depots are placed north of the Kansas Line so an abundant supply of ammunition will ready to go forward when required. Meanwhile, the engineers are equally tested. The 2nd Engineering Battalion must transform the hole-torn road leading through the Mundung-ni valley into a highway capable of carrying Sherman tanks.

The Communists have earlier taken precautions to make the road impassable by creating obstacles, including the usual menacing mines, but they have also pushed huge rocks from the heights. The engineers, working without their bulldozers, which are out of operation and in for repairs, plod forward. When possible the obstacles, such as craters, are repaired. Others are detonated, but if all else fails, the engineers modify the route and swerve it to the stream bed until it can be again diverted back upon the road. The engineers, by working without their mechanized equipment, draw less attention from the enemy.

During the first few days of October, the 2nd Division units deploy at their respective jump-off points and await the signal to attack. Meanwhile, the commanders spend countless repetitive hours going over the attack strategy. The 72nd Tank Battalion is informed that the roads are prepared to shuttle the armor through the Mundung-ni valley and that at those points too tight for passage, the engineers had sculptured the slopes with explosives to remove the jagged rocks.

In the 23rd Regimental zone, Task Force Sturman, established two days prior to the assault, is formed as yet another diversion to knock the enemy on Heartbreak Ridge, while simultaneously protecting the right flank. It is to drive through the Sat'ae-ri valley to pound against the enemy on the east slope of the ridge. The task force is built from a composite of units, including a French platoon and a company-sized contingent created out of the 2nd Division's security units. The task force is further bolstered by the 2nd Reconnaissance Company and the 23rd Tank Company.

As dawn breaks on 4 October, the troops of the 2nd Division begin final preparations for the attack as the armor begins to roll toward the respective starting lines. However, while the divisional assault is not scheduled until late on the night of the 5th, Task Force Sturman bolts ahead and moves northward through the Sat'ae-ri valley to distract the enemy. And the task force is not the only distraction. Forty-nine fighter bombers arrive to bomb and strafe the enemy's positions.

On 5 October, the stage is finally set for Operation TOUCHDOWN. The entire 2nd Division is lined up and ready to charge to the end zone, known as Heartbreak Ridge. During the afternoon, a thunderous, earth-shattering artillery bombardment commences. Meanwhile, as TF Sturman grinds ahead in the Sat'ae-ri valley, the 72nd Tank Battalion has its engines at the ready to plow through the Mundung-ni Valley and lead the way to the objectives, Hills 867, 1005, 980 and 1040, on the western sector of the valley. They are to be seized by the 9th Regiment, operating on the Divisional left flank.

In the meantime, the 23rd Regiment prepares to advance against the obstinate prize, Hill 931, and the ridge stretching from there to the west, but its task doesn't halt there. The 23rd is to position itself from where it can pivot to either move to secure an objective west of Hill 851, known as Hill 520, or to directly attack Hill 728, or bolster the attack of the 38th Regiment against it, depending on the progress of the offensive. The 38th Regiment is assigned responsibility for securing Hill 485. Through some luck, elements of the 38th Regiment on the previous day had detected that Hill 485 had been abandoned by the enemy.

In the late afternoon of 5 October, the artillery preparation commences. Later, just prior to the jump-off at 2100, Marine night fighter squadrons arrive and plaster the enemy positions with a combination of rockets and napalm, adding streams of machine gun fire that rivet the slopes. The tank-infantry forces move out in a wide-sweeping strike that finds cracks in the defenses. On the left, the 3rd Battalion, 9th Infantry, encounters only nominal op-

position as it drills toward Hill 867, while the 1st Battalion pushes toward Hill 666 and encounters similar resistance.

On the west the 3rd Battalion, 9th Infantry, presses toward Hill 867. Doggedly, the offensive continues through the dark of night in an all-out effort to end the stalemate. The 1st Battalion drives toward Hill 666. The full-throttle advance continues to progress throughout the following day and no serious problems develop with resupply. On 7 October, Hill 867, defended by the N.K. 3rd Regiment, 12th Division, falls to the 3rd Battalion, but there is no pause in the fight. On the following day, Hill 960 is secured by the 3rd Battalion, while the 1st Battalion evicts the occupants of Hill 666. Coupled with the progress of the 38th Regiment, by the 8th, the 2nd Division achieves five of its objectives. The rapid progress signals the fast approaching demise of the now temporary invincibility of the Communists on Heartbreak Ridge.

The 23rd Regiment, snagged in a quagmire since the initial attack commenced, receives the sparks necessary to break out from the abominable positions before the area is transformed into a graveyard. The developing strategy to disrupt the security of the enemy's galvanized lines unfolds well in the zone and the absence of an artillery bombardment and air strikes on Hill 931 underscores the ruse. The defenders are anticipating a leisurely night, unaware that the 23rd is finally on the move. The property value of the hill rises steeply.

The attack maintains the element of surprise as the attached French platoon gives all outward appearances of driving against Hill 931, while the 1st Battalion, 23rd Regiment, advances in the direction leading to Hill 851. All the while, the 2nd Battalion creeps quietly up the slopes of the real target, Hill 931, in a stealth move coordinated with the guns of the 37th FABn, the latter awaiting the signal to commence firing. Over the course of the operation, each enemy bunker yet undestroyed is marked for oblivion by the artillery. As the 2nd Battalion encroaches the target, every available piece of artillery goes into action, sending an enfilade of fire upon the slopes with tremendous effectiveness. The mortars, which had inflicted about eighty-five percent of the casualties on the 23rd Regiment, begin to be silenced.

Meanwhile, the infantry charges toward the crest, using flame throwers as they climb, taking out other bunkers previously unmolested by the artillery. The momentum of the charge stuns the defenders as the 2nd Battalion rolls forward like an assembly line to finish the project with their rifles and grenades. The attack continues in lop-sided fashion. The enemy is unable to return any punishing fire. While the enemy is being eliminated, the regiment sustains only light casualties into the early morning hours of the 6th. By about 0300, about one-half of the hill is controlled by the 2nd Battalion. The enemy, however, still attempts to thwart the inevitable. A strong counterattack is

Two U.S. troops rush through heavy fire and smoke.

mounted. The 2nd Battalion, in anticipation of the attack, is fully prepared and repulses it handily prior to dawn.

At the crack of dawn on the 6th, still in the zone of the 23rd Regiment, the attack is reinitiated. As the 2nd and 3rd Battalions grind forward, a link is made with the French battalion. Some resistance re-

mains, but the powerful thrust of the combined strength of the three regiments clears the hill by about noon.

Back in the 38th Regiment's zone of operations, after occupying Hill 485 on the 4th, the regiment's 1st Battalion focuses on Hill 728, which it secures by about noon. Meanwhile, the 2nd Battalion moves against Hill 636, which is secured on the following day. The seizure of the two hills proves to be a key achievement during the early stages of the operation. It gives the 38th Regiment dominating positions from which to shepherd the engineers while they continue to complete the last leg of the pathway for the tanks. And, it permits the 38th Regiment to provide an umbrella of cover fire.

In conjunction with the seizure of the second objective, Hill 636, the 72nd Tank Battalion is attached to the 38th Regiment. The tankers, led by Lt. Colonel John O. Woods, assist the regiment in the quest to seize several more targets, beginning with Hill 605 farther north and from there Hill 905–Hill 974, which stretches northwest from Hill 636 to Hill 1220 along the Kim Il Sung Mountain range. In addition, Hill 841 north of Hill 974 falls into the zone of the 38th Regiment.

On the 9th, from newly gained positions at Hill 960, northwest of Hill 867, the 9th Regiment continues to advance northwest to secure Hill 1005, beyond Hill 666. Some stubborn resistance occurs at the objective as the troops close upon the crest, but the close-quartered fighting rises to a crescendo of fury following an order to fix bayonets. The cold steel of the regiment's bayonets overcomes the grenades and burp guns of the defenders. The hill falls, further shrinking the enemy's tenacious stranglehold on the high ground. In the meantime, the ROK 8th Division, which is advancing against Hill 1050, pounces upon it and secures it on 10 October.

By 10 October, the engineers finish the task of removing the obstacles and laying the road, which acts as a draw-bridge for the armor to plow deep into the enemy's lair, something totally unexpected by the Communists. While the tanks of the 72nd Tank Battalion surge forward, supported by a contingent of engineers and an infantry detachment (Company L), they stumble upon the vanguard of the Chinese 204th Division (68th Army) while they are leisurely relieving elements of the N.K. V Corps in the vicinity of the village of Mungdung-ni. Suddenly the Communists come under an avalanche of fire that totally catches them off-guard. As the Chinese break for safer positions, the tank-infantry force pursues.

During the running fight, the troops sustain casualties as they bolt through Mungdung-ni, but the Chinese sustain high casualties. During the exchange, the tanks continue to penetrate deeper and in conjunction with the advance, the tanks are spaced from where they can provide cover for one another while simultaneously pounding the enemy positions. The operation succeeds in severing the enemy supply lines on the western side of Heartbreak Ridge.

The loss of the supply line also hampers the ability to bring in fresh troops, which adds another spike into the enemy's defenses, which are tumbling but not yet toward a total collapse. As the tanks plow forward, the 2nd Battalion, 38th Infantry, launches an attack against Hill 605, but there, the enemy refuses to budge.

Company L, 38th Regiment, encounters fierce resistance in the vicinity of Mundung-ni. To break the impasses and get the platoon on the advance, Sergeant Tony K. Burris singlehandedly advances through the fire to destroy the obstacle. Burris tosses a bunch of grenades and takes out 15 of the enemy force. The fighting continues into the following day, while the 3rd Battalion presses ahead. On the 9th, at the next ridge in the path, Burris again takes action and leads a contingent to the crest, but he becomes wounded en route. Upon reaching the summit, he is again wounded. Undaunted, he stands to expose the enemy position and provide guidance for a 57-mm rifle team. The machine gun nest is quickly destroyed.

The attack resumes, but Burris refuses evacuation. He settles for emergency aid on the spot, then participates in the attack. Again, a wall of enemy fire stalls the advance. Burris, ignoring his wounds, lunges forward to take on the machine gun nest and he succeeds in destroying it and the 6-man crew. Afterward, Burris bolts to the next nest. He moves to within grenade throwing range and tosses it to eliminate the nest, but in the process, enemy fire cuts him down with a mortal wound. The remainder of his command secures Hill 605 on Heartbreak Ridge. Sergeant Tony Burris is awarded the Medal of Honor posthumously for his extraordinary heroism and courage in the face of the enemy.

Also on the 9th, while Hill 605 falls to the 2nd Battalion, the 1st Battalion strikes a fatal blow against Hill 900 to bring it down and under the control of the 38th Regiment. Nevertheless, in this region of hills and more hills, the 38th Regiment remains on the attack while the tanks scour the valley on a search and destroy mission. Two other objectives remain in the zone, Hills 974 and 1220 in the Kim II Sung Mountain range. They fall on 12 and 15 October, respectively.

The tanks make full use of the paths modified by the engineers, roaring through the valley and inflicting devastating punishment. Thanks to the lightning strikes of the 72nd Tank Battalion during five brutal days, the enemy loses about 350 bunkers on or near Heartbreak Ridge. The combined actions of the 72nd Tank Battalion and TF Sturman in the Mundung-ni and Sat'ae-ri Valleys respectively seal the fate of the Communists by encircling Heartbreak Ridge with an armored picket fence. The defenders are left with no hope of relief and only two options: surrender or fight to the last man. They choose the latter.

On the 10th at Heartbreak Ridge, the 23rd Regiment moves to dispose of the remaining resistance on the final objective, Hill 851, which by this time is defended by North Koreans and by Chinese elements who had escaped the fury of the tanks near Mungdung-ni. The 1st and 3rd Battalions, supported by the French Battalion, close the clamps on the obstinate defenders who choose not to capitulate.

In conjunction with the attack to gain the hill, the 2nd Battalion moves from Heartbreak Ridge to Hill 520, slightly south of the village of Mungdungni. However, some enemy forces still hold parts of Hill 520. The hostile ground is to be seized by Company G. The 3rd Platoon is delegated as the unit to spearhead the attack.

Company G, 2nd Battalion, led by Lt. Riddle (acting commander) is bolstered by Companies E and F. Company F is posted from where it can pass through the positions of Company G to continue the assault, and Company E is deployed nearby on a separate ridge about 500 yards to the south. From its positions, Company E is to provide cover fire.

One small hill stands between the attackers and the target on the top of Hill 520, which is flat ground. During the afternoon at about 1300—following an artillery barrage, heavy machine gun fire and recoilless rifles that pound the hill—the platoon moves hurriedly to the knoll under cover fire from other elements of Company G. The number of defenders remains unknown, making it difficult to determine if one platoon is sufficiently strong enough to reduce the resistance, but a direct attack is still considered as the most effective route. The Fluor Spar Valley there is inundated with mines.

The platoon, led by Corporal David W. Lamb, comes under severe enemy fire, much of which originates on the south side of the hill, but the platoon advances to the knoll unscathed. While maneuvering to eliminate the enemy positions, the platoon is forced to take incoming fire from the enemy, but other dangers also lurk; friendly fire behind them is also stroking the terrain.

One man, PFC Harry Schmidt, stands out amid the platoon. He wears a bright yellow band around his waist, marking him as a prime target, but essentially, his daring is actually a beacon for the U.S. support weapons that follow the yellow band to identify the exact location of the advancing platoon.

The enemy maintains their positions and as one squad swings to the left side of the objective, enemy fire brings it to a halt. After several of the troops are wounded, a call is made for reinforcements. In the meantime, the main body of the platoon comes under more fire and some casualties are incurred at the knob in front of the hill. The 1st Platoon, led by Lt. Jay M. Gano, is thrown into the fight. However, Gano, new to the outfit, delegates temporary command to Private Cliff R. High, who has been in charge of the platoon, to maintain his position and give Gano a little time to gather combat experience. Nevertheless, as the 1st Platoon begins its sprint toward the 3rd Platoon, several men are struck and one is literally restrained by Private High. Meanwhile, the remainder of the platoon under Gano continues moving ahead until Gano is killed.

As the 1st Platoon stalls, without leadership, other problems develop as the machine gun up front with Corporal Lamb expends its ammunition at just about the same time some North Koreans bolt from their concealed bunkers on the hill. Urgent calls are placed by Lamb and support fire pours upon the hill, but ineffectively, striking above the enemy. As the platoon members begin to withdraw, pursuit is given by the Communists, but unexplainedly, they halt and head back up the hill. Suddenly, the 3rd Platoon is obscured by smoke and the objective is not visible either. Lieutenant Riddle orders machine guns posted at the jump-off point to commence firing at the suspected positions on Hill 520 and the targets are apparently hit effectively; word reaches Riddle that the fire was on target.

Afterward, Private High again moves ahead with the 1st Platoon, passing wounded troops who are moving back toward the main line. Meanwhile, Corporal Lamb is in the process of receiving more ammunition. Both Lamb and High prepare to take the next move to gain the hill; however, enemy fire still pounds the positions to rack up more casualties. With a combined strength of less than twenty men, Lamb and High advance about thirty yards before encountering machine gun fire, but the contingent continues to push and fortuitously the fire is not well-aimed.

As they cover about thirty remaining yards, the enemy begins to use grenades, one of which wounds Corporal Lamb. Before the attack can stall, one soldier, Corporal Arne Severson, clasps his machine gun and defies the fire. He advances with his weapon blazing. The enemy takes Severson out with a grenade just as he reaches the slope. Despite having sustained two broken legs, a determined Severson is able to establish a position from which he continues to fire at the enemy. As the attack fails to make more progress, Severson is retrieved by others and pulled back to the main body.

Although progress remains slow and plagued with complications, the remaining able-bodied men of the two platoons launch a second assault to gain the hill, and in the process, Private High is downed by a grenade and knocked unconscious. His troops erroneously assume he had been killed and head back to the line of departure, but soon they are astonished to see High appear back at the line. A new attack is prepared by Private High. The attack is initially bolstered by the arrival of three flame throwers. Unfortunately, one of the men carrying the weapons is wounded as the attack jumps off and the other two turn out later to be inoperable, again leaving the task of destroying the bunkers to the infantry.

Eventually, Private High and several others take out an obstinate bunker (eastern side of the hill), then move to the south side of the hill where other enemy bunkers stall the attack. One particular bunker remains unscathed despite intense efforts to eliminate it. Although the bunker remains active, it is kept at bay by riflemen. But yet another bunker comes to life. Soon after, it is silenced by a grenade, opening the way to the top of the hill. Amazingly, Private Schmidt is still wearing his bright yellow waistband as the troops ascend the hill. Three bunkers are encountered, but each is unmanned. Once the troops reach the top of the hill, eight enemy troops are detected as they attempt to escape to the northwest.

Soon after, on the north side of the hill, the enemy command post is discovered. The troops also spot eight soldiers there and quickly accept their surrender. At another bunker, not known to the Americans, surprisingly, four troops emerge and surrender. Some of the defenders are able to escape, but the hill itself falls to Company G at 1600 following a harrowing three-hour battle.

While the 2nd Battalion takes and maintains the security of Hill 520, the 1st Battalion, 23rd Regiment and the French Battalion plod forward to reduce Hill 851. The cost is thirty casualties, most of which are minor.

The North Koreans and Chinese desperately toil to hold Hill 851, but their resources have weakened greatly at Heartbreak Ridge since the opening of the full offensive on 5 October. The 23rd Regiment, which had sustained heavy casualties while bogged down during the first couple of weeks, is exhibiting ferocity as they advance. Although the hill in question is but a speck of battered ground, to the 2nd Division it is the summit to be gained in honor of all the troops who had fallen there.

During the 11th and 12th, the 2nd Battalion and the French contingent press ahead, again in small but methodical steps, eliminating obstacles as they move. In a coordinated maneuver, the 3rd Battalion bolts to the east-west spur that stretches from Hill 520 (held by the 1st Battalion) and the 2nd Battalion's objective, Hill 851, to threaten the hill from the west and alert the enemy of their presence, to again bolster the main attack. During the night of the 12th-13th, the two attacking battalions establish night positions and prepare to reinitiate the advance on the following day.

On 13 October, the North Koreans and the Chinese defenders on Hill 851 are greeted at dawn by the first glimmer of daylight and the uninvited French Battalion, led by Lt. Colonel Ralph Monclar, which pounces upon the foe and gains the coveted prize for the 2nd Division.

The grim path to victory had taken thirty days, most of which were consumed with horrendous combat and horrific casualties on both sides, but in the case of the enemy, they are much more severe. The 2nd Division sustains more than 3,700 casualties, with about 1,800 inflicted on the 23rd Regiment (including the attached French contingent), primarily from the deadly mortar fire that dominated the ridges for weeks. The U.S. Army estimates that about 25,000 casualties had been inflicted upon the enemy at Heartbreak Ridge during the period 13

September through 15 October. The defending units were composed of the N.K. 6th, 12th, and 13th Divisions and the Chinese 204th Division.

The 2nd Division had also been supported by Fifth Air Force; however despite 842 sorties that delivered about 250 tons of bombs on suspected positions, the enemy had so brilliantly constructed the bunkers that most were unscathed and had to be destroyed by direct hits. Nevertheless, the air power played a vital part in the victory by disrupting enemy movements and assisting in suppressing enemy artillery. In the end, similarly as it had been through the ages, it was the infantry that had to finally take out the obstacles one by one.

For most of the world, Heartbreak Ridge will be remembered as one more barren piece of valueless ground in the Korean wilderness, but to the 2nd Division, it is not retained as a passing dreadful memory. Rather, it and the recently hard-fought contest for Bloody Ridge will be indelibly etched in their hearts. At a cost of nearly 4,000 casualties, for the 2nd Division its losses had hallowed the ground on Heartbreak Ridge. Operation TOUCHDOWN had crumbled the resistance and carried the 2nd Division across the finish line and helped to write the newest chapter in its history.

With the capture of Heartbreak Ridge, the X Corps sector is no longer under the observation of the enemy and the lines in the sector are aligned with IX Corps.

September 13 *In the X Corps sector, 1st Marine Division zone,* the 1st Marines jump off and advance at 0900, six hours late due to a lack of sufficient ammunition and supplies, as well as an ongoing evacuation mission to get wounded Marines to medical facilities. Company F, 2nd Battalion, 7th Marines, is relieved by the 2nd Battalion, 1st Marines, south of Hill 749 (Objective Baker) at 1100. Afterward, the task of relieving the remaining two companies begins. The North Koreans are deeply entrenched in bunkers. The 7th Marines are on the opposite slope of Hill 749, about 400 yards from where the 1st Marines expected the troops to be, based on a report.

In the meantime, the 3rd Battalion, 1st Marines, is unable to push closer to its objective, Hill 751, because of fire from enemy controlled Hill 749. Elements of the 2nd Battalion continue to hold. At 1600, the advancing 3rd Battalion remains several hundred yards short of the 2nd Battalion. Finally, at about 2025, the two units are joined. However, the night does not remain calm. The Marines are subjected to mortar attacks and several counterattacks. Hill 749 remains under Communist control throughout the night.

In other activity, the Marines have had difficulty getting re-supplied; however, on this date, the 1st Marines receive a bonus, dubbed Operation WINDMILL. Just prior to 1600, four choppers, transporting the landing point section (20 by 40 feet), and soon after, seven helicopters each transporting about 800 pounds of ammunition and

A U.S. mortar team fires upon Hill 931, north of 894. It is the highest peak on what becomes known as Heartbreak Ridge. The battle for the ridge continues from September 13 to October 15.

A contingent of the 2nd Division (Fire Direction and Control Team) are deployed from where they can observe the crest of Hill 931 (Heartbreak Ridge).

supplies, depart to deliver to the 1st Marines. The 11th Marines contributes to the historic operation by laying smoke to help cover the flights as the choppers move at low altitude.

The first chopper arrives at 1610 and the cargo, suspended in a net, is unloaded. The chopper then takes off, transporting five wounded Marines and two others in litters. One of the Marines on the flight receives medical attention back at X-83 within thirty minutes after being wounded. The operation, which includes twenty-eight flights, ends in a space of two and one-half hours. In addition, the Marines receive 18,848 pounds of supplies and 74 wounded are evacuated. The Marines had been working on such a transport system since 1947, but this is its first trial, one that changes military transport forever.

September 14 *In the X Corps sector, 1st Marine Division zone,* the attack to secure Hill 749 continues. At 0800, the 2nd and 3rd Battalions, 1st Marines, inch forward against artillery, mortar and machine gun fire to eliminate the North Koreans on the northern slope of the hill. The concealed bunkers are slowly eliminated one by one. During the engagement, PFC Edward Gomez, an ammunition bearer, moves forward with a rifle squad to ensure his machine gun is supplied with ammunition. An enemy grenade is tossed into the area containing Gomez and other Marines of Company E, 2nd Battalion. To save the others, Gomez grabs the grenade and throws himself in the trench to take the full shock of the grenade. Gomez survives and becomes a recipient of the Medal of Honor for his actions, above and beyond the call of duty.

While the 2nd Battalion gains only about 325 yards, it is sufficient to give the 3rd Battalion breathing room to surge to the crest of Hill 751. The day's grueling pace does not totally eliminate the resistance north of Hill 749.

In Air Force activity, a plane attached to the 8th Bombardment Group Squadron, 3rd Bomber Group, executes strikes against an enemy train in the vicinity of Yangdok. The pilot of the B-26, Captain John S. Walmsley, Jr., scores damage, but the train, laden with supplies, is not destroyed and Walmsley's ammunition had been expended. Rather than depart the area, he calls for assistance and another B-26 arrives. Walmsley stays and uses his searchlight (experimentally attached to his plane) to illuminate the target. He dives in at extremely low altitude, making his aircraft a lucrative target, so he can blast the area with his searchlight. Walmsley makes the pass but is hit by enemy fire and he crashes into a mountain. Captain Walmsley is awarded the Medal of Honor for his extraordinary heroism above and beyond the call of duty. (*See also* **September 13–October 15 1951** THE BATTLE OF HEARTBREAK RIDGE.)

September 15 *In the X Corps sector, 1st Marine Division zone,* the 2nd and 3rd Battalions, 1st Marines, prepare again to knock out the resistance that continues to impede progress, but the North Koreans seem to have an endless supply of ammunition and countless concealed log bunkers. An artillery bombardment is requested to precede the assault of the 2nd Battalion, but the enemy guns are not silenced. Once again, the Marines advance at 1710, but they come under walls of fire. The crossfire is so intense, the Marines are forced to withdraw under cover fire of the 11th Marines' artillery. The enemy tactic (crossfire) is dubbed the "North Korean T Formation."

In related activity, the 5th Marines move from the Hays Line into position to pass through the 3rd Battalion, 1st Marines, on the 16th. In the meantime, Company F, 2nd Battalion, engages a strong entrenched force on Hill 749. A forward platoon is hit with overwhelming strength and compelled to pull back. Corporal Joseph Vittori and two others, during the withdrawal, race through the retreating column to engage the advancing enemy. The trio encounters a force and in a close-quartered fight, the Marines prevail.

At that time, an un-manned machine gun is covered by Vittori. He moves from point to point to cover the flanks and pours fire upon the enemy, while Marine casualties continue to climb. Nonetheless, Vittori, mortally wounded, holds his ground.

The 1st Korean Marine Regiment and the Division Recon Company are to assume responsibility for the 5th Marines' vacated positions along the Hays Line. At midnight (15th-16th), the 2nd Battalion is nearly smothered by a forceful assault, but the Marines meet the attack with even more ferociousness. The battle continues into the daylight hours. Meanwhile, the 3rd Battalion, 1st Marines, near Hill 751 comes under a tenacious attack.

In the ROK 8th Division zone along the left flank, the entire division moves against enemy-held Hill 854. Some progress is made as the South Koreans force one of the three defending North Korean battalions to abandon their positions during the contest that continues into the following day.

In Air Force activity, General Otto P. Weyland informs General Vandenberg that the continuing growth of the strength of the Communists (Russian and Chinese) in the air is reaching epidemic proportions. At this time, the Air Force still does not have enough Sabre jets to counter the threat due to Washington's refusal to provide more planes. Weyland proclaims that the Communists are in position to expand MiG Alley straight down to Pyongyang if they are not stopped.

During the month of September, FEAF loses three F-86 Sabre jets, one P-51 Mustang, one F-80, and one F-84. Intelligence has ascertained that the Communists (with the belief they have greatly weakened the U.S. Air Force) have initiated a massive program to restore the airfields in North Korea. If the work is completed, MiG Alley would be expanded to the point that the Communists would be fighting for air superiority. More Sabres are not forthcoming, but an operation to destroy the airfields will be initiated. The first three fields, strung between MiG Alley and Pyongyang, become the first priority. The fields are Namsi, Taechon, and Saamcham. Subsequent reports by the Chinese indicate that the three fields come under 119 attacks.

September 16 General Van Fleet arrives in the 2nd Division sector and the 1st Marine Division sector to confer with the commanders and to check on the condition and morale of the units. At this time, Van Fleet instructs the respective Corps commanders to "firm up his line by 20 September and to plan no further offensives after that date."

In the X Corps sector, 1st Marine Division zone, at one minute after midnight (15th-16th), the Marines are alerted to another night without sleep as Communist artillery begins to ring the perimeter of the 2nd Battalion, 1st Marines. The booming sounds of 76-mm, 105s and 122-mm shells are accompanied by mortar fire. The screeching sounds of North Korean whistles and blaring bugles signal the arrival of yet another night attack. The exhausted Marines, still able to fight despite their diminished numbers from casualties, become galvanized. The ground runs red as the Communists come against the lines in successive waves. The Communists penetrate, slightly against weaker parts of the line, but as the Marines there are compelled to give some ground, one man, Corporal Joseph Vittori, plows through the line of retreat to lead a counterattack. In addition, Vittori bolts from one foxhole to the next to man machine guns , while others there fall from wounds. Neither Vittoli, nor the other Marine are willing to become the vanquished. Every wave that strikes is shattered and by 0400, the North Korean force, estimated at regimental strength, temporarily runs out of troops for the next wave.Corporal Vittoli is killed during the final minutes of the fight. When Corporal Vittori's body is recovered, more than 200 dead Communists are counted at his front. Corporal Vittori is awarded the Medal of Honor posthumously for his extraordinary courage in the face of the enemy.

The North Koreans also strike the 3rd Battalion positions at Hill 751. This attack also occurs slightly after midnight, but not with the same intensity. Nevertheless, the attacking force of about 150 troops is also repelled. Later, at 0830, the 1st Battalion, 1st Marines, moves out to pass through the 2nd Battalion to finish the fight. Enemy resistance along the ridge line running to Hill 749 still has a powerful punch. Nonetheless, the 1st Battalion plows forward in yet one more grueling day of combat. At 1800, it concludes. Hill 749 (Objective Baker) is secured. The Marines establish night positions with both Hill 749 and 751 in their possession. Lt. Colonel Horace E. Knapp had been wounded and evacuated on the previous day. He had been replaced on this day by Lt. Colonel John E. Gorman.

Also, during the first part of the afternoon, the 5th Marines commence an attack to seize Objective Dog, a hill mass about 1,000 yards distant. The attack is spearheaded by Company F, 2nd Battalion, 5th Marines, which drills forward on a path that runs between Hill 680 and 673 (Kanmubong Ridge) and leads directly into yet another enemy crossfire. The advance, short of the objective, is halted at 1700 to evacuate wounded and get a well-needed pause.

Another unit, Company, D, requests a signal to identify the positions of Company H. A white phosphorous grenade is used; however, planes on a mission to strike enemy-held Hill 980 on Kanmubong Ridge mistake the signal as a target location. Company H is struck by napalm and strafing machine gun fire. No casualties are incurred thanks to a last-minute recogni-

tion panel that is spotted in the nick of time. By this time, it is too late to reinitiate the attack. It is suspended until 0400 on the following day.

During the four-day contest to secure Objective Baker (Hill 749), the Marines sustain 90 killed, 714 wounded and 1 missing. The North Koreans lose 771 killed (counted) and 81 POWs; however the estimate of enemy killed is reported as more than twice the number counted. There will be no pause for relaxation for the Marines.

In Naval activity, one of the jets (F2H) crash lands on the carrier USS *Essex* (CV 9), causing damage and loss of life. Four men are missing, three are killed and 27 others sustain injuries.

In other activity, the Photo Unit, 1st Marine Aircraft Wing, relocates from Pusan to Yongil Man, Korea.

September 17 *In the X Corps sector, 1st Marine Division zone,* the 5th Marines reinitiate the attack to secure Hill 812. The attack, scheduled for 0400, is postponed until 0700. The vanguard again is Company F and the delay in jumping off, surprisingly, gives the Marines an advantage. The enemy is spotted while still eating breakfast. At about the same time, the positions are sent to the 11th Marines and an artillery bombardment prompts the Communists to abort the meal. The attacking unit advances swiftly until it gets caught in the expected crossfire. At about 0830, Company E leapfrogs ahead with one platoon of Company F. Air strikes are requested, but again no planes arrive.

By 1100, progress remains extremely slow. Lt. Colonel Stiff concludes that it will take a full-powered push to win the prize. Bolstered by a preliminary artillery bombardment, the platoon from Company F lunges against the flank, while Company E plows straight ahead. The enemy is totally unprepared along the flank and the attack severs the resistance there. Within about thirty-six minutes, the Marines climb to the summit and following gruesome, close-quartered fighting, the Marines prevail. The quest for Hill 812 proves to be the spear that pierces the spine of the resistance.

From Hill 812, Company E bolts westward along the ridgeline that links with Hill 980 and prepares to seize it, but permission is denied because the North Koreans still hold Hill 1052 and from there, the new prize would be imperiled. Company E is directed to withdraw 600 yards toward Hill 680. In the meantime, while the Marines establish defensive positions, the enemy left at Hill 980 continues to shell the perimeter in conjunction with enemy-held Hill 1052. Company E holds along the ridgeline that leads to Hill 980, while Company F deploys around Hill 812. Meanwhile, the 1st Marines hold the area north of Hill 751, but the regiment is not linked to the 2nd Battalion.

September 18–21 1951 *In the X Corps area, 1st Marine Division sector,* pursuant to Operation Order 27–51, Hill 854 is to be secured, either by relief of the ROK 8th Division if it is in their hands or by attack, if still controlled by the Communists during the operation to relieve the South Koreans. The

On 18 September, Sherman M4 tanks bolster the 2nd Division in the vicinity of Hill 1179 (Taeu-san) near Pia-ri. By 21 September, the 2nd Division sector stabilized, but fighting did not cease.

1st Marine Division begins to stretch its line farther east to relieve the ROK 8th Division in a complex troop reformation. The ROK 8th Regiment, after being relieved, is to in turn relieve the ROK 5th Division on the far left. Afterward, the ROK 5th Division is to redeploy in a newly created zone to the left of the 1st Marine Division. The operation is completed by 21 September.

The North Koreans still control much of Hill 854, giving the Marines the task of clearing the remaining resistance there. On the 20th, the 1st Battalion, 1st Marines, relieves two battalions of the ROK 10th Regiment near Hill 854 without incident; however, eleven casualties are incurred due to friendly mines. The Marines move ahead using maps from the ROKs that fail to correctly identify where mines had been placed. In addition, the 3rd Battalion, 1st Marines relieves two battalions of the 21st ROK Regiment. The 3rd Battalion, 1st Marines, schedules an attack to clear the southwest ridgeline for the afternoon; however, it is postponed due to lack of expected air cover. Slightly after 1700, the battalion jumps off and it also becomes victimized by friendly mines just as Company H reaches a point about fifty yards from the line of departure. One man is killed and another is wounded. Consequently, the attack is suspended to await engineers who can eliminate the problem. The attack is reinitiated on the following day. In the meantime, the Marines direct the ROKs to find the mines they planted and eliminate them.

September 18   *In the X Corps sector, 1st Marine Division zone,* the 2nd Battalion, 5th Marines, come under attack at 0430. Company E's positions are hit hard, compelling the unit to give some ground. The Commu-

nists launch another assault at 0840, but it fails. The North Koreans maintain constant artillery bombardments against the Marine positions throughout the day. The 1st Marine Division reports casualties for this day as 16 killed and 98 wounded. Most of the day's casualties are sustained by the 2nd Battalion. Other than the artillery fire, the day remains tranquil. The Marines also pass the night (18–19) with little activity. Nonetheless, at dawn, the Communists break the silence.

In Naval activity, CTG 95.9 (attached to CTF 95) initiates a two-day mission against Wonsan. The enemy positions in the area are attacked by planes as well as naval surface guns and rockets. The British carrier HMS *Glory* (CVL) had moved from the east coast of Korea to the west coast to participate in this mission.

September 19   *In the Eighth Army area,* Fifth Air Force executes missions to support the crossing of the Naktong River near Waegwan by the 24th Division. Also, The 1st Cavalry Division crashes through the enemy lines.

In the X Corps sector, the entire line, except for the sector covered by the 2nd Division, is now stable. (*See also,* **September 13–October 15 1951** THE BATTLE OF HEARTBREAK RIDGE.)

In the 1st Marine Division zone, the enemy still controls Hills 980 and 1052. Between the two hills and the Marines stands "The Rock," a 12-foot-high granite knob on the ridgeline about 700 yards west of Hill 812. The North Koreans hold the western side, while the Marines hold the top and the eastern side. The northern slope is the only area able to provide some protection to the Marines.

The 2nd Battalion, 5th Marines, desperately need sand bags, barbed wire and other items. Thanks to new additions, in the afternoon the Transport Helicopter Squadron has 10 helicopters execute 16 flights to deliver more than 12,000 pounds in about one hour.

In other activity, the 1st Battalion, 5th Marines, relieves the 1st and 2nd Battalions, 1st Marines, then deploy to the right of the 2nd Battalion, 5th Marines. The 1st Battalion's line extends eastward along the ridge toward the Soyang-gang. In conjunction, during the day, the Marines continue to fortify their positions, hindered primarily by long-range artillery fire.

In other activity, the 3rd Battalion, 1st Marines, reinitiates the mission to clear Hill 854. In what has become habitual, the requested planes, due to arrive at 0700, arrive overhead at 1040. The four Air Force F-15s strike their targets and leave the area. At 1220, subsequent to an artillery barrage, Company H again leads the way. Enemy resistance remains firm, prompting the vanguard to request another air strike; however, the Marine Air Wing is not in direct coordination with the Marines. Fifth Air Force planes never arrive. Absent the air strikes, the Marines call upon the artillery and mortars.

The advance remains sluggish against the ferocious resistance, but the Marines grind forward toward the peak. At 1745, word is passed back from Company H that the hill is under Marine control. The battle for Hill 854, which erupted on the previous day, cost the 3rd Battalion, 1st Marines, 64 casualties, including those affected by friendly mines and of the total, nine are killed. The Communists' dead, according to actual count at the hill, amounts to 159. The additional number of killed and wounded, estimated by the Marine Corps, stands at 150 and 225, respectively.

Also, Marine Fighter Squadron 323 (VMF 323) departs the USS *Sicily* (CVE 118) en route to Kangnung, from where it will reinitiate land-based operations.

In Naval activity, the USS *Toledo* (CA 133), the USS *Craig* (DD 885) and USS *Parks* (DD 884) initiate a bombardment of enemy positions at Wonsan, prior to an air strike by planes attached to the HMS *Glory* (CVL).

September 20   This date marks a significant turning point in the war. The strategy for the remainder of the conflict changes from a war consumed with perpetual movement to a conflict based on position. It had long ago been decided in Washington, D.C., not to fight for complete victory and now as the Eighth Army has achieved extraordinary success and is beginning to peak, defensive lines become the new way of conducting the war. As of this day, X Corps is to cease offensive attacks and according to General Van Fleet's order of 18 September, to "firm up the existing line and to patrol vigorously in front of it." Meanwhile, the IX Corps remains engaged at Heartbreak Ridge.

In the X Corps sector, 1st Marine Division zone, at 0315, the North Koreans strike the Marine positions on the eastern side of "The Rock" as part of a plan to regain Hill 812. The enemy initially pounds the area with artillery and mortar fire, but right after, the Communists close against a platoon of Company E, 2nd Battalion. The Marines ignore the fire of the burp guns and grenades and mount a counterattack, but the North Koreans push the platoon back. The Communists occupy the lost ground and take aim on Company E.

Another counterattack is mounted at 0500. Company E drives directly into the enemy's front while Company F duplicates its strategy at Hill 812 and strikes the

An enemy bunker after being reduced by the 7th Marines. An enemy casualty is on the lower left. Also, the tree fragments are casualties of Marine artillery.

Marines on Hill 884 receive supplies on 20 September, delivered by a Sikorsky helicopter.

Communists' flank. The North Koreans are caught off guard by 2nd Platoon's strike against their flank. The resistance vaporizes as the Communists bolt for their side (west) of The Rock. The North Koreans lose 60 killed.

By this date, the Marines, since the operation began on 11 September, have secured three of the four objectives; however, Objective Charlie, the ridgeline in the 1st Korean Marine Regiment zone, northwest of Hill 1052, still needs to be seized. As the Marines prepare to take the remaining objectives, everything changes and quite suddenly. Division Operation Order 26–51 places an immediate halt to offensive operations. As it turns out, the fight for The Rock becomes the final chapter in the nine-day battle and it is the last "action of mobility" for the Marines in Korea.

In Naval activity, the USS *Orleck* (DD 886) bombards enemy positions at Wonsan. Targets hit include an ammunition depot and one sampan. A directive is received by Fast Carrier Task Force (TF-77) that 20 September is the final day the task force will be required to supply close-air support missions.

In other activity, Marine Squadron VMF-323 arrives at Itami Air Base, Japan, from the USS *Sicily.* The squadron will depart for Korea on the 24th and begin operation from Pusan.

September 21 Operation SUMMIT *In the X Corps sector,* at Hill 884, the Marines introduce a new tactic of getting troops from an assembly area to the front. At 1030, after a one-half hour delay due to fog, a contingent of Marines attached to the 1st Shore Party Battalion is transported by helicopter to Hill 884 to clear two separate landing sites to receive what becomes the first fighting force delivered by helicopter to a battlefield.

Two helicopters, each transporting one team, hover over their respective landing sites, which stand about 100 yards from each other at a point on the hill several hundred yards from the crest. The Marines assigned to the task, using knotted ropes that dangle dangerously from the helicopters, slither about thirty feet down the ropes during high winds. The initial part of the operation succeeds within about forty minutes.

These are the only two sites on the hill capable of handling such an operation. Each encompasses an area of about 50 square feet and both contain two sides of the landing space that terminate at a sheer cliff. Within minutes after the sites are cleared, the waiting helicopters of HMR-161 zoom into action at Field X-83. With the exception of some temporary minor communication problems between X-83 and the landing point team, the operation is flawless. Within three and one-half hours (flight time), 224 Marines and almost 18,000 pounds of supplies and equipment are transported about fourteen miles and delivered to the battlefield.

One contingent includes a heavy machine gun platoon from the 2nd Battalion, 7th Marines. The well-oiled operation brings a helicopter above the respective landing sites every thirty seconds and the time spent there hovering averages about twenty seconds, while five Marines with full gear descend the ropes. The identical trip without the use of the helicopters would have taken fourteen hours and required supplies to be carried by laborers.

The final part of the mission, the task of laying a telephone line between the Reconn Company on Hill 854 and the 1st Marines command post about eight

An M16 multiple-gun motor carriage maneuvers through mud in the vicinity of Kumsong on 21 September. Infantry in the background and a jeep move in opposite directions.

miles to the rear of the hill, is also a success. The time to lay each line takes about fifteen minutes.

General Byers, USA, X Corps commander, is among many who congratulate HMR-161 and the participants in the operation. Byers commentst: "Your imaginative experiment with this kind of transport is certain to be of lasting value to all the services." Another commenting on the tremendous achievement is Major General Gerald C. Thomas, who remarks: "Operation SUMMIT, the first helicopter borne landing of a combat unit in history was an outstanding success. To all who took part, well done."

The team responsible for the blueprint that had to be created within a twenty-four hour period included Lieutenant Colonel George W. Herring (commanding officer of HMR-161); Lt. Colonel William C. Mitchell (Herring's executive officer); Major Ephraim Kirby Smith (Reconn Company CO) and Lt. Richard C. Higgs (acting division embarkation officer).

In the 1st Marines zone, an enemy force launches a probing assault against the lines of Company G, 3rd Battalion, during the early morning hours. The attack is repelled; however, during the fight, a grenade is tossed into a foxhole occupied by Corporal Jack Davenport and one other Marine. Davenport, in an effort to save the other Marine's life, takes the brunt of the explosion by covering the grenade with his body. Corporal Davenport is awarded the Medal of Honor posthumously for his courage under fire and his selfless sacrifice to save the life of another.

In Naval activity, Marine Squadron VMF-212 departs Itami Base, Japan, aboard the USS *Rendova.*

September 23 *In the X Corps sector, 1st Marine Division zone,* the Marine Reconnaissance Company deployed at Hill 884 is relieved by the 1st Marines.

In other activity, Marines in forward observation

The French Battalion attached to the U.S. 2nd Division occupies Hill 931 (Heartbreak Ridge) on 23 September.

posts place a call to the Navy and the USS *New Jersey* responds. Enemy positions that had been spotted by the observers are struck by the big 16-inch guns of the *New Jersey* (BB-62), which hits its targets more than twenty miles away. The 2,000-pound shells destroy ammunition depots, artillery positions and troop formations. The Marine patrols also receive hefty support from the artillery of the 1st Marine Division and U.S. Army units that are attached, which add extra punch to the patrols.

The North Koreans are greeted by the *New Jersey* a few additional times when called by the 1st and 3rd Battalions, 1st Marines, while on patrol through the end of the month. This is the first use of the Navy's guns in support of the 1st Marine Division since the latter part of 1950. The naval bombardments are sometimes able to break up counterattacks before they can be initiated. The Marines are appreciative of the naval fire power supporting them along their front, which is spread about thirteen miles in the mountains of the Korean wilderness and partly northwest of the Punch Bowl, where it linked with the ROK 5th Division.

In Air Force activity, a group of eight B-29 Superfortresss, attached to the 19th Bomber Group, strike and destroy the center span of the Sunch'on rail bridge. The bombers use the SHORAN bomb system (airborne radar device coordinated with two ground beacon stations), which prove to be unaffected by the extremely heavy cloud cover.

September 25   *In Naval activity,* a contingent of F-84s spot sixteen MiG-15s near Sinanju, but no fight erupts. Later a larger group, composed of 36 F-84s, encounters 16 MiG-15s in the same general area and yet another group of 37 F-84s encounters about 100 MiG-15s. Combat ensues and the carrier planes report the destruction of five MiGS and five others damaged. The carrier planes sustain one plane damaged.

In Air Force activity, the Chinese reinitiate their participation in the air battles. They (with 32 MiGS) join with the Russians to increase the number of MiGS against the already outnumbered Sabre jets of the Americans. Far East Air Forces planes, while on the attack to destroy bridges at the Ch'ongch'on River battle, come under attack. During the following month, ten separate air battles occur between Chinese pilots in their MiGS and Americans in their Sabres. Afterward the Chinese will report the destruction of 20 downed American planes and another 10 damaged. These records show a marked difference from those maintained by Far East Air Forces, which for the identical period report 40 MiGs destroyed and U.S. losses at seven F-86s, two F-84s, five B-29s, and one RF-80.

A contingent of the 336th Fighter-Interceptor Squadron, 4th Fighter-Interceptor Group, led by Major Richard D. Creighton, is one of the units that encounter the enemy this day. Creighton spots one MiG and attacks. The MiG becomes damaged and Creighton again fires to bring the plane down in the vicinity of Anju.

September 27   General Matthew Ridgway suggests (to the Chinese Communists) that site of cease fire talks be relocated from Kaesong to a site near the No-Man's Land village of Songhyon.

In the X Corps sector, 1st Marine Division zone, helicopters again take combat troops to the front. A daytime exercise is initiated in preparation for a genuine movement after dark. Subsequent to dark, Operation BLACKBIRD commences. Six helicopters (HRS-1) lift Company E, 2nd Battalion, 1st Marines, from a dry stream bed in the vicinity of Hill 702 and transport the unit (more than 200 troops) to the northwestern rim of the Punch Bowl. The landing site, encompassing an area of 50 by 100 feet, is prepared by the 1st Shore Party Battalion. The entire operation, including a round-trip of 13 miles, takes place in less than two and one-half hours, despite traveling a circuitous route to prevent the enemy from observing the operation.

After the troops arrive and begin the one-mile march to the front, one Marine is wounded by a mine. Shortly thereafter, it is determined that the entire area is mined, causing the march to be aborted. The operation experienced other problems. The pilots had been temporarily blinded by the glare on their windshields and the trip through the mountain passes became dangerous due to the nasty terrain and the artillery flashes. After assessing the results, it was concluded that transferring troops during darkness would be restricted to friendly territory. Operation BLACKBIRD is the only time troops are lifted in the darkness during the entire conflict.

In Air Force activity, a C-124A Globemaster aircraft, during an operation known as PELICAN, transports its initial cargo, 30,000 pounds of aircraft parts, from Japan to Kimpo Airfield in Korea.

September 28   *In Air Force activity,* a reconnaissance plane (RF-80) remains in the air for slightly more than fourteen straight hours on a combat mission over Korea, thanks to airborne fuel tankers. The RF-80, while in flight, is refueled repeatedly by two separate KB-29M tankers.

In Naval activity, the HMAS *Murchison,* while moving along the Han River, comes under fire from artillery, mortars and small arms. The vessel sustains some slight damage and one man is wounded.

September 29   *In the United States:* The draft numbers for the month of November are elevated on this day from 33,700 to 39,000. The Marines will take 10,000 for November and for the following month, 9000.

September 30   General Van Fleet proclaims in a statement the reasoning for his strategy: "My basic mission during the past four months has been to destroy the enemy, so that the men of Eighth Army will not be destroyed." Van Fleet states that it is "imperative" to eliminate as many weapons as possible and "mandatory" that the high ground be controlled. By controlling the high ground at the cost of "losing a comparative few, we saved other thousands." Van Fleet notes that Eighth

A B-26 bomber on a mission over North Korea.

Army estimates of enemy casualties from 25 May through 25 September amounts to 188,237. At the close of his statement, General Van Fleet notes: "The Communist forces in Korea (as the Eighth Army autumn campaign begins) are not liquidated, but they are crippled."

In the X Corps sector, 1st Marine Division zone, the Marines have, since the 20th, been under orders to restrict their actions to patrols. However, from the 20th until this day, the Marines have exhibited no passiveness. Casualties for the period include 59 killed, 331 wounded and 1 missing. Enemy losses number 505 killed (counted) and 2327 prisoners. Marine casualties for September stand at 1,822, and the 1st Korean Marine Corps Regiment has sustained 594. North Korean losses for September stand at 2,799 killed (counted) and 557 prisoners.

In Air Force activity, Brigadier General Joe W. Kelly assumes command of Far East Air Forces Bomber Command. He succeeds Brigadier General Robert H. Terrill.

October   During this month, the U.N. forces in Korea at the maximum reaches 236,871, U.S. Army; 21,020, Fifth Air Force; 30,913, U.S. Marines (including 5,386 officers and enlisted men of the 1st Marine Air Wing). The ROK forces total 286,000 troops and from other nations, the combined total equals 32,172. The forces are composed of four corps and fourteen divisions deployed along a front that extends about 123 miles across the Korean peninsula. Enemy forces along the front total 600,000 men, including reserves and units deployed to fill in as reinforcing units.

In numbers, each side hovers around 600,000; however on the field, the enemy greatly exceeds the U.S.-U.N. forces, because more than twenty five percent of the Allied forces are behind the lines in duties such as maintenance and administration.

In the Eighth Army sector, the units are essentially operating on a defensive mode.

In the X Corps sector, 1st Marine Division zone, activity is limited to patrols. The activity for the entire month is greatly reduced from previous months, so much so that Division, rather than maintain a daily diary, merely splits the month into two parts. Nonetheless, while the enemy continues to evade, when contact is made, they are engaged. The ratio of casualties for October stands at 20 to 1 in favor of the Marines. During the previous month, the ratio had been 4 to 1. *In Air Force activity,* by this time the Communists are building their confidence in the air, with flights being initiated by Russian and Chinese pilots. Meanwhile, the U.S. air strength remains at a disadvantage due to the shortage of Sabres. The shortage, however, does not prevent the FEAF from continuing its missions. On this day, the MiGs intercept a flight of Sabres and lose two against no U.S. losses during the ongoing campaign to destroy or damage North Korean airfields.

In related activity, a contingent of four F-86 Sabre jets, attached to the 4th Fighter Interceptor Group and led by Lieutenant George L. Jones, encounters and engages a pair of M-15 MiGs in the vicinity of Tokch'on this morning. Jones downs one of the MiGs.

October 2 *In Naval activity,* Task Element 95.11 (Task Group 95) receives orders directing its aircraft to initiate the daily bombing of the area along the northern bank of the Han River west of Yesong Gang. In addition, spotter planes are to be provided for the warships that are bombarding enemy positions in the vicinity of Han Point.

In Air Force activity, during Operation SNOWBALL on October 1–3, C-119s, attached to the 315th Air Division, test a new tactic. The planes drop 5-gallon drums of napalm behind enemy lines.

In air combat between F-86 Sabre jets and Communist MiGs, the Communists lose six planes. One of the MiGs is downed about 15 miles east of Uiju by Colonel Francis S. Gabreski, the commanding officer of the 4th Fighter Interceptor Wing. Another MiG is downed by Colonel George J. Ola, 4th Fighter-Interceptor Group. The U.S. sustains no losses.

Also, Captain Paul W. Bryce, Jr. (4th Fighter-Interceptor Group) finds two MiGs on either side of his F-86 just as he is departing the area near Chongju at about 1500. Bryce begins to climb, moving directly toward the enemy planes, and passes the one of the MiGs so closely that his Sabre jet begins to vibrate violently, but as he passes, the MiG sustains greater shock and the plane breaks up. Bryce had not fired his machine guns. The enemy pilot is observed ejecting from his plane before it crashes.

Captain George W. Dunn of the 334th Fighter Interceptor Squadron, 4th Fighter-Interceptor Group, spots a trio of three MiGs taking two other Sabres under attack near Sonchon. Dunn drives into the MiGs, lets go with a long burst of machine gun fire and strikes one of the enemy planes in the wing and fuselage. The enemy pilot

General Matthew Ridgway (commander-in-chief, U.N.), on left, confers with Major General Claude B. Ferenbaugh, commander 7th Infantry Division on 2 October.

attempts to evade Dunn, but to no avail. Dunn stays on his tail and again opens fire. The burst pounds the cockpit and afterward, the MiG still remains in flight, momentarily. The plane begins to climb, but soon after, it rolls to the left, then spins uncontrollably and crashes.

On this same day, Dunn, still leading his flight, encounters another band at a point about 15 miles southeast of the Sui Ho Reservoir. He engages a damaged MiG and downs it to receive one-half of a victory, sharing it with his wingman, who damaged the plane and then passed it without being able to finish it off.

October 3 *In the I Corps sector,* Operation COM-MANDO commences. Major General (later Lieutenant General) John W. O'Donnell, in command of I Corps since relieving General Milburn, directs the operation, which is intended to fortify the defensive line and secure the Jamestown Line. In addition, the operation is designed to improve the rail lines from Seoul to Ch'orwon and Kumwa. The operation is completed successfully by 15 October.

In Air Force activity, a flight of F-80s attached to the 8th Bomber wing are intercepted by a band of MiGs while on a mission. The pilots report a probable three MiGs downed against no U.S. losses. *In Naval activity,* Operation RETRIBUTION commences. The HMS *Black Swan* (PF) moves up the Han River to draw fire, while 11 planes of TE 95 lurk nearby. Once the enemy exposes its positions, the planes swoop down and plaster the positions, inflicting damage to the defenses and casualties to the Communists troops.

October 4 *In the X Corps sector,* the 2nd Division is engaged in fierce fighting in the area west of the Punch Bowl.

October 5 *In Naval activity,* the USS *Firecrest* (AMS 10), while operating off Hungnam, receives fire from shore batteries. No casualties are sustained, but the vessel has some slight damage. In related activity, Task Element 77.14, composed of the USS *New Jersey* (BB 62), USS *Helena* (CA 75), USS *Small* (DD 838) and the USS *Hanson* (DD 832), bombard enemy positions in the Hamhung–Hungnam area. The mission is the first naval bombardment of the area since X Corps troops abandoned it in December.

In Air Force activity, a four-plane contingent of F-86s, 336th Fighter-Interceptor Squadron, 4th Fighter-Interceptor Group, led by Major Richard D. Creighton, encounter a band of three MiG-15s near Taech'on. Creighton downs on plane. The MiG crashes but the pilot ejects.

October 6 *In Air Force activity,* a four-plane patrol of F-86s, attached to the 336th Fighter-Interceptor Squadron (4th Fighter-Interceptor Group) come under attack in the vicinity of Sinanju by a large force of MiG-15s. Lieutenant Arthur L. O'Connor moves against the six enemy planes that are firing at two Sabre jets below his plane. He leads his element into the middle of the fight to disrupt the MiG air attack and he then moves against the MiGs that are attacking a con-

tingent of B-26 bombers who arrive on target. During the tenacious fight, O'Connor's wingman's aircraft gets hit and he attempts to pull back, with MiGs on his tail. O'Connor disengages his dog fight and heads to protect his wingman. Once again O'Connor is able to disrupt the enemy. Several of the MiGs are damaged, but none are downed. O'Connor and his wingman make it safely back to their base.

In Naval activity, a contingent of friendly guerrillas operating on the west coast of Korea near Pungchon withdraws under some protective fire from a British warship, the HMS *Amethyst.*

October 7 *In Naval activity,* Rear Admiral J.J. Clark, commanding officer Carrier Division 5, replaces Rear Admiral John Perry (commander Carrier Division 1) as commander, Fast Carrier Task Force 77. The USS *Ernest G. Small* (DD 838) sustains heavy damage after striking a mine off Hungnam. Nine crewmen are killed and 18 others are wounded.

October 8 *In Air Force activity,* in one encounter with MiGs, a Sabre jet knocks one down. No losses are sustained by the U.S. unit.

In Naval activity, Rear Admiral C.F. Espe, USN, replaces Rear Admiral T.B. Hill as commander, Amphibious Group 1 and Amphibious Task Force 90.

October 9 Sergeant Tony Burris, 38th Regiment, 2nd Division, is killed during action against the enemy. Burris is posthumously awarded the Medal of Honor. (*See also,* **September 13–October 15 1951** BATTLE OF HEARTBREAK RIDGE.)

October 10 After delaying since late August, the Communists respond to General Ridgway's requests to resume the peace talks. Since the talks had stalled, the U.S.-U.N. forces had succeeded in gaining much of the high ground along the front. The new positions seem to convince the Chinese that the ground will not be retaken and it probably would help to end the stalled talks.

In Air Force activity, Far East Air Forces acknowledges an ancient Chinese anniversary, the overthrow of the Manchu Dynasty in 1911. The planes drop leaflets for the benefit of the Communist troops and they broadcast over the radios.

In Naval activity, Task Group 95.9 commences an air and surface attack against Kojo Island. Also, the USS *Small* (DD 838), en route from Hungnam to Sasebo, Japan, strikes a mine and sustains severe damage (loses its bow); however, the crew is able to keep the ship afloat with the remainder kept water-tight.

October 11 *In the X Corps sector, 1st Marine Division zone,* Operation BUMBLEBEE commences. At 1000, as part of the operation in which the 7th Marines at Won-tong-ni participate, the 3rd Battalion is lifted by helicopter and transported to the division's center along the front. The operation involves 156 flights by 12 helicopters. The distance from Field X-77 to the front lines is about 17 miles and the duration of time is about 10 to 12 minutes, with the helicopters landing at one-minute intervals and spending an average of seventeen seconds unloading the troops.

The helicopters are beginning to play a much larger part in the war in Korea. In just under six hours, 959 fully equipped men and equipment are transported. The total amount of weight transported during the operation amounts to 229,920 pounds. In conjunction, the remainder of the 7th Marines (1st and 2nd Battalions) move by overland routes to the front to complete relief of the 5th Marines.

In Naval activity, Kojo again comes under attack by Task Group 95.9. Also, the USS *Renshaw* (DDE 499), while operating off Songjin, comes under fire from enemy shore guns. The vessel sustains some minor damage and one crewman sustains a slight wound. The enemy fire was unexpected, as the area had been quiet for a few months.

October 12   By this date, the new line, Jamestown, is secure. An offensive to establish the line had commenced during the previous month by five divisions, the 1st Cavalry (IX Corps), 3rd, Infantry (I Corps), 25th Infantry (I Corps) and the ROK 1st Division (X Corps) along with the 1st British Commonwealth. The offensive advanced to extend the line three to four miles from the vicinity of Kaesong to Ch'orwon.

Also, friendly guerrillas operating from the island of Sinmi-do on the west coast of Korea abandon the island after Communist pressure makes their positions untenable.

In Air Force activity, during continuing operations to damage and destroy airfields in North Korea, one MiG is destroyed, with no U.S. losses.

October 13   Typhoon Ruth arrives and inflicts much destruction in the Japan-Formosa-Korea region and its force hinders naval and air operations for several days.

In the IX Corps sector, Operation NOMAD and POLAR commences. It is designed to secure phase lines, later designated the Missouri Line. The operation is carried out with the 24th U.S. Division, supported by ROK forces. It is completed by 22 October.

In the X Corps sector, 1st Marine Division zone, from 1 October to this date, 87 North Korean troops surrender to the 1st Marine Division. (*See also,* **September 13–October 15 1951** THE BATTLE OF HEARTBREAK RIDGE.)

October 14   *In the X Corps sector, 1st Marine Division zone,* the Marines maintain only patrols through October 31; however, while the infantry penetrates further into enemy territory, other patrols include tanks and when necessary, all units receive artillery support and air cover.

October 15   The U.S. 2nd Division seizes Heartbreak Ridge (*See also,* **September 13–October 15 1951** THE BATTLE OF HEARTBREAK RIDGE).

In the X Corps sector, 1st Marine Division zone, ur-

gent calls for help arrive for a beleaguered ROK unit that had become surrounded while operating in the IX Corps sector. The ROKs had sustained casualties and had expended most of their ammunition. Marine helicopters are dispatched (Operation WEDGE) to assist the isolated contingent. Six helicopters (HRS-1) arrive with 19,000 pounds of ammunition and evacuate 24 wounded troops.

October 16   *In the X Corps sector, 1st Marine Division zone,* a contingent of the 1st Battalion, 7th Marines, advances against North Korean fortifications in the high ground near Changhang. The Communists raise fierce resistance and pound the attacking force with artillery, mortars and machine gun fire, but to no avail. The objective is breached just prior to 1540. By 1700, all resistance is eliminated. The Marines withdraw after determining that the area is untenable due to booby traps and mines. They sustain three killed and 18 wounded. The Communists sustain 35 killed (counted).

In Air Force activity, a contingent of 16 Sabre jets commanded by Major Richard D. Creighton, 336th Fighter Interceptor Squadron, while escorting fighter bombers on a mission near Sinuiju, prepares to leave the area and return to base due to being low on fuel. Just as the formation prepares to turn, Major Creighton spots a huge force of MiG-15s that number about 100 and are closing against the fighter bombers.

Creighton's Sabres, at a higher elevation, abort their departure and dive to tackle the 100 MiGs. While the MiGs focus on the Sabres, the fighter bombers complete their mission. In the meantime, the skies become consumed with the opposing planes. The clashes spread south for about 100 miles reaching down toward Pyongyang. During the encounter, four MiGs are downed and three others are damaged. During the same aerial donnybrook, four of the planes under Major Franklin L. Fisher drive into an eight-plane formation. He downs one of the MiGs and just as he is running out of ammunition, MiGs close on him, but he is able to take evasive action and then he downs a second MiG.

Aware that the fighter bombers have completed their task and that the Sabres are nearly running on fumes, Creighton orders his command to disengage. No U.S. losses occur. An Air Force publication noted that a total of nine MiGs are destroyed on this day, but still there are no U.S. losses. Also, Colonel Benjamin S. Preston, Jr., 4th Fighter-Interceptor Group, closes on two MiGs and damages one, then as it begins to dive, Preston again scores and downs the MiG about 7 miles east of Sinuiju.

In other activity, B-29s execute thirty-one day and night sorties on the 16th-17th. The Superfortresses concentrate on rail bridges and marshaling yards, but the airfield at Samchang is also hit.

In yet other activity, a flight of four F-86 Sabres attached to the 334th Fighter-Interceptor Squadron, 4th Fighter-Interceptor Group, encounters and engages a group of eight MiGs in the vicinity of P'anp Yong

Dong. Lieutenant Orren H. Ohlinger heads right into the enemy formation, takes the second in line and opens fire. The MiG slows from the hits, permitting Ohlinger to pour more fire and finish it off.

Also, a flight of four Sabre jets, attached to the 334th Fighter-Interceptor Squadron, 4th Fighter-Interceptor Group, encounters and engages a band of two MiGs in the vicinity of Sinanju. Lieutenant John J. Burke and his element leader attack the pair. Burke scores a hit on his target and it is shot from the sky. Also, Lieutenant Merlyn E. Hroch, attached to the 334th Fighter-Interceptor Squadron, 4th Fighter-Interceptor Group, while on patrol with three other Sabre jets, spots a MiG that attacks two other F-86s. Hroch moves against the MiG and opens fire. It sustains damage, but the enemy pilot evades destruction by heading into the sun. Nevertheless, Hroch's wingman takes over and blasts the aircraft from the sky. It plummets to the earth about 10 miles from Pyongyang.

October 17   *In the X Corps sector, 1st Marine Division zone,* a contingent of the 1st Korean Marine Corps Regiment attacks separate Communist strongpoints in the area northwest of Hill 751 and south of Hill 1052. The contingent, bolstered by tanks and artillery, eliminates twenty-five fortified bunkers. During the operation, 15 enemy troops are killed (counted) and three others are captured.

In Naval activity, the USS *Samuel N. Moore* (DD 747), while operating off Hungnam, is hit by enemy shore gun fire. The vessel sustains damage to the steering engine room and casualties are inflicted. One man is killed and two others are wounded.

October 19   *In Air Force activity,* C-54s evacuate sick and wounded from Korea. The troops are transported to Tachikawa Air Base, Japan, from where they are then moved aboard C-54s to a new 1,000 bed medical facility opened this day by the U.S. Army at Camp Drew, north of the airbase.

October 21–30 1951   More than 100 MiGs are spotted each day in the skies over North Korea, the first time the Communists have initiated sorties there. During this period, the engagements between the Air Force and the Communists cost the loss of three F-86 Sabre jets. The Communists lose five MiGs.

October 21   *In the IX Corps sector,* elements of the 24th Division seize the high ground in the area just south of Kumson.

October 22   *In the X Corps sector,* 1st Marine Division zone, the Marines execute Operation BUSH-BEATER to clear the enemy from the east flank of the division. A contingent of the 1st Battalion, 1st Marines, is airlifted by helicopters (HMR-161) to the target zone. The troops drive westwardly toward the Soyang-gang River in coordination with a simultaneous operation by the Marine Reconnaissance Company, which is closing from the opposite direction. Other similar operations are executed during October. One code-named HOUSEBURNER is carried out literally, as the Marines attempt to destroy as many huts as possible to ensure that the enemy is not able to use them during the frigid Korean winter.

In Air Force activity, in response to word of a B-29 being shot down, two SA-16s, attached to the 3rd Air Rescue Squadron, speed to the scene and retrieve the entire 12-man crew of the downed aircraft. The rescue marks a record. It is the highest number of men retrieved on any single day of the war.

Also, another B-29, piloted by Captain Lyle B. Bordeaux (30th Bombardment Squadron, 19th Bombardment Group) takes extremely heavy fire while on a bombing mission over the airfield at Taech'on. The plane's controls begin to fail, but Bordeaux keeps her in the air. Enemy fighters also arrive and the machine gun fire wounds several crew members. Bordeaux, aware of the dire circumstances, maintains his composure and although the craft continues to lose altitude, he refuses to land in enemy territory or abandon the wounded. He makes it back to the vicinity of Seoul and continues to circle a small island until all of the crew bails out. As the last man out, Bordeaux jumps from an elevation of about 1,000 feet.

October 23   The USS *Helena* (CA 75) is hit by enemy shore gunfire while operating off Hungnam. The vessel sustains some damage and four crewmen sustain slight injuries.

In Air Force activity, the 30th Bomber Wing strikes Namsi Airfield and ignites a furious and costly air battle. FEAF launches nine B-29s to strike Namsi Airfield, located between MiG Alley and Pyongyang. One of the bombers is forced to return to base. The mission is protected by a force of 55 F-84s attached to the 49th and 136th Fighter Bomber Wings. In addition, F-86 Sabre jets fly overhead at a higher elevation to intercept any MiGs that might arrive.

MiGs encounter and engage the Sabres, preventing the Sabres from protecting the B-29s. As the F-86s fight off the MiGs, numbered at about 100, and down two, other MiGs strike the B-29s and F-84s. The bombing force is hit by a contingent of about fifty MiGs and it is not certain whether they are a part of the force that engages the Sabres or a totally separate band. Nonetheless, the MiGs are an overmatch for the ThunderJets and their straight wings.

The Communists score heavily upon the force. Without the Sabres there, the MiGs easily penetrate the protective formation and succeed in shooting down three of the B-29s. Of the remaining five bombers, three receive such tremendous damage that they make emergency landings in either Korea or Japan.

One of the seriously damaged bombers is piloted by Lieutenant William E. Reeter (372nd Bombardment Squadron, 307th Bombardment Wing). Reeter and seven of his crew are badly wounded, but he retains command and decides not to bail out due to the wounded on board. His action saves the crew from capture or worse. The plane remains in formation to receive further protection en route back to a base. During the encounter, three separate fires erupt aboard the aircraft, but all are extinguished. The plane successfully makes an emergency landing in Korea.

Also, Colonel Albert C. Prendergast, commander, 136th Fighter-Bomber Wing, flying a Republic F-84E in the mission, expends all of his fuel and is forced to bail out, but he dies in the failed attempt. The B-29 gunners claim the downing of three MiGs and the F-84E pilots also claim three. One F-84 is also shot down during the air battles. The engagement is referred to as the Battle of Namsi.

General Vandenberg, aware of the disaster and the slaughter of the B-29s, rethinks his position about not sending more Sabres. It becomes evident that if more Sabres don't arrive, the outnumbered Americans will soon run out of B-29s and their crews. Consequently, Vandenberg orders the dispatch of 75 F-86 Sabre jets to Korea. Air Defense Command gets the directive to fill the slots at once. The new arrivals will be F-86Es, a newer version, and Vandergrift also orders a crew and crew chief for each plane. The planes will be deployed primarily with the 51st Fighter Interceptor Wing, but some move to the 4th Fighter Interceptor Wing.

Experienced airmen of the 4th Wing move to the 51st to help them with the transition to the Sabre jets. One of the veterans is Colonel Francis S. Gabreski. He assumes command of the 51st Wing. Far East Air Forces, with their new additions, will have a complement of 165 Sabres. Nevertheless, not all of the planes will be available for combat. In addition, the pleas of General Otto P. Weyland have finally doubled his force, but the odds remain great. The Communists have more than 550 MiGs that can attack and then run across the Yalu River, which the Sabres are forbidden to cross.

October 24 *In Air Force activity,* the Far East Air Forces campaign to bomb North Korean airfields continues. On this day, an 8-plane contingent attacks the field at Sunch'on and during the mission a force of about 70 MiGs intercepts the formations. The Americans shoot down two MiGs, one by gunners on the B-29s and another by Colonel Harrison R. Thyng, attached to the 4th Fighter Interceptor Wing. However, the Communists down another of the B-29s. The loss prompts General Weyland, commanding officer, Far East Air Forces, to suspend B-29 attacks for two days. Afterward, the daylight raids are reinitiated.

October 25 The peace talks that had been aborted by the Communists on 23 August 1951 are renewed this day. The location is changed from Kaesong to Panmunjom, a small village slightly north of the 38th Parallel. The talks are held in tents because the village has no houses.

In Air Force activity, F-51 Mustangs execute a large amount of sorties against enemy forces in the I Corps sector and report that the strikes account for about 200 enemy casualties.

In other activity, while on a rescue mission to re-trieve a downed pilot in enemy territory, an H-5 helicopter is hit by enemy fire and forced to make an emergency landing. The men evade capture by making it to concealed positions, where they remain unscathed until the following day. On the 26th, two additional helicopters arrive at the scene and rescue all four men.

In Naval activity, Marine planes attached to VMF-312 attack targets, including rails and locomotives near Myong-dong. A band of eight MiGs attack the Corsairs, but the enemy pilots' poor marksmanship fails to do the Marines' F4U4Bs any harm. Afterward, the pilots spot another group of MiGs, numbering 16, but again are spared damage.

October 26 U.N and Communist representatives at Panmunjom concur on a line of demarcation (spelled out on the 23rd) and sign an agreement by initialing maps that designate the respective positions, which essentially is listed as "a line linking up the farthest points of repeated contacts up to 2,000 yards forward of the United Nations MLR" (Main Line of Resistance, front lines). General Van Fleet, Eighth Army commander, pursuant to the cease fire, directs his corps to maintain "aggressive defensive actions until a full armistice is concluded."

The line of demarcation is to remain in effect for thirty days; however, Van fleet insists that if a full cease-fire is not in place by 27 November, the agreed upon line would become subject to modification in conjunction with positions at that time.

October 27 *In the X Corps sector, 1st Marine Division zone,* the 1st Marines dispatch a reconnaissance contingent to estimate the strength and positions of an enemy force detected north of the 1st Battalion's lines. The intelligence gathering continues for three days and on the following day, an attack is launched to eliminate the problem. Also, the 1st Marine Division initiates use of an airfield at Sokchori, located in the ROK I Corps sector.

In Air Force activity, B-29s, on a final daylight raid of the medium bombers, knock out six MiG-15s, a high mark for a single day for the gunners. The Superfortresses are protected by F-84s and RAAF Meteors during the raid against Sinanju, but all the planes are downed by the B-29s. Three other MiGs are damaged.

Up until the last week in October, only six B-29s had been lost, but during this one week, five have been destroyed and another eight sustain heavy damage. The losses force FEAF to halt daylight attacks by B-29s. The daylight attacks by the Superfortresses will not resume until 19 September 1952.

In other activity, during the day's missions, the 67th Fighter-Bomber Squadron, 18th Fighter-Bomber Group, attacks the rails at Kuni-ri and subsequently, the formation moves against a troop center at Youndong. One of the men in Captain Richard D. Anderson's command is shot down by antiaircraft fire. Anderson remains overhead to protect the other pilot and while doing so, enemy fire also hits his plane. Nevertheless, he remains in the area. Meanwhile, an H-5 helicopter from the 3rd Air Rescue Squadron, escorted by fighters, arrives and rescues the pilot.

October 28 *In the IX Corps sector, 1st Cavalry Division zone,* enemy fire stalls Company G, 3rd Battalion, in the vicinity of Chong-dong. Lieutenant Lloyd Burke moves on his own to end the blockage. He drives against several bunkers and throws grenades into each of them. Following that action, Burke returns to get a rifle, then heads back and eliminates the defenders in a second bunker and moves again toward a third. The contingent that had been stalled bolts up and advances, but soon after, yet another bunker stalls progress. Burke sets out one more time and on this trek he brings a light machine gun and several boxes of ammunition. His gun eliminates about 75 more enemy troops before he expends all the ammunition. However, he sends for more ammo and reinitiates the one-man wrecking crew's advance.

By this time he is wounded, but not enough to halt his attack. He carries the light machine guns in his arms as he drives forward. A machine gun position and two mortar positions fall victim to his marksmanship, as well as about 35 additional enemy troops, bringing the count to more than 100 killed. The men in the command, about 35, are stunned by Burke's fearlessness. They are inspired to drive forward and continue the attack. Lieutenant Burke becomes a recipient of the Medal of Honor for his extraordinary heroism and leadership in the face of the enemy.

In Air Force activity, a patrol of the 336th Fighter-Interceptor Squadron, 4th Fighter-Interceptor Group, encounters MiGs in the vicinity of Taech'on. During the engagement, one MiG is downed by First Lieutenant Robert H. Moore.

October 29 *In the X Corps sector, 1st Marine Division zone,* the USS *New Jersey* and the USS *Toledo* support the actions during the last two weeks of October. By the end of the month, the *New Jersey* executes 11 missions and the *Toledo* participates in 41 missions. On this day, the USS *Toledo* receives a message from General Gerald Thomas: "Your accurate and effective fire during period 24–29 October made an important contribution to operations of this division. Many thanks and come again."

In Naval activity, the USS *Osprey* (AMS 28) is hit and damaged by enemy shore batteries at Wonsan. No fatalities occur, but one crewman is badly wounded.

October 30 *In the X Corps sector, 1st Marine Division zone,* the 1st Battalion, 1st Marines, dispatches Company C, led by Captain John R. McMahon, to eliminate enemy positions on a ridge to its front. The contingent sweeps along the ridge destroying bunkers as it advances. The North Koreans manage to threaten the attack by pouring mortar and small arms fire; however, the Marines quickly find protective cover and pull back under the support fire of artillery fire, air strikes and heavy machine gun fire. The operation costs the company one man wounded. The Marines destroy about 40 enemy bunkers. The North Koreans lose 65 killed (counted).

In Naval activity, the British destroyer HMCS *Cayuga,* operating off the west coast of Korea, comes under fire from enemy shore guns on Amgak Island and sustains some slight damage.

October 31 *In the X Corps sector, 1st Marine Division zone,* the 3rd Battalion, 1st Marines, pursuant to orders from General Thomas, uses Communist tactics against the enemy. They initiate an artillery attack to signal a night assault; however, as the guns silence, the Marines use a North Korean bugle signal to trip up the Communists. The bunkers empty as the North Koreans answer the call to man the open trenches to prepare to defend. Instead of Marine infantry, the Communists are greeted by mortar and artillery fire. Estimated casualties amount to 47 killed and 48 wounded.

In other activity, the 1st Marine Division, for the month of October, reports 50 killed, 2 missing and 2 missing in action. The figures include the Korean Marines. Enemy casualties are reported as 709 killed (counted) and an estimated count of 2,377 killed. The number of enemy wounded is estimated at 4,927. The Marines also capture 571.

In Air Force activity, subsequent to a successful experiment with the C-124A during the latter part of September (Operation PELICAN), the plane returns to the United States. The plane's performance convinces the leaders of the 315th Air Division that it would require the services of a squadron of the C-124A Globemasters in Korea.

In other activity, the Air Defense Section of the Marine Tactical Air Control Squadron 2 relocates to Pohang and is placed under the control of Marine Ground Control Interceptor Squadron 1. The squadron continues to operate as the Tactical Air Direction Section.

November 1951–May 1952 The Chinese, unlike the U.S., do not rotate individual pilots in a fashion such as a particular number of missions. Rather, like the Russians, they rotate entire units. Between November of this year and May of 1952, the Chinese rotated 17 MiG-15 regiments and one La-11 regiment. The practice gives, in this instance, combat experience to about 450 pilots, but it also at times places inexperienced pilots up against the American Sabre pilots. In the air duels that do occur, with few exceptions, the Americans prevail, against both the Chinese and the Soviets.

November 1 At this time, about 208,000 enemy troops face Eighth Army, but in reserve, the enemy has nine Chinese armies totaling about 235,000 troops and with four North Korean Corps in reserve, the force is strengthened by another 138,000. The U.N. forces, composed primarily of U.S. troops, number about 195,000; however, many of these are support troops.

In the X Corps sector, 1st Marine Division zone, the Marines continue to remain active along their front, the eastern portion of the X Corps zone, but activity is restrained to patrols. Nevertheless, the Marines are aware that enemy units — including the 1st, 15th and 19th N.K. Divisions — remain to their front. Throughout November, the Marines maintain responsibility for the eastern sector of X Corps zone in east-central Korea.

In Air Force activity, Colonel Harrison R. Thyng assumes command of the 4th Fighter Interceptor Wing.

November 2   *In Air Force activity,* Lieutenant Colonel George L. Jones (334th Fighter-Interceptor Squadron, 4th Fighter-Interceptor Group) and one other pilot, while on a mission near Sonch'on, spot two MiGs. Jones fires at one and damages it, but before he can finish the plane off, he expends his ammunition. With smoke blowing from its wing the MiG begins to dive, and Jones' wingman, Lieutenant Richard A. Pincoski, takes aim and finishes it. Both pilots share the kill.

A victory ship unloading cargo unto a DUKW at Inchon on 3 November. The DUKW will carry its cargo directly to waiting rail cars.

Other types of cargo also arrive in Korea, including this net full of turkeys for the upcoming traditional dinner on Thanksgiving Day.

— *In the United States:* The Defense Department calls for a January draft of 59,600 men.

November 3   An SA-16, flying to retrieve a downed pilot, comes under intense fire and its mission is aborted. The helicopter, attached to the 3rd Air Rescue Squadron, moves to the Korea Bay and defies the 6 to 8 foot waves to land and retrieve another downed pilot without harm.

November 4   *In the I Corps sector,* the 1st King's Own Scottish Borderers (British Commonwealth Division), holding positions on Hill 355 subsequent to its seizure during the previous month, comes under a surprise night attack by the Chinese. The positions first come under a bombardment that lasts about three hours and it is followed by an attack signaled by the whistles and bugles that direct the Chinese foot soldiers to charge toward the perimeter with total disregard to the barbed wire.

The British are forced to surrender some ground when elements of Company B are overwhelmed, but later, during the early morning hours of the 5th, the positions are regained and the Chinese are driven back. By dawn, the British control the hill; however, in yet another of the fights on a hill with no lasting value, the British lose 7 killed, 87 wounded and slightly more than 40 missing.

In Air Force activity, a large group of MiGs, composed of about 60 planes, attacks a formation of 34 F-86s in the skies near Sinanju. Following the air duels, two of the MiGs are downed and three others are damaged. The U.S. reports no losses. Captain William F. Guss, USMC, attached to the USAF 4th Fighter Squadron, knocks down one MiG to become the first Marine pilot to down a Chinese MiG.

In Naval activity, an F9F-2 plane crashes through the barricades on the USS *Antietam* (CV 36), causing damage and injuries to the crew. Four men are killed and ten others are injured, one severely. In addition, two planes are destroyed and six others sustain varying degrees of damage.

November 5   *In the United States:* Lt. General Lemuel Shepherd (commander Fleet Marine Force, Pacific) is appointed on this day as commandant of the Marine Corps, scheduled to succeed General Clifton B. Cates. Shepherd assumes the position on 1 January 1952. General Cates does not retire upon the end of his term as commandant. He is appointed as commanding officer, Marine Corps Schools, Quantico.

November 6   Chinese Communists flying jet fighter planes and Soviet medium bombers strike the island of Taehwa-do in the Yalu Gulf. It is the initial confirmation of Chinese pilots flying Soviet bombers (TU-2s).

In Air Force activity, a contingent of eleven enemy twin-engine light bombers strike friendly-held Taehwa-do Island in what is the first confirmed air-to-ground action by an enemy light bomber contingent since the outbreak of the war. The Communists mount a night amphibious raid and seize the islands of Ka-do and Tan-do on the west coast of Korea.

November 7–8 1951 *In the X Corps sector, 1st Marine Division zone,* the artillery of the 11th Marines is especially busy as they fire in coordination with the 90-mm rifles of the 1st Marine Tank Battalion in an effort to destroy enemy fortified positions. The two-day continuous bombardment pounds 34 known artillery positions and 25 bunkers. The attack also concentrates on 22 machine gun positions and several supply dumps. The two U.S. units aggressively pound the enemy positions throughout the month, but the Communists have actually been able to augment their fortified positions to make them less accessible to the artillery attacks.

November 8 A group of F-86s and F-80s spots a large formation of MiGs that numbers more than 100 planes; however, only a small number choose to take on the outnumbered American planes. The U.S. loses one F-86. The enemy loses one MiG and one other is damaged.

Also, Marine Squadron VMF-214 departs Itami aboard the USS *Lenawee* (PA-195) at Kobe, Japan.

November 9 *In the X Corps sector, 1st Marine Division zone,* preparations are made to celebrate the birthday of the Marine Corps, which falls on the following day. Orders (OP-nO 50–51) arrive instructing the division to arrange for a massive bombardment of a particular position from where the enemy is able to observe Marine lines.

In Air Force activity, eleven stranded crewmen of a downed B-29 are rescued by a C-47 that lands on the beach on Paengnyong-do Island located off the southwest coast of North Korea. The 19th BG attacks marshaling yards at Hwang-ju, Kowon, and Yangdok; the Saamcham Airfield; and a barracks area. In other night attacks, 98th BW B-29s bomb Taech'on Airfield, fly five close support sorties and a leaflet sortie, and strike Hungnam.

In Naval activity, U.S. warships engaged in minesweeping operations at Wonsan Harbor west of Mo-do and Sin-do Islands come under fire from enemy shore batteries before the mission is completed.

November 10 *In the X Corps sector, 1st Marine Division zone,* enemy positions on Hill 1052 are greeted by a thunderous bombardment in celebration of the Marine Corps' Birthday, which is on this day. Eighty-three Marine planes in coordination with the 11th Marines' artillery and the division's tanks, mortars and machine guns light up Hill 1052 like a Christmas tree. The USS *Los Angeles* joins in the celebration and adds its big guns. The Marines, in the spirit of the day, deliver 50,000 leaflets to the hill, each extending an invitation for the enemy to join the Marines for their birthday dinner that evening. Twenty North Koreans surrender; however, it is uncertain whether the unusual invitations had anything to do with it.

November 11 *In the X Corps sector, 1st Marine Division zone,* along the Minnesota Line, the 5th Marines relieves the 1st Marines. This operation becomes the largest helicopter lift (Operation SWITCH) of troops since the inclusion of helicopters in the Marine operations. About 2,000 troops are moved by helicopters, which deliver 950 troops to Hill 884; another 952 Marines are transported from the hill to Field X-83. The entire operation is completed in about ten hours, another tactical historic first for the U.S. Marines. Hill 884 soon becomes known as "Helicopter Hill."

In Naval activity, the USS *Gloucester* (PF 22) comes under fire while operating off Hungnam. One man is killed and 11 others are wounded.

November 12 General Ridgway instructs General Van Fleet to halt all Eighth Army offensive action, except those required to bolster the main line of defense (Operation RATKILLER). In addition, Eighth Army is to establish outposts at positions 3,000 to 4,000 yards to the front of the MLR. The 155-mile line extends from the Yellow Sea in the west to the Sea of Japan in the east. The I Corps, commanded by Lt. General John W. O'Daniel, holds the left, followed by IX Corps (Major General Willard G. Wyman) and to the right, the X Corps (Major General Clovis E. Byers), followed by the ROK I Corps. The activity across the entire front during November and December of this year remains relatively light.

In the I Corps sector, the South Korean 1st Division mounts continual probes with tank-infantry forces, but no major battles develop. The raids continue until 16 December.

In Naval activity, the USS *New Jersey* (BB 62), operating on the west coast of Korea, commences its final bombardment of enemy troop positions. The gunners receive guidance from an air spotter attached to the HMS *Sydney* (CVL).

Also, the USS *Los Angeles* (CA 135), operating on the east coast of Korea, provides fire support to the Marines and the ROK I Corps, each engaged at the front. The U.S. Navy estimates enemy casualties at about 105 to 140; its reports state that 27 bunkers are destroyed and an undeterminable number of other bunkers are damaged.

In yet other activity, Rear Admiral H.E. Regan assumes command of Carrier Division 17 (Hunter Killer Group). He relieves Captain J.L. Kane.

— *In Japan:* Marine Fighter Squadron VMF 214 departs Japan en route to the U.S. and its base at El Toro (Marine Corps Air Station), California.